economics
for business

4
edition

economics
for business

IAN FRASER
JOHN GIONEA
SIMON FRASER

The McGraw·Hill Companies

Sydney New York San Francisco Auckland
Bangkok Bogotá Caracas Hong Kong
Kuala Lumpur Lisbon London Madrid
Mexico City Milan New Delhi San Juan
Seoul Singapore Taipei Toronto

National Library of Australia Cataloguing-In-Publication Data
Author: Fraser, Ian, 1950-
Title: Economics for business / Ian Fraser, John Gionea, Simon Fraser.
Edition: 4th ed.
ISBN: 9780070998438 (pbk.)
Notes: Includes index.
Target Audience: For tertiary students.
Subjects: Economics.
        Economics—Case studies.
        Australia—Economic conditions.
        Australia—Economic conditions—Case studies.
        Australia—Economic policy.
        Australia—Economic policy—Case studies.
Other Authors/Contributors: Gionea, John.
                 Fraser, Simon John, 1961-
Dewey Number: 330

Published in Australia by
McGraw-Hill Australia Pty Ltd
Level 2, 82 Waterloo Road, North Ryde NSW 2113
Acquisitions editor: Michael Buhagiar
Development editors: Amanda Evans and Fiona Howie
Art director: Astred Hicks
Cover and internal design: Em&Jon Design
Production editor: Laura Carmody
Permissions editor: Haidi Bernhardt
Copyeditor: Gillian Armitage
Proofreader: Ross Blackwood
Indexer: Michael Ramsden
Typeset in CaeciliaCom-45Light 9.5/13pt by diacriTech, India
Printed in China on 70gsm matt art by iBook Printing Ltd

CONTENTS IN BRIEF

CONTENTS IN FULL

PART 3

FUNDAMENTAL MACROECONOMIC CONCEPTS

PART 4

PART **5**

Contents in full

PART 6

ECONOMIC POLICIES

PART 8

ABOUT THE AUTHORS

IAN FRASER
Royal Melbourne Institute of Technology

Dr Ian Fraser recently retired from the post of Director of the RMIT International College. At RMIT University Ian had many other roles including Deputy Dean and Associate Dean (International and Commercial Liaison) in the Faculty of Business. Ian has extensive experience in research consultancies, seminar presentations, board positions and business leadership. He has co-authored several books in the areas of economics, international trade, and banking and finance, and provided consulting services for several global enterprises, including Mobil and Ericsson.

He holds degrees in economics and education and postgraduate qualifications in management (B Econs (Monash), B Education (Melb), MBA (UNE), and a PhD from RMIT). He has worked as a lecturer and facilitator in vocational and higher education in Australia and overseas. Ian has been involved as a lecturer, manager and negotiator on behalf of RMIT University in China, Japan, Singapore, Vietnam and Indonesia, as well as Australia. In 2007 Ian was awarded a PhD for his thesis on 'Strategy Formation in Chinese Universities'.

JOHN GIONEA
Royal Melbourne Institute of Technology

Dr John Gionea has taught in the area of Economics and International Business for some 18 years at various universities in Melbourne (RMIT, Swinburne), China (Wuhan), Romania (Bucharest), and Denmark (Aarhus), following more than 20 years of experience in the private and government sectors.

Unlike many other practitioners in the business area, John has shown a steady interest in research, consulting, training and teaching at various levels (TAFE, undergraduate and postgraduate), and his contribution to this book is the result of a sustained effort to bring together extensive practical experience and diverse theoretical skills.

John is a former consultant to the United Nations Economic Commission for Europe and the author of *International Trade and Investment: An Asia-Pacific Perspective*, also published by McGraw-Hill Australia (2005).

SIMON FRASER

Simon Fraser graduated with a Bachelor of Economics (Hons) from Monash University. He also has a Graduate Diploma of Education and a Masters of Business, in which he examined Australian–Vietnamese culture and its impact on business relationships. Simon is currently pursuing doctoral studies part-time.

He worked as Industrial Officer for a Victorian Teachers Union and then started teaching part-time at RMIT University in Industrial Relations in 1987. In 1988, he commenced full-time teaching in the School of Business Studies, teaching Business Economics, International Trade and Finance and Comparative Business Cultures. In 1996 he was appointed Head of the Department of Business Studies for RMIT College Penang, the university's off-shore campus in Malaysia.

He left RMIT University in 1997 to pursue a career in international development, and has undertaken consultancies for the World Bank, Asian Development Bank, AusAID and the United Nations Development Program. He has lived and worked in Indonesia, Malaysia, Laos PDR, Tajikistan, Vietnam, India, Sri Lanka, Vanuatu and Guyana, as well as travelling extensively throughout the Asia-Pacific region, including Papua New Guinea, Thailand, Cambodia, Timor Leste, PR China, South Korea, East Timor, Bhutan, the Philippines and also South Africa and parts of South America.

PREFACE

Economics for Business 4e follows the success of the previous three editions, with the second edition being a category winner in the Australian Publishing Association's Awards for Excellence in Educational Publishing.

The authors have maintained the book's user-friendly style, making the study and understanding of basic principles of micro- and macroeconomics easy and rewarding.

Economics for Business has been specifically written for students studying introductory economics in vocational and postgraduate programs as a terminal course over one or two semesters. It is ideal for students of the Advanced Diploma of Accounting in the **FNS10 Financial Services Training Package** and for introductory economics units at undergraduate level. It also provides a good foundation for students who will progress to further studies in economics in business-related programs.

This fourth edition incorporates the events, developments and regulatory changes that continue to transform Australia's national economy in a world of change. The authors have gone to great lengths to discuss such important current aspects of the Australian economy as:

* the nature, causes and consequences of the global financial crisis (GFC)
* the rapid recovery of the Australian economy following the impact of the GFC
* the resilience shown by the Australian economy in the post-East Asian crisis period, when experiencing continuous growth in spite of issues such as the regional and global slowdown in the early 2000s, the terrorist events of 11 September 2001 and the GFC
* the reform of Australia's tax system, including the goods and services tax (GST) and the mining tax
* the further decline in the unemployment rate in Australia in a low inflation environment
* the strong rise of the Australian dollar as major countries engaged in a 'currency war' in the aftermath of the GFC
* improvements in Australia's financial system and its competition policy framework
* the growing significance of Australia's external sector.

This edition retains the Link to International Economy and Link to Business studies, providing new examples of the workings of the Australian economy in an international context. In line with suggestions from a number of lecturers using this textbook, many examples in the Links refer to events in other economies (e.g. in the United States, Europe, China, India, Japan, Indonesia and Vietnam) impacting on the Australian economy.

IAN FRASER
JOHN GIONEA
SIMON FRASER

ACKNOWLEDGMENTS

A new edition is a daunting and time-consuming task, which would not be possible without the joint effort, assistance and support from a number of people and organisations. McGraw-Hill Australia and the authors would like to thank Andrew Tomadini from the International Trade in Services section and Ryan Oswin from the Balance of Payments section at the Australian Bureau of Statistics for advice on the new format of Australia's balance of payments.

We would also like to thank those who provided valuable feedback on the text at various stages of this fourth edition's development:

- Maralyn McDowell—QUT International School
- Grant Altoft—Southbank Institute of TAFE
- John Lodewijks—University of Western Sydney
- Joy Nicholas—Box Hill TAFE.

Ian Fraser wishes to thank Jim Brown of Haileybury College for introducing him to the study of economics, Mike Hall of the Reserve Bank for introducing him to the practice of economics and Dr Lilai Xu for introducing him to China. Ian also wishes to thank Morgan Blackthorne for providing the photograph of him on page xvi.

Thanks also go to the reviewers of the previous editions of the text: Jeff Morris, North Point Institute of TAFE; Bob Schunke, Adelaide Institute of TAFE; John Calabro, Holmesglen Institute of TAFE; Ron Lipson, Victoria University of Technology; Fe'ama Brass, South East Metropolitan College of TAFE; Bernie Boschman, Barton Institute of TAFE; Daniel Meers, Kangan Batman Institute of TAFE; Brian Bragg, South Western Sydney Institute of TAFE; Helen Summers, Northern Melbourne Institute of TAFE; Steven Phelan, Moreton Institute of TAFE; James Mulheran, Sydney Institute of Technology; Julian Chong, Swinburne University of Technology; Paul Croft, TAFE NSW, South Western Sydney Institute; Sue Fisher, TAFE NSW, Western Sydney Institute; Ray Lum Mow, Sydney West International College; Bob Nelson, La Trobe University; Joy Nicholas, Box Hill Institute of TAFE; and Pat Walsh, International College, Queensland University of Technology.

The authors would also like to thank the staff at McGraw-Hill for their assistance with the development and production of this book. Our gratitude goes to our publisher Michael Buhagiar for his inspiration and consideration in developing this edition and for finding a way around various snags and pitfalls; to development editor Amanda Evans for her encouragement, professionalism, problem-solving and friendly demeanour at all times; to Fiona Howie for coordinating the review process; to Gillian Armitage for her detailed copyediting; to production editor Laura Carmody for her patient and methodical project management during production; to Astred Hicks for overseeing the cover and internal design process; to permissions editor Haidi Bernhardt for her thorough permissions management; and to Lisa McNeil for marketing and promotional aspects.

We are grateful to our families and colleagues, without whose support and understanding this book would not have been possible.

IAN FRASER

JOHN GIONEA

SIMON FRASER

WHAT'S NEW IN THIS EDITION?

In this fourth edition of *Economics for Business* a number of improvements have been made to the overall pedagogical structure and organisation of the book:

- The textbook structure has been reorganised, including the elimination of two old topics and the inclusion of a new topic (**Chapter 10—Aggregate demand and aggregate supply**) and two new appendixes on financial modelling techniques.
- As part of the reorganisation process, the chapter on **National income, expenditure and product** from the previous edition has been split into two new chapters—**Chapter 9 (Measuring the economy's size and growth)** and **Chapter 10 (Aggregate demand and aggregate supply)**.
- At the same time, new financial modelling techniques such as break-even analysis, net present value and yield curves are now covered in the **Appendix to Chapter 6** and **Appendix to Chapter 16**.
- A substantially revised **Chapter 16 (Wealth creation)** aims to provide basic information about the process of wealth creation in Australia and enable students to apply the principles of economics to their future business and personal lives.
- A new section in **Chapter 2 (Economic systems)** discusses a number of fundamental issues related to the economies in transition from centrally-planned systems to market-based economies.
- **Part 7 (Australia in the international economy)** has been expanded to include geographic and sectoral trends in Australia's foreign direct investment.
- **Chapter 18 (The balance of payments)** presents Australia's balance of payments according to the new format compiled by the Australian Bureau of Statistics (ABS) from September 2009, based on the sixth edition of the International Monetary Fund's *Balance of Payments and International Investment Position Manual* (BPM6).
- 'Australia's national competitiveness rankings' are discussed in **Chapter 20 (Structural change)** (pp. 422–4), where the main findings of the most recent annual reports of the World Economic Forum on Australia's current business and microeconomic competitiveness and Australia's prospects in terms of growth competitiveness are summarised.
- Review questions have been moved to the end of each chapter and new applied questions and exercises have also been added to the end-of-chapter material, which has been extensively revised and updated.

This edition also features new and revised data and information on contemporary issues, including:

- detailed treatment of the CPI and its components and how the Reserve Bank uses the CPI for monetary policy purposes
- explanations of the GFC, its causes and consequences for financial regulation
- sovereign risk, systemic risk, and systematic and unsystematic risk
- risk and the rate of return, negative gearing, basic information on the stock market for first-time investors and an update on the issues affecting superannuation in Australia
- the role of the RBA, APRA and the implementation of Basel 111
- the basic model of banking and an update on Islamic banking practices.

E-STUDENT

ONLINE LEARNING CENTRE

The Online Learning Centre (OLC) that accompanies this text helps you get the most from your course. It provides a powerful learning experience beyond the printed page. The premium content areas, which are accessed by registering the code at the front of this text, provide you with extensive online resources. Instructors have additional access to an instructor-specific resource area.
www.mhhe.com/au/fraser4e

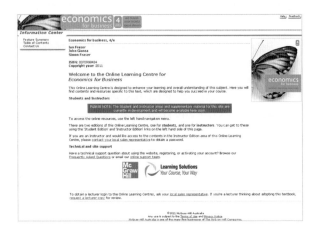

EBOOK

Economics for Business 4e is also available as an eBook. A powerful search engine means eBook users can easily locate topics while interactive features allow you to insert notes or highlight specific content. Users can share their notes with others and lecturers can link eBook content directly to other resources such as digital study guides.

POWERPOINT® PRESENTATIONS

A set of PowerPoint presentations summarises the key points of each chapter. They can be downloaded as a valuable revision aid.

E-INSTRUCTOR

INSTRUCTOR RESOURCE MANUAL

The Instructor Resource Manual features comprehensive lecture notes, teaching ideas and examples, as well as suggested solutions to discussion questions and case problems. This manual is an ideal resource for busy teachers and can be used together with the PowerPoint presentations as part of a powerful teaching package.

POWERPOINT® PRESENTATIONS

For instructors, this text comes complete with a full suite of colour PowerPoint presentations that distil key concepts from each chapter of the book. Present these in classes to reinforce key economic principles to your students and distribute them as class notes.

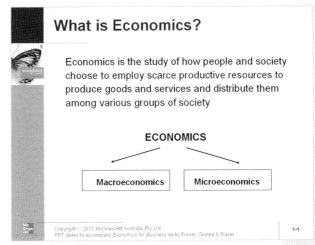

EZ TEST

EZ Test Online is a powerful and easy-to-use test generator for creating paper or digital tests. It allows easy 'one click' export to course management systems such as WebCT and Blackboard, and straightforward integration with Moodle.

EZ Test Online gives instructors access to the testbanks of this text and a range of others from one point of entry and also permits them to upload or edit their own questions. More information is available via the Online Learning Centre.

TESTBANK

A bank of test questions written specifically for this text lets instructors build examinations and assessments quickly and easily. The testbank is available in a range of flexible formats: in Microsoft Word®, in EZ Test Online or formatted for delivery via Blackboard or WebCT.

ARTWORK LIBRARY

Illustrations and graphs from the text are available in an online artwork library as digital image files. Instructors have the flexibility to use them in the format that best suits their needs.

TEXT AT A GLANCE

Economics for Business 4e is a pedagogically rich learning resource. The features below have been designed to guide and assist your learning as you use this text.

CHAPTER OPENER

Learning objectives
Each chapter begins with a numbered list of objectives that outline the topics covered within the chapter.

Introduction
The introduction sets the scene for the content covered in each chapter.

IN THE TEXT

Learning objectives
Chapter objectives are located in the margin of the text at the beginning of each relevant section of the chapter.

Example
This feature provides a clear explanation of a particular aspect of a theory using examples.

Margin definitions
Key terms appear in bold type in the text, and are defined in the margin.

Link to Business and Link to International Economy
Mini case studies based on real and hypothetical situations are given throughout with short-answer questions to illustrate the theory covered in the text.

LEARNING OBJECTIVES
After studying this chapter, you will be able to:

1. explain the significance of marginal revenue and marginal cost
2. distinguish between the long run and short run
3. distinguish between fixed cost and variable cost
4. state the law of diminishing returns
5. describe the different profit-maximising positions for a monopolist and a perfectly competitive firm
6. given a cost and revenue table, calculate and explain the profit-maximising positi...
7. defin...
8. distin...

INTRODUCTION

In previous chapters we have identified various economic systems. We have also closely examined individual markets and how they operate. Our study of markets introduced the concepts of supply and demand.

In this chapter we look at a model that illustrates how the economy operates. In a capitalistic, mixed economy like that of Australia, money is used by households, businesses and government to buy and sell goods and resources in markets, to pay and collect taxes, and to borrow and lend in financial markets. All these flows can be envisioned schematically in a flow diagram, which enables us to see the interaction between incomes and payments in the economy. The circular flow is shown to be critical in understanding how we measure economic activity and how we assess the size of the economy.

LEARNING OBJECTIVE 2
Describe the three basic economic questions

THE BASIC ECONOMIC QUESTIONS AND OPPORTUNITY COST

Since resources are limited (scarcity) and wants are unlimited, we must choose how to make optimum economic use of resources. These choices that we make on a daily basis are

---

EXAMPLE

Assume that, in the short run, the size of the factory remains the same (is held constant). In order to increase output, the factory owner may add more machinery, more raw materials, more labour. The owner may change inefficient work practices, extend working hours, shorten lunch breaks or offer incentives to work harder.

---

opportunity cost
the sacrifice, or forgone alternatives, in choosing to satisfy one need or want rather than another

Opportunity cost is the sacrifice, or forgone alternatives, in choosing to satisfy one need or want rather than another.

For example, assume you had $100 and spent it on dinner for two at a restaurant. To an accountant, the cost of the meal would be $100. To an economist, the cost is everything else you can no longer buy with that $100 because you spent it at a restaurant. The opportunity cost of the dinner was several CDs, reducing your credit card bill, enrolling in a short course,

---

ONE PRODUCER, ONE PRODUCT: WHO BENEFITS?

As you will see in your study of economics, in theory the most efficient way of producing a product, let's say breakfast cereal, is to have one producer (a 'monopolist') producing one product, provided that the producer operates with the interests of consumers as a top priority. In some countries governments create monopolies by providing licences to favoured groups of producers. Frequently these favoured groups are related to, or are business friends of, those in government.

QUESTIONS
1. Compare the relative power of consumers in a command economy and a market economy. Can you think of any examples?
2. Describe how governments in a command economy and a market economy would deal

LINK TO BUSINESS

POLAND—EUROPE'S 'STAR' TRANSITION ECONOMY

LINK TO INTERNATIONAL ECONOMY

Poland, a former centrally-planned economy, has pursued a policy of economic liberalisation since 1990 and today stands out as a success story among transition economies. Poland joined the European Union in 2004, and it is also a member of the WTO, OECD and NATO.

From 1990 to 2000 Poland's economy grew at an average annual rate of 4.7 per cent, and from 2000 to 2008 at an average rate of 4.4 per cent (the corresponding growth rates for the Euro area were 2.1 and 2.8 per cent). One should note that during the recent global financial crisis, Poland has been the only OECD member economy, other than Australia, to avoid a recession.

As a result of strong economic growth, Poland's GDP per capita (PPP) grew from US$5250 in December 1991 to US$17 275 in December 2008, but it is still only around half the level of the Euro area. Poland's inflation in recent years has been kept under control, varying between a high of 4.8 per cent in August 2008 and a low of 2 per cent in August 2010. From 1990 until August 2010, Poland's unemployment rate averaged 13.80 per cent.

According to Trading Economics consultants, from 1998 until 2010, Poland's average benchmark

SUMMARY

1. Chapter 1 introduced you to the basic economic concepts used by economists to understand issues relating to production, distribution and consumption.
2. The key issue is to try to satisfy unlimited needs and wants in an economy when there are limited or finite resources available.
3. The problem of scarcity forces us to make a choice, and every choice we make imposes costs known as opportunity costs.
4. The three basic economic questions that every economy tries to solve, given limited resources and unlimited wants, are:
   (a) what to produce
   (b) how to produce
   (c) for whom to produce.
5. Scarcity and choice are presented in a simple model known as production possibility theory, which illustrates the range of choices that a two-output economy can make to produce maximum outputs.
6. Production possibility theory was introduced using both static and dynamic assumptions to illustrate a range of situations inside and outside the frontier.

KEY TERMS				
basic economic problem		labour	6	productivity	14
basic economic problem	8	land	6	resources	5
capital	6	needs	7	scarcity	5
consumption	8	opportunity cost	10	static analysis	11
dynamic analysis	11	production	8	wants	7
enterprise	6	production possibility frontier	12		
factors of production	6	production possibility schedule	11		

REFERENCES

1. Charles W. Hill, *International Business*, International edn, McGraw-Hill-Irwin, New York, United States, 2004.
2. See ‹www.apsc.gov.au/annualreport/0809/index.html›, accessed 4 November 2010, for the Annual Australian Public Service Report which details financial arrangements and key sectors where the APS is intricately involved in the Australian economy.
3. Philip Lewis, Anne Garnett, Kim Hawtrey and Malcolm Treadgold, *Issues, Indicators and Ideas: A Guide to the Australian Economy*, Pearson Education Australia Pty Limited, South Melbourne, 2003.
4. ‹www.oecd.org/document/60/0,3343,en_2649_34533_1942460_1_1_1_1,00.html#tbw›, accessed 4 November 2010.
5. John Jackson and Ron McIver, *Macroeconomics*, 7th edn, McGraw-Hill Australia, Sydney, 20...

REVIEW QUESTIONS

1. How would you describe a market economy?
2. What distinguishes a market economy from a command economy?
3. Is there a role for government intervention in the Australian economy?
4. Can you identify other distinguishing elements in economic systems?
5. Briefly consider the economies of France, North Korea, South Korea, Brunei, Switzerland, Cuba, Poland, Denmark and Mongolia. What type of economic system would you classify them as?

...onomy where the government
...duces the goods and services for
...market coordinates the economic
...wer.

APPLIED QUESTIONS AND EXERCISES

1. Complete the following table to summarise the effects of various economic developments listed in Column (1) on aggregate demand:
   (a) Indicate in Column (2) one to two major components of aggregate demand that are likely to be affected by each economic development. Use the letters from the formula of aggregate demand as follows: *C*—personal consumption, *I*—private investment, *G*—government expenditure, *X*—exports, *M*—imports.
   (b) Indicate in Column (3) the impact of each economic development on aggregate demand, by using + for an

---

Break-even analysis   Appendix to Chapter 6

APPENDIX TO CHAPTER 6: BREAK-EVEN ANALYSIS

After the completion of this chapter you should have a better idea of the relationship between company revenues, costs and profits. As you are aware from media reports, profits often appear to be used as an indicator of the success of an organisation.

A person starting a new business often asks, 'At what level of sales will my company make a profit?' Established companies that have suffered through some rough times might have a similar question. Others ask, 'At what point will I be able to draw a fair salary from my company?'

The break even is the level of activity at which total revenues equal total costs. At the break-even point, the firm neither makes a profit, nor a loss. The break-even analysis calculates a break-even point based on fixed costs, variable costs per unit of sales, and revenue per unit of sales.

the break even
the level of activity at which total revenues equal total costs point

Knowledge of the break-even point analysis is useful to the management of both small and large businesses when deciding whether to introduce new product lines, change sales prices on established products, or enter new market areas.

To illustrate how break-even analysis can help management make decisions, we will use MAS Spectrometers Ltd as an example.

MAS Spectrometers Ltd specialises in producing and exporting spectrometers, instruments used to control industrial and medical processes and to monitor pollution. The relevant data for this business are:

- Unit selling price: $5000
- Unit variable costs: $4000
- Total monthly fixed costs: $120 000.

END OF CHAPTER

Summary
Each chapter ends with a summary to reinforce the theories learnt in the chapter.

Key terms
All key terms in a chapter are listed at the end of each chapter in alphabetical order.

References
Relevant sources used for research are listed at the end of each chapter.

Review questions
A list of revision questions at the end of every chapter is designed to test students' grasp of the principles explored in the chapter.

Applied questions and exercises
End-of-chapter exercises and case studies give students concrete examples of concepts discussed in the chapter. Extended exercises are given in relevant chapters.

Appendixes
An appendix with additional information to expand on the theory covered in the chapter is provided after Chapters 6 and 16.

1

ECONOMIC CONCEPTS AND SYSTEMS

Chapter 1

Economic concepts

LEARNING OBJECTIVES

After studying this chapter, you will be able to:

1. distinguish between microeconomics and macroeconomics
2. distinguish between positive and normative economics
3. in general terms, describe the contributions made to economic theory by leading economists
4. discuss and illustrate the problem that scarcity poses for an economy
5. describe the three basic economic questions
6. illustrate the concept of scarcity using a production possibility frontier
7. use production possibility theory to construct a production possibility frontier.

INTRODUCTION

Economics is the study of people in the ordinary business of life.

Source: Alfred Marshall, Principles of Economics:
An Introductory Volume, Macmillan, London, 1890.

In this chapter, some fundamental economic concepts will be introduced. These concepts are essential for any further study of economics and provide the basis on which the science of economics is built. The student needs to understand the concepts of scarcity and production possibility analysis, and the basic economic problems of what to produce, how to produce and who receives the outputs that are produced. This leads to a wider perspective of the interrelationships between economics, decision making in business and politics, and the means to satisfy human needs and wants.

Students will understand the methods that economists use to try to solve the basic economic problems in order to maximise individual satisfaction (in economics this is referred to as 'utility') and general economic welfare. Economics is a fundamental part of our everyday life and has implications for decisions at all levels of society, from government and corporations to households and individuals. The study of economics should improve our understanding of how an economy works, so we can maximise our own economic welfare and individual satisfaction and make informed economic decisions.

With a firm understanding of the basic economic concepts developed in this chapter, you will be able to deepen your appreciation of broader issues in economics in later chapters in this text. In turn, this will enable you to assess the structure and function of economics in the Australian community, to judge the performance of our key economic decision makers, and to understand shifts in economic thinking.

In economics, distinctions are often drawn between various dimensions of economics, most notably between:

LEARNING OBJECTIVE 1
Distinguish between microeconomics and macroeconomics

- microeconomics, which is the part of economics which examines the behaviour of basic elements in the economy, including individual markets and agents (such as consumers and firms, buyers and sellers) and the decisions that individuals make as they interact when trying to maximise their individual welfare
- macroeconomics, which addresses issues affecting the entire national and international economy and includes major issues such as unemployment, inflation, economic growth, the labour force, macroeconomic management including monetary and fiscal policies and prices and incomes policies.

Macroeconomic issues are dealt with in later chapters in this text.

In addition, we need to understand the distinction between positive and normative economics. Positive economics describes and explains economic phenomena and events. It attempts to describe the causal relationship that may exist between economic activities and outcomes and attempts to test economic theories. As such it purports to be value-free. For example, a positive economic theory may describe the relationship between interest rate rises and economic activity in the housing market, but it does not assert what the interest rate should be, just that there is a relationship.

LEARNING OBJECTIVE 2
Distinguish between positive and normative economics

If positive economics describes 'what is', normative economics describes 'what ought to be' and has values associated with economic statements and analysis such as what the economy ought to be like and what policies ought to be implemented. If positive economics describes the relationship between housing and interest rates, normative economics may say that 'credit card interest rates ought to be lowered because they're too high'. It is a value statement because it cannot be proven true or false. Normative economic analysis is used considerably in such areas as developing public policy and inequality and poverty measurements.

LEARNING OBJECTIVE 3
In general terms, describe the contributions made to economic theory by leading economists

LEADING ECONOMISTS

ECONOMIST	AREA OF RESEARCH	KEY POINTS
Adam Smith (1723–90)	Scottish philosopher and political economist	Wrote first 'modern' work on economics—*An Inquiry into the Nature and Causes of the Wealth of Nations* (1776). His book *The Theory of Moral Sentiments* discusses the nature and motive of morality and provides a background to his work on economics.
		Developed the concept of the role of 'the invisible hand' which stated that an individual does not contribute to society because they desire to promote public interest and economic welfare and wellbeing, but instead that societal wellbeing is enhanced because people pursue a policy of self-interest, of individual economic welfare and economic wellbeing.
		'It is not from the benevolence of the butcher, the brewer, or the baker, that we expect our dinner, but from their regard to their own interest.'
David Ricardo (1772–1823)	Classical economist	Developed the Law of Comparative Advantage with Adam Smith.
		An opponent of protectionism at the national economic level, he believed that free trade maximised individual and national economic welfare.
		Published *On the Principles of Political Economy and Taxation* in 1817.
Karl Marx (1818–83)	Economic and political theories of Socialist and Communist economic systems	Argued that there were inherent conflicts within a capitalist economic system as the class system that evolved under capitalism would lead to (revolutionary) change and bring in a new economic and political structure called a 'worker's state'.
		Publications include: *The Manifesto of the Communist Party* (1848) and *Capital* or *Das Kapital* (Volume 1 published 1867 and Volumes 2 (1885) and 3 (1894) published after his death by his collaborator Joseph Engels).

continued ↘

ECONOMIST	AREA OF RESEARCH	KEY POINTS
John Maynard Keynes (1883–1946)	Macroeconomic theory	Argued that the key to providing economic stability was through the control of aggregate demand and this necessitated a larger and growing role for governments in the economy in cases of inadequate aggregate demand.
		Believed the government has an economic and social responsibility to intervene in the market.
		Published *The General Theory of Employment, Interest and Money* (1936).
John Kenneth Galbraith (1908–2006)	Keynesian	Adjusted basic economic principles to account for market developments such as the market power of large and increasingly global corporations that were able to act as price makers rather than price takers. (These terms are explained in Chapter 5.)
		Published *The Affluent Society* (1958) and *The Age of Uncertainty* (1977).
Milton Friedman (1912–2006)	Nobel Prize winner in economics	Oversaw return to neoclassical economic theory and the power of the free and unfettered market.
		Promoted 'monetarism' which advocated a smaller role for government intervention in the market and a focus on the control of the money supply.
Paul Krugman (1953–)	Nobel Prize winner in economics	One of the most influential economists and contributors to economic debate in the world today.
		Interests include international trade, economies of scale and consumer behaviour.
		Follower of Keynesian economics (among other influences).
		‹www.krugmanonline.com›.

These are understandably brief summaries of key economic intellectuals and practitioners, and readers may wish to delve deeper into the writings of these economists to further their understanding of the development of economic theories and leading economists in the history of the science. In addition, readers' attention is drawn to other economists who have influenced the development of economics and implementation of economic theories. These include David Hume (1711–76), Thomas Robert Malthus (1766–1834), John Stuart Mill (1806–73), Jean Baptiste Say (1767–1832), and Jeffrey Sachs (1954–) who has an interest in development economics and poverty alleviation, author of *The End of Poverty*, and Joseph Stiglitz (1943–) former World Bank economist, Nobel Prize winner and author of *Globalisation and its Discontents*.

LEARNING OBJECTIVE 4
Discuss and illustrate the problem that scarcity poses for an economy

resources
inputs used in the production of goods and services for consumption to satisfy our needs and wants

scarcity
the relationship between unlimited needs and wants and the limited supply of resources available to satisfy those needs and wants

factors of production
the resources (land, labour, capital and sometimes enterprise) used to produce goods and services

land
any naturally occurring endowment that an economy has at its disposal

labour
any productive physical and mental activity

capital
any good used in the production process to produce other goods

enterprise
the ability to combine the three other factors of production to produce goods and services to satisfy consumption demands

SCARCITY

Every economy is endowed with what we call **resources**, which are inputs used in the production of goods and services for consumption to satisfy our needs and wants. The issue of **scarcity** is crucial in understanding economics. Our needs and wants are unlimited and we will never be able to completely and wholly satisfy them; but in any economy the level of resources and the ability to produce goods and services for consumption are limited. We inevitably have to make choices in the way we use our resources.

FACTORS OF PRODUCTION

These resources, or **factors of production** as they are often called in economic texts, are land, labour and capital. Sometimes, enterprise is included as a fourth factor of production.

Land

Land is defined as any naturally occurring endowment that an economy has at its disposal. This includes for example, soils, crops, mineral deposits, forests, ocean harvests, flora and fauna.

Labour

Labour is considered to be any productive physical and mental activity. Shop assistants, fast food workers, sales representatives, teachers, engineers and surgeons are all examples of the labour factor of production.

Capital

Capital is any good used in the production process to produce other goods. It includes commercial buildings like supermarkets, the car and mobile phone used by a sales representative, interactive whiteboards, classroom furniture and libraries used by teachers, computers used by engineers, and scalpels and operating theatres used by surgeons.

Capital is produced by combining land and labour.

Enterprise

Enterprise is the ability to combine the three other factors of production to produce goods and services to satisfy consumption demands. An entrepreneur, a chief executive officer of a corporation and a business manager all have special skills that are used to produce goods and services for a profit. Profit is the residual return to the entrepreneur after total costs have been deducted from revenue.

Characteristics of factors of production

These factors of production—land, labour, capital and enterprise—have some essential characteristics:

* They are scarce. At any point of time, there is a fixed, finite amount of the resource which is insufficient to satisfy the demands for it (see 'Applied questions and exercises—Hybrid cars' later in this chapter).
* They have alternative uses. Any factor of production can be used to satisfy needs and wants, but not at the same time. A choice among the alternatives becomes necessary. A building in the city could be used as office space, student residential

accommodation, expensive and exclusive apartments, or converted to a casino, a library, restaurants or an amusement arcade. It could be any one or all of these over time, but it cannot be all of them at the same time.

- The quantity of a resource varies. Countries have different amounts of resources, which affects production and consumption decisions. The quantity of resources is relatively fixed but it can change over time as new resources are discovered or populations increase. A country with a rising birth rate is in the long term increasing its labour resource, which will in turn place increased demands on other resources such as housing, education and health services.
- The quality of a resource varies. The productivity of resources can vary in different economies. The quality of resources can be altered through the application of new technology, education and training. Policies to encourage students to complete their secondary schooling and undertake tertiary studies are attempts to improve the quality of the labour resource.

A choice must be made by individuals and by societies in confronting the problem of limited resources but unlimited needs and wants.

NEEDS AND WANTS

Our **needs** are the things that are necessary for survival: food, shelter and clothing. The goods and services that supply them are basic and essential. Once our needs are satisfied, we turn to satisfying our **wants**, buying the more complex commodities that improve the quality of our lives.

Imagine a student with a limited income, who purchases generic brand food, lives in cheap rental accommodation, and buys clothes at chain stores. If the student experiences a sudden increase in income (inheritance, finishing study and getting a well-paid job) they will still satisfy their needs but will satisfy their wants (desires) as well. The former student may be able to now eat at restaurants, take out a mortgage on a house, and purchase expensive fashionable clothing by shopping at exclusive boutiques.

needs
things that are necessary for our survival: food, shelter and clothing

wants
more complex commodities that improve the quality of our lives

Characteristics of needs and wants

The importance of needs and wants is:

- They are unlimited. We will never completely satisfy all of our individual or society's needs and wants. There will always be a new model car, the latest fashions, and chic holiday destinations. Our needs and wants will always be with us and are limitless.
- They are recurrent. Some needs and wants are recurrent; they have to be satisfied again and again. Examples are coffee first thing in the morning (is this a need or want?), lunch every day, going out on Saturday nights.
- They are complementary. Satisfaction of some needs and wants requires the consumption of more than one good or service. In order to satisfy the want of listening to music, you must 'consume' both a compact disc and a compact disc player. Each product by itself is virtually useless. Additional examples are a mobile phone and SIM card, and petrol for a car.
- They change. An individual's needs and wants change over time. A 10-year-old has little interest in playing pool, drinking beer and listening to music in a noisy smoke-filled pub. But after eight years or so, their wants will have changed. A 28-year-old may be more interested in a well-paid job with good promotion prospects, purchasing

a house or apartment and building up an investment portfolio. So our needs and wants change over time as our experiences, expectations and abilities to satisfy them change. On retirement, a 60-year-old may be interested in holidays, cruise ships or playing golf and maximising their leisure time.

Satisfying needs and wants

The economic process of satisfying needs and wants has three steps: it uses resources in production, distribution and consumption (Figure 1.1).

Figure 1.1
The three-step process of satisfying needs and wants

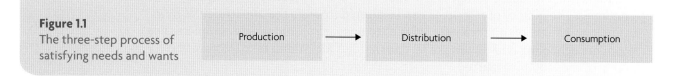

Production → Distribution → Consumption

Production

production
the process of combining the resources of land, labour, capital and enterprise to produce goods and services

Production is the process of combining the resources of land, labour, capital and enterprise to produce goods and services. Production can be labour-intensive, with a high ratio of labour to capital; or capital-intensive, with a high ratio of capital to labour. The choice depends on the amount of factors of production in the economy, the cost and availability of capital, the skill and education levels of labour, and the particular type of production taking place. A large, cheap, well-educated labour force may be a more profitable alternative than expensive technology and machinery.

Distribution

The resources and goods and services that have been produced have to be distributed to the people who want them. How goods and services are distributed is often highlighted as one of the key distinguishing characteristics of different types of economic systems (together with the ownership of resources) and it will be examined further in the next chapter.

Consumption

consumption
the process of using up goods and services

basic economic
problem
the questions of what to produce, how to produce and for whom to produce arise because of scarcity

Finally, the goods and services are consumed. This **consumption** raises questions of who should have access to the goods and services. With a finite level of resources, there must be some way of allocating the limited goods and services among the unlimited needs and wants of a society. The answer to this question will also be covered in the next chapter in more detail, but for now, let's say that various economic systems decide the issue of consumption by either allocating limited goods and services according to the price mechanism or through substantial government intervention as the two extremes.

LEARNING OBJECTIVE 5
Describe the three basic economic questions

THE BASIC ECONOMIC QUESTIONS AND OPPORTUNITY COST

Since resources are limited (scarcity) and wants are unlimited, we must choose how to make optimum economic use of resources. These choices that we make on a daily basis are attempts to solve the **basic economic problem(s)**.

WHAT TO PRODUCE

What needs and wants can be satisfied with scarce productive resources, all of which could be used to make a variety of alternative goods and services? What will be the composition of output? Who decides on what the final output of goods and services will be that an economy produces over a given period with given resources?

HOW TO PRODUCE

What is the desirable and economically 'best' method of production? The choice between capital-intensive and labour-intensive methods is determined by the quantity and quality of resources available in an economy.

For example, compare agricultural practices in Australia and Indonesia. Australia has tended to use capital-intensive processes because of the higher cost of labour and the greater efficiency of capital (machinery) over labour on large tracts of land. In Indonesia, where the plots of land are much smaller, labour is considerably cheaper and is used in preference to expensive and often inappropriate machinery. Another example may be to compare the costs of production in the TCF (textile, clothing and footwear) industries in Australia, relative to China. If you were a manufacturer of clothing garments, would you think it economically cheaper to produce garments in Australia or China?

FOR WHOM TO PRODUCE

Who should have access to the limited goods and services that are produced, and how does an economy allocate these limited goods and services?

For instance, given medical resources are limited, society must decide whether to provide them on the basis of need, or of ability to pay. Australia has a system whereby those who cannot afford to pay, but still have a need to access medical services, become part of the 'public health system' while those on higher incomes or with greater capacity to take out health insurance are part of the 'private health system'.

OPPORTUNITY COST

Every time a decision is made about production, distribution or consumption, there is a cost. However, economists use the term 'cost' in a special sense. The 'opportunity cost' as it is referred to in economics, is the economic consequence of any decision and highlights the nature of scarcity and choice (see Figure 1.2 overleaf).

Opportunity cost is the sacrifice, or forgone alternatives, in choosing to satisfy one need or want rather than another.

For example, assume you had $100 and spent it on dinner for two at a restaurant. To an accountant, the cost of the meal would be $100. To an economist, the cost is everything else you can no longer buy with that $100 because you spent it at a restaurant. The opportunity cost of the dinner was several CDs, reducing your credit card bill, enrolling in a short course, seeing five films, a night out at a nightclub with friends, saving the money, buying books, new clothes, going to the dentist or donating to charity.

This illustrates the concepts of scarcity (the limited amount of money), the need to make a choice, and the costs associated with the choice made. Every day such choices are made. How to get to university—you could drive, ride a bike, walk or catch public transport. Do you take lunch, buy it or go without? And if you buy it, what do you buy from the range of choices available?

opportunity cost
the sacrifice, or forgone alternatives, in choosing to satisfy one need or want rather than another

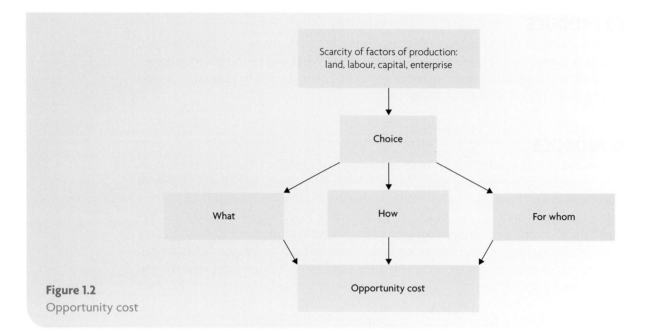

Figure 1.2
Opportunity cost

Another example is a large tract of forest: should it be conserved or logged? The opportunity cost of conservation is potential export income, the loss of timber workers' jobs, processed timber for housing, the use of cleared land for sporting fields etc. The opportunity cost of logging is the loss of an area for recreation for campers and bush-walkers, and potentially endangering native species of flora and fauna.

**LINK TO
BUSINESS**

DECISIONS, DECISIONS!

Assume you have recently come into some inheritance from a deceased aunt who left you A$20 000. You need to decide whether to take an overseas trip, pay off your credit card, or purchase a small portable coffee machine that enables you to fulfil your dreams of becoming a barista.

QUESTIONS
1. How will you decide which option to adopt?
2. What factors will you take into account in making your decision—for and against?
3. Identify some more opportunity costs of deciding to become a barista?

**LINK TO
INTERNATIONAL
ECONOMY**

WATER POWER

The Three Gorges Dam Project in Hubei Province in Central China is essentially a flood mitigation project to stop the annual flooding of the Yangtze River. But it also generates electricity.

Estimates indicate that the project which became commercially operational in 2008 is expected to generate 84.7 billion kilowatt hours of electricity per year. This is enough to power 18 cities of 1 million people. Operation of the project is expected to reduce China's consumption of imported coal by 50 million tonnes per year, thus reducing the discharge of 2 million tonnes of sulfur dioxide and 10 000 tonnes of carbon monoxide each year. Additional generators are to be installed by 2011. However, the project also sets records for the number of people displaced (more than 1.2 million), number of cities and towns flooded (13 cities, 140 towns, 1350 villages), and length of reservoir (more than 600 kilometres).

QUESTIONS
1. What factors of production are involved in building the Three Gorges Dam?
2. What needs and wants are being met by the project?
3. Explain the impact of the project on the question of 'how to produce electricity?'.
4. What are the opportunity costs of building the dam and shifting to hydro-electricity?
5. List two possible effects of the project on Australia (hint: one is to do with the ozone layer).

ILLUSTRATING SCARCITY: PRODUCTION POSSIBILITY THEORY

LEARNING OBJECTIVE 6
Illustrate the concept of scarcity using a production possibility frontier

In order to understand the workings of the economy, economists often employ models to illustrate a concept. The models are a simplified version of the real thing, and they are based on a set of (often unrealistic) assumptions.

Production possibility theory is the first model we examine, which demonstrates the problems of scarcity, choice and opportunity cost. We start with a **static analysis** of the production possibility model and proceed to **dynamic analysis**. The difference between the two models is the element of time. The static model assumes a fixed amount of resources at a given point in time, while the dynamic model allows for change over time.

static analysis
assumes a fixed amount of resources at a given point in time

dynamic analysis
assumes that the amount of resources will change over time

THE STATIC PRODUCTION POSSIBILITY MODEL
This static model analyses an economy at a fixed point in time and depends on five crucial assumptions:

1. There is a fixed quantity of resources.
2. The economy uses these resources to produce only two goods.
3. The resources can be used interchangeably to produce either good.
4. The economy uses all the resources; there are no resources left over.
5. Resources are used at maximum efficiency; there is no wastage, no idle capacity.

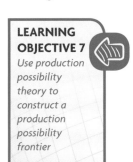

LEARNING OBJECTIVE 7
Use production possibility theory to construct a production possibility frontier

The **production possibility schedule** is a table that shows the various amounts of the two goods that can be produced, given the above assumptions. Ignore the unrealistic nature of the assumptions that an economy can produce only two commodities which both use the same inputs. Remember it is a simplified model used to illustrate a theory.

Table 1.1 overleaf shows the production possibilities. From the table we can see that, with a given quantity of inputs (factors of production), if the economy devoted all its resources to producing CD players, 800 CD players would be produced, but there would be no computers. This is shown as production possibility A. There are no computers because the fixed quantity of resources at our disposal cannot be used to produce both CD players and computers at the same time. It is one or the other   we need to make a choice and there will be an opportunity cost in any choice we make.

production possibility schedule
a table showing the various amounts of two goods that can be produced, given the five assumptions

Table 1.1   Production possibility schedule in a two-output economy

PRODUCT	A	B	C	D	E
Computers	0	100	200	300	400
CD players	800	600	400	200	0

Alternative production possibilities are indicated at output E, where this economy is producing 400 computers but no CD players. At production possibility D, 300 computers and 200 CD players are produced. In moving from point E to point D, we gained 200 CD players, but the opportunity cost of doing so was 100 computers.

If this economy reaches point C, but requires more CD players, it has to give up some computers to produce the additional CD players. Such is the nature of scarcity, choice and opportunity cost. The more we want of one product, the more we have to give up of the other product.

The production possibilities can be shown graphically and the maximum output levels are indicated by a line known as the **production possibility frontier** (sometimes referred to as the production possibility curve). The frontier shows the maximum efficient level of output combinations that are available to this economy with a finite level of resources. It also allows us to measure the opportunity cost of any economic decision. We place computers on the vertical axis and CD players on the horizontal axis (Figure 1.3).

production possibility frontier
a line indicating the maximum output levels on a production possibility graph (also known as the production possibility curve)

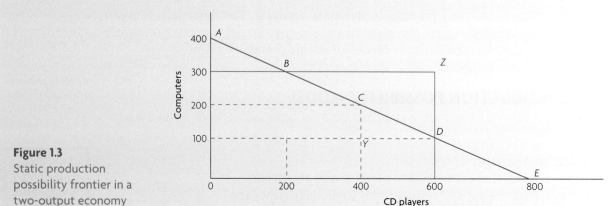

Figure 1.3
Static production possibility frontier in a two-output economy

Given our assumptions, the economy in static production possibility theory cannot produce unlimited outputs. Points such as Z are impossible with fixed resources and factors of production. Point Z shows a production possibility of 600 CD players and 300 computers.

However, if we were to produce 600 CD players, with limited resources we could only produce a maximum of 100 computers (point D). Alternatively if we were producing 300 computers, the maximum resources available allow 200 CD players to be produced, not the 600 indicated by point Z. So points outside the production possibility frontier are not possible using existing resources and technology.

If an economy is producing at a point within the production possibility curve, point Y, it is not producing at the most efficient level in order to maximise output. The economy is satisfying fewer needs and wants than it could be. Causes for the economy to be at Point Y could include unemployed or underemployed resources, and inefficient use of resources.

At point Y, this economy is producing 100 computers and 400 CD players, but if the decision was made to produce 100 computers it should be producing 600 CD players, or if it decided to produce 400 CD players it should produce 200 computers. Production at a point inside the frontier indicates that the economy has fewer goods than it could produce.

THE DYNAMIC PRODUCTION POSSIBILITY MODEL

This model allows for changes that occur in an economy's level of resources over time. We can therefore alter some of our earlier assumptions:

- The quantity of resources will change over time.
- We continue with the assumption that only two goods are produced.
- The resources can be used interchangeably to produce either good, but may be more efficient in producing one or the other.
- The economy uses all the resources; there are no resources left over.
- Resources are used at maximum efficiency, with no wastage or idle capacity.

For example, when populations increase, new resources are discovered, or new and better technology is applied to production we will see that the production possibility curve will shift. The quantity and quality of resources in every economy change over time and when this does occur, the production possibility curve will shift (Figure 1.4).

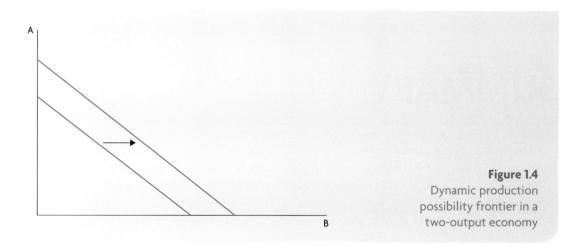

Figure 1.4
Dynamic production possibility frontier in a two-output economy

When the quantity and/or quality of resources increase over time, the economy can produce more goods and the entire curve shifts outwards. However, the opposite is also true. Over time resources are used up, or perhaps the birth rate falls; the available resources are reduced and the curve shifts inwards, indicating that fewer goods and services can be produced.

Note that a change in resources or technique of production may affect the production of one product only. In this case, the production possibility frontier shifts on one axis only (see Figure 1.5 overleaf).

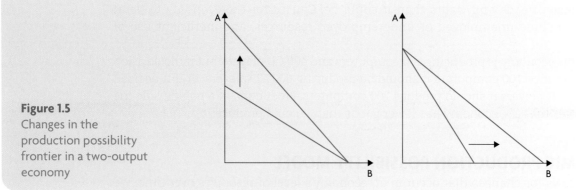

Figure 1.5
Changes in the production possibility frontier in a two-output economy

Production possibility theory illustrates that increasing levels of output enable greater levels of consumption and satisfaction of consumers' needs and wants.

Living standards are able to increase thanks to rising **productivity**, which is a measure of what can be produced for each hour of work. The main reasons for rising productivity are innovations and the use and application of technology. Between 1904 and 2004 Australia's production per hour worked grew by 1.8 per cent per year on average. Over 100 years this adds up to a 600 per cent increase. As a result of this growth in productivity Australians could enjoy shorter hours of work and more holidays or increased incomes and access to a larger range of goods and services as examples of the benefits of higher productivity.

productivity
a measure of what can be produced for each hour of work

SUMMARY

1. Chapter 1 introduced you to the basic economic concepts used by economists to understand issues relating to production, distribution and consumption.
2. The key issue is to try to satisfy unlimited needs and wants in an economy when there are limited or finite resources available.
3. The problem of scarcity forces us to make a choice, and every choice we make imposes costs known as opportunity costs.
4. The three basic economic questions that every economy tries to solve, given limited resources and unlimited wants, are:
   (a) what to produce
   (b) how to produce
   (c) for whom to produce.
5. Scarcity and choice are presented in a simple model known as production possibility theory, which illustrates the range of choices that a two-output economy can make to produce maximum outputs.
6. Production possibility theory was introduced using both static and dynamic assumptions to illustrate a range of situations inside and outside the frontier.

KEY TERMS

basic economic problem	8	labour	6	productivity	14
capital	6	land	6	resources	6
consumption	8	needs	7	scarcity	6
dynamic analysis	11	opportunity cost	9	static analysis	11
enterprise	6	production	8	wants	7
factors of production	6	production possibility frontier	12		
		production possibility schedule	11		

REVIEW QUESTIONS

1. What is economics a study of?
2. Using examples, explain the following terms:
   (a) land
   (b) labour
   (c) capital
   (d) enterprise.
3. What is the difference between needs and wants?
4. What differences can you highlight between microeconomics and macroeconomics?
5. Look at how your needs and wants have changed over time. List your needs and wants five years ago and what you anticipate they will be in five years time.
6. If resources are limited but our wants are unlimited, can we ever be economically 'happy'?
7. How do accountants and economists differ in their concepts of 'cost'?
8. What is the opportunity cost of reading this textbook?
9. Can you think of examples of a good where there is no opportunity cost?
10. Is pollution a scarce good?
11. How does an economy like Australia's solve the basic economic question(s) of What, How and For whom?
12. List three economic decisions involving choices you have made today.
13. Why is scarcity fundamental in a study of economics?
14. Why does a point inside the production possibility frontier represent unemployment?
15. What factors in a dynamic production possibility curve will allow the curve to shift outwards over time?
16. Describe the essential characteristics of the factors of production.
17. Describe the production processes involved in the operation of a fast food outlet.
18. Assume you are alone on an island and that for every hour you work, you can collect either one fish or two coconuts.
   (a) Draw your production possibility frontier based on working eight hours per day.
   (b) What is the opportunity cost of two coconuts?
   (c) Assume you take two hours off to make a ladder so now you can collect four coconuts per hour. Describe what you have done in terms of your dynamic production possibility frontier using the correct economic terminology.
   (d) What was the opportunity cost of building the ladder?
   (e) What has happened to your productivity?
   (f) What choices do you now have that you did not have before?

APPLIED QUESTIONS AND EXERCISES

HYBRID CARS

Most hybrid vehicles use an internal combustion engine alongside a battery-operated electric system as an alternative source of power. Hybrid technology is environmentally friendly, but that does not necessarily mean it is always the best option for the consumer.

PROS

- Environmentally friendly: hybrid cars have lower emissions of greenhouse gases and have less impact on the environment.
- Lower operating costs: due to increasing petrol prices batteries and alternate sources of power are a cheaper option.
- Efficient performance: hybrid cars perform better than petrol-powered cars because they use two sources of power. There is an internal combustion engine for slower speeds and an electrical system for faster speeds.
- Government incentives: some governments around the world have implemented schemes to encourage consumers to purchase hybrid cars instead of petrol-run cars.

CONS

- Cost: hybrid cars are expensive and require a high initial investment due to costly batteries and having two engines.

- High-risk batteries: costly high-voltage batteries can be dangerous, especially in accidents.

Source: Naik, Abijit, 'Hybrid Cars Pros and Cons' <www.buzzle.com/articles/hybrid-cars-pros-and-cons.html>, accessed 4 November 2010.

QUESTIONS

1. What factors of production are involved in the construction, purchase and use of hybrid cars?
2. Explain the concept of scarcity and how it relates to the example above.
3. What social needs and wants are implied?
4. What is produced by using conventional cars, not a hybrid variety?
5. Explain the opportunity costs arising from purchasing a more expensive hybrid car over a conventional car.

BLUNDSTONE FACTORY TO CLOSE

In January 2007 it was reported in the Tasmanian *Mercury* that the Blundstone boot factory in Hobart would close with production shifting offshore to Thailand and India. The major reason offered was that price increases in raw materials, for example, fuel and labour, together with inflation and decreasing tariffs made it unprofitable for the company to continue to operate in Australia. Rising production costs and an inability to pass this on to the consumer led to the closure.

QUESTIONS

Your answers to questions 1 and 2 should refer to the concepts of factors of production, needs and wants, and the basic economic questions.

1. Why has Blundstone decided to close down Australian operations in favour of overseas manufacturing?
2. What impact will shifting manufacturing offshore have on the consumer?
3. What is the opportunity cost of using manufacturing machinery to produce the boots instead of local labour in Hobart?
4. Explain the impact at a national level of the overseas manufacture of Blundstone Work Boots in terms of the dynamic production possibility model.

Chapter 2

Economic systems

LEARNING OBJECTIVES

After studying this chapter, you will be able to:

1. explain why scarcity is common to all economic systems
2. describe different economic systems and how they attempt to overcome the problem of scarcity
3. discuss the distinguishing characteristics of market-based and centrally-planned economic systems
4. identify different forms of ownership of economic resources
5. identify different allocative mechanisms
6. describe the distinguishing features of economies in transition from centrally-planned to market-based economies.

INTRODUCTION

economic system
the way a nation organises its economic activities to solve the issue of scarcity and the basic economic problems

An **economic system** is the way a nation organises its economic activities to solve the issue of scarcity and the basic economic problems of what to produce, how to produce and for whom to produce. Although every economy is faced with scarcity of resources, different economic systems develop and adopt different methods to overcome scarcity and maximise the economic welfare of the society.

The two economic systems presented in this chapter are a market economy and a centrally-planned economy. These are theoretical models: in reality, most economic systems are mixed economic systems, displaying some of the characteristics of both market and centrally-planned economies. Since the 1980s many former centrally-planned economies have adopted a more market-oriented structure as a result of disappointing economic performance. These are known as emerging market economies or transition economies such as those found in eastern Europe.

Economic systems are distinguished from each other according to their methods of organising economic activities, the extent of government intervention into the economy, the ownership of the factors of production, and the means of allocating goods and services throughout the economy.

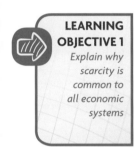

LEARNING OBJECTIVE 1
Explain why scarcity is common to all economic systems

SCARCITY AND ECONOMIC SYSTEMS

Chapter 1 showed that every economy faces the problem of scarcity of resources (factors of production). Despite the limited amounts of resources available, our wants are unlimited and so we must make a choice about which needs and wants will be satisfied and how we go about this. The methods of solving the basic economic problems create an economic system.

Every economic system attempts to operate on the production possibility frontier to maximise the output and welfare of the economy and its individuals. Moreover, economic systems are attempting to extend the production possibility frontier in order to increase the welfare of the society. As we know from Chapter 1, any economic decision imposes an opportunity cost. Any attempt to produce more of one commodity can only be gained by producing less of another.

The choices that are made and how they are made is the essence that distinguishes economic systems. Economic decision making attempts to promote economic welfare and wellbeing. How is this best achieved?

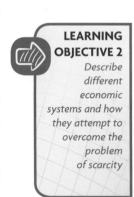

LEARNING OBJECTIVE 2
Describe different economic systems and how they attempt to overcome the problem of scarcity

- Supporters of a market economic system believe it is best achieved by maximising individual liberty and economic freedom. It is a system that emphasises efficiency over equity, and rewards individual effort.
- Supporters of a centrally-planned economy believe it is best achieved through the active economic intervention of the government. In the trade-off between efficiency of the system and equitable distribution and consumption of the goods and services that are produced, equity prevails.

The choice of an economic system is as much political as economic. It is an expression of the society's values. Which system is better? The answer rests on your values and what you think is important.

THE MARKET ECONOMIC SYSTEM

LEARNING OBJECTIVE 3
Discuss the distinguishing characteristics of market-based and centrally-planned economic systems

A **market economy** is also referred to as a capitalist economy or private enterprise economic system.

The reasons for the term 'market economy' are evident. A market is where buying, selling and exchange take place; so a market economy allocates resources and distribution of goods and services (buying, selling and exchange) throughout the economy with minimal control and regulation.

The five key elements that distinguish a market economy from other types of economic systems are:

1. The factors of production are in private ownership.
2. Economic decision making is decentralised.
3. Economic motivation is self-interest (profit for companies, utility (or satisfaction) for consumers).
4. The allocative mechanism is price.
5. Efficiency is valued over equity.

Remember, though, that we are describing a pure market economy; in the real world few economies approach this extreme as there will be state ownership of resources, government economic activity and not all goods are allocated simply through the price mechanism.

market economy
an economy where resources are allocated and goods and services distributed with minimal control and regulation

LEARNING OBJECTIVE 4
Identify different forms of ownership of economic resources

PRIVATE OWNERSHIP

In a market economy the individual is free to own land and capital resources, and buy and sell the factors of production—land, labour, capital and enterprise. Individuals are considered to own their own labour, which they can sell for a wage if they desire. The **private ownership** of economic resources and the factors of production can be passed on to future generations, sold to overseas buyers or used (or not used) for any purpose the owner decides. There is no government directive on resource use which is entirely the individual's decision (within legal limits of course).

The reason behind this high level of individualism is that individuals are considered the best judge of their own welfare. Individuals are thought to be able to make the best decisions on how to use or dispose of their resources, including decisions such as whether to sell their labour (be employed), for how much (a wage) and for how long (the opportunity cost and trade-off between work and leisure).

private ownership
the factors of production can be possessed by individuals as their private property (the evidence of which is a legal title) and others can be denied the use of these assets

DECENTRALISED DECISIONS

In the extreme form of market economy, economic decision making is left to the individual. There is no government intervention in the market, and all economic **decisions are decentralised**. The role of the state is restricted to providing a legal system and enforcing the

decentralised decisions
decision making is left to the individual and there is no government intervention in the market

law, national security, and administering a framework by which trade and commerce can take place within the market.

For example, such a state would not set minimum wage levels. The employers, the buyers of labour, would have to offer a sufficient wage to the sellers of labour to induce them to work. If the wage that was offered was too low, people would value their leisure over work; employers would have to improve their offer to get people to work. (Overtime, for example, is paid at a higher hourly rate as a reward and incentive from employers to employees.)

SELF-INTEREST

self-interest
maximising individual economic welfare at the expense of any attempts to directly maximise collective welfare

The third distinguishing element of the market economy is that the individual is economically driven and motivated through the pursuit of **self-interest**. Maximising individual economic welfare is at the expense of any attempts to directly maximise collective welfare. Market economists assert that maximising individual welfare will ensure collective welfare is achieved as a consequence.

profit
revenue minus cost

The economic motivation for producers is **profit**. They produce and sell goods and services, using the factors of production available to them, for more than it cost to produce. This profit (revenue minus cost) is theirs to spend, save or use to generate more goods and services and (hopefully) produce more profit.

utility
the satisfaction provided through goods and services

The consumer is motivated by what economists call **utility** or satisfaction. Goods and services are purchased because they provide the consumer with utility. But consumers' ability to purchase is constrained by their level of income. The more goods and services you wish to purchase, the more income you need, which generally means selling more labour, which will mean less time to consume the goods and services you wish to purchase. It is a case of scarcity and opportunity cost once again.

LEARNING OBJECTIVE 5
Identify different allocative mechanisms

ALLOCATION BY PRICE

price
a means of allocating limited goods and services among unlimited wants according to consumers' ability to purchase

Price is a reliable, efficient and non-interventionist means of allocating limited goods and services among unlimited wants. Perhaps everyone would like to own the latest model BMW for example, but the car company cannot produce enough cars for everyone. It must allocate its limited and scarce resources (the number of cars produced) among our unlimited demands. Price is the allocative mechanism used. If you have the means to purchase the car, and wish to do so, and there is one available, then you purchase the car. The price system is a method of allocating the scarce commodity to a restricted number of consumers. Alternatives to allocating scarce numbers of cars amongst competing consumer demand could be to hold a lottery or form a queue (first come, first served).

EFFICIENCY IS VALUED

efficiency
means using resources to produce the goods and services on which we place the highest value

Finally, because individuals are motivated by self-interest and attempt to maximise their individual welfare, they are more efficient in their economic decision making. Production decisions are based on efficiency outcomes to produce greater profits. Consumption decisions are also driven by concerns of **efficiency** and the need to get the best return on expenditure.

THE COMMAND ECONOMIC SYSTEM

A command economic system is radically different from a market economy. A **command economy** is also called a centrally-planned economy. Currently the only true command economies are perhaps Cuba, Myanmar (Burma) and North Korea while previously The People's Republic of China, Vietnam and the former Soviet Union would have been characterised under this system. Table 2.1 shows how such economies differ from market economies but even in these countries' economies, there are market economic aspects.

In a command economy, the allocation of resources and distribution of goods and services—in fact, all economic decision making—is planned and managed by a central planning authority.

By way of contrast, the five key elements which distinguish a command economy from other types of economic systems are:

1. The means of production are in state ownership.
2. Economic decision making is centralised.
3. Economic motivation is collective welfare.
4. Allocative mechanisms other than price (non-price) are used.
5. Equity is valued over efficiency.

command (centrally-planned) economy
all economic decision making is planned and managed by a central planning authority

Table 2.1 **Characteristics that distinguish market and command economies**

CHARACTERISTIC	MARKET ECONOMY	COMMAND ECONOMY
Resource ownership	Individual	The state
Economic decision making	Individual buyers and sellers (decentralised)	State planning authorities (centralised)
Economic motivation	Self-interest (profit and utility)	Collective welfare
Allocative mechanism	Price	Queues
Economic priority	Efficiency	Equity

state ownership
in a command economy, the state owns the productive resources

STATE OWNERSHIP

In a command economy the state owns the productive resources. **State ownership** means that the government owns the land and capital factors of production, and it directs labour to work in designated occupations, producing goods and services deemed necessary for maximising state economic welfare. Individuals are not free to own, buy or sell the factors of production.

In the absence of private ownership, the state provides essential commodities, for example housing, transport, medical services etc which are allocated to the members of the society.

LEARNING OBJECTIVE 4
Identify different forms of ownership of economic resources

CENTRALISED DECISIONS

All economic **decisions are centralised** in the hands of the central planning authorities. Output and prices are not determined by the interactions of buyers and sellers, but by the state authorities. The authorities decide the goods and services that will be produced and

centralised decisions
all economic decisions are handled by the central planning authorities

which factors of production will be used. They set quotas for production and wage rates, and individuals cannot negotiate higher salaries. Food prices are fixed by the state planners, especially for essential commodities. Economic life appears to be regulated, ordered and secure, with the state guaranteeing employment and equal access to goods and services.

COLLECTIVE WELFARE

collective welfare
the state decides which goods and services will be produced and allocates them equitably among the members of the economy as a whole

The third distinguishing characteristic of a command economy is that the economic motivation of society and the planning authorities is to maximise **collective welfare** over individual welfare. Central planners believe that an economic system motivated by the pursuit of self-interest will maximise the welfare of some individuals at the expense of others and the greater society as a whole. The state decides which goods and services will be produced and allocates them equitably among the members of the economy as a whole, rather than individually. An individual's level of income should not be a deciding factor in their ability to purchase goods and services.

> **LEARNING OBJECTIVE 5**
> *Identify different allocative mechanisms*

ALLOCATION BY NON-PRICE MECHANISMS

A command economy uses **non-price allocative mechanisms** to distribute a limited amount of goods and services among unlimited wants. While a market economy produces, for example, a wide variety of cars to satisfy many desires, wants, income levels and abilities to purchase, a command economy tends to produce a cheaper generic item that might be available to everyone if they are prepared to wait long enough.

non-price allocative mechanisms
distributing a limited amount of goods and services among unlimited wants through means other than price (e.g. making people wait in line for them)

If cheap basic goods are given priority over luxuries, more commodities can be produced with scarce resources and hence satisfy more consumer demands. The range of choices is restricted, but the ability to satisfy demand is increased.

A typical allocative mechanism is queuing; it does not matter whether you are a labourer or a surgeon, the same product is supplied at the same price if you are prepared to spend time queuing for it.

EQUITY IS VALUED

equity
the equal distribution of goods and services to all members of a command economy

The final distinguishing element is a belief in the equitable distribution of goods and services to all members of the economy. But **equity** and collective welfare are achieved at a cost of efficiency. To take the example of queuing, highly productive workers waste time standing in a queue instead of producing more goods and services.

THE NORTH KOREAN ECONOMY

LINK TO INTERNATIONAL ECONOMY

North Korea is one of the world's most centrally-planned and least open economies and faces myriad chronic economic problems. These problems are compounded by severe food shortages since floods in 2007, lack of arable land, inefficient collective farming practices, and shortages in fuel. In a departure from strict economic control, in 2002 the government permitted limited private farmers' markets to sell some commodities and private farming to boost agricultural production. These policies were reversed in 2005 and a centralised food rationing system was reintroduced.

South Korea has predicted that North Korea's economy will shrink again due to trade sanctions that could force the country into crisis. It estimates that North Korea has posted economic growth in only one year of the past five and it still struggles with severe food shortages.

QUESTIONS

1. Describe the costs and benefits of loosening government control over private farmers' markets and practices.
2. List some of the benefits that could be provided through reducing military expenditure in North Korea.
3. Why do you think centrally-planned economies are inherently inefficient at producing goods and services that satisfy people's needs and wants?

THE MIXED ECONOMY

Nowadays there are no pure market economies or command economies. Most countries have mixed economies, which combine elements of market forces with state intervention and planning to varying proportions. A **mixed economy** can be defined as a market economy in which both private sector firms and firms owned by the government take part in economic activity. The proportions of public and private enterprise in the mix vary widely between countries. Since the 1980s the public role in most mixed economies has declined as privatisation of public entities has been pursued by many governments.[1]

The Australian economy leans more towards pure capitalism over central planning but has important differences. In Australia, the government plays an important role in promoting economic stability and growth, in providing certain goods and services that would be underproduced or not produced at all by the market system, and in modifying the distribution of income.[2] A comparison of tax collections in Australia when social security contributions are included, with other OECD countries showed that the tax burden in Australia in 2007 was 33.3 per cent of gross domestic product (GDP) compared to an OECD average of 35.8 per cent. This is lower than in most transition economies and in some Western economies with higher levels of central planning (sometimes referred to as 'socialist' economies) such as Sweden (2007—48.3 per cent) and Denmark (2007—48.7 per cent). At the same time, the share of the Australian Government's taxation in GDP is higher than the corresponding indicator in economies with less interventionist governments such as the United States and Japan, both 28.3 per cent in 2007.[3, 4]

Jackson and McIver noted that private ownership and reliance on the market system do not always go together, nor do central planning and public ownership.[5] Such historical exceptions have been provided by **National Socialism** in Germany under Hitler, the former Yugoslav economy and post-World War II Sweden. Nazi Germany's economic system has been called variously national socialism or **authoritarian capitalism**, characterised by a high degree of government control and direction combined with private ownership of resources.

Yugoslavia's **market socialism** was characterised by public ownership of resources, coupled with increasing reliance on market forces to coordinate economic activity. Sweden's government has a high degree of intervention in stabilising economic activity and in redistributing income, while around four-fifths of economic activity is conducted in the private sector.

mixed economy
a market economy in which both private sector firms and firms owned by the government take part in economic activity

National Socialism
a right wing political ideology that tried to amalgamate elements of both left- and right-wing ideologies into an economic and political structure

authoritarian capitalism
an economic system that has a high degree of government control and direction combined with private ownership of resources

market socialism
an economic system that combines public ownership of resources with increasing reliance on market forces to coordinate economic activity

LEARNING OBJECTIVE 6

Describe the distinguishing features of economies in transition from centrally-planned to market-based economies

emerging market economies
economies in a process of transition from being command economies to being more market-oriented in their approach to answering the basic economic questions

EMERGING MARKET ECONOMIES

Since the 1980s many countries have chosen to shift their economic systems to a more market-oriented approach in pursuit of more rapid economic growth and higher living standards. Many countries that were part of or under the influence of the former Soviet Union have chosen to change their economic systems.

Emerging market economies include current and former command economies in Europe and East Asia. The International Monetary Fund (IMF) describes emerging market economies as transition economies, classifying them in the following groups:[6]

- Transition economies in Europe and the former Soviet Union:

    — Central and Eastern Europe (CEE): Albania, Bulgaria, Croatia, Czech Republic, Macedonia, Hungary, Poland, Romania, Slovak Republic, Slovenia.
    — Baltics: Estonia, Latvia, Lithuania.
    — Commonwealth Independent States (CIS): Armenia, Azerbaijan, Belarus, Georgia, Kazakhstan, Kyrgyz Republic, Moldova, Russia, Tajikistan, Turkmenistan, Ukraine, Uzbekistan.

- Transition economies in Asia: Cambodia, China, Laos, Vietnam.

The IMF and various economists such as Pugel[7] and Fisher and Gelb,[8] have generally agreed on the main steps required in the transition process:[9]

- *Liberalisation.* The process of allowing most prices to be determined in free markets and lowering trade barriers that had shut off contact with the price structure of the world's market economies.
- *Macroeconomic stabilisation.* Primarily the process of bringing inflation under control and having it lowered over time, after the initial burst of high inflation that follows from liberalisation. This process requires discipline in fiscal and monetary policy and progress toward sustainable balance of payments.
- *Restructuring and privatisation.* The processes of creating a viable financial sector and reforming the enterprises in these economies to render them capable of producing goods that could be sold in free markets and of transferring their ownership into private hands.
- *Legal reform.* Establishing a legal system with contract laws, property rights and appropriate competition policies.

The general belief was that liberalisation and macroeconomic stabilisation could be undertaken fairly quickly along with the privatisation of small-scale enterprises. At the same time, it was expected that the privatisation of large-scale enterprises and legal institutional reforms would intensify at a later stage and take a longer time.

Different approaches to transition

Countries such as Poland and the Czech Republic adopted a 'shock therapy' approach to the transition to a market-oriented economy. This approach included:

- rapid price and trade liberalisation, accompanied by a determined stabilisation program to restore or maintain price stability
- the immediate opening of markets
- privatisation of most state-owned companies
- reform of the tax system, legal system, the financial sector, and the civil sector.

MANUFACTURING IN CHINA

China began opening its economy to the outside world in 1978. Since then some 200 million people have been raised out of poverty and a substantial middle class has developed. The reserve army of underemployed agricultural labour is slowly being absorbed into manufacturing industries as China develops its low-cost labour advantage in global supply chains. In 2002, 50 per cent of the parts needed by General Motors and Ford globally were manufactured in China.[10]

LINK TO INTERNATIONAL ECONOMY

QUESTIONS

With 1.2 billion people, China represents a potential market for many manufactured goods.

1. Why have Ford and General Motors established manufacturing plants in China?
2. Why has the Chinese Government supported the development of manufacturing in China?
3. If you were considering in which country to establish a car manufacturing plant, what factors would you take into account in making a choice between Australia and China?

The Czech Republic's ex-President Vaclav Havel said, 'It is impossible to cross a chasm in two leaps'.

In contrast, China has taken a much more cautious approach because of the need to limit the negative effects of introducing market forces to previously protected parts of the economy and society. China's former leader Deng Xiao-Ping described this approach as 'feeling the stones to cross the river'.

FREE MARKET OR GOVERNMENT INTERVENTION

One way of defining a type of economic system is by the extent of government involvement. Those who value the efficiency of an economic system over equity have a strong conviction and preference for the free market; they believe that government should minimise its intervention in the economy to select functions that only the government can provide. Free marketeers believe that the free, unfettered market will fulfil economic functions and provide maximum individual, collective and economic welfare.

Other economists, called interventionists, see a much wider role for government to assist in and regulate resource allocation, ownership of production and distribution of goods and services. They insist that the government is better equipped, and less encumbered by the pursuit of self-interest, to decide where and how resources should be directed, what production levels should be and who should share in the benefits of production.

WHICH SYSTEM IS BEST?

This question has interested economists, economic planners, politicians and others for many years. It is best answered with more questions. How do we measure 'best'? What criteria do we use to judge 'best'? Each system has advantages and disadvantages, and the answer depends on what the society thinks is important—its values.

POLAND—EUROPE'S 'STAR' TRANSITION ECONOMY

LINK TO
INTERNATIONAL
ECONOMY

Poland, a former centrally-planned economy, has pursued a policy of economic liberalisation since 1990 and today stands out as a success story among transition economies. Poland joined the European Union in 2004, and it is also a member of the WTO, OECD and NATO.

From 1990 to 2000 Poland's economy grew at an average annual rate of 4.7 per cent, and from 2000 to 2008 at an average rate of 4.4 per cent (the corresponding growth rates for the Euro area were 2.1 and 2.8 per cent). One should note that during the recent global financial crisis, Poland has been the only OECD member economy, other than Australia, to avoid a recession.

As a result of strong economic growth, Poland's GDP per capita (PPP) grew from US$5250 in December 1991 to US$17 275 in December 2008, but it is still only around half the level of the Euro area. Poland's inflation in recent years has been kept under control, varying between a high of 4.8 per cent in August 2008 and a low of 2 per cent in August 2010. From 1990 until August 2010, Poland's unemployment rate averaged 13.80 per cent.

According to Trading Economics consultants, from 1998 until 2010, Poland's average benchmark interest rate was 9.04 per cent reaching an historical high of 24 per cent in March of 1998 and a record low of 3.50 per cent in June 2009.

Poland had a government budget deficit in 2008 equivalent to 3.71 per cent of the gross domestic product (GDP).

The solid growth of the Polish economy is attributed by economic analysts to rising private consumption, a jump in corporate investment, good macroeconomic management and European Union funds. Since 2004, European Union membership and access to European Union structural funds have provided a major boost to the economy.

MARKET SYSTEMS
Advantages

- Individuals can judge their own activities. They are best able to decide when to work, how much to work, how often, and for what remuneration.
- Individuals can decide how to dispose of their own income.
- By avoiding state intervention in the economy, the market system avoids introducing inefficiencies into the system, which impose an economic cost on the individual and hence on society.
- The state must secure some of the individual's income through taxation to support its bureaucracy. By minimising state intervention, the economy minimises the amount spent on administration and hence maximises individual welfare.
- A market system, driven by profit and utility, will develop the most efficient means of producing, distributing and consuming goods and services.

Disadvantages

- Market systems create inequalities of wealth and lead to a concentration of market power in select groups.
- Market power results in exploitation of the economically poorer and less powerful.
- Often individuals do not know what is best for them.

- Disadvantaged groups—migrants from a non-English speaking background, single parents, youth, long-term unemployed, those lacking desired skills and educational qualifications—are unfairly treated by a market economic system.
- Inherited wealth is not based on economic considerations such as skill and entrepreneurial ability and is unfair.

COMMAND ECONOMY
Advantages

- Abundant provision of collective goods such as education, health, public transport and recreational facilities.
- The government provides employment security.
- Everyone is given equal opportunity and not disadvantaged because of lack of wealth.
- Wasteful competition can be avoided.

Disadvantages

- The system is grossly inefficient and wastes vast amounts of output through inefficiency, poor planning and bottlenecks in production.
- Decision making is cumbersome when it is not motivated by profit.
- Allocating goods and services by means such as queuing is a waste of human resources.
- There is a lack of financial incentives for workers and entrepreneurs.
- The system does not respond quickly to shocks.

ONE PRODUCER, ONE PRODUCT: WHO BENEFITS?

As you will see in your study of economics, in theory the most efficient way of producing a product, let's say breakfast cereal, is to have one producer (a 'monopolist') producing one product, provided that the producer operates with the interests of consumers as a top priority. In some countries governments create monopolies by providing licences to favoured groups of producers. Frequently these favoured groups are related to, or are business friends of, those in government.

LINK TO
BUSINESS

QUESTIONS
1. Compare the relative power of consumers in a command economy and a market economy. Can you think of any examples?
2. Describe how governments in a command economy and a market economy would deal with a monopoly to ensure that the interests of consumers are protected.
3. Would you expect a monopolist in the breakfast cereal example above to act in the best interest of consumers or the monopolist?
4. Is there anything wrong with government providing a licence to create a monopoly to a relative or business friend if the welfare of consumers is maintained?

SUMMARY

1. All economies are constrained by scarcity and the need to make a choice in economic decisions. As a result, different economic systems have evolved specific characteristics that distinguish different types of economic systems.
2. The two main models of economic systems are termed market and command economies. In fact, nearly all economies are mixed: they display characteristics of both market and command economies. Five key elements are applied to distinguish between the two theoretical models.
3. In the 1990s there was a massive transition by command economies towards a more market-oriented economic structure. These economies can be described as emerging market economies.
4. No economic system is 'good' or 'bad'. Our evaluation of an economic system depends on the criteria that we use to assess its performance.

KEY TERMS

authoritarian capitalism	23	efficiency	20	non-price allocative mechanisms	22
centralised decisions	21	emerging market economies	24	price	20
collective welfare	22	equity	22	private ownership	19
command economy	21	market economy	19	profit	20
decentralised decisions	19	market socialism	23	self-interest	20
economic system	18	mixed economy	23	state ownership	21
		National Socialism	23	utility	20

REFERENCES

1. Charles W. Hill, *International Business*, International edn, McGraw-Hill-Irwin, New York, United States, 2004.
2. See <www.apsc.gov.au/annualreport/0809/index.html>, accessed 4 November 2010, for the Annual Australian Public Service Report which details financial arrangements and key sectors where the APS is intricately involved in the Australian economy.
3. Philip Lewis, Anne Garnett, Kim Hawtrey and Malcolm Treadgold, *Issues, Indicators and Ideas: A Guide to the Australian Economy*, Pearson Education Australia Pty Limited, South Melbourne, 2003.
4. <www.oecd.org/document/60/0,3343,en_2649_34533_1942460_1_1_1_1,00.html#tbw>, accessed 4 November 2010.
5. John Jackson and Ron McIver, *Macroeconomics*, 7th edn, McGraw-Hill Australia, Sydney, 2004.
6. International Monetary Fund, *IMF Transition Economies: An IMF Perspective on Progress and Prospects*, 3 November 2000, <www.imf.org/external/np/exr/ib/2000/110300.htm#I>, accessed 4 November 2010.
7. T.A. Pugel, *International Economics*, 12th edn, McGraw-Hill-Irwin, New York, United States, 2004.
8. Stanley Fischer and Alan Gelb, 'Issues in socialist economy reform', *Journal of Economic Perspectives*, 5, 1991, pp. 91–105.
9. Based on International Monetary Fund, *IMF Transition Economies: An IMF Perspective on Progress and Prospects*, 3 November 2000, <www.imf.org/external/np/exr/ib/2000/110300.htm#I>, accessed 4 November 2010.
10. Ming Zeng and Peter J. Williamson, 'The Hidden Dragons', *Harvard Business Review*, October 2003.

REVIEW QUESTIONS

1. How would you describe a market economy?
2. What distinguishes a market economy from a command economy?
3. Is there a role for government intervention in the Australian economy?
4. Can you identify other distinguishing elements in economic systems?
5. Briefly consider the economies of France, North Korea, South Korea, Brunei, Switzerland, Cuba, Poland, Denmark and Mongolia. What type of economic system would you classify them as?
6. Can you envisage an economy where the government owns resources and produces the goods and services for the economy while the market coordinates the economic system? Justify your answer.

7. In what circumstances would a market economy be considered ineffective?

8. Research question: See what you can find on the internet about the economic performance of an emerging market economy such as China, Vietnam, Hungary or the Czech Republic.

9. According to research by the IMF and various economists, which of the following measures is *not* a required feature of the process of transition from a command economy to a market-based one?
   (a) liberalisation of most prices
   (b) immediate lowering of inflation
   (c) restructuring of the financial sector
   (d) reform of the legal system (e.g. contract laws, property rights).

10. List the areas of government involvement in the Australian economy.

11. What have been the advantages to consumers of selling previously government-owned enterprises in Australia?

12. Are there areas where you think there should be more, or less, government intervention? Why?

13. Often a by-product of manufacturing or other economic activity is the generation of pollution. Can pollution be controlled with more or less government intervention?

14. Construct a table to show additional advantages and disadvantages of the two different types of economic systems.
   (a) How many of your criteria involve value judgments?
   (b) Is it possible to assess an economic system without making value judgments?

APPLIED QUESTIONS AND EXERCISES
DEREGULATION OF STATE-OWNED ENTERPRISES
NEW ENERGY MARKET AFTER DEREGULATION

When the Western Australian Government reformed the way electricity was generated and distributed, a new wholesale electricity market was established.

The aim of the reforms was to offer consumers a choice of competitively priced energy products and services, and to attract private investment into the market. Under this deregulation, the state's electricity assets would continue to be owned by the government.

To foster competition, Western Australia's primary electricity business, Western Power, was separated into four businesses.

1. Verve Energy—generation business producing electricity at power stations and supplying this electricity to retailers.

2. Synergy—retail business purchasing electricity from suppliers and selling it to customers.

3. Western Power—networks business managing the distribution of electricity from suppliers to consumers.

4. Horizon Power—regional business responsible for all of the functions of generating or procuring, transmitting and retailing electricity to customers.

The deregulation allowed competing generators to offer electricity into a market for sale to retailers who in turn purchased electricity for their customers.

The purpose of competition was to bring more choices for consumers, including innovative solutions.

Source: <www.verveenergy.com.au/subContent/homePageInfo/ electricityMarket/energyDeregulation.html>, accessed 4 November 2010.

QUESTIONS

1. Why did Western Australia want to deregulate the energy sector and state-owned enterprises?

2. Who benefits from the industry deregulation of the energy market?

3. Do you think state ownership of economically productive resources and essential services should be controlled by the state or be in the hands of the private sector?

4. Could private ownership generate greater efficiency and profits for the purchaser? How?

5. An area of similarity between modern mixed market and command economies is the role that the state plays in the welfare of the citizens.
   (a) What areas of welfare are provided by the state?
   (b) How does the state in a market economy pay for its welfare programs?
   (c) What areas of welfare could be provided by the private sector?

CUBA

Cuba is an example of a country with strong state-backed regulation of the economy. However, in recent years there has been a slight loosening of control to increase economic and enterprise efficiency in an attempt to alleviate serious shortages of consumer goods and services. Despite these new changes, Cuba still struggles to improve living standards as measured by GDP per capita. The UNDP Human Development Index ranks Cuba at 95 out of 182 countries with GDP per capita at US$6876.

Since the 1990s, there has been a loss of Soviet aid which has compounded production difficulties. Since late 2000, Venezuela has been providing oil on preferential terms and Cuba has been paying for the oil, in part, with the services of Cuban personnel in Venezuela including medical professionals.

Source: <http://hdrstats.undp.org/en/countries/country_fact_sheets/ cty_fs_CUB.html>, accessed 4 November 2010.

QUESTIONS

1. With limited resources, how is Cuba paying for its imported oil products?
2. How would you measure 'standard of living?' Is the measurement the same in a market and centrally-planned economy?

CENTRAL ASIA—TAJIKISTAN

With the collapse of the former Soviet Union in 1991, of the former 15 Soviet Republics, Tajikistan was left as one of the poorest countries in the region with an estimated 60 per cent of the population living below the poverty line, poorly developed infrastructure, limited industry and a reliance on agricultural production for labour employment and export income. The problem of transition from a centrally-planned economy to one with market-based reforms was exacerbated by hyperinflation, the collapse of industrial production and a civil war (1992–97) as well as large external debt. Tajikistan depends on aid from Russia and Uzbekistan and on international humanitarian assistance for much of its basic subsistence needs.

QUESTIONS

1. Define transitional or emerging market economies.
2. Explain the goals that the government would be hoping to achieve in moving towards a more market-oriented system.
3. Why might foreign investors be attracted to invest in the Tajik economy?

2

THE PRICE
MECHANISM

Chapter **3**

Demand, supply and equilibrium

LEARNING OBJECTIVES

After studying this chapter, you will be able to:

1. construct a demand and supply curve from a demand and supply schedule
2. explain the laws of demand and supply and their relationship to price and quantity
3. describe the reaction of price to excess demand and excess supply
4. explain the differences between movements along a curve and shift of the curve
5. explain the significance of the conditions of demand and supply
6. explain the importance of equilibrium price and quantity.

INTRODUCTION

A thorough understanding of the interaction of demand and supply, and price and quantity is essential in any study of markets and microeconomics. This chapter begins with an explanation of demand and supply and shows the implications of the interaction of demand and supply on price and quantity. The chapter will also show how equilibrium is established in the market and how it is restored in a situation of disequilibrium, such as excess demand or excess supply. Finally, we distinguish between movements along a demand or supply curve, which are caused by a change in price, and shifts of the demand or supply curve, which are caused by a change in the conditions of demand or supply.

DEMAND

Whenever various goods and services are purchased, consumers are showing their demand for those products. However, it is essential to distinguish demand—or, more correctly, effective demand—from the simple notion of desire for a commodity.

EFFECTIVE DEMAND

In economics, when we talk of demand for a commodity we are really talking about effective demand, which has three distinguishing characteristics:

1. the desire to buy the commodity
2. the ability to buy the commodity at the given price
3. the willingness to buy the commodity at the given price at a point in time.

When individuals purchase a good or service they are showing their demand or preference for that product (desire), at that price (ability), at that time (willingness).

To say that demand for tomatoes is 50 kilograms is meaningless because there is no mention of the price of tomatoes, nor of a timeframe. Is it 50 kilograms per week, per month, at 50 cents per kilo or $5 per kilo?

We can therefore define **effective demand** as the amount of a commodity that will be purchased at a given price by consumers at a point in time.

effective demand
the amount of a commodity that will be purchased at a given price by consumers at a point in time

DEMAND SCHEDULE

For example, examine the demand for ice-cream shown in Table 3.1 overleaf. Such a table is called a **demand schedule**. It shows how many ice-creams would be purchased over a range of prices at a particular time.

If the price of an ice-cream is $1.20, then only 5000 would be purchased by the population of this city. However, if the same ice-cream is priced at $0.80, then 10 000 ice-creams would be purchased and consumed.

The graph in Figure 3.1 overleaf represents the market demand for ice-cream in a city at various prices at a point in time. From the information contained in the demand schedule, we can construct a market demand curve.

demand schedule
shows the amount of a commodity that would be purchased over a range of prices at a particular time

Table 3.1   **Demand schedule for ice-cream (March)**

PRICE PER ICE-CREAM ($)	QUANTITY DEMANDED (Q_d)
1.40	2 500
1.20	5 000
1.00	7 500
0.80	10 000
0.60	12 500
0.40	15 000
0.20	17 500

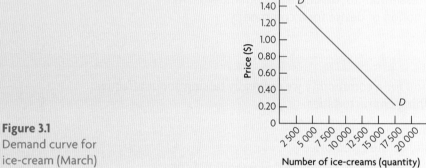

Figure 3.1
Demand curve for ice-cream (March)

MARKET DEMAND CURVE

A **market demand curve** is simply a summation of all the **individual demand curves** that exist in that city. Individuals normally exhibit different demand curves, reflecting different and varied scales of preference for a product at various prices. Some people are willing to purchase a particular product at high prices, while others prefer to spend their money on alternative products. If we were able to ask every individual how much of a product they would be willing to purchase at a range of prices, we would get a lot of small, individual demand curves at each price.

The demand schedule in Table 3.2 illustrates this connection between individual demand and market demand. It shows that the market demand is simply the aggregate (or sum of) the individual demand curves. We can represent this graphically (Figure 3.2).

The graphs in Figure 3.2 show that all the demand curves, both individual and market, have the same characteristic of sloping downwards from left to right. Why is this? It reflects the inverse relationship between the price of the product and the quantity demanded at that price.

At higher prices, we are less willing or less able to purchase the commodity, or purchase it in great numbers. We may have alternative uses for our money, or we do not think the

Table 3.2   Individual and market demand schedule for ice-cream

PRICE PER ICE-CREAM ($)	GRIFFIN	LUCY	ALEX	MARKET
1.40	1	0	0	1
1.20	5	2	3	10
1.00	10	4	6	20
0.80	15	6	9	30
0.60	20	8	12	40
0.40	25	10	15	50
0.20	30	12	18	60

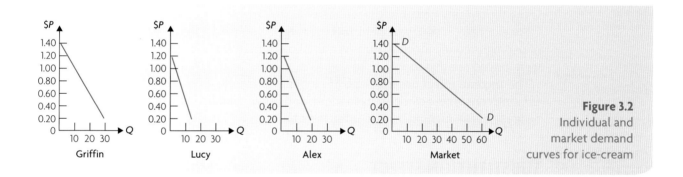

Figure 3.2
Individual and market demand curves for ice-cream

commodity is sufficiently valuable or essential to pay a high price for it. In the demand schedule in Table 3.2 we can see that when ice-creams were $1.40 each, only Griffin was willing to buy one. Lucy and Alex were not. As the price of ice-cream decreased, Griffin bought more ice-creams and Lucy and Alex entered the market by buying ice-creams at lower prices.

The lower the price of the commodity, the more we are willing to purchase.

THE LAW OF DEMAND

The **law of demand** then states that there is an inverse (indirect) relationship between price and quantity demanded.

$$\text{As } P\uparrow, Q_d\downarrow$$
$$\text{As } P\downarrow, Q_d\uparrow$$

where P represents price and Q_d represents quantity demanded.

Your own experiences should show this to be true and support this inverse relationship between P and Q_d. If, for example, the price of ice-creams were to double overnight, would you purchase as many? Alternatively, if the price of ice-creams were to fall by half, would you buy more?

This simple analysis of course ignores many factors, such as income levels, price of substitutes, fashion, etc. Later, we shall examine the effect on the demand curve when these factors are included in the analysis and are allowed to change. But initially we can confidently state that, **ceteris paribus**, when the price of a product increases, the quantity demanded will decrease; and when the price of the product decreases, the quantity demanded will increase. Ceteris paribus means that if we hold all but one variable constant and vary the remaining one, we can observe the impact of the changes.

This is due to the income effect and the substitution effect.

INCOME EFFECT

When the price of a good falls, consumers' purchasing power increases. Their real income (as opposed to their money income) has increased. Note the important distinction between real income and money income.

Money income is the actual amount of money you have in dollars and cents. **Real income** is the purchasing power of that money.

For example, if you were paid $500 per week, you might think that you were well paid and had a high money income. However, if a box of matches cost $50 and all other commodities were priced relative to this, then your real income would be quite low.

The **income effect** describes people's behaviour in response to an increase in income. So, existing consumers can purchase more, and other consumers, who were previously excluded because of the high price, can enter the market.

SUBSTITUTION EFFECT

The **substitution effect** suggests that as the price of a good changes, consumers will cease purchasing it and buy closely related or **substitute goods**. As an example, suppose the price of butter increases. Substitutes are able to satisfy a similar demand. Common substitute products are tea for coffee, and margarine for butter. When the price of butter increases, consumers may decide to purchase a substitute product instead, and so demand for butter falls. Recall the earlier relationship between price and quantity in Table 3.2 on the previous page.

So, as the price of a product changes, the combination of the income and substitution effects will ensure that more (or less) of the product will be purchased as the price falls (or rises).

SUPPLY

So far we have been concerned with consumers, identifying the law of demand and the close relationship between price and quantity demanded. Let's now turn our attention to supply, and the relationship between the amount that producers supply and the price of the product.

Producers in the economy are in business to make a profit and try to do so by satisfying consumer demand for goods and services. However, producers have a very different relationship with price than consumers.

ceteris paribus
all things being equal

money income
the actual amount of money a consumer has in dollars and cents

real income
the purchasing power of money income

income effect
the effect of changes in income on people's ability to spend

substitution effect
as the price of a good changes, consumers will cease purchasing it and buy closely related or substitute goods

substitute goods
goods that serve a similar purpose to a desired good and are able to satisfy a similar demand

Supply is defined as the ability and willingness of producers to offer for sale a good or service at a certain price at a certain point in time.

Supply is not simply the amount of goods in existence. Earlier we noted the distinction between desire and effective demand, and so it is with supply. Producers must be willing and able to offer the goods for sale at various prices. The higher the price that the commodity can sell for, ceteris paribus, the greater the profit the producer will make, and the more producers are willing to offer for sale, or supply to the market.

For suppliers, the opposite is the case. The lower the selling price of the good, the less will be supplied to the market by producers. Why? Producers may not be able to cover costs of production when the price is low, or they may be able to switch their productive efforts into alternative profit-making areas.

LAW OF SUPPLY

The **law of supply** states that the quantity supplied will vary directly with the price of the product.

$$\text{As } P\uparrow, Q_s\uparrow$$
$$\text{As } P\downarrow, Q_s\downarrow$$

where P represents price and Q_s represents quantity supplied.

SUPPLY SCHEDULE

We can construct a supply schedule and supply curve to illustrate this relationship. How much ice-cream would producers supply to a market at various prices? This information is contained in the supply schedule shown in Table 3.3.

The **supply schedule** shows the amount of ice-cream that producers are willing and able to supply at various prices. For example, at the high price of $1.40 per ice-cream, suppliers are willing to supply 17 500 ice-creams. As the price decreases to $1 and then to $0.60, suppliers would supply to the market 12 500 and 7 500 ice-creams respectively.

Table 3.3   **Supply schedule for ice-cream (March)**

PRICE PER LITRE ($)	QUANTITY SUPPLIED (Q_s)
1.40	17 500
1.20	15 000
1.00	12 500
0.80	10 000
0.60	7 500
0.40	5 000
0.20	2 500

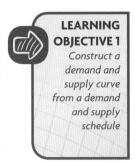

LEARNING
OBJECTIVE 1
*Construct a
demand and
supply curve
from a demand
and supply
schedule*

SUPPLY CURVE

This can be represented graphically by constructing a market supply curve with the information contained in the supply schedule. Once again, price is measured on the vertical axis and the quantity on the horizontal axis. The supply curve shows the direct and positive relationship between quantity supplied and price (Figure 3.3).

The market supply curve has a positive slope and is opposite to the demand curve, that is, it slopes upwards from left to right. The higher the price, the greater the incentive to supply more. The **market supply curve** is simply the sum or aggregate of **individual supply curves**.

In Table 3.4 we assume that the total amount of ice-cream in the market is supplied by three producers. Figure 3.4 shows the same information graphically.

An increase in the price per litre of ice-cream, with all other factors held constant, results in more ice-cream being supplied. A decrease in the price per litre of ice-cream, with all other factors held constant, results in less ice-cream being supplied.

market supply curve
*the sum or aggregate
of individual supply
curves*

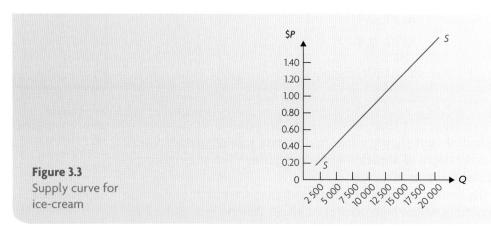

Figure 3.3
Supply curve for
ice-cream

**individual supply
curves**
*producers normally
exhibit different
supply curves,
reflecting preferences
about the quantities
of production at
various price levels*

Table 3.4   **Individual and market supply schedule for ice-cream**

	PRODUCER A	PRODUCER B	PRODUCER C	MARKET
1.40	8000	3500	6000	17500
1.20	7000	3000	5000	15000
1.00	6000	2500	4000	12500
0.80	5000	2000	3000	10000
0.60	4000	1500	2000	7500
0.40	3000	1000	1000	5000
0.20	2000	500	—	2500

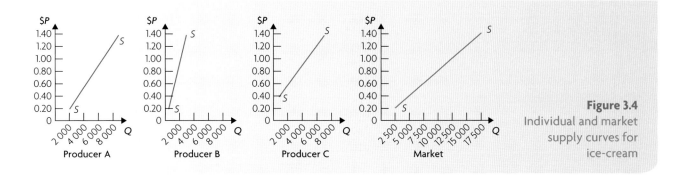

Figure 3.4
Individual and market
supply curves for
ice-cream

PRICE DETERMINATION BROUGHT ABOUT BY THE INTERACTION OF DEMAND AND SUPPLY

With a clear understanding of the basic principles and operation of demand and supply, we turn our attention to the interaction of demand and supply, price determination and the concept of **equilibrium**.

If we combine the demand and supply schedules for ice-cream in Tables 3.1 (p. 34) and 3.3 (p. 37), we get the figures shown in Table 3.5 below, which can be plotted on the one graph. There is one price in Table 3.5 where the quantity demanded is equal to the quantity supplied. This is known as the **equilibrium price**, and the equilibrium quantity can be seen graphically as the point where the demand and supply curves intersect (Figure 3.5 overleaf).

The equilibrium price represents a unique position on the schedule and graph: it is the only price where quantity demanded is equal to quantity supplied, that is, at 80 cents and 10 000 ice-creams.

equilibrium
refers to a situation where the quantity demanded and the quantity supplied is in balance at a particular price

equilibrium price
the price at which the quantity demanded is equal to the quantity supplied

Table 3.5   **Demand and supply for ice-cream**

PRICE PER ICE-CREAM ($)	DEMAND FOR ICE-CREAM (Q_d)	SUPPLY OF ICE-CREAM (Q_s)
1.40	2 500	17 500
1.20	5 000	15 000
1.00	7 500	12 500
0.80	10 000	10 000
0.60	12 500	7 500
0.40	15 000	5 000
0.20	17 500	2 500

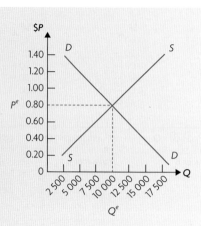

Figure 3.5
Demand and supply
equilibrium for
ice-cream

**LEARNING
OBJECTIVE 3**
Describe the
reaction of
price to excess
demand and
excess supply

DISEQUILIBRIUM AND EXCESS SUPPLY (I.E. SURPLUS)

What will happen in the event of a price change?

If price were to increase, there would be two immediate effects. Recall the law of demand and law of supply.

$$\text{As } P\downarrow, Q_d\uparrow$$
$$\text{As } P\downarrow, Q_s\downarrow$$

equilibrium quantity
*the quantity
demanded and
supplied at the
equilibrium price*

Looking at Figure 3.6, P_e and Q_e are the initial equilibrium price ($0.80) and **equilibrium quantity** (10 000) and P^1 is the new, higher price ($1.20); Q_d^1 and Q_s^1 are the new quantities demanded (5000) and supplied (15 000).

Because of the price increase, producers supply more ice-cream to the market, expecting to sell it and make greater profits. They have moved along their supply curve from point E (equilibrium) to point H, the point where the $1.20 line intersects the supply curve. In this instance, the triangle bounded by G, E and H constitutes excess supply.

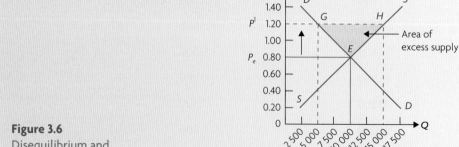

Figure 3.6
Disequilibrium and
excess supply

CONSUMERS

However, at the higher price, consumers actually demand less of the product than at the earlier equilibrium price. They have moved along their demand curve from point E (equilibrium) to point G, the point where the $1.20 price line intersects the demand curve.

These **disequilibrium conditions** are known as **excess supply** (or surplus). The amount of excess supply is equal to the quantity between Q_d^1 and Q_s^1. Producers are supplying an amount equal to the distance $0–Q_s^1$, but only a fraction of that quantity, measured by the distance $0–Q_d^1$, is being consumed. The market is now in a state of disequilibrium.

Consumers have ceased consuming an amount equal for the distance $Q_d^1–Q_e$ and switched to alternative, substitute goods, and producers now find they have a build-up of unwanted, unpurchased stock. No consumers will purchase it at that high price.

disequilibrium conditions
all situations other than market equilibrium

excess supply
when the quantity supplied is greater than the equilibrium level

PRODUCERS

What will be the producers' reaction? How will they eliminate the excess supply? Having a build-up of stock, they find it is better to sell their goods at a lower price than not to sell them at all (examples are sales by ski shops at the end of the ski season and summer stock clearance sales by clothing retailers).

Producers respond to an excess supply of goods by lowering the price, which decreases the amount being supplied while encouraging further consumption of a now cheaper product. Let's assume they decrease the price to P^2, equivalent to $1.00 in the demand and supply schedule contained in Table 3.5 (p. 39). In Figure 3.7, as the price has decreased from P^1 to P^2, consumers have increased consumption by an amount equal to the distance from $0–Q_d^1$ to $0–Q_d^2$, an increase in the amount $Q_d^1–Q_d^2$.

The amount supplied, moreover, has decreased from $0–Q_s^1$ to Q_d^2, a decrease in production by an amount equal to the distance between Q_s^1 and Q_s^2. Once again, recall the laws of demand and supply:

$$\text{As } P\downarrow, Q_d\uparrow$$

$$\text{As } P\downarrow, Q_s\downarrow$$

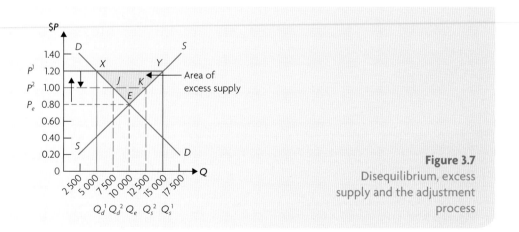

Figure 3.7
Disequilibrium, excess supply and the adjustment process

INTEREST RATES AND RETAIL SALES

LINK TO BUSINESS

Assume that Bank A increases its interest rates for housing mortgages. This means that households that have borrowed money from Bank A via a mortgage to finance the purchase of a house have less money to spend after making their monthly repayments. If they are not able to increase their income, they will have to save less or spend less.

QUESTIONS

1. How might this affect spending in grocery stores?
2. How might it affect spending in expensive designer clothing stores compared to spending in so-called '$2 Shops'?
3. How might the stores react?
4. How might other banks react to the rise in interest from Bank A?

Consumers have moved along their demand curves from point X to point J, and producers have moved along their supply curves from point Y to point K.

However, we are still in a state of disequilibrium with excess supply represented by the distance $Q_d^2-Q_s^2$. Producers find that a further decrease in price to P_e will restore equilibrium in the market with the amount supplied equal to the amount being demanded.

LEARNING OBJECTIVE 3
Describe the reaction of price to excess demand and excess supply

DISEQUILIBRIUM AND EXCESS DEMAND (I.E. SHORTAGE)

excess demand
when the price of a good falls below the equilibrium level

Excess demand results when the price falls below the equilibrium level, as Figure 3.8 shows.

The market is initially in equilibrium, with demand equal to supply at P_e and Q_e. Assume a price decrease to P^1, below the market clearing level ($0.40, for example) in Table 3.5 (p. 39).

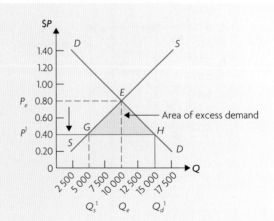

Figure 3.8
Disequilibrium and excess demand

At the new price below the equilibrium price, there is little incentive for producers to supply the market with the goods. As they divert resources into other productive efforts, the quantity supplied decreased from $0–Q_e$ to $0–Q_s^1$. Producers have moved along the supply curve from point E to point G. In this instance, the triangle bounded by G, E and H constitutes excess demand.

CONSUMERS

However, because the price has decreased, consumers wish to purchase more. Demand has increased from $0–Q_e$ to $0–Q_d^1$. Consumers have moved along the demand curve from point E to point H.

The market is once again in a state of disequilibrium. However, this time it is known as excess demand (or a shortage) equal to the amount between Q_s^1 and Q_d^1. This unsatisfied demand makes consumers willing to pay more, offering prices above P^1 to ensure they are able to purchase the limited amount of commodities being produced. The higher price being offered to producers is an incentive for them to produce more as they realise there is a large unsatisfied demand consisting of consumers who are willing to pay a higher price.

PRODUCERS

However, the higher price now being asked by producers is a disincentive for some consumers and so some demand will cease. Let us assume P^2 was the new price charged by producers as consumers bid against each other and forced up the price (Figure 3.9). P^2 is still too low for the market to clear and restore equilibrium. There is still a situation of excess demand, albeit less than at P^1.

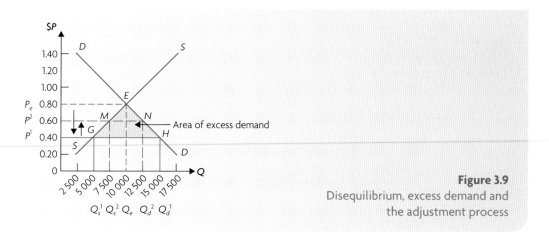

Figure 3.9
Disequilibrium, excess demand and the adjustment process

Excess demand is now the distance between Q_s^2 and Q_d^2 as production has increased from $0–Q_s^1$ to $0–Q_s^2$ and producers have moved along their supply curve from point G to point M, while demand has fallen from $0–Q_d^1$ to $0–Q_d^2$. This is shown by the movement along the demand curve from point H to point N.

A continued state of excess demand cannot exist. Consumers continue to pressure producers by offering higher prices for the limited quantity of goods, and hence producers increase production. Eventually, in a market economy, the market will clear as the quantity demanded equals the quantity supplied at the equilibrium price.

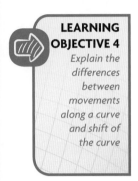

MOVEMENTS ALONG THE CURVE AND SHIFTS OF THE CURVE

So far our analysis has concentrated only on price changes and the reaction of producers and consumers. All other factors were held constant. This means that the demand and supply curves did not shift, but rather we had movements along the curves which were due to price changes.

There is a critical distinction between these two factors. There is only a movement along the curve when the price changes. The curve does not shift.

So in Figure 3.6 (p. 40), when the price increased from P_e ($0.80) to P^1 ($1.20), consumers moved along their demand curve from point E to point G and producers moved along their supply curve from point E to point H. Figure 3.10 extends the analysis by reducing price from $1.20 to $1.00. When the price decreased to P^2 ($1.00), consumers moved along their demand curve from point G to point J, while producers moved along their supply curve from point H to point K.

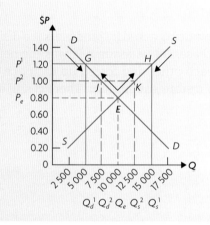

Figure 3.10
Movements along the curve and shifts of the curve

In this case, we say that there has been a decrease in quantity demanded (contraction) and an increase in quantity supplied (expansion).

When the conditions of demand and supply change (as opposed to a price change), the curve itself will shift (as opposed to movements along the curve).

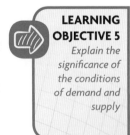

CONDITIONS OF DEMAND

There are many factors known as **conditions of demand** that may cause the demand curve to shift. Note that in each of the following cases (except the substitution effect, which we have already analysed) the price remains unchanged, and so there are no movements along the curve. Instead, the curve shifts. These movements are summarised in Table 3.6 at the end of this section (p. 49).

CHANGE IN TASTES

Another name for this is fashion. Fashion has a major effect on consumption patterns. It introduces an element of time and suggests that over time demand for certain types of goods changes. We may no longer demand them, irrespective of any price drops (Figure 3.11). Assume body piercing was no longer fashionable and fewer people undertook to have piercing, the shift in the demand curve would look like this:

conditions of demand
factors that may cause the demand curve to shift

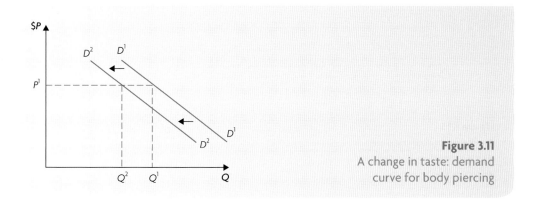

Figure 3.11
A change in taste: demand curve for body piercing

IMPROVEMENTS IN TECHNOLOGY

As technology develops, our demand patterns change. Vinyl records have been replaced by compact discs and then iPods, and traditional cameras (SLRs) have been replaced by digital cameras and image-collecting mobile phones, as the quality and capabilities of new technologies improve (Figure 3.12).

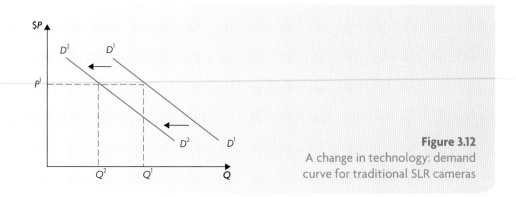

Figure 3.12
A change in technology: demand curve for traditional SLR cameras

REAL INCOME

Another name for real income is purchasing power, as we discussed in connection with the income effect. As our real income increases, we are able to make different types of purchases. We can afford to buy more goods, and/or a higher quality of goods, than before.

Higher real income increases our consumption of certain goods, and these are known as normal goods. **Normal goods** are those that we consume more of when our income increases. **Inferior goods** are those that we decrease our consumption of when our income increases.

For example, as our real income increases, we may switch our purchase from cheap wine (inferior good) to champagne (normal good) (Figure 3.13).

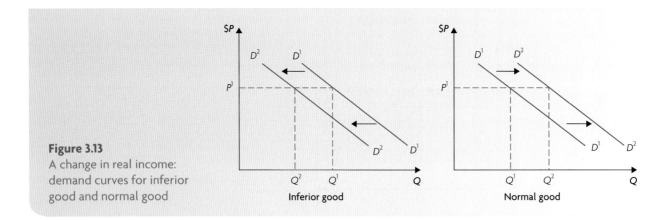

Figure 3.13
A change in real income:
demand curves for inferior
good and normal good

CHANGE IN POPULATION

An increase in the population will lead to an increase in demand for all types of production. Even more specific is a change in the demographics of a population. As certain age or gender groups increase or decrease, demand for products purchased by those particular demographic groups will change (Figure 3.14).

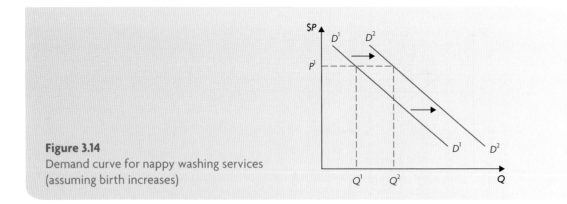

Figure 3.14
Demand curve for nappy washing services
(assuming birth increases)

CHANGE IN THE PRICE OF SUBSTITUTES

We mentioned substitute products when we referred to the substitution effect. Substitute goods are alternative goods that can be used for the same purpose, for example butter and margarine. Although they are different goods, they can serve the same purpose whether as a spread or used in cooking. Muesli and porridge are also often cited as examples of substitute goods.

A change in the price of one good affects the demand for the other. For example, an increase in the price of coffee will likely lead to an increase in demand for tea.

When the price of one product changes, there will be a shift along the demand (or supply) curve. And, as a result of the substitution effect, the curve for the substitute product will also shift. This is the important distinction between a change in price, which causes a movement along the curve, and a change in the conditions of demand, which causes the curve itself to shift (Figure 3.15).

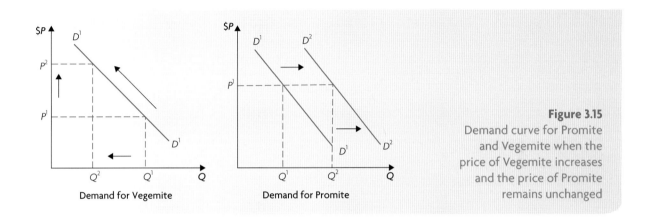

Figure 3.15
Demand curve for Promite and Vegemite when the price of Vegemite increases and the price of Promite remains unchanged

A CHANGE IN THE PRICE OF OTHER GOODS

A general increase in the price of all commodities will decrease our real income and leave less money available for spending. Another consideration is the notion of complementary goods.

Two or more products are said to be **complementary goods** when an increase in the price of one causes a decrease in demand for the other. Examples are a desktop computer and a monitor, gin and tonic, Blu-ray DVD player and Blu-ray DVDs etc.

Complementary goods are 'consumed' together, not in isolation. An increase in the price of compact disc players will reduce demand for them, and therefore fewer compact discs will be purchased even though their price is unchanged (Figure 3.16).

complementary goods
two or more products are said to be complementary goods when an increase in the price of one causes a decrease in demand for the other

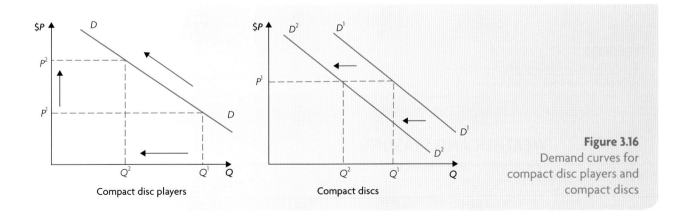

Figure 3.16
Demand curves for compact disc players and compact discs

EXPECTATIONS OF THE FUTURE

With the expectation of a worsening economy and/or potential unemployment, people may decrease their expenditure, particularly on highly priced items or items requiring credit commitments. Savings will increase.

Expectations of full employment and confidence in the economy encourage people to make large purchases and enter into debt or credit obligations (Figure 3.17). Expectations of future government policies may also affect consumption decisions.

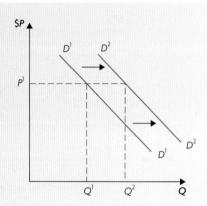

Figure 3.17
Demand for white goods (fridge, washing machines etc) because of expectations of economic improvement

ADVERTISING

Advertising is an attempt to induce consumers to buy the advertised brand—shifting the demand curve for that product to the right—while reducing spending on competitors' brands—shifting the demand curve for their products to the left (Figure 3.18).

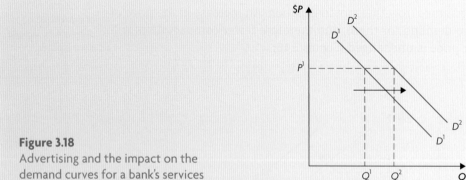

Figure 3.18
Advertising and the impact on the demand curves for a bank's services

WEATHER AND SEASONS

The seasons have a profound effect on demand and consumption patterns. During the colder winter months, expenditure rises for raincoats and umbrellas, shifting the demand curve to the right; in summer, the demand for ice-cream increases, shifting the curve to the right (in winter to the left). If you were a producer of ice-cream, what would be your response in the

Table 3.6   **Summary of changes in demand**

FACTOR	CHANGE	EFFECT	RESULT
Price	Increase	Movement left along the demand curve	Contraction of quantity demanded
	Decrease	Movement right along the demand curve	Expansion of quantity demanded
Change in taste	Increase in demand for a product	Shift of demand curve to right	Increase in demand
	Decrease in demand for a product	Shift of demand curve to left	Decrease in demand
Technology	Technological advancement	Shift of demand curve to right	Increase in demand
	Old technology displaced	Shift of demand curve to left	Decrease in demand
Real income	Increase	Shift of demand curve to right	Increase in demand
	Decrease	Shift of demand curve to left	Decrease in demand
Changes in population	Increase	Shift of demand curve to right	Increase in demand
	Decrease	Shift of demand curve to left	Decrease in demand
Change in price of substitutes	Increase	Shift of demand curve to right	Increase in demand
	Decrease	Shift of demand curve to left	Increase in demand
General price change (complementary goods)	Increase	Shift of demand curve to left	Decrease in demand
	Decrease	Shift of demand curve to right	Increase in demand
Expectations of future price changes	Increase	Shift of demand curve to right (buy now)	Increase in demand
	Decrease	Shift of demand curve to left (defer purchase)	Decrease in demand
Advertising	Increase in influence	Shift of demand curve to right	Increase in demand
	Decrease in influence	Shift of demand curve to left	Decrease in demand
Climatic changes	Increased preference for products	Shift of demand curve to right	Increase in demand
	Decreased preference for products	Shift of demand curve to left	Decrease in demand

THE CHEMIST WAREHOUSE

LINK TO
BUSINESS

The Chemist Warehouse began operating throughout Australia to compete with established pharmacy chains and is now the largest pharmacy retailer in Australia, employing over 4000 people. As well as providing dispensary services, the Chemist Warehouse stocks health and beauty products, medicines and medical aids and veterinary products. As well as retail, the Chemist Warehouse provides internet and distance dispensing. The Chemist Warehouse claims that aggressive pricing and larger trade volume turnover allows it to offer goods at lower prices than its competitors.

QUESTIONS

1. Explain the impact of the Chemist Warehouse on the supply of pharmacy services throughout Australia.
2. What combination of two graphs would you use to illustrate the above pharmacy market situation?
   (a) Show a movement along the demand curve to the right for Chemist Warehouse.
   (b) Shift the supply curve to the right for Chemist Warehouse and explain how this could come about.
   (c) Shift the supply curve to the left for other pharmacies and explain how this could come about.
   (d) Shift the demand curve to the right for Chemist Warehouse, and show a movement along the demand curve to the left for other pharmacies. Explain how this could occur.
3. What factor would have been the main determinant for these changes in the retail pharmacy market?
   (a) Chemist Warehouse provides normal goods, while other pharmacy chain stores provide inferior goods.
   (b) Changes in the prices of substitute products.
   (c) Changes in retail costs of Chemist Warehouse and other pharmacy chain stores.
   (d) Changes in consumer preferences and tastes.
   (e) Bigger advertising expenditure and internet exposure by Chemist Warehouse.
   (f) Changes in prices of alternative products.

colder winter months to a decrease in demand for ice-cream? If you produced umbrellas, what would you do to counter a decrease in demand during the summer months?

Remember, when the demand curve actually shifts, we say there has been an increase or decrease in demand. But when there is movement along the curve, we describe this as an increase or decrease in the quantity demanded.

Table 3.6 on the previous page summarises changes in demand that may cause the demand curve to shift.

CONDITIONS OF SUPPLY

conditions of supply
factors that may cause the supply curve to shift and lead to an increase or decrease in supply

Similarly to demand, there are many factors known as **conditions of supply** which may cause the supply curve to shift and lead to an increase or decrease in supply. We will list some of them, and they are summarised in Table 3.7.

Table 3.7   **Summary of changes in supply**

FACTOR	CHANGE	EFFECT	RESULT
Price	Increase	Movement right along supply curve	Expansion of quantity supplied
	Decrease	Movement left along supply curve	Contraction of quantity supplied
Changes in technology	Advances	Shift of supply curve to right	Increase in supply
	Lapse in technology	Shift of supply curve to left	Decrease in supply
Production costs	Increase	Shift of supply curve to left	Decrease in supply
	Decrease	Shift of supply curve to right	Increase in supply
Price of alternative goods	Increase	Shift of supply curve to left (for existing production)	Increase in supply of new product
	Decrease	Shift of supply curve to right	Increase in supply
Climatic changes	Good season	Shift of supply curve to right	Increase in supply
	Bad season	Shift of supply curve to left	Decrease in supply

IMPROVEMENTS IN TECHNOLOGY

Technological improvements enable suppliers to supply a greater quantity of goods at the same (or decreased) cost. Examples include reductions in the cost of computer components, improved mobile phone capacity and applications, better farming techniques, new types of high-yielding seed varieties, improved production line management, increased automation. In these cases, the supply curve shifts to the right (Figure 3.19).

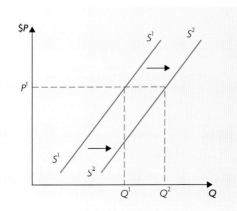

Figure 3.19
Supply curve shift as a result of improvements in technology

A CHANGE IN PRODUCTION COSTS

A closely related situation occurs when production costs change. If the price of one or more of the factors of production (land, labour, capital and enterprise) changes, costs of production cause a shift in the supply curve. Increasing wage rates may cause a shift in the supply curve to the left, as companies are forced to use alternative products that have lower labour costs or change to more capital-intensive production. Cheaper raw materials—due to a decrease in import tariffs, for example—cause a rightward shift in the supply curve (Figure 3.20).

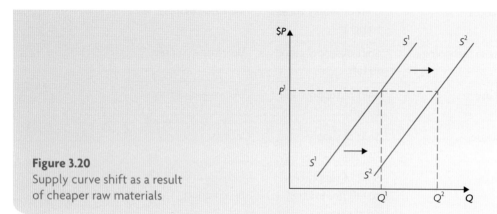

Figure 3.20
Supply curve shift as a result of cheaper raw materials

A CHANGE IN THE PRICE OF ALTERNATIVE PRODUCTS

Raw materials may be used to produce different products. If the price of one finished good increases, production will be shifted into that commodity, reducing the supply of others. For example, land may be used for raising beef or growing wheat. If the price of wheat increases relative to the price of beef, then farmers will offer less land for beef and increase the amount of land under cultivation for wheat (Figure 3.21).

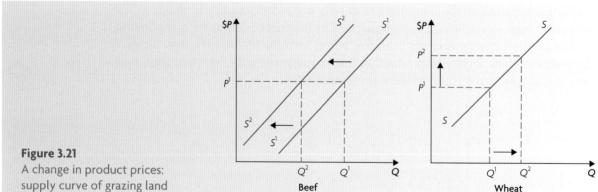

Figure 3.21
A change in product prices: supply curve of grazing land

WEATHER AND SEASONS

Droughts, storms and other climatic factors can all affect the supply of goods onto the market. A drought will reduce the supply of agricultural produce, for example, while an unusually favourable growing season may give farmers greater returns (Figure 3.22).

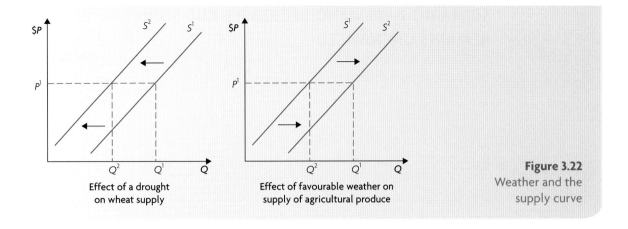

Figure 3.22
Weather and the
supply curve

Effect of a drought
on wheat supply

Effect of favourable weather on
supply of agricultural produce

CHANGES IN EQUILIBRIUM PRICE AND QUANTITY

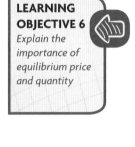

LEARNING OBJECTIVE 6
Explain the importance of equilibrium price and quantity

The discussion of disequilibrium, excess demand and excess supply showed that disequilibrium was a temporary phenomenon. Through the interaction of supply and demand, the perfect market ensures that equilibrium price and quantity are restored. However, as we have just observed, sometimes the demand or supply curves shift. This creates a new equilibrium position, with a changed equilibrium price and quantity.

Four such situations can arise. There are implications for equilibrium price and quantity when changes in demand and supply interact.

SCENARIO 1—DEMAND INCREASES AND SUPPLY REMAINS UNCHANGED

Where demand has increased, for example, due to a population increase as a result of a rise in birth rates and migration, a new equilibrium price and quantity are established, both higher than the previous equilibrium price and quantity (Figure 3.23).

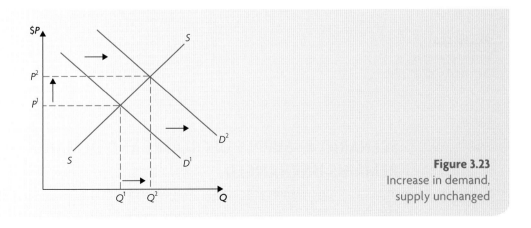

Figure 3.23
Increase in demand,
supply unchanged

SCENARIO 2—DEMAND DECREASES AND SUPPLY REMAINS UNCHANGED

In this case, a new equilibrium price and quantity are established, which are both less than the previous equilibrium levels (Figure 3.24).

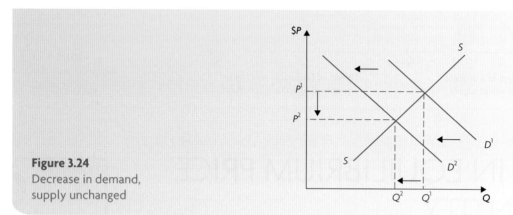

Figure 3.24
Decrease in demand, supply unchanged

SCENARIO 3—SUPPLY INCREASES AND DEMAND REMAINS UNCHANGED

Where the conditions of supply change, resulting in an increase, the supply curve shifts to the right. If the demand curve remains unchanged, a new equilibrium price is established, which is lower than the previous equilibrium price, and the equilibrium quantity is higher (Figure 3.25).

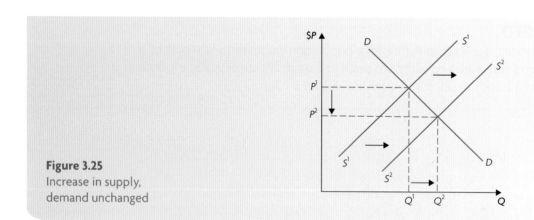

Figure 3.25
Increase in supply, demand unchanged

SCENARIO 4—SUPPLY DECREASES AND DEMAND REMAINS UNCHANGED

This situation leads to a new equilibrium with a higher price, and a decrease in the amount supplied (Figure 3.26).

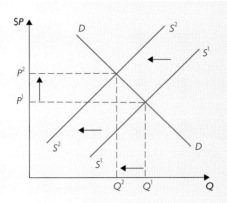

Figure 3.26
Decrease in supply,
demand unchanged

CONDITIONS OF DEMAND AND SUPPLY

Assume you own a small retail bakery in a local shopping complex.

QUESTIONS
How would the following changes affect your sales? See if you can illustrate these effects using demand and supply curves.

1. An increase in income tax that reduces after-tax incomes.
2. A health campaign emphasising the benefits of eating wholemeal and multi-grain bread.
3. The impact this would have on your sales of white bread.
4. A drought in the wheat-producing areas reduces the supply of wheat to bakeries across the country.
5. A new competitor opens a bakery that also specialises in cakes and coffee.

LINK TO
BUSINESS

RUSSIAN FIRES 2010 AND WHEAT SUPPLY

Massive fires in Russia during August 2010 wiped out an estimated 25 per cent of Russia's wheat crop which prompted the government to ban the export of all wheat from Russia. It was predicted that this would impact on Australian markets with benefits for Australian wheat producers, and increased prices for consumers as higher grain costs would drive up the cost of bread. Higher prices for wheat and other grains were also predicted to have a big impact on the agriculture industry as farmers look to change from other crops such as corn to a more profitable yield of wheat while prices are high.

QUESTIONS
1. Explain what happened to the conditions of supply for wheat.
2. Draw a diagram to illustrate the above scenario using equilibrium price and quantity analysis to show how the fires in Russia impact on the price and quantity of wheat.
3. Illustrate how a natural disaster, such as the fires in Russia, could impact on the price of Australian wheat.
4. Show what will happen to the supply curve for corn if the predictions above held true.

LINK TO
INTERNATIONAL
ECONOMY

SUMMARY

1. Demand, or effective demand, is different from desire. Effective demand has three characteristics. Consumers must:
    (a) desire to purchase the commodity
    (b) be willing to purchase the commodity
    (c) be able to purchase the commodity.
2. The demand schedule is a table constructed to show the quantity of a commodity demanded at different prices. From this information we derive the demand curve, which is a graphic representation of the demand schedule and illustrates the quantity of a product that will be purchased by a consumer at different prices.
3. The market demand curve for a product is the aggregate of all individual demand curves for that product. The law of demand states that demand varies inversely with the price of the product. An increase in price will lead to a decrease in quantity demanded, and a decrease in price will lead to an increase in quantity demanded.
4. Supply, or effective supply, is the quantity of a product that producers are willing and able to offer in exchange for money in the market. The supply schedule is a table showing the quantity of a product that will be supplied by a producer at different prices. From this information we derive the supply curve, which is a graphic representation of the supply schedule and illustrates the quantity of a product that will be supplied by a producer at different prices.
5. The law of supply states that the supply of a commodity will vary directly with the price of a commodity. An increase in price encourages producers to supply more goods, while a decrease in price leads to a decrease in quantity supplied.
6. A movement along the demand curve is caused only by a change in price.
    (a) A decrease in price will lead to a movement along, rightwards and down the demand curve; it therefore represents an increase in the quantity demanded, or an expansion of demand.
    (b) An increase in price will lead to a movement along, leftwards and up the demand curve; it therefore represents a decrease in the quantity demanded, or a contraction in demand.
7. A movement along the supply curve is caused only by a change in price.
    (a) A decrease in price will lead to a movement along, leftwards and down the supply curve, and therefore a decrease in the quantity supplied or a contraction in supply.
    (b) An increase in price will lead to a movement along, rightwards and up the supply curve, and therefore an increase in the quantity supplied or an expansion of supply.
8. A shift of the demand curve is caused by a change in the conditions of demand.
    (a) A shift of the demand curve to the right means that there is an increase in demand. More is demanded by consumers at the existing price.
    (b) A shift of the demand curve to the left means that there is a decrease in demand. Less is demanded by consumers at the existing price.
9. Conditions of demand include:
    (a) changes in personal tastes
    (b) changes in technology
    (c) changes in real income
    (d) changes in the size of the population and the demographic composition
    (e) changes in the price of substitutes/complementary goods
    (f) future expectations
    (g) advertising
    (h) weather and climatic factors.
10. A shift of the supply curve is caused by a change in the conditions of supply. It is not caused by a change in the price of the product. As the conditions of supply change, the supply curve will shift, resulting in a change in supply.
    (a) A shift of the supply curve to the right means that there is an increase in supply and more is supplied at the existing price.
    (b) A shift of the supply curve to the left means that there is a decrease in supply and less is supplied at that price.

11. Conditions of supply include:
    (a) improvements in technology
    (b) a change in production costs
    (c) a change in price of alternative products
    (d) weather and climatic factors.

12. The price mechanism is the process whereby adjustments in price ensure equilibrium between supply and demand in all free markets. The equilibrium price is the price at which the market is just cleared, that is, where there is no excess demand or excess supply.

13. If demand is greater than supply, the market is in a state of disequilibrium, which cannot be sustained. This is known as a situation of excess demand. The market will eliminate excess demand by increasing price. The price increase will lead to movements along the demand and supply curves, reducing quantity demanded and increasing quantity supplied until equilibrium is restored.

14. If supply is greater than demand, it is known as excess supply. The market will clear the excess supply by decreasing the price. The price decrease means movements along the demand and supply curves downwards, reducing quantity supplied and increasing quantity demanded until the excess supply no longer exists and equilibrium is restored.

KEY TERMS

ceteris paribus	36	equilibrium quantity	40	market supply curve	38
complementary goods	47	excess demand	42	money income	36
conditions of demand	45	excess supply	41	normal goods	46
conditions of supply	50	income effect	36	real income	36
demand schedule	33	individual demand curve	35	substitute goods	36
disequilibrium conditions	41	individual supply curve	38	substitution effect	36
effective demand	33	inferior goods	46	supply	37
equilibrium	39	law of demand	35	supply schedule	37
equilibrium price	39	law of supply	37		
		market demand curve	34		

REVIEW QUESTIONS

1. Identify whether the following statements are true or false. Be prepared to justify your answer.

    (a) The market demand curve is the sum of individual demand curves. True or False?

    (b) The demand curve slopes downward from right to left. True or False?

    (c) The law of demand highlights the direct relationship between price and quantity. True or False?

    (d) The substitution effect only works when the price increase is high. True or False?

    (e) An increase in money income will always increase our real income. True or False?

    (f) The quantity supplied will move in the same direction as price. True or False?

    (g) The supply curve has a positive slope and always moves in the opposite direction to the demand curve. True or False?

    (h) The market supply curve will depend on the number of individual producers. True or False?

    (i) A position of disequilibrium such as excess demand will eventually force prices down. True or False?

    (j) Price readjustments and excess supply ensure that a cheaper price and small quantity will be produced. True or False?

    (k) Disequilibrium cannot persist when price and quantity are flexible variables. True or False?

    (l) A government fixing price below equilibrium ensures everyone is able to buy the good. True or False?

    (m) Movements along the supply curve are caused by changes in the conditions of demand. True or False?

    (n) Normal goods are superior to inferior goods in price and quality. True or False?

    (o) Complementary goods are the opposite of substitute goods. True or False?

    (p) An increase in the price of a product with alternative uses will lead to less of it being produced. True or False?

    (q) A recession would be likely to cause a shift to the left in the supply curve. True or False?

2. Distinguish between desire and demand.

3. Distinguish between a demand schedule and a demand curve.

4. What is the law of demand?

5. Explain the income effect and the substitution effect. How are they related to the law of demand?

6. Define supply.

7. 'The higher the price, the more producers will supply.' What is meant by this statement?

8. What is disequilibrium? Why can a state of disequilibrium not persist in a free market?

9. Under what conditions can the equilibrium price change? Illustrate your answers.

10. Distinguish between a movement along a demand or supply curve, and a shift of that curve.

11. How will a rise in real income affect the demand for normal goods and inferior goods?

12. Use an example to show the effect of a declining birth rate on the demand for crèches.

13. What is the difference between substitute goods and complementary goods?

14. Plus/minus: We are in the mobile phone retail market. Using the supply–demand theory, show the likely effect of the following market developments on the equilibrium price and quantity for mobile phones. Use the (+) sign for a likely increase and the (−) sign for a likely decrease. Support your choices with supply–demand curves:

MARKET DEVELOPMENTS (CETERIS PARIBUS)	EQUILIBRIUM PRICE (+/−)	QUANTITY (+/−)

   (a) a decrease in the rate of immigration

   (b) a ban on mobile phone stores advertising to consumers

   (c) a government increase in the GST on all technology products from 10 to 15 per cent

   (d) a health report linking constant mobile phone use with hearing impairment

   (e) improved, more efficient capital-intensive methods to produce cheaper mobile phones

   (f) an ageing population

   (g) a decrease in personal income tax

   (h) a decrease in tariffs on imported mobile phones.

15. Consider the graph in Figure 3.27 showing the demand and supply of rental housing.

   (a) What could have caused the supply curve to shift to the right?

   (b) What is the result of such a shift?

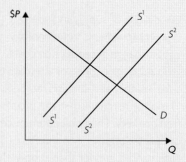

Figure 3.27
Demand and supply of rental housing

16. Under what condition could there be an increase in quantity bought and sold, but no change in the equilibrium price? Draw a graph of price and quantity to illustrate your answer.

17. 'For a limited time only, prices on all bedding has been slashed by 50%' so reads the advertisement in the local daily newspaper. Using your understanding of demand and supply, how will this price cut affect the demand for bedding? Why would stores adopt such pricing practices?

APPLIED QUESTIONS AND EXERCISES
AUSTRALIAN MIGRATION

In recent years in Australia there has been considerable debate and argument about the arrival of refugees into Australia—so-called 'Boat People', who are a small percentage (approximately 1.5 per cent) of the overall level of Australia's migration intake. Aside from political debate, there is considerable economic debate about the benefits and costs of refugees and migrants to the Australian economy.

Some groups want lower immigration in order to reduce infrastructure pressures on cities like Sydney and Melbourne and because of fears that migrants cause unemployment.

On the other side are people who are concerned about the consequences of Australia's ageing population and the impact this will have on the workforce. In particular, skilled migration is viewed as a valuable source of labour:

In 2008–09, more than 171 000 migrants were granted visas under the Skill and Family Streams of Australia's Migration Program. In this same period nearly 670 000 people received temporary entry visas to Australia to undertake specific work or business, or to entertain, play sport, have a working holiday or study. In addition to this, 13 507 humanitarian entrants were granted visas to enable them to live in Australia to rebuild their lives, having fled persecution or suffering.

Immigration affects the demand side of Australia's economy through:

- migrants' own spending (food, housing and leisure activities)
- business expansion (investment to produce extra goods and services)
- expansion of government services (health, education and welfare).

It also affects the supply side of the economy through:

- labour, skills and capital introduced into Australia
- new businesses developed by migrants
- migrant contributions to technology
- adding productive diversity through knowledge of international business markets.

Source: Australian Immigration Fact Sheet, <www.immi.gov.au/media/fact-sheets/04fifty.htm>, accessed 5 November 2010.

QUESTIONS

1. Australia has an ageing population. Without an increase in migration rates, what will be the effect on the demand curve for each of the following products and/or services?
   (a) child care
   (b) home care
   (c) restaurants
   (d) nursing homes
   (e) car registrations
   (f) organised overseas travel and tours
   (g) lawn bowling clubs and facilities.
2. How will an increase in overseas students' temporary resident visas affect the demand curve for housing rentals?
3. Using supply curves, illustrate why some people think increased migration will lower wages. Extend the analysis to show the effect of changes in demand that occur with increased migration.
4. Select five goods regularly used in your household. Using demand and supply analysis and extending from individual to market curves, illustrate the effect of an increase in migration to Australia.
5. Some opponents of increases in migration cite the adverse impacts on the environment.
   (a) Why do they argue this?
   (b) Do you agree with their argument?
   (c) What business opportunities could arise as a result?
6. If we wanted to shift the supply curve for labour to the right, what substitutes are there for increased migration?

FARMERS' MARKETS AND SUPERMARKETS

A Farmers' Market is a predominantly fresh food market that operates regularly within a community, at a focal public location that provides a suitable environment for farmers and food producers to sell farm-origin and associated value-added processed food products directly to customers.

Farmers' markets run in direct competition with the major supermarkets such as Coles, Woolworths, Safeway and IGA.

Source: <www.farmersmarkets.org.au/about/definition>, accessed 5 November 2010.

QUESTIONS

1. Explain the impact on the demand for fresh food produce sold at local farmers' markets if supermarkets drastically reduce prices of fresh food produce.
2. Illustrate using demand and supply curves for farmers' markets and supermarkets.
3. What has been the impact of farmers' markets on local greengrocers?

OVERWEIGHT AUSTRALIANS

In 2004, 16 per cent of men and 17 per cent of women were obese. Also 43 per cent of men and 25 per cent of women were overweight. The National Health Survey conducted in 2007–08 revealed that the situation has worsened with 42.1 per cent of adult males and 30.9 per cent of adult females classified as overweight and 25.6 per cent of males and 24 per cent of females classified as obese.

QUESTIONS

1. Using demand analysis, describe the impact of this trend on:
   (a) demand for larger-sized clothing
   (b) demand for cosmetic surgery
   (c) demand for low-fat diet products
   (d) weight loss programs such as Jenny Craig and Weight Watchers.
2. Using supply analysis explain the impact of this trend on:
   (a) supply of seats per passenger aircraft
   (b) permissible population densities per floor in high-rise buildings and elevators
   (c) ratio of staff to patients in hospitals
   (d) women-only health and fitness centres.

Chapter 4

Price and income elasticity

LEARNING OBJECTIVES

After studying this chapter, you will be able to:

1. define elasticity of demand and elasticity of supply
2. explain the connection between elasticity of demand and the slope of the demand curve
3. calculate simple elasticities using the total revenue method
4. distinguish between price elasticity, income elasticity and cross elasticity of demand
5. explain different factors that affect the elasticity of demand
6. explain different factors that affect the elasticity of supply.

INTRODUCTION

Our study of demand and supply in Chapter 3 showed that changes in the price of a product alter the quantity demanded and quantity supplied. Recall that the laws of demand and supply state that when the price increases, the quantity demanded decreases and the quantity supplied increases. We know there will be a change in the quantity, but will it change by a small or large proportion?

Producers in particular need to understand the concept of elasticity. In so doing, they will have an idea of the likely responsiveness by consumers to changes in the price of the product.

There are various kinds of elasticities:

- Price elasticity of demand and supply measures the responsiveness of demand and supply to changes in the price of a product.
- Income elasticity of demand measures the responsiveness of demand for a product to changes in a person's income.
- Cross elasticity of demand measures the responsiveness of the quantity demanded for one good, when the price of another good changes.

The simplest method of evaluating the elasticity of demand for a product is to use the total revenue method. It quickly determines whether demand is elastic, inelastic or of unit elasticity.

Many factors can affect the elasticity of demand and supply. Several examples will be used to show how elasticity can change over time, how it can respond readily (elastic) or not very readily (inelastic) to price changes.

price elasticity of demand
the degree of responsiveness of demand quantity for a product to a change in the price of that product

ELASTICITY OF DEMAND

Price elasticity of demand is the degree of responsiveness of demand quantity for a product to a change in the price of that product.

If the price were to increase, by how much would demand decrease? Similarly, if the price were to decrease, what would be the size of the increase in demand?

We can highlight five possibilities in measuring price elasticity of demand, each of which has a distinctly sloped demand curve and is a reflection of different consumer responses to a change in price. We will discuss them in turn, and Table 4.1 (p. 65) summarises the various possibilities of price elasticity of demand and the effects on revenue.

LEARNING OBJECTIVE 1
Define elasticity of demand and elasticity of supply

PERFECTLY INELASTIC DEMAND

When a price change causes no change in the demand for the product (an exceptional case), then the elasticity of demand is equal to zero ($E_d = 0$) and the demand curve between the two prices is drawn as a vertical line. It is rare for products to have a perfectly inelastic demand curve, but drugs of addiction and essential medicines are examples. The price increase P^1 to P^2 has not led to a decrease in quantity demanded (Figure 4.1 overleaf).

LEARNING OBJECTIVE 2
Explain the connection between elasticity of demand and the slope of the demand curve

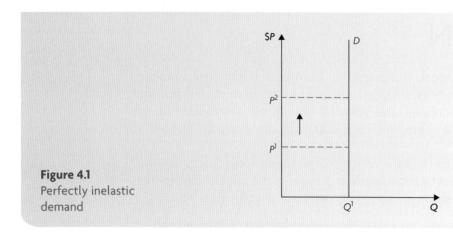

Figure 4.1
Perfectly inelastic
demand

INELASTIC DEMAND

inelastic demand
where a change in
price causes a less-
than-proportionate
change in the
quantity demanded

Inelastic demand is where a change in price causes a less-than-proportionate change in quantity demanded. Then the elasticity of demand is greater than zero but less than one ($0 < E_d < 1$). Demand is said to be inelastic (not responsive) and the demand curve is steeply sloped. Figure 4.2 shows a considerable increase in price that is not matched by a proportionate decrease in the quantity demanded.

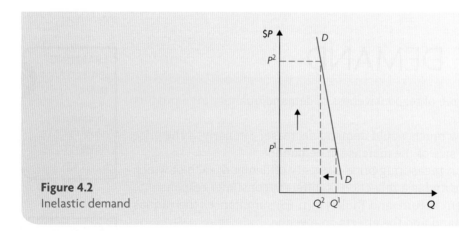

Figure 4.2
Inelastic demand

UNIT ELASTICITY

unit elasticity of
demand
where a change in
price leads to an
equal change in
quantity demanded

Where a change in price leads to an equal change in quantity demanded, we have **unit elasticity of demand**. Unit elasticity is equal to one ($E_d = 1$). The demand curve for unit elasticity is at a 45-degree angle, showing that a 20 per cent increase in price will lead to a 20 per cent decrease in quantity demanded (Figure 4.3).

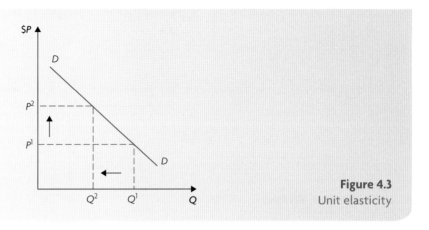

Figure 4.3
Unit elasticity

ELASTIC DEMAND

Elastic demand is where a change in price leads to a more-than-proportionate change in quantity demanded. The elasticity of demand is greater than one ($E_d > 1$). Demand is said to be elastic (responsive) to the change in price, and the slope of the demand curve is much flatter. Figure 4.4 shows that a small increase has led to a larger-than-proportionate change in quantity demanded.

elastic demand
where a change in price leads to a more-than-proportionate change in quantity demanded

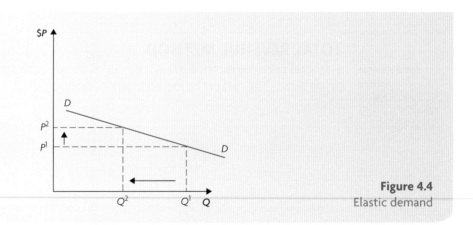

Figure 4.4
Elastic demand

PERFECTLY ELASTIC DEMAND

Where a change in price (increase) leads to demand for the product ceasing altogether, then the elasticity of demand is said to be equal to infinity (E_d = infinity). That is, consumers are so responsive to a price change that, should the price increase, then all consumers would stop purchasing the product. The new price line P^2 (Figure 4.5 overleaf) does not intersect the demand curve, indicating that the quantity demanded ceases. Like perfectly inelastic demand, it is a rare case.

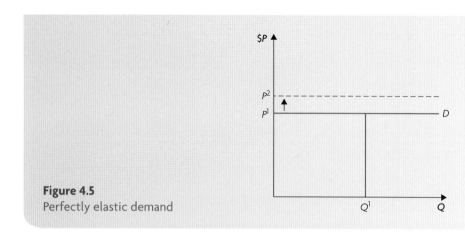

Figure 4.5
Perfectly elastic demand

**LEARNING
OBJECTIVE 3**
*Calculate simple
elasticities using
the total revenue
method*

MEASURING PRICE ELASTICITY OF DEMAND

The simplest way to measure price elasticity, and hence the responsiveness of consumers to a change in price, is known as the total revenue method. This will show us whether demand is inelastic, unitary or elastic.

TOTAL REVENUE METHOD

**total revenue
method**
*finds total revenue
by multiplying the
quantity sold by
the selling price*

The **total revenue method** finds total revenue by multiplying the quantity sold by the selling price. This is the total revenue accruing to the seller. It is expressed as:

$$TR = P \times Q$$

where TR = total revenue
P = price
Q = quantity.

The total revenue also represents the total outlay of buyers at each price as prices change.

Remember that price elasticity of demand measures the responsiveness of consumers to a change in price. So to gauge the price elasticity of demand we have to compare the total revenue at one price with the total revenue at another price.

Demand schedule

Consider the demand schedule for milk shown in Table 4.1.

If demand is inelastic (unresponsive) then, as the price increases, quantity demanded will decrease less than proportionally. Total revenue as a result will increase and it would be in a producer's interest to charge the higher price for the product.

Table 4.1 shows this at the lower prices. When the price increased from 20 to 30 cents per litre, the quantity demanded decreased, as we would expect. However, the total revenue increased because of the inelastic demand for milk at that lower price. The inelasticity of demand for milk continues if we compare 30 cents per litre with 40 cents per litre. Quantity

Table 4.1   **Demand schedule for milk**

PRICE PER LITRE ($)	QUANTITY DEMANDED	TOTAL REVENUE	ELASTICITY
1.00	18 000	18 000	
			Elastic
0.90	22 000	19 000	
			Elastic
0.80	27 000	21 000	
			Elastic
0.70	33 000	23 000	
			Elastic
0.60	40 000	24 000	
			Unitary
0.50	48 000	24 000	
			Inelastic
0.40	58 000	23 000	
			Inelastic
0.30	70 000	21 000	
			Inelastic
0.20	84 000	16 000	

demanded decreased from 70 000 to 58 000 litres, yet total revenue increased from $21 000 to $23 000.

The inelastic demand for milk continues from 40 cents to 50 cents. As a result of the increase in price, quantity demanded has decreased, yet total revenue has increased from $23 000 to $24 000. It would appear that it is in this producer's interest to charge 50 cents per litre and produce 48 000 litres of milk in order to maximise profits.

If the producer continued to charge higher prices in the hope or expectation of greater revenue, we can see the implications of this when faced with elastic demand for the product.

If demand is elastic, an increase in price will result in a decrease in total revenue.

This is shown in Table 4.1 by increasing the price from 70 to 80 cents. The quantity demanded decreases, as we would expect, from 33 000 to 27 000 litres. However, total revenue falls from $23 000 to $21 000.

In desperation at falling profits, the producer may try to increase the price, hoping to increase total revenue. If the demand is elastic, then the opposite will be the case. For example, by increasing the price from 80 to 90 cents, quantity demanded will decrease from 27 000 to 22 000 litres; and as a result of the responsiveness of consumers to a change in price, total revenue falls further from $21 000 to $19 000.

Note that total revenue does not change when the price is between 50 and 60 cents.

Unit elasticity means that a change in price has led to a proportionate change in quantity demanded—48 000 to 40 000 litres.

Total revenue remains at $24 000. It would probably be in this producer's interest to charge 60 cents and produce 40 000 litres of milk; this level of output earns the greatest total revenue for the least effort.

Demand curve

The figures in Table 4.1 (p. 65) can be drawn as a demand curve (Figure 4.6). It highlights two important aspects of the demand curve and elasticity.

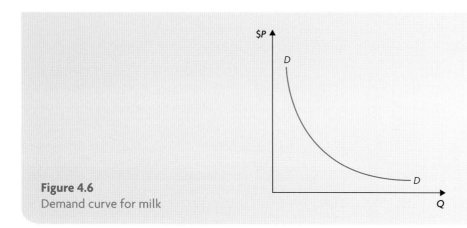

Figure 4.6
Demand curve for milk

- The variability of elasticity over a range of prices. Elasticity varies over the different prices in a demand schedule, which reflects consumers' behaviour and response to a range of price changes. We can make the general observation from Table 4.1 that, for this product, demand tends to be elastic at higher prices and inelastic at lower prices.
- Elasticity and slope of the curve. Elasticity is not always indicated by the slope of the curve, despite our initial generalisations in Figures 4.1 to 4.5.

The appearance of Figure 4.6 indicates that, at the higher prices, demand is inelastic; that is, the curve is quite steep. However, from the demand schedule in Table 4.1 we know this not to be the case. Also, at the lower prices, the flatness of the demand curve appears to indicate elastic demand. We know that this is also incorrect and opposite to what we calculated in Table 4.1.

Remember that the slope of the demand curve is based on absolute changes in price and quantity. Elasticity is a measure of the relative changes in price and quantity.

Do not fall into the trap of suggesting a certain type of elasticity is shown only by the slope of the curve. It is essential to calculate the elasticity using the total revenue method when comparing the elasticity of demand over the range of two or more prices:

- When P↑, and TR↓, demand is elastic (a flatter curve)
- When P↑, and TR↑, demand is inelastic (a steeper curve)
- When P↑, and TR is constant, demand is unit elastic (a 45 degree curve).

Consider the three demand curves shown in Figures 4.7 to 4.9, which highlight the shortcomings of estimating elasticity based on the appearance of the slope of the curve. In each case the slope is the same, and the price increase is the same, from $4 to $5.

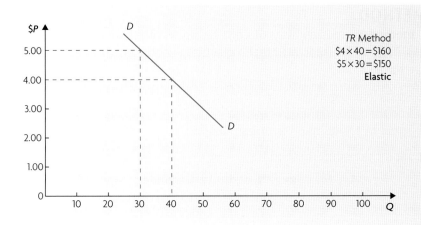

Figure 4.7
Total revenue method
for elastic demand

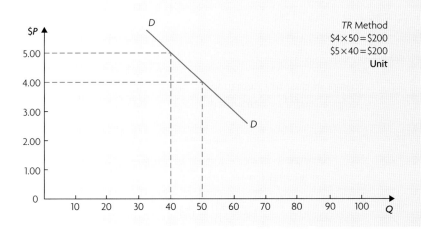

Figure 4.8
Total revenue method
for a demand of unit
elasticity

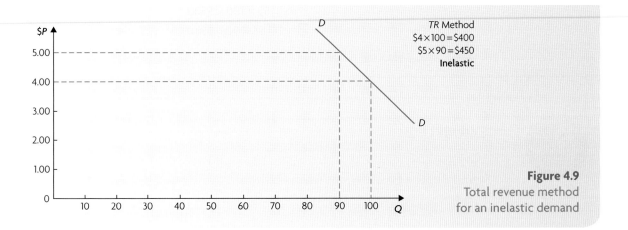

Figure 4.9
Total revenue method
for an inelastic demand

POINT METHOD

point method
used to find the elasticity coefficient, which shows what kind of elasticity a product has

The **point method** is another way of calculating whether demand is elastic, inelastic or unitary. This method is used to find the elasticity coefficient, which tells us what kind of elasticity we have:

- If the coefficient is greater than 1.0, demand is elastic.
- If it is less than 1.0, demand is inelastic.
- If it is equal to 1.0, demand is unitary elastic.

The formula for the point method is:

$$E_d = \frac{\text{percentage change in quantity demanded, between two points}}{\text{percentage change in price between two points}}$$

EXAMPLE 1

If the original price was $5 and 100 units were sold, what is the elasticity of demand when price changes to $6 and 90 units are sold?
Using the point method:

(a) percentage change in quantity demanded

$$\frac{\text{change in quantity demanded}}{\text{original quantity demanded}} \times \frac{100}{1} = \frac{10}{100} \times \frac{100}{1} = 10$$

(b) percentage change in price

$$\frac{\text{change in price}}{\text{original price}} \times \frac{100}{1} = \frac{1}{5} \times \frac{100}{1} = 20$$

$$E_d = \frac{10}{20} = 0.5$$

Elasticity is less than one, therefore demand is inelastic.
Alternatively, the total revenue method:

$$\$5 \times 100 = \$500$$
$$\$6 \times 90 = \$540$$

Demand is inelastic.

EXAMPLE 2

The original price was $5 and 100 units were sold; when the price increased to $6, 40 units were sold. The elasticity of demand using the point method is as follows:

(a) percentage change in quantity demanded

$$\frac{\text{change in quantity demanded}}{\text{original quantity demanded}} \times \frac{100}{1} = \frac{60}{100} \times \frac{100}{1} = 60$$

(b) percentage change in price

$$\frac{\text{change in price}}{\text{original price}} \times \frac{100}{1} = \frac{1}{5} \times \frac{100}{1} = 20$$

$$E_d = \frac{60}{20} = 3$$

The elasticity coefficient is greater than one, therefore demand is elastic. To confirm this, check the total revenue method:

$$\$5 \times 100 = \$500$$
$$\$6 \times 40 = \$240$$

Demand is elastic.

Two other demand elasticity measurements need to be mentioned before we turn our attention to the elasticity of supply. These are known as income elasticity of demand and cross elasticity of demand.

INCOME ELASTICITY OF DEMAND

This type of elasticity measures the responsiveness of quantity demanded for a particular product to changes in a person's income.

We normally expect the **income elasticity of demand** to be positive, that is, an increase in income would cause an increase in demand; or if not positive, then equal to zero, that is, an increase in income would cause no change in demand.

The only exception is for inferior goods (Chapter 3), where the elasticity may be negative. That is, when income increases, the demand for the good decreases.

CROSS ELASTICITY OF DEMAND

Cross elasticity of demand measures how the quantity demanded of one good responds to changes in the price of another good. These goods can be either substitute goods or complementary goods (Chapter 3).

When the elasticity is positive, the goods are substitutes. A rise in the price of one good causes an increase in the demand for the substitute good. For example, an increase in the price of wine may lead to an increase in the demand for beer.

When the elasticity is negative, the goods are complementary. A rise in the price of one good causes a decrease in demand for the complementary good. For example, when the price of compact disc players increases, the demand for compact discs will decrease.

ELASTICITY OF SUPPLY

Price elasticity of supply measures the responsiveness of producers to any price changes. It not only shows whether they will supply more or less to the market when the price changes, but also measures how much more or less. If producers are very responsive to price changes,

LEARNING OBJECTIVE 4

Distinguish between price elasticity, income elasticity and cross elasticity of demand

income elasticity of demand

measures the responsiveness of quantity demanded for a particular product to changes in a person's income

cross elasticity of demand

measures how the quantity demanded of one good responds to changes in the price of another good

LEARNING OBJECTIVE 1

Define elasticity of demand and elasticity of supply

price elasticity
of supply
measures the
responsiveness of
producers to any
price changes

then supply is elastic. Alternatively, if producers are not very responsive to price changes, the supply is inelastic.

As for elasticity of demand, there are five distinct elasticities of supply, each with its unique supply curve that reflects the producers' response to a change in price.

PERFECTLY INELASTIC SUPPLY

Where a change in price does not lead producers to supply additional quantities of goods, the elasticity of supply is said to be zero and the supply curve is vertical ($E_s = 0$), as shown in Figure 4.10.

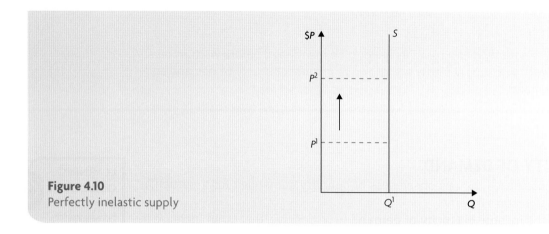

Figure 4.10
Perfectly inelastic supply

INELASTIC SUPPLY

inelastic supply
where the quantity
supplied is relatively
unresponsive to price
changes

Where the quantity supplied is relatively unresponsive to price changes, we have a situation of **inelastic supply.** The supply curve is inelastic ($0 < E_s < 1$). In this case, the supply curve is steeply sloped. Figure 4.11 shows that a considerable increase in price will not induce producers to supply a large increase in quantity.

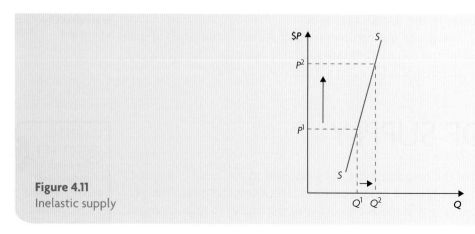

Figure 4.11
Inelastic supply

UNIT ELASTICITY

Where a change in price leads to a proportionate change in quantity supplied, we have **unit elasticity of supply.** Unit elasticity is equal to one ($E_s = 1$). The supply curve is on a 45-degree angle (Figure 4.12).

unit elasticity of supply
where a change in price leads to a proportionate change in quantity supplied

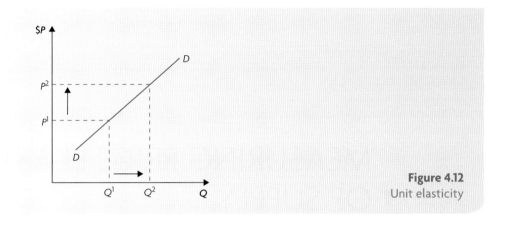

Figure 4.12
Unit elasticity

ELASTIC SUPPLY

Where the quantity supplied is more than proportionate to the change in price, we have a situation of **elastic supply.** The elasticity of supply is greater than one ($E_s > 1$) and the supply curve has a flatter slope (Figure 4.13).

elastic supply
where the quantity supplied changes more than proportionately to the change in price

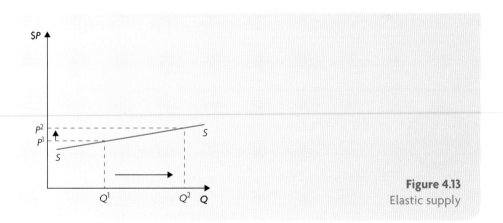

Figure 4.13
Elastic supply

COMPLETELY ELASTIC SUPPLY

Where a change in price of a good causes supply to change dramatically, in this case ceasing altogether, we have **completely elastic supply.** Elasticity of supply is said to be infinite ($E_s = $ infinity) and is shown as a horizontal line (Figure 4.14 overleaf). If the price decreases from P^1 to P^2, supply of the good ceases. This price is too low to sustain any producers in the market.

completely elastic supply
where supply of the good will cease when the price decreases

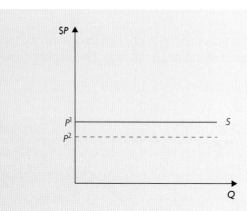

Figure 4.14
Completely elastic supply

MEASURING PRICE ELASTICITY OF SUPPLY

To calculate the elasticity of supply we use the point method, so the procedure is similar to our earlier calculations of elasticity of demand. However, we substitute elasticity of supply for elasticity of demand.

$$E_s = \frac{\text{percentage change in quantity supplied}}{\text{percentage change in price}}$$

Again:

- Where the coefficient is greater than 1.0, supply is elastic.
- Where it is equal to 1.0, supply is unitary.
- Where it is less than 1.0, supply is inelastic.

EXAMPLE 1

There is a price increase from $100 to $102 and an increase in supply from 200 to 250.

(a) percentage change in quantity supplied

$$\frac{\text{change in quantity supplied}}{\text{original quantity supplied}} \times \frac{100}{1} = \frac{50}{200} \times \frac{100}{1} = 25$$

(b) percentage change in price

$$\frac{\text{change in price}}{\text{original price}} \times \frac{100}{1} = \frac{2}{100} \times \frac{100}{1} = 2$$

$$E_s = \frac{25}{2} = 12.5$$

The elasticity coefficient is greater than one, so supply is elastic (Figure 4.15).

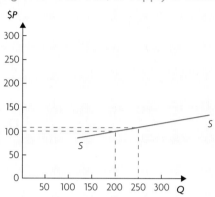

Figure 4.15
Elastic supply

EXAMPLE 2

There is a price increase from \$100 to \$102 and an increase in quantity supplied from 200 to 202.

(a) percentage change in quantity supplied

$$\frac{\text{change in quantity supplied}}{\text{original quantity supplied}} \times \frac{100}{1} = \frac{2}{200} \times \frac{100}{1} = 1$$

(b) percentage change in price

$$\frac{\text{change in price}}{\text{original price}} \times \frac{100}{1} = \frac{2}{100} \times \frac{100}{1} = 2$$

$$E_s = \frac{1}{2} = 0.5$$

The elasticity coefficient is less than one, so supply is inelastic (Figure 4.16).

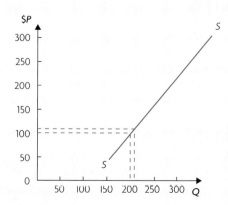

Figure 4.16
Inelastic supply

EXAMPLE 3

There is a price increase from $100 to $102 and an increase in quantity supplied from 200 to 204.

(a) percentage change in quantity supplied

$$\frac{\text{change in quantity supplied}}{\text{original quantity supplied}} \times \frac{100}{1} = \frac{4}{200} \times \frac{100}{1} = 2$$

(b) percentage change in price

$$\frac{\text{change in price}}{\text{original price}} \times \frac{100}{1} = \frac{2}{100} \times \frac{100}{1} = 2$$

$$E_s = \frac{2}{2} = 1$$

Because the elasticity coefficient is equal to one, supply is said to have unit elasticity (Figure 4.17).

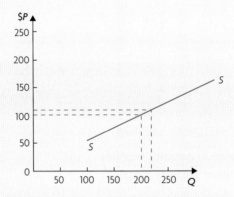

Figure 4.17
Unit elasticity

LEARNING OBJECTIVE 5
Explain different factors that affect the elasticity of demand

FACTORS AFFECTING ELASTICITY OF DEMAND

Consumers' responses to price changes are determined by many influences. Elasticity of demand is also affected by several factors concerning the commodity, the consumer and/or the price itself. We discuss six of these factors below.

AVAILABILITY OF SUBSTITUTES

Substitute goods are goods that can be used in place of other goods for the same purpose. Rice Bubbles and Corn Flakes are considered substitutes as breakfast cereal.

Products that are close substitutes for others are very price-sensitive because a change in price of one will cause a change in the buying habits of consumers. So when the price of one breakfast cereal (Rice Bubbles) increases, consumers switch to purchasing an alternative breakfast cereal (Corn Flakes). Rice Bubbles in this case would be said to have an elastic demand curve. The greater the number of substitute products available, the greater the elasticity of demand.

There is a distinction, however, between the price sensitivity of consumers to the market as a whole, and to individual producers in the market. If the market retail price for petrol increases, consumers have little choice but to pay the higher price. However, if one individual producer increases its price, consumers will probably switch to the other, cheaper brands. Petrol, because of the lack of substitutes, has an inelastic demand. However, particular brands of petrol, or petrol stations on opposite sides of a street, are close substitutes and tend to be highly elastic.

ELASTICITY OF DEMAND FOR HOME LINE TELEPHONE SERVICES

With the growth in mobile telephone adoption rates, the demand for home line telephone rental is declining. Whereas previously home lines were also used for internet connection, the expansion of mobile and wireless technology means that home line telephones are increasingly becoming unnecessary and seen as a duplication of services with consumers paying for two services (home phone and mobile) when they are able to do with one service.

LINK TO
BUSINESS

QUESTIONS

1. Draw a diagram illustrating the demand for traditional home phone line rental services to show the impact of mobile phone and wireless technology on traditional home phone line rental.
2. Explain what has happened to the conditions of demand for traditional home phone line rental.
3. How would you expect this change to affect the pricing of traditional home phone line rental?
4. List the products and services that are complementary to:
    (a) traditional home phone line rental
    (b) mobile phones in the home with wireless connection.
5. Would you describe the demand for mobile phones as elastic or inelastic? Give a reason for your answer.

ESSENTIAL COMMODITIES

The extent to which the commodity is a necessity is another factor determining its elasticity of demand. Examples are bread, rice, milk and essential medicines. Consumers always need the product, regardless of its price. Commodities such as bread or rice can be fundamental to our diet and a price rise is unlikely to lead to a significant decrease in quantity demanded. Demand is said to be inelastic for these commodities.

HABIT OR DESIRABILITY

For such commodities as tobacco products, alcohol and drugs of addiction, demand tends to be inelastic. Consumers purchase the product through force of habit or necessity, and pay quite high prices to do so.

With an inelastic demand curve, products in these categories tend to attract a significant amount of tax as a way of raising revenue for the government. Such income for the government is virtually guaranteed; people will continue to buy the product regardless of the increased price resulting from tax charges, and so the demand for the product is said to be inelastic.

TOTAL OUTLAY AND INCOME

Where the outlay on a good is only a small proportion of income, we would expect demand to be inelastic. An increase in the price of toothpicks from 40 to 60 cents a packet is a 50 per cent increase. However, not many consumers would baulk at paying an extra 20 cents. Demand is inelastic.

Where the outlay is large, a small percentage increase can actually mean a significant price increase. A 5 per cent price increase on a $30 000 car is an extra $1500. In this instance, demand would be elastic.

Because of the absolute amounts involved, a 50 per cent increase in the price of toothpicks (inelastic) has a much smaller effect than a 5 per cent increase in the price of a motor car (elastic).

COMPLEMENTARY PRODUCTS

While substitute products are considered interchangeable, complementary products are used together. To consume one product you must consume both. Separately, each product is virtually useless. Demand for a compact disc is only a small fraction of the cost of buying a compact disc player. Generally, if you can afford the player, you can afford some discs.

TIME

The time of the year can affect purchasing patterns. As winter approaches, we start to buy the latest ski equipment, paying higher prices because it is essential to have proper equipment and the latest fashion accessories.

In summer we buy little snow-skiing equipment and switch our consumption patterns to T-shirts, surfboards and factor-30 sunscreen.

During summer, we defer the purchasing of ski gear and therefore it is elastic, while during winter demand for ski gear tends to be inelastic.

ELASTICITY OF DEMAND IN THE PETROL RETAIL MARKET

LINK TO BUSINESS

There has long been concern that the retail price of petrol tends to increase on weekends (Friday to Sunday) and is cheaper during the week (especially Wednesday).

QUESTIONS
1. Describe the price elasticity of demand for petrol and the reason for your answer.
2. Why would petrol station retailers adjust prices in this way? Would it have anything to do with the number of consumers, the location of the petrol stations and the amount of money they have to spend?

LINK TO INTERNATIONAL ECONOMY

UNDERSTANDING PRICE ELASTICITY OF DEMAND

An understanding of price elasticity of demand is essential for producers. They need to know and understand consumers' likely responses to proposed price changes. A producer would ideally like an inelastic demand curve. In situations of inelastic demand, industries tend to be carefully monitored by government bodies such as the Australian Competition and Consumer Commission (see Chapter 7); such products as electricity, water and gas have in the past been supplied to consumers by government monopolies (see Chapter 6).

FACTORS AFFECTING ELASTICITY OF SUPPLY

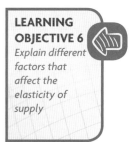

LEARNING OBJECTIVE 6
Explain different factors that affect the elasticity of supply

The influences on elasticity of supply are similar to those on elasticity of demand.

TIME

Depending on the product, some producers are able to respond quickly to price changes, while other producers are constrained in the immediate future by previous production decisions.

In agriculture, time is required to increase output: farmers must wait for crops to grow and ripen, or for the right growing season or climatic conditions. By contrast, in a factory, overtime can provide a ready response to changes in price and supply constraints.

In a shirt factory, for example, the quantity supplied is relatively elastic because it is fairly easy to increase production in a short time by adding more labour inputs and raw materials, running additional shifts, and increasing overtime etc (see Figure 4.18(a) overleaf). With orchids, on the other hand, the quantity supplied is relatively inelastic because of the time it takes to increase production (see Figure 4.18(b) overleaf).

ABILITY TO STOCKPILE OR STORE OUTPUT

We see that different products, such as shirts and orchids, exhibit different elasticities because of the time factor. In addition, the elasticity of supply can change for a product as production decisions are altered.

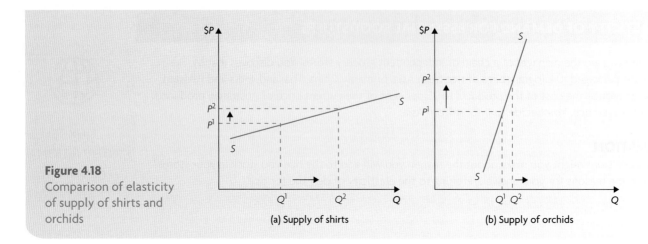

Figure 4.18
Comparison of elasticity
of supply of shirts and
orchids

(a) Supply of shirts

(b) Supply of orchids

If the products can be stored—like wool and wheat—they can be withdrawn from sale when the price is low, in the expectation of a higher price at some time in the future. Of course, other factors need to be taken into account when stockpiling goods, such as storage costs and public opinion considerations of the effect of withdrawing products from consumer circulation.

EXCESS CAPACITY

Supply is more elastic when there is excess capacity and the producer can increase production quickly to take advantage of rising prices. When there is idle machinery, unused factory space and the possibility of overtime, production may quickly be increased.

However, when the producer and firm are operating at total capacity to produce goods, supply usually becomes inelastic.

BUSINESS EXPECTATIONS

A firm that is able to forecast market trends accurately can benefit from price changes. However, it needs to know how long the price change will last. If the price change is considered to be long term, with a degree of permanence, the producer will tend to increase output, reflecting an elastic supply curve. On the other hand, if the price changes are considered transitory, supply will be more inelastic.

ELASTICITY OF DEMAND AND SUPPLY FOR CARS IN INDIA

LINK TO
INTERNATIONAL
ECONOMY

Maruti Suzuki India Ltd is India's biggest carmaker and will boost production capacity 46 per cent due to increased economic growth and higher demand for cars from the market. Maruti currently builds 1.2 million vehicles a year, but with a new factory at Manesar, near New Delhi, it will be able to make as many as 1.75 million vehicles annually.

It is predicted that industry-wide car sales could double in India by 2015 and Maruti plans to spend 35 billion yen ($416 million) to build this new factory to keep up with demand. Ford Motor Co. and Volkswagen AG are also building plants and introducing new models in India, which will pose a challenge to Maruti's 50 per cent market share.

Mercedes Benz, Audi and BMW have also benefited from this high demand as the demand for luxury cars in the Indian market has also been increasing in recent years.

Source: <www.bloomberg.com/news/2010-09-07/maruti-suzuki-to-raise-india-capacity-as-demand-rises-beyond-expectation-.html>, accessed 5 November 2010.

QUESTIONS

1. If you were the manager of the Maruti Suzuki India plant:
   (a) What decisions might you make about the price of your vehicles to customers to maintain a high demand and sales volume?
   (b) What decisions might you make about the production capacity of your car plant?
   (c) What competition, if any, do you face from luxury carmakers?
   (d) What do you consider to be the elasticities of demand for luxury vehicles and the cheaper, more generic Maruti Suzuki models?

Give reasons for your answers, referring to the concept of elasticity of supply and demand.

ELASTICITY OF DEMAND FOR AND SUPPLY OF WATER

LINK TO BUSINESS

In 2003 severe water restrictions were introduced in several Australian cities after six years of drought. In Victoria, after significant rains during 2009 and 2010, water restrictions were eased. The watering of lawns, previously banned as part of the restrictions, was permitted any time with a bucket, watering can or hose fitted with a trigger nozzle, and automatic watering systems could be programmed to operate between specific times on alternate days. In addition during restrictions, the price of water to consumers was increased and by 2010 this was yet to be reduced.

QUESTIONS

1. Describe the elasticity of demand for water for the following. Illustrate using diagrams.
   (a) household users
   (b) football club ovals
   (c) car washes
   (d) market gardeners
   (e) rice farmers in the Riverina.
2. Describe how the restrictions would affect demand for the following. Illustrate using diagrams.
   (a) pebbles and pavers
   (b) garden designers
   (c) lawnmowers
   (d) manufacturers of water tanks
   (e) front loader versus top loader washing machines.
3. How would you describe the elasticity of supply of water? Give reasons for your answer.
4. Why do you think that the government has not decreased the price of water to the consumer following the easing of restrictions? What could be a possible consequence of reducing the price of water?

SUMMARY

1. Elasticity is an important concept for consumers and producers. Producers, especially, need to be conscious of elasticity in any pricing decisions they make. For price-sensitive goods, and goods for which there is an elastic demand, any price increase will, in fact, lead to a fall in total revenue.

2. There are five types of price elasticity of demand. They range from perfectly inelastic, where the consumer is unresponsive to price changes, to perfectly elastic, where the consumer is highly responsive. In between, we identified three other elasticities, reflecting a variety of responses by the consumer, which could be due to the product, the availability of substitutes, the size of the price change, and a range of other factors.

3. It is important to calculate the price elasticity of demand using either the total revenue method or the point method. The elasticity cannot be indicated with certainty by the slope of the curve. Income elasticity of demand and cross elasticity of demand are two additional methods of assessing aspects of elasticity.

4. Price elasticity of supply measures the responsiveness of producers to a change in the price of the product. Supply can range from inelastic or unresponsive to price changes through to highly responsive or elastic to price changes. We usually use the point method to calculate the elasticity of supply.

5. A considerable range of factors affects the elasticity of supply and demand. They include the availability of substitutes, the time of the year, the extent to which the commodity is essential, the ability to stockpile or store output, and excess capacity.

KEY TERMS

completely elastic supply	71	income elasticity of demand	69	price elasticity of supply	70
cross elasticity of demand	69	inelastic demand	62	total revenue method	64
elastic demand	63	inelastic supply	70	unit elasticity of demand	62
elastic supply	71	point method	68	unit elasticity of supply	71
		price elasticity of demand	61		

REVIEW QUESTIONS

1. Identify whether the following statements are true or false. Be prepared to justify your answer.

   (a) You can always tell the elasticity of demand by the slope of the demand curve. True or False?

   (b) Income elasticity suggests that, the higher our income, the more goods we have to buy because of the income effect. True or False?

   (c) The total revenue used in conjunction with the slope of the curve indicates elasticity of demand. True or False?

   (d) A producer would prefer consumers to have very elastic demand curves. True or False?

   (e) According to cross elasticity of demand, when the elasticity is positive, the goods are complementary. True or False?

   (f) If the supply curve of a producer is elastic, a price increase would result in an increase in total revenue. True or False?

   (g) A perfectly inelastic supply curve is the same as a perfectly inelastic demand curve. True or False?

   (h) If the elasticity coefficient is greater than one, and the total revenue increases with a price change, supply must be elastic. True or False?

   (i) If close substitutes are available, demand will be highly elastic. True or False?

   (j) Demand for drugs of addiction is highly inelastic. True or False?

   (k) Governments will impose a tax on a product that has an elastic demand because it is a certain way of raising revenue. True or False?

   (l) Inelastic demand is the same as elastic supply. True or False?

   (m) Wool must have an inelastic demand. That is why we stockpile so much of it. True or False?

2. In Table 4.2, calculate the price elasticity of demand for each price increase.

Table 4.2: Price elasticity of demand

PRICE $	QUANTITY Q	TOTAL REVENUE TR	ELASTICITY E
5.00	5		
4.00		60	
3.00	40		
2.00		120	
1.00	80		

3. Explain why the slope of the curve is not always a good indicator of the price elasticity of demand.
4. As a producer, what demand curve would you like consumers of your product to have? Why?
5. You run a small grocery store in an inner suburb. Your customers are mostly low- to middle-income wage earners. Rises in the costs of running your store are beginning to erode your already small profit. Two friends have offered you vastly different advice. One said to increase your prices and another said to decrease your prices. Why have your friends offered different solutions to the same problem?
6. How will the following price changes affect total revenue?
   (a) a price rise and elastic demand
   (b) a price rise and elastic supply
   (c) a decrease in price and inelastic demand
   (d) a fall in price and elastic demand.
7. List the major factors affecting the elasticity of demand. How elastic is the demand for the following products?
   (a) sausages
   (b) caviar
   (c) newspapers
   (d) salt
   (e) cigarettes
   (f) an overseas trip to (i) New Zealand (ii) Europe
   (g) Jim Beam whisky
   (h) rice.
8. Explain the distinguishing elements of:
   (a) price elasticity of demand
   (b) income elasticity of demand
   (c) cross elasticity of demand.

9. Using your understanding of elasticity, explain why governments prior to the 1990s provided essential services such as electricity, gas and telecommunications.
10. Assume that you are a government adviser and wish to impose a tax that will have minimal impact on low-income earners. What sort of goods would you select? Conversely, you wish to impose a tax that would maximise revenue earning for the government. What sort of goods would you select?
11. The elasticity of supply can change over a period of time. Why is this the case? Illustrate your answer with diagrams showing the different possible elasticities.

APPLIED QUESTIONS AND EXERCISES
ALCOPOPS

In 2008, the Commonwealth Government increased taxes on pre-mixed alcoholic drinks by 70 per cent. Estimates were that the new tax would raise A$2 billion over four years. In addition to raising new revenue, the new tax was aimed at reducing consumption of alcohol, particularly among teenage girls, as part of a preventative health program to tackle binge drinking.

QUESTIONS

1. How would you describe the elasticity of demand for pre-mixed drinks or 'alcopops'?
2. When the government introduced the new tax, what goal was it trying to achieve in terms of the demand curve for pre-mixed drinks?
3. Assuming the government's tax was successful, what would be the impact on the demand curve for cheap cask wine?
4. Alcopops were sold at licensed supermarkets, hotel bottle shops and chain liquor outlets. Assuming a reduced demand for alcopops because of the new tax, describe a possible impact on the demand curve for labour at chain liquor outlets and hotel bottle shops who do not have the same ability to diversify and sell a range of non-alcoholic products.

ELASTICITY OF SUPPLY AND DEMAND IN THE SKIING INDUSTRY

The Australian skiing industry operates out of a very narrow seasonal base—approximately three months in a good season. In a good year, providers of accommodation, ski hire and tow operators stand to benefit from increased usage of services and more people taking part in ski and après-ski activities. In a poor year, with the late arrival of snow and the early finish to the season, and hence fewer visitors to the ski slopes, many operators need to meet their operating costs plus profits in a shorter period of time.

QUESTIONS

1. Draw a diagram to illustrate the effect of a poor supply of snow and short season on demand for resort accommodation.

2. With a reduced ski season, how would you describe the elasticity of demand for ski hire facilities?

3. Illustrate two possible outcomes by reducing the hiring price to encourage more customers or increasing price to increase total revenue.

4. The introduction of snow-generating machines can extend the ski season. What will be the impact on the supply curve of restaurants on the mountain by extending the ski season?

3

MARKET STRUCTURES

Chapter **5**

Market structures and the Australian capitalist economy

LEARNING OBJECTIVES

After studying this chapter, you will be able to:

1. describe the four main market structures in a capitalist economy
2. explain the distinguishing characteristics of these four market structures
3. distinguish between a price taker and a price maker
4. distinguish between a homogeneous product and a heterogeneous product
5. identify the market structures to which various Australian industries belong
6. explain what is meant by product differentiation, how it occurs and why
7. describe various types of barriers to entry facing a firm in an imperfect competitive market structure.

INTRODUCTION

LEARNING OBJECTIVE 1
Describe the four main market structures in a capitalist economy

Chapter 1 introduced the idea that different economic systems have developed in attempts to solve the basic economic problems. Two basic types of economic systems were presented, market (capitalist) and command (centrally planned). Each system grapples with the notion of scarcity of resources and the competing solutions to the problems of what to produce, how to produce and for whom.

A capitalist system is the type of economic system we have in Australia. Within capitalism, different **market structures** have evolved. These structures are identified by factors such as the number of buyers and sellers, the nature of the product, the availability of information, the ability to enter and leave the market, the forms of competition and the mobility of resources.

While still operating within a capitalist economic system, Australia has the following market structures:

- perfectly competitive markets
- monopolies
- monopolistic competition
- oligopolies.

This chapter describes and explains the distinct characteristics of these four different market structures.

market structures
different types of markets, identified by factors such as number of buyers and sellers, nature of the product, availability of information, ability to enter and leave, forms of competition and mobility of resources

THE CAPITALIST ECONOMY

Two major characteristics distinguish a capitalist economic system from a command system:

- Individual private ownership of resources or the factors of production. This contrasts with communal ownership in primitive economies, and ownership by the state in command economies.
- Broadly speaking, the extent of government intervention in the economy is assumed to be minimal in pure capitalist economies. Government intervention does not exist in primitive economies. In command economies, government authorities plan and implement economic decisions across the whole economy.

Australia, like most other economies, is in fact a **mixed economy**. That is, we have private enterprise as the economic basis for decision making and allocating goods and services among competing wants, but government involvement in allocating resources in the Australian economy accounts for approximately 25 per cent of economic activity.

Command-type economies also have government and private activity in the economy, but the proportions may be reversed when compared with the capitalist economic system. That is, there may be 70 per cent government activity and 30 per cent private activity accounting for economic output.

The Australian economy can variously be called a capitalist economy, a private enterprise economy, a mixed economy or a market economy. All these terms, in effect, describe the same basic economic market structure.

mixed economy
an economy with a mixture of private enterprise and government intervention

MARKET ECONOMY

market economy
*one in which major
decisions concerning
both the production
and distribution
of goods and
services are made
in accordance with
the market forces of
demand and supply*

A **market economy** is one in which major decisions concerning both the production and distribution of goods and services are made in accordance with the market forces of demand and supply. The required elements for a market to exist are:

- producers who are willing and able to exchange goods and services for payment (and profit)
- consumers who are willing and able to purchase goods and services by payment and receiving utility (satisfaction)
- an agreed price that represents the value placed upon the goods and services by the producer and consumer.

However, the form and substance that these markets can take is varied. It is impossible to describe fully all the different market structures operating in Australian industries. A single producer dominates some industries, in other industries there are thousands. In what follows, we provide a theoretical description of each of the four market structures: perfect competition, monopoly, monopolistic competition and oligopoly.

To decide the exact location of an industry within a particular market structure requires flexibility in thinking and is to some extent arbitrary.

Perfect competition is often claimed to be the most efficient economic structure because of the high levels of economic efficiency it achieves. It does this through allocative efficiency, in that goods and services are allocated in the most efficient ways to maximise consumer utility and producer profits. In the next chapter we will see that in the short run and long run, price will be equal to marginal cost and allocative efficiency is achieved. Moreover, productive efficiency will be achieved in the long run as the market moves towards equilibrium output.

Pareto optimality

Pareto optimality is an economic principle developed by the Italian economist Vilfredo Pareto (1848–1923). The principle states that given an amount of resources and alternative uses for them, if a change in the allocation makes at least one person better off, without making anyone else worse off, then there has been a Pareto improvement. When no further changes can be made in the allocation of the resources to improve outcomes, then Pareto efficiency or Pareto optimality has been achieved.

PERFECT (PURE) COMPETITION

perfect competition
*a hypothetical model
of an economy which
provides the basis
of many economic
theories and models*

Perfect competition rarely exists in practice, but it is illuminating to examine it. A perfectly competitive market has seven distinguishing characteristics:

1. a large number of buyers and sellers
2. a homogeneous product
3. perfect knowledge
4. perfect mobility
5. freedom of entry and exit
6. absence of non-price competition
7. the firm is a price taker.

A LARGE NUMBER OF BUYERS AND SELLERS

A main feature of pure competition is very large numbers of buyers and sellers, so that no individual is able to exercise any influence over the price in the market. With a large number of competing sellers, no individual seller will attempt to sell goods above the market price. No one would buy them when cheaper products were available. Similarly, no seller will sell goods below the market price and miss out on the extra income to be gained. Each seller provides only a small fraction of market supply.

A HOMOGENEOUS PRODUCT

With a **homogeneous product** (standardised product) any particular producer is indistinguishable from other producers. There is no branding or specific labelling. Producer A's goods are identical in shape, form and price to Producer B's, Producer C's, Producer D's, and so on. If the buyers can distinguish the product of any one firm in any way, then the element of perfect competition is destroyed. Because it is a homogeneous product and there are a large number of sellers, the consumer is indifferent to the specific producer of the product.

PERFECT KNOWLEDGE

In a perfectly competitive market it is assumed that every buyer and seller is fully acquainted with all the conditions in the market, in particular the price, quality and availability of the product.

PERFECT MOBILITY

No producer in an industry has any specific locational or geographic advantage over others. Moreover, factors of production are free to move throughout the industry or between industries, as the owner believes appropriate in his or her search for profit.

FREEDOM OF ENTRY AND EXIT

New producers are free to enter any industry and existing producers are free to leave the industry. There are no **barriers to entry**, whether financial, legal, technical or political, to prohibit or prevent firms entering the industry and selling their products. Anyone who wishes to enter a particular industry and compete can do so. No one is excluded on the grounds of legality, government prohibition, union claims, patent copyrights, resource ownership or other reasons.

ABSENCE OF NON-PRICE COMPETITION

Because it assumes an identical product and many sellers in the market, this market structure is accompanied by an absence of non-price competition; that is, there is no competition on the basis of factors such as product quality, special design features, advertising and accompanying sales promotion. If all firms in the industry produce indistinguishable (homogeneous) products, advertising would be an unnecessary expenditure (and cost thus reducing profit), so firms do not attempt to use advertising to create brand loyalty. Because of the assumption of perfect knowledge, consumers know that all the products have the same features.

LEARNING OBJECTIVE 2
Explain the distinguishing characteristics of the four main market structures in a capitalist economy

homogeneous product
a standardised product whose producer is indistinguishable from other producers

barriers to entry
means of preventing new firms entering an industry through legal, economic, financial or technical means

THE FIRM IS A PRICE TAKER

Because there are a large number of firms in each industry, and no firm can therefore exercise any influence over price, each firm is said to be a **price taker**. That is, it must take the going market price for the goods. Because each firm is contributing only a fraction to total market output, increasing or decreasing output will have no measurable effect on total supply and therefore the price. The producer cannot adjust the price, but rather must adjust to any price changes.

For example, if there were 50 000 firms in a particular industry, each producing 50 units of output, then total output would be 2 500 000. If one firm were to halve its output to 25 units, total output would be reduced to 2 499 975, a negligible change.

These assumptions and distinguishing characteristics that underlie perfect competition are unrealistic. Few markets are perfectly competitive, but there are some close approximations:

- fruit and vegetable markets
- stock exchanges
- betting rings at racetracks
- the global financial market.

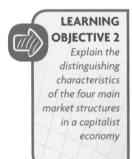

AN EXAMPLE OF PERFECT COMPETITION: FRUIT AND VEGETABLE MARKETS

Large numbers of buyers and sellers

A visit to any large wholesale or retail market, such as the Adelaide Central Market, shows that this characteristic holds true. At the Queen Victoria Market in Melbourne, for instance, there are 1000 sellers in an area equal to a city block. It is estimated that up to 30 000 shoppers visit the market in a week, depending on the time of year. The Queen Victoria Market also competes with the Prahran Market, Preston Market, South Melbourne Market and others selling fresh food, produce, meats, fish and deli items.

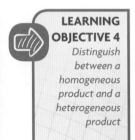

A homogeneous product

You buy a pumpkin from stall A or stall B or stall C. In quality it is indistinguishable from other pumpkins. Producers have begun to attach stickers to their products in an attempt to distinguish them from others and therefore destroy this element of homogeneity.

Perfect knowledge

If you were prepared to walk up and down every aisle and compare price and quality of the goods, you could, for example, obtain perfect knowledge of the range of goods, the types of goods and the prices. In fact, this is not practical. At the Queen Victoria Market, for instance, it would take a long time, given the number of sellers. In addition, prices tend to change according to the time of day and some sellers will bargain over prices.

Perfect mobility

There is no advantage in the particular location of a stall at the market. The density of people ensures that no position is special. The geography of the market changes. One week a particular stall sells fruit, another week vegetables, depending on the anticipated demand.

Freedom of entry and exit

You are free to become a stallholder at a market provided there is space for you and you pay the rent demanded for your space. No one forces you to attend each week and sell produce, and you are allowed to exit the market when you see fit. Consumers are free to shop there or at any other market.

Absence of non-price competition

Individual sellers at a market do not spend money on advertising. With so many competing sellers offering identical produce, it would be a waste of money. Shoppers tend to buy from regular sellers or shop around to get the best price.

The firm is a price taker

The firm has no ability to influence the price set in the marketplace. It has to accept the price set by the market. If a firm charges too high a price, its competitors will undercut it with a lower price, and consumers will buy from the competitor (assuming no quality differences).

MONOPOLY

At the other extreme of the four types of market structures is a monopoly, which provides the sharpest contrast to perfect competition.

A **monopoly** is a situation where there is one seller or one buyer in the market. Five major elements distinguish a monopoly from other market structures:

- one seller
- one product
- price maker
- barriers to entry
- minimal advertising expenditure.

monopoly
a situation where there is one seller or one buyer in the market

ONE SELLER

The defining characteristic of a monopoly market is that there is only one producer in the market. That is, the firm is the industry. The firm does not have any competitors in production.

ONE PRODUCT

In a monopoly there is only one product, for which there are no close substitutes. This places the monopolist in a unique and powerful position in the market. Not only is it the only producer in the market, but there are no close substitute products and so consumers are forced to take it or leave it: they either buy the product from the monopolist or survive without it.

LEARNING OBJECTIVE 3
Distinguish between a price taker and a price maker

PRICE MAKER

The monopolist is a **price maker**. In the absence of competitors, market power enables the monopolist to set the price, largely avoiding the interactive forces of demand and supply. The monopolist is responsible for and controls the quantity supplied. Therefore, given a downward-sloping demand curve, the monopolist can determine the price of the product by manipulating the quantity of output.

price maker
a firm is a price maker when it is able to set the price in the marketplace

BARRIERS TO ENTRY

The monopolist's ability to block entry of potential firms is another characteristic that distinguishes it from perfect competition. The monopolist can prevent new firms entering the industry through legal, economic, financial or technological means.

MINIMAL ADVERTISING EXPENDITURE

As the only producer, with no competition or close substitute goods, the monopolist does not need to advertise to promote its products or to encourage expenditure by consumers. Any advertising that takes place is usually to promote awareness and public relations.

LEARNING OBJECTIVE 5
Identify the market structures to which various Australian industries belong

TYPICAL MONOPOLIES

Traditionally, monopolists have controlled industries that are considered essential. In Australia, governments have usually controlled the essential industries. Previously federal or state governments had monopolies in areas such as telecommunications (Telstra, formerly Telecom), gas and electricity, postal communications, water supply and public transport.

In the 1990s, government economic policy and direction moved to loosen government control. Governments that previously excluded new entrants through legislation passed laws and encouraged new firms to enter the industry in order to provide competition in price and quality. This is dealt with further in Chapter 7.

Sometimes regulatory bodies are formed to coordinate the activities of many individual producers and act as a monopolist on their behalf, either by setting prices or restricting (stockpiling) supply. Examples are the Australian Wool Corporation and the Australian Wheat Board.

EXAMPLE OF A MONOPOLY: AIRPORTS

There are very few private monopolistic companies in Australia today. For many years Telstra enjoyed what is known as a 'government monopoly'. In 1991 Optus was selected to bring competition into the long-distance telecommunications market, and it has changed the market structure in this industry. Australia Post enjoys elements of monopoly in the delivery of postal services though it faces competition from private parcel delivery services. Companies controlling airports enjoy what is a natural monopoly and have come under criticism for misuse of market power.

One seller

International airlines generally land at one airport only in each state—Melbourne is Tullamarine, Sydney Airport, Darwin International, Brisbane (and Cairns) International Airports etc. So only one international airport and supporting services is generally provided in each state.

One product

Most airports provide the same services to international airlines and customers: check-in facilities, parking and shops.

Price maker

The controlling airport authority determines all fees and service charges such as parking fees. Customers have no alternative but to park within the airport precinct and pay the stated parking fees, which many people consider exhorbitant.

Barriers to entry

There were legal barriers to entry, because the government prohibited any firm from competing with the airport. Moreover, there are considerable financial and locational barriers to entry regarding the airport infrastructure (such as car parks, baggage handling facilities, trolleys, check-in counters etc). To set up a rival airport without using existing infrastructure would be financially prohibitive.

Minimal advertising

During any period of monopoly the company has little reason to advertise as there is no competition.

MONOPOLISTIC COMPETITION

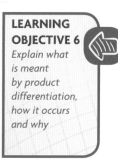

LEARNING OBJECTIVE 6
Explain what is meant by product differentiation, how it occurs and why

In between perfect competition and monopoly are two remaining market structures that present more realistic scenarios: monopolistic competition and oligopoly.

Monopolistic competition is a type of market structure where a large number of firms produce close, but not perfect, substitutes. The producers distinguish their output and themselves through product differentiation or geographical fragmentation.

Product differentiation is the process whereby real or imagined differences are created in products that are in effect identical. This is done through advertising, packaging and quality, among other things.

When a firm that has many competitors promotes its product as being slightly different and somehow 'better' than those of its competitors, it can establish customer loyalty or brand loyalty. The firm is then in a position to exert some influence over the price of the product. The retail trade in clothing is an example of a monopolistically competitive industry. There are seven distinguishing characteristics of monopolistic competitors:

monopolistic competition
where a large number of firms produce close, but not perfect, substitutes

product differentiation
the process whereby real or imagined differences are created in products that are in effect identical

1. varying numbers of buyers and sellers
2. heterogeneous products
3. imperfect knowledge
4. imperfect mobility
5. barriers to entry
6. absence of price competition
7. limited price control.

VARYING NUMBERS OF BUYERS AND SELLERS

The number of buyers and sellers varies in particular industries. Each firm produces a small share of the total output.

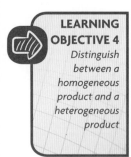

LEARNING OBJECTIVE 4
Distinguish between a homogeneous product and a heterogeneous product

heterogeneous products
products that have been differentiated from each other and can in most cases be clearly identified with a particular firm

HETEROGENEOUS PRODUCTS

Firms produce **heterogeneous products**, which in most cases can clearly be identified with a particular firm. Usually this results from product differentiation and the way the product is packaged, labelled or advertised. Note the contrast with perfect competition, where the products were homogeneous, or indistinguishable.

Heterogeneity involves not only the physical characteristics of the product, but also factors such as the geographic location of the store, credit availability, customer service—in fact, the total package of benefits offered to the consumer as an inducement to buy. The products are close but not perfect substitutes.

IMPERFECT KNOWLEDGE

Unlike perfect competition, which unrealistically assumed perfect knowledge on the part of producers and consumers, monopolistic competition assumes imperfect knowledge. Consumers are rarely in a position to evaluate all prices, qualities and additional benefits of a particular good. It is too time-consuming and costly.

Consumers tend to rely on the information given to them by the producers rather than searching it out for themselves.

IMPERFECT MOBILITY

It is generally acknowledged that there is some rigidity in the movement of the factors of production and they are not perfectly mobile. The factors of production are not totally transferable across industries as perfect competition assumes. In addition, there are locational advantages in some industries. Shipping agents, for example, prefer to be located near the docks, not in the countryside. Aircraft freight forwarders can usually be found close to airports. Consequently, some firms have a locational advantage over others in the same industry.

LEARNING OBJECTIVE 7
Describe various types of barriers to entry facing a firm in an imperfect competitive market structure

BARRIERS TO ENTRY

Sometimes the barriers to entry are insurmountable, sometimes not. Generally, however, entry is easier, but not as easy as in perfect competition; and survival is difficult, but not as difficult as in perfect competition.

Generally the barriers to entry are financial. A firm entering the market has to advertise to inform consumers and gain market share by wooing customers away from existing producers. Usually the advertising required to generate customer awareness is expensive, and firms without large financial resources are excluded from the market. In addition, a new entrant needs sufficient financial resources to spend on product research and development, which are essential for it to appear to have created a new and differentiated product.

ABSENCE OF NON-PRICE COMPETITION

Because of product differentiation, there tends to be substantial competition in areas other than price in monopolistically competitive industries. Competition revolves around perceived quality differences in the products, advertising and associated services. The desirability of a product over its competitors is highlighted through non-price variables.

LIMITED PRICE CONTROL

Price control is limited. Monopolistically competitive producers have limited control over price changes. Because they have competitors they cannot make the price like a monopolist. However, product differentiation offers a small margin where they may be able to raise their price above competitors' prices. Consumers apparently recognise some differences between the various sellers' products and are often willing to pay a marginally higher price for a differentiated product that they perceive as superior.

MONOPOLISTIC COMPETITION AND EXCESS CAPACITY

Excess capacity refers to when a firm is producing a lower level of output than it is capable of producing. In certain situations, increasing the scale of output will reduce overall per unit costs of production. In monopolistic competition output may be less than that of more efficient perfectly competitive firms. Excess capacity may arise in cases when there is an increase in demand and firms may need to invest to meet the increase in demand over and above existing capacity to do so. Particularly in cases when demand is not forecast to be constant, firms may elect to maintain excess capacity, rather than invest in increasing productive capacity.

MONOPOLISTIC COMPETITION: RETAIL CLOTHING TRADE AS AN EXAMPLE

The retail clothing industry is a good example of a monopolistically competitive industry. There are many in the industry whose products are close, but not perfect, substitutes. They have been able to distinguish their products: a different cloth, a different style, a different fashion, and available at different locations. Their advertising attempts to highlight the differences. The particular characteristics are examined below.

LEARNING OBJECTIVE 5
Identify the market structures to which various Australian industries belong

Varying number of buyers and sellers

The number of buyers and sellers depends on economic factors, the time of the year, and regular changes in fashion. Each firm produces a small percentage of the total output. In the retail clothing trade some large well-known chains sell both women's and men's clothing, but as a percentage of the total output their contribution is small. Prominent women's wear retailers, usually found in shopping centres and other high traffic volume places, include Witchery, Portmans, Katies, Esprit, and Country Road. They make up, however, a surprisingly small segment of the total number of women's wear retailers.

Heterogeneous products

A product can clearly be identified with a particular firm. This is done through packaging, advertising and labelling. All clothing items have a label to distinguish the particular brand from close substitutes, and often the label is visible when the item is worn—a red tab on a pair of jeans, the number of stripes on a pair of running shoes, a motif on a shirt pocket.

Imperfect knowledge

As consumers, we are not in a position to evaluate all the prices and qualities and benefits of a particular article of clothing we may wish to buy. The number of stores in a city, as well as all the suburban outlets, means we cannot acquire perfect knowledge. We either shop in a selected area that we are familiar with, or go to larger stores with a bigger range of goods.

Imperfect mobility

In this industry, the location of the retail outlet can be critical. Retail clothing traders require high customer volume and traffic. Customers usually browse when shopping for clothes. For every 10 people that enter a clothing shop, only one may buy. Hence it is essential for traders to be located in areas or centres with a large number of potential customers.

Barriers to entry

After creating a new and distinguishable product you must sell it. This means incurring the additional expenses of advertising and informing the consumer, or positioning the retail outlet in an area with high customer traffic, usually with high rental costs. As we saw in Chapter 3, when demand is greater than supply, price increases, so when demand for shop rental in areas with high customer traffic exceeds the supply of available shops, rents must increase. A producer must have the financial resources to be able to support such expenses.

Also, fashions change frequently. A clothing retailer must have up-to-date information and a constant turnover of stock to stay in business.

Absence of non-price competition

Although price is important in the eyes of the consumer, clothing retailers tend to compete in non-price areas. Quality is often highlighted in this industry. Some retailers offer inducements: buy a suit, get a free shirt. There are regular sales of old stock, where prices are discounted to make way for new fashions; or the price per unit may decrease, the greater the quantity you buy.

Price control is limited

Product differentiation enables the trader to charge slightly different prices for the product. The ability to do so, however, depends on the availability of substitutes and the reputation of the brand name. Where clothing fashions are concerned, although there may be close substitute products, you would expect little variation in price. But if there is customer brand loyalty, consumers will pay a higher price.

OLIGOPOLY

oligopoly
*where a market
has relatively
few suppliers*

The remaining market structure, known as an **oligopoly**, is a market that has relatively few suppliers, usually six or fewer. Price differences are generally minimal within oligopolies, and most competition takes place in non-price areas, such as advertising.

In Australia, industries such as insurance, banking and retailing can be characterised as oligopolies. In oligopolistic industries there tends to be a high degree of concentration; that is, a substantial portion of output is produced by a limited number of producers.

There is also a great interdependence among all the firms. When one firm makes a decision, the others evaluate it closely. The actions and reactions of the other firms must be anticipated in any pricing or output decisions.

The five characteristics of an oligopolistic market structure are as follows:

1. few suppliers and producers
2. products are close substitutes
3. a degree of control over price
4. difficult market entry
5. significant non-price competition.

FEW SUPPLIERS AND PRODUCERS

A monopolist is a sole producer in a market, and a duopoly has two producers. In an oligopoly there must be at least three producers. A small number of firms dominate the market. There are fewer producers than in a market with perfect competition or monopolistic competition—in those market structures each firm held a fairly small share of the market.

In an oligopoly a small number of producers can account for up to 70 or 80 per cent of the output. The remaining small percentage of output is produced by a small number of fringe firms, smaller both in size and in share of output.

With a few large firms dominating the market, their policies are interrelated. Because each of these large firms contributes a substantial portion to total output, when one firm attempts to improve its market share, it does so at the expense of the others. Such actions can be financially dangerous, inviting retaliation in the form of a price war (discussed further below).

PRODUCTS ARE CLOSE SUBSTITUTES

Depending on whether the industry is producing raw materials or finished goods, this market structure varies in the area of substitutes and product differentiation. If the oligopolists are producing raw materials, such as minerals, then the product is virtually uniform. In the area of finished goods, where the consumer is the direct recipient of the good, the product is highly differentiated. An example is the car industry.

A DEGREE OF CONTROL OVER PRICE

The degree of the interdependence among the dominant firms and the extent of product differentiation have a direct influence on the ability of a firm to manipulate price. Oligopolists may tacitly agree not to alter prices significantly or frequently.

If a firm lowers price in an attempt to grab market share, other firms have no option but to match the price reduction. They may even undercut the first firm to try to force it out of the market. A protracted **price war** is a serious drain on finances—a firm cannot run at a loss forever. A firm that uses prices as its main selling point in the marketplace must be confident that it has the financial resources to beat its rivals.

If a firm raises its price above competitors, rival firms may not follow the price increase. The firm would then lose market share as it prices itself out of the market and virtually hands over its customers to its competitors. The sensitive nature of pricing in an oligopolistic market means that there is potential for collusion among oligopolistic firms in the industry (more of this in Chapter 7).

Collusion is where the firms in an oligopolistic market make an arrangement regarding the price of the product or somehow divide the market share. In effect, by joining together

price war
involves the use of pricing as a competitive weapon

collusion
where the firms in an oligopolistic market make an arrangement regarding the price of the product or somehow agree on how to divide the market share between them

they act as a monopolist in their pricing practice. Alternatively, the oligopolists may agree to set quotas.

The potential for collusion in oligopolistic industries has drawn close government attention to monitor competition. Generally, even in the absence of any collusive agreements between firms, there is little variation in price between them. Compare petrol prices in Australia and watch how they change on each day of the week.

In oligopilistic market structures, firms can engage in predatory pricing. This is the practice of selling the firm's output at a very low price to drive out competition or prevent new potential firms from entering the market. The firm is willing to forgo profits in the short run to maximise its market position of power in the long run. It is an attempt to create a barrier to entry because if existing or potential new firms cannot match the price, they will go out of business or direct their resources into a different industry.

DIFFICULT MARKET ENTRY

Without substantial financial backing, market entry into an oligopoly is a formidable prospect. Without substantial investment funds or ownership of raw materials or patents, for instance, a new entrant is at a decisive cost disadvantage. A new firm must battle against the existing firms, which all desire to keep it out: a further division of the market means less for all the existing firms.

Initial costs may be considerable. It is not possible to start small and build up a business over time. The industry may be a specialised one where the skills and techniques of low-cost production are learned over time. This works against new entrants because they lack the skills. Entry is not impossible, but it is difficult.

SIGNIFICANT NON-PRICE COMPETITION

There is keen competition between products in non-price dimensions. Firms in oligopolistic industries frequently spend considerable amounts on advertising and other promotional activities, such as sponsorship of events with high public exposure.

For example, car manufacturers have high advertising budgets to promote their products' superiority over rivals. Soft-drink manufacturers spend millions in sponsorship deals and media blitzes to induce consumers to drink Brand X instead of Brand Y or Z.

LINK TO BUSINESS

OLIGOPOLY AND THE PRISONER'S DILEMMA

In oligopolistic markets, each firm knows that its level of profit will depend on the actions of other firms in the same market, i.e. its competitors. This gives rise to 'the prisoner's dilemma' with respect to pricing and levels of output. In game theory, people's behaviour is studied in how they react to certain situations and the prisoner's dilemma is an example of how difficult it is to cooperate, even when it is in both player's best interest to do so. Applying this to market behaviour illustrates that oligopolistic (and duopolistic) firms will select their own strategy to dominate the other in the short term to maximise individual gain. In so doing, eventually equilibrium is reached whereby they are both worse off than if they had adopted a non-dominant strategy.

COMPETITION IN THE VIDEO/DVD/CD GAMES BUSINESS

Assume you own a video/DVD/CD games store and you are considering opening additional stores to increase your revenue and local market share. You have two competitors within a 5 kilometre radius—one in the main street, one in a new housing area. Your store is located on a highway next to four fast food chain stores and a petrol station.

LINK TO
BUSINESS

QUESTIONS
1. What type of market structure are you in?
2. Are all three video/DVD/CD games competitors operating in the same market?
3. Are you selling a homogeneous or heterogeneous product?
4. What can you say about the knowledge of consumers?
5. Can you do anything about barriers to entry to your market?
6. Can you identify any possible areas of non-price competition?
7. List three opportunities for product differentiation.
8. Will there be any impact on the market structure if the petrol station starts offering to rent videos/DVD/CD games?

EXAMPLE OF AN OLIGOPOLY: MOBILE PHONES

In 2010 the mobile phone market in Australia exhibited the characteristics of an oligopoly.

LEARNING OBJECTIVE 5
Identify the market structures to which various Australian industries belong

Few suppliers
Telstra is the major player together with Optus, Vodafone, Hutchison, Virgin, AAPT and other smaller suppliers.

Products are close substitutes
The essential services provided are access to mobile phone lines via infrastructure like telephone towers. However, each provider offers specific services to subscribers to differentiate them from other service providers.

A degree of control over price
One area where there is little evidence of competition is in the area of price. Australian prices for mobile phone services are among the highest in the world. Competition is focused on service and lifestyle or fashion issues, contacts, download rates and price per minute call charges.

Difficult market entry
The cost of establishing a mobile phone network is very high. The owners of Telstra, Optus, Virgin and Vodafone and others have invested large amounts of capital into the development of mobile phone infrastructure.

Significant non-price competition
Mobile phone companies advertise extensively and maintain major sponsorships in order to promote themselves and to differentiate their products in the minds of consumers. This considerable expenditure is aimed at gaining more customers and increasing market share at the expense of rivals.

THE PUBLIC TRANSPORT SYSTEM IN MELBOURNE

LINK TO BUSINESS

In 1999 the state government owned and operated public transport system in Melbourne was sold by the government to private operators. After being put to international tender, the right to operate the suburban and country train and suburban tram systems was awarded to National Express, Connex and Yarra Trams.

The reason behind the government divesting itself of these economic public transport resources was the view that the private sector would generate improved services at lower cost. In the first few years following 'privatisation' some improvements were evident such as a fall in late and cancelled services, an increase in service levels and passenger traffic.

In December 2002 National Express handed its tram and train services back to the government because it could not continue to pay for the losses involved in running the system.

In 2004 the government announced that two private companies would run the public transport system in Melbourne—there would be one tram and one train company (private monopolies under government regulation, as opposed to government monopolies).

In 2010, at the expiration of the initial contract awarded to Connex, Metro replaced Connex as the provider of train services to suburban Melbourne.

QUESTIONS

1. Describe the history of Melbourne's public transport in terms of monopoly and oligopoly.
2. How would you describe the latest arrangement in terms of:
   (a) number of sellers
   (b) nature of the product
   (c) freedom of entry and exit
   (d) price control?
3. Do you think consumers will be better off? Why?
4. If Metro were to increase the price of train tickets, what alternatives would customers have?

ILLEGAL INTERNATIONAL DRUG CARTELS

LINK TO INTERNATIONAL ECONOMY

The organisations involved in trafficking of cocaine from South America have traditionally been highly organised. During the 1980s, the groups involved were even dubbed 'cartels'. A cartel is a consortium of businesses whose combined domination of an industry is so complete that they can collaborate to set prices and otherwise manipulate the market to their mutual benefit.

*Source: <www.unodc.org/pdf/research/wdr07/WDR_2007_2.3_coc_usa.pdf>,
accessed 5 November 2010.*

In Colombia, South America, the three main cartels were the Medellin Cartel, the Cali Cartel and the Norte del Valle Cartel. Individually and collectively, they attempted to manipulate the quantity of illegal cocaine they exported and the prices that the drug would sell for. While they made billions of dollars, they also operated within an environment of mistrust, violence, bribery and assassinations.

QUESTIONS

1. Describe the market structure for cocaine in terms of:
   (a) number of buyers and sellers
   (b) nature of the product
   (c) degree of knowledge of the participants
   (d) mobility of resources
   (e) degree of freedom of entry and exit
   (f) non-price versus price competition
   (g) who the price taker is.
2. Is the global market for illegal drugs such as cocaine perfectly competitive, a monopoly, monopolistically competitive or an oligopoly? Give three reasons for your answer. Additional information can be found at ‹www.unodc.org›, accessed 5 November 2010.

SUMMARY

1. A capitalist economic system has developed different market structures as it has evolved over time.
2. While a perfectly competitive market is a more abstract model than what really exists in the economy, it provides a useful starting point to distinguish one market structure from another. Perfect competition is characterised by:
   (a) a large number of buyers and sellers
   (b) a homogeneous product
   (c) perfect knowledge
   (d) perfect mobility
   (e) freedom of entry and exit
   (f) no non-price competition
   (g) the firm being a price taker.
3. A monopoly is at the opposite extreme, characterised by:
   (a) one seller
   (b) one product with no close substitutes
   (c) the firm being a price maker
   (d) significant barriers to entry
   (e) minimal non-price competition (i.e. advertising).
4. With the absence of real perfect competition and a growing movement away from monopolistic industries, particularly in the government sector, we are left with two market structures which describe the current state of many industries in the Australian economy.
5. The characteristics of monopolistic competition are:
   (a) varying numbers of buyers and sellers
   (b) heterogeneous products
   (c) imperfect knowledge
   (d) imperfect mobility
   (e) barriers to entry
   (f) no non price competition
   (g) limited control over price.

6. The final example is of an oligopolistic market structure:
   (a) few producers
   (b) products are close substitutes
   (c) a degree of control over price
   (d) difficult market entry
   (e) significant non-price competition.

KEY TERMS

barriers to entry	87	market structures	85	price maker	89
collusion	95	mixed economy	85	price taker	88
heterogeneous products	92	monopolistic competition	91	price war	95
homogeneous product	87	monopoly	89	product differentiation	91
market economy	86	oligopoly	94		
		perfect competition	86		

REVIEW QUESTIONS

1. Identify whether the following statements are true or false. Be prepared to justify your answer.
   (a) Most markets in Australia are perfectly competitive because of the large number of buyers. True or False?
   (b) All products in perfectly competitive markets are homogeneous. True or False?
   (c) In a perfectly competitive market, all the prices for a product will be negotiable. That is why we say the firm is the price taker—it must take the price the customer offers. True or False?
   (d) There is no such thing as a monopolistic producer because all products have substitutes. True or False?
   (e) A monopoly will usually attract new firms because of the profits that can be made. True or False?
   (f) Monopolies usually produce essential commodities and so are usually run by governments. True or False?
   (g) Product differentiation will always exist in monopolistically competitive markets. True or False?
   (h) Because of product differentiation, a producer in a monopolistically competitive market has a large degree of control over price. True or False?
   (i) Advertising is wasted expenditure because consumers know of product differences in monopolistically competitive markets. True or False?
   (j) Collusion is a refined form of competition and is legal in certain industries in Australia. True or False?
   (k) Products are easily distinguishable in oligopolistic industries. True or False?
   (l) A new firm would initially find it difficult to enter the car manufacturing industry, but would survive in the long run because of the amount of profits that can be made and shared. True or False?

2. Distinguish between heterogeneous goods and homogeneous goods.

3. What type of market structure would you say applied to the petroleum industry? Why?

4. If the perfectly competitive market rarely exists, what is the purpose of studying it?

5. Why would a perfectly competitive firm not decrease its price to increase market share?

6. How would you distinguish a market economy from other economic systems? Do you believe similar market structures exist in non-capitalist economic systems?

7. The telecommunications market in China is dominated by three state run corporations—China Telecom (fixed line and broadband internet), China Unicom (GSM, local and long distance calls and CDMA network) and China Mobile (mobile and multimedia services). Do you think consumers in China would benefit by opening the market to competition? Why?

8. Since China's entry into the World Trade Organization in 2001, foreign operators are gradually being allowed access to the Chinese market for telecommunication services. How will this change the telecommunications market structure in China?

9. 'Non-price competition is the method used by oligopolists to increase market share.' What is meant by this statement?

10. What is a price taker?

11. What is a price maker? Are oligopolists price makers?

12. 'Product differentiation exists in all industries and in all markets.' Do you agree with this statement? Why or why not?

13. Why would firms avoid price wars in an oligopoly? Can you think of circumstances when a price war would be advantageous? How would this affect the consumer in the short term and the long term?

14. What is collusion? Do you think it should be illegal, or is it simply an example of non-competitive behaviour by firms ensuring their survival in the industry?

15. Why will there always be product differentiation in monopolistic competition?

16. 'The greater the total number of firms in the industry, the more competitive the industry will be.' Do you agree with this statement? Why or why not?

17. Which market structure do you think the following industries belong to? Why?
    (a) steel
    (b) petroleum
    (c) stock exchange
    (d) railways
    (e) television
    (f) daily newspapers
    (g) toothpaste
    (h) cement
    (i) egg farms
    (j) diamond mining.

18. The Australian Institute of Petroleum states: 'The Australian refining sector is a price taker. Domestic prices are closely linked to relevant international prices.'

    Source: <www.aip.com.au/pricing/facts/Weekly_Petrol_Prices_Report. htm>, accessed 5 November 2010.

    Do you agree that the Australian refining sector is a price taker and does not dictate terms and process to the retail petrol consumer?

APPLIED QUESTIONS AND EXERCISES

HOME HARDWARE

Bunnings warehouse is a leading retailer of home improvement and outdoor living products and a major supplier of building materials throughout Australia and New Zealand. With over 180 stores, in 2009–10 sales reached in excess of $A6.4 billion. Originating in Western Australia in the 1880s, Bunnings continued to expand and with acquisitions of McEwans in Victoria and South Australia spread through eastern Australia. Bunnings offers a wide range of additional services to the industry in all facets of do-it-yourself building, garden supplies and a variety of hardware services.

QUESTIONS

1. How would you describe Bunnings—a monopoly or oligopoly? Give reasons for your answer.

2. Describe the change taking place in the structure of the market for home hardware in terms of:
   (a) number of sellers
   (b) nature of the product—homogeneous or heterogeneous
   (c) knowledge
   (d) mobility
   (e) freedom of entry and exit
   (f) price control.

3. What is your prediction for the future of smaller home hardware stores?

24 HOUR CONVENIENCE STORES

7-11 originally began in Australia as a store that would sell grocery items and that would open from 7 am to 11 pm—outside of normal trading hours for mainstream stores. The first store opened in 1977, and in 1978 the company quickly expanded to 24 hour operations. Also in 1978 the company introduced selling petrol as an additional product line. In 1981, the first Sydney store opened and in 1982, the first store in Brisbane commenced operations. In May 2010, 7-11 announced that it had acquired Mobil Fuels' retail businesses.

QUESTIONS

1. Describe the market structure for 24 hour retailing in Australia.

2. Describe the market structure for petrol in Australia.

3. What new entrants are you aware of in the 24 hour convenience store market? Has this changed the market structure?

4. What are the consequences for small corner stores that usually service a community within a small radius if they cannot operate extended hours trading?

Chapter **6**

Contemporary market capitalism: Price and output determination in different market structures

LEARNING OBJECTIVES

After studying this chapter, you will be able to:

1. explain the significance of marginal revenue and marginal cost
2. distinguish between the long run and short run
3. distinguish between fixed cost and variable cost
4. state the law of diminishing returns
5. describe the different profit-maximising positions for a monopolist and a perfectly competitive firm
6. given a cost and revenue table, calculate and explain the profit-maximising position
7. define and explain economies of scale
8. distinguish between internal and external economies of scale
9. explain the significance of a kinked demand curve and how it arises.

INTRODUCTION

Chapter 5 introduced the four market structures that exist in a capitalist economy: perfect competition, monopoly, monopolistic competition and oligopoly. Here we expand on that rudimentary analysis by showing how firms in each of the four market structures make decisions about price and output as they attempt to maximise their individual profits.

Some additional and useful economic concepts are incorporated into the analysis, such as the law of diminishing returns, economies of scale and diseconomies of scale.

Each of the four market structures is unique and faces different problems in its attempts to maximise its profit.

PRICE AND OUTPUT DETERMINATION: PERFECT COMPETITION

Chapter 5 described perfect competition as a market structure in a capitalist economy with the following characteristics:

- a large number of buyers and sellers
- homogeneous products
- perfect knowledge
- perfect mobility
- freedom of entry and exit
- absence of non-price competition
- the firm is a price taker.

Even though there are few instances of perfect competition, it is our starting point in evaluating how a firm attempts to maximise its profit and determine the quantity of output that it will produce.

REVENUE

Revenue is calculated by multiplying the price of a product by the quantity sold.

When the market comprises a large number of firms, no individual firm is able to exercise any influence over price. Moreover, the output of each individual firm is a small contribution to the total market output. The firm is a price taker, which means it must accept the prevailing market price. Any attempt by an individual firm to sell at a higher price will cause demand to cease altogether.

Similarly, no firm sells at less than the market price because it would be selling the product at a price below the going market rate and not earning as much revenue as it could.

Each firm faces a perfectly elastic demand curve, as Figure 6.1 overleaf shows. Although the market demand curve is downward-sloping, the individual demand curve facing the firm is horizontal.

When consumers purchase a product at a given price, they are showing their demand or preference for that product. This demand can also be viewed as revenue for a firm.

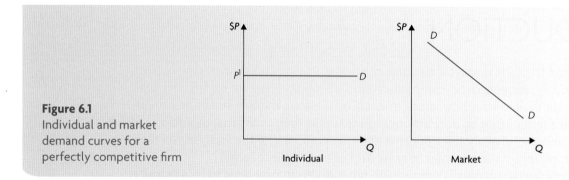

Figure 6.1
Individual and market
demand curves for a
perfectly competitive firm

The money you pay for a product is the same as the revenue the firm receives. However, this revenue can be measured in three different ways, which are listed in Table 6.1. They are average revenue, total revenue and marginal revenue.

Table 6.1   **Demand and revenue schedule for a perfectly competitive firm**

QUANTITY DEMANDED Q (SOLD)	PRODUCT PRICE $	AVERAGE REVENUE AR	TOTAL REVENUE TR	MARGINAL REVENUE MR
0	41	—	0	41
1	41	41	41	41
2	41	41	82	41
3	41	41	123	41
4	41	41	164	41
5	41	41	205	41
6	41	41	246	41
7	41	41	287	41
8	41	41	328	41
9	41	41	369	41
10	41	41	410	41

Average revenue

average revenue
total revenue divided by the quantity sold

If the product price that the consumer pays is unchanged in a perfectly competitive market, **average revenue** must be the same as the price. This is expressed as an equation:

$$AR = TR \div Q$$

where AR = average revenue
TR = total revenue
Q = quantity.

In Table 6.1, average revenue is unchanged at $41, which is also the selling price of $41.

$$\$41 \div 1 = \$41$$
$$\$82 \div 2 = \$41$$
$$\$123 \div 3 = \$41$$

Total revenue

Total revenue, as its name implies, is the total amount of revenue that a firm receives from selling a given quantity of goods.

In Table 6.1, marginal revenue is a constant amount of $41. This is because we are examining a perfectly competitive market where the price is fixed at $41. With each additional unit sold, total revenue must rise by $41. (This factor will change in different market structures, as we will see later in this chapter.) Marginal revenue is also a comparative measurement. It compares total revenue when the quantity sold is one ($41) with total revenue when the quantity sold is two ($82), or with total revenue when the quantity sold is eight ($328), or with total revenue when the quantity sold is nine ($369). That is why the marginal revenue column is offset between the two figures in the total revenue column.

$$TR = P \times Q$$

where TR = total revenue
P = price
Q = quantity.

In Table 6.1, total revenue is cumulative and increases by a constant amount, that is, the selling price of $41. Each additional unit sold adds the same amount to total revenue.

$$\$41 \times 4 = \$164$$
$$\$41 \times 5 = \$205$$
$$\$41 \times 6 = \$246$$

Marginal revenue

Marginal revenue is a crucial measurement for a firm contemplating producing and selling additional output, or trying to decide how much to produce. It is the addition made to total revenue by the sale of one additional unit.

Demand and revenue

The relationship between demand and revenue is shown in Figure 6.2 overleaf. We can see that the total revenue curve increases by constant amounts. The perfectly elastic demand curve (for the consumer) is equal to the average and marginal revenue curves for the firm, which is also equal to the price.

COSTS

Every firm must pay costs associated with production. In economics the costs are divided into short-run and long-run costs. The distinction between them is somewhat blurred

total revenue
the total amount of revenue that a firm receives from selling a given quantity of goods

marginal revenue
the addition made to total revenue by the sale of one additional unit

LEARNING OBJECTIVE 1
Explain the significance of marginal revenue and marginal cost

LEARNING OBJECTIVE 2
Distinguish between the long run and short run

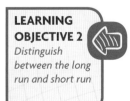

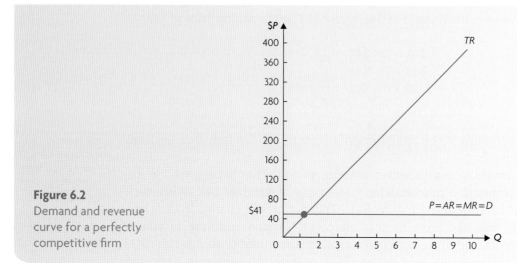

Figure 6.2
Demand and revenue curve for a perfectly competitive firm

because it depends on the particular industry under examination. However, the short run is usually defined in this way:

The **short run** is a time period whereby a firm is not able to vary its inputs of factors of production. In the short run, the firm is constrained by a given amount of capital and labour. The **long run**, as the name implies, is a longer period of time. The long run is the time period sufficient for a firm to be able to vary the quantities of its factors of production.

During one week, for example, a firm has a certain amount of resources at its disposal—machinery, raw materials, and labour. This is the short run. During a year, a firm may alter the types of input it uses, maybe less machinery and more labour. This is the long run. But, as stated earlier, the short-run and long-run periods vary in particular industries. The short run and long run for a city clothing retailer are vastly different from those for a major steel producer. This chapter will focus on short-run costs associated with a firm's production. The short run shows more economic dynamism than the long run.

LEARNING OBJECTIVE 3
Distinguish between fixed cost and variable cost

Fixed costs

Fixed costs are costs that the firm incurs irrespective of any level of output. Sometimes called overhead costs, they include, for example, rent on factory space and interest on borrowed capital. Even if the firm produces nothing, it must pay these fixed costs.

Variable costs

Variable costs are those costs directly associated with the level of production. Variable costs increase with the level of output. The more you produce, the more your variable costs increase. Variable costs include the cost of raw materials, wages paid to labour, and fuel and power charges.

Total cost

Total cost is simply the addition of fixed and variable cost for each level of output.

It is expressed as an equation:

$$FC + VC = TC$$

where FC = fixed cost
      VC = variable cost
      TC = total cost.

Marginal cost

The final measurement of cost is marginal cost, which is similar to marginal revenue. Marginal revenue was defined as the addition to total revenue made by the sale of one more unit. **Marginal cost** is the addition to total cost through producing one additional unit.

Marginal revenue and marginal cost are critical concepts for a firm to understand, and ideally each firm should be able to calculate the marginal revenue and marginal cost measurements. In deciding the quantity of output, or whether to increase production and output, a firm must evaluate whether additional production will cost more than the revenue to be gained by selling the additional output. That is, will marginal cost be greater than marginal revenue, or vice versa? To maximise its profits, the firm needs to know the answer. Table 6.2 details the various costs associated with different levels of production.

We can make some important observations regarding the figures in Table 6.2. First, note the variable costs. As output increases, variable costs also increase, as we would expect. To increase output, you need additional raw materials, extra electricity and so on. However, variable costs do not increase by the same amount for each increase in output. Initially, the variable costs increase by smaller amounts, up to the third unit of output in Table 6.2, after which they increase by larger amounts.

marginal cost
the addition to total cost through producing one additional unit

Table 6.2   **Short-run cost schedule for a perfectly competitive firm**

QUANTITY Q	FIXED COST FC	VARIABLE COST VC	TOTAL COST TC	MARGINAL COST MC
0	35	—	35	
1	35	24	59	24
2	35	40	75	16
3	35	60	95	20
4	35	85	120	25
5	35	115	150	30
6	35	155	190	40
7	35	210	245	55
8	35	285	320	75
9	35	380	415	95
10	35	505	540	125

REDUCING COSTS THROUGH CALL CENTRES

3 Messaging offers businesses a call centre service whereby it answers calls on behalf of the business. Whereas previously a business may have required a designated person(s) and section within an office to answer calls this is now undertaken by 3 Messaging.

QUESTIONS

1. Explain the nature of fixed and variable costs.
2. Identify the fixed costs in call centres such as 3 Messaging and by an individual firm.
3. Explain how allocating this service of call centres could contribute to a company's profitability.
4. Why would a firm choose to use a call centre rather than use their own personnel?

**LEARNING
OBJECTIVE 4**
*State the law
of diminishing
returns*

**law of diminishing
returns**
*if you hold one
factor of production
constant while
adding more of the
variable factors of
production, then
output per unit of
input will initially
increase before
output begins to
decrease per unit
of input*

Law of diminishing returns

This alteration in the rate of increase of variable costs is a demonstration of the **law of diminishing returns**. It can be stated thus:

If you hold one factor of production constant while adding more of the variable factors of production, then output per unit of input will initially increase before output begins to decrease per unit of input.

Comparing costs

The second point to note in Table 6.2 (p. 107) is that even at zero units of output, the firm has still incurred costs of $35. This distinction between fixed costs and variable costs is important. The firm has some control over variable costs, but it has no control over fixed costs. Whenever the Reserve Bank lifts official interest rates, firms have no option but to pay this higher interest on borrowed funds. Figure 6.3 shows the breakdown of fixed, variable and total costs, while Figure 6.4 shows the marginal cost curve.

EXAMPLE

Assume that, in the short run, the size of the factory remains the same (is held constant). In order to increase output, the factory owner may add more machinery, more raw materials, more labour. The owner may change inefficient work practices, extend working hours, shorten lunch breaks or offer incentives to work harder.

Initially, productivity may increase (measured, for example, as a decrease in per unit cost) but there is a point where further increases in productivity are not possible. With the size of the factory space fixed, extra workers may simply get in each other's way instead of producing more. Machines may not be fully utilised, and overcrowding results in a decrease in productivity.

The factory owner must make more factory space available if productivity is to increase again. But this can only happen in the long run, when all factors of production can be altered.

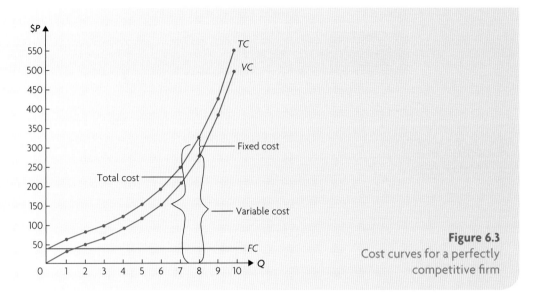

Figure 6.3
Cost curves for a perfectly competitive firm

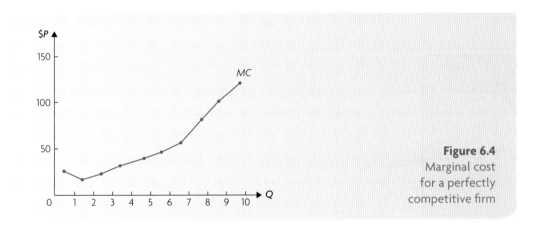

Figure 6.4
Marginal cost for a perfectly competitive firm

MAXIMISING SHORT-RUN PROFIT FOR A PERFECTLY COMPETITIVE FIRM

A firm is in business to make a profit, which is the difference between the total costs it incurs in production and the total revenue it receives from selling its output. It must decide at what level of output it will make the greatest profit. There are two different methods for calculating the profit-maximising level of output: by total cost and total revenue; and by marginal cost and marginal revenue.

Total cost–total revenue method

In Table 6.3 we bring together some of the data contained in Tables 6.1 (p. 104) and 6.2 (p. 107).

LEARNING OBJECTIVE 5
Describe the different profit-maximising positions for a monopolist and a perfectly competitive firm

Table 6.3   **Earning the greatest profit**

QUANTITY Q	FIXED COST FC	VARIABLE COST VC	TOTAL COST TC	TOTAL REVENUE TR	+PROFIT −LOSS
0	35	—	35	—	−35
1	35	24	59	41	−18
2	35	40	75	82	+7
3	35	60	95	123	+28
4	35	85	120	164	+44
5	35	115	150	205	+55
6	35	155	190	246	+56
7	35	210	245	287	+42
8	35	285	320	328	+8
9	35	380	415	369	−46
10	35	505	540	410	−130

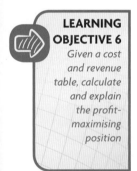

LEARNING OBJECTIVE 6

Given a cost and revenue table, calculate and explain the profit-maximising position

The firm should produce at the level of output where it earns the greatest profit. In Table 6.3, this is an output level of six units, where the total profit, the difference between total cost and total revenue, is $56.

At output levels zero and one the firm makes a loss of $35 and $18 respectively. As production increases from two to five units of output, each increase in production makes a successively larger level of profit, from $7 to $55. At seven units of output, the firm is still making a profit of $42 but this is less than $56, the profit at six units of output. Likewise with output of eight units, where profit is reduced to $8. If the firm produces nine or 10 units of output, it makes a loss of $46 or $130.

Figure 6.5 shows graphically that the firm should produce at the level of output where the distance between total cost and total revenue is greatest.

The area where the TR curve lies above the TC curve represents output levels where the firm makes profits. The output levels where the two curves intersect (points A and B) represent break-even points. At these points the firm does not make any profit, but it does not incur any losses. At point A, the initial costs have been offset from revenue gained by increasing production. At point B, all the profit earned by an output level of 28 has been cancelled out because costs are increasing more rapidly than revenues.

Marginal cost–marginal revenue method

In Table 6.4 we reproduce the marginal revenue and cost information contained in Tables 6.1 (p. 104) and 6.2 (p. 107). The marginal cost–marginal revenue method suggests that a firm should increase production so long as the addition to total revenue is greater than the addition to total cost. Ideally, the firm produces that level of output where marginal revenue is equal to marginal cost. If this is not possible, then the firm produces up to the point where marginal revenue is still greater than marginal cost but they are almost equal.

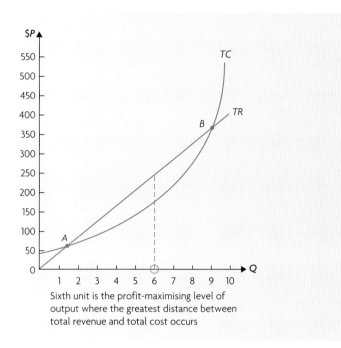

Figure 6.5
Profit-maximising level
of output for a perfectly
competitive firm

Sixth unit is the profit-maximising level of
output where the greatest distance between
total revenue and total cost occurs

In Table 6.4 we see that this occurs at six units of output. The addition to total cost, that is, the marginal cost of the sixth unit, was $40, but the addition to total revenue, the marginal revenue, was $41. So by producing the sixth unit, the firm made $1 profit for that sixth unit of output. At output levels below this, the cost of production was far less than the revenue to be gained, so the firm maximised profits by increasing production. At output levels of seven and above, the cost

Table 6.4   **Marginal revenue and marginal cost for a perfectly competitive firm**

QUANTITY Q	MARGINAL COST MC	MARGINAL REVENUE MR	+PROFIT −LOSS
0	—	—	—
1	24	41	+17
2	16	41	+25
3	20	41	+21
4	25	41	+16
5	30	41	+11
6	40	41	+1
7	55	41	−14
8	75	41	−34
9	95	41	−54
10	125	41	−84

of production starts to diminish the profit earned earlier. Although from Figure 6.5 (p. 111) we can see that the firm is still making a profit, it is less with each subsequent level of production above seven.

This information is shown graphically in Figure 6.6. The firm will produce that level of output where marginal revenue is equal to marginal cost (*MR* = *MC*), or where the two marginal curves intersect.

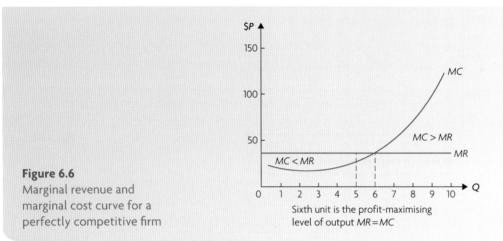

Figure 6.6
Marginal revenue and marginal cost curve for a perfectly competitive firm

We can show how the selling price of the product can alter the profit-maximising level of output. The perfectly competitive firm has no control over price; if the price changes, the firm must alter its output decision to continue to maximise its total profits. In Table 6.5 and Figure 6.7 we have reproduced the earlier, unchanged cost schedules but have decreased the selling price to $31. In Table 6.6 and Figure 6.8 (p. 114) we repeat the earlier marginal cost measurement with the new marginal revenue schedule.

Table 6.5   **Cost and revenue schedule for a perfectly competitive firm (price $31)**

QUANTITY Q	FIXED COST FC	VARIABLE COST VC	TOTAL COST TC	TOTAL REVENUE TR	+PROFIT −LOSS
0	35	—	35	—	
1	35	24	59	31	−28
2	35	40	75	62	−13
3	35	60	95	93	−2
4	35	85	120	124	+4
5	35	115	150	155	+5
6	35	155	190	186	−4
7	35	210	245	217	−28
8	35	285	320	248	−72
9	35	380	415	279	−136
10	35	505	540	310	−230

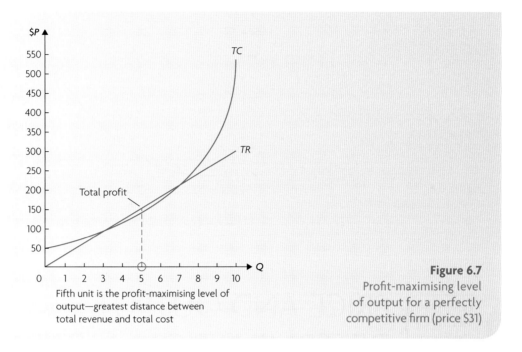

Figure 6.7
Profit-maximising level
of output for a perfectly
competitive firm (price $31)

Fifth unit is the profit-maximising level of
output—greatest distance between
total revenue and total cost

Table 6.6   **Marginal cost and marginal revenue schedule for a perfectly
competitive firm (price $31)**

QUANTITY Q	MARGINAL COST MC	MARGINAL REVENUE MR	+PROFIT −LOSS
0			
1	24	31	+7
2	16	31	+15
3	20	31	+11
4	25	31	+6
5	30	31	+1
6	40	31	−9
7	55	31	−24
8	75	31	−44
9	95	31	−64
10	125	31	−94

The numbers in Table 6.6 show that if the selling price is $31, the profit-maximising level of output is five units. If the firm continues production up to six units and does not adjust output to the new price, it loses $9, as can be seen from the marginal revenue marginal cost schedule. Or, if we look at Table 6.5, it would lose the potential for $5 profit at five units of output plus incur a loss of $4—a total loss of $9.

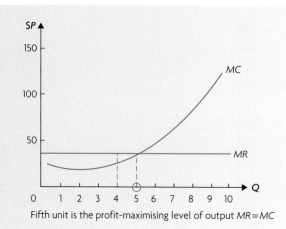

Figure 6.8
Profit-maximising
output

Fifth unit is the profit-maximising level of output $MR = MC$

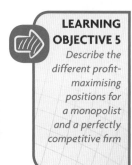
PRICE AND OUTPUT DETERMINATION: MONOPOLY

A monopoly is at the opposite end of the market structure spectrum from perfect competition. Instead of many sellers in the market, a monopolist is the only seller. The monopolist is the industry. A pure monopoly is said to exist when there is only one seller of a good for which there are no close substitutes.

Pure monopoly is rare for several reasons. There are substitutes for most products, although they may not be close substitutes: candles for electricity, letters instead of phone calls, faxes and emails.

PUBLIC UTILITIES

Most monopolies are public utilities. That is, they are usually controlled by, or answerable to, a federal or state government. The National Broadband Network will be a monopoly created by the federal government. Currently Australia Post is one of the few remaining government-owned monopolies in Australia. Management of water resources, an essential and finite resource, has largely been contracted out to international and Australian private sector firms.

BARRIERS TO ENTRY

Monopolies owe their existence to barriers to entry. In perfect competition, we assume that there are no barriers to entry or exit, but a monopolistic market structure is different. These barriers might include:

- control over essential raw materials
- protection by patents or copyright in production processes

- protection from imported competing goods by tariffs, quotas, embargoes or subsidies
- the size of the market, which may limit production to one firm.

ECONOMIES OF SCALE

In many industries, production costs are cheaper for longer production runs. The resulting savings are called economies of scale. Obviously, the economies are related to the size of the market, but per-unit cost can be lowered by increasing the size of output.

For example, if a machine costs $10 000 and you produce 50 units the average per-unit cost of the machine is $200. If you produce 500 units, the average per-unit cost of the machine becomes $20.

Economies of scale occur more often in oligopolies, and are discussed in more detail later in this chapter.

EXAMPLES OF MONOPOLIES

As already stated there are few instances of monopolies in Australia today, especially non-government monopolies. Now Telstra is no longer a monopoly, it faces competition from Optus and a range of other providers in the provision of services to customers. However, Telstra still controls the telecommunication infrastructure, and the other companies pay to use it. Thus Telstra faces competition in the customer service part of the market, but is a near monopolist in the provision of the infrastructure. Australia Post, in 2009, celebrated 200 years as Australia's oldest continually operating organisation and is still considered a government business enterprise.

PRICE AND OUTPUT

Unlike perfect competition, the monopolist does not face a perfectly elastic, horizontal demand curve which is equal to average revenue, marginal revenue and price. Because the monopolist represents the industry, the market demand curve for the industry is the same demand curve facing the monopolist, as in Figure 6.9.

The monopolist has considerable market power and, unlike the perfectly competitive firm, is not a price taker. In fact, a monopolist is known as a price maker. (Assume for the moment that the monopolist is not restricted in its behaviour by government bodies such as the Australian Competition and Consumer Commission, which is discussed in Chapter 7.)

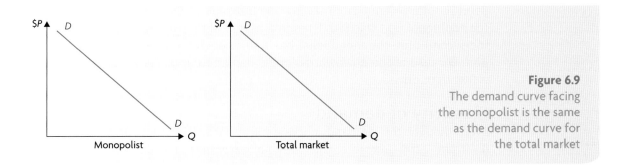

Figure 6.9
The demand curve facing the monopolist is the same as the demand curve for the total market

As price maker, the monopolist has very different revenue curves from those of perfect competition. The monopolist maximises profit by selecting the output where marginal cost is equal to marginal revenue. The monopolist's revenue schedule is shown in Table 6.7.

Table 6.7   **Revenue schedule for a monopolist**

QUANTITY Q	PRICE ($) AVERAGE P/AR	TOTAL REVENUE TR	MARGINAL REVENUE MR (+PROFIT) (−LOSS)
1	100	100	
2	90	180	(180 − 100) +80
3	80	240	(240 − 180) +60
4	70	280	(280 − 240) +40
5	60	300	(300 − 280) +20
6	50	300	(300 − 300) 0
7	40	280	(280 − 300) −20
8	30	240	(240 − 280) −40
9	20	180	(180 − 240) −60
10	10	100	(100 − 180) −80

Marginal revenue

For the perfectly competitive firm, marginal revenue was equal to the selling price, but for a monopolist marginal revenue is less than the selling price. This is a vital distinction in its price and output determination.

In Figure 6.10, suppose a monopolist moves along the demand curve from Point A to Point B. At point A, it was selling one unit at $100; at B, it is selling two units at $90. While the average revenue is equal to the selling price, $100 in the case of A and $90 in the case of B, what is the marginal revenue? In perfect competition it would also be equal to price and average revenue. However, in a monopoly, we find that marginal revenue is less than the selling price.

Recall that marginal revenue is the addition to total revenue from selling one more unit. At point A, total revenue from selling one unit was $100. At point B, total revenue from selling the additional unit was $90. Therefore marginal revenue is $180 − $100 = $80. In order to sell the second unit, the monopolist has had to decrease price, including the price on the first unit, because of the downward-sloping demand curve. For a monopolist, marginal revenue is less than price.

Elasticity of demand

Even though the demand curve (and hence the price and average revenue curves) does not fall below zero, the marginal revenue curve does. This draws on our study of

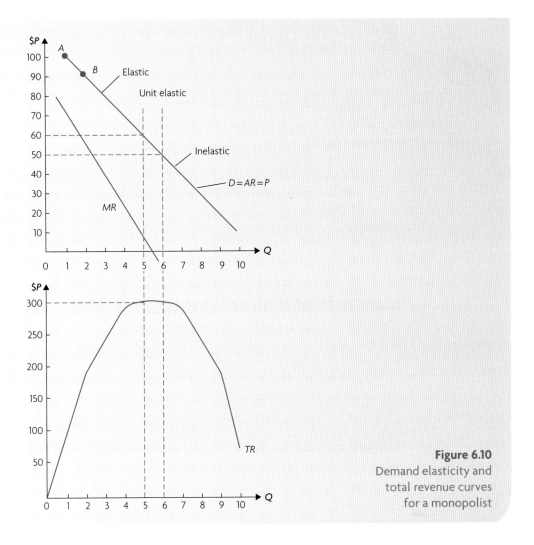

Figure 6.10
Demand elasticity and total revenue curves for a monopolist

elasticity in Chapter 4. Using the total revenue method, when demand is elastic (inelastic), a price decrease will increase (decrease) total revenue.

In Figure 6.10 every price reduction from $100 to $60 results in an increase in total revenue. Every price reduction from $40 to $10 results in a decrease in total revenue. Total revenue is unchanged between $60 and $50. Therefore demand is elastic in the price range $100 down to $60, unit elastic between $60 and $50, and inelastic between $40 and $10.

Where demand becomes inelastic, marginal revenue becomes negative and total revenue decreases with further price decreases, as Figure 6.10 shows. A profit-maximising monopolist avoids the inelastic section of the demand curve.

The elastic nature of demand is equated with the total revenue curve. Total revenue will increase, by decreasing amounts, from output of one unit through to output of five units. When total revenue is at its greatest, marginal revenue is equal to zero, and when demand becomes inelastic, total revenue actually decreases.

CATERING AT SPORTING GROUNDS

LINK TO
BUSINESS

Major sporting grounds provide catering and beverages during sporting events. In so doing, they can display many monopolistic characteristics in the range and variety of goods on offer, particularly alcoholic beverages.

QUESTIONS
1. List the monopolistic characteristics of a sporting ground's beverage suppliers.
2. Are there any close substitutes for the services provided by the sporting ground?
3. Why are patrons restricted in the types of food and beverages they are allowed to bring into the ground?

MARGINAL REVENUE AND MARGINAL COST

A monopolist, like a firm in perfect competition, chooses that level of output where marginal revenue is equal to marginal cost, as shown in Figure 6.11. However, the price that the monopolist charges for the product is indicated by the demand curve.

Thus, to sell output $0-Q_m$ (4), the monopolist selects price P_m (70). Like a firm in perfect competition, the monopolist would not choose output Q_y (7.1) or Q_x (2). At Q_x marginal revenue is greater than marginal cost, and the monopolist increases total revenue and profit by increasing production. Similarly at output Q_y, where marginal cost is greater than marginal revenue, the monopolist finds profits diminishing at that level of output.

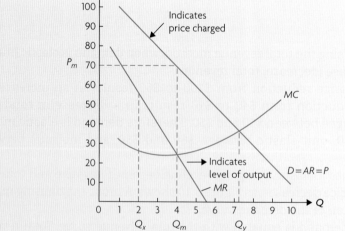

Figure 6.11
Profit-maximising price and output for a monopolist

THE MICROSOFT BUSINESS MODEL UNDER THREAT

The Microsoft business model involves software owned by the company, developed by in-house teams with frequent upgrades, already installed on new computers. Its dominant position in the market has enabled high profits for more than two decades. Microsoft's business model is under threat from open-source licensed software such as Linux. Open-source licences involve a completely different philosophy with use and improvement of software open to anyone. The source code that drives the software can be modified by anyone using the software. Many large entities including the British Government are investigating switching to Linux. When one city government switched to Linux, it caused Microsoft losses in excess of US$30 million in lost licences, training and support.

IBM provides consulting and support services to Linux applications, as well as to proprietary applications such as those of Microsoft.

Microsoft has responded to this threat to its dominant position by:

- stressing dangers to security from open source
- cutting prices on their software
- introducing 'shared source licensing', which enables large clients to gain access to source codes.

Open-source software seems to work well for general applications such as web servers or operating systems but not so well for specialised applications such as video editing or large databases, which require highly developed software.

QUESTIONS

1. Describe the main fixed and variable costs of Microsoft.
2. Are there barriers to entry to Microsoft's market?
3. What is the impact of Linux on the key elements of the Microsoft business model?
4. Describe the likely impacts of open-source software on the competitive position of Microsoft.
5. How can Microsoft react to the threat?

LINK TO
INTERNATIONAL
ECONOMY

PRICE AND OUTPUT DETERMINATION: MONOPOLISTIC COMPETITION

As we know from Chapter 5, monopolistic competition implies a market structure that is essentially competitive, although it lacks some of the characteristics of perfect competition.

Most notably, firms compete through product differentiation. The products are no longer homogeneous, as in perfect competition, but heterogeneous, as firms attempt to make their products different—or at least appear different in the eyes of the consumer—from those of their competitors. Monopolistically competitive firms produce variations of the same product. Variations include style or design features, materials, functional features and perceived differences that are created through marketing and advertising.

Because of product differentiation, firms in this market structure have a limited control over price, but in seeking to maximise profits there are distinct differences between this market structure and perfect competition and monopoly.

The demand curve facing a monopolistically competitive firm is elastic, but not perfectly elastic as in perfect competition. The firm, unlike a monopolist, is not a price maker. It must take into account the selling price of its product with regard to the selling price of its competitors' products, which are slightly differentiated.

If a monopolistically competitive firm raises the price of its product, it will lose some customers to its competitors. Loyal customers will maintain some sales, but overall sales will fall. Alternatively, if it lowers price, it will attract customers away from competitors.

Monopolistically competitive firms tend to engage in substantial non-price competition in the form of advertising and sales promotion. The intended effect is to make the demand curve more inelastic (that is, tending to vertical across a range of prices) and/or push the demand curve to the right, as in Figure 6.12.

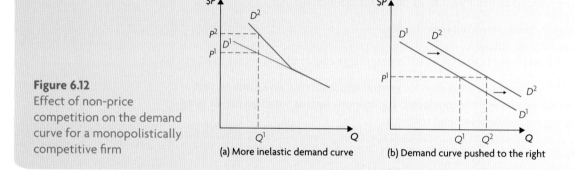

Figure 6.12
Effect of non-price competition on the demand curve for a monopolistically competitive firm

(a) More inelastic demand curve

(b) Demand curve pushed to the right

The greater the ability of a firm in monopolistic competition to create product differences, either real or imagined, the greater the firm's ability to control prices. With successful product differentiation, backed up by advertising and marketing, consumers cease to perceive other firms' products as close substitutes and the successful firm will be able to raise prices. In an industry with a large number of rivals, though, this may not be possible.

The greater the number of firms in the industry and the less effective the product differentiation, the more elastic the demand curve facing the firm.

PRICE AND OUTPUT DETERMINATION: OLIGOPOLY

The final study of price and output determination is applied to oligopolistic industries. Oligopoly is the market structure characterised by a few large firms dominating the market.

The firms can be producing homogeneous products like aluminum or petroleum products, or clearly differentiated products such as cars, cigarettes and beer. Indeed, when the product is homogeneous like petrol, firms try to differentiate in other areas such as services, image and product range offered to the consumer. For example, petrol used to be super or standard; now varieties include super, unleaded, ultra and premium, and there is also LPG.

Milk used to be a homogeneous product in a multi-use glass bottle. Now there are many varieties of milk—with added calcium, added flavours, reduced cholesterol or fat, or treated to extend shelf life—and they are branded and promoted as separate products.

Oligopolies arise partly because of economies of scale (mentioned above). The efficient production of a low-cost product may only be possible with a relatively small number of producers. If there are many producers, the high costs of production lead to inefficiency, and as some firms fail and close down or merge, an oligopolistic structure evolves.

ECONOMIES OF SCALE

Economies of scale can be internal or external, and there are also diseconomies of scale which likewise can be internal or external.

Economies of scale exist when total production costs increase at a slower rate than the increase in the quantity of output. This is another way of saying that per-unit costs or average costs decrease when you increase the size of output.

LEARNING OBJECTIVE 7
Define and explain economies of scale

Internal

Internal economies of scale are cost reductions within the firm irrespective of changes in other firms within the industry.

When a firm increases the scale of production, it can specialise in the use of the factors of production. Firms may receive purchasing discounts for bulk orders of raw materials, which lowers the per-unit cost so the firm can offer the product to the consumer at a cheaper price than competitors. Large expenditure on advertising may result in concession rates. Because the firm has a large number of workers, some can specialise in specific tasks in line with their training and experience, which brings about greater productivity and cost savings. Previously wasted by-products of production may be reused and sold instead of thrown away, while smaller firms find that their small quantities of by-products are insufficient for reuse or further processing.

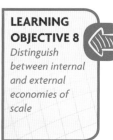

LEARNING OBJECTIVE 8
Distinguish between internal and external economies of scale

economies of scale *when total production costs increase at a slower rate than the increase in the quantity of output*

External

External economies of scale arise when the size of the industry as a whole increases and firms benefit from per-unit cost reduction. Unlike internal economies, which benefit only the individual firm, external economies benefit all the firms in the industry. A particular firm may not itself increase its size of operations, but it receives benefits because it belongs to an expanding industry.

External economies of scale can occur when large firms attract other firms that provide inputs to set up nearby. Many firms in an industry tend to 'agglomerate' or locate themselves in a close geographical area. External economies of scale can occur when:

- suppliers of raw materials are local
- transport distances are reduced
- international export markets are accessible
- skilled, trained labour is available
- a large market demand exists in the area.

External economies of scale are the result of services provided by other firms or the government and are outside the immediate control of the firm gaining the advantage.

QUEENSLAND RAIL AND ECONOMIES OF SCALE

LINK TO BUSINESS

From 1 July 2010, Queensland Rail was split into two distinct companies—Queensland Rail providing passenger rail services and QR National which provides freight and coal freight services.

QR National is one of Australia's largest railway operators and is expected to be among the largest companies listed on the Australian Securities Exchange (ASX). The business operates within the resources sector and focuses on coal and mineral haulage across Queensland, New South Wales and Western Australia.

QR National is also one of Australia's largest freight transport companies and had freight tonnages of 248 million tonnes recorded during the 2008–09 financial year.

Over the past five years, QR National's coal and freight businesses have grown significantly, both organically and through acquisition, with freight tonnages increasing by 41 per cent from 176 million tonnes in 2004–05 to 248 million tonnes in 2008–09.

QR National provides large-scale supply chain solutions to a diverse Australian customer base and has a fleet of more than 700 locomotives and 16 000 wagons,

QR National has over 9000 employees with a high standard of engineering and technical capability developed over 145 years.

Source: <www.qrnational.com.au/Corporate/Pages/AboutQRNational.aspx>, accessed 5 November 2010.

QUESTIONS

1. Summarise the Queensland Government's objective in selling off a profitable government enterprise.
2. Describe the external economies of scale for Queensland Rail that can arise by keeping the two entities as one rather than separating the two divisions.
3. Describe the internal economies of scale for QR National and coal producers that may be achieved through the public float of QR National.

DISECONOMIES OF SCALE

diseconomies of scale
cost increases per unit of output which result from increasing production

Diseconomies of scale are cost increases per unit of output which result from increasing production.

Internal

Internal diseconomies of scale usually arise when a firm becomes too big to manage its operation efficiently and productively.

As a firm gets larger, it may be unable to manage its operation effectively. Bottlenecks in production can occur. Breakdowns in lines of communication with authority, and an increasing feeling of alienation among staff may occur as they are given more specialised, and hence repetitive, tasks to perform. The costs of communication within the firm increase as there are more people to be kept informed. A lack of effective management and coordination leads to internal disarray and rising per-unit costs, with increasing inefficiency.

External

External diseconomies of scale arise as a result of the expansion of a group of firms or the industry as a whole.

As delivery orders increase, there is increased congestion, pollution and traffic jams, which leads ultimately to increased transport costs. Increased production may lead to increases in noise pollution and pollution of air, water and soil. The resulting ecological and environmental problems impose a cost on society to clean up the pollution that has been caused.

Economies and diseconomies of scale are most notable in oligopolistic industries and are a serious consideration in the firms' decisions about price and output. In addition, because of the small number of firms in the industry, price changes by an oligopolistic firm are closely monitored by competitors.

THE KINKED DEMAND CURVE

Our earlier studies of demand have assumed that the demand curve will be a straight line. Whether elastic or inelastic, the demand curve is uniformly shaped. Oligopolies provide an exception to this in that their demand curves may be kinked or bent. This **kinked demand curve** can arise with price changes and the behaviour of the other firms in the industry.

Imagine three large firms in an industry, each with equal market share, as shown in Figure 6.13. If firm A cuts its price, the other two firms, B and C, will most likely follow. They cannot afford to be selling at a higher price and would lose market share. (Recall: as $P\downarrow$, $Q_d\uparrow$.) So in the case of a price decrease, the remaining firms will also cut their price out of necessity.

However, if firm A raises its price, firms B and C will take this as an opportunity to gain market share by keeping the price of their goods constant (or raising the price by less).

If your firm is part of an oligopoly, in the event of a price decrease it will stay on its individual demand curve D^A, D^A. This demand curve applies only if you quote a price below the existing price P^1. If you increase the price above P^1, say, to P^2, your competitors will not follow and your demand and quantity sold will fall dramatically. The demand you have lost has been taken up by rival firms.

A profit maximiser in this industry chooses the level of output and charges the price where the kink occurs. This ensures relative price stability.

LEARNING OBJECTIVE 9
Explain the significance of a kinked demand curve and how it arises.

kinked demand curve
the demand curve in oligopolies may be kinked or bent due to price changes and the behaviour of the other firms in the industry

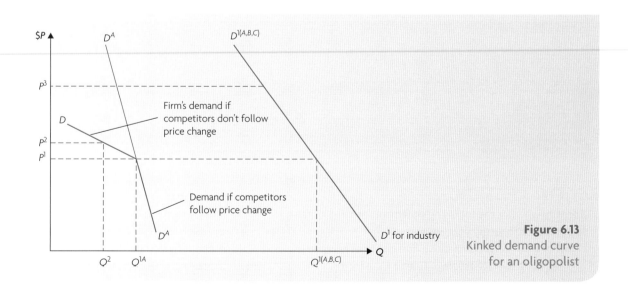

Figure 6.13
Kinked demand curve for an oligopolist

The kinked demand curve is also explained by way of elasticity. Above the kink, that is, at prices above P^1, demand is elastic. A price increase will lead to a greater than proportional decrease in demand. A price decrease is usually a short-term measure and the ensuing price war may be disastrous for the profit levels of all the firms.

Oligopolists try to avoid price competition. Instead they have been known to enter into price agreements, or market-sharing agreements, known as collusion (which is illegal) or engage in non-price competition.

Non-price competition covers the whole package of services offered to the consumer, such as favourable financing or after-sales service. Price competition can occur to prevent new firms, which initially may not be able to reap economies of scale, from entering the industry.

SUMMARY

1. This chapter explored the price and output decisions made by firms in each of the four market structures explained in Chapter 5. Each firm is assumed to maximise profits and so makes decisions on price and output decisions that aim to maximise the individual firm's profit.
2. Perfectly competitive firms are largely victims of what the market dictates. They are price takers and must accept the market price as given. They will produce the level of output where marginal cost is equal to marginal revenue.
3. Monopolists are price makers and can charge prices above the level of a perfectly competitive firm. With no rivals, they wield enormous market power.
4. Monopolistic competition places constraints on the ability of a firm to charge prices in excess of competitors. However, firms in this market structure engage in considerable non-price competition, such as product differentiation, in an attempt to distinguish their goods from those of their competitors and thus charge a higher price.
5. Oligopolies are also hampered in their ability to fix their own price and quantity of output. When an oligopolist decreases its price, other firms in the industry are likely to follow. If an oligopolist raises its price, however, other firms will attempt to gain market share. This is why an oligopolist is faced with the kinked demand curve.

KEY TERMS					
average revenue	104	fixed costs	106	short run	106
break-even point	127	kinked demand curve	123	total cost	106
contribution margin (CM)	128	law of diminishing returns	108	total revenue	105
diseconomies of scale	122	long run	106	variable costs	106
economies of scale	121	marginal cost	107		
		marginal revenue	105		

REVIEW QUESTIONS

1. Identify whether the following statements are true or false. Be prepared to justify your answer.
   (a) For a perfectly competitive firm, marginal revenue is equal to average revenue. True or False?
   (b) Fixed cost decreases as output increases. True or False?
   (c) Due to the law of diminishing returns, variable costs initially increase by decreasing amounts. True or False?
   (d) A perfectly competitive firm will maximise profits by producing where marginal revenue equals marginal cost. True or False?

(e) A monopoly exists because there are no substitute products available. True or False?

(f) A monopolist is faced with a highly elastic demand curve. True or False?

(g) Monopolists select the level of output where marginal cost is equal to marginal revenue. True or False?

(h) Marginal revenue for a monopolist is equal to price as for a perfectly competitive firm. True or False?

(i) Firms in monopolistically competitive industries engage in substantial product differentiation. True or False?

(j) Non-price competition has little or no effect on the shape and slope of the demand curve in monopolistic competition. True or False?

(k) Product differentiation is a waste of resources for monopolistically competitive firms because they are price takers. True or False?

(l) Monopolistic competitors are firms that produce homogeneous products and try to distinguish them in the eyes of the consumer. True or False?

(m) Oligopolies are the natural result of industries with high production costs when the market size is small. True or False?

(n) Whenever an oligopolistic firm increases the size of output it will achieve economies of scale. True or False?

(o) A profit-maximising oligopolist will attempt to operate on the kinked section of its demand curve where other firms cannot follow. True or False?

(p) Oligopolistic firms can increase in size and output up to a certain point before they start achieving diseconomies of scale. True or False?

2. Explain what is meant by economies of scale. For an industry you are familiar with:

(a) list five examples of internal economies of scale that a firm in that industry may benefit from

(b) list five examples of external economies of scale.

3. Explain briefly, using diagrams, how a perfectly competitive firm with a given cost and revenue structure can determine if it is operating to maximise its profits in a perfectly competitive market.

4. Why is a perfectly competitive firm faced with a perfectly elastic demand curve?

5. Table 6.8 sets out certain information related to the costs and revenue for a perfectly competitive firm:

(a) fill in the missing information

(b) construct a diagram showing the marginal revenue and marginal cost curves

(c) at what level would you advise the firm to produce? Why?

The selling price per unit is $50.

6. What are the two desired effects on the demand curve if a monopolistically competitive firm differentiates its product through advertising? What limitations are there on achieving the desired aim?

7. Explain what is meant by the law of diminishing returns. How does it apply to production costs in the short run?

8. Explain how an oligopolist can be faced with a kinked demand curve.

9. 'Advertising doesn't benefit the consumer. It simply adds to the cost of the product.' What does this statement mean? Do you agree?

10. Do you think it was reasonable that in the past, most monopolies were controlled by governments, restricting entry into the market? What are some of the implications

Table 6.8: Costs and revenue for a perfectly competitive firm

QUANTITY	FIXED COST	VARIABLE COST	TOTAL COST	TOTAL REVENUE	+/– MARGINAL COST	MARGINAL REVENUE
0				—		
1	10		20	50		
2		40				
3			70			
4		100				
5		150				
6					200	
7		495				

of allowing private ownership of monopoly industries, for example the supply and management of water resources?

11. Explain what is meant by the short run and the long run in economies. Do all firms have the same short-run and long-run periods?

APPLIED QUESTIONS AND EXERCISES
AIR CHARTER SERVICES

Direct Air <http://directair.com.au> provides air charter services throughout Australia with a head office in Melbourne and offices in Perth, Darwin and Alice Springs. The company competes in a crowded market for air services, ranging from large domestic and international providers such as Qantas and Virgin Blue and a multitude of smaller, specialist air charter companies. Direct Air made a business decision that in order to expand its business it needed to open new offices to attract additional clientele.

QUESTIONS

1. What type of market structure does Direct Air operate in?
2. What barriers to entry exist for a firm wishing to enter the air charter market?
3. In terms of economies of scale, what would be the advantages of Direct Air joining with another similar company?
4. What fixed costs and variable costs face Direct Air in seeking to expand its operations?

APPENDIX TO CHAPTER 6: BREAK-EVEN ANALYSIS

After the completion of this chapter you should have a better idea of the relationship between company revenues, costs and profits. As you are aware from media reports, profits often appear to be used as an indicator of the success of an organisation.

A person starting a new business often asks, 'At what level of sales will my company make a profit?' Established companies that have suffered through some rough years might have a similar question. Others ask, 'At what point will I be able to draw a fair salary from my company?'

The **break-even point** is the level of activity at which total revenues equal total costs. At the break-even point, the firm neither makes a profit, nor a loss. The break-even analysis calculates a break-even point based on fixed costs, variable costs per unit of sales, and revenue per unit of sales.

break-even point
the level of activity at which total revenues equal total costs

Knowledge of the break-even point analysis is useful to the management of both small and large businesses when deciding whether to introduce new product lines, change sales prices on established products, or enter new market areas.

To illustrate how break-even analysis can help management make decisions, we will use MAS Spectrometers Ltd as an example.

MAS Spectrometers Ltd specialises in producing and exporting spectrometers, instruments used to control industrial and medical processes and to monitor pollution.

The relevant data for this business are:

- Unit selling price: $5000
- Unit variable costs: $4000
- Total monthly fixed costs: $120 000.

The break-even point can be:

(a)   calculated from a mathematical (algebra) equation
(b)   calculated by using 'contribution margin' analysis
(c)   derived from a break-even graph.

(A) MATHEMATICAL (ALGEBRA) EQUATION

From the start, we can assure you that this is very simple maths, nothing to worry about. The break-even point can be expressed in terms of dollars, or in terms of units.

THE BREAK-EVEN POINT IN DOLLARS
The break-even equation is:

$$\text{Break-even sales} = \text{Variable costs} + \text{Fixed costs}$$

The break-even point in dollars is found by expressing variable costs as a percentage of the unit selling price. To get this for MAS Spectrometers we divide the unit variable cost ($4000) by the unit selling price ($5000), which comes to a percentage of 80 per cent.

We note the value of the unknown level of sales where we break even with 'X'.
The starting equation is:

$$X = 0.80X + \$120\ 000$$

We shift 0.80X to the left side of the equation (with a minus sign, of course):

$$X - 0.80X = \$120\ 000, \text{ and then we have}$$
$$0.2X = \$120\ 000$$

Now we can calculate the value of X:

$$X = \$120\ 000 \div 0.2 = \$600\ 000$$

Therefore, MAS Spectrometers should sell for $600 000 to break even.

THE BREAK-EVEN POINT IN UNITS

The break-even point in units can be calculated directly from the algebra equation by using unit selling prices and unit variable costs. The calculation is:

$$\$5000X = \$4000X + \$120\ 000$$
$$(\$5000X - \$4000X) = \$120\ 000$$
$$\$1000X = \$120\ 000$$
$$X = \$120\ 000 \div 1000$$
$$X = 120 \text{ units}$$

Therefore, it appears that MAS Spectrometers must sell 120 units to break even. We will check the accuracy of the figure as follows:

Sales (120 × $5000)		$600 000
Total costs		
• Variable (120 × $4000)	$480 000	
• Fixed	$120 000	$600 000
NET PROFIT		$0

(B) BREAK-EVEN CALCULATION USING CONTRIBUTION MARGIN

contribution margin (CM)
the amount of revenue remaining after deducting variable cost

Contribution margin (CM) is the amount of revenue remaining after deducting variable cost. In the case of MAS Spectrometers, the contribution margin is calculated as follows:

$$\text{Sales } (\$1\ 000\ 000) - \text{Variable costs } (\$4000 \times 200) = \$200\ 000$$

The contribution margin is available to cover fixed costs and to contribute profit to business.

Given that contribution margin equals total revenues less variable costs, it follows that at break-even point, the contribution margin must equal total fixed costs.

One common way of expressing the contribution margin is a per-unit basis. The formula for contribution margin per unit is:

Contribution margin per unit = Unit selling price – Unit variable cost

At MAS Spectrometers, the contribution margin per unit is $1000, calculated as:

$5000 – $4000 = $1000

It tells us that for every unit sold, the firm will have $1000 to cover fixed costs and contribute to profit.

When we use the contribution margin per unit method, the formula to calculate the break-even point in units is:

Fixed costs ÷ Contribution margin per unit = Break-even point in units

Therefore, the calculation of the break-even point in units at MAS Spectrometers is:

$120 000 ÷ $1000 = 120 units

(C) GRAPHIC PRESENTATION

In the graph in Figure 6.14, sales volume in units is recorded alongside the horizontal axis, while both total sales and total costs (fixed plus variable) in dollars are recorded on the vertical axis.

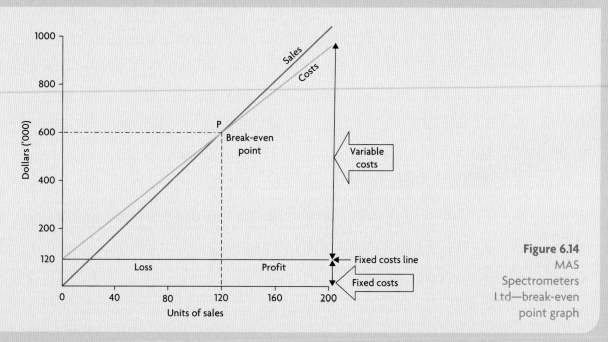

Figure 6.14
MAS Spectrometers Ltd—break-even point graph

We will construct the graph in a number of steps:

- We plot the total sales starting at zero activity level. For each unit of spectrometer sold total revenue increases by $5000. At 40 units sold, sales revenue reaches $200 000 and at the upper level of activity (200 units) total sales reach $1 000 000.
- We plot the total fixed costs line by a horizontal line at $120 000. It stays the same at every level of activity.
- The total cost line starts at the fixed cost line at zero activity and increases the amount by the variable cost of $4000 for each extra unit. At 40 units the total variable cost is $160 000 and the total cost is $280 000 (which includes the fixed cost of $120 000). At 200 units, total costs make $920 000.
- We determine the break-even point from the intersection of the sales line and the costs line. The break-even point in dollars is found by drawing a horizontal line from the break-even point to the vertical axis ($600 000). The break-even point in units is determined by drawing a vertical line from the break-even point to the horizontal axis (120 units). At this sales level, the firm will cover costs, but makes no profit.
- In addition to identifying the break-even point, the break-even graph shows both the profit and loss areas. Thus, the amount of profit or loss at each level of sales can be derived from the total sales and total costs lines.

Such a graph is especially useful in management meetings, because the effects of a change in any major elements of the graph (e.g. revenue, costs, volume) can be promptly illustrated. For instance a 10 per cent increase in sales revenue due to a 10 per cent increase in price will change the shape of the sales line. At the same time, the effects of an increase of wages on total costs can be quickly assessed.

Economic literature identifies a few limitations of break-even analysis:

- It assumes there are no changes in costs over the time period.
- It assumes a constant selling price.
- When more than one type of product is sold, total sales will be in a constant sales mix. This complicates the analysis, because different products will have different cost relationships.
- The analysis does not allow for changes in market conditions in the time period—e.g. entry of a new competitor.

Notwithstanding such limitations, break-even analysis is a common management tool for modern firms. It may take a little bit of time to understand, but you should make an effort to grasp this concept—people really do this in business and if you can tell a potential employer that you are able to do this, it will increase your chances in the job market.

REVIEW QUESTION

Outline a couple of methods by which one can determine the break-even point.

APPLIED QUESTIONS AND EXERCISES

1. Peter's Mowers Ltd manufactures and exports lawn mowers. The unit selling price is $700, variable costs total $420 and fixed costs are $140 000. Calculate the break-even point in units using:
   (a) A mathematical (algebra) equation
   (b) Contribution margin per unit.

Chapter **7**

Government market intervention in the Australian economy

LEARNING OBJECTIVES

After studying this chapter, you will be able to:

1. identify key market failures that may justify government intervention
2. explain how governments attempt to overcome market power
3. distinguish between private goods and public goods
4. identify externalities in production
5. explain how competition is maintained and resources allocated efficiently
6. discuss how an economy is managed and economic fluctuations are minimised
7. explain various forms of anti-competitive behaviour regulated by the Australian Competition and Consumer Commission
8. distinguish between vertical agreements and horizontal agreements.

INTRODUCTION

market power
the ability to exert control over the price or quantity side of the marketplace

In a competitive market structure, consumers' welfare is maximised when no firm has excessive **market power** and firms are unable to manipulate market forces. However, imperfections in a market system often prevent consumers from maximising their welfare. Monopolistic competition and particularly oligopolies and monopolies allow firms to maximise their own welfare at the expense of the consumer.

To overcome this market power, governments actively participate in the regulation of the economy. Their need to do so arises out of the competitive market system's inability to maximise consumer welfare and the system's five areas of potential failure:

1. inequality and the price system
2. public goods
3. externalities in production
4. monopoly power and inefficient resource allocation
5. economic fluctuations.

Through legislation, government statutory authorities are empowered to oversee and prohibit certain types of behaviour by firms if it is deemed to lessen competition. They can also monitor price changes to ensure they are not excessive.

The degree and level of government involvement in the economy is an ongoing debate. Australian political parties have divergent opinions on the extent to which the government should become involved, ranging from minimalist to interventionist.

Regardless of the political ideology of the government of the day, all Australian governments have acted to correct various perceived failures of the market system.

LEARNING OBJECTIVE 1
Identify key market failures that may justify government intervention

WHY INTERVENE?

The analysis in previous chapters of microeconomic demand and supply behaviour, and the behaviour of firms in a competitive capitalist market system, suggests that goods and services should be produced efficiently and in line with consumer preferences. The growth of imperfect competitive market structures, such as monopolies and oligopolies, indicates that this might not always be the case. Private monopolies may produce a level of output where marginal cost and marginal revenue intersect, but charge a higher price than would be possible under perfect competition. Oligopolies may enter into (illegal) market-sharing or price-fixing arrangements that impede the free working of the market system, restrict consumer choice, or ensure that oligopolists are able to charge a price for goods in excess of a competitive price.

NEGATIVE OUTCOMES

Constant striving for high levels of growth and output to achieve economies of scale has produced a range of negative side effects that, many argue, are not dealt with adequately by a purely competitive market system. Negative economic outcomes such as poverty, income inequality, pollution, and environmental and ecological degradation are just some of the problems that have given rise to active government intervention in the maintenance and workings of the Australian market economy.

A market economy is viewed by many observers as being unable to produce desirable outcomes without active government intervention. The desire for high rates of economic growth, efficiency in production, equitable access to goods and services, and attempts to overcome certain flaws in a competitive market economy, have led to varying degrees of government intervention and involvement in the economy.

MINIMALIST OR INTERVENTIONIST?

The major Australian political parties traditionally held different views on the role of the government in the working of the economy and the desirable level of intervention to ensure that the economy performs at the 'best' level.

TWO VIEWS

In the past, the Australian Labor Party believed in taking an active role in the management of the economy and redistributing income on an equitable basis. Labor supporters believe that the government's role is to promote 'managed' growth in line with society's best interests.

The Liberal and National Country Parties support a minimalist role for government in the economy. The market, it is argued, is the most efficient and equitable means of allocating goods and services. While conservatives certainly believe there is a role for government in the economy, they see it as much less interventionist. The dynamics of a market economy will produce solutions for problems that arise, and many problems are largely due to government interference in the first place.

These respective economic ideologies could historically be paralleled with two major schools of economic thought. The Australian Labor Party has always been more Keynesian in its approach, following the economic doctrine of J.M. Keynes[1] that was first espoused in the 1930s after the Great Depression (the Cambridge School). The Liberal Party follows the neoclassical tradition of David Ricardo[2] and Alfred Marshall of the 1800s, and more recently Paul Samuelson and Milton Friedman[3] (the Chicago School).

CONVERGENCE

The doctrine of economic rationalism (sometimes called neo-liberalism) held centre stage for much of the 1990s and into the 2000s, with the result that differences between the major parties have lessened. In Australia there are two fundamental beliefs that underlie economic rationalism. The first is a belief that individual freedom should be a fundamental goal of society and government intervention in the free market diminishes individual freedom. The second is that privately-owned organisations that pursue profits are more efficient than government-owned organisations because they have to compete in the marketplace. The minor parties have been a voice in the economic wilderness advocating a more interventionist role for government to remedy adverse economic outcomes. The Greens in particular have approached economic policy with a new agenda placing environmental considerations at the forefront of economic decision making.

Notwithstanding political differences on the extent of intervention, the major Australian political parties agree that there is a role for the government to play in economic participation.

Two principal reasons why government intervention is necessary are:

1. to overcome market failure
2. to overcome market power.

OVERCOMING MARKET FAILURE

market failure
occurs when the market system itself may fail to provide adequately for all members of society

Market failure comes about when the market system itself may fail to provide adequately for all members of society. Several examples of **market failure** can be recognised, and the following five are discussed below, with ways of overcoming them:

1. the (re)distribution of income
2. public goods and services
3. externalities in production
4. maintaining competition
5. managing the economy.

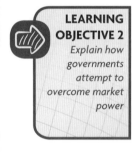

LEARNING OBJECTIVE 2
Explain how governments attempt to overcome market power

THE PRICE SYSTEM AND THE (RE)DISTRIBUTION OF INCOME

The essence of the price system is a person's ability to pay. A market economy produces a vast array of goods and services which are available to be purchased, provided you have the means to do so, that is, the money and income (effective demand).

WINNERS AND LOSERS

In a system of flexible wages, principles of supply and demand, when applied to labour, ensure that those who have skills that are in high demand but short supply can receive income considerably higher than other workers. The market system is good at rewarding those people who are in demand, whether through inherent skills or specific training. (Recall that when there is excess demand, prices will increase—in this case wages are the price of labour.)

But we are not all equally endowed with the same skills, level of education or access to education. Those who do not have skills that are in demand, or who have skills that are in abundance, receive much lower wages. Their economic purchasing power is decreased—excess supply, prices (wages) go down. If wages cannot be lowered sufficiently, unemployment may result.

Economically disadvantaged groups, if left to the will of the market, might find survival difficult—the aged, the single parent with dependent children, the physically and mentally disadvantaged, new migrants, those from a non-English speaking background, and the unemployed. Poverty for people in these groups is a reality in Australia.

HELPING THE VULNERABLE

Governments in Australia attempt to solve this problem by trying to maintain price stability, with low inflation rates. In addition, they provide relief and assistance to disadvantaged groups, such as the unemployed and single parents, in the form of pensions, rent assistance, job retraining, benefits and special allowances. Medicare ensures a minimum access to health services regardless of ability to pay, while those who can pay may opt for additional private health services. Government-funded schools ensure equal access to education, while some consumers prefer to send their children to non-government schools and pay higher fees. Minimum wage rates ensure access to a degree of financial security, particularly within an award system and a guaranteed income for certain types of employment.

REDISTRIBUTION THROUGH TAXES

These benefits to low-income earners have to be paid for, and in Australia this is done through the taxation system. Income tax in Australia is a **progressive tax**: the higher your income, the greater percentage of it you must pay as tax. For example, tax rates in 2010–11 are shown in Table 7.1. The differential rates are intended to bring about some degree of income equality, with the wealthier members of society sharing their good fortune and ability to earn higher levels of income with those who are less economically fortunate.

progressive tax
the higher your income, the greater percentage of it you must pay as tax

Table 7.1   **Tax rates for Australian Residents, 2010–11**

THE FOLLOWING RATES APPLY FROM 1 JULY 2010	
TAXABLE INCOME ($)	**TAX ON THIS INCOME**
$1–$6000	Nil
$6001–$37 000	15 cents for each dollar over $6000
$37 001–$80 000	$4650 + 30 cents for each dollar over $37 000
$80 001–$180 000	$17 550 + 37 cents for each dollar over $80 000
Over $180 000	$54 550 + 45 cents for each dollar over $180 000
The above rates **do not** include the Medicare levy of 1.5 per cent.	

Source: Australian Tax Office, <www.ato.gov.au/individuals/content.asp?doc=/content/12333.htm>, accessed 8 November 2010.

As well as the progressive tax system, there is a variety of tax offset arrangements for groups such as low income families, pensioners and self-funded retirees. These arrangements are aimed at reducing the income tax payable by these groups.

Despite a progressive income tax regime in Australia, we should note that there are some **regressive taxes**. The government imposes a uniform goods and services tax which applies to most goods and services in Australia. If your annual income is $100 000, you pay the same dollar amount of tax on goods and services as a person whose annual income is $25 000. The two incomes are vastly different, yet those who receive them pay the same tax. In this case, the higher your income, the smaller the tax as a percentage of that income. Any uniform tax increase on a product hits low-income earners more than higher-income earners. For further discussion of taxation policy and issues, in particular the introduction of a goods and services tax (GST), see Chapter 20.

regressive tax
the lower your income the greater the percentage you pay in tax

LEARNING
OBJECTIVE 3
*Distinguish
between private
goods and
public goods*

PROVISION OF PUBLIC GOODS AND SERVICES

In a market economy a firm will produce goods and services to sell and make a profit. If individuals want the product and have the ability to pay for it, they can do so. These are **private goods** to be consumed by the individuals as appropriate.

Private goods are subject to the principle of exclusion, which means that those who are not willing or able to pay for the good are excluded from consuming it. **Public goods**, on the other hand, are goods that cannot be withheld from one individual without withholding them from the whole of society.

private goods
goods that are consumed by those individuals who are willing and able to pay for them; if you cannot pay for them you cannot consume them

PUBLIC GOODS

A public good is produced and consumed communally, or not at all. These goods would not be produced under the price system because they do not conform to the **exclusion principle**. There is no effective way of excluding consumers who do not pay.

Some examples of public goods are national defence, streetlights and police protection. There is no way of excluding an individual from national security once a defence force is in place; a streetlight bestows light on all; and we all receive equal protection and fair treatment from the police.

The provision of public goods, or **collective goods** as they are sometimes known, is known as the **free-rider effect**. Free-riders receive the benefit provided by the goods without having to pay. Because a private firm is not a charity but is in business to make money, and because of the free-rider effect, the government undertakes the provision of these services. Society as a whole ultimately pays for these services through the taxation system.

public goods
goods that cannot be withheld from one individual without withholding them from the society as a whole

exclusion principle
people who do not pay for a good or service can be excluded from consuming it

collective goods
another name for public goods

EXTERNALITIES IN PRODUCTION

In undertaking production, firms may also produce **externalities**, or **spillovers**. These are the negative by-products of production.

The most obvious example is pollution associated with production. Unless firms are forced to pay attention to these externalities, they can ignore them. The costs are borne by those who suffer from the pollution. When a firm dumps waste into a river, people who use the river for fishing, swimming, recreation or drinking suffer as a result.

When a firm can avoid paying for negative externalities, it can produce its goods at a lower cost. The direct purchaser of the good gains the benefit of a cheaper good, but society as a whole bears the cost. Because firms try to maximise profits by minimising costs, this is an unfortunate market failure.

Governments intervene by imposing strict requirements on firms with regard to pollution, emission and noise levels to minimise the cost to society. There may be penalties for ignoring regulations or incentives to conform; the government may impose taxes on behaviour that creates loss of welfare or pay subsidies for firms' activities that increase welfare.

free-rider effect
the provision of public goods (e.g. military forces, police, street lighting, street cleaning), from which people cannot be excluded from consuming just because they have not paid

In this instance, governments intervene and attempt to reallocate resources in line with activities that benefit society as a whole.

externalities (spillovers)
the negative by-products of production

MAINTAINING COMPETITION AND EFFICIENT RESOURCE ALLOCATION

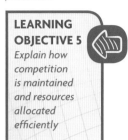

LEARNING OBJECTIVE 5
Explain how competition is maintained and resources allocated efficiently

In market-oriented economies most political parties agree that a competitive market economy is best at allocating resources efficiently and producing goods and services in line with consumer preference. However, the attraction of economies of scale means that successful companies are likely to grow larger and become able to exercise monopoly or market power.

CONTROLLING MONOPOLIES

The growth of monopolies and their associated market power disrupts the efficient workings of a competitive system. Faced with a relatively inelastic demand curve, a monopolist can restrict output and therefore create an artificial shortage and charge a higher price (see Figure 7.1). Alternatively, the monopolist may decide to charge a high price and produce the appropriate level of output (see Figure 7.2 overleaf).

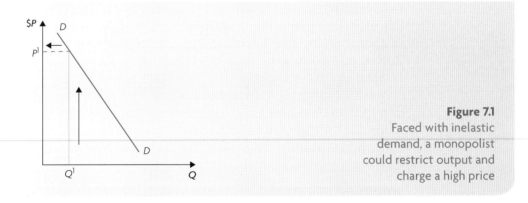

Figure 7.1
Faced with inelastic demand, a monopolist could restrict output and charge a high price

Because a monopolist is not faced with a competitive environment, this situation could persist, to the detriment of consumers. Resources are allocated in line with the monopolist's wishes, not the desires of society as a whole. Whether this misallocation of resources and market failure arises or not, governments intervene in three different ways, because they consider a lower price and/or greater quantity of output is socially desirable:

1. government ownership
2. legislation and regulation
3. price setting.

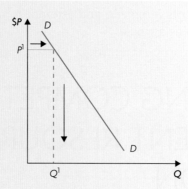

Figure 7.2
Faced with inelastic demand, a monopolist could charge a high price in order to restrict consumption

Government ownership

Natural monopolies are situations where technical or technological factors, or economies of scale, dictate that one firm should provide the goods. In the past in these cases, governments have usually taken over the production themselves.

In the past, electricity, gas and water services, rail transport and telecommunications have all been government monopolies. However, successive federal and state governments in the 1980s, 1990s and early 2000s sought to increase efficiency in these industries by allowing competition and deregulating those industries. For example, in Australia in many states, electricity, gas and railways have been sold to private operators.

Legislation and regulation

In recognising the allocative efficiency of a market system achieved through competition, government can legislate to ensure that competition in industries is maintained. It regulates and prohibits anti-competitive behaviour. For example, privatisation of industries like electricity production has usually included legislation to establish a regulatory body to control prices. The Australian Competition and Consumer Commission (the ACCC) was formed in 1995 to administer the federal *Trade Practices Act 1974* (now superseded by the *Competition and Consumer Act 2010*) and other Acts.

The ACCC attempts to ensure competition and fair trade in the marketplace to the benefit of consumers, business and the community. The ACCC also regulates national infrastructure industries with primary responsibility to ensure that individuals and businesses comply with the Commonwealth's competition, fair trading and consumer protection laws.

CHINA'S PLANNING AGENCY TO REGULATE PRICES

LINK TO
INTERNATIONAL
ECONOMY

China's top economic planning agency, the National Development and Reform Commission (NDRC), has urged Chinese authorities to increase supervision in order to stabilise prices in food, transportation and tourism during the holiday periods. The aim is to crack down on price rigging, including circulating misleading or false information about price hikes, commodity hoarding or forcing up prices of grain, cooking oil, meat, eggs and dairy products.

Departments have also been asked to ramp up measures to regulate prices of public transportation and in the tourism industries, while curbing arbitrary price hikes and irregular charges.

Source: <www.chinadaily.com.cn/china/2010-09/10/content_11287731.htm>, accessed 5 November 2010.

QUESTIONS
1. Why is a government agency involved in price regulation of essential commodity items?
2. What would be the impact on price of commodity hoarding?
3. In a capitalist, free market economy, should there be a role for a body such as the National Development and Reform Commission to regulate prices?

PRICE SETTING

In situations of a private monopoly, the government may force the monopolist to behave like a perfectly competitive firm in its price and output levels.

For example, consider the monopolist in Figure 7.3. A monopolist allowed to act without government interference would produce output $0–Q^1$, where the marginal revenue and marginal cost curves intersect (point C). However, as we know, they would charge price P^1 for that level of output (point A). If the government sets a maximum price P^2 for the good, at that price where the marginal cost curve cuts the demand curve (point B), price will decrease from P^1 to P^2, output will increase from Q^1 to Q^2, and the firm will move down the demand curve from point A to point B.

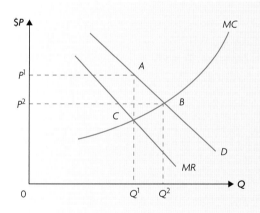

Figure 7.3
Setting a maximum monopoly price

MANAGING THE ECONOMY AND MINIMISING ECONOMIC FLUCTUATIONS

LEARNING OBJECTIVE 6
Discuss how an economy is managed and economic fluctuations are minimised

A market economy is characterised by a business cycle of boom and recession. The economy soars on the wave of prosperity, a boom period such as the Australian economy experienced in the 1950s and 1960s. Then it comes to a crashing halt, in a recession such as that of the 1970s and 1980s. The period of the 1990s was one of growing prosperity after a severe recession at the start of the decade. This long 'boom' continued in the first part of the 21st century before the world economy was caught in the grip of the global financial crisis.

BOOMS

The two major economic ills, inflation and unemployment, fluctuate in booms and recessions. During booms, when economic prosperity is high and economic growth is increasing, inflation usually increases as well.

If the inflation is due to excess demand, the government can try to reduce the excessive spending that is causing the inflationary pressure. It can cut its own spending and try to decrease private sector spending as well. Measures include tax increases, which reduce individuals' spending money and hence demand, and a tight monetary policy with higher interest rates, which increase the cost of borrowing, or some combination of the two.

RECESSIONS

During a recessionary period, the government can adopt the opposite policy: it can try to stimulate demand and encourage spending. This spending creates new demand for goods and services and, hopefully, further spending, creating further demand and employment. The effect is cumulative, creating additional demand and employment.

Unfortunately, in the second half of the 20th century this policy led to inflation and a need to reverse the process. Governments would spend money on public work programs and offer incentives or inducements to the private sector in the hope that it would also begin to spend and thus cure the recession. A loose monetary policy with lower interest rates encourages private sector borrowing and increases investment spending.

This is, of course, a simplistic view but it serves to highlight the role governments take in trying to even out the cycle and lessen the harmful effects of a severe recession or sustained period of inflation. This subject is dealt with in detail in Chapters 8 and 9.

LEARNING OBJECTIVE 2
Explain how governments attempt to overcome market power

OVERCOMING MARKET POWER

There are many critics of the theories of competitive market capitalism. The assumptions that competition and an unfettered marketplace will ensure maximum economic welfare for society may be true, but today a competitive marketplace is the exception, not the norm. Market power can be defined as the ability to exert control over the price or quantity side of the marketplace.

Critics argue that competitive market capitalism has now evolved into contemporary market capitalism, perhaps a more realistic description of the capitalist economies in the world today. Transnational corporations, huge oligopolistic structures wielding significant market power, are commonplace. Consumers have little choice as firms exhibit non-competitive behaviour in attempts to gain market share from competitors, enter into arrangements with competitors, or attempt to eliminate all competition from the market. Economists such as J.K. Galbraith[4] have written extensively about these industrial market structures.

THE AUSTRALIAN EXPERIENCE

Since the mid 1970s legislation has been enacted in Australia with the primary aim of maintaining competitive behaviour and restricting uncompetitive practices.

Imperfect markets exist in capitalist economies in the form of monopolistic competition, oligopolies and monopolies, and producers have varying degrees of power. As we saw in

Chapter 6, this arises out of barriers to entry, economies of scale, differentiated products, or market dominance by a small number of large firms. In these cases, governments may intervene in the market. They may intervene actively by prohibiting certain anti-competitive behaviour, or passively by watching industries to ensure competition is maintained.

In 1995 the Australian Competition and Consumer Commission (ACCC) and the National Competition Council (NCC) were established. The ACCC was created through the merger of the Trade Practices Commission and the Prices Surveillance Authority. The NCC was intended to provide state, territory and federal governments with the economic benefits of a national policy of competition and consumer protection. While the ACCC has responsibility for fostering competition across the whole country, the NCC conducts reviews and research, and it advises and makes recommendations in relation to policy and pricing.

The ACCC and the NCC emerged from the findings of the National Competition Policy Review, chaired by Professor Fred Hilmer (the Hilmer Report). The report's vision was for a national competition policy whereby federal, state and territory governments cooperate to ensure national uniformity of rules of market conduct.

The Australian Competition and Consumer Commission

The ACCC is an independent statutory authority that attempts to foster competition and encourages fair trading practices in all Australian markets. It is also charged with the responsibility for price surveillance in certain markets. The overall objective of the ACCC is to make markets work, and it is mostly occupied with enforcing compliance with the *Competition and Consumer Act 2010* (Cwlth) through the court system.

But the ACCC also has a pivotal role in encouraging competition by prohibiting anti-competitive conduct and unfair trading practices. It provides education and information services to business to ensure they are aware of and comply with the legislation. The ACCC's website can be found at <www.accc.gov.au>, accessed 5 November 2010.

The National Competition Council

The NCC is a review and advisory body. It reviews intergovernment agreements including anti-competitive regulation, structural reform of government monopolies and competitive neutrality. It assesses the progress of state and territory governments in implementing the national competition policy reforms in electricity, gas, water and road transport. (Under the principle of competitive neutrality, government businesses should not have competitive (dis)advantages relative to private sector organisations simply because of government ownership. It means that private and government businesses compete on a similar footing.)

The NCC provides policy advice to all levels of government to assist them in meeting Competition Policy Agreement obligations that were signed at the Council of Australian Governments (COAG) in April 1995. The NCC promotes microeconomic reform, reform in public utility structures, and removal of anti-competitive legislation. It encourages competition between states, and competitive neutrality between government and the private sector.

restrictive trade practices
any actions by a firm that aim to restrict or limit competition

LEARNING OBJECTIVE 7
Explain various forms of anti-competitive behaviour regulated by the Australian Competition and Consumer Commission

RESTRICTIVE TRADE PRACTICES

Restrictive trade practices are any actions by a firm that aim to restrict or limit competition and therefore reduce the effectiveness of the price mechanism. In Australia many of these practices are covered by the *Competition and Consumer Act.*

Sometimes restrictive trade practices are considered to be in the public interest and are therefore allowed. An example is the restriction on entry into medical practice to those with qualifications.

Some types of restrictive practices are not allowed. Firms may not act in ways designed to limit competition. Two methods of doing this are called vertical agreements and horizontal agreements. In both instances, price competition is prevented, the entry of new firms is restricted, and/or consumer choice is limited. The remainder of the chapter examines these and other types of restrictive practices.

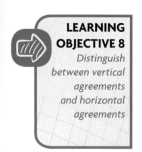

LEARNING OBJECTIVE 8
Distinguish between vertical agreements and horizontal agreements

vertical agreements
an agreement between firms involved in different stages of the production process, designed to limit competition

horizontal agreements
agreements between firms in the same industry at the same level of production, designed to limit competition

cartel
firms that enter into collusive agreements or engage in other discriminatory practices

price fixing
a horizontal arrangement that arises when firms in an industry agree on a recommended price for the goods

VERTICAL AGREEMENTS

Vertical agreements take place between firms involved in different stages of the production process. A manufacturer may impose conditions on a wholesaler who may in turn place constraints on a retailer. A manufacturer may be selective in its choice of retailers, allowing them access to markets denied to other retailers. Retailers may agree to purchase exclusively from a certain wholesaler.

HORIZONTAL AGREEMENTS

Horizontal agreements are made between firms in the same industry at the same level of production. They are a form of collusion whereby firms agree to sell goods collectively at a certain price. The firms may agree to divide certain markets among themselves, with each firm agreeing not to poach customers outside its designated area.

Collusion is usually restricted to oligopolistic industries. Because of the large number of firms in monopolistic competition, it is difficult to arrange and maintain.

CARTELS

The firms that enter into collusive agreements—such as setting price, output and market share—or engage in other discriminatory practices are known as a **cartel**.

The best-known cartel is OPEC, the Organization of the Petroleum Exporting Countries. Economic history shows that cartels do not last for extended periods. If they are operating in Australia, they either get caught or the temptation to cheat on other cartel members is too great. The cartel breaks down and a degree of competition is restored. International cartels like the government-related OPEC or the private diamond cartel headed by DeBeers have been able to survive for long periods of time in part due to the involvement of governments, which have been able to maintain a degree of discipline among the members of the cartel.

PRICE FIXING

Price fixing (a horizontal arrangement) arises when firms in an industry agree on a recommended price for the goods. They may also reach agreements on the extent and amount of price discounting.

Simply agreeing with competitors to fix prices is illegal, irrespective of the prices involved, the duration of the agreement or the success of the agreement.

The ACCC investigated major windscreen manufacturers and found that, over an 18-month period, senior representatives met on six occasions and agreed on the discounts off catalogue prices for windscreens. The purpose of the agreement was to stop price discount wars that were taking place. The agreement had no lasting effect, but the ACCC imposed fines totalling $195 000.

RESALE PRICE MAINTENANCE

In **resale price maintenance** a supplier directly sets a price below which a retailer cannot sell goods, or acts indirectly by threatening to cut off supply if the retailer sells below that supplier's stated price. It is prohibited by the Act (section 48).

A supplier may recommend a resale price, but the price actually charged is the retailer's decision. Resale price maintenance is a vertical arrangement. Suppliers of products sometimes impose a specified resale price in order to maintain brand positioning. It is illegal to cut off, or threaten to cut off, supply to a retailer because it discounts goods or sells them below the price set by the supplier.

However, in certain circumstances, a supplier can refuse to supply if a retailer sells the product below the retailer's cost (called loss leading). This does not apply to seasonal clearance sales. A supplier may specify a maximum price for resale.

resale price maintenance *when a supplier directly sets a price below which a retailer cannot sell goods, or acts indirectly by threatening to cut off supply if the retailer sells below that supplier's stated price*

PRICE DISCRIMINATION

Price discrimination occurs when a supplier charges different purchasers different prices for goods of the same grade and quality.

Price discrimination is unlawful only if it substantially lessens competition (section 49). In most cases, discounts offered by suppliers to certain buyers are legal. They only become illegal when the supplier has substantial market power and uses discounting to competitors to deliberately harm particular businesses.

price discrimination *when a supplier charges different purchasers different prices for goods of the same grade and quality*

EXCLUSIVE DEALING

Exclusive dealing is the supply of goods to a purchaser on the condition that it does not deal with the supplier's competitor(s), nor stock the competitor's goods. The purchaser cannot be restricted territorially or limited as to whom it sells the goods (section 47). There are two types of exclusive dealing:

1. In full line forcing, a supplier refuses to supply goods or services unless the intending purchaser agrees to refuse or limit the amount it buys from a competitor of the supplier. This will result in a substantial lessening of competition.
2. Third line forcing is not subject to the test of 'substantially lessening competition' as above. It is the supply of goods or services on condition that the purchaser buys goods and services from a particular nominated third party. It covers situations where the purchaser is refused supply because it will not agree to that condition.

An example of this was an action against a Sydney car dealer and its finance manager. The company was offering special deals on the condition that finance was arranged through a particular credit provider.

exclusive dealing *the supply of goods to a purchaser on the condition that it does not deal with the supplier's competitor(s), nor stock the competitor's goods*

PRIMARY BOYCOTTS

Primary boycotts are agreements between two or more competitors to refuse to deal, or limit their dealings, with another supplier or class of competitors.

primary boycotts *agreements between two or more competitors to refuse to deal, or limit their dealings, with another supplier or class of competitors*

For example, a manufacturer may consider a distributor as unsuitable for its products. It can refuse to supply its own products but cannot seek support from other manufacturers to also refuse to supply the distributor. Two or more competitors cannot force or threaten another firm not to deal with a customer. Such activities are illegal.

SECONDARY BOYCOTTS

secondary boycotts
actions that hinder supplies to or from a firm where it is intended to damage the firm substantially or bring about a lessening of competition in the market

Secondary boycotts are actions that hinder supplies to or from a firm where it is intended to damage the firm substantially or bring about a lessening of competition in the market.

For example, if a trade union is in dispute with a manufacturer, another union supplying the manufacturer with goods might refuse to do so in order to bring pressure on the manufacturer to agree to the first union's demands. This is prohibited (section 45D).

One of the best-known examples of a secondary boycott was the so-called Mudginberri case in 1986. A dispute arose between Mudginberri and the Meat Workers Union. Members of the Meat Inspectors Association refused to cross the union picket line and inspect the meat. The Meat Workers Union was found to have engaged in a secondary boycott. The union was required to pay total fines and damages of more than $1 700 000.

MISUSE OF MARKET POWER

A corporation with substantial market power (e.g. market share) is prohibited from using that market power in ways that will lessen competition, and from acting in ways that damage or eliminate competitors (actual or potential), prevent entry into the market, or deter a person from engaging in competitive market behaviour (section 46).

misuse of market power
using market power in ways that will lessen competition, acting to damage or eliminate competitors, prevent entry into the market or deter a person from engaging in competitive market behaviour

Examples are refusing to deal with a business or offering to conduct business on unrealistic terms. The supplier does not have to supply everyone in the market. The onus is on the customer to show that the supplier's action deterred or prevented the business from entering and competing in the market. Provisions against **misuse of market power** now extend to trade between Australia and New Zealand.

MERGERS

mergers
where two or more firms join together to become one firm

Mergers (where two or more firms join together to become one firm) are not allowed where the merger would result in the firm being in a position to dominate the market, or where as a result of the merger there would be a substantial lessening of competition. This applies especially if the firm is already in a position of dominance (section 50).

PENALTIES

The *Trade Practices Act 1974* (Cwlth) was enacted to monitor potentially restrictive trade practices and to take action when they are found. If guilty, firms and individuals were initially penalised up to $250 000 for companies and $50 000 for individuals.

In 1993 the maximum penalties were greatly increased. Penalties for anti-competitive conduct, which had not changed since the Act was introduced in 1974, were increased to $10 million for corporations and up to $500 000 for individuals.

On 1 January 2011, the *Trade Practices Act* was superseded by the *Competition and Consumer Act 2010*. The main restrictive trade activities that are prohibited by the new Act are described opposite with examples.

BE AWARE OF THE *COMPETITION AND CONSUMER ACT*

Consider the following business scenarios:

1. An oil company supplying petrol to retailers requires the retailers to purchase its oil and lubricants and to sell only tyres and accessories from its subsidiary companies.
2. A building products company wants to take over one of its competitors, which has been waging a two-year price war by taking advantage of its superior quality assurance.
3. A company supplying crockery all over Australia insists on retailers charging the same price wherever it is sold, and withholds supply from any retailer that refuses to comply.
4. A trade union representing dock workers who are on strike calls on truck drivers and ships' crews to refuse to supply services that relate to the company with which it is in dispute.

QUESTION

Use your knowledge of the *Competition and Consumer Act* to provide advice on each of the situations.

LINK TO BUSINESS

SUMMARY

1. Because of various failures of competitive market capitalism, and the rise of imperfect competition, governments play an active role in the Australian economy.
2. Such failures include income inequality, hence the need for income redistribution through the tax and social welfare system. Governments also undertake the provision of essential services, which a market system would be unable or unwilling to provide due to the free-rider effect. Where there are externalities in production such as pollution, governments provide the economic incentive to minimise such waste.
3. Governments try to maintain competition and allocative efficiency by minimising the potential effects of monopoly power. They also attempt to minimise the harmful effects of economic fluctuations such as booms and recession.
4. The Australian Competition and Consumer Commission and the National Competition Council were established to regulate anti-competitive behaviour. The *Competition and Consumer Act* monitors any behaviour by firms that is intended to decrease competition while increasing market power. These government bodies act in the interests of the individual consumer and the welfare of society as a whole.

KEY TERMS					
cartel	142	market failure	134	progressive tax	135
collective goods	136	market power	132	public goods	136
exclusion principle	136	mergers	144	regressive tax	135
exclusive dealing	143	misuse of market power	144	resale price maintenance	143
externalities (spillovers)	137	price discrimination	143	restrictive trade practices	141
free-rider effect	136	price fixing	142	secondary boycotts	144
horizontal agreements	142	primary boycotts	143	vertical agreements	142
		private goods	136		

REFERENCES

1. John Maynard Keynes (1883–1946). His major work was *The General Theory of Employment, Interest and Money*, 1936. He brought about a transformation in economics, both theory and policy, laying the foundations for what is now called macroeconomics.

2. David Ricardo (1772–1823). His most important work was *The Principles of Political Economy and Taxation*, 1817, which dominated English classical economics for the next 50 years.

3. Milton Friedman (1912–2006), well-known American economics professor and leading member of the 'Chicago School'. His many publications included *Inflation: Causes and Consequences* (1963) and *The Great Contraction* (1965). He made contributions to the theory of distribution, but his main work was on the quantity theory of money.

4. John Kenneth Galbraith (1908–2006), a leading American political economist. His many works included *The Economic Discipline* (1967) and *The New Industrial State* (1967).

REVIEW QUESTIONS

1. Listed below are some examples of government intervention in the economy. Give one argument for and one argument against each form of intervention.
   (a) pensions for older people
   (b) unemployment benefits
   (c) provision of police at football games
   (d) provision of art galleries
   (e) free tertiary education
   (f) provision of a public health system
   (g) tariffs on imports of clothing and footwear
   (h) subsidised primary and secondary education.

2. Identify whether the following statements are true or false. Be prepared to justify your answer.
   (a) The progressive income tax system in Australia ensures a more equitable distribution of wealth for low-income earners. True or False?
   (b) The free-rider effect means consumers are able to be excluded from the consumption of public goods. True or False?
   (c) Subsidies and taxes are methods used by governments to ensure that production decisions take into account society welfare in minimising externalities. True or False?
   (d) Monopolies are the most efficient in production. That is why governments control many monopolistic industries. True or False?
   (e) In recessionary periods, governments spend on public works programs to try to influence economic activity. True or False?
   (f) Government legislation is aimed at maintaining competitive market behaviour and minimising the growth of imperfect markets and uncompetitive practices. True or False?
   (g) Vertical agreements are arrangements made between firms in the same industry and at the same level of production. True or False?
   (h) Collusion can exist in any of the four main types of market structures but is found most commonly in monopolistic competition. True or False?

3. What is meant by 'allocative efficiency of the price mechanism'?

4. Distinguish between mergers and cartels.

5. What are the five areas that justify government intervention in the economy to overcome market failure?

6. In what way does the government attempt to redistribute income? What is the reason for doing this?

7. Why won't private firms supply collective goods?

8. What do you understand by the term 'market failure'?

9. What is the free-rider effect? How is it related to the exclusion principle?

10. What is the difference between a primary boycott and a secondary boycott?

11. Explain six types of restrictive trade practices.

12. If competition is the basis for a competitive capitalist economy, do you think it is contradictory that the government interferes and restricts the behaviour of large, powerful, competitive firms?

13. Why is it necessary for governments to make and enforce environmental regulations?

14. Discuss the following statement: 'Pollution isn't a problem. When the pollution gets bad enough, a company will make it economically worthwhile to clean up the mess.'

15. Why will government control of emission levels provoke conflict with business?

16. Discuss the following statement: 'There is no need to take into account future generations in economic development. As supply of a resource decreases, price will increase and so demand will decrease.'

17. In what ways have government and business adapted to meet environmental concerns?

18. Business practices in the past have led to environmental and land degradation in some sectors. Is there a role for governments to play in eliminating this? How? What are the costs to business and consumers in adhering to government regulations? What are the costs of ignoring regulation?

APPLIED QUESTIONS AND EXERCISES
CABCHARGE

Cabcharge has admitted to breaching the former *Trade Practices Act* by abusing its position of market dominance. Cabcharge admitted that in refusing requests from competitors to process Cabcharge cards on its electronic payments system, it had taken advantage of its dominant position in the market. Moreover, Cabcharge admitted to 'predatory pricing' because it installed fare meters in taxis at cost or below cost, thus eliminating rivals. The settlement consisting of penalties and costs amounted to A$15 million.

For further details go to: <www.accc.gov.au/content/index.phtml/itemId/948779>, accessed 5 November 2010.

QUESTIONS

1. How did Cabcharge take advantage of its market position?
2. In what way were competitors disadvantaged?
3. How does competition reduce price and raise customer service?

ACCC MAINTAINS OPPOSITION TO NAB ACQUIRING AXA

The National Australia Bank is proposing to acquire AXA Asia Pacific Holdings Limited's Australian and New Zealand businesses. The issue for the ACCC is that the NAB and AXA business operations overlap in several areas including life insurance, superannuation, financial planning and advisory services and their concern is that the proposed merger could result in a substantial lessening of competition, even though NAB and AXA proposed to restructure some elements of their businesses by divesting some of AXA's operations to IOOF Holdings Limited.

The basis upon which the ACCC reached its decisions is outlined in a Public Competition Assessment which is available on the ACCC's website, <www.accc.gov.au/publiccompetitionassessments> and also on <www.accc.gov.au/content/index.phtml/itemId/946139>, accessed 5 November 2010.

QUESTIONS

1. What are the ACCC's competition concerns?
2. How do mergers as proposed lessen competition and make the consumer worse off?

4

FUNDAMENTAL MACROECONOMIC CONCEPTS

Chapter **8**

The circular flow

LEARNING OBJECTIVES

After studying this chapter, you will be able to:

1. explain what is meant by the five-sector model of the economy
2. describe the five-sector circular flow of income model, building it up from two sectors to five sectors and including the major money flows
3. outline the role of each sector of the economy, explaining its relationship with the other four sectors
4. use the model to explain the equal flows of income, production and expenditure.

INTRODUCTION

In previous chapters we have identified various economic systems. We have also closely examined individual markets and how they operate. Our study of markets introduced the concepts of supply and demand.

In this chapter we look at a model that illustrates how the economy operates. In a capitalistic, mixed economy like that of Australia, money is used by households, businesses and government to buy and sell goods and resources in markets, to pay and collect taxes, and to borrow and lend in financial markets. All these flows can be envisioned schematically in a flow diagram, which enables us to see the interaction between incomes and payments in the economy. The circular flow is shown to be critical in understanding how we measure economic activity and how we assess the size of the economy.

THE FIVE SECTORS

LEARNING OBJECTIVE 1
Explain what is meant by the five-sector model of the economy

A modern economy operates by a complex interaction between a very large number of units, varying in size and in the nature of goods or services they provide. In order to examine the operation of the economy as a whole, it is easier if we group the different units into sectors.

A sector is an area of the economy whose component parts can readily be identified as performing similar functions in the economy. The economy's sectors interact with each other, a process that is described by using aggregates or total data on the economy.

A widely accepted classification divides the economy into five sectors:

1. The *household sector* consists of consumers: those individuals who buy the goods and services provided by the other sectors of the economy to satisfy their personal needs and wants. A large proportion of the household sector also provides the labour or human effort that goes into the production of those goods and services.
2. The *business sector* consists of production: the countless individual firms that undertake the production of goods and services.
3. The *financial sector* consists of firms that specialise in financial services—banks, credit unions, building societies, finance companies. They act as intermediaries between people or firms with surplus funds and those who wish to borrow them.
4. The *government sector* consists of all government authorities at national, state and local level. Some government services are 'collective goods' provided free of charge but paid for by taxpayers; others are sold to consumers by 'government enterprises' just like the output of private firms.
5. The *overseas sector* (or the external sector) is the rest of the world with whom our economy has business relations by way of trade and financial transactions.

Initially, we will look only at the first two—household and business. We can understand some important points from this simplified analysis. Once those points are clear, we will progressively add the other three sectors.

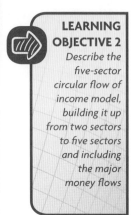

THE SIMPLE CIRCULAR FLOW MODEL

ASSUMPTIONS

Like any model in economics, the simplified version of the **circular flow model** is based on certain assumptions:

- The economy consists of only two sectors, the **household sector** and the **business sector**. This means that there is no government sector and government intervention in economic activities, and the economy lacks both a financial sector and an overseas sector.
- The household sector owns all the resources (i.e. land, labour, capital and enterprise).
- There is no saving by either households or firms. This means that all income received by households (consumers) is spent on goods and services, and all income received by businesses is paid out for the use of productive resources. There are no undistributed profits.
- All production is carried out by businesses that produce only finished ('final') goods and services used directly for consumption purposes, therefore there is no investment, there is no overseas trade. This is a **closed economy** where all goods and services available to consumers are produced by local firms using local resources. All business sales are to local consumers using locally earned income.
- There are no resource inventories.

In this simplified model the households sell their resources to the business sector. Land (real estate sales, office rent), labour (work) and capital (machinery, materials) all provide examples of households selling resources to business. Note also that households gain income from such sales. These are listed in Table 8.1.

circular flow model
a diagram representing the flow of products and resources between businesses and households in exchange for money

household sector
owns all the resources (labour, land, capital, enterprise), sells them to the business sector and earns a factor income (e.g. wages, rent, interest, profit) for contributing resources to production

business sector
consists of the individual firms that undertake the production of goods and services

closed economy
an economy that is isolated from the rest of the world

Table 8.1   **The incomes from resources**

RESOURCE	INCOME
Land	Rent
Labour	Salaries and wages
Capital	Interest
Enterprise	Profit

MARKETS

The business sector uses the resources provided by households to produce goods and services. Producers sell those goods and services to distributors for income. Distributors in turn sell goods and services to consumers for income. Together, producers and distributors make up business. Consumers are individuals in households. There is interaction between households and business in the exchange of resources for rent, salaries and wages, interest or profit, and the exchange of goods and services for payment.

Such interaction occurs through markets. While there are many markets, there are only two types:

- resource or factor markets, named from factors of production, another name for resources
- product markets, which deal in output from production; also called goods and services or commodity markets.

We shall use the terms **resource market** and **product market**.

Resource (factor) markets are where households sell resources to business, or business buys resources from households. Product markets are where businesses sell goods and services to households, or households buy goods and services from businesses.

FLOWS IN THE SIMPLE MODEL

We can express the relationship between the household sector and the business sector in a diagram. Figure 8.1 presents not only the two sectors, but also the four flows of transactions that take place between them.

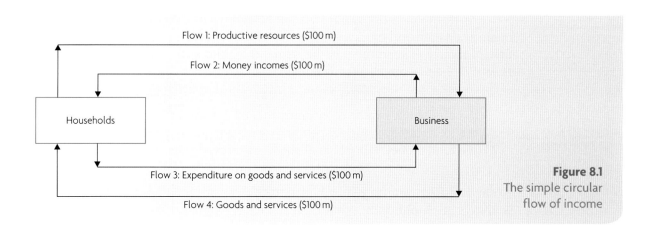

Flow 1: Productive resources ($100 m)

Flow 2: Money incomes ($100 m)

Households

Business

Flow 3: Expenditure on goods and services ($100 m)

Flow 4: Goods and services ($100 m)

Figure 8.1
The simple circular flow of income

Flow 1

This represents the flow of productive resources through the economy, measured over a period of time (e.g. a year), including land and natural resources, labour and enterprise, and capital. The clockwise flow moves from the household sector, which sells or supplies the resources, into the producers' sector, which purchases these productive inputs so that final goods and services can be produced.

Flow 2

This represents the money payments that the business sector makes to the households in the form of rent, wages, interest and the distribution of profits. These payments constitute business demand for the factors of production. The direction of this flow is shown in Figure 8.1 by the anti-clockwise arrow running from the business sector to the household sector.

Flow 3

This is consumption spending by households on final goods and services produced by businesses. This anti-clockwise flow represents the goods and services demanded and purchased by households with the income obtained by selling the services of their resources in flow 2.

Flow 4

This is the clockwise flow of final goods and services produced by businesses and sold to households. When measured over a period of time, it is equal in value to the level of spending in flow 3. In most countries the flow of production is measured by an indicator called gross domestic product (GDP), which is explained in more detail in the following chapter.

Circular flows

You can see that this process is circular. If you think about it, you will realise why this has to be. Households have no means of buying goods and services unless they receive income from selling resources. Similarly, the business sector has no means of buying resources, if it is unable to sell its goods and services.

Hence, this money-using, pure market economy has a clockwise flow of money payments made against an anti-clockwise flow of resources, goods and services. The clockwise circular flow of money expenditures is the demand for the anti-clockwise circular supply. In fact, flows 1, 2, 3 and 4 are all exactly equal in value.

This means that the money value of resources supplied (e.g. $100 million):

> = the total money value of incomes paid by businesses (e.g. $100 million)
> = the total money value of spending by households (e.g. $100 million)
> = the total money value of final goods and services produced (e.g. $100 million).

As depicted in Figure 8.1 (p. 153), the size of each flow would remain constant from day to day and from year to year, while all resources are fully used. In other words, the model is always in 'equilibrium'—that is, in a state of balance. (This concept is discussed further below.) In the real world, this static state of the economy would only be accidental: the value of income, spending and production fluctuates from year to year and even during the same year. To explain this and to make the model more realistic and more useful, we will have to relax the assumptions of the two-sector economy and introduce a modified five-sector version.

THE FIVE-SECTOR MODEL

DEFICIENCIES IN THE SIMPLE MODEL

The main objection to the simple circular flow model is that it assumes that every dollar received as income (i.e. flow 2) is spent by households on the consumption of final goods and services produced within the country.

In the real world, such a model is misleading:

- It disregards the possibility that some households and businesses will save part of their income with financial institutions (banks, finance companies), which, in turn, may then lend out some of these savings to businesses for purchasing machinery and equipment, or for financing investment. Households may also borrow money.
- It fails to acknowledge that governments collect various taxes from households to finance their spending on areas such as roads, administration, education and health.
- It disregards Australia's overseas trade in goods and services, involving revenue from exports and expenditure on imports.

In other words, each nation's circular flow of money can suffer 'leakages' (money **outflows**), or benefit from 'injections' (money **inflows**) in the three sectors that are left out of the simple circular flow model: the financial sector, the government sector and the overseas sector.

We will try to rectify the failings of the simple model by adding the three missing sectors, and we will examine their impact on the operation of the economy as a whole.

outflows
leakages from the flow of income (e.g. savings, taxes and imports)

inflows
injections into the flow of income (e.g. investments, government spending, exports)

THE FINANCIAL SECTOR

The reasons for having a **financial sector** will be discussed in Part 5. For our purposes here, the financial sector reflects two very important economic issues: savings and investment.

LEARNING OBJECTIVE 3
Outline the role of each sector of the economy, explaining its relationship with the other four sectors

Savings

Consider our observation above that some income is saved and not spent. If income is not spent, it must be saved. So **savings** can be defined as that part of income that is not spent,

i.e. total income (Y) = consumption spending (C) + saving (S)

Most people save with banks; some savings go to other financial institutions such as building societies or credit unions. Because savings are income not currently used to purchase goods and services from the business sector, savings represent a leaking of funds from the circular flow of income, and will diminish that flow.

Table 8.2 illustrates this. It shows the impact of savings on spending, output and income when households save 10 per cent of their income in each production cycle. (The value of production, income and consumer spending in Year 1 equals $100 million, as in the simple flow model. Saving starts in Year 2.)

financial sector
this third sector of the economy has savings as a leakage from the flow of income and investment as an injection in the flow of income

savings
a leakage or withdrawal from the circular flow of income defined as that part of household income not spent on current consumption

Table 8.2   **Effects of savings on spending, production and income**

TIME PERIOD	PRODUCTION ($ MILLION)	HOUSEHOLD INCOME ($ MILLION)	CONSUMER SPENDING/ BUSINESS INCOME ($ MILLION)	HOUSEHOLD SAVING ($ MILLION)
Year 1	100	100	100	0
Year 2	100	100	90	10
Year 3	90	90	81	9
Year 4	81	81	73	8

Table 8.2 shows that, as consumer spending falls, production and incomes continue to fall. Unless something else happens, the economy will contract and may enter into a recession. Fortunately the financial sector does not lock up our savings, and the potentially adverse effects of saving are offset by the financial sector's investment operations.

Investment

investment
the process of increasing capital; therefore, it represents that part of production which is not used for current consumption

As we all know, business may update equipment, acquire machinery and improve materials in the production process. It may also expand its product inventories (stock of goods) to enable it to profit from strong increases in demand. Either way, business is spending to increase levels of production. Such spending is called **investment**. The first is capital investment and the second inventory investment.

Note that this is not the most common use of the word 'investment'. For most of us, investment is putting money in the bank, buying shares or similar activities. In economics, however, investment is the process of increasing capital. In other words, investment is that part of production which is not used for current consumption,

i.e. total income (Y) = consumption of goods and services (C) + investment (I)

Saving is a leakage from the circular flow, while investment is an injection of funds into it. The level of saving within the economy is determined by the decisions of a very large number of individuals depending on various factors, such as the level of income, the level of interest rates and consumer expectations.

The level of investment spending results from the decisions of the many entrepreneurs within the business sector, depending on factors such as the level of business income and profits, business confidence and expectations, and government measures in the area of taxation and interest rates.

The relative levels of saving and investment within the economy in a given period (e.g. one year) determine the state of the economic activity. Because saving and investment levels are decided by different people, savings may be equal to, less than or greater than the value of investment for a period of time.

As Table 8.3 shows, the three-sector model of the economy can have one of three outcomes.

Table 8.3   **The financial sector's impact on overall economic activity**

SAVINGS (S) ($ BILLION)	INVESTMENT (I) ($ BILLION)	SAVINGS AND INVESTMENT	MACROECONOMIC EFFECTS
15	15	S = I	Economy in equilibrium
15	25	S < I	Economy expands
15	10	S > I	Economy contracts

government sector
this fourth sector in the five-sector economy involves governments influencing the equilibrium level of national income by the use of taxation (T) which is a leakage and government spending (G) which is an injection

The five-sector circular flow of income, including the financial sector, is shown in Figure 8.2.

THE GOVERNMENT SECTOR

In our discussion of the **government sector**, it is important to note that government is used in its most general sense. No particular government is referred to, nor any particular aspect of government activity. All modern economies have some degree of government intervention.

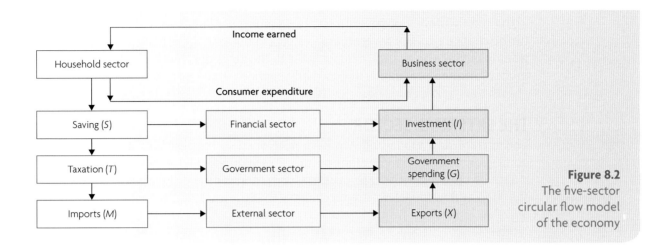

Figure 8.2
The five-sector circular flow model of the economy

The government sector contributes further outflows (taxes) and inflows (government spending) to the circular flow.

Taxes

The government imposes taxes (T) of various kinds. Direct **taxation** is imposed on the household sector (income tax) and the business sector (company tax), as are indirect taxes (sales tax, import duties).

Taxation is leakage of funds because it effectively reduces the level of household **disposable income** and the level of business funds for production purposes.

Like savings, taxes have the effect of lowering consumption expenditure and business investment.

taxation
a compulsory payment to government; therefore, a leakage of funds from the circular flow of income

disposable income
income available for a household to spend

Government spending

Government spending (G) represents an injection of funds into the circular flow. It includes expenditure on collective goods and services (e.g. wages to public servants) and on goods and services provided by the business sector. Other government injections into the circular flow include transfer payments to the household sector (e.g. pensions, unemployment benefits).

The overall effect of the government sector on the circular flow (i.e. overall economic activity) depends on the relative levels of government revenue from taxes and government spending (Table 8.4).

Table 8.4   **Impact of the government sector on overall economic activity**

GOVERNMENT TAXATION (T) ($ BILLION)	GOVERNMENT SPENDING (G) ($ BILLION)	GOVERNMENT TAXATION AND SPENDING	MACROECONOMIC EFFECTS
130	130	$T = G$	Economy in equilibrium
120	130	$T < G$	Economy expands
130	125	$T > G$	Economy contracts

The relative levels of government taxes and spending partly depend, as we will see in future chapters, on the government's efforts to manage the economy. The government might want to produce no change, a fall or a rise in the flows presented above: productive resources, money incomes, production of goods and services, and consumer expenditure.

THE EXTERNAL SECTOR

The circular flow model that we have developed so far describes a closed economy where domestic economic activity alone occurs. This is unrealistic, because the Australian economy is heavily involved with other countries and their markets. By adding the external sector to the circular flow model, we are recognising that the Australian economy is an **open economy** and that Australia's business relations with the rest of the world have an increasing impact on the state of the Australian economy.

open economy
a five-sector economy (i.e. one with an external sector) where imports are a leakage and exports are an injection to the income flow

These issues will be discussed fully in Part 7. For now, we need only concern ourselves with an outline of the main outflows and inflows of funds related to the overseas sector and their impact on overall economic activity. The main inflows of funds generated by the overseas sector include:

- exports of goods and services to other countries by the home economy's business
- foreign investment undertaken in Australia and income payments to Australian residents (e.g. interest, dividends).

Because these activities earn income for the Australian economy, they are an injection of funds into the circular flow.

Australia's business relations with the rest of the world also determine outflows of funds for purchases of imported goods and services by households, government and the business sector, for Australian investment overseas, and for income payments to overseas residents. Income spent abroad in this way is seen as a leakage, thereby lowering the flow of domestic spending.

To simplify things, we regard all inflows of funds as exports (X) and all outflows of funds as imports (M); see Figure 8.2 (p. 157).

As with other leakages and injections, there is no reason why imports must necessarily be equal to exports in a given year. The people making decisions to buy Australian exports of goods and services are located overseas.

The impact of the overseas sector on the economic activity is summarised in Table 8.5. If exports are greater than imports, then the circular flow increases. If imports are greater than exports, then the circular flow decreases.

Table 8.5   **Impact of the overseas sector on overall economic activity**

IMPORTS (M) ($ BILLION)	EXPORTS (X) ($ BILLION)	EXTERNAL BALANCE	MACROECONOMIC EFFECTS
150	120	Trade deficit ($M > X$)	Economy contracts
150	170	Trade surplus ($M < X$)	Economy expands
150	150	Balanced trade $M = X$	Economy in equilibrium

With this we have completed the examination of the five-sector circular flow model (Figure 8.2) which is relevant to all modern economies such as Australia.

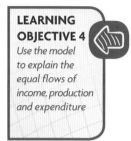

LEARNING OBJECTIVE 4
Use the model to explain the equal flows of income, production and expenditure

INFLOWS TO AND OUTFLOWS FROM THE ECONOMY: AN OVERVIEW

A little time taken now to consolidate this discussion of the three additional sectors of the economy will help us to understand aggregate demand and other macroeconomic concepts in Chapter 10.

EXAMPLE

Imagine a tank of water (see Figure 8.3). There is a pipe high on one side and another low on the opposite side. Water flows into the tank through the high pipe and out through the low pipe. Table 8.6 shows various situations and the consequences that arise. As we have shown in our discussion of the financial, government and external sectors in the economy, circular flows are similar. Situations and their consequences are shown in Table 8.7.

Table 8.6   **Effects of inflows and outflows on a tank of water**

SITUATION	WATER LEVEL
Inflows = Outflows	No change
Inflows > Outflows	Rises
Outflows > Inflows	Falls

Table 8.7   **Effects of inflows and outflows on the circular flow of income**

SITUATION	CIRCULAR FLOWS
Inflows = Outflows	No change
Inflows > Outflows	Increase
Outflows > Inflows	Decrease

You can see that the economy's size depends on the level of outflows and inflows. It follows that, if there is a policy to change the size of an economy (such as growth to employ more people), then adjustments to the outflows and inflows are likely to give effect to that policy. These effects are illustrated in Figure 8.3.

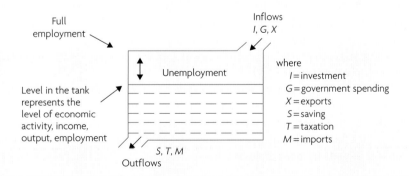

where
  I = investment
  G = government spending
  X = exports
  S = saving
  T = taxation
  M = imports

Figure 8.3
The flows in the economy

EQUILIBRIUM

equilibrium in circular flow
a situation where total injections in the economy are equal to total leakages (the outflows and inflows are in balance)

Economists refer to the situation of no change in the flows as **equilibrium in circular flow**—a very important concept and one that we pursue in the next chapter. For now, note that there are different levels of equilibrium in the economy. For instance, the concept was introduced in Part 2 where we discussed market equilibrium. Our current use of the term refers to overall equilibrium in the economy. Overall economic equilibrium exists because there is balance in all three of the sectors that we have added to the simple two-sector circular flow diagram. At equilibrium, aggregate demand (or total expenditure) equals aggregate supply, that is, the sum of the leakages equals the sum of injections:

$$\text{i.e.} \quad S + T + M = I + G + X$$

disequilibrium
a situation where the total injection of funds in the economy is out of balance with the total leakage of funds

If the economy is to go out of balance (**disequilibrium**), then the balance between households and business or within any of the other three sectors must be upset. If the total injection of funds is less than the total leakage of funds:

$$\text{i.e. if} \quad S + T + M > I + G + X$$

income and production will be greater than spending and supply will be greater than demand. Therefore, production will be decreased and unemployment will result, as the level of income falls to a lower equilibrium.

If the total injection of funds is greater than the total leakage of funds:

$$\text{i.e. if} \quad S + T + M < I + G + X$$

income and production will be less than spending, and supply will be less than demand. As a result, the excess demand will attract an upward adjustment in the levels of production and income within the business sector in response to the higher level of spending.

The economic reality shows that macroeconomic equilibrium is only short-lived: the level of economic activity fluctuates most of the time. The causes and effects of disequilibrium in the circular flow, as applied at macroeconomic level, will be examined later in this book.

BUSINESSES AND HOUSEHOLDS IN THE FIVE-SECTOR MODEL

LINK TO
BUSINESS

The circular flow model emphasises the important role played by the business sector in our economy. Entrepreneurs in the business sector buy or hire the productive resources (land, capital, labour) in the factor market. They take a risk in deciding what goods and/or services to produce, how much, how, and for whom. They coordinate the other three factors of production. In this process they create jobs in the economy. They do not do this for nothing. Their reward is profit.

Businesses are instrumental in expanding the economy when they spend money for new investment in equipment and technology (*I*) and when they sell Australian-made goods and services to other countries (*X*).

The household sector is at least as important as the business sector. It performs a dual role in the economy: it provides labour and other resources to firms, permitting the production of goods and the generation of incomes; and it also provides the consumers who exchange their income for final goods and services. About 60 per cent of Australia's expenditure on goods and services is made by individual consumers.

Even the leakages from the income of the household sector are important. Savings (S) are converted by the financial sector into investment (I), which is used for the expansion of production in the business sector and the creation of new jobs. The amount of income collected by the government as tax (T) is spent by the government for the provision of goods and services benefiting the entire society (e.g. defence, police, public works). The household sector is vital to any economy.

QUESTIONS

1. What is the role of the business sector in the financial and external sectors?
2. What is the effect of savings on the circular flow?
3. What is the importance of the three leakages in the circular flow?

SAVINGS VERSUS GROWTH

Economic experts agree that, over recent decades, the low level of savings in Australia has been one of the weak points for Australia's macroeconomic performance. To address this issue, the Australian Government initiated various measures, such as:

- The 1996 Budget's 'super tax', meant to raise $500 million in revenue from the superannuation of high-income earners with more than $70 000 in wages and super benefits.
- The 1997 Budget's 'savings rebate' in the form of a $2 billion tax cut for existing savers, was phased in from July 1998.
- The Budgets in 2002–03 and 2004–05 placed a special emphasis on boosting net investment savings. For instance the 2004–05 Budget provided an enhanced government superannuation co-contribution scheme and a reduction in the superannuation surcharge, worth $2.7 billion over four years, expected to boost incentives to save.
- The 2010–11 budget announced an increase in employer super contributions to 12 per cent by 2019.

LINK TO
INTERNATIONAL
ECONOMY

Such measures were meant to help the government to fulfil its commitment to balance the budget—but not only that. The increased private savings generated by such measures were expected to provide a number of economic benefits, such as the reduction in Australia's reliance on foreign debt; more investment and jobs; and a rise in the speed limits to growth that had held Australia back over the 1980s.

Generally, these objectives have been met, except for Australia's reliance on foreign debt, which is a long-lasting issue of the Australian economy.

THEORIES ABOUT SAVINGS AND GROWTH

Why do increased savings lead to increased growth? The usual explanation relies on a model built by the United States economist Robert Solow, which assumes that all resources are fully employed in an economy that is closed to the outside world. Another United States economist, Martin Feldstein, extended this view by showing that, despite the current economic globalisation, there is still a close connection between domestic savings and domestic investment.

However, a number of studies have concluded that any links between growth and savings run in the opposite direction. One of the best examples of the new thinking is a 1993 World Bank report, *The East Asian Miracle: Economic Growth and Public Policy*, which concludes that 'growth drives savings rather than the other way round'. A similar conclusion was drawn by two United

continued ↘

continued

States experts, Christopher Carrol and David Weil, in a separate study of four Asian countries (Japan, South Korea, Singapore and Hong Kong): in all four cases, growth was high early and savings were high later.

An Italian economist, Antonella Palumbo, intervened in the debate. Palumbo said that we should look at the importance of some other factor, such as a phase of intense industrial development, rather than 'a temporal coincidence between high growth rates and high savings'. World Bank studies showed that more prosperous developing countries (e.g. South Korea, Malaysia) tend to cover a larger share of their investment needs with local savings and rely less on foreign savings. These countries with higher savings and investment rates have also recorded greater growth rates. It is often argued that higher domestic savings are needed in Australia to ease pressures on the current account deficit. A counter-argument is provided by John Pitchford of the Australian National University. Pitchford argues that the current account deficit (i.e. the deficit in the external sector of the open economy) is not a big problem, provided we make productive use of investment that draws on the global pool of savings.

Such arguments seem to support the view that more evidence should be produced with regard to the link between savings and growth before the finance sector is allowed to make further demands on the Budget.

Sources: Based on Brian Toohey, Australian Financial Review, *13 March 1997; Dwight H. Perkins, Steven Radelet, Donald R. Snodgrass, Malcolm Gillis and Michael Roemer*, Economics of Development, *5th edn, W.W. Norton & Company, Inc., New York, United States, 2001, pp. 380–2.*

SUMMARY

1. The two-sector circular flow of income is a basic model of the economy which shows the household and business sectors and the resource and product markets. This model ignores the existence of the financial, government and overseas sectors. According to this model outflows (leakages) are equal to inflows (injections) and the economy will always be in a state of equilibrium.
2. The five-sector model of the circular flow of income includes households, firms, financial, government and external sectors. The model shows how equilibrium or disequilibrium occurs in the economy, depending on the net difference between total leakages and total injections.
3. An open economy represented by the five-sector circular flow model is illustrated in a flow diagram, to show:
   (a) the flow of resources and of goods and services in exchange for money
   (b) outflows of savings into the financial sector where they are converted into investment
   (c) outflows of taxes collected and used by the government sector for expenditure on collective goods and services plus transfer payments (e.g. social security payments)
   (d) flows of goods, services and money between the domestic economy and the rest of the world.

KEY TERMS

business sector	152	equilibrium in circular flow	160	open economy	158
circular flow model	152	financial sector	155	outflows	155
closed economy	152	government sector	156	product market	153
disequilibrium	160	household sector	152	resource (factor) market	153
disposable income	157	inflows	155	savings	155
		investment	156	taxation	157

REVIEW QUESTIONS

1. Outline the four flows in the simple circular flow of income.
2. Briefly explain the assumptions of the simplified circular flow model.
3. Explain the role of the household sector and business sector in the simple circular flow model.
4. Why must consumption equal income in the simple circular flow of income? Explain.
5. Outline the limitations of the two-sector circular flow of income.
6. Why is saving regarded as a leakage from, and investment an injection into, the circular flow of income?
7. What is the impact of a government budget surplus on the circular flow model?
8. Explain, with reference to the circular flow model, the impact of exports on production and employment in Australia.
9. Outline the concept of equilibrium in the circular flow of income.
10. In your opinion, which sector is more important to the economy: the business sector or the household sector? Explain.

APPLIED QUESTIONS AND EXERCISES

1. Outline the way in which the five-sector circular flow of income can explain rises and falls in the levels of GDP, employment and unemployment.
2. 'Savings are a leakage from the circular flow, therefore they are a negative factor for the economy.' Do you agree with this statement? Why or why not?
3. Assume you are the owner-manager of a company that manufactures car components in a five-sector economy.

Explain the likely effects on the economy of each of the following developments (ceteris paribus):
   (a) The total value of your annual sales rises from $10.5 million to $13.0 million.
   (b) You borrow $1 million for the purchase of new equipment.
   (c) Your annual company tax paid to the taxation office increases from $1.2 to $2.0 million.
   (d) You make export sales to South Korea and New Zealand worth $1.8 million.

4. For two consecutive years, the Bucksland economy has recorded the following values regarding its circular flow (Table 8.8):

Table 8.8: Bucksland's circular flow values

	YEAR 1 B$ MILLION	YEAR 2 B$ MILLION
X	60	85
G	300	315
S	50	45
M	75	70
T	305	315
I	40	40

   (a) What will be the net impact of all these items on Bucksland's economy?
   (b) Which sector has the largest contribution to the changes in the economy's situation?
   (c) Which two of the six items could be most easily manipulated in order to restore the equilibrium?

Table 8.9: Gross savings/GDP ratio and the gross capital formation as a percentage of GDP

ECONOMY/GROUP	GROSS SAVINGS AS A % OF GDP		GROSS CAPITAL FORMATION (GCF)[1] AS A % OF GDP	
	1995	2008	1995	2008
Australia	23	29	24	29
The Euro Area	15	16	21	22
United Kingdom	15	15	17	17
United States	15	14	18	18
New Zealand	18	16	23	24
China	43	54	42	44
Malaysia	34	38	44	22
Singapore	52	46	34	31
Republic of Korea	36	31	38	31
East Asia and Pacific[2]	39	48	40	40

[1]Gross capital formation is outlay on additions to fixed assets of the economy (e.g. land improvements, machinery and equipment purchases, construction works), and net changes in inventories.
[2]Only low and medium income economies.

Source: Compiled from World Bank, World Development Indicators 2010.

5. Table 8.9 on the previous page shows the gross savings/ GDP ratio and the gross capital formation as a percentage of GDP in a number of selected economies and groups of economies. Examine the figures in the table and explain the following:

(a) The link between gross savings and gross capital formation and how it could be explained with the help of the circular flow of income model.

(b) Why the two kinds of ratios are not identical in each individual economy/group.

(c) Why the levels of the two ratios tend to be higher in East Asian economies compared to developed economies.

6. After reading the Link to international economy on 'Savings versus growth' on page 161, answer the following questions:

(a) According to most experts, which version of the circular flow model shows a more direct link between domestic savings and economic growth: the simple circular flow model or the open economy model?

(b) What do you think will happen to the savings/GDP ratio in South-East Asian countries over the next decade: is it likely to stay high, as it was prior to the East Asian crisis, or is it expected to decline? Is this likely to affect East Asia's economic growth? Explain.

Chapter 9

Measuring the economy's size and growth

LEARNING OBJECTIVES

After studying this chapter, you will be able to:

1. define gross domestic product (GDP) and its main features
2. describe the three approaches to the calculation of GDP
3. distinguish between nominal GDP (GDP at current prices) and real GDP (GDP at constant prices)
4. explain how nominal GDP figures can be adjusted to account for changes in the macro price level
5. identify a few shortcomings of GDP as a measure of economic activity and economic welfare
6. explain the role of GDP in comparing various economies in terms of size and growth
7. identify other important measures of the macro economy
8. describe and explain the business cycle and outline the causes of fluctuations in the economy
9. explain the links between expenditure and income ('the multiplier effect')
10. understand how the global financial crisis has impacted on the economies of Australia and New Zealand.

INTRODUCTION

Economic activity is made up of the productive activities, the income-earning activities and the spending activities of individuals, groups of individuals, firms and governments.

As explained in the previous chapter, the level of national income is subject to a set of interacting forces pulling it in opposite directions: leakages (saving, taxes and imports) reduce it, and injections (investment, government spending and exports) increase it.

At the level of a firm, the measurement of the firm's flow of income and expenditure is needed by the firm's management to assess the economic health (e.g. profit or loss) of the firm in a particular period of time. Also, by examining its accounts over a longer period of time, the firm's management can detect if the firm's business is growing or declining, at what rate, and can identify some immediate causes for the firm's performance. On this basis, the firm's management can make intelligent decisions on future strategies which are deemed to improve the firm's business performance.

At the level of a national economy, we have a system of national income accounting, which is a system used to measure the level of aggregate production, income and expenditures for a nation at some point in time and to explain the immediate causes of that level of performance.

At the same time, by comparing the national income accounts over a number of years we can plot the long–run course (e.g. growth, decline or stagnation) the national economy has been following.

Finally, based on the information provided by the national income accounts, the government will be able to formulate and implement macroeconomic policies (e.g. fiscal, monetary and other policies discussed in Part 8) to improve the performance of the economy as a whole.

In this chapter we will discuss a number of outputs from the national accounts that can be used to get an indication of the size of economic activity and its growth over time. Statistics of this type enable year by year comparisons of an economy or the comparison of one economy with another.

We will learn later on, in Chapter 21, how governments use this sort of information in order to establish the level of economic activity and to develop economic policies aimed at achieving their economic objectives.

LEARNING OBJECTIVE 1
Define gross domestic product (GDP) and its main features

gross domestic product (GDP)
the market value of all final goods and services produced in the economy during a year

GROSS DOMESTIC PRODUCT

The national accounts provide us with aggregate measures of what is happening in the economy. These broad aggregates include indicators such as total production, total spending, total income and total employment.

The main output from the national accounts used to assess the economy's overall performance is called the **gross domestic product (GDP)**. GDP is the market value of all final goods and services produced in the economy during a specific period (e.g. a year or a quarter).

For instance, in the financial year 2008–09 Australia's GDP in current prices amounted to around A$1.25 trillion. Therefore, that was the size of the Australian economy in that year expressed in Australian dollars.

Let's explain in more detail the meaning of the above definition of GDP.

GDP—A MONETARY MEASURE

GDP measures the market value of a period's output in monetary terms. As we know, each year the economy produces a large number of goods and services to satisfy the unlimited needs and wants of its population. Goods use various weights and measures in different systems (e.g. metric, British, American). Services or 'intangibles' have different measures to goods (e.g. phone calls are measured in minutes).

This way, a physical measurement of total production is impossible, and GDP must be a monetary measure, which can provide us with a meaningful idea of its relative worth from one period to another.

'Market value' is the total value of the production of goods and services in a specific period valued at the market prices of the same period.

For instance in Table 9.1, the GDP of a hypothetical economy is made up of three products: crude oil, cars and telecom calls. By looking at outputs only, in two consecutive years, we are not sure about the performance of the economy. Especially as the output of crude oil declines, while the other two have a slight increase.

Table 9.1   **GDP made up of heterogenous outputs by using money prices, two consecutive years, $ million (hypothetical data)**

	ACCOUNTING UNIT	ANNUAL OUTPUT	AVERAGE MARKET PRICE ($/UNIT)	MARKET VALUE ($ MILLION)
YEAR 1 OUTPUTS				
(1) Crude oil	Barrels	10.0 million	50	400
(2) Cars	Units	0.5 million	10 000	5000
(3) Telecom calls	Minutes	2000 million	0.18	360
GDP Year 1				**5860**
YEAR 2 OUTPUTS				
(1) Crude oil	Barrels	8.0 million	40	320
(2) Cars	Units	0.55 million	10 000	5500
(3) Telecom calls	Minutes	2100 million	0.2	420
GDP Year 2				**6240**

However, when we attach price tags to each of the products, we can calculate the market value of the aggregate production in the hypothetical economy. The total market value of the three products increases from $5860 million to $6240, an annual growth rate in current prices of 6.5 per cent.

GDP COUNTS ONLY FINAL GOODS AND SERVICES

An important point to retain is that GDP counts only the value of **final goods and services**.

On the other hand, *intermediate goods and services* are goods and services that are subject to further processing, manufacturing or resale. To avoid double counting of products or services which are sold more than once, GDP includes only the market value of final goods and services and ignores the cost of intermediate goods and services. Otherwise, the value of GDP would be unduly inflated.

final goods and services
finished goods and services that are being purchased for final use

An example will give you a better idea of this concept. Suppose there are six stages of production in getting a writing pad into the hands of a student, who is the ultimate or final user (see also Table 9.2):

- Firm 1 (a tree farm) sells trees to a logging company at $0.50 per unit. Firm 1 pays out $0.50 to the owners of wages, rents, interest and profits.
- Firm 2 processes the trees into logs and sells the logs to Firm 3 (a pulp mill) at $1.10 per unit. The **value added** of $0.60 is used by the logging company to pay wages, rents, interest and profits.
- Firm 3 processes the logs into pulpwood and sells it to a paper manufacturer at $1.80 per unit, with a value added of $0.70 paid to the owners of resources.
- Firm 4 manufactures writing pads and sells them to a stationery wholesaler at $2.70 per unit, with a value added of $0.90 per unit.
- Firm 5 (stationery wholesaler) sells writing pads to a retail stationery store at $3.20 per unit, with a value added of $0.50 per unit.
- Firm 6 (stationery retail store) sells the writing pad to a student (the 'final user') at $4 per unit, with a value added of $0.80 per unit.

value added

the market value of a firm's output less the value of its intermediate goods and services

Table 9.2   **Value added in a six-stage process to produce writing pads**

(1) PRODUCTION STAGE	(2) PRODUCT	(3) SALE PRICE OF PRODUCT ($)	(4) VALUE ADDED ($)
Firm 1, Tree farm	Trees	0.50	0.50
Firm 2, Logging company	Logs	1.10	0.60
Firm 3, Pulp mill	Pulpwood	1.80	0.70
Firm 4, Paper manufacturer	Writing pad	2.70	0.90
Firm 5, Stationery wholesaler	Wholesale service	3.20	0.50
Firm 6, Retail stationery store	Retail service	4.00	0.80
Value added (total income)			4.00

At each stage, the difference between what a firm has paid for the product and what it receives for sale is paid out as wages, rent, interest and profits for the resources used by that firm in helping to produce and distribute the writing pad.

The values of the first five transactions are not included in GDP. When a student buys the writing pad for his or her studies, the final purchase price ($4) is added to GDP as a consumer expenditure.

non-productive transactions

transactions where no production of goods or services occurs (e.g. purely financial transactions, and second-hand sales)

Exclusion of non-productive transactions

As discussed before, GDP is a measure of the annual production of the economy. For that reason, any **non-productive transactions** must be carefully excluded from the calculation of GDP.

The main types of non-productive transactions include:

- purely financial transactions
- second-hand sales.

Purely financial transactions consist of:

(a) public transfer payments—Public transfer payments are social security government payments in return for which recipients make no contribution to current production. Examples are social welfare payments, veterans' benefits, other types of pensions and unemployment benefits. They are not included in GDP, because they do not represent production of any new or current output, and their inclusion would artificially overstate the size of production.

(b) private transfer payments—Private transfer payments (e.g. transfer payments from overseas parents to their children studying in Australia) are excluded because they do not involve production. They are simply a transfer from one individual to another.

(c) trading in financial securities (e.g. bonds or stocks)—Trading in financial securities are excluded from GDP because they represent only the exchange of certificates of ownership (stocks) or indebtedness (bonds) and not current production.

Approaches to measuring GDP

There are three different approaches to the determination of GDP. They are based on the statistical identity Income = Expenditure = Production ($I = E = P$), explained by the circular flow model (see Chapter 8).

Expenditure approach: GDP(E)

One way of looking at GDP is as the sum of all the expenditures involved in taking the total output off the market. The expenditure method (**GDP(E)**) uses what is spent on outputs as a measure of those outputs. With this method, GDP is measured at the point of spending on consumption and investment by the private sector and by the government. The value of exports must be added because the spending by overseas customers on Australian goods and services is injected into the Australian economy. But the value of imports must be deducted, because spending by Australians on goods and services produced overseas is a leakage to other economies (see Table 9.3 overleaf). Therefore, GDP measured by the expenditure method is:

$$GDP(E) = C + I + G + (X - M)$$

where the letters stand for the following components:

- *C*—**personal consumption expenditure**. This component comprises total spending by households for durable goods (e.g. cars, appliances, furniture etc), non-durable consumer goods (e.g. food, clothing, soap, petrol) and services (e.g. legal advice, medical treatment, entertainment, education). This is expenditure on Australian-produced as well as imported final goods and services. As Table 9.3 shows, it is the largest component, accounting in 2008–09 for approximately 54 per cent of GDP(E). (A long-term average ratio would be more like 60 per cent.)

LEARNING OBJECTIVE 2
Describe the three approaches to the calculation of GDP

GDP(E)
a version of GDP which measures GDP as the sum of all the expenditures involved in taking that total output off the market

personal consumption expenditure (C)
expenditure on locally produced as well as imported final goods and services

Table 9.3   **Australian gross domestic product using the expenditure approach, 2008–09, $A billion, and per cent**

GDP(E) COMPONENT	AMOUNT (A$ BILLION)	PER CENT OF GDP(E)
Household consumption (C)	679.8	54
Gross private domestic investment (I)	294.4	23
Total government expenditure (G), out of which:	**278.6**	**22**
• Government consumption (G^1)	213.8	17
• Government investment (G^2)	64.8	5
Gross national expenditure (GNE = C + I + G)	1252.8	99
Net exports (X – M) resulting from:	**6.1**	**1**
• Exports (X)	284.7	23
• Imports (M)	278.6	22
Gross domestic product (E)* (C + I + G + X – M)	1258.9	100

* ABS identifies most of the times a statistical discrepancy is involved in estimating GDP. For the purposes of this topic, a statistical discrepancy calculated by the ABS of around A$14 billion has been distributed proportionately across GNE categories to ensure consistency of GNE with GDP.

Source: Adapted from Australian Bureau of Statistics, <www.abs.gov.au>, accessed 8 November 2010, cat. no. 5206032.

gross private investment expenditure (I)
expenditure by the private sector on capital goods and services (not including the transfer of paper assets or second-hand tangible assets)

government purchases of goods and services (G)
component of aggregate demand, which consists of government consumption (also known as G^1) and government investment (known as G^2) and excludes all government transfer payments

exports (X)
expenditure on domestically produced goods and services by overseas governments, firms and individuals

imports (M)
expenditure by domestic consumers on goods and services produced overseas

- **I—gross private investment expenditure.** This is expenditure by the private sector on capital goods and services (e.g. machinery, equipment, tools, building and construction, changes in stocks and inventories). It tends to be the most volatile component of aggregate demand. The share of this component in 2008–09 shown in Table 9.3 comes to 23 per cent of total GDP(E), however, over the last two decades or so, it has been as low as 12–13 per cent.

- **G—government purchases of goods and services.** This includes a consumption component (e.g. wages and salaries of public servants, goods such as stationery) known as G^1 and an investment component (e.g. purchase of fixed assets, provision of hospitals, schools, power, transport, roads) known as G^2. In 2008–09, G^1 was around 17 per cent and G^2 was about 5 per cent. Generally, since the early 1970s, total government expenditure ($G^1 + G^2$) has represented approximately 20 to 25 per cent of Australia's GDP(E). As discussed above, government spending excludes all government transfer payments (e.g. unemployment benefits, pensions), because they do not reflect any current production.

- **X—exports.** This is expenditure on domestically produced goods and services by overseas governments, firms and individuals. Table 9.3 shows that, in 2008–09, exports of goods and services accounted for around 23 per cent of Australia's GDP (up from about only 9 per cent in the early 1960s).

- **M—imports.** This is expenditure by domestic consumers on goods and services produced overseas. The total value of imports of goods and services must be estimated, and subtracted from C + I + G + X, to avoid an overstatement of total production in Australia. The same table indicates that Australian imports of goods and services in 2008–09 accounted for around 22 per cent of Australia's GDP, which is more than double the corresponding level of the early 1960s.

In general, 'net exports' (X – M) in Australia represent a negative figure (–1 to –2 per cent of aggregate demand), which means that they are reducing GDP. ABS data (cat. no. 5206032) indicates that over the last 30 years or so, small trade surpluses were recorded in only five financial years (1980, 1992, 1997, 2002 and 2009).

Income approach: GDP(I)

Another way of measuring GDP is to add up all the income derived from the production of goods and services, in order to obtain **GDP(I)**. Relatively reliable statistics are available on incomes, particularly from tax returns By definition, GDP(I) should provide the same amount as the expenditure method described above. In practice, however, measurement errors will make the two figures slightly off when reported by national statistical agencies.

Total income can be subdivided according to various schemes, leading to various formulae for GDP measured by the income approach. A common one is:

$$GDP(I) = COE + GOS + GMI + T_{P \& M} - S_{P \& M}$$

where
  COE = Compensation of employees
  GOS = Gross operating surplus
  GMI = Gross mixed income
  $T_{P \& M}$ = Taxes on production and imports
  $S_{P \& M}$ = Subsidies on production and imports.

ABS data illustrating this approach is presented in Table 9.4.

GDP(I)

a version of GDP which measures GDP as the sum of income derived or created from the production of the GDP, the main source of data being tax returns

Table 9.4   **Australian gross domestic product using the income approach, 2008–09, A$ billion, and per cent**

GDP(I) COMPONENTS	AMOUNT (A$ BILLION)	PER CENT OF GDP(I)
Compensation of employees (COE):	**607.5**	**48**
• Wages and salaries	541.3	43
• Employers' social contributions	66.2	5
Gross operating surplus (GOS):	**422.1**	**34**
• Non-financial corporations (private)	236.4	19
• Non-financial corporations (public)	15.9	1
• Financial corporations	59.6	5
• General government	26.4	2
• Dwellings owned by persons	83.8	7
Gross mixed income (GMI)	**95.1**	**8**
• Taxes less subsidies on production and imports $(T_{P \& M} - S_{P \& M})$	120.8	10
• Statistical discrepancy	7.6	1
• GDP(I)* $(COE + GOS + GMI + T_{P \& M} - S_{P \& M})$	1253.1	100.0

Source: Adapted from Australian Bureau of Statistics, <www.abs.gov.au>, accessed 8 November 2010, cat. no. 5206034.

A few words about each category included in the GDI(*I*) formula:

- Compensation of employees (COE) is the largest income category, accounting in 2008–09 for around 48 per cent of all GDP(*I*). It comprises primarily the wages and salaries that are paid by employers (e.g. businesses and government) to suppliers of labour, as well as employers' social contributions (e.g. superannuation payments and compensation payments).
- Gross operating surplus (GOS) is the surplus (often incorrectly referred to as 'profit'*) due to owners of incorporated enterprises. More precisely, the GOS is the excess of the gross output value over the sum of intermediate consumption, wages, salaries and supplements and indirect taxes less subsidies.

  The above 'profit' denomination is not technically correct, because only a subset of total costs are subtracted from gross output to calculate GOS. Net operating surplus is then calculated by subtracting depreciation allowances from operating surplus. (Depreciation can be defined as the reduction in value of an asset through wear and tear.) Therefore, a more accurate statement of the total income of an enterprise is made only after the deduction of 'depreciation' from GOS.

  Table 9.4 (p. 171) shows that GOS's share in GDP(*I*) in 2008–09 was around 34 per cent. The same table lists four categories of enterprises with a GOS: private non-financial corporations, public non-financial corporations, financial corporations and general government.
- Gross mixed income (GMI) is the same measure as GOS, but for unincorporated businesses. This often includes most small businesses.
- Taxes less subsidies on production and imports ($T_{P \& M} - S_{P \& M}$)

We can note at this stage that the sum of COE, GOS and GMI represents in fact the income of all of the factors of production in the economy. Thus, the three categories are called the 'total factor income', which measures the value of GDP at factor (basic) prices. The difference between basic prices and final prices (those used in the expenditure calculation) is those total taxes and subsidies that the government has levied or paid on that production. So adding taxes less subsidies (also called 'negative indirect taxes') on production and imports converts GDP at factor cost to GDP(*I*).

Production approach: GDP(P)

With the production approach, the value of GDP is measured at the point where goods and services leave the producers. GDP using the production approach is derived as the sum of gross value added for each industry, at basic prices, plus taxes less subsidies on products.

GDP measured by this method is known as **GDP(P)**.

GDP(P)
a version of GDP measured at the point where goods and services leave the producers

Integration of the three approaches

While each of the three approaches should, conceptually, deliver the same estimate of GDP, if the three measures are compiled independently using different data sources, then different estimates of GDP result.

This probably does not surprise you, since we are dealing here with large-scale calculations across the whole of the Australian economy.

However, the Australian national accounts estimates have been integrated with annual balanced supply and use tables. This way, annual estimates using the *I*, *E* and *P* approaches are identical for the years for which these tables are available. These tables have been compiled from 1994–95, up to the year preceding the latest complete financial year.

Prior to 1994–95, and for quarterly estimates for all years, the estimates using each approach are based on independent sources, and there are usually differences between the *I*, *E* and *P* estimates. Nevertheless, for these periods, a single estimate of GDP has been compiled.

The equivalence of income, production and expenditure

EXAMPLE

Let's imagine a retail electronics store. A customer pays $900 in exchange for a TV set. The customer's purchase is a sale for the retailer/producer of the same value ($900). The money received by the retailer is paid out in wages, rent, interest and profit, this money being income to all the owners of the factors of production—land, labour, capital and enterprise.

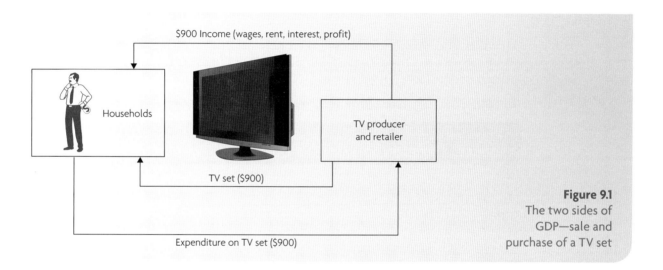

Figure 9.1
The two sides of GDP—sale and purchase of a TV set

If we extrapolate this transaction to the level of the whole economy, where thousands of such transactions, involving various goods and services, take place each day, we will understand the meaning of a fundamental equation in economics:

$$\text{total expenditure} = \text{GDP} = \text{total income}$$

NOMINAL (MONEY) GDP VERSUS REAL GDP

You will recall that GDP is not a physical amount, but a money or market value of all final goods and services produced in a period of time (quarter or year).

The problem is that GDP is a price-times-quantity figure (actually a sum of 'n' price-times-quantity figures) and, as such, any growth of GDP can be due to an increase in the physical quantity (which is objective), but also to an increase in prices (which can be misleading, because a lot of the additional value might be just the result of inflation).

Therefore, even if the physical output did not change in terms of the number of units produced or in its composition from one year to the next, GDP would probably have a different dollar value because the prices per unit of output changed.

Let's explain with a very simple example.

LEARNING OBJECTIVE 3
Distinguish between nominal GDP (GDP at current prices) and real GDP (GDP at constant prices)

EXAMPLE

We have an economy which produces only two products (X and Y). Table A below shows figures for total value and composition of GDP in Year 1 at current prices (e.g. as set at the moment of each transaction during the reference period).

Table A   **Year 1 (GDP at current prices)**

PRODUCT	(1) PRICE (IN DOLLARS)	(2) QUANTITY	VALUE (1) × (2)
X	3	10	30
Y	5	20	100
GDP			130

The GDP 'at current prices' is also called 'nominal GDP' or 'money GDP'. Assume that in Year 2, X's price rises to $4 and Y's to $6, but output quantities stay the same. The nominal GDP as illustrated by Table B(1) will rise to $120, which is an increase of $30, or, some 23 per cent!

Table B(1)   **Year 2 (GDP at current prices/nominal GDP)**

PRODUCT	(1) PRICE (IN DOLLARS)	(2) QUANTITY	VALUE (1) × (2)
X	4	10	40
Y	6	20	120
GDP			160

23 per cent is a fabulous annual growth. The question is: Did our economy actually grow in size by almost one quarter? Not really. As we said, output quantities (10 for 'X' and 20 for 'Y') did not change, so there is no real growth and the increase in the value of GDP (at current prices) is only the result of the price increases, or what economists call 'inflation'.

Fortunately, national income accountants have been able to resolve this problem by selecting a point of reference or 'base year' and by keeping prices in all other years constant. The deflating or inflating of nominal GDP eliminates the distorting effect of price changes.

In our example, in Table B(2) we keep prices in Year 2 constant and we notice that, because output quantities did not change, the total **real GDP** will stay unchanged from Year 1.

real GDP
GDP at constant prices (e.g. inflated or deflated to account for price-level changes)

Table B(2)   **Year 2 (GDP at constant prices/real GDP)**

PRODUCT	(1) PRICE (IN DOLLARS)	(2) QUANTITY	VALUE (1) × (2)
X	3	10	30
Y	5	20	100
GDP			130

It is clear now that our economy was in a stagnant position in Year 2 compared to Year 1. There was no real GDP growth. It is obvious that nominal GDP figures can be misleading when used to measure the changes in economic activity, especially when prices experience large variations.

This above example, consisting of only two goods and two prices, is very simple to understand. We realise that the situation in the real economy is much more complex, given that we deal with thousands and thousands of goods and services at different prices, with quantities and prices changing from year to year at various rates.

How will national income accountants convert nominal GDP to real GDP at the level of the whole economy?

Inflating and deflating GDP

We understand now that the value of different years' outputs (GDPs) can be compared only if the value of money itself does not change because of inflation or deflation. GDP is a price-times-quantity figure. As discussed above, a GDP figure that reflects current prices is called 'GDP at current prices' or **nominal GDP**. However, it is the quantity of goods and services produced and distributed to households that affects their standard of living, not the size of the figure on the price tags of these goods.

In order to represent the real growth of GDP national income, statisticians deflate nominal GDP when prices are rising and inflate it when prices are falling.

They will do this by deriving a general price index that estimates overall changes in the price level.

Price indexes

Let's have a short break and discuss briefly a few basic things about price indexes. A price index is a single number calculated from a set of prices. Such a price index is nothing more than a level measured relative to a fixed point of reference, called **base year**.

To understand the concept of price indexes and how they assist the calculation of real GDP we will assume that we have an economy which produces one product only, product 'X'. Table 9.5 overleaf uses as base year 'Year 1'. In column (1) we have the number of units produced in the economy in three consecutive years. Prices per unit in the three years are listed in Column (2). In Column (3) we will calculate and insert the price index in each year. The price index in Year 1 (base year) is set by convention as 100.

When in Year 2, the price increases from $4 to $5, we can calculate the price index in Year 2 through the formula:

$$\text{Price index} = \frac{\text{Price in any given year}}{\text{Price in base year}} \times 100$$

Therefore the price index in Year 2 will be

$$\text{Price index (Year 2)} = \frac{\$5}{\$4} \times 100 = 125$$

Similarly, in Year 3, when the price increases to $7 per unit, the price index becomes

$$\text{Price index (Year 3)} = \frac{\$7}{\$4} \times 100 = 175$$

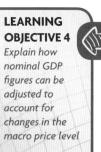

LEARNING OBJECTIVE 4
Explain how nominal GDP figures can be adjusted to account for changes in the macro price level

nominal GDP
GDP measured at current prices (e.g. dollars of the period)

base year
the year containing the reference price level and output relative to which price levels or outputs in other periods are measured

Table 9.5   **Adjusting nominal GDP (hypothetical data)**

| | (1) | (2) | (3) | (4) | (5) |
YEAR	UNITS OF OUTPUT	PRICE ($/UNIT)	PRICE INDEX (YEAR 1 = 100)	NOMINAL GDP, $ (1) × (2)	REAL GDP, $
1	10	4	100	40	40
2	12	5	120	60	50
3	15	7	140	105	75

We know that the nominal GDP is a price-times-quantity figure, so in Column (4) we will calculate the $ values for the nominal GDP (at 'current prices') resulting in $40 (Year 1), $60 (Year 2) and $105 (Year 3).

As we said before, in order to calculate the real GDP (at 'constant prices'), we will have to deflate/inflate the nominal GDP in Column (4) with the price index in Column (3). The simplest and most direct method is by dividing the price index numbers in Column (3) into the corresponding nominal GDP in Column(4).

This will bring us to:

$$\text{Real GDP (Year 1)} = \frac{\$40}{100} \times 100 = \$40$$

(Note: Because of the conventional price index of 100 in the base year, real GDP in the base year is always equal to nominal GDP in the same year. In other words in the base year there is no inflation.)

$$\text{Real GDP (Year 2)} = \frac{\$60}{120} \times 100 = \$50, \text{and finally,}$$

$$\text{Real GDP (Year 3)} = \frac{\$105}{140} \times 100 = \$75$$

In conclusion, the above calculations related to Table 9.5 should give us a basic understanding of price indexes and of how the process of adjusting the nominal GDP to real GDP via price indexes takes place.

Now we can make a step further to the real economy.

REAL GDP IN THE REAL ECONOMY

It should be most clear by now that while nominal GDP reflects changes in both output and prices, real GDP figures allow us to make a better estimate of changes in real output.

As mentioned before, at the level of the whole economy, the national income accountants adjust the level of nominal GDP through much broader price indexes to cover all goods and services operating in the economy.

In Australia, two types of national accounts based price index are published. The first type is referred to as chain price indexes which are calculated by a complex chain-weighted geometric series for all expenditure components and sub-components of gross domestic product (GDP). The components are: government consumption, household consumption, private capital formation, public capital formation, and imports and exports of goods and services.

Chain price indexes use as their weights the volumes of expenditure in the previous financial year (ending 30 June).

The second type of price index is referred to as **implicit price deflators (IPDs)**, which are compiled at the same levels as the chain price indexes, but which use for their weights the volumes of expenditure in the current period.

Both chain price indexes and IPDs are compiled quarterly and are published by the Australian Bureau of Statistics (ABS) roughly two months after the reference period.

Table 9.6 provides us with the 'real economy' illustration of the inflating and deflating processes over a recent nine-year period.

The general price index for the whole economy in Table 9.6 is the implicit price deflator (IPD) listed in Column (2) with the base year in 2007–08. Because the long-term trend has been for the price level to rise, the issue is to inflate the pre-2007–08 figures because nominal GDP in Column (3) understates the real output of those years. Column (4) shows what GDP would have been in the selected nine years if the 2007–08 price level had prevailed. By the same token, the rising price level has caused the nominal GDP figure in 2008–09 to overstate real output, hence the nominal GDP had to be reduced/deflated.

implicit price deflator (IPD) *a broadly based measure of the average level of prices in the economy based on consumer goods and services, investment goods and services, goods and services purchased by the government, and goods and services exported and imported*

Table 9.6   **General price level (IPD), nominal GDP ($ billions) and real GDP ($ billions), annual figures, from 2000–01 to 2008–09**

(1)	(2)	(3)	(4)
YEAR	IMPLICIT PRICE DEFLATOR INDEX (2007–08 REFERENCE YEAR)	GDP(E) CURRENT PRICES ($ BILLIONS)	REAL GDP(E) CONSTANT 2007–08 PRICES ($ BILLIONS)
2000–01	76.3	708.9	928.5
2001–02	78.7	759.2	964.1
2002–03	80.9	804.4	994.6
2003–04	83.5	865.0	1035.8
2004–05	86.9	925.9	1065.2
2005–06	91.2	1000.8	1097.9
2006–07	95.8	1091.3	1139.3
2007–08	100.0	1181.8	1181.8
2008–09	105.2	1258.9	1197.2

Source: Compiled from ABS, Australian National Accounts: National Income, Expenditure and Product, cat. no. 5206032.

One should note that the price level index used in the adjustment process in Table 9.6 is not the consumer price index (CPI),which is widely reported in news media. As explained in more detail in Chapter 12, CPI measures the price of a 'market basket' of consumer goods and services.

By contrast, IPDs (and, for that matter, chain price indexes) include, as mentioned above, not only consumer goods and services, but also investment goods, goods and services purchased by government, and goods and services exported and imported.

In conclusion, given that real GDP adjusts for changes in the price level, by inflating/deflating nominal GDP, it is a superior measure of the level of macroeconomic activity.

LINK TO BUSINESS

THE INFORMAL ECONOMY

An informal economy is economic activity that is neither taxed nor monitored by a government, contrasted with a formal economy.

Economists agree that there exists a relatively large and apparently expanding underground sector in our economy. Some participants in this sector are engaged in illegal activities such as gambling, prostitution, loan-sharking and illegal drugs. For obvious reasons, persons receiving income from such illegal businesses choose to conceal their incomes.

However, not all informal economy comes from illegal activities (e.g. 'black market'). Many participants in the informal economy are in legal activities, but do not fully report their incomes, for tax-evasion reasons:

- A waiter may under-report tips from customers.
- A businessperson may record only a portion of sales receipts for the tax collector.
- One tradesman fixes the roof of a neighbour in return for babysitting services. The value of the exchange via 'barter' is unreported.
- A worker who wants to retain unemployment or other welfare benefits, may obtain an 'off-the-books' or 'cash-only' job so there is no record of his or her work activities.

In situations of an inflationary environment and declining real incomes, the incentive has become greater to receive income in forms (for example, cash and barter) that cannot be easily discovered by the taxation department.

The informal economy is thus not included in that government's GDP figures and thus official estimates of GDP are generally regarded as an understatement.

Although the informal economy is often associated with developing economies, all economic systems contain an informal economy in some proportion.

Estimates about the size of 'the informal/underground economy' in Australia vary between 5 and 10 per cent of GDP. Internationally, estimates of a United States-based database, NationMaster, about the size of the informal economy varied between around two-thirds of GDP in countries like Georgia and Bolivia, to close to 13 per cent in New Zealand, just under 9 per cent in the United States and around 3 per cent in Canada.

Source: <www.nationmaster.com/graph/eco_inf_eco-economy-informal>, accessed 8 November 2010.

LEARNING OBJECTIVE 5
Identify a few shortcomings of GDP as a measure of economic activity and economic welfare

LIMITATIONS OF GDP

As discussed above, GDP is a reasonably accurate measure of national economic performance. However, for various reasons, GDP measurement has a number of limitations:

- The above discussion about 'the informal economy' identifies such a limitation, which makes us reasonably believe that the official calculation of GDP understates the true value of total economic activity.
- The exclusion of non-market transactions from GDP (e.g. voluntary work for charities, household production, child care, do-it-yourself home repairs and services) may be regarded as an inconsistency in the calculation of GDP (e.g. similar paid activities are included in GDP). It also understates the true value of total production.
- GDP is a quantitative rather than qualitative measure. To the extent that product quality has improved over time, GDP understates improvement in our material wellbeing.

- GDP data provides no information regarding the composition and allocation of total output. At the same value of GDP, one economy may provide a diversified and well-balanced production of capital and consumer goods, while another economy's production may be heavily concentrated on military goods. In one economy GDP may be more evenly distributed among households, while in another, a large proportion of national income is concentrated in a few hands. In short, GDP measures the size of total output, but does not reflect changes in the composition and distribution of output that might also affect the economic wellbeing of society.
- A larger GDP involves most often the 'negative externalities' discussed in Chapter 7 such as pollution caused by steel mills, chemical plants or coal-fuelled power stations. The spillover costs associated with the production of the GDP are currently not deducted from total output and, hence, GDP overstates our national economic welfare.

Over the recent decades, there have been many attempts to replace or supplement the GDP indicator with alternative concepts emphasising social welfare, such as:

- Human Development Index (HDI)—HDI uses per-capita GDP (as an indicator of standard of living) and then factors in indicators of life expectancy and education levels.
- Genuine Progress Indicator (GPI) or Index of Sustainable Economic Welfare (ISEW)—The GPI and the ISEW attempt to address many of the above criticisms by taking the same raw information supplied for GDP and then adjusting for income distribution, adding for the value of household and volunteer work, and subtracting for crime and pollution.
- Gini coefficient—in economics, the Gini coefficient measures the disparity of income within a nation.

LEARNING OBJECTIVE 6
Explain the role of GDP for comparing various economies in terms of size and growth

Notwithstanding the above limitations of GDP, GDP remains an extremely useful measure of national economic performance. As we will show in the next sections, GDP provides a good tool not only for measuring the size of an individual economy, but also for comparing various economies in terms of size and growth.

GDP—INTERNATIONAL COMPARISONS

In each country, national income accounting uses the respective national currency: yen in Japan, euros in France, rupiahs in Indonesia. In order to compare GDP in various countries, international organisations such as the World Bank convert GDP in national currencies to United States dollar values.

Table 9.7 overleaf lists comparative 2008 GDP data for the world's largest 10 economies, plus a few other selected economies in the Asia-Pacific region, including Australia. Data is in current United States dollars. Dollar figures for GDP are converted from domestic currencies using single year official exchange rates. It appears that in 2008 Australia, with a GDP size of around US$925 billion, and 1.6 per cent of the world's GDP, ranked 13th in the world, and third in size in the Asia-Pacific region next to Japan and China.

Table 9.7 indicates that the largest economy in the world is by far that of the United States, with almost a quarter of the world's GDP. In 2009, the United States' GDP was almost three times larger than Japan's and about 115 times that of New Zealand. The Australian GDP was only about 6.5 per cent of the size of that of the United States, which is less than the GDP of the United States' third largest state GDP, that of the state of New York.

LINK TO
INTERNATIONAL
ECONOMY

continued ↘

continued

Table 9.7   **Comparative GDP data, current US$ values and per cent shares of world GDP, 2009**

WORLD RANKING	ECONOMY	GDP US$ BILLION	% OF WORLD GDP
1	United States	14 256	24.5
2	Japan	5 067	8.7
3	China	4 985	8.6
4	Germany	3 347	5.7
5	France	2 649	4.5
6	United Kingdom	2 175	3.7
7	Italy	2 113	3.6
8	Brazil	1 572	2.7
9	Spain	1 460	2.5
10	Canada	1 336	2.3
11	India	1 310	2.2
12	Russian Federation	1 231	2.1
13	Australia	925	1.6
14	Mexico	875	1.5
15	Republic of Korea	832	1.4
18	Indonesia	540	0.9
32	Thailand	264	0.5
40	Malaysia	192	0.3
43	Singapore	182	0.3
53	New Zealand	125	0.2

Source: Adapted from World Development Indicators database, World Bank, 1 July 2010, <http://siteresources.worldbank.org/DATASTATISTICS/Resources/GDP.pdf>, accessed 5 November 2010.

This method of comparing GDPs in United States dollars obtained from the conversion of national currencies via official exchange rates has been criticised for its large dependence on official exchange rates, which are not only volatile, but in some countries can be artificially manipulated by government authorities.

Over the last two decades or so, international organisations such as the World Bank and the IMF started to use a new method for calculating GDP, called 'the purchasing power parity (PPP)'. This method is presented in Chapter 25. However, the official exchange rate conversion seems to be the method preferred by international organisations.

ECONOMIC GROWTH

Economic growth is the increase in value of the goods and services produced by an economy. GDP is a useful macroeconomic measure again, because economic growth is conventionally measured as the per cent rate of increase in real gross domestic product, or GDP. As a measure of economic growth, GDP has all the advantages and drawbacks of that level variable.

economic growth
increase in value of the goods and services produced by an economy

The formula of economic growth rate in a particular year (say 2009) is:

$$\text{GDP growth 2009} = \left(\frac{\text{GDP2009}}{\text{GDP2008}} - 1 \right) \times 100\%$$

EXAMPLE

Bucksland's real GDP in 2008 was $120 billion and, in 2009, real GDP went up to $126 billion. What is Bucksland's annual growth rate in 2009?
We apply the above formula:

$$\text{GDP growth 2009} = \left(\frac{126}{120} - 1 \right) \times 100\% = 5\%$$

Figure 9.2 presents the average of annual real GDP growth rates over 2000–08 and in 2009 in selected developed economies and groups including Australia.

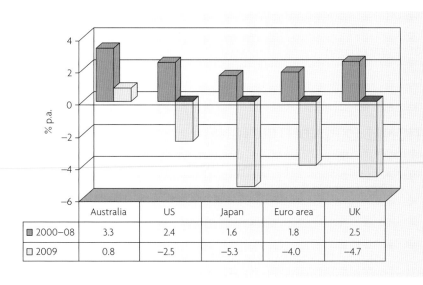

	Australia	US	Japan	Euro area	UK
■ 2000–08	3.3	2.4	1.6	1.8	2.5
☐ 2009	0.8	−2.5	−5.3	−4.0	−4.7

Figure 9.2
Comparative real GDP growth rates in Australia and selected developed economies and groups, annual average 2000–08 and 2009 (per cent per annum)
Source: World Bank, 2010 World Development Indicators, Table 4.1; OECD Economic Outlook, May 2010.

It appears that, among the selected developed economies, Australia's economy has recorded a leading performance in terms of economic growth, in the period preceding the global financial crisis. During 2009, which was the year most affected by the crisis, Australia was the only economy in the sample to record a positive economic growth. A more detailed analysis of Australia's performance during the financial crisis compared to that of New Zealand is presented at the end of this chapter. At the same time, a broader discussion of the theory and practice of economic growth is undertaken in Chapter 25.

LEARNING OBJECTIVE 7
Identify other important measures of the macro economy

OTHER NATIONAL ACCOUNTS

As discussed before, the size of the Australian economy is typically described in terms of GDP.

In addition to GDP, several other national accounts are reported in economic literature, because they are important measures of the macro economy.

We will discuss briefly a few such measures:

- national turnover of goods and services (NTGS)
- gross national expenditure (GNE)
- net domestic product (NDP)
- gross national income (GNI).

NATIONAL TURNOVER OF GOODS AND SERVICES (NTGS)

national turnover of goods and services (NTGS)
the total market supply of final goods and services $(GDP + M)$

National turnover of goods and services (NTGS) is the total market supply of final goods and services $(GDP + M)$. We know that GDP is the total market value of final goods and services. However, we also know that the total amount of goods and services does not include only Australian-made goods and services, but also imported goods and services. We found that part of expenditure made by households (C), private investors (I) and government (G) is spent on imports of goods and services. Therefore we may describe the total annual amount of goods and services as the sum of GDP and imports (M) of final goods and services. This total flow, referred to as national turnover of goods and services is thus the total market supply of final goods and services. The formula for national turnover is:

$$NTGS = (GDP + M)$$

GROSS NATIONAL EXPENDITURE (GNE)

gross national expenditure (GNE)
equals the sum of domestic consumption, investment and government expenditures $(C + I + G)$.

Gross national expenditure (GNE) equals the sum of domestic consumption, investment and government expenditures $(C + I + G)$. Thus GNE represents total domestic demand for goods and services. The formula for GNE is:

$$GNE = C + I + G$$

It is usually different from GDP because expenditures on imports are included, but exports (goods produced within the economy, but sold outside of it) are not.

Since: $NTGS = (GDP + M) = (GNE + X)$

Then: $GDP = NTGS - M = GNE + X - M = C + I + G + (X - M)$

NET DOMESTIC PRODUCT (NDP)

We can recall that GDP is not entirely a measure of newly produced output, because it includes the estimated value of the capital goods required to replace those worn out in the production process. The measurement designed to correct this deficiency is called **net domestic product (NDP)**.

NDP is an annual measure of the economic output of a nation that is adjusted to account for depreciation, calculated by subtracting depreciation from the GDP.

Therefore, the formula for the net domestic product is:

$$NDP = GDP - depreciation \text{ (also known as consumption of fixed capital)}$$

According to ABS, 'consumption of fixed capital' in 2008–09 amounted to around $198 billion.

Therefore, Australia's NDP in 2008–09 was:

$$NDP = \$1253 \text{ billion} - \$198 \text{ billion} = \$1055 \text{ billion}$$

Thus, NDP estimates how much the country has to spend to maintain the current GDP. If the country is not able to replace the capital stock lost through depreciation, then GDP will fall. In addition, a growing gap between GDP and NDP indicates increasing obsolescence of capital goods, while a narrowing gap means that the condition of capital stock in the country is improving.

net domestic product (NDP)
the economic output of a nation that is adjusted to account for depreciation, calculated by subtracting depreciation from the gross domestic product

GROSS NATIONAL INCOME (GNI)

Gross national income (GNI) was formerly called gross national product (GNP). The difference between GDP and GNI is that GDP defines its scope according to location, while GNI defines its scope according to ownership. GDP is product produced within a country's borders; GNI is product produced by enterprises owned by a country's citizens. The two would be the same if all of the productive enterprises in a country were owned by its own citizens, but foreign ownership makes GDP and GNI non-identical. Production by Japan's Toyota Motor Co. in Australia counts as part of Australian GDP, but does not affect Australia's GNI (it is part of Japan's GNI). On the other hand, production by BHP Billiton in a subsidiary in the United Kingdom counts as part of Australia's GNI, but not as Australia's GDP. (This production is part of the United Kingdom's GDP.)

GNP may be much less than GDP if much of the income from a country's production flows to foreign persons or firms. But if the people or firms of a country hold large amounts of the stocks and bonds of firms or governments of other countries, and receive income from them, GNP may be greater than GDP. For most countries, however, these statistical indicators differ insignificantly.

According to the ABS, in 2008–09, Australia's gross national income was around $1205 billion, which is lower than GDP(I) at $1253 billion. The difference between the two figures represents the net income (e.g. interest and dividends) payable to non-residents. (See more details about net income in Chapter 18.)

gross national income (GNI)
comprises the total value produced within a country (i.e. its gross domestic product) together with its income received from other countries (notably interest and dividends), less similar payments made to other countries

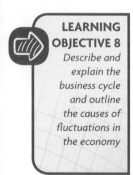

LEARNING OBJECTIVE 8

Describe and explain the business cycle and outline the causes of fluctuations in the economy

THE BUSINESS CYCLE

In Chapter 8 we learnt that in the real world the level of economic activity (GDP) fluctuates all the time.

Business cycles are inherent in market economies. Historical and empirical evidence indicates that, while individual business cycles vary considerably in duration and intensity, all have four phases: expansion, peak, contraction and trough. Figure 9.3 shows the usual pattern of the business cycle.

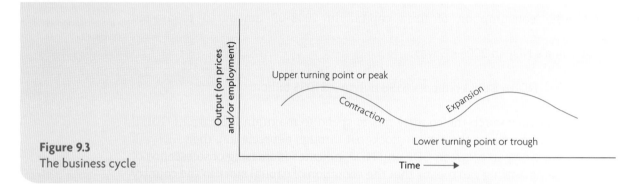

Figure 9.3
The business cycle

PEAKS AND TROUGHS

business cycle

the recurrent 'ups and downs' in the level of growth in economic activity that extend over a period of several years

period of the cycle

a complete business cycle, experienced when the level of economic activity has fluctuated between peak and peak, or conversely, between trough and trough

peak

the phase of the business cycle during which the economy reaches its maximum after rising during an expansion

An economy is considered to have experienced a complete business cycle when the level of economic activity has fluctuated between peak and peak, or conversely, between trough and trough. This is called the **period of the cycle**.

As we have seen, not all peaks reach the same heights. Nor do all troughs plummet to the same depths.

To move from a **peak** to a **trough**, the economy goes through a contraction phase. If the peak represents high economic activity, then the economy must contract for it to be undergoing low economic activity at its trough.

Likewise, to move from a trough to a peak, the economy goes through an expansion phase, a change from a period of low economic activity to a period of high economic activity. Remember, the economy continues to grow (unless economic circumstances are really desperate), but the rate of growth varies.

In Figure 9.3, the peak is labelled the upper turning point. This is because it represents the point at which the expansion phase becomes a contraction phase, that is, the economy turns from being expansionary to being contractionary. Similarly, the trough is called the lower turning point. It represents the point at which the contraction phase becomes an expansion phase, that is, the economy turns from being contractionary to being expansionary. A term related to the contractionary phases of the business cycle is that of **recession**. A descriptive definition of recession is 'a downturn in the business cycle during which output, sales and employment decline'.

However, although the level of output growth may fall in our economy, prices tend to be inflexible or 'sticky' in a downward direction. The price level is likely to fall only if the recession is severe and prolonged; this is how a depression occurs.

Other terms used in business cycle analysis are *ceiling* and *floor*. In Figure 9.3, there are two peaks and one trough. The right peak is not as high as the left peak. Some analysts call the highest upper turning point (in Figure 9.3, the left one) the ceiling, and the lowest turning point, the floor. Because it is highly unlikely that successive upper turning points will have the same **amplitude**, such terminology helps to clarify descriptions of the business cycle.

A further point should be noted about the business cycle: not all movements are in the one direction. In an expansion phase, some indicators rise a lot, others rise a bit, and some fall. A contraction phase may see some indicators falling and others rising. Generally though, an expansion phase sees the key indicators (output, prices, employment) rising and a contraction phase sees the key indicators falling. Moreover, again in general, indicators that fall most during contraction tend to rise most during expansion.

EXPLAINING FLUCTUATIONS

Various explanations have been offered to explain the fluctuations of business activity:

- Major innovations (e.g. railways, motor vehicles and computers) have a profound impact on investment and consumption spending—and therefore on output, employment and price levels.
- Random events, such as wars and political turmoil, raise spending on military items at the expense of consumer goods. When peace is restored, there is a drastic reduction in military production and a strong upsurge in consumption spending as resources are shifted to the production of consumer goods.

Although there is a diversity of opinion about the causes of business fluctuations, there is general agreement that the immediate determinant of the level of national output and employment is the level of total expenditure. Total expenditure may change frequently and significantly over time, and this subsequently induces fluctuations in total economic activity.

THE MULTIPLIER

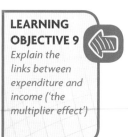

LEARNING OBJECTIVE 9
Explain the links between expenditure and income ('the multiplier effect')

A critical concept in understanding the relationship between expenditure and income is the so-called **multiplier effect**. The multiplier effect may be described as the chain reaction that results from changes in the level of expenditure. The multiplier quantifies the amount by which income is changed by a change in expenditure.

To explain this concept, we first have to summarise a few related indicators.

MARGINAL PROPENSITY TO CONSUME (MPC)

The **marginal propensity to consume (MPC)** is the proportion of any change in disposable income that is consumed:

$$MPC = \frac{\text{change in consumption}}{\text{change in disposable income}}$$

If an increase in income of $500 results in an increase in consumption of $300, then

$$\text{MPC} = \frac{300}{500} = \frac{3}{5} = 0.60$$

MARGINAL PROPENSITY TO SAVE (MPS)

Similarly, the **marginal propensity to save (MPS)** is the proportion of any change in disposable income that is saved:

marginal propensity to save (MPS)
the proportion of any change in disposable income that is saved

$$\text{MPC} = \frac{\text{change in saving}}{\text{change in disposable income}}$$

Since any income earned is either spent or saved it follows that:

$$\text{MPC} + \text{MPS} = 1$$

That is, if MPC = 0.60, then MPS = 0.40.

MULTIPLIER EFFECT

Shifts in total expenditure, whatever the underlying cause, give rise to even larger changes in total income and output. This is referred to as the multiplier effect.

For instance, if intended investment rises by $5 billion and the resulting change in total income amounts to $10 billion, the multiplier is 2.

We have to examine why there is a multiplier effect and what determines the size of the multiplier. To begin, we refer to the national income equation explained earlier in this chapter. You will remember this as:

$$Y = C + I + G + (X - M)$$

where Y = national income
C = consumption spending
I = private investment spending
G = government spending
X = export spending
M = imports

It is clear that any change in spending changes income. And, of course, any change in income brings about a change in spending, or induced change in income. But income is not the only factor in spending. People can increase or decrease their spending while their income remains unchanged. This is known as an autonomous change in spending.

These observations apply to the national income equation. A shift in consumption, private investment, government spending or net exports causes a shift in the same direction in income. This is illustrated in Figure 9.4. An expenditure shift of $5 billion (from EE to E^1E^1) brings about an income shift of $10 billion (from N to N^1). The ratio of $10 billion to $5 billion is the ratio of 2:1. Therefore, the multiplier is 2. In Figure 9.4, the multiplier is 2 because of the slope of EE, the spending schedule. The slope of EE is known as the marginal propensity to consume (MPC). If the MPC had been 3:4, then the multiplier would have been 4 and a $5 billion rise in spending would have brought about a $20 billion rise in income.

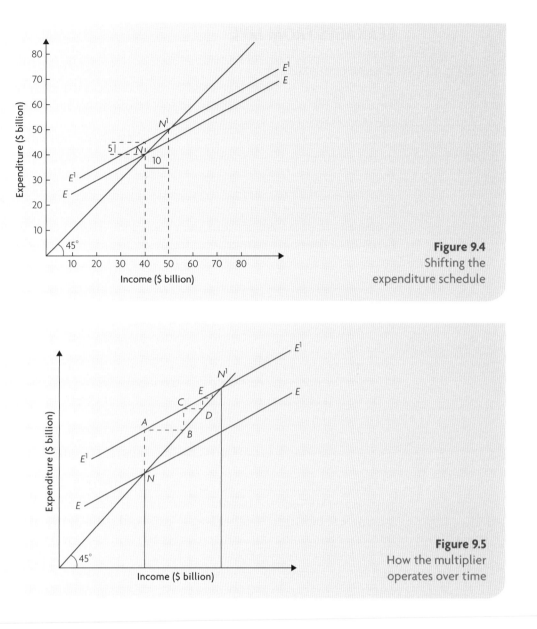

Figure 9.4
Shifting the
expenditure schedule

Figure 9.5
How the multiplier
operates over time

In real economic situations, the multiplier's effect is not instantaneous. It takes time for such an effect to work through the economy. This is explained in Figure 9.5.

How the multiplier operates over time

Assume the periods in Figure 9.5 are quarters (as they are in Australia's national accounts). Planned spending is increased (NA) this quarter. Income is increased (AB) next quarter. Planned spending is then increased (BC) the quarter after that, creating an increase in income of CD. And so on until N^1 is reached.

Note that NA = AB but BC = $\frac{1}{2}$ AB. That is because the MPC is 1:2 and only half of the increased income is spent. This also illustrates that the effect on income decreases over time until N^1 is reached.

If only half the increased income is spent, where does the other half go? An economic way of asking the same question is: What determines the size of the MPC?

LEAKAGES FROM MPC

Since the MPC is the propensity to consume or spend, what we do with our income establishes the size of the MPC.

The first leakage from increased income is tax, because income attracts tax. Thus, the amount of the taxation must be deducted from available income to establish how much of the increased income is available to be spent.

The second leakage is savings, an income earner's alternative to spending in disposing of increased income. If the additional income earned is saved and not spent, then the MPC is reduced.

As explained above, there is in fact a complementary concept to MPC that helps to explain the relationship between spending (consumption) and saving. This is known as marginal propensity to save (MPS). It refers to people's inclination to save any extra income that they earn. Since the only two outcomes from earning income are consuming and saving,

$$MPC + MPS = 1$$

The third leakage from increased income is spending on imports. It underlines the fact that the MPC (and, of course, the MPS) refers to uses of income, not where income is spent, if indeed it is.

On the other hand, the multiplier refers to the effect of an increase in domestic income on domestic production. That is why spending on imports gets round the multiplier, reducing its effect in the domestic economy and therefore reducing its effect on income.

These leakages also explain the relationship of the MPC to the multiplier. The multiplier (M) is thus the reciprocal of MPS,

$$\text{i.e. } M = \frac{1}{MPS} \text{ or } \frac{1}{(1 - MPC)}$$

If MPS (or MPC) changes, so does the multiplier. More specifically, the larger the MPC the smaller the MPS and the larger the multiplier. Hence, the effects of an increase in spending on income will be larger. Another way of expressing this is to say that the smaller the leakages into tax, savings and imports, the larger the multiplier will be.

John Maynard Keynes observed, 'a fundamental law … that [people] are disposed, as a rule and on the average, to increase their consumption as their income increases, but not by as much as the increase in their income'.[1] In this statement, Keynes alerts us to the other major point that we need to discuss about the relationship between spending and income.

Keynes sets out that point like this. At any income level, the proportions of income consumed and saved are constant. Further, the proportions of an increase in income that are consumed and saved (MPC and MPS respectively) are also constant at any income level. However, the proportion of total income consumed, known as the average propensity to consume, falls as income increases.

Because these changes are not simultaneous but work their way through the economy over time, what happens in one period influences the outcome in another. More particularly, increased spending in one period increases income in a subsequent period by a factor equivalent to the multiplier. Moreover, if income = expenditure = output, production will also be increased by that same factor.

One brief observation brings this discussion to an end. Throughout this chapter, we have discussed increases brought about by the multiplier. That focus arises from the fact that, most commonly, economic growth is occurring and the multiplier must be operating to increase income.

There is nothing automatic about this. The multiplier may operate negatively, compounding a drop in spending into a much higher drop in income and leading to a further significant drop in spending and so on. This may in fact happen in the contraction stages of the business cycle; it most certainly did happen in the greatest contraction period that economists have measured—the 1930s Depression.

This merely reflects an adage that has developed around discussions of the business cycle—'What goes up must come down'. And this discussion may provide another explanation for the fluctuations that take place in economic activity.

LEARNING OBJECTIVE 10
Understand how the global financial crisis has impacted on the economies of Australia and New Zealand

AUSTRALIA, NEW ZEALAND AND THE GLOBAL FINANCIAL CRISIS

LINK TO INTERNATIONAL ECONOMY

We have read a lot about the global financial crisis (GFC). One wonders how the economies of Australia and New Zealand have been impacted by the GFC. We'll try to find out the answer in the following brief comparative analysis.

The fact is that Australia and New Zealand are not only located in the same geographic region, but they share a common colonial heritage, and have established very close political and economic relations, formalised progressively since 1983 in the framework of the Australia New Zealand Closer Economic Relations Trade Agreement (ANZCERTA).

Table 9.7 (p. 180) showed that the Australian economy is over seven times larger than that of New Zealand. However, given their high degree of economic integration, one would expect that the two trans-Tasman economies would have experienced comparable issues and performance in the context of the GFC.

GFC'S REGIONAL IMPACT

International economic organisations like the IMF and the OECD, along with private consultants and analysts like Trading Economics and John Forster (2010), have noted that both economies have been able to ride out the GFC better than many other major developed economies. Among the reasons advanced for this performance one can mention:

- In both Australia and New Zealand, the effects of the global crisis appeared more slowly than observed elsewhere. The relatively small scale of the two economies, especially in the case of New Zealand, represented an advantage.
- Australian and New Zealand financial institutions largely escaped the worst of the problems besetting institutions in the United States, the United Kingdom, Ireland and Germany.
- The housing markets in Australia and New Zealand did not collapse to the same extent as elsewhere, which has prevented further drains on the banks via non-performing mortgages.
- Both economies, especially Australia, are closely linked with Asia, especially China, and China's fiscal stimulus package, which has maintained the Chinese economy's strength, has helped the exports of primary products of Australia and, to a lesser extent, those of New Zealand.
- In addition, sound macro-management in both economies, before and during the crisis, including significant fiscal incentives to consumers and the business sector combined with monetary policy stimulus (e.g. low interest rates), cushioned the blow from the global crisis.

THE BUSINESS CYCLES

Figure 9.6 overleaf presents the comparative quarterly growth of real GDP in Australia and New Zealand over a nine-quarter timeframe, which is a good illustration of the business cycles in the two economies.

continued ↘

continued

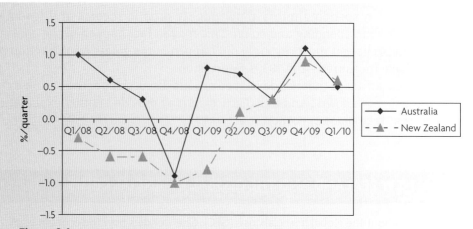

Figure 9.6

Australia and New Zealand, comparative real GDP quarterly growth, over the period between quarter 1, 2008 and quarter 1, 2010 (per cent per quarter)

Source: Adapted from <www.tradingeconomics.com>, accessed July 2010.

It appears that, over the period, both economies reached their lowest point in the business cycle in the fourth quarter of 2008. However, during the nine-quarter period, New Zealand has recorded a total of five consecutive quarters of negative growth, while Australia experienced only one quarter of negative growth (−0.9 per cent) in the December quarter, 2008.

Following the December quarter, 2008, Australia's economy recovered to reach in the fourth quarter of 2009 a growth rate of 1.1 per cent. This was Australia's fastest pace since March 2007, underscoring the RBA's decision of early March 2010 to boost borrowing costs for the fourth time in five meetings.

New Zealand started its recovery in the second quarter of 2009, and experienced four consecutive quarters of positive growth with a high of 0.9 per cent real GDP growth (what a coincidence!) in the fourth quarter, 2009.

In March 2010, RBA's governor, Glenn Stevens, the first Group of 20 central banker to increase interest rates (in October 2009), said that Australia's economy was running at or near 'trend' after skirting the global recession of 2009.

In early June 2010, New Zealand's Reserve Bank Governor, Alan Bollard said: 'The economy has entered its second year of recovery with growth becoming more broad-based.'

Australia's average of real GDP growth rates over the nine-quarter period was a positive 0.5 per cent, while the corresponding average for New Zealand was a negative growth of 0.2 per cent, which would indicate that by the end of the March quarter, 2010, New Zealand's real GDP had not yet reached the pre-crisis level.

INFLATION AND LABOUR MARKETS

As known from Keynes theory, strong economic growth tends to fuel inflation, while, in a contractionary/recessionary environment, inflation tends to fall. Table 9.8 presents the quarterly change in inflation represented by the consumer price index (CPI). It appears that Australia and New Zealand recorded comparable levels of inflation. Australia tended to outpace New Zealand in terms of inflation growth in 2008, but the Australian inflation level dropped faster than that of New Zealand in 2009. In the first quarter, 2010, the level of inflation in Australia was slightly higher than in New Zealand, but still within Australia's inflation target range of 2 to 3 per cent on average over the cycle.

Table 9.8   **Comparative quarterly inflation and unemployment rates in Australia and New Zealand, from quarter 1, 2008 to quarter 1, 2010, per cent per quarter**

PERIOD	QUARTERLY CPI CHANGE (% PER QUARTER)		QUARTERLY UNEMPLOYMENT RATE* (% PER QUARTER)	
	AUSTRALIA	NEW ZEALAND	AUSTRALIA	NEW ZEALAND
Q1/08	4.2	3.4	4.1	3.9
Q2/08	4.5	4.0	4.2	3.9
Q3/08	5.0	5.1	4.2	4.3
Q4/08	3.7	3.4	4.5	4.6
Average 2008	4.35	3.98	4.25	4.18
Q1/09	2.5	3.0	5.3	5.1
Q2/09	1.5	1.9	5.6	5.9
Q3/09	1.3	1.7	5.8	6.5
Q4/09	2.1	2.0	5.6	7.1
Average 2009	1.85	2.15	5.58	6.15
Q1/10	2.9	2.0	5.3	6
Average 9 quarters	3.08	2.94	4.95	5.24

*quarterly average of monthly data.

Source: Adapted from <www.tradingeconomics.com>, accessed July 2010.

In terms of unemployment, Table 9.8 suggests that during the crisis Australia showed more resilience and a slower growth in unemployment rates compared to New Zealand. Again, the stronger economic growth in Australia over the last six quarters of the period has certainly contributed to a healthier situation in the labour market.

THE ASIAN LINK

Apart from specific structural differences, one reason listed by analysts for the slightly better performance of Australia during the GFC is that, although both economies have increased their trade links with the fast-growing Asian region, the Australian economy has benefited more from this relationship, due to deeper complementarities between the mineral-resource rich Australian economy and the mineral-resource deficient Asia.

According to an IMF working paper published by Yan Sun in May 2010, the share of emerging Asia (China, Republic of Korea, India, Taiwan, Singapore, Hong Kong) in Australia's exports has increased from around 29 per cent in 2000 to over 44 per cent in 2009. The corresponding shares in New Zealand's exports were 15 per cent in 2000 and 20.5 per cent in 2009.

POST-CRISIS PROSPECTS

Yan Sun's paper finds that the main negative impact of the global crisis is likely to come through higher cost of capital under tighter global financial conditions. At the same time, strong demand for commodities from emerging Asia, especially for Australia, could increase the return to capital and thereby support investment and capital accumulation.

continued ↘

continued

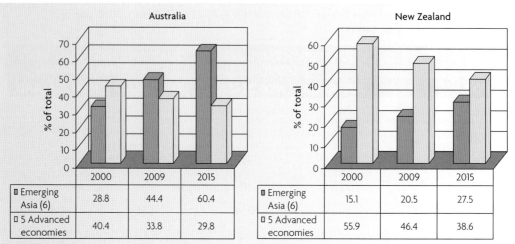

Figure 9.7

Comparative per cent share of six economies in emerging Asia and five advanced economies in total exports of Australia and New Zealand, 2000, 2009 and 2015

Note: Emerging Asia: China, Republic of Korea, India, Taiwan, Singapore, Hong Kong. Five advanced economies: United States, Japan, United Kingdom, Germany, New Zealand/Australia.

Source: Adapted from Yan Sun, Potential Growth of Australia and New Zealand in the Aftermath of the Global Crisis, IMF, May 2010, WP/10/127.

Yan Sun's projections for the shares of emerging Asia in total exports by 2015 are over 60 per cent for Australia and close to 30 per cent for New Zealand. New Zealand has an additional 'derived benefit' from Australian growth, given that Australia is expected to stay as New Zealand's leading export market taking over almost one quarter of New Zealand's exports.

The IMF working paper estimates potential growth, over the medium term, of about 3 per cent for Australia and 2 per cent for New Zealand, which is higher than that of many other advanced economies, reflecting partly their strong linkages to fast-growing Asia.

OECD's *Economic Outlook* of May 2010 has comparable projections: Australia's real GDP is expected to increase by 2.4 per cent in 2010 and 3.5 per cent in 2011, while New Zealand's economic growth rate is projected at 1.5 per cent in 2010 and 2.7 per cent in 2011.

REFERENCES

1. J. Forster, *The global financial crisis—Implications for Australasian business*, Wiley, Milton Qld, 2010.
2. Yan Sun, *Potential Growth of Australia and New Zealand in the Aftermath of the Global Crisis*, IMF working paper, May 2010, WP/10/127WP/10/127, <www.imf.org/external/pubs/cat/longres.cfm?sk=23899.0>, accessed 8 November 2010.
3. New Zealand, *2010 Article IV Consultation Preliminary Concluding Statement of the IMF Mission*, 29 March 2010, <www.imf.org/external/np/ms/2010/032910.htm>, accessed 8 November 2010.
4. *OECD Economic Outlook*, Annex Table 1, May 2010.

QUESTIONS

1. Outline a few factors which have assisted the Australian and New Zealand economies to avoid the worst effects of the GFC.
2. Identify the peak(s) and the trough(s) for Australia and New Zealand over the nine-quarter period.
3. Are the developments in real GDP, CPI, and unemployment in the two economies consistent with the Keynes theory? Why or why not? Briefly explain.
4. Discuss the importance of the Asian link for the two economies during the financial crisis and in the post-crisis period.

SUMMARY

1. The national accounts provide us with aggregate measures of what is happening in the economy through indicators such as GDP, total spending and total income.

2. GDP is the market value of all final goods and services produced in the economy during a period of time, regardless of who owns the factors of production (e.g. domestic or foreign owners). To avoid double counting, GDP does not include intermediate products. Second-hand sales and non-productive transactions are also excluded from the calculation of GDP.

3. GDP may be calculated by three approaches:

   (a) Expenditure approach: GDP is determined by adding consumer purchases of goods and services (C), gross investment spending by businesses (I), government purchases of goods and services (G) and net exports ($X - M$) that is:

   $$GDP = C + I + G + (X - M)$$

   (b) Income approach: A common formula for the income approach is:

   $$GDP(I) = COE + GOS + GMI + T_{P\&M} - S_{P\&M}$$

   Where
   COE = Compensation of employees
   GOS = Gross operating surplus
   GMI = Gross mixed income
   $T_{P\&M}$ = Taxes on production and imports
   $S_{P\&M}$ = Subsidies on production and imports.

   (c) Production approach: GDP(P) is derived as the sum of gross value added for each industry, at basic prices, plus taxes less subsidies on products.

4. A GDP figure that reflects current prices (e.g. prices existing during the time period of production) is called nominal GDP. However, we are more interested in the real GDP calculated at constant prices (prices existing in a base year), which eliminates the influence of inflation.

5. To achieve the adjustment between the nominal GDP and the real GDP we may use a broad price index such as the GDP price chain index or implicit price deflators (IPDs). Real GDP is computed by dividing nominal GDP for year X by year X's broad price index and then by multiplying the result by 100.

6. GDP measures the size of the economy. By converting the real GDP value expressed in the national currency into United States dollars, we can compare the sizes of various economies (e.g. Australia's GDP is over seven times larger than that of New Zealand, but it accounts for only around 6.5 per cent of that of the United States).

7. The annual percentage change in real GDP in a nation is regarded as the economic growth of that nation. Prior to the GFC, Australia recorded generally higher economic growth rates than other major economies (e.g. United States, Euro area, United Kingdom, Japan). Australia's GDP has also been more resilient during the GFC.

8. GDP is a reasonably accurate measure of national economic performance. However, it is a less than perfect measure, mainly because it excludes a number of factors such as:

   (a) the informal ('underground') economy
   (b) non-market transactions (e.g. voluntary work for charities, household production, child care, do-it-yourself home repairs and services)
   (c) information regarding the composition and allocation of total output
   (d) the spillover costs associated with the production of the GDP etc.

9. In addition to GDP there are other national accounts reported in economic and media reports such as:

(a) National turnover of goods and services (NTGS)—the total market supply of final goods and services (GDP + M).

(b) Gross national expenditure (GNE)—equals the sum of domestic consumption, investment and government expenditures (C + I + G).

(c) Net domestic product (NDP)—the economic output of a nation that is adjusted to account for depreciation, calculated by subtracting depreciation from the gross domestic product (GDP – depreciation/consumption of fixed capital).

(d) Gross national income (GNI)—comprises the total value produced within a country (i.e. its gross domestic product) together with its income received from other countries (notably interest and dividends), less similar payments made to other countries.

10. The term *business cycle* refers to the recurrent 'ups and downs' in the level of growth in economic activity that extend over a period of several years. Business cycles vary greatly in duration and intensity. The four phases of the economic cycle are: expansion, contraction, peak and trough. A recession is technically defined as at least two consecutive quarters of real GDP decline.

11. The multiplier is the factor that causes greater increases in income than in spending. The relationship between the multiplier and the marginal propensity to consume (MPC) underlines the notion that increases in spending produce greater increases in income.

KEY TERMS

amplitude	185	gross domestic product (GDP)	166	net domestic product (NDP)	183
base year	175	gross national expenditure (GNE)	182	nominal GDP	175
business cycle	184	gross national income (GNI)	183	non-productive transactions	168
economic growth	181	gross private investment		peak	184
exports (X)	170	expenditure (I)	170	period of the cycle	184
final goods and services	167	implicit price deflator (IPD)	177	personal consumption	
GDP(E)	169	imports (M)	170	expenditure (C)	169
GDP(I)	171	marginal propensity to consume (MPC)	185	real GDP	174
GDP(P)	172	marginal propensity to save (MPS)	186	recession	185
government purchases of goods		multiplier effect	185	trough	185
and services (G)	170	national turnover of goods and		value added	168
		services (NTGS)	182		

REFERENCE

1. John M. Keynes, *General Theory of Employment, Interest and Money*, Macmillan, London, United Kingdom, 1936, p. 96.

REVIEW QUESTIONS

1. Why is GDP calculated as the market value (price-times-quantity) of the total outputs in a certain period and not as a sum of actual physical volumes of production? Discuss.

2. Why should GDP(I) equal GDP(E)? Briefly explain.

3. Why do national accountants use for the calculation of economic growth of a nation the real GDP and not the nominal GDP? Briefly discuss.

4. 'GDP is a perfect measure of the size of the economic activity of a nation in a specified period.' Do you agree with this statement? Why or why not?

5. Outline the main difference(s) between the GDP and the GNI.

6. 'Business cycles are inherent in market economies.' Do you agree with this statement? Explain your answer.

7. What factor is generally regarded as the immediate determinant of the level of national output and employment? Discuss.

8. Outline the main factors suggested by experts as explanations for the business cycle?

9. What do you think people mean when they say about the business cycle 'what goes up, must come down'?

10. Define the concept of 'multiplier'. What is the relationship between the multiplier and the MPC?

APPLIED QUESTIONS AND EXERCISES

1. The following list presents a number of goods and services. Circle YES if you think one item should be included in the value of GDP or circle NO if you think that item should be excluded from the GDP calculation.

(a) A Toyota car produced in June 2009
   and sold in March 2010   YES/NO

(b) Peter from 'Jim's Mowing' does the
   lawn around the house of a cousin
   on a contractual basis   YES/NO

(c) The sale of a used TV set at a garage sale   YES/NO

(d) The payment of a government pension
   to a retired worker   YES/NO

(e) The sale of Telstra shares to a Telstra
   phone subscriber   YES/NO

(f) The birthday gift of a cheque of $20 sent
   by a grandmother to her grandchild   YES/NO

2. The country of Bucksland produces wine and edible oil, and it has published the following macroeconomic data, where quantities are in litres, and prices are dollars per litre.

GOOD	2009		2010	
	QUANTITY	PRICE	QUANTITY	PRICE
Wine	500	$3	600	$4
Edible oil	2000	$2	2000	$3

What was Bucksland's economic growth rate in 2010?

3. We stated above that 'ABS data (cat. no. 5206032) indicates that over the last 30 years or so, small trade surpluses were recorded in only five financial years (1980, 1992, 1997, 2002 and 2009)'. Considering economic developments you may be aware of as having occurred in Australia and overseas, outline a couple of likely reasons for the net trade surplus recorded by the Australian economy in 2009.

4. By convention, Australian national accounts treat government spending on the salaries of teachers and university lecturers as government consumption (G^1). Some experts argue that such spending should be treated as 'government investment' or (G^2). If you were one of that group of experts, how would you argue your case? Discuss.

5. Which items listed below would you classify as consumption spending and which as investment spending?
   (a) The construction of a house that will be occupied by its owner.
   (b) The purchase of a new computer for your business.
   (c) A restaurant bill from a wedding reception function.
   (d) A shipping company ordering a new ship.
   (e) The purchase of a flat to rent out.
   (f) The construction of a factory building using money borrowed from a bank.

6. Complete the following table to summarise the effects of various economic developments on aggregate demand. Indicate one to two major components of aggregate demand (AD) that are likely to be affected by the economic development. Use the letters from the formula of the GDP(*E*)/AD as follows:
   - *C* (personal consumption)
   - *I* (private investment)
   - *G* (government expenditure)
   - *X* (exports)
   - *M* (imports).

   Also indicate the likely change in the level of aggregate demand (all things being equal) using either + (means AD increases) or − (means it will decrease).

ECONOMIC DEVELOPMENTS	COMPONENTS OF AGGREGATE DEMAND (C, I, G, X, M)	+/− CHANGE IN LEVEL OF AD
(a) An increase in indirect taxes		
(b) Higher levels of domestic private investment		
(c) Higher levels of saving		
(d) A fall in the budget deficit		
(e) An increased outflow of Australian investment overseas		
(f) Higher spending by foreigners on Australian-made goods and services		
(g) A decline in the budget surplus		
(h) A reduction of personal income tax		
(i) An increased inflow of foreign investment in Australia		

7. Online exercise. The table opposite presents in column (2), Japan's quarterly real GDP per cent changes from quarter 1/2008 to quarter 1/2010 as recorded by the United States-based consultancy Trading Economics, www.tradingeconomics.com/Economics/GDP-Growth.aspx?Symbol=JPY, 13 July 2010.

   (a) Task 1: Check the Trading Economics' website and update the table with the corresponding figures for the three remaining quarters of 2010. If there are any revisions of data for previous semesters update accordingly.

   (b) Task 2: Use an Excel spreadsheet to produce a line graph on Japan's real GDP per cent changes over the 12 quarters.

   (c) Task 3: Indicate in column (3) the phase of Japan's business cycle in each quarter by using the following symbols: E = Expansion; C = Contraction; P = Peak; T = Trough; U = unclear.

   (d) Task 4: Check if Japan's economy has experienced a recession or more during the 12-quarter period. If this is so, when did this happen? Explain.

QUARTER/ YEAR	REAL GDP PER CENT CHANGE PER QUARTER	BUSINESS CYCLE PHASE
(1)	(2)	(3)
Q1/08	1.2	
Q2/08	−4	
Q3/08	−4.3	
Q4/08	−9.6	
Q1/09	−15.8	
Q2/09	6.9	
Q3/09	0.4	
Q4/09	4.6	
Q1/10	5	
Q2/10	?	
Q3/10	?	
Q4/10	?	

Chapter 10

Aggregate demand and aggregate supply

LEARNING OBJECTIVES

After studying this chapter, you will be able to:

1. discuss briefly the Keynesian view of equilibrium
2. explain what is meant by aggregate demand
3. understand the relationship between the price level and aggregate demand and how it shapes the aggregate demand curve
4. describe the main non-price level factors that cause the aggregate demand to shift
5. outline the main historical views on the aggregate supply curve
6. distinguish between short-run and long-run aggregate supply
7. identify the main determinants of supply
8. explain the aggregate demand–aggregate supply model and how it impacts on economic activity
9. discuss the main changes in the aggregate demand–aggregate supply macroeconomic equilibrium.

INTRODUCTION

In Chapter 3 we examined the implications of the interaction of demand and supply on the price and quantity of a single product in an individual market (e.g. computers, cars, grain etc.). We have also learnt how equilibrium is established in the market and how it is restored in a situation of disequilibrium, such as excess demand or excess supply.

Our analysis in this chapter is now in terms of aggregates—that is, in terms of the economy as a whole.

Although the aggregate demand and aggregate supply curves will look somewhat like single product demand and supply curves, 'in large scale', the variables being measured and the underlying rationales for the curves are completely different. At the same time, the axes of our diagrams will be the overall price level (P)—reflecting the implicit price deflator (IPD)—and real GDP (Q), rather than the price of a single product X and units of product X.

The aggregate demand–aggregate supply model will provide us with some basic analytical tools and a means of organising our thinking about the macroeconomic conditions encountered by our economy. The model will enable us to describe the fluctuations in our aggregate measures of the level of real output and the price level, and suggest some of the possible causes.

LEARNING OBJECTIVE 1
Discuss briefly the Keynesian view of equilibrium

THE KEYNESIAN VIEW OF EQUILIBRIUM

Until the Great Depression of the 1930s, classical economists based their analysis of the fluctuations of national income on a principle established by the 19th century economist Jean Baptiste Say. According to Say's theory, there could be no long-term disequilibrium between aggregate demand and aggregate supply, because supply created its own demand. In other words, the production of goods and services (supply) generates an equal amount of total spending (demand) for these goods and services and thus general overproduction was impossible. In situations of disequilibrium, prices fall to stimulate demand, wages fall to stimulate employment, and interest rates fall to allow an extra saving to be taken up in investment in capital goods. The classical theory was based on the principle of 'leaving the economy alone to fix its own problems', or laissez-faire.

In his *General Theory of Employment, Interest and Money* (1936), J.M. Keynes refuted the classical theory by demonstrating that supply does not guarantee that the generated income will be entirely spent on the produced output. The Keynesian model is based on the principle that aggregate demand (or total expenditure) determines the level of total production, income and employment.

A shortfall in aggregate demand causes a downward adjustment of supply, and the equilibrium level of income is lowered to a new level where supply is again equal to demand, with some resources (including labour) being unemployed in the process.

Because aggregate demand is such a fundamental concept in the determination of production, income and employment levels, we will discuss in more detail the components that make up this macroeconomic indicator and the factors that can influence it.

AGGREGATE DEMAND

LEARNING OBJECTIVE 2
Explain what is meant by aggregate demand

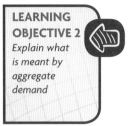

As discussed in Chapter 9, one important method for calculating the gross domestic product (GDP) is by the expenditure approach, or more exactly by adding consumer purchases of goods and services (C), gross investment spending by businesses (I), government purchases of goods and services (G) and net exports (X – M). That is:

$$GDP(E) = C + I + G + (X - M)$$

This is exactly the same way we defined GDP in the previous chapter. Any discrepancy between what was produced and what consumers actually bought was accounted for by changes in inventories. Now we are using the same categories as categories of demand.

Aggregate demand can be broadly defined as the total expenditure on domestically produced goods and services. In other words, aggregate demand is the total demand for goods and services in the economy.

aggregate demand
the total expenditure on domestically produced goods and services

It is quite possible that, in a given period, the aggregate demand by households (C), private businesses (I), government agencies (G) and foreigners (X – M) will not be exactly equal to the total production that firms had expected to sell.

So when we refer to total demand for goods and services, we are indicating the amount of goods and services that are sold in the economy. The question is: Who are they sold to?

USERS OF GOODS AND SERVICES

The main users of goods and services are the three major sectors in the economy: the private sector (households and businesses), the government sector and the external sector.

- Households (consumers) use goods and services for survival (food, doctors), entertainment (stereos), security (insurance), education (books), and so on. Their use is final: that is, the good or service is not used further along the economic system. Once purchased, it is put to use.
- Businesses use goods and services to begin, increase or improve production. For example, a factory is extended using construction goods and building services; a computer database replaces an old filing cabinet; a stockbroker sets up practice in rented office space.
- Governments use goods and services to enable their administrations to operate and to carry out projects. This category includes both capital (use in further production) and consumption (final use) purchases of government—federal, state and local.
- In the external sector, exporters sell Australian goods and services overseas to make profits. This is the only destination of goods and services that is external to the economy.

THE EFFECTS OF IMPORTS

As we saw in the previous section, it is also possible to bring goods and services into the economy from external sources—through imports. This may or may not affect demand for domestic goods and services. It affects demand if the imported goods and services are the same as, or similar to, domestic goods and services; they compete with each other. But if the imported goods and services are not otherwise available in the economy, then they are not in competition with domestic goods and services.

Note that non-competing imported goods and services may still affect aggregate demand. A potential user of domestic goods and services (by definition also a potential contributor to aggregate demand) has limited resources to purchase goods and services. If a domestic firm decides to buy expensive equipment that is produced exclusively overseas, it may have to postpone the purchase of other smaller items that can be procured domestically.

So imports always have potential to threaten domestic aggregate demand. For this reason, they must be balanced against exports to assess the net effect of external activity or aggregate demand. We subtract imports into the economy from exports out of the economy to obtain that net effect (net exports).

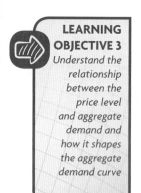

LEARNING OBJECTIVE 3
Understand the relationship between the price level and aggregate demand and how it shapes the aggregate demand curve

AGGREGATE DEMAND CURVE

The **aggregate demand curve** shows the amount of goods and services—real domestic output—that domestic consumers, private businesses, the government and foreign buyers will collectively want to purchase at each possible price level.

It is important to recognise that goods and services are used by households for consumption (C), by private firms for investment (I), and by government for both consumption (G^1) and capital investment (G^2). They are also used in exports (X), although the effect of imports (M) has to be acknowledged.

Ceteris paribus (all other things being equal), the lower the average level of prices in the economy (IPDI—implicit price deflator index), the larger will be the level of real domestic output purchased. Therefore, other things being equal, the aggregate demand curve shows an inverse relationship between the price index level and the level of real GDP.

As shown in Figure 10.1, the aggregate demand curve slopes downwards and to the right, same as the demand curve for a single product discussed in Chapter 3. What are the main reasons for this shape? It is interesting to note that the reasons causing the down-sloping shape of the aggregate demand curve are not the same as for the down-sloping demand curve for a single product market (e.g. income and substitution effects).

In Figure 10.1, all prices are falling (on average), so the rationale for the substitution effect (e.g. a product becoming cheaper relative to substitute products) is not applicable anymore.

aggregate demand curve

the amount of goods and services—real domestic output— that domestic consumers, private businesses, the government and foreign buyers will collectively want to purchase at each possible price level

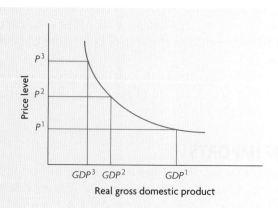

Figure 10.1
The aggregate demand curve

At the same time, an individual's demand curve for a specific product assumes the consumer's income to be fixed, while the aggregate demand curve implies varying aggregate incomes.

The reasons for the downward slope of an aggregate demand curve include:

- interest rate effect
- real balances or wealth effect
- net exports effect.

INTEREST RATE EFFECT

The **interest rate effect** is the impact on total spending (real GDP) caused by the direct relationship between the price level and the level of interest rates. Assuming that the supply of money in the time period relevant to the aggregate AD curve remains fixed, at a high price level:

- individual households have to spend more money for their purchases of goods and services (and alternatively will buy fewer goods and services)
- the cost of borrowing (e.g. nominal interest rates) will increase, which will discourage households from buying big-ticket items such as homes, cars, electronic equipment
- businesses cut back on investment projects because of the rising cost of borrowing
- investors and lenders require compensation for the impact of price level on the purchasing power of their funds through increases in the interest rate they charge for such funds
- all in all, higher interest rates will reduce both consumption and investment purchases that are interest rate sensitive, therefore total spending (real GDP) will decline.

Conversely, a reduction in the general level of prices (say in a recession) will reduce the demand for money and the cost of borrowing (e.g. nominal interest rates will decrease), which will tend to increase both personal consumption and investment. (This relationship is discussed in more detail in Chapter 23 on monetary policy.) Therefore, the lower level of prices or interest rates will tend to cause an increase in the level of aggregate demand.

interest rate effect
the impact on total spending (real GDP) caused by the direct relationship between the price level and the level of interest rates

REAL BALANCES OR WEALTH EFFECT

The **real balances or wealth effect** indicates that a higher price index level reduces the real value or purchasing power of accumulated financial assets (e.g. savings or bonds), held by households and causes them to cut back on their consumer spending.

A household might feel comfortable about buying a new car or a boat if the real value of its financial assets is, say, $80 000. But if inflation causes the real value of these asset balances to decline to, say, $60 000, the household members may decide to defer their purchase.

Conversely, a decline in the price level increases the real value of the household's wealth to, say, $100 000, and household members are more willing and able to spend.

real balances or wealth effect
the impact of changes in the price level on consumer wealth and ultimately on consumer spending and aggregate demand

NET EXPORTS EFFECT

The **net exports effect** is the impact on total spending (real GDP) caused by the inverse relationship between the price level and the level of exports.

net exports effect
impact on total spending (real GDP) caused by the inverse relationship between the price level and the level of exports

As discussed before, exports and imports are important components of aggregate demand. Volumes of our exports and imports depend, among other things, on the relative prices in Australia and abroad.

A higher domestic price level tends to make Australian goods more expensive compared with foreign goods, which will tend to reduce volumes of exports and increase volumes of imports. Consequently, a rise in the domestic price level will tend to reduce the net exports component of Australian aggregate demand.

In summary, the net exports effect suggests that an increase/decrease in Australia's price level relative to other countries reduces/increases the net exports component of aggregate demand. Therefore, the net exports effect on the aggregate demand curve is caused by the inverse relationship between the price level and the net exports of an economy.

Figure 10.2 summarises the three main reasons for which the aggregate demand curve is downward-sloping.

Figure 10.2
Reasons for a downward-sloping aggregate demand curve

Main effects	Impact of price level changes on the aggregate demand (AD)
Interest rate effect	(a) Higher price level → Higher interest rates → AD decreases (b) Lower price level → Lower interest rates → AD increases
Real balances effect	(a) Higher price level → Lower real balances → AD decreases (b) Lower price level → Higher real balances → AD increases
Net exports effect	(a) Higher price level → Lower net exports → AD decreases (b) Lower price level → Higher net exports → AD increases

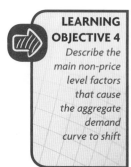

LEARNING OBJECTIVE 4
Describe the main non-price level factors that cause the aggregate demand curve to shift

determinants of aggregate demand
an assortment of ceteris paribus factors other than the price level that affect aggregate demand, but which are assumed constant when the aggregate demand curve is constructed

DETERMINANTS OF AGGREGATE DEMAND

In the previous section, we found that changes in the price level in the economy cause changes in the level of spending by consumers, businesses, government and foreign buyers. The negatively sloped aggregate demand curve captures the inverse relationship between the price level and the aggregate demand.

Given the inverse relationship between the price level (e.g. implicit price deflator (IPD)) and the level of real domestic output, we can predict the direction of real domestic output; that is, an increase in the price level, other things being equal, decreases the quantity of real domestic output demanded, while, conversely, a decline in the price level will increase the level of real output desired. This inverse relationship is represented graphically as point-to-point movements along a stable aggregate demand curve.

As was the case in our discussion on individual demand curves in Chapter 3, we must distinguish between changes in real GDP demanded, caused by changes in the price level, and changes in aggregate demand, caused by changes in one or more of the non-price level determinants listed in Figure 10.3.

The **determinants of aggregate demand** can be defined as an assortment of ceteris paribus factors other than the price level that affect aggregate demand, but which are assumed constant when the aggregate demand curve is constructed.

The specific ceteris paribus factors are commonly grouped by the four broad expenditure categories—consumption spending, investment spending, government spending, and net exports spending.

Should any specific aggregate demand determinant change, it must affect the aggregate demand curve through one of the four aggregate expenditures.

Similarly to other determinants, aggregate demand determinants shift the aggregate demand curve. A change in any of the determinants can either increase or decrease the aggregate demand. An increase in aggregate demand is depicted graphically by a rightward shift in the aggregate demand curve. A decrease in aggregate demand is illustrated by a leftward shift (see Figure 10.4).

It means that, at the same price level, consumers desire to buy more or fewer goods and services than before. Therefore, the changes in the level of real GDP(E) resulting from changes

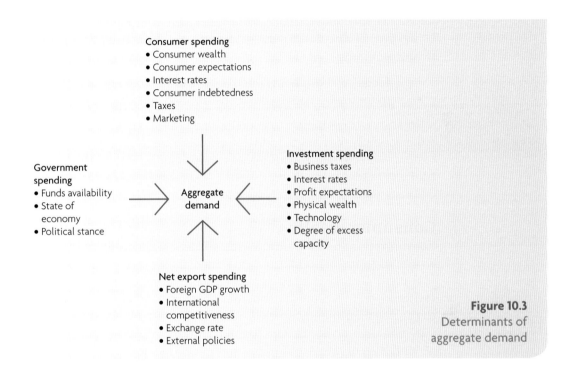

Figure 10.3
Determinants of aggregate demand

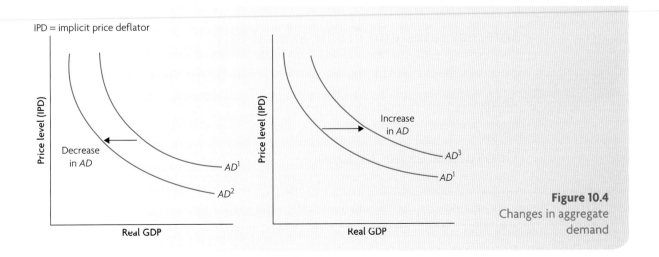

Figure 10.4
Changes in aggregate demand

in its main components (consumer spending, private investment spending, government spending, and net export spending) are this time caused by various factors other than the price level.

As each component of aggregate demand is influenced by a variety of factors, in the next section we will briefly review the influence of these non-price level determinants on the various components of aggregate demand, and, in the final analysis, on aggregate demand as a whole.

CONSUMER SPENDING (C)

Consumer spending is easily the largest single component of aggregate demand (about 55 to 60 per cent of Australia's aggregate demand). There are two types of consumption spending in any economy:

- induced consumption, which results from a change in income
- autonomous consumption, consumption spending that is independent of income.

Domestic consumers may collectively alter their purchases of goods and services independently of changes in the price level, due to changes in one or several non-price level factors such as: real consumer wealth, consumer expectations, level of consumer savings, consumer indebtedness and taxes.

Consumer spending is dependent on a number of factors, which we will examine in turn.

Consumer wealth

Consumer wealth represents the stock of assets accumulated by consumers such as physical wealth (e.g. land or buildings), and financial assets (bank accounts, stocks and bonds).

A sharp decline in personal assets (e.g. due to the decline in the price of assets in a recession) will discourage consumer spending and aggregate demand, and, ceteris paribus, the aggregate demand curve will shift to the left.

In exchange, an increase in the real value of consumer wealth, without an increase in the general level of prices, will encourage consumer spending, and the aggregate demand curve will shift to the right.

Please note that this factor is different from the above 'wealth effect', which assumes a fixed demand curve and which results from a change in the price level.

Interest rates and credit availability

The level of consumption expenditure is also affected by the cost (i.e. the level of interest rates) and the availability of consumer credit. The more credit that is available in the economy and the easier it is to get, the higher consumer spending is likely to be. In Australia, loans are readily available through formal application to financial institutions or through credit cards, a fact that tends to push consumer spending to higher levels.

Consumer expectations

Consumer spending is also usually altered by changes in consumer expectations about their future.

If consumers are confident and feel secure about their economic future, they are likely to spend for big dollar items such as houses, cars, consumer electronics, travel overseas, which will increase aggregate demand and will shift the aggregate demand curve to the right.

'Saving for a rainy day', however, is a significant attitude among householders, especially when the economy contracts and economic prospects are grim. Economic depression brings widespread unemployment and a significant drop in consumer confidence. This has the effect of lowering the level of aggregate demand and economic activity. The graphical illustration will be a shift of the aggregate demand curve to the left.

Marketing

Heavy advertising, particularly on the electronic media, not only influences consumers in their choice of brands, but actually brings new consumers of a product range into the market. The overall effect is to increase consumer spending.

Marketing also creates and sustains fashions, which in turn influence people to buy. The entertainment market, from DVDs to toys and computerised games, provides examples of fashions—and hence consumer spending—under constant change. The car market, where new model releases are heavily promoted, is a further example.

PRIVATE INVESTMENT SPENDING (I)

Among the components of aggregate demand, private investment expenditure is considered to show the greatest fluctuations. For this reason, private investment spending probably influences aggregate demand more than any other component. We will look at the major determinants of private investment expenditure.

Business taxes

Business decisions regarding private investment expenditure are largely based on the commercial principle of profitability. Government policies regarding rates of company tax, indirect taxes (e.g. sales tax) and incentives affect business perceptions. These policies alter the profitability of undertaking productive activity and may thus influence the level of private investment expenditure.

Governments offer incentives in order to influence the amount and direction of investment. East Asian governments, for instance, have encouraged private investment through various incentives such as tax breaks and cheap credit.

Interest rates

Private investment expenditure is predominantly financed by borrowings from the financial sector. Therefore the cost (represented by interest rates) and availability of credit are important factors in determining the level of private investment expenditure. The assumption here is that investment requires borrowing. The assumption is valid, since few potential investors have sufficient capital to proceed without borrowing. It also highlights the direct relationship between savings and investment, which was emphasised in an earlier section.

High interest rates discourage investment in another way. The opportunity cost of investing is also high when the funds could earn high levels of interest on deposit with a financial institution or converted to government securities.

Business confidence and expectations

Business confidence primarily relates to business expectations concerning:

- the general economic outlook, particularly anticipated levels of demand and unemployment
- the anticipated rate of return (profit) on investment.

The return on investment is clearly also dependent on the level of aggregate economic activity. Broadly defined, rate of return is the profit generated by an investment as a proportion of the initial investment. If this ratio is high, the investment is likely to proceed on the assumption that high profits will result.

Physical wealth

Physical wealth refers to capital goods (e.g. equipment, tools etc.) possessed by the business. This determinant works for investment spending much as it does for consumption spending. In this case, wealth is capital, the object of investment. The business sector will be less inclined to invest in capital goods, if it has only recently purchased a lot of capital goods through investment. A big expansion in the amount of capital is bound to cause (eventually) a decline in investment and aggregate demand, illustrated graphically with a leftward shift of the aggregate demand curve.

Technology

Advances in technology enhance the need to invest in capital (e.g. new equipment to implement the new technology). New technologies will increase investment spending and aggregate demand, determining a shift of the aggregate demand curve to the right.

INFLUENCES ON GOVERNMENT SPENDING (*G*)

According to the Keynesian model, government spending is regarded as autonomous—that is, expenditure independent of income.

According to the World Bank, general government consumption in Australia represented in 2008 around 18 per cent of GDP, unchanged from 1980. This level of government spending was comparable to that of other industrial countries like Germany, Canada and Japan, and lower than that of France, Sweden and Denmark. It was considerably higher than the level recorded in developing East Asia and the Pacific, at only some 13 per cent of GDP. (See more details in the Link to International Economy later in this chapter.) We will look at the determinants of government expenditure below.

The level of funds available

The primary determinant of government expenditure is the level of funds available to the government sector from taxation receipts and government borrowings.

LINK TO
BUSINESS

CHANGES IN GDP

The production possibility frontier model in Chapter 1 pointed out that a nation can produce more goods and services to satisfy more needs and services over a period of time only if it has access to more productive resources or if it can improve the quality of its resources through better technology and raise its productive efficiency. Such developments enable our production possibility frontier to move outwards. However, we have just seen that another important determinant of a nation's output is the level of total final spending on its production, or aggregate demand. It is fluctuations in the level of aggregate demand that help cause GDP to fall sometimes, and at other times to rise.

Among the components of aggregate demand, private investment spending has varied in Australia over the last two decades or so between 12 and 19 per cent of GDP(*E*). Private investment spending has a major role to play. If a car component supplier spends $2 million for new equipment, this will increase the nation's productive potential by mobilising more and better quality resources (capital, labour), and at the same time contributes to a higher aggregate demand by its spending for the acquisition of those productive resources. The owners of the productive resources (e.g. Australian equipment suppliers and workforce) may spend most of their income in Australia, causing an increase in the size of the national cake.

However, the size of Australia's aggregate demand does not depend only on what Australian companies produce, sell and spend in Australia. Given that Australia is a mixed economy with a growing external sector increasingly integrated in the global economy, Australia's aggregate demand is strongly influenced by its performance in the external sector. Also, we should not disregard the contribution that government spending (especially government investment) makes to the size of aggregate demand. We will examine the contribution of these two sectors in the following sections of this chapter.

The state of the economy

The level of government expenditure is also determined by the state of the economy. The level of aggregate economic activity influences both the receipts and the expenditure of the government sector. In periods of recession, for instance, taxation receipts are reduced, and expenditure on social security (particularly unemployment benefits) is increased. Reduced taxation receipts cause government expenditure to decrease unless the government sector offsets its reduced taxation revenue by increasing government borrowings.

The state of the economy also influences the macroeconomic policies of government and thereby influences the level of government expenditure. In periods of contracting economic activity, for instance, government attempts to stimulate the level of aggregate demand by expansionary macroeconomic policies. The government sector generally increases its level of expenditure, which, in these circumstances, is most likely to be funded by government borrowings.

Political stance

The level of government expenditure is also influenced by the government's political ideology with regard to the size and role of government in a market capitalist system. The Howard Coalition government in Australia, for instance, reduced the relative level of social expenditure compared to the previous Labor governments. A government of socialist orientation in Sweden, Austria or France would spend more on social security than its right-wing counterpart.

INFLUENCES ON NET EXPORT SPENDING ($X - M$)

If the external sector is represented in the circular flow as exports minus imports, the causes of change in exports and imports will explain the influences on net export spending. What, then, causes change in exports and imports? We examine below three major factors.

The world economy (foreign GDP)

Since both exports and imports are dealings with economies outside Australia, what is happening in those economies is relevant to the value of our exports and our imports. Significantly for net export spending, moreover, both the general trends in the world economy—such as high inflation—and specific trends in particular economics such as a drop in Japanese steel demand—may profoundly affect the Australian economy.

Take, for example, Australian trade with Japan. Assume inflation in Australia is higher than in Japan and in competitors' markets. Before long, Japanese importers shift their preference from Australian goods to similar products offered by other foreign suppliers. Also, Japanese goods increase their market share in Australia at the expense of domestic suppliers. If Australian inflation is lower than that in other countries, including Japan, there may be more demand for the Australian goods in Japan because of the lower prices Australian exporters can offer.

Australia tends to reflect worldwide patterns of economic activity. Thus, when world demand falls—especially in major economies such as the United States, Japan and the European Union—demand in Australia falls. If world demand is down, export values fall to reflect falls in both the quantity and the prices of exports. On the other hand, during the 1990–92 international recession, Australian exports kept growing. This was due to the strong demand in East Asian countries, which experienced continuous economic growth during that period. We examine the impact of the currency crisis in East Asia in Chapter 19. What about the broader economic crisis in East Asia? How is it affecting the Australian economy? We examine a few aspects of this relationship in the Link to International Economy later in this chapter.

International competitiveness

This is affected by efficiency throughout the economy. High labour productivity and efficient use of capital are the keys to achieving efficiency. Australia's long distances and sparse populations make capital efficiency imperative, especially as other economies that deal with Australia do not have such chronic problems.

The exchange rate, which values Australia's dollar against other currencies, also determines cost competitiveness because it influences export and import prices. (A complete discussion of these issues can be found in Chapter 19.) In brief, a high exchange rate means high export prices, which puts more pressure on domestic costs to maintain competitiveness. The high exchange rate also reduces prices of imports, which may mean that they sell better in Australia.

The critical combination for aggregate demand is where exports increase and imports decrease. So, a relatively lower Australian dollar may have a positive influence on net export spending.

Government's external policies

Any activity of government that promotes exports and limits imports will affect net export spending. The balance between export incentives (e.g. tax concessions, export grants), on one hand, and protectionist measures (e.g. tariffs, quotas) or liberal import policies, on the other, is therefore critical for net export spending and the aggregate demand.

HOW DOES THE STRUCTURE OF DEMAND VARY INTERNATIONALLY?

LINK TO INTERNATIONAL ECONOMY

In its annual report on World Development Indicators covering over 200 countries, the World Bank produces an interesting table on the 'Structure of demand', which is in fact the GDP(E) by its main components.

For comparison purposes, the table below brings together 2008 data on the structure of demand for five advanced economies and five emerging market economies in Asia. Notwithstanding the statistical difficulties faced by the World Bank in collecting such data, especially in developing countries, where the quality of government accounting systems tends to be weak, Table 10.1 provides us with a few interesting findings:

Table 10.1   **Structure of demand**

ECONOMY/ GROUP	HOUSEHOLD FINAL CONSUMPTION (% OF GDP)	GENERAL GOVERNMENT FINAL CONSUMPTION (% OF GDP)	GROSS CAPITAL FORMATION (% OF GDP)	EXPORTS OF GOODS AND SERVICES (% OF GDP)	IMPORTS OF GOODS AND SERVICES (% OF GDP)
ADVANCED ECONOMIES					
United States	71	16	18	12	15
Euro area	57	20	22	41	39
Japan	56	18	24	18	16
Australia	55	18	29	21	23
New Zealand	58	19	24	29	30
Average five economies/ groups	59	18	23	24	25
EMERGING ASIAN ECONOMIES					
China	34	14	44	37	28
India	54	12	40	23	28
Indonesia	63	8	28	30	29
Malaysia	46	12	22	110	90
Thailand	56	12	29	77	74
Average five economies	51	12	33	55	50

Source: Compiled from World Bank, 2010 World Development Indicators, Table 4.8.

- Private consumption (C) in the five advanced economies averages 59 per cent, compared to only 51 per cent in the five Asian emerging economies. Does this reflect the differences in income per capita and consumer spending?
- The contribution of government consumption (G^1) to GDP tends to be higher in the group of advanced economies (18 per cent), compared to Asian emerging economies (only 12 per cent). This might surprise at first sight, but it might be a reflection of a broader tax base in advanced economies. A lower government consumption ratio does not mean less regulation and in fact emerging and developing economies all around the world tend to be highly regulated with potentially negative impact on business.
- The next component **gross capital formation**, brings together private investment (I) and government investment (G^2), therefore all investment in the economy. Asian emerging economies have a much higher expenditure on this component than advanced economies. This is due to a traditionally high ratio of savings in Asian countries at both private and government level, with savings being converted by the financial system into investment. It also reflects the attraction of Asian economies for foreign investors.
- The contribution of the external sector to GDP tends to be much more important in Asian emerging economies on both exports and imports. Net exports are positive in the Asian

gross capital formation
outlays on additions to fixed assets of the economy (e.g. land improvements, machinery and equipment purchases, construction works), and net changes in inventories

continued ↘

continued

group (and the percentage would be much higher if we included in the analysis the 'Asian tiger economies' of Singapore, Hong Kong and the Republic of Korea, which are well known for their aggressive exports, but are already classified internationally as 'high income' and 'advanced' economies). On the other hand, the contribution of net exports to GDP in advanced economies is quite low and the average of 'net exports' is negative.

- In other words, advanced economies tend to depend more than Asian economies on their domestic markets and less on foreign economies. On the other hand, the recovery of Asian economies in the recent global financial crisis has been made more difficult by the synchronous crisis in the world's advanced economies, which proves once more the close economic interdependence in a global economy.

QUESTIONS

1. Which component of Australia's aggregate demand is more important for Australia's economic growth: personal consumption, or gross investment formation? Explain your choice.
2. United States and Japan, two of the world's largest economies, show a relatively small contribution of the external sector to aggregate demand. Why? Discuss.
3. 'Indonesia's above-average share of private consumption in GDP among the five Asian economies indicates that consumers in Indonesia have a higher income and purchasing power compared to the other four Asian economies.' Is this statement true? Why, or why not?

AGGREGATE SUPPLY

In the first part of this chapter we learned that aggregate demand is the total demand for goods and services in an economy. But the aggregate demand curve alone does not tell us the equilibrium price level or the equilibrium level of output. In order to obtain this information, we need to add the aggregate supply curve to the diagram containing the aggregate demand curve.

aggregate supply (AS)
the total value of all goods and services produced within the economy in a particular time period

Aggregate supply (AS) can be defined as the total value of all goods and services produced within the economy in a particular time period. It is also known as total output.

The shape of the supply curve—at least in the short term—is upward sloping, just like that of an individual product supply curve, discussed in Chapter 3. However, as in the case of the aggregate demand and market demand curves, the theory of the market supply curve does not directly apply to the theory of the **aggregate supply curve**. The shape of the market supply curve is upward sloping because profit-maximising firms will be encouraged to supply more when market price rises. The same rationale does not fully apply to the aggregate supply curve, because in this case we consider the general price level in the economy and if this level rises it means that not only selling prices of most goods and services in the economy will rise, but also the prices of inputs in the production process.

aggregate supply curve
a graphical representation of the relationship between real production and the price level

Ceteris paribus, the relationship between the price level and real GDP is generally seen to be direct or positive output, where a higher level of prices (GDP deflator or implicit price deflator) will determine a higher level of domestic output, while a lower level of prices will cause a lower level of domestic output.

HISTORICAL VIEWS OF THE AGGREGATE SUPPLY CURVE

Historically, economists have differed in their views in relation to the shape of the aggregate supply curve. We will briefly note a few characteristics of the classical view and of the Keynesian view, to finish with the so-called 'Keynesian—neo-classical synthesis'.

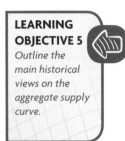

LEARNING OBJECTIVE 5
Outline the main historical views on the aggregate supply curve.

The classical view of aggregate supply

Classical and neo-classical economists believe strongly in the concepts of supply and demand in all markets. Whilst they are prepared to believe that markets might not be in equilibrium in the short run, they believe that all markets clear (i.e. supply equals demand) in the long run.

Classical economists think that in the long run the aggregate supply curve is vertical at the full-employment level (Figure 10.5(a)). This view is based on two assumptions:

1. The economy usually operates at its full-employment level, with absolutely no spare capacity.
2. The selling prices of products and production costs are flexible and change rapidly in order to maintain a full-employment level of output.

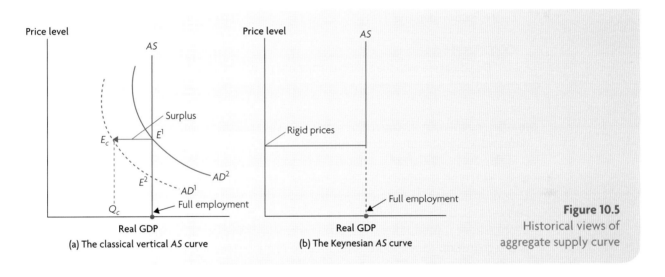

(a) The classical vertical *AS* curve

(b) The Keynesian *AS* curve

Figure 10.5
Historical views of aggregate supply curve

Classical and neo-classical economists contend that the full-employment level of real production is maintained regardless of the price level, which creates a vertical, or perfectly elastic, aggregate supply curve. Should the price level rise or fall, the economy moves up and down along the curve and real production remains unchanged (Figure 10.5(a)).

The Keynesian view of aggregate supply

J.M. Keynes' theory reflects the context of the Great Depression of the early 1930s. Keynes argued that price and wage inflexibility meant that unemployment can be a prolonged feature of the economy. An economy trapped in a depression or severe recession cannot achieve full employment for many years without an increase in aggregate demand, which assumes a proactive government management supported by strong government spending.

CAN SUPPLY CREATE ITS OWN DEMAND?

Figure 10.5(a) illustrates why classical economists believed in the self-correction of markets. The economy is in equilibrium at E^1 and real output is at full employment level. Let's suppose a severe decrease in investment spending due to a drop in business confidence, which causes a decline in aggregate demand and a shift of the aggregate demand curve to the left from AD^1 to AD^2. As a result of this shift, aggregate supply will exceed aggregate demand with $E^1 > E_c$, which will generate a large accumulation of inventories. In order to eliminate unsold inventories resulting from the decline in aggregate demand, business firms will temporarily cut production and reduce their prices. At E_c (denoting the level of output in a period of crisis), the decline in aggregate output will also affect prices in factor markets (e.g. labour market). Prices of production inputs, including that of labour (wages) will go down. Would workers accept a reduction in wages? Yes. They will, because not only their wage rates will go down, but also the prices of consumer goods they purchase, which will keep their purchasing power and living standards almost unchanged. Owners of other factors of production (e.g. land, capital) will likewise accept lower prices. As a result, due to the fall in prices, there will be a downward movement along AD^2 from E_c to a new equilibrium point in E^2. In conclusion, E^1 and E^2 represent points along a classical vertical aggregate supply curve, AS, which would be a justification for the classical view that 'supply creates its own demand'.

QUESTION

1. Do you agree with the statement 'Supply creates its own demand'? Why, or why not?

In brief, Keynesian theory argues that, in a severely recessed economy, increases in aggregate demand will boost production rather than prices.

Figure 10.5(b) illustrates a basic Keynesian aggregate supply (AS) curve (sometimes referred to as 'extreme Keynesian'). The obvious feature is that the curve is shaped like a reverse L, with a horizontal segment joining a vertical segment at a sharp corner. The horizontal segment of the curve reflects the Keynesian notion that a decline in demand leads to a decline in real production, primarily because prices remain constant. The vertical segment is a recognition that the total quantities of resources are fixed and that total production is ultimately limited, which results in full employment. Keynes has also adopted the classical view that, at full employment level, any increase in aggregate demand will not increase domestic output any more, but will fuel inflation.

While this reverse-L shaped curve captures the original essence of Keynesian economics, the Keynesian view has evolved over the years, in conjunction with contributions from other economists who have adopted the general framework of Keynesian theory. The following section is such an example.

The three ranges of the aggregate supply curve

We will further discuss an eclectic or general view of the way the shape of the aggregate supply curve varies in relation to fluctuations in real GDP. It is sometimes referred as the 'Keynesian–neo-classical synthesis'.

The aggregate supply (AS) curve presented in Figure 10.6 indicates the level of real GDP produced at each possible price level. It has the following three distinct ranges or segments:

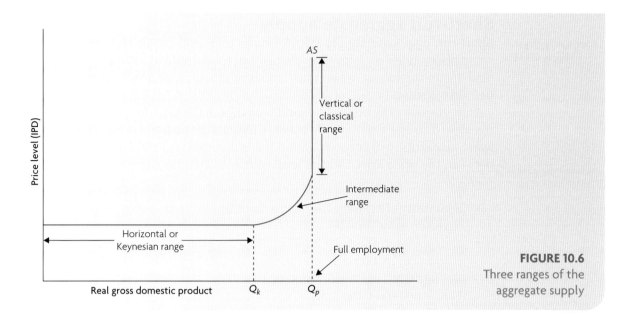

FIGURE 10.6
Three ranges of the aggregate supply

1. A horizontal or Keynesian range, up to Q_k.
2. An intermediate range, between Q_k and Q_p (the full employment output or 'potential output' as opposed to 'actual output').
3. A vertical or classical range.

A few brief notes on each range of the aggregate supply curve:

- Within the Keynesian range, the price level is constant for an economy in severe recession. In this range there is much unemployment of labour and excess plant capacity.
- In the intermediate range the price level rises moderately as the resource markets become progressively tighter and demand for real GDP rises. This is the rising segment of the aggregate supply approaching the full employment output level (Q_p).
- The classical range occurs at Q_p. This is the vertical segment of the aggregate supply curve, which represents an economy at full employment output. The level of real GDP remains constant, while the price level rises when there are further increases in aggregate demand.

We will refer again to this curve when we discuss later in the chapter the equilibrium shifts resulting from aggregate demand shifts.

SHORT-RUN VERSUS LONG-RUN AGGREGATE SUPPLY

We mentioned above that the relationship between the level of prices in the economy and the level of the real GDP is generally positive. In order to explain further the rationale behind this relationship as illustrated in the aggregate supply curve, we will have to distinguish between short-run and long-run aggregate supply.

We introduced the concepts of short run and long run at the microeconomic level in Chapter 6. Now we are discussing these concepts in a macroeconomic context, at the level of the entire domestic economy.

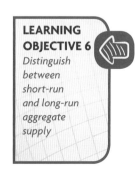

LEARNING OBJECTIVE 6
Distinguish between short-run and long-run aggregate supply

Short-run aggregate supply

short-run aggregate supply (SRAS) *total real production available in the economy when prices in the economy can change, but the prices (e.g. nominal wages) and productivity of all factor inputs (e.g. wage rates, labour productivity and technology level) are assumed to be held constant*

Short-run aggregate supply (SRAS) shows total real production available in the economy when prices in the economy can change, but the prices (e.g. nominal wages) and productivity of all factor inputs (e.g. wage rates, labour productivity and technology level) are assumed to be held constant.

As in the case of aggregate demand, a change in the price level results in a movement along the short-run aggregate supply curve. The slope of the SRAS curve depends on the degree of spare (underutilised) capacity within the economy. Figure 10.7(a) illustrates the relationship between the price level and the level of real GDP in the short-run aggregate supply. In this scenario:

- input prices (e.g. wages, equipment, technology) are assumed to be fixed and are based on price level P^1
- an increase in the price level will improve profits and encourage firms to expand real output. For instance, when the price level P^1 increases to P^2, the real GDP moves along the short-run aggregate supply curve to the right from point A^1 (corresponding to Q^2) to A^2 (corresponding to Q_p).

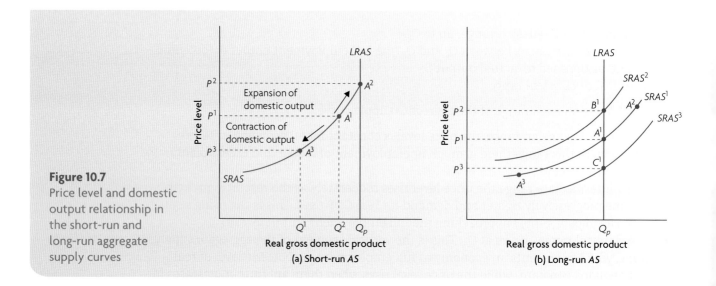

Figure 10.7
Price level and domestic output relationship in the short-run and long-run aggregate supply curves

Alternatively, a decrease in the price level from P^1 to P^3 will cause a contraction in real output. Therefore, the short-run aggregate supply curve is assumed to slope upwards.

Economic literature identifies four models which can explain the upward sloping shape of the short-run aggregate supply curve: the sticky wage model, the worker misperception model, the imperfect information model, and the sticky price model.

Let's explain briefly how these four factors determine the shape of the SRAS:

1. The sticky wage model is based on the labour market. When the price level in the economy rises, the wage the workers receive cannot adjust immediately (e.g. are 'sticky') and as a result real wages fall. When real wages fall, labour becomes cheaper. When labour becomes cheaper, firms can afford to hire more labour. When firms hire more labour, real output increases.

2. The worker misperception model, also based on the labour market, shows that workers may not immediately be aware of the existence of a higher price level. Changes in the price level do not immediately change nominal wages. When firms increase nominal wages, workers—due to misperceptions—believe that real wages also increase. When workers believe that real wages increase, workers provide more labour. When workers provide more labour, real output increases.

3. In the imperfect information model neither the worker nor the firm has complete information about the labour market. That is, neither is better informed than the other about the real wage, the nominal wage, or the price level. When the overall price level rises, producers mistake it for a relative increase in the price level. When the relative price level rises, the real wage earned by producers rises. When the real wage earned by producers rises, the amount of labour supplied by producers increases. When the amount of labour supplied by producers increases, real output increases. Therefore there is a direct relationship between the price level and the real output.

4. In the sticky prices model the mutual relationship between the price level and the level in real output can be summarised by the following two events:

   a) First, when firms expect a high price level, they set their relatively sticky prices high. Other firms follow suit and set their prices high as well. Thus, a high expected price level leads to a high actual price level. When the expected price level is high, producers produce more output, as the incentive for production is also high.

   b) Second, when the level of output is high, the demand for goods and services is also high. When the demand for goods and services is high, the price charged for goods and services rises. When the price charged for goods and services is high, firms set their relatively sticky prices high. When some firms set their relatively sticky prices high, other firms follow suit. Thus, the overall price level increases.

Again, the relationship between the price level and real output level is direct, which contributes to a positive slope of the SRAS.

The long-run aggregate supply (LRAS)

The **long-run aggregate supply** differs from the SRAS in that no input prices are assumed to be constant. Thus, LRAS is a measure of a country's potential output. The LRAS concept is linked strongly to that of the production possibility frontier (PPF) discussed in Chapter 1.

The long-run aggregate supply curve is vertical reflecting the independent relations between the price level and aggregate real production, where output is fixed by the factors of production, namely capital and labour. In the long run, the ability of an economy to produce goods and services to meet demand is based on the state of production technology and the availability and quality of factor inputs (e.g. land, labour, capital).

long-run aggregate supply (LRAS) *represents the relationship between the price level and output in the long run, when both prices and average wage rates can change*

DETERMINANTS OF SUPPLY

In the previous section we examined how changes in the price level determine changes in the level of real output. At the same time, as in the case of aggregate demand, there are factors, other than the price level, that can cause changes in aggregate supply. They are called **determinants of aggregate supply**.

Determinants of aggregate supply represent an assortment of ceteris paribus factors, other than the price level, that cause changes in the short-run and long run aggregate supply. These factors are assumed constant when the short-run and long-run aggregate supply curves

LEARNING OBJECTIVE 7 *Identify the main determinants of supply*

LINK TO BUSINESS

FLEXIBLE WAGES AND THE LONG-RUN AGGREGATE SUPPLY CURVE

As mentioned above, in the long run nominal wages are assumed to be fully flexible in response to changes in the price level.

Figure 10.7(b) shows the implications of this assumption for aggregate supply. The economy is operating at its potential level of output (Q_p) and at the initial price level P^1, meeting in point A^1. In the long run, a price level rise from P^1 to P^2 will increase nominal wages, which will cause a shift of the $SRAS^1$ to the left to $SRAS^2$. Conversely, a decrease in the price level from P^1 to P^3 will reduce nominal wages and shift the $SRAS^1$ to the right to $SRAS^3$. All three intersections points A^1, B^1, and C^1 are on the vertical line. Therefore we can assume that $LRAS$ curve is vertical.

determinants of aggregate supply
an assortment of ceteris paribus factors, other than the price level, that cause changes in the short-run and long-run aggregate supply

are constructed. Changes in any of the aggregate supply determinants cause the short-run and/or long-run aggregate supply curves to shift. While a wide variety of specific ceteris paribus factors can cause the aggregate supply curves to shift, they can be grouped into four broad categories:

1. resource quantity
2. resource quality
3. resource prices, and
4. the legal and institutional environment.

Let's review a few aspects of each of these factors.

Changes in resource quantity

A society's production possibility curve shifts outwards when the resources available to it increase. Shifts to the right in the production possibilities curve translate into shifts to the right of our long-run aggregate supply curve. Increases in the quantity of domestic resources (e.g. land, labour, capital, entrepreneurial ability) lower input prices and, as a result, per-unit production costs fall, and the short-run aggregate supply curve moves to the right. Thus, at any given price level, firms collectively produce and offer for sale more real domestic output than before. Conversely, declines in the quantity of resource supplies increase input prices and reduce the economy's ability to produce output, shifting the economy's short-run and long-run aggregate supply curves to the left.

Let's review a few examples of the impact of changes in resource quantity on aggregate supply.

Land

More land resources could become available through discoveries of mineral deposits, irrigation of land, or technological innovation. An increase in the supply of land resources will lower the price of land inputs and thus lower per-unit production costs. For example, the relatively recent discovery that widely available materials at low temperatures can act as superconductors of electricity is expected eventually to reduce per-unit production costs by reducing electricity loss during transmission. This lower price of electricity will increase both short-run and long-run aggregate supply.

On the other hand are the widespread loss of agricultural land through salinity and the nation's loss of topsoil through intensive farming. Eventually, each of these problems may increase input prices and shift the long-run and short-run aggregate supply curves to the left.

Labour

An increase in the availability of labour resources reduces the price of labour; while a decrease raises labour's price.

The size of the labour force can increase through natural growth of population or via immigration.

Reasons for a declining population and workforce include emigration, wars, famines, diseases and natural disasters.

Shifts in the supply of labour also affect the potential output of society. For example, the immigration of employable workers from abroad has historically increased the availability of labour in Australia. Conversely, the great loss of life during World War I greatly diminished the post-war availability of labour in Australia, tending to raise per-unit production costs and reduce the potential output level.

Capital

Changes in the economy's stock of capital is the most important influence on the quantity of capital. These changes are brought about through a combination of investment and depreciation. Investment adds to the capital stock and depreciation reduces it. Investment has the curious role of affecting both the aggregate demand curve, as one of the main four components of GDP(E), and the aggregate supply curves, by influencing the capital stock.

An increase in the quantity of capital stock takes place when the society will save more and will direct a bigger proportion of savings towards the purchase of capital goods.

At the same time, short-run and long-run aggregate supply declines when the quantity of the nation's stock of capital diminishes. For example, in the depths of the Great Depression of the 1930s, Australia's capital stock deteriorated because new purchases of capital were insufficient to offset the normal wearing out and obsolescence of plant and equipment.

Long-run and short-run aggregate supply tends to increase when society adds to its stock of capital. Such an addition would happen if society saved more of its income and directed the savings towards the purchase of capital goods. In much the same way, an improvement in the quality of capital reduces production costs and increases short-run and long-run aggregate supply. For example, businesses have over the years replaced poor-quality equipment with new, superior equipment.

Entrepreneurial ability

Finally, the amount of entrepreneurial ability available to the economy can change in time and shift the aggregate supply curve. More individuals with entrepreneurial aspirations involved in new business ventures will tend to shift the aggregate supply curves to the right.

Changes in resource quality

The second major determinant of the aggregate supply curves is the quality of resources. If the quality of labour, capital, land and entrepreneurship changes, then the SRAS and LRAS curves shift. An improved quality increases aggregate supply and a decline in quality decreases aggregate supply.

- Land quality can be improved through mechanisation, fertilisers and chemicals application and improved land management techniques (e.g. crop rotation).
- Labour can improve its quality through education, training and multi-skilling. Higher quality labour, brought about by more education, is more productive and causes the aggregate supply to increase.

- Capital quality can be improved through research and development. Improvements in technology will affect aggregate supply favourably via increases in productivity. Technology generally affects the quality of capital, but can also peripherally affect the quality of labour, land, and entrepreneurship. In modern times, technology has invariably advanced, causing increases in the quality of capital and thus increases in aggregate supply. It is, however, possible for a technological step backwards that would cause a decrease in the quality of capital and aggregate supply (e.g. eastern European countries under communism in the post-World War II period).
- Entrepreneurial ability can be promoted through management and training education and via media publicity.

Resource price

The third major aggregate supply determinant is resource price. The price of resources affects the cost of producing output and thus the price level charged for an existing quantity of real production. This determinant only affects the short-run aggregate supply. Because the long-run aggregate supply is independent of the price level it is also unaffected by changes in resource prices and production cost.

Three of the more important resource prices that influence production cost and shift the SRAS curve are:

Wages

Wage payments to labour are usually at the top of any list of resource prices.

Around 70 per cent of all business costs are wages or salaries. All else being equal, changes in wages have a significant impact on per-unit production costs and on the location of the aggregate supply curve.

Economy-wide changes in wages shift the SRAS curve. Higher wages, by increasing production cost, cause a decrease short-run aggregate supply. Lower wages, by decreasing production cost, cause an increase short-run aggregate supply.

Prices of imported resources

A decrease in the prices of imported raw materials (e.g. crude oil) and equipment will decrease production costs and increase aggregate demand. Conversely, an increase in import prices will decrease aggregate supply and cause a shift of the aggregate supply curve to the left.

Exchange rate fluctuations will also affect prices of imported resources. If the Australian dollar gets stronger in relation to other foreign currencies, our imports will be encouraged and our exports will be discouraged, impacting unfavourably on domestic output (see Chapter 19 for more details on exchange rates).

Market power

A change in the degree of market power of sellers of resources can also affect input prices and short-run aggregate supply. For instance a reduction in the market power of OPEC in the oil sector during the mid 1980s reduced the cost of manufacturing and transporting in the Australian economy, contributing to an increase in the Australian aggregate supply.

At the same time, a change in the use of union market power may also affect the location of the aggregate supply. Some observers believe that unions exploited their market power to achieve large increases in award pay rates in the 1970s, or to control wage increases throughout much of the 1980s. This would have had a negative effect on the short-run aggregate supply, which would have shifted to the left. In exchange, an increase in productivity (e.g. real output per unit of input) should be beneficial for both the short-run and long-run aggregate supply.

Figure 10.11(a) (p. 223) illustrates shifts in short-run aggregate supply. A favourable change in the determinants of supply (e.g. lower production costs through lower costs of imported resources) will cause a shift of the short-run aggregate supply to the right from AS^1 to AS^3, determining a higher aggregate supply and a lower level of prices.

Legal and institutional environment

Changes in the legal and institutional setting in which businesses collectively operate can make or break aggregate supply. In brief, government measures meant to promote business activity will be positive for aggregate supply with a change of the AS curve to the right, while measures making business less attractive will affect the level of domestic production and will cause a shift of the AS curve to the left.

The main influences in this area include:

- changes in taxes and subsidies
- changes in the extent of regulation.

Tax reductions (e.g. excise and payroll tax, corporate tax) combined with government subsidies will favour an increase in aggregate supply and a shift to the right of the aggregate supply in the short and long run. Conversely, tax increases and subsidy cuts will affect negatively aggregate supply.

Excessive regulation increases business costs and causes a decline in aggregate supply. However, the potential loss to production must be traded off against any benefits derived from regulation.

Figure 10.8 summarises the main determinants of aggregate supply discussed above.

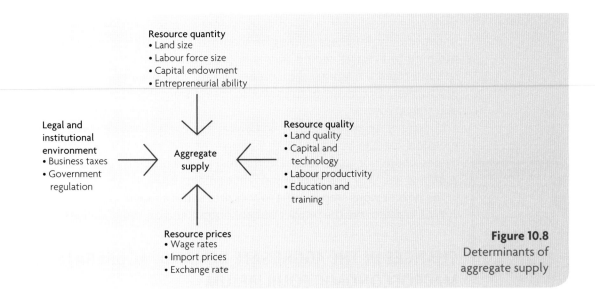

Figure 10.8
Determinants of aggregate supply

LEARNING
OBJECTIVE 8
*Explain the
aggregate
demand–
aggregate supply
model and
how it impacts
on economic
activity*

AGGREGATE DEMAND AND AGGREGATE SUPPLY EQUILIBRIUM

We learnt in Chapter 2 that the intersection of the demand for and the supply of a particular product would determine the equilibrium output of that good.

Similarly, as illustrated in Figure 10.9, macroeconomic equilibrium occurs where the aggregate demand curve, AD, and the aggregate supply curve, AS, intersect. In our case, the intersection of the two curves at equilibrium point E lies to the left of the long-run aggregate supply curve and potential output (Q_p). The equilibrium real domestic output and price level are Q_e and P_e respectively. If suppliers in Australia had decided to produce a larger domestic output such as Q^2, it would be unable to dispose of that output; that is, aggregate demand would be insufficient to take that domestic output off the market.

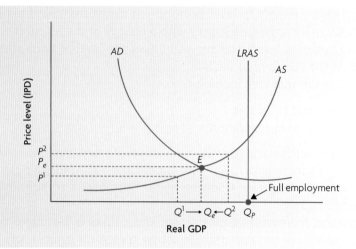

Figure 10.9
The aggregate demand and aggregate supply model

Faced with unwanted inventories and costs and falling profits, businesses would be forced to reduce prices and cut back on output to the equilibrium point, as indicated by the leftward-pointing arrow.

Alternatively, if businesses had only produced domestic output Q^1, they would find that their orders could not be filled quickly enough and their inventories would be drawn down unexpectedly. Business managers would react by hiring more people and by producing more output. Prices would increase (but just, because we are only at the beginning of the intermediate range) and profits would rise because sales of output would exceed production. Domestic output would rise to equilibrium, as shown by the rightward-pointing arrow.

At point E, aggregate supply will equal aggregate demand, with no upward or downward pressure for the price level to change. At macroeconomic equilibrium, sellers neither overestimate nor underestimate the real GDP demanded at the prevailing price level. The economy will stay (but not for long) in equilibrium.

The next obvious step in our analysis is to shift the aggregate demand and aggregate supply curves and observe the impact on real output and on the price level.

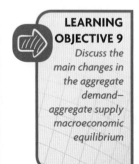

LEARNING
OBJECTIVE 9
*Discuss the
main changes in
the aggregate
demand–
aggregate supply
macroeconomic
equilibrium*

CHANGES IN THE AGGREGATE DEMAND–AGGREGATE SUPPLY MACROECONOMIC EQUILIBRIUM

Similarly to the market disequilibrium at the microeconomic level discussed in Chapter 3, the aggregate demand–aggregate supply macroeconomic equilibrium can be disrupted by shifts of either the aggregate demand curve or aggregate supply curve. Such shifts, as indicated before, can be caused by changes in the determinants of aggregate demand (listed in Figure 10.3, p. 203) or aggregate supply (Figure 10.8, p. 219) respectively.

We will start by examining the aggregate demand shifts.

Equilibrium shifts arising from aggregate demand shifts

We will do our analysis by shifting the aggregate demand curve along the three ranges of the aggregate supply curve (Figure 10.10) and observing the impact of such shifts on the real GDP and the price level, and the correlated effects on inflation and unemployment.

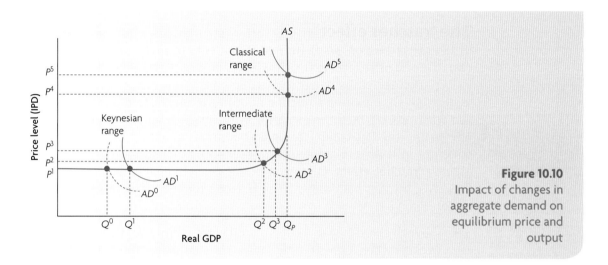

Figure 10.10
Impact of changes in aggregate demand on equilibrium price and output

The Keynesian (horizontal) range

We have a recessionary environment with a high level of unemployment and excess plant capacity. Prices are weak reflecting the poor aggregate demand. In order to have an increase in aggregate demand, the economy requires a positive change in the determinants of aggregate demand. Let's suppose that people become more optimistic in their expectations about future economic conditions and their job prospects. We listed this determinant in Figure 10.3 as 'consumer expectations'. Consumers decide to spend more of their current incomes. The resulting increase in aggregate demand will shift the aggregate demand curve along the horizontal aggregate supply curve from AD^0 to AD^1. The increased level of aggregate demand will be met through increased domestic output (Q^1), without increased production costs and with no effect on the general level of prices (the price level remains at P^1).

The intermediate range

Increased 'profit expectations' from the business sector will contribute to an increased aggregate demand, which records a shift from AD^2 to AD^3 and creates an increase in real GDP (Q^2 to Q^3), as well as additional employment with a corresponding reduction in unemployment. The downside is that pressure is placed on labour and other resource markets. Bottlenecks (obstacles to output flows) develop, when some firms, say in the steel sector, have no unused capacity, and cannot fill all their orders for steel. This will hold up production in the car sector and building industry, large users of steel. Steel firms, experiencing labour shortages, will raise the price of steel, which will increase production costs in the car and building industries. Increased production costs are passed on by car manufacturers and building firms as higher prices, determining a higher price level in the economy (P^2 to P^3). Domestic output is still increasing in this range, but not as smoothly as in the horizontal range.

The classical (vertical) range

This range occurs when the economy reaches full employment. It corresponds to the production possibility curve of Chapter 1. In this range further domestic output growth is not possible with the existing level of resources, and any increase in aggregate demand (AD^4 to AD^5) will only produce pure inflation. Inflation, which was no problem in the Keynesian range, and only a minor problem in the intermediate range, becomes a chronic problem in the classical range.

The 'ratchet effect'

In the above section we examined the effects of increases of aggregate demand on the real GDP and price level in the three segments of the aggregate supply curve. The question is, 'What of decreases in aggregate demand?'. The theory would predict that a decrease in demand should bring a decline in both the real output and price level. However, there is a complicating factor in situations of decline in aggregate demand which makes such effects unclear. The complication is that prices of both products and resources tend to be sticky, or inflexible in a downward direction, at least in the short term. Economists talk about a '**ratchet effect**' (a ratchet being a mechanism that permits us to crank a wheel forwards, but not backwards.) The reasons for the inflexibility of prices include various factors such as:

ratchet effect
the result of the tendency for prices of both products and resources to be individually 'sticky' or inflexible in a downward direction, leading to a loss in the downward flexibility of the general level of prices

- the high share of wage costs in total costs of firms and the tendency to hire more workers when higher output levels are attained
- a desire to not reduce workforce morale and productivity through redundancies
- firms with monopoly power may resist price cuts and use large cuts in production and employment instead
- price changes are often costly to implement (think of the need for customer notifications, record updates, new brochures etc.).

Equilibrium shifts arising from aggregate supply shifts

Now we consider a stationary aggregate demand curve and changes in the aggregate supply curve, caused by one or several determinants listed in Figure 10.8 on page 219 (e.g. resource quantity, resource quality, resource prices, legal and institutional environment). All factors listed in Figure 10.8 can cause changes in the short-run aggregate supply. However, only a couple of factors can change the long-run aggregate supply (e.g. productivity and changes in the legal and institutional environment), with a couple of other factors being only possible determinants (e.g. prices of imported resources, or market power).

Given the profit-maximisation objective of private firms, one of the paramount factors for a change in aggregate supply is represented by production costs. If costs (e.g. wages, materials from domestic or foreign suppliers etc.) increase, firms respond by decreasing their output (and employment) or by increasing their prices, or both. In Figure 10.11(a) we have AS^1 shifting to the left to AS^2, meaning that less real GDP will be supplied (Q^1 to Q^2) and the price level increases from P^1 to P^2. This is a situation of 'stagflation' where both the price level and unemployment level increase. The reverse happens when production costs go down.

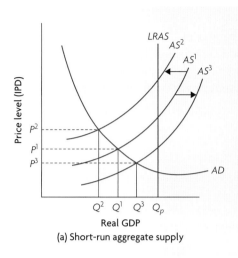

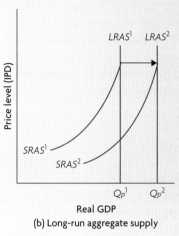

Figure 10.11
Changes in short-run and long-run aggregate supply curves

(a) Short-run aggregate supply

(b) Long-run aggregate supply

Domestic output rises (Q^1 to Q^3), and the price level drops (P^1 to P^3), which is a beneficial outcome for both businesses and consumers.

What about the long-run aggregate supply (*LRAS*)? Can it shift as well? Yes, although it might be at a slower pace. Remember again the production possibilities curve of Chapter 1. An increase in the quantity of resources (e.g. labour, stock of capital) and/or quality of resources (e.g. improvements in productivity and efficiency through technological innovation) would shift *LRAS* outward. Government regulation promoting competition within markets or between markets and stimulating the pace of innovation can also contribute to a shift of *LRAS* outwards. In Figure 10.11(b), following the presence of one or several of the above factors, there is a shift in the long-run aggregate supply from $LRAS^1$ to $LRAS^2$, which increases the full employment output level (or economy potential) from Q_p^1 to Q_p^2.

SUMMARY

1. John Maynard Keynes rejected the classical theory that the economy self-corrects in the long run to full employment. The key in Keynesian theory is aggregate demand, rather than the classical economists' focus on aggregate supply.
2. The aggregate demand (AD) curve shows the level of real domestic output that will be purchased at each possible price level.
3. The rationale for the down-sloping aggregate demand curve is based on the interest rate effect, the real balances effect, and the net exports effect.
4. The determinants of aggregate demand include factors, other than price, that are causing shifts of the aggregate demand:

CONSUMER SPENDING	INVESTMENT SPENDING	GOVERNMENT SPENDING	NET EXPORT SPENDING
• Consumer wealth	• Business taxes	• Funds availability	• Foreign GDP growth
• Consumer expectations	• Interest rates	• State of economy	• International competitiveness
• Interest rates	• Profit expectations	• Political stance	
• Consumer indebtedness	• Physical wealth		• Exchange rate
• Taxes	• Technology		• External policies
• Marketing	• Degree of excess capacity		

5. The aggregate supply curve shows the levels of real domestic output that will be produced at various price levels.

6. A complete view of the shape of the AS curve is represented by the aggregate supply curve with three ranges:

   (a) The Keynesian (horizontal) range—In a recessionary environment, production costs and price level are stable.

   (b) The intermediate range—Price level rises as GDP level rises towards the full employment level.

   (c) The classical (vertical) range—Coincides with the full employment output. Any AD increases fuel inflation.

7. Reasons for the upward-sloping short-run AS curve include:

   (a) the sticky wage model

   (b) the worker misperception model

   (c) the imperfect information model, and

   (d) the sticky price model.

8. The shape of the long-run aggregate supply is vertical.

9. Short-run aggregate supply (SRAS) shows total real production available in the economy when prices in the economy can change, but the prices (e.g. nominal wages) and productivity of all factor inputs (e.g. wage rates, labour productivity and technology level) are assumed to be held constant.

   The determinants of aggregate supply (e.g. factors, other than price) include:

   (a) resource quantity (e.g. labour force size, capital endowment)

   (b) resource quality (e.g. technological innovation, changes in productivity)

   (c) resource price (e.g. wages and prices of material inputs)

   (d) legal and institutional environment (e.g. business taxes and government regulation).

10. Long-run aggregate supply (LRAS) represents the relationship between the price level and output in the long run, when both prices and average wage rates can change.

    The long-run aggregate supply curve is vertical reflecting the independent relations between the price level and aggregate real production, where output is fixed by the factors of production, namely capital and labour.

11. The intersection of the aggregate demand and short-run aggregate supply curve determines the equilibrium price level and real domestic output in the short-run aggregate supply.

12. The aggregate demand curve may change as a result of changes in any of its determinants. Given short-run aggregate supply, rightward shifts of aggregate demand increase real domestic output and employment, and increase the price level.

13. The ratchet effect reflects the fact that prices are flexible upwards, but relatively inflexible downwards.

14. A favourable change in the condition of determinants of SRAS (e.g. improved technology) will cause a shift to the right of the aggregate supply curve. Conversely, a negative determinant (e.g. higher prices of imported materials) will cause a shift of the SRAS curve to the left.

15. An increase in the quantity of resources (e.g. labour, stock of capital) and/or quality of resources (e.g. improvements in productivity and efficiency through technological innovation) would shift LRAS outward.

KEY TERMS

aggregate demand	199	determinants of aggregate demand	202	net exports effect	201
aggregate demand curve	200	determinants of aggregate supply	216	ratchet effect	222
aggregate supply (AS)	210	gross capital formation	209	real balances or wealth effect	201
aggregate supply curve	210	interest rate effect	201	short-run aggregate supply (SRAS)	214
		long-run aggregate supply (LRAS)	215		

REFERENCE

1. John M. Keynes, *General Theory of Employment, Interest and Money*, Macmillan, London, United Kingdom, 1936, p. 96.

REVIEW QUESTIONS

1. Distinguish between the short-run and the aggregate-run supply curve.
2. Outline the main features of the three ranges of the aggregate supply curve.
3. 'Aggregate demand curve is negatively sloped.' What does it mean?
4. Explain why the rationale for a downward sloping aggregate demand curve is different from that for the demand curve for a single product.
5. Outline the main changes in the AD-AS macroeconomic equilibrium.
6. Unemployment can be caused by a leftward shift of aggregate demand or a leftward shift of aggregate supply. Which problem can be easier to resolve? Discuss.
7. How can the government stimulate Australia's aggregate demand? Should government stimulus be exercised throughout the business cycle or only in a certain phase? Discuss.
8. What category of determinants can have a stronger contribution to the increase of domestic output—resource quantity or resource quality? Discuss.
9. 'Private investment can make or break Australia's aggregate demand.' Do you agree with this statement? Explain your answer.
10. Outline the concept of the 'ratchet effect'.
11. Distinguish between short-run aggregate supply (SRAS) and long-run aggregate supply (LRAS).
12. Outline a few favourable determinants of the SRAS.
13. 'The determinants of the shifts in the aggregate demand curve are the same with the determinants/ conditions of demand for a single product discussed in Chapter 3.' Explain the concept of 'consumer wealth' and how 'consumer wealth' can impact on aggregate demand.
14. Why is 'investment spending' the leading component of aggregate demand?
15. Can government spending influence aggregate demand?
16. Why is GDP growth in other economies important for Australia's economic growth?
17. Show how an imported good or service may affect aggregate demand even though it does not directly compete with a domestic good or service.
18. What are the factors which influence the net export spending?

APPLIED QUESTIONS AND EXERCISES

1. Complete the following table to summarise the effects of various economic developments listed in Column (1) on aggregate demand:

   (a) Indicate in Column (2) one to two major components of aggregate demand that are likely to be affected by each economic development. Use the letters from the formula of aggregate demand as follows: *C*—personal consumption, *I*—private investment, *G*—government expenditure, *X*—exports, *M*—imports.

   (b) Indicate in Column (3) the impact of each economic development on aggregate demand, by using + for an increase of aggregate demand, or, – for a decrease in aggregate demand.

COLUMN (1) ECONOMIC DEVELOPMENT	COLUMN (2) AD COMPONENT (C, I, G, X, M)	COLUMN (3) +/– AD CHANGE
An increase in indirect taxes		
Higher levels of consumer saving		
An increased inflow of foreign investment in Australia		
A decline in the budget surplus		
Higher spending by foreigners on Australian-made goods		

2. The table overleaf presents the real GDP and the real GDP deflator for Bucksland over 2006–10.

   Based on these indicators establish the range of the AS curve for Bucksland by filling each box in Column (4) with one of the letters:

   K = Keynesian range

   I = Intermediate range

   C = Classical range

COLUMN (1) YEAR	COLUMN (2) REAL GDP INDEX (2005 = 100)	COLUMN (3) GDP PRICE DEFLATOR (2005 = 100)	COLUMN (4) RANGE OF AS CURVE K/I/C
2006	95	95	
2007	98	95	
2008	101	96	
2009	105	102	
2010	105	110	

3. The following table presents macroeconomic data about Malaysia's economy (real GDP, inflation, unemployment) over 2003–08.

	REAL GDP CHANGE (% P.A.)	GDP DEFLATOR (2000 = 100)	U/E RATE (% P.A.)
2003	5.8	104.8	3.6
2004	6.8	111.1	3.5
2005	5.3	116.3	3.5
2006	5.8	120.8	3.3
2007	6.2	126.7	3.2
2008	4.6	139.8	3.3

Source: Compiled from ADB data at <www.adb.org/Documents/Books/ Key_Indicators/2009/xls/MAL.xls>, accessed 9 November 2010.

(a) Outline the situation of the Malaysian economy over 2007–08.

(b) What can you conclude has happened to aggregate demand and/or aggregate supply in Malaysia in 2007 and 2008 in order to have created these changes in the output level and price level?

(c) Outline the likely reason(s) for the relatively stable level of unemployment, despite a high real GDP growth.

4. Table 10.2 presents the structure of Malaysia's GDP(*E*)/ aggregate demand (AD) by the main components.

Table 10.2: Components of Malaysia's AD as percentage of GDP(*E*), 2007, 2008

	2007	2008
Private consumption	45.8	45.2
Government consumption	12.2	12.5
Gross domestic capital formation	21.7	19.1
Exports of goods and services	110.5	103.6
Imports of goods and services	90.2	80.5

Source: Compiled from ADB data at <www.adb.org/Documents/Books/ Key_Indicators/2009/xls/MAL.xls>, accessed 9 November 2010.

(a) Which component of Malaysia's aggregate demand appears to have had the highest contribution to Malaysia's GDP change in 2008?

(b) Identify two or three likely factors, other than price, from the list below, which would have contributed to the changes in Malaysia's GDP(*E*) growth and composition:
   • increase in consumer spending
   • higher private and government investment
   • strong foreign demand for Malaysian exports
   • a reduction of personal income tax
   • a decrease in government spending.

5. What is an Australian 'super-resource tax' likely to affect: aggregate supply, aggregate demand, or both? Discuss.

Chapter **11**

The labour force

LEARNING OBJECTIVES

After studying this chapter, you will be able to:

1. define unemployment
2. explain how unemployment is measured by the Australian Bureau of Statistics
3. describe the main types of unemployment and the two main approaches to measuring unemployment
4. compare the unemployment rates in Australia and other countries
5. suggest the main causes and effects of unemployment
6. examine how demographic factors will influence the future workforce and government social policies.

INTRODUCTION

In this chapter, we examine one of the most divisive issues in our society—unemployment. It is divisive because a considerable proportion of Australian households are directly affected by it and a whole lot more indirectly so. There is conflict about it at every level of society: within households, small businesses, large corporations and government authorities.

Any discussion about unemployment raises fear because of people's uncertainty and anxiety about it and confusion because of the unsatisfactory explanations for its existence. These issues are dealt with here.

Unemployment appears in the same part in this text as inflation because they are both key indicators of the state of the economy. Indeed, broadly speaking, an economy cannot be said to be progressing unless these two aspects are under control.

The study of unemployment provides insights into the use of economic indicators to evaluate an economy. The problems of unemployment that face Australia indicate that economic trends can become entrenched. Our response to this particular question gives us significant information about Australia's approach to economic management.

A brief word on the title of this chapter. If the core issue in this chapter is unemployment, why is the chapter called 'The labour force'?

labour force
all persons aged 15 years and over who, during the reference week, were employed or unemployed (as defined)

There are many aspects of work and employment that must be included in any worthwhile analysis of unemployment. This body of information, concepts and interpretations is best described under the broader heading of the **labour force**, a social and economic entity that exists separately from the study of unemployment. For example, participation rates and the composition of the workforce, as well as unemployment, are both central to other economic and social issues. An understanding of the concepts and data collected under the heading of 'The labour force' helps us to interpret the realities of unemployment in Australia in the 2000s.

LEARNING OBJECTIVE 1
Define unemployment

DEFINING UNEMPLOYMENT

As shown in the previous chapter, over the past few decades employment in Australia has grown significantly in the services sector, particularly in the property and business division and the accommodation, cafes and restaurant division, while manufacturing has suffered a steady decline in employment. This shift in labour demand has resulted mainly from new technology, microeconomic reforms (such as tariff reductions, industrial relations reforms) and internationalisation of product markets.

unemployment
a situation where some people are willing and able to work, but are unable to find paid employment

Unemployment can be defined as a situation where some people are willing and able to work, but are unable to find paid employment. It is measured in various ways.

EMPLOYMENT SERVICES AND STATISTICS

There are two official sources of information about unemployment in Australia: the *Labour Force Survey*, published by the Australian Bureau of Statistics (ABS), and **Centrelink**, a statutory authority reporting to the Minister for Family and Community Services (DFACS).

Centrelink
a statutory authority reporting to the Minister for Family and Community Services (DFACS)

Since 1 May 1998 a new regime introduced by the Australian Government has cut back on government involvement in the delivery of employment services by making more use of market forces and the private sector. The system has involved Centrelink and

JOB SERVICES AUSTRALIA

Job Services Australia began in 1998 as 'Job Network' after the dissolution of the Commonwealth Employment Services (CES). In 1996–97, the Australian Federal Parliament passed legislation to combine the functions of the CES and the Department of Social Security. As a result Centrelink was created to provide monetary welfare support to people across Australia. The delivery of employment services was tendered out to Job Network organisations whose primary responsibility was to assist people into work.

In 2009, the Labor Government renamed the program 'Job Services Australia'.

Job Services Australia is a competitive $4 billion industry with organisations competing for contracts through tenders.

Agencies contracted under Job Services Australia include Mission Australia, The Salvation Army, Max Employment, Workways Australia and the Jobfind Centres Australia.

The peak industry bodies for Job Services Australia members are National Employment Australia (NESA) which represents all employment and employment-related service providers, and Jobs Australia, which represents the not-for-profit sector.

LINK TO BUSINESS

Job Network (currently Job Services Australia), and has offered a different approach to job placement in Australia. (See the above Link to Business for details.)

There are differences between the unemployment statistics published by the ABS and those on job seekers produced by Centrelink. The ABS exists to gather and analyse statistics, whereas Centrelink and other agencies exist to find and promote employment. In other words, they have different objectives in analysing and publishing unemployment statistics.

Job Network
a national network of over 100 private and community organisations dedicated to finding jobs for unemployed people, particularly the long-term unemployed

ABS statistics

The ABS statistics on unemployment result from regular household surveys. *The Labour Force Survey* (LFS) is the most widely used source of labour force statistics. The LFS was conducted quarterly from 1960 to November 1977 and monthly from February 1978. The survey is designed to produce reliable estimates of employment and unemployment at the national and state levels.

A properly selected random sample of 35 000 residences is used, with the occupants interviewed between Day 6 and Day 12 of each month. One-eighth of the sample residences are changed for each survey. This method has the merit of constantly changing the total base while ensuring continuity (for example, to provide accurate data on long-term unemployed). Defence and diplomatic personnel and overseas visitors are specifically excluded from the surveys because they would distort the statistics. Survey information is used to classify the labour force status of the population according to the concepts and definitions recommended by the International Labour Organization (ILO).

The survey week of any particular ABS statistic on unemployment—and other ABS economic statistics—can be critical, though the science of statistics suggests that any particular week is 'typical' or 'normal'. The number of unemployed is estimated from the results of those surveys. The limitations of the ABS survey include:

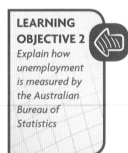

LEARNING OBJECTIVE 2
Explain how unemployment is measured by the Australian Bureau of Statistics

- the size of the sample is very small and gives little information on non-sampled areas
- the very narrow definition of 'people unemployed' is likely to understate the size of unemployment

- the measure is subject to error (e.g. due to inaccurate answers in the survey)
- there is a time lag between the collection and publication of data
- 'discouraged workers' often carry out voluntary work, assist with domestic duties, or become voluntarily inactive over long periods of time. These persons form the so-called hidden unemployed which significantly understates the 'real' unemployment figures.

Centrelink statistics

Centrelink, in contrast to the ABS, actually counts those registered for unemployment benefits. Unemployment statistics provided by Centrelink are based on the unemployed persons registered with it seeking full-time employment.

There are a number of reasons why the unemployment statistics from the ABS *Labour Force Survey* cannot be directly compared to the Centrelink/DFACS job seeker data. In accordance with international standards, the ABS classifies a person as unemployed if he or she was not employed in the week before the interview, had actively looked for work and was available for work. The Newstart Allowance and Youth Allowance series count people in receipt of an allowance who may be employed part-time (within an income test limit). As discussed in the next section, the ABS classifies a person as *employed* if, among other things, he or she has worked for one hour or more during the survey period.

There are also limitations in Centrelink information. The main cause for an underestimation of the actual unemployment figure is the unwillingness of some people to register at a Centrelink branch due to:

- the social stigma attached to being unemployed
- a preference to look for employment themselves
- not being eligible for unemployment benefits (e.g. unemployed married person whose spouse is working).

For consistency, our discussion will focus more on ABS analyses than on Centrelink figures. The ABS has rigorously pursued a comprehensive and consistent approach in developing its statistics. We can be confident of its information, even if we disagree with some of the discussion of its results.

THE CRITERIA FOR UNEMPLOYMENT

Most importantly, a mix of ABS and Centrelink statistics may prove unnecessarily complicated in highlighting issues relevant to unemployment.

The ABS classifies a person as 'employed' if they did at least one hour of work for pay or profit during the survey week, or if they worked at least 15 hours in an unpaid position on a family farm or in a family business. Those not in this category are then categorised either as 'not in the labour force' or 'unemployed'.

The ABS uses international criteria to define unemployment in a specified period. The definition is detailed and strict. The unemployed are those who:

- are aged 15 and over
- were not employed during the survey week
- had actively looked for full- or part-time work (by writing, telephoning, answering newspaper advertisements, checking Centrelink noticeboards) at any time in the four weeks up to the end of the survey week.

But this is not enough to qualify as unemployed. In addition, the person must be in one of three categories:

1. available for work in the survey week, or would have been available except for temporary illness
2. waiting to start a new job within four weeks from the end of the survey week and would have started in the survey week if the job had been available then
3. waiting to be called back to a job from which they had been stood down without pay for less than four weeks up to the end of the survey week for reasons other than bad weather and plant breakdown.

TYPES OF UNEMPLOYMENT

There are three broad types of unemployment: cyclical, non-cyclical and long-term unemployment.

CYCLICAL UNEMPLOYMENT

Cyclical unemployment (demand-deficient unemployment) is caused by a deficiency in the level of aggregate demand. It happens because of the normal fluctuations that occur in the business cycle over time. Therefore, it can be identified in the 'contraction' and 'trough' phases of the business cycle. At the depth of the Great Depression (1931–32), cyclical employment in Australia reached 30 per cent of the workforce.

NON-CYCLICAL UNEMPLOYMENT

Non-cyclical unemployment is not related to any phase of the business cycle. It includes various forms of unemployment which we will look at in turn.

Frictional unemployment

Frictional unemployment is so named because it results from lags or frictions in the price mechanism, which slows down adjustment in the labour market. Most frictional unemployment is temporary and includes people who are in the process of changing jobs, those in seasonal occupations and school leavers looking for their first job. Even when there is full employment[1] (i.e. minimum flexible unemployment) there is always some frictional unemployment.

Structural unemployment

Structural unemployment (often referred to as technological unemployment) is caused by adjustment in the industrial structure of the economy. Changes in demand for some types of goods cause some factories to reduce their production and put off labour. Developments in technology increase the demand for certain types of skilled labour, while some of the unskilled lose their jobs. Examples of structural unemployment have been:

- robots have replaced labour in motor vehicle assembly
- word processor operators have replaced typists
- computers have replaced labour in typesetting.

cyclical unemployment
unemployment caused by the lack of jobs during a contraction/ recession

LEARNING OBJECTIVE 3
Describe the main types of unemployment and the two main approaches to measuring unemployment

non-cyclical unemployment
unemployment that is not related to any phase of the business cycle (includes such forms as frictional, structural and seasonal unemployment)

frictional unemployment
unemployment caused by the normal search time required by workers with marketable skills who are changing jobs, initially entering the labour force, or re-entering the labour force

structural unemployment
unemployment caused by a mismatch of the skills of workers out of work and the skills required for existing job opportunities (often referred to as 'technological unemployment')

During times of boom (as in 2000–01 and 2005–07), cyclical unemployment decreases as more jobs become available and the demand for labour increases. During downturns and recessions (as in 1992–03, 2008–09), the level of aggregate demand weakens, demand for labour falls and so cyclical unemployment increases.

Seasonal unemployment

seasonal unemployment
unemployment resulting from a seasonal down-turn in business activity that is independent of the business cycle

Seasonal unemployment results from the seasonal nature of production in some commodities, particularly in a number of areas of primary production such as sheep shearing and fruit picking.

LONG-TERM (HARD-CORE) UNEMPLOYMENT

Some members of society are essentially unemployable. Such people may have become unemployed for cyclical or non-cyclical reasons, or may never have worked since leaving school. They remain in the unemployment pool because they are the people least suited to employment—because of lack of education, poor physical or mental abilities, or negative attitude to work.

long-term (hard-core) unemployment
when a person is unemployed for 12 months or more

Long-term (hard-core) unemployment is defined as unemployment of 12 months or more.

In Australia, long-term unemployment is principally a problem for people towards the end of their working life: older age groups tend to have longer periods of unemployment.

Hard core unemployment tends to increase in periods of economic downturn.

For instance, during the recession of the early 1990s, the number of people who were long-term unemployed almost trebled, peaking at around 320 000 in 1993. Over this period, the proportion of unemployed who had been out of work for at least 12 months rose from one in five to one in three.

The 2008 GFC-related downturn has seen the number of long-term unemployed increase from 70 000 to around 100 000. An increase in the average duration of unemployment (from 28 to 36 weeks over the year to December 2009) suggests that the unemployed found it increasingly difficult to obtain work.

ABS (cat. no. 6291.0) annual estimates in August 2010 placed the number of long-term unemployed at 109 800, accounting for around 0.9 per cent of the total workforce and around 17.4 per cent of total unemployment. The average duration of long-term unemployment was estimated at 34.5 weeks. However, some 45 300 of unemployed people were listed under 'very long-term unemployment' (e.g. 104 weeks or more).

UNDEREMPLOYMENT

Underemployed workers are employed people who want, and are available for, more hours of work than they currently have.

underemployment
when people who have part-time jobs would prefer to work more hours, or full-time

Underemployment is most common in periods of recession or contraction. A survey in April 1993, when the economy was just coming out of a serious recession, showed that of the estimated 1.78 million employed part-time, about 528 700 would have preferred to work more hours. It was also reported that in August 2003, 25 per cent of part-time workers wanted to work more hours (ABS cat. no. 6105.0, table 4.4).

ABS data indicate that since 2000, underemployed workers have outnumbered unemployed people. In May 2010, for instance, there were 837 000 underemployed workers and 610 000 unemployed people. The underemployment rate was 7.2 per cent compared with the unemployment rate of 5.2 per cent.

Unlike the unemployment rate, which rises and falls with the business cycle, historically, the underemployment rate has tended to rise in economic downturns, but not recover as quickly when the economy begins to improve.

Underemployment is another example of understating the unemployment rate because the official figure counts all part-time workers as equal to fully employed workers. Technological development and relatively high wage costs have been major contributors to underemployment in Australia.

Hidden unemployment

Official unemployment statistics tend to exclude a large number of people who are willing to work but are not actively seeking employment. As mentioned above, these people could be classified as the **'hidden unemployed'**. Because they are not actively seeking employment, mainly because of the depressed state of the labour market, or the lack of adequate facilities or services (e.g. affordable child care), they are not included as part of the labour force. ABS information showed that in the early 1990s more than 700 000 people were in this category, which was almost as many as those officially recognised as being unemployed.

During the global recession in 2009, many employees made agreements with employers to reduce working hours, which helped save jobs and meant the unemployment rate did not fall as much as predicted.

'hidden unemployed' *people who are willing to work but are not actively seeking employment, because of the depressed state of the labour market or the lack of adequate facilities or services*

FULL EMPLOYMENT

It is not possible for the entire labour force to be employed at any one time. The natural rate of unemployment occurs when there is full employment in the economy (demand and supply for labour are in equilibrium). The natural rate of unemployment only includes frictional, structural, seasonal and hard-core unemployment. Cyclical unemployment is not included.

The natural rate of unemployment is often referred to in Australia as the Non-Accelerating Inflation Rate of Unemployment (NAIRU). The NAIRU is that level of unemployment that can be achieved using expansionary macroeconomic policy, without causing inflation. Since the unemployment at the NAIRU is structural unemployment, it follows that microeconomic policies are needed to reduce unemployment any further.

The natural rate of unemployment can vary over time. In the late 1960s and 1970s the natural rate was between 1 and 2 per cent. Currently, the natural rate of unemployment is considered to be around 5 per cent. During the economic boom of 2005–07 the natural rate of unemployment fell as structural unemployment was reduced.

MEASURING UNEMPLOYMENT

There are two approaches to measuring unemployment. The first is direct measures of unemployment, such as the number of unemployed people and the **unemployment rate** (i.e. the percentage of the labour force regarded as unemployed). The second, the labour force participation rate, represents the percentage of the population 15 years and over who are either actively employed as part of the labour force or are actively seeking paid employment. Together, these two types of statistics provide a clear picture of the state of labour markets at any one time. We will look at the direct measures first.

unemployment rate *the percentage of people in the labour force who are without jobs and are actively seeking jobs*

DIRECT MEASURES

The direct measures of unemployment use three simple equations.

The first two show that the number of unemployed people and the unemployment rate are a product of two factors: the number of people in jobs and the size of the labour force:

$$U = LF - J$$

$$UR = \frac{U}{LF} \times 100$$

where:

- U is the number of unemployed people
- UR is the unemployment rate
- LF is the size of the labour force
- J is the number of people in jobs (employed persons).

EXAMPLE

In Australia in August 2010 there were 11 258 200 employed persons and the labour force was 11 870 800. Using our two formulas, we get:

$$U = 11\,870\,800 - 11\,258\,200 = 612\,600 \text{ unemployed persons}$$

$$UR = \frac{612\,600}{11\,870\,800} \times 100 = 0.0516 \times 100 = 5.2 \text{ per cent}$$

Note that the unemployment rate is a proportion of the labour force, not a proportion of the population. As an economic indicator, the unemployment rate gives us a picture of what proportion of those eligible and willing to work are unable to do so.

The third direct measure reminds us that labour markets are not static—they are continually changing, with inflows and outflows of labour into and from the pool of unemployed. Inflows into the workforce consist of people who have quit a job voluntarily and are looking for another, people who have been sacked or retrenched, school leavers, immigrants and other new entrants into the workforce, and people who have decided to re-enter the workforce after a period absent from it.

The formula for measuring inflows and outflows is:

$$U_t = U_{ut-1} + I_t - O_t$$

where:

- U_t is the end of period unemployment level
- I_t and O_t are respectively inflows and outflows over the period t.

EXAMPLE

Suppose at the end of the previous year total unemployment was 767 000, inflows into the workforce during the current year totalled 50 000 and outflows totalled 20 000. The number of unemployed at the end of the current year will be:

$$U_t = 767\,000 + 50\,000 - 20\,000 = 797\,000$$

INDIRECT MEASURES

The **labour force participation rate**, an indirect measure of unemployment in the economy, measures the proportion of the working age population either 'employed' or 'actively looking for work'. The participation rate is calculated as follows:

$$LFPR = \frac{J + PLW}{CV_{15+}}$$

labour force participation rate *for any group, the labour force expressed as a percentage of the civilian population in the same group*

where:

- *LFPR* is the labour force participation rate
- *J* is the number of people in jobs (employed persons)
- *PLW* is the number of persons looking for full-time and part-time work
- CV_{15+} is number of the civilian population aged 15 and over.

EXAMPLE

In the above calculation, in August 2010 the number of employed persons in Australia was 11 258 200. At the same date the 'number looking for work' (the total of those looking for full-time or part-time work) was 434 400. The civilian population aged 15 and over was 17 878 500. We can calculate the labour force participation rate as follows:

$$LFPR = \frac{11\ 258\ 200 + 434\ 400}{17\ 878\ 500} = \frac{11\ 692\ 600}{17\ 878\ 500} \times 100$$

$$= 0.654 \times 100$$

$$= 65.4 \text{ per cent}$$

The participation rate tends to increase when job opportunities increase and vice versa, reflecting job seekers' confidence. For instance, in late 1992 and early 1993 the unemployment rate was at record highs of 11 per cent; the participation rate reached a low of 62 per cent in April 1993. By comparison, in August 2008 the unemployment rate was only 4.2 per cent and the participation rate was 65.5 per cent.

The goal of full employment

As we will discuss in Chapter 21, one of the fundamental macroeconomic objectives of any responsible government is that of 'full employment'. Full employment does not mean 'zero per cent unemployment'. This is because both frictional and structural unemployment are present even at the best of times.

Specifically, the full-employment rate, sometimes called 'the natural rate of unemployment' is equal to the total of the rates of frictional and structural unemployment.

In June 2010 a senior Treasury officer, David Gruen, told a Senate committee it was 'a long-standing practice' to regard full employment as 5 per cent, although there was 'a reasonable band of uncertainty around that number'.

Full employment refers to the lowest *sustainable* rate of unemployment. That is, the lowest rate to which unemployment can fall before shortages of labour lead to excessive wage increases and start pushing up the rate of inflation.

In economics jargon, this is the 'non-accelerating inflation rate of unemployment' (NAIRU) employment.

One has to note that in the 1950s, 1960s and early 1970s full employment (and the NAIRU) was regarded as an unemployment rate no higher than 2 per cent.

HOW ABS DATA CAN BE DOWNRIGHT MISLEADING

Paul Kerin of the Melbourne Business School noted in *The Weekend Australian* how ABS media reports on economic statistics can be downright misleading.

For instance, in the 11 March 2010 media release about the Australian labour force in February 2010, the ABS stated that 'the seasonally adjusted unemployment rate rose 0.1 percentage points' (e.g. from 5.4 per cent to 5.5 per cent). Resulting media headlines included 'Unemployment up as part time jobs fall' (ABC) and 'Employment reality check' (Crikey). At the same time, the ABS 'trend' data for the same month indicated that the Australian unemployment rate went down from 5.6 per cent to 5.5 per cent.

The problem is that ABS reports produce three sets of statistics: original, seasonally adjusted and trend. ABS knows that 'seasonally adjusted data' are inferior to 'trend' movements as indicators of what is really happening, and are often not statistically significant anyway.

Seasonally adjusted statistics are better than original (raw) statistics because they adjust for seasonal patterns, such as school leavers entering the job market after the school year ends. But 'irregular' influences make seasonally adjusted monthly statistics notoriously volatile and unreliable.

The ABS's 'Guide to Interpreting Time Series' recognises that in seasonally adjusted data, irregular variation generally dominates period-to-period movements, obscuring the trend, and warns of the adverse impact that reliance on seasonally adjusted movements may have for business decisions, policy advice, commentary and analysis.

It recommends that those using its statistics for the purpose of monitoring underlying trends should pay attention to its explicit trend estimates, which apply statistical techniques to minimise the impact of irregular influences. Because they 'represent the fundamental, or underlying behaviour of the series' the guide indicates they are generally more suitable for most business planning decisions and policy advice and, as a result, ABS reports emphasise trend rather than seasonally adjusted series.

Although the 11 March labour force media release stated that 'the seasonally adjusted unemployment rate rose 0.1 percentage point', it did not mention that the more reliable and relevant trend unemployment rate fell by 0.1 percentage point. And it did not indicate that the seasonally adjusted movement was not statistically significant.

However, on 11 March, the ABS reported that the seasonally adjusted number of unemployed rose 10 700, but not that this was statistically insignificant, or that trend unemployment was down 8300. It reported that seasonally adjusted part-time employment fell by 11 000 (which the ABC used in its reports), but not that this was statistically insignificant, or that the trend was up 14 900.

Therefore, business people, economic researchers and economics students, be critical and selective about ABS reports and look as much as possible for 'trend' estimates.

UNEMPLOYMENT CHANGES

Unemployment was a major problem for Australia's economy throughout the last quarter of the 20th century. After a low annual average of 1.9 per cent over 1940–41 to 1973–74, Australia's unemployment rate has climbed to an average of 7.6 per cent over 1974–75 to 1999–2000.

Figure 11.1 shows the most important changes in the ABS trend estimate of the underemployment rate for persons from August 2000 to August 2010. Over the 10-year period the trend rate reached a first peak of 7.4 per cent in November 2001 (up from 6.6 per cent in August 2000), then it reached a low of 5.9 per cent in May 2008. The GFC brought the unemployment trend rate up again to 7.9 per cent in August 2009. The trend fell again thereafter in line with increased Australian economic activity.

Figure 11.1 shows also that unemployment trend rates for males tend to be consistently below the corresponding rates for female employees. Over the 10-year period, the gap between female unemployment rates and those for male employees has only slightly declined from 3.7 percentage points in August 2000 to 3.5 percentage points in August 2010.

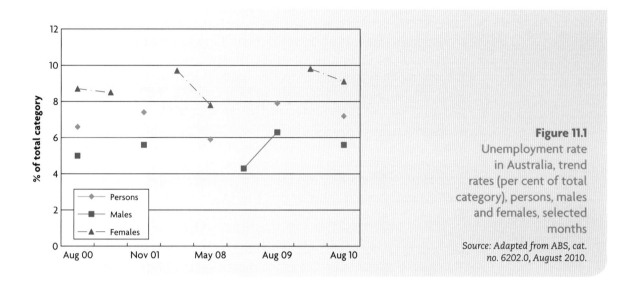

Figure 11.1
Unemployment rate in Australia, trend rates (per cent of total category), persons, males and females, selected months
Source: Adapted from ABS, cat. no. 6202.0, August 2010.

Although the unemployment rate over the 2000s has generally trended down, it is still regarded by experts as the most significant economic and social problem facing policy makers in Australia in the new millennium.[2]

A clear trend in Australian employment is the growth in the share of part-time jobs. Figure 11.2 indicates that while total employment in Australia has increased by around 2 million persons between 1999 and 2009, part-time employment has increased its share of total employment from around 26 per cent to almost 31 per cent. (Part-time employment's share was under 23 per cent in 1991.)

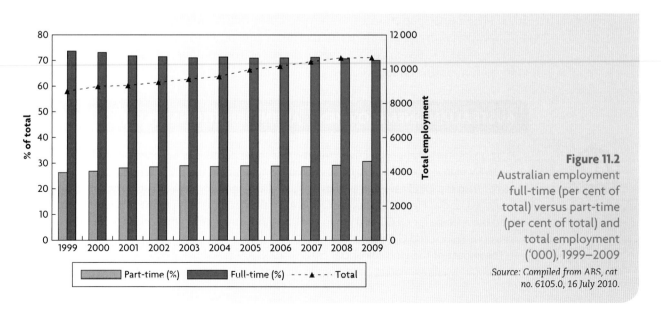

Figure 11.2
Australian employment full-time (per cent of total) versus part-time (per cent of total) and total employment ('000), 1999–2009
Source: Compiled from ABS, cat. no. 6105.0, 16 July 2010.

Research on the Australian labour market has revealed a number of other key characteristics:

- A higher proportion of the total unemployed is now concentrated in the middle-aged groups: middle-aged unemployment accounts for a significantly higher proportion of the unemployed than youth unemployment.
- Cyclical changes have involved sharp increases in the rate of unemployment, whereas reductions in the rate of unemployment have taken much longer to occur.
- As in other OECD countries over recent decades, a most striking change in the Australian labour force was the dramatic increase in female labour force participation. Between May 1970 and August 2008, the seasonally adjusted female participation rate increased from 37.9 per cent to 58.7 per cent. This increase is associated with an increase in part-time work.
- Youth unemployment rates are higher than in the late 1980s. In December 2003, 24.2 per cent of females and 17.6 per cent of males aged 15 to 19 not in education were looking for work. These figures were lower than the peak figure of 37 per cent for the female rate in 1993–94 and the 30 per cent for the male rate in 1992–93, but moderately higher than those in 1989–90 (18 per cent for females and 14 per cent for males). The ABS seasonally adjusted unemployment rate for August 2009 was 11.9 per cent for 15 to 24-year-olds (includes young people in education looking for work). Young people tend to be one of the most affected groups in economic slow-downs and this was also the case in the GFC. The underemployment rate for young people (aged 15–24), jumped from 11.0 per cent in May 2008 to 14.8 per cent in August 2009 (with young females recording above average rates).
- As explained above, much of Australian unemployment consists of people who will be unemployed for quite a long time.

In relation to the prospects of the Australian labour force market, recent studies indicate that the age profile of the working population is undergoing a shift towards a greater proportion of older workers and a relative scarcity of new entrants. The labour force aged 60 to 64 is anticipated to almost double by 2016, compared to 1998. The overall labour force participation rate is projected to decline to 60.6 per cent in 2016, from around 64 per cent in 2003. Male participation rates are projected to fall for all age groups except those 60 years and over. In contrast, female participation is projected to increase in all age groups, except those aged 15 to 19 years and 65 years and over. (See more on demographic prospects in the final section of this chapter.)

AUSTRALIAN UNEMPLOYMENT: AN INTERNATIONAL PERSPECTIVE

LINK TO INTERNATIONAL ECONOMY

From an international perspective, over the last three decades or so, unemployment has been relatively high in Australia. Australia's unemployment rate in the 1990s tended to be somewhat higher than the OECD average. However, Australia's unemployment situation has gradually improved, and as Figure 11.3 shows in 2008 Australia fared better in terms of unemployment rate than the average for OECD as a group and corresponding rates in the United States, the United Kingdom, France and Germany.

The impact of the global financial crisis of 2008–09 saw slowing economic growth and deteriorating labour market conditions in most countries around the world. Among the

LEARNING OBJECTIVE 4
Compare the unemployment rates in Australia and other countries

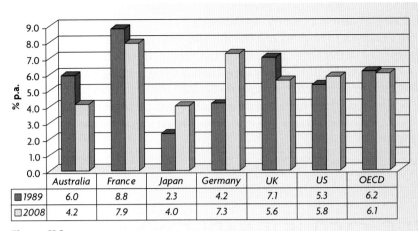

	Australia	France	Japan	Germany	UK	US	OECD
■ 1989	6.0	8.8	2.3	4.2	7.1	5.3	6.2
□ 2008	4.2	7.9	4.0	7.3	5.6	5.8	6.1

Figure 11.3

Average annual unemployment rate, Australia, OECD, selected OECD member economies 1989–2008, per cent per annum

Source: Adapted from Organisation for Economic Cooperation and Development, Factbook 2010: Economic and Social Statistics.

countries of the Organisation for Economic Cooperation and Development (OECD), the average unemployment rate rose from 6.1 per cent in 2008 to 8.3 per cent in 2009. Australia was one of the least affected countries in the OECD over this period, with the harmonised unemployment rate rising just 1.3 percentage points to 5.6 per cent. This was less than the rises experienced in Canada (2.1), New Zealand (2.2), the United Kingdom (2.0) and the United States (3.5).

However, the OECD's *Employment Outlook* of May 2010 reported that in 2009, 21 per cent of Australians in the prime working age group (25 to 54) were unemployed or outside the labour force. Of the 27 OECD countries the IMF terms 'advanced', Australia ranked 20th on that key indicator. Switzerland was top, with only 13 per cent of its prime working age people not in jobs.

East Asian countries such as Malaysia, Thailand and Indonesia, which have experienced a long period of strong economic growth and shortages of skilled workers, are now facing a serious unemployment problem in the wake of the Asian financial crisis and the GFC (see Table 11.1).

Table 11.1   **Unemployment rates in selected developing Asian countries, 2000, 2009 (per cent)**

	2000	2009
China	3.1	4.3
Indonesia	7.2	8.1
Malaysia	3.0	3.7
Thailand	3.6	1.5
Sri Lanka	7.6	5.6
Philippines	11.2	7.5

Source: Adapted from Asian Development Bank, <www.adb.org/statistics>, accessed 1 October 2010.

continued ↘

continued

As growing unemployment in a country like Indonesia is likely to generate increased illegal migration of the workforce to neighbouring countries like Malaysia and Singapore, Australia may expect to receive some of this wave of desperate boat people. There is another negative effect of the crisis for Australia. Many Australians who have been working or doing business in Indonesia for many years have been forced to return to Australia because of the unstable political and economic conditions in Indonesia, putting a further strain on Australia's social security system. That is why a normalisation of the situation in East Asia is of direct interest to Australia and to the world economy as a whole.

LEARNING OBJECTIVE 5
Suggest the main causes and effects of unemployment

CAUSES OF UNEMPLOYMENT

According to Keynes, unemployment is fundamentally caused by lower than optimum aggregate demand. With a lower demand for goods and services, businesses require fewer staff to satisfy that demand. This can have the effect of reducing demand even more, as unemployed people do not spend as much as employed people. Private investment will decline as well. Obviously, this cause is generally referred to as so-called cyclical unemployment.

Keynes argued that it was the role of government to stimulate aggregate demand by spending money on government services and infrastructure. This 'pump-priming' expenditure would stimulate the demand–employment spiral and lead to greater employment, which in turn would lead to further increases in aggregate demand. We have to note that contractionary (e.g. anti-inflationary) government policies may also contribute, at least in the short term, to higher unemployment. For instance, a Budget surplus reduces aggregate demand, and high interest rates reduce the incentive to consume.

Among the non-cyclical unemployment in modern economies, a particular concern is represented by structural unemployment, which, as explained above, is unrelated to the business cycle. OECD studies show that, in some countries, structural unemployment has risen since 1990 from levels that were already high. This group of countries includes three of the major European Union members, Germany, France and Italy. In other countries, such as the United Kingdom, Ireland, the Netherlands and New Zealand, falls in structural unemployment either began or continued.

EXPLANATIONS FOR STRUCTURAL UNEMPLOYMENT

There are two standard economic explanations for structural unemployment. As explained above, structural unemployment is mainly due to fundamental changes in the structure of labour demand—specifically, the kind of jobs that the economy offers. Technological change, the development of new industries and the demise of old ones, globalisation and geographic shifts in manufacturing, all create new kinds of jobs and cause many old ones to disappear. Most often the new industries are more capital-intensive and require sophisticated technological skills. The result is that less-educated workers cannot compete and so they join the ranks of the structurally unemployed. Demand for labour is also diminished by rising labour costs (e.g. higher minimum wages, mandated employer contributions), with the result that employers tend to hire fewer staff.

DOES TECHNOLOGY GENERATE INCREASED UNEMPLOYMENT?

LINK TO
BUSINESS

A difficult question. The Luddites during the Industrial Revolution believed so, and their protest against technological change went as far as the destruction of new equipment.

The well-known economist Wasili Leontief expressed his concern about the undesirable distributional effects of technological advancements across income groups.

However, in their 1986 research, R.H. Mabry and A.D. Sharplin concluded that: 'Those who argue that the production of more goods and services with fewer inputs will produce long-term unemployment are wrong—and, thankfully, few in number.'

Nathan Rosenberg, a specialist in the history of technology, pointed out in a testimony before a United States congressional committee on technology and unemployment that: 'Our present employment difficulties lie elsewhere than in the sphere of technology-generated unemployment.'

Looking at ABS employment statistics in a couple of 'technology-heavy' Australian sectors we find that:

- Employment in the Australian media technology and telecommunications industry increased from 222 600 in February 1990 to 251 600 in February 2007.
- Employment in the Australian financial and insurance services industry increased from 365 200 in February 1990 to 408 600 in May 2007.

Certainly, the technology–employment relationship has to be looked at with due care, but everyone would agree that the return to cottage industries is no viable solution for the future of employment.

A second explanation for structural unemployment blames social welfare programs for eroding the incentives to find a new job quickly. In Europe, for example, where unemployment is higher than in the United States, unemployment assistance lasts for many months and pays a large percentage of the worker's last salary, so that the lifestyle of the unemployed is not immediately affected. Assistance with health insurance, housing and food makes the newly unemployed less enthusiastic in looking for a job.

The issues are similar in Australia. The Howard Government argued that the dramatic increase in labour-market spending in the first half of the 1990s had simply not been cost-effective. Their approach emphasised two strategies: helping the unemployed in their job search; and tightening social security assistance to encourage the unemployed to increase their efforts to find work. The general outcome has been good, with the unemployment rate going under 6 per cent in 2004.

Explanations for the growing unemployment in East Asian countries are complex and cannot be discussed here in detail. It appears that some weak economic fundamentals—in particular, large account deficits, high dependence on short-term capital inflows, and increasing evidence of rising levels of non-performing loans, to some degree associated with overbuilding—adversely affected the value of their currencies and business confidence. Thus those economies were vulnerable to a reversal of capital inflows. Foreign investment has slowed down in most affected economies and 'disinvestment' has even suspended the implementation of a number of mega-projects, with the net result of a lower demand for labour.

The Phillips curve: The trade-off between unemployment and inflation

Following pioneering empirical work in the late 1950s, a British economist, A.W. Phillips, identified an inverse statistical relationship between the unemployment rate and the rate of inflation; that is, high rates of inflation are accompanied by low rates of unemployment, and vice versa. The graphical representation of this relationship is known as the Phillips curve.

Figure 11.4(a) shows what the expected relationship should look like. Figure 11.4(b) shows the relationship between the two economic indicators for the 1961 to 1969 period. The line generalising on the data portrays the expected inverse relationship.

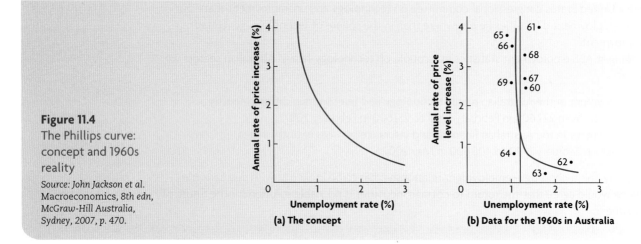

Figure 11.4
The Phillips curve: concept and 1960s reality

Source: John Jackson et al. Macroeconomics, 8th edn, McGraw-Hill Australia, Sydney, 2007, p. 470.

(a) The concept

(b) Data for the 1960s in Australia

On the basis of this empirical evidence, economists believed that a stable, predictable trade-off existed between unemployment and inflation. Using the Phillips curve, economists came to believe that they could advise governments on the opportunity cost—in terms of inflation—of achieving any employment target. The concept seemed to provide governments that were experiencing considerable unemployment with a low level of inflation as a sort of consolation prize, which might represent a solid basis for economic recovery and higher employment.

However, events of the 1970s and early 1980s were clearly at odds with the trade-off between the inflation rate and the unemployment rate that the Phillips curve embodied.

Following the international energy crisis of the early 1970s, caused by five big hikes in OPEC's crude oil prices, many countries, including Australia, experienced both more inflation and more unemployment. This is known as 'stagflation', a combination of 'stagnation' and 'inflation'.

Stagflation put in doubt the credibility of the Phillips curve trade-off. Later statistics showed that a trade-off relationship still existed, but with the entire curve moving steadily to the top right corner of the diagram (Figure 11.5).

The shift of the Phillips curve to the right would show a less desirable position of the curve, where the trade-off occurs at much higher rates of inflation and levels of unemployment. More traditional economists recommend that incomes policies (such as wage controls) be used to counter the trend. But monetarists argue that they will not work and that there is really no trade-off relationship after all. According to the latter, the true long-term relationship between unemployment and the rate of inflation lies along a vertical line, on which no trade-offs are possible.

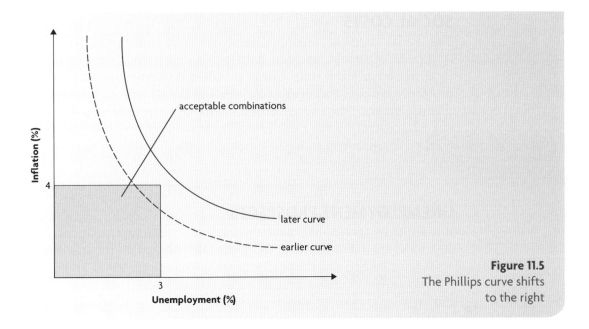

Figure 11.5
The Phillips curve shifts
to the right

EFFECTS OF UNEMPLOYMENT

Unemployment is associated with a number of economic and social costs. First, as explained in Chapter 1, unemployment represents an under-utilisation of a major resource, the labour force, resulting in a loss of potential production and income.

ECONOMIC COSTS: GDP GAP

The economic cost of unemployment to society is called the GDP gap. This can be calculated as the difference between the potential GDP (what GDP would be if the economy were 'fully' employed) and the actual GDP.

Therefore the GDP gap is the dollar value of final goods and services not produced because there is unemployment. In other words, the GDP gap may be regarded as the opportunity cost of unemployment. As a rule of thumb, the GDP gap widens when the unemployment rate rises and narrows when the unemployment rate falls.

Unemployment also exerts a considerable impact on the expenditures and revenues of both state and federal governments. Unemployment represents an additional cost to the government budget (unemployment benefits, labour-market programs), while taxation revenue (income, sales and company tax) is reduced as a result of lower levels of income, spending, sales and profits. Governments may be forced to bring down larger deficit budgets in order to stimulate demand and thus incur a corresponding increase in public indebtedness.

Unemployment brings about a loss of income and hence widens the gap in terms of income distribution. It affects mostly older people and teenagers. For instance, in July 2003 teenagers had an unemployment rate of 13 per cent and a participation rate of 57 per cent, compared with an adult unemployment rate of 6 per cent and participation rate of 80 per cent. In general, unemployment has a negative impact on the standards of living of the population.

SOCIAL COSTS

The social costs of unemployment are also substantial. Unemployment can cause sociopolitical unrest, as seen with marches by the unemployed in France and street riots in Indonesia. Crime rates, suicides, domestic violence, family break-up, health problems, poverty, and drug and alcohol abuse all tend to increase during periods of high unemployment. Studies have linked unemployment to mental illnesses such as depression and to increasing use of health services. These in themselves impose a greater cost burden on the community in terms of funding health and welfare services, law enforcement and other community services.

UNEMPLOYMENT PROSPECTS

It is generally agreed that the main reason for the sharp rise in unemployment in the early 1990s was the fall in demand for goods and services. In the late 1980s, for instance, when aggregate demand was strong, the unemployment rate fell to 5.8 per cent.

It has been calculated that if the workforce keeps growing at around 1.5 per cent and productivity growth measures about 1.5 to 2.0 per cent, annual average GDP growth of at least 3.5 per cent will be required just to stop unemployment rising again. If unemployment is to trend downwards, growth would have to rise to 4 per cent. It seems that the Howard Government's objective for real GDP growth set in December 1997 at 4 per cent per annum, if achieved and sustained, might bring unemployment back to lower historical levels (see also Chapter 25).

Of course for such economic growth to be sustainable, it will have to be accompanied by solid microeconomic reform in a number of sectors of the Australian economy, including the labour market. Otherwise, we will have a repetition of the boom–bust cycle of the late 1980s and early 1990s.

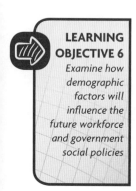

LEARNING OBJECTIVE 6

Examine how demographic factors will influence the future workforce and government social policies

DEMOGRAPHIC PROSPECTS AND THE LABOUR FORCE

It is obvious that the future size and composition of the Australian labour force is very much determined by demographic factors. Basically, changes in population distribution and composition are the result of the interaction of the three components of population change: births, deaths and migration.

Population change (PC) may be simply expressed by the following equation:

$$PC = B - D +/- NM$$

where:
B = number of births
D = number of deaths
NM = net migration.

The difference between the number of births and deaths represents the natural growth of population, while net migration is the general balance of the inward and outward movement of population in a given period (normally one year).

According to the ABS, **net overseas migration** is the addition (or loss) to the population of Australia arising from the difference between those leaving permanently or on a long-term basis, and those arriving permanently or long term. The annual net overseas migration figure is also adjusted to account for the estimated number of people who change their travel intentions, for example, people who come to Australia intending to stay short term (less than 12 months) but who decide to stay longer, or vice versa. These people are called 'category jumpers'.

Australian demographic data indicates that Australia will experience further ageing of its population over the next four decades due to the decline in the total fertility rate (TFR) of Australian women and increased population longevity.

Australia's net overseas migration has some offsetting effect on the rate of Australia's population ageing. Net migration tends to fall during economic downturns, partly because permanent and long-term temporary departures increase, and partly because governments have adjusted migrant intakes.

In February 2010 the Federal Treasury issued the *2010 Intergenerational Report, Australia to 2050: Future Challenges*. The report shows that even with slower population growth the total Australian population is projected to be 35.9 million people by 2050.

A few findings of the report:

- By 2050, nearly one-quarter of Australia's population will be aged 65 and over, compared with 13 per cent in 2010.
- The proportion of working age people will continue to decline. This means that there will be only 2.7 people of working age for every person aged 65 and over, compared with five people in 2010 and 7.5 in 1970. (If this occurs, it will be important for Australia to make the most of its labour force by increasing the rates of participation in employment, and also increasing the levels of participation of those who are currently working and are willing and able to work more hours.)
- Ageing and health pressures are projected to result in an increase in total government spending from 22.4 per cent of GDP in 2015–16 to 27.1 per cent of GDP by 2049–50. As a consequence, spending is projected to exceed revenue by 2¾ per cent of GDP in 40 years' time.
- Australia must dramatically raise productivity if it is to meet the challenges of an ageing population.

In response to these challenges, the Federal Government launched in February 2010 a $43.4 million Productive Ageing Package to provide training support to older Australians planning to stay in the workforce.

The increase in the level of taxes normally required by such demographic developments will not be a popular solution for any future Australian Government. Taxation will probably provide only part of the solution.

net overseas migration
the addition (or loss) to the population of Australia arising from the difference between those leaving permanently or on a long-term basis, and those arriving permanently or long term

SUMMARY

1. In this chapter, we have looked at the labour force in Australia from the point of view of both employment and unemployment. The labour force participation rate is compared with the unemployment rate, the point being that both statistics should be interpreted together to get an accurate picture of the situation in the labour force at any one time. This has given us perspectives on what has been achieved in this important economic indicator and where the failures have been.

2. Until 30 April 1998, both agencies involved in unemployment statistics (ABS and CES) were federal agencies, and unemployed people were assisted by the Commonwealth Employment Service (CES) and the Department of Social Security. Since then a new regime, incorporating Centrelink and Job Network/Job Services Australia, commercialises the task of finding work for the unemployed, with the focus on results.

3. The three broad types of unemployment are cyclical, non-cyclical and long term. Cyclical unemployment is caused by a deficiency in the level of aggregate demand. Non-cyclical unemployment can be frictional, structural or seasonal. Long-term (hard-core) unemployment is a growing problem in Australia.

4. From an international perspective, Australia has a middle ranking among OECD members in terms of unemployment rates. A major concern is that 21 per cent of Australians in the prime working age group (25 to 54) were unemployed in 2009 or outside the labour force. The rapid globalisation of East Asia has made the goal of maintaining full employment a more complex undertaking.

5. The main cause of unemployment appears to be a deficient demand for goods and services. Other causes include: technological change (contributing to structural unemployment), increased labour costs, lack of private investment, and anti-inflationary economic policies.

6. There are economic and sociopolitical effects of unemployment. The main economic effect is the wastage of labour resources. Other economic effects include: loss of income for many individuals, a widening gap in terms of income distribution, adverse effects on the Federal Budget and lower living standards. The non-economic effects include sociopolitical unrest, personal health problems, plummeting of morale and family disintegration.

7. A steady reduction in the unemployment rate will depend very much on a sustainable economic growth of around 4 per cent per annum.

8. The 'ageing' of Australia's population will contribute to a declining proportion in total population of the working age group (15 to 64) and to a tripling in the proportion of the 85-plus age group, which will raise further challenges to government policies.

REFERENCES

1. In statistical terms, full employment is defined in terms of a zone where relatively few people are unemployed. The full employment zone in Australia in the 1950s and 1960s was 1 to 2 per cent. In the 1990s it was reasonable to expect governments to attain a level of 4 to 5 per cent.

2. R. Dornbusch, P. Bodman, M. Crosby, S. Fischer and R Startz, *Macroeconomics*, McGraw-Hill Australia, Sydney, 2002, p. 152.

REVIEW QUESTIONS

1. Define unemployment and comment on key points in the definition.

2. Explain and justify the official sources of data on unemployment in Australia.

3. What are the main changes in unemployment in the 2000s?

4. What effect has part-time work had on employment levels in Australia in recent years?

5. Explain recent trends in structural unemployment in OECD countries.
6. What are the main costs of unemployment?
7. Discuss the likely impact of demographic changes in Australia on Australia's labour force and on government policy. What measures, other than tax increases, could the government adopt without affecting the standard of social welfare?
8. In Australia, who is eligible to receive unemployment benefits? Why?
9. What are the limitations of the unemployment records of ABS and Centrelink?
10. What is the difference between the unemployment rate and the labour force participation rate?
11. Explain how an increase in the number of people employed can actually worsen the unemployment rate.
12. What is cyclical unemployment? How is it different from non-cyclical unemployment?
13. Differentiate between frictional and structural unemployment.
14. Differentiate between hidden unemployment and underemployment.
15. How does Australia's unemployment situation rate among OECD countries? Discuss.
16. What is the likely impact of the East Asian slow-down on Australia's economy?
17. What is the opportunity cost of unemployment?
18. What measures can be taken to reduce structural unemployment?
19. What happened in the 1970s and early 1980s to render the Phillips curve theory less useful?
20. What is the likely impact of an average long-term economic growth rate of 4 per cent per annum on Australia's unemployment as a whole and on the types of unemployment (cyclical, structural, 'hard-core')?

APPLIED QUESTIONS AND EXERCISES

1. From the main indicators of the Australian labour force market in Table 11.2, calculate the following:
   (a) the unemployment rate
   (b) the number of persons 'looking for work'.
2. Collect annual data about Australia's unemployment rate and inflation (CPI) rate for the period 2000 to 2010. Draw a Phillips curve based on the data, plotting the CPI on the vertical axis and the unemployment rate on the horizontal axis. Does the Phillips curve for the above period show a trade-off between inflation and unemployment? Discuss.

Table 11.2: Australian labour market, leading indicators

Civilian population aged 15 and over	15 930 700
Labour force	9 672 200
Participation rate (per cent)	63.6
Part-time employed persons	2 736 000
Full-time employed persons	6 936 200
Unemployed	571 700

Source: Adapted from the Australian Bureau of Statistics, Labour Force, Australia, cat. no. 6202.0, June 2004.

3. Table 11.3 shows international comparisons of unemployment over about four decades in Australia and four other OECD countries.
   (a) Which of the five nations has achieved the best performance over the whole period and which one has shown the worst performance? Discuss the possible reasons.
   (b) Plot column graphs showing Australia's unemployment rate in the 1990s and the 2000s against the other four nations. Label all data and axes and head the graph appropriately.
   (c) Suggest three possible reasons for the marked increase in average unemployment rates in all five nations since the 1960s.

Table 11.3: Comparative unemployment rates (per cent) in Australia, United States, United Kingdom, Japan and France, 1960s–2000s

PERIOD	AUSTRALIA	UNITED STATES	UNITED KINGDOM	JAPAN	FRANCE
1960s	1.8	4.6	1.6	1.3	1.5
1970s	3.6	6.1	3.5	1.7	3.8
1980s	6.1	7.3	9.4	2.5	9.0
1990s	8.6	5.5	7.8	3.3	10.9
2000–09	5.5	5.5	5.4	4.7	8.8

Source: Compiled from OECD, Economic Outlook, various editions.

Chapter 12

Inflation

LEARNING OBJECTIVES

After studying this chapter, you will be able to:

1. define inflation
2. explain some of the consequences of inflation
3. explain some of the causes of inflation and show that inflation is an economic indicator of fluctuations in the economy
4. explain how inflation is measured by the Australian Bureau of Statistics
5. discuss the use of the consumer price index to express real monetary values in the economy
6. explain the indicators of consumer price inflation used by the Reserve Bank
7. describe inflation changes in previous economic periods and suggest reasons for those changes
8. discuss the effects on the economy of differences between Australia's inflation rate and those of its major trading partners.

INTRODUCTION

In Australia during the 1950s and 1960s, prices were relatively stable and, apart from some brief 'hiccups', the inflation rate was low. However, in the early 1970s inflation rates rose to high levels as a result of sharp rises in oil prices and large wage increases and continued at high levels into the 1980s. Figure 12.1 illustrates that over the period from 1998 to 2007 inflation trended upward. The global financial crisis (GFC) in 2008 brought about a dramatic reduction in both the rate and trend. Note that the upper limit of the Reserve Bank's target range for underlying inflation is 3 per cent.

Figure 12.1 illustrates the consumer price index from 1994 to 2010.

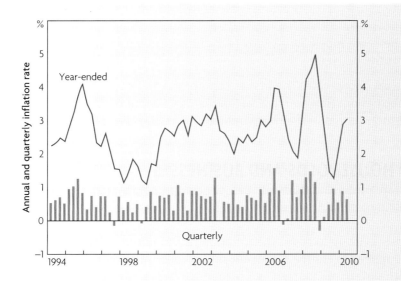

Figure 12.1
Consumer price index, Australia, 1994–2010, per cent change per annum
Note: RBA estimate excludes interest charges prior to September quarter 1998 and is adjusted for the tax changes associated with the new tax system. Source: Reserve Bank, Statement on Monetary Policy, August 2010, Graph 73, <www.rba.gov.au/publications/smp/2010/aug/pdf/0810.pdf>, p 49, accessed 15 October 2010. Data supplied by Australian Bureau of Statistics and Reserve Bank of Australia.

One of the objectives of economic policy is the maintenance of relatively low rates of inflation. As we shall see, inflation can lead to social and political problems as well as economic problems.

inflation
a persistent increase in the general level of prices

WHAT IS INFLATION?

LEARNING OBJECTIVE 1
Define inflation

Inflation can be defined as a persistent increase in the general level of prices.

'Persistent' alerts us to one important feature of inflation: it occurs over several periods. 'General' alerts us to another: inflation occurs throughout the economy, with the prices of many items rising in the same period. Inflation reduces the value of money because each dollar buys less. The opposite of inflation is **deflation** when prices are falling. Deflation is usually associated with recessions or depressions when demand is very weak. An example of

deflation
a situation of falls in the general price level

persistent deflation is Japan where prices have fallen or not changed very much throughout most of the 1990s and 2000s.

Another situation is **stagflation** when inflation is combined with rising unemployment. Australia was in this situation in the late 1970s reflecting rigidities in the social and economic structure. The economic reforms from 1983 produced a more competitive and efficient economy without the problems of deflation or stagflation.

ANNUAL RATE

A brief note is appropriate here to avoid confusion about inflation rate periods. Australia's consumer price inflation rate is announced quarterly. That rate indicates that prices have risen by the amount of the inflation rate on those prices three months ago. To derive an annual inflation rate, there are two approaches:

1. multiply the figure for the previous quarter by four, on the grounds that it represents the previous three
2. compare the latest index figure with 12 months earlier and derive the percentage change over the full year.

Both methods are acceptable. The first is sometimes preferred because it is based on the most recent information. However, the second is more accurate because it uses the actual change from 12 months ago to the latest quarter.

EFFECTS ON HOUSEHOLDS AND BUSINESSES

For households, an annual inflation rate of 5 per cent means that an item that cost $1 a year ago is now likely to cost $1.05. A car that cost $20 000 a year ago is now likely to cost $21 000, an increase of 5 per cent.

Note the phrase 'is likely to cost'. The inflation rate is not automatic; nor is it binding. No one compels a supplier to charge 5 per cent more when inflation is 5 per cent. The inflation rate is an after-the-event measure. It is a measure of what has happened to prices after the period in which those prices were charged for the goods or services.

Price is determined by buyers and sellers. The inflation rate may be 5 per cent, but the price on a particular item may be 7 per cent higher than last year. Moreover, on another item in the same store, the price may be only 2 per cent higher than last year. The inflation rate is very much an average increase in prices.

Business is also affected by inflation. Here, we must think in bigger amounts. Let's say the price of a piece of machinery was $100 000 a year ago. Annual inflation of 5 per cent suggests that it will now be priced at $105 000. The business has to find an extra $5 000 in addition to what it would have paid a year ago, if it wishes to purchase the equipment now.

INCREASED COSTS

Given that many pieces of equipment cost a great deal more than the $100 000 used in our example, you can see how great an impact inflation has on a business. Assume that Qantas, Australia's international airline, pays $400 million for one jumbo jet. Admittedly, jumbo jets are made in the United States, so we are not talking domestic prices here. But assume that world inflation is 5 per cent. In these circumstances, Qantas would find its jumbo jet could cost $420 million one year later—$20 million more. If the value of the Australian dollar (AUD) falls against the United States dollar (USD) the cost of the plane, in Australian dollars, will be even higher. On the other hand if the AUD increases against the USD, then the cost will be lower in AUD (see Chapter 19).

Nor are equipment purchases the only issue here. General cost pressures, which rising prices represent, feed claims for higher wages. So, business not only faces increases in costs of materials and equipment; in an inflationary economy it also has to deal with rising wage costs.

The government sector is not immune from increased purchasing costs in an inflationary situation either. Governments in Australia spend billions of dollars a year on purchases of equipment and materials. If the inflation rate is 5 per cent, and it applies generally, a government's inflation bill is enormous. If the expenditure is $10 billion, the cost of total deferral for 12 months at 5 per cent annual inflation is $500 million.

CONSEQUENCES OF HIGH LEVELS OF INFLATION

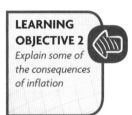

LEARNING OBJECTIVE 2
Explain some of the consequences of inflation

Earlier we noted that high rates of inflation can have serious social, economic and political consequences. Some of the effects of rapid inflation are:

- It can penalise people on fixed incomes, like pensioners and self-funded retirees, because their income does not rise as rapidly as prices, so they are able to buy fewer goods and services.
- Inflation tends to redistribute income from low-income groups to higher-income groups because low-income groups have fewer real assets like property, which might rise in price, and are in jobs where it is difficult to get a pay rise to help offset the effects of inflation.
- People lose faith in currency as a store of value and often borrow as much as possible to invest in 'real' assets like gold, houses and antiques, the price of which tends to rise faster than the general inflation rate.
- Forecasts of the rate of return on capital investments become unreliable, and this makes businesses unwilling to undertake long-term projects. Because of this, future living standards may not be as high as they would have been.
- If the rate of inflation in Australia is higher than those of our major trading partners, our ability to compete in world markets is damaged.
- High inflation rates generate concern in the Reserve Bank for the reasons set out above and lead to higher interest rates.

Different groups in society have different abilities to protect themselves from the effects of inflation. Powerful entities—trade unions, large companies, wealthy individuals—may be able to increase their share of national income at the expense of weaker groups—pensioners, the unemployed, and other groups that depend on social welfare. Thus, persistently high inflation can threaten social and political stability.

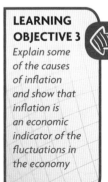

LEARNING OBJECTIVE 3
Explain some of the causes of inflation and show that inflation is an economic indicator of the fluctuations in the economy

CAUSES OF INFLATION

There is no single cause of inflation. Rather, at any given time, a number of factors interact to cause inflation. For example, a fall in the exchange rate may lead to an increase in the price of imports, which causes a general rise in the rate of inflation. Trade unions may react to this by seeking higher wages, which leads to an increase in the costs of businesses, which causes them to raise the prices of their goods and services. This scenario has happened frequently in Australia.

The main causes of inflation are:

demand-pull inflation

when suppliers of labour, goods and services seek to take advantage of excessive demand in the domestic economy by raising their prices

cost-push inflation

if wages increase faster than the rate of increase in productivity, companies may find it necessary to raise prices to maintain profitability

- External factors, such as changes in exchange rates or changes in the price of goods. An example is oil prices during periods of instability in the Middle East or disruptions to food supplies caused by droughts or floods.
- Excessive demand in the domestic economy. An example of this is a mining boom which increases demand for labour and goods and services including items ranging from big trucks to accommodation for mine workers. Suppliers of labour, goods and services seek to take advantage of the situation by raising their prices. This is usually described as **demand-pull inflation**. It is sometimes associated with excessive rates of growth in the money supply.
- If wages increase faster than the rate of increase in productivity, companies may find it necessary to raise prices to maintain profitability. This is known as **cost-push inflation**.
- Government-induced price rises can cause the general rate of inflation to increase. For example, rises in indirect taxes such as those on alcohol and tobacco raise the retail price of goods and services.

As we have seen, what people think about prices can actually affect the level of inflation, creating a self-fulfilling prophecy: when people expect inflation to rise, they increase their prices, thus ensuring that inflation increases. In Australia, although inflation rates were very low for most of the 1990s, it took many years for inflationary expectations to fall to levels that matched the actual inflation rate.

RUSSIA BANS WHEAT EXPORTS

LINK TO INTERNATIONAL ECONOMY

In 2010 unusually hot weather, drought and forest fires led the Russian Government to ban the export of wheat. At the time Russia was a significant exporter of wheat in the world. At the same time heavy rain in Canada, one of the world's largest wheat exporters, prevented crops being sown in some regions. Wheat prices in global markets jumped by 50 per cent in June as panic buying saw traders and speculators competing to lock in future supplies.

QUESTIONS
1. List two reasons why the global price of wheat jumped in 2010.
2. Explain why panic buying can become a 'self-fulfilling prophecy'.

INFLATION AFFECTS BOTH INDIVIDUALS AND BUSINESSES

LINK TO BUSINESS

For the individual, it is important to remember that inflation tends to redistribute wealth away from low-income people with little bargaining power, no assets and limited ability to borrow, and towards people on higher incomes, who tend to have all these things. Speculators who can convert borrowed funds into assets that appreciate faster than the rate of inflation tend to become business heroes—at least for as long as their cash flow is sufficient to meet the repayments on their borrowings.

For businesses, inflation is usually associated with rising costs. Firms that sell essential products or have strong brand loyalty can usually pass on higher costs in the form of higher prices. Inflation also requires businesses to watch their cash flow, because:

- Costs of inputs to the business in the form of parts, materials and labour are all rising.
- Interest costs may also be rising.
- Forward planning becomes difficult because rising money values are difficult to predict. This affects pricing and investment decisions.

However, inflation makes it easier to conceal wrong business decisions because the rise in nominal values disguises losses. Businesses that borrow heavily to finance speculation in assets during inflationary periods have to watch the attitude of financial markets carefully. In the past, inflationary periods usually ended with higher interest rates, forcing companies that had borrowed heavily to collapse because their cash flows were insufficient to service their borrowing costs.

QUESTIONS
1. Assume you are an investor in the stock market in a period of 10 per cent inflation. Describe the characteristics of companies that you would prefer to invest in.
2. If you expected interest rates to increase rapidly, what changes would you make to your investment portfolio?

MEASURING INFLATION

LEARNING OBJECTIVE 4 Explain how inflation is measured by the Australian Bureau of Statistics

Inflation can only be identified if it is measured. We have to be confident that prices are indeed rising before we can claim that inflation exists. We have to measure the extent of inflation before we can explain what is causing it.

Measuring inflation is also important in enabling us to evaluate significant features of the economy. It is clear from Chapter 3 that prices are one of the critical outcomes in an economy. Prices, for example, are one of two components of markets, the other being quantities. Both demand and supply curves represent combinations of prices and quantities for different groups of sellers and buyers.

PRICE INDICES

For business and government, committed as they are to outputs for making profits (business) or for providing services (government), there are some income measures that can compensate for inflation. Business can react to higher costs by increasing prices and governments can increase taxes, though both responses are, of course, inflationary in themselves. This can lead to an inflationary spiral where higher costs lead to higher prices and so on.

Note also that neither business nor government has unlimited flexibility in increasing their income. People may not purchase products or services if the price is too high. Business is sensitive to this because it affects profits. Governments respond to this because they face elections where they have to justify their provision of services to the people.

The most common way of measuring inflation is by **price indices**. Indices are statistics that measure the change in a variable over time. For inflation, the variable is price. The aim is to measure changes in price over a 12-month period (for an annual inflation rate).

price indices *measurements of the changes in prices over time*

Calculating a price index

A price index is calculated by establishing some base price, and then comparing it with prices 12 months ago and with current prices. The change in price is calculated by checking the price 12 months ago and the current price against the price in the **base period**. When making comparisons between retail sales this year and last year, economists are interested in the 'real' change: the change in dollar-values adjusted for inflation. The dollar-value terms are referred to as **nominal values**. When they have been adjusted they are called **real values**.

By convention, the price in the base period is identified as 100. Let's assume the base period was five years ago. If the price index number 12 months ago was calculated to be 112 and the current price is $115, all the following statements would be correct:

- inflation was 12 per cent over the four-year period to 12 months ago: 112 − 100
- inflation was 15 per cent over the five-year period to now: 115 − 100
- inflation was 2.7 per cent over the 12-month period to now:

$$\frac{115 - 112}{112} \times 100$$

The first two statements should be clear because they include the base price of 100. You may be a little puzzled by the last, which does not use the base figure. Both figures relate to the common starting point—the base price of 100.

The advantage of basing the calculation on a common point is demonstrated when two statistics are related to a common point: other statistics can be related not only to the common point but also to each other using the common point.

This is like comparing people's heights using a ruler against a wall. Each person's height from the floor is measured and then the measured points are compared. The floor is the common point, or base point, in the calculation. We confidently say that one person is X centimetres taller than another without saying what each person's height is.

One further observation on these three statements about price changes: the index numbers are restated as percentages. We can do this because the base point is expressed as the point 100 and in fact this is the reason for the convention. To say that the base point is 100 and another chosen point is 112 is the same as saying that the base point is 100 per cent and the second point related to that is 112 per cent. Although index numbers are widely used for inflation statistics, the common way of expressing price changes in economics is in percentages.

Advantages

Price indices adjust market or current prices to real terms, thus removing the effect of inflation from calculations. Because they give realistic values to the component prices of such important economic statistics as aggregate demand and gross domestic product, they are integral to a proper understanding of economic trends over time. Awareness of the operation of price indices therefore deepens our appreciation of major changes in the economy.

Choosing which prices to measure

Now we have explained how indices work in identifying price changes, the next question is: what prices are we talking about? Consider the range of prices, even in a relatively small economy like Australia's. Every time something is bought and sold, price is involved.

Although it is beyond the scope of our discussion to detail these measures, there are indices of resource prices, producer prices, distributor prices and consumer prices in Australia.

Some are government or official indices; others are calculated and published by private organisations and universities. All are used, to a greater or lesser degree, by governments, by businesses, by political, social and economic lobby groups, and by individual citizens to show the effects of price changes for whatever purpose they are seeking to pursue.

Any assertion about price change in the economy should say what prices are referred to. Consider consumer prices. If inflation has been causing price rises throughout the economic system, consumer prices may or may not reflect that fact precisely.

Say, for example, there has been a rise in resource prices to the producer. The producer sells to the distributor at a higher price. That higher price may just cover the increase in costs, or it may be well above that increased cost level. The distributor in turn covers the increased cost by increasing the price to the consumer. In this situation, the consumer price increase must cover the increased prices charged by the resource owner, the producer and the distributor.

The two most commonly used measures of inflation in Australia are the GDP deflator and the CPI.

GDP DEFLATOR

The most broad-ranging measure of inflation is the **implicit price deflator index (IPDI)**—or, as it is more commonly known, the GDP deflator. This series of indices is issued annually by the Australian Bureau of Statistics (ABS). The GDP is the total market value of all final goods and services produced in the economy in any given year.

The **GDP deflator** measures a broad range of prices, including consumer prices, at various stages of the economic process. For example, the GDP deflator measures prices paid by consumers and producers for items such as energy, equipment and raw materials. The specific application of the GDP deflator is to take the total market value of production and to remove the inflation caused by price changes to identify the 'real' change in GDP. Thus it enables us to identify the 'real' rate of growth in the Australian economy. Refer to Chapter 9 for detailed information on the GDP deflator.

LEARNING OBJECTIVE 5
Discuss the use of the consumer price index to express real monetary values in the economy

implicit price deflator index (IPDI)
a measure of inflation calculated on a broad range of prices at various stages of the economic system

GDP deflator
a measure of inflation calculated on a broad range of prices at various stages of the economic system

THE CONSUMER PRICE INDEX

By far the most often-quoted and the most widely used measure of inflation is the **consumer price index (CPI)**. The ABS defines the CPI as the measurement of quarterly changes in the price of a 'basket' (or group) of goods and services that account for a high proportion of expenditure by the CPI population group (i.e. metropolitan households of wage and salary earners).

Two points about the CPI are highlighted by this definition:

- It is a quarterly statistic. Whatever measure is devised for inflation, it is important that it be calculated frequently.
- It represents price changes in a basket of goods and services. This enables prices in one period to be compared with prices in another period, the user being confident that prices of the same goods and services are being considered.

consumer price index (CPI)
the measurement of quarterly changes in the price of a 'basket' of goods and services that account for a high proportion of expenditure

Typical goods and services

The contents of the basket are changed on a five-year basis to reflect changes in the way consumers spend their money. For instance in the 2005–10 basket education expenses were separated from recreation expenses, in recognition of the growth of privately funded secondary and tertiary education and the increasing burden this places on household expenditures. By making such changes, the ABS recognises the significance of these items in the expenses of the average Australian metropolitan household.

As living standards rise, patterns of consumption change with a greater proportion of income being spent on services. For example, in Australia, households are spending a larger proportion of their income on communication devices, consequently communication is now an important category of household spending.

Typical households

The categories used in the CPI are based on the results of the Household Expenditure survey which is the only authoritative source of data on the expenditures of different types of households in each of the capital cities. Only the spending patterns of households in cities are considered in constructing the basket of goods and services because they are 'typical' in that the vast majority of Australians live in large cities. The purchasing patterns of non-metropolitan households are excluded from CPI surveys because the ABS considers them to be different from metropolitan households. Table 12.1 illustrates the weights used in the 2005–10 version of the CPI. It is an indication of the prosperity of Australian households that there is little difference between the percentages of household income spent on food (15.44) compared to recreation (11.55) plus alcohol and tobacco (6.79).

Table 12.1   Weights used in the 2005–10 CPI

	%
Alcohol and tobacco	6.79
Housing	19.53
Health	4.7
Transportation	13.11
Household contents and services	9.61
Financial and insurance services	9.31
Recreation	11.55
Food	15.44
Communication	3.31
Clothing and footwear	3.91
Education	2.73

Source: *Australian Bureau of Statistics*, Consumer price index,
15th series weighting patterns, *cat. no. 6430.0.*

Wage and salary households only are included because most Australians belong to such households. Non-wage households have spending habits significantly different from those of wage households because they depend either on wealth or on age pensions or social security benefits. The need to be representative justifies excluding non-wage households from the CPI surveys. While these points arise directly from the definition of the CPI, other decisions about the structure of the CPI also give insights into the processes of measuring inflation.

Each quarter, the ABS collects about 100 000 prices from Australia's capital cities. These are classified into 90 groupings under 11 broad headings:

1. food
2. alcohol and tobacco
3. clothing and footwear
4. housing: rent, electricity and gas, and house purchase prices
5. household contents and services: items such as glass and tableware, towels and linen, hairdressing and personal care services
6. transportation: public transport, taxis and other private transport not owned by the household, and the cost of running one or more cars
7. financial and insurance services: items such as real estate agents' fees and taxes on transfers, house and motor vehicle insurance, and interest rates on deposits and loans
8. recreation: domestic and international holiday travel and accommodation, audio visual and computer equipment and pet expenses
9. communication: mainly telecommunication expenses
10. education: preschool, primary, secondary and tertiary school fees
11. health: hospital and medical services, pharmaceuticals, dental services.

The data that is used to create the CPI is collected at least once every three months. Frequent price observations are made of items that have volatile prices such as petrol, fresh foodstuffs and holiday travel. It thus produces a reasonably clear picture of what is happening to prices paid by consumers in capital cities.

Reserve Bank measures of inflation

The Reserve Bank has developed measures of inflation which it uses in implementing monetary policy targeted at maintaining inflation in a band between 2 and 3 per cent. These are the 'trimmed mean' and the 'weighted median' (see Chapter 23 for details).

The 'trimmed mean' is calculated by ordering the CPI expenditure categories by the magnitude of their price change for the quarter and taking the expenditure weighted average of the middle 70 per cent of price changes. The 'weighted median' is the price change in the middle of this ordering.

The purpose is to remove short-term volatility from the measures of inflation in order to identify the trend in the underlying inflation rate of consumer prices.

LEARNING OBJECTIVE 6
Explain the indicators of consumer price inflation used by the Reserve Bank

TRENDS IN INFLATION
Historical and international comparisons

Figure 12.2 overleaf provides a long-term perspective on inflation in Australia from 1960 to 2010. It illustrates the unusually long period of rapid inflation between 1970 and 1990. In this period inflation peaked at more than 16 per cent in 1975 and apart from a brief period did not fall below 6 per cent per annum until the 1990s. The lower rate of inflation reflects economic and industrial relations reforms conducted in the 1980s and 1990s which helped to create a more competitive and productive economy.

Figure 12.2 shows that Australia's inflation rate, as measured by the CPI, trended downward during the 1980s and has been fairly stable since 1990, apart from the introduction of the goods and services tax in 2001 and the lead-up to the GFC in 2007. Since 2001 the inflation

LEARNING OBJECTIVE 7
Describe inflation changes in previous economic periods and suggest reasons for those changes

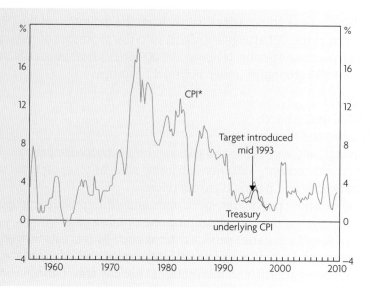

Figure 12.2

Inflation over the long run, per cent change from previous year

* Excludes interest charges prior to September quarter 1998.
Source: Australian Bureau of Statistics and Reserve Bank of Australia, <www.rba.gov.au/monetary-policy/about.html>, accessed 14 October 2010.

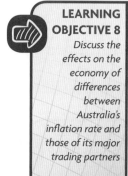

LEARNING OBJECTIVE 8

Discuss the effects on the economy of differences between Australia's inflation rate and those of its major trading partners

rate in Australia has been higher than that of its major trading partners, the United States and Japan, with the exception of the period from 2005–08 for the United States. Figure 12.3 compares Australia's CPI with inflation in the United States and Japan since 2000.

Such comparisons of inflation are useful for economic planners:

- International comparisons, showing rates of inflation in the countries with which Australia trades, illustrate Australia's inflation performance against other economies, and also draw attention to the importance of price changes in trade. It is possible, for example, for Australia's inflation rate to rise because of high-priced imports from another country whose inflation rate is higher than Australia's, or because of a fall in the Australian dollar exchange rate which makes imports more expensive in Australian dollar terms. Changes in the relative prices of Australian goods in other countries can raise or lower their competitiveness. Similarly higher inflation in countries supplying goods to Australia can make their products less competitive against Australian produced goods.

Figure 12.3

Inflation rates in Australia, United States and Japan, 2000–10, per cent per annum change in consumer prices

Source: Compiled from Reserve Bank, Statistics, Tables G2 and I2.

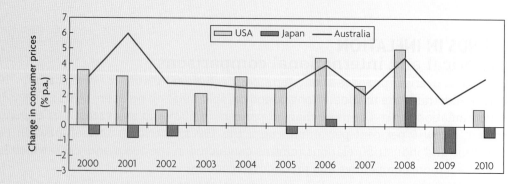

Table 12.2   Average annual inflation rates 1969–2009

YEAR	ORIGINAL DOLLAR VALUE	$ VALUE IN 2009	AVERAGE ANNUAL INFLATION RATE
1969	100	990	5.9
1979	100	391	4.6
1989	100	175	2.8
1999	100	137	3.2
2007	100	106	3.1
2008	100	102	1.8

Source: Reserve Bank of Australia Inflation calculator.

- Historical comparisons show the trend in prices in the Australian economy over a long period, providing context and perspective for the inflation rate at any particular time.

  Table 12.2 illustrates inflation rates over different periods of time using a calculator created by the Reserve Bank. For example if you started working and paying into a superannuation fund in 1969 and retired in 2009 you needed to generate an average annual return of 5.9 per cent over the 40-year period just to match the depreciation in the value of your money caused by inflation. On the other hand if you started working in 1989 the inflation rate you needed to better the 20-year mark is 2.8 per cent. If the returns after tax on your superannuation do not match the rate of inflation then the real value of your funds is shrinking. See Chapter 16 for more details.

Australian trends since the 1990s

Inflation fell in Australia in the early 1990s with onset of a severe recession. It proved to be the most difficult period for the Australian economy since the Great Depression of the 1930s. A recession is a period of low economic growth characterised by low demand and therefore high unemployment.

CHICKEN EXPORTS TO CHINA

You export chicken meat to China. Your competition comes from Thailand, Indonesia and Japan. Your costs suddenly rise because of a shortage of grain in Australia because of drought.

QUESTIONS

1. Explain the impact of this change on your business.
2. Avian flu strikes the chicken industries of Thailand and Indonesia.
   (a) Explain the impact of this on the price of chicken meat in China.
   (b) Explain the effects on your business.

LINK TO
INTERNATIONAL
ECONOMY

If demand is low, there is little incentive for producers and distributors to increase their prices. In fact, they keep prices low to try to sell more output. So a recession represents a sustained period of minimal price increases.

This is a situation where demand-pull inflation is not operating. A feature of high demand is high prices, because consumers want the output and have the means to pay for it. On the other hand, low demand means that consumers consider carefully whether to spend at all, and the exact price to pay.

The high unemployment associated with the recession made trade unions cautious about seeking higher wages. In this economic environment, many wage increases were gained only at the expense of reductions in the number of employees.

Figure 12.4 illustrates the composition of inflation over the period 2000–10. It shows that food prices increased by 46 per cent over the decade and that the costs of housing, health, alcohol, tobacco and education all rose by more than 50 per cent. Increases in government taxes and charges were the main cause of price rises for tobacco and alcohol. Increases in health insurance, the medicare surcharge and health care costs in general pushed up prices in the health category by 65 per cent. Increases in charges for places at universities and TAFE colleges as well as rising school fees raised education costs by 68 per cent over the decade. An underlying housing shortage and the tax-driven investor demand helped to increase housing costs by 57 per cent.

Increases in government taxes and charges were the result of two factors:

1. the adoption of a user-pays philosophy by all levels of government in Australia
2. the slow rate of growth of wages, preventing the federal government from relying on fiscal drag (see Chapter 21) to generate revenue faster than the rate of growth of incomes in the economy.

Higher food and alcohol costs may reflect the duopoly situation in Australia, with two major companies dominating retail activities like supermarkets and liquor stores and seeking to extend their dominance to petrol retailing.

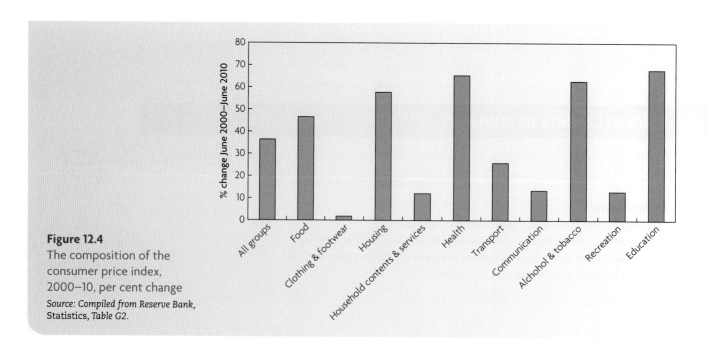

Figure 12.4

The composition of the consumer price index, 2000–10, per cent change

Source: Compiled from Reserve Bank, Statistics, Table G2.

The Bureau of Statistics also provides data on inflation rates for 'tradeable' and 'non-tradeable' items. Tradeables are items whose prices are mainly determined on the world market. In general the inflation rate for tradeable items is lower than for non-tradeable items reflecting the higher degree of competition in world markets. The price in Australia of tradeables can be affected by exchange rate changes (a fall in the dollar makes imports more expensive), by changes in tariffs and by discounting, for example, to stimulate demand in an economic downturn.

Figure 12.5 illustrates the rate of inflation for these two categories for the period 2000–10.

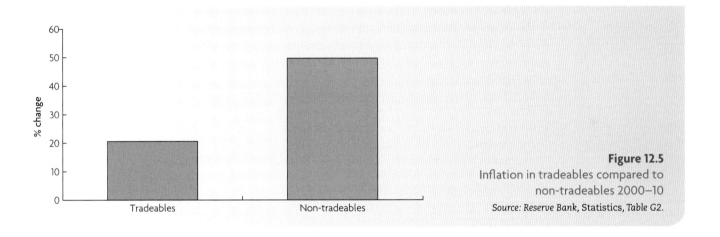

Figure 12.5
Inflation in tradeables compared to non-tradeables 2000–10
Source: Reserve Bank, Statistics, Table G2.

Figure 12.6 illustrates the relationship between interest rates and consumer prices in Australia over this period. Changes in interest rates tend to reflect changes in people's inflationary expectations as well as other, more short-term factors. Usually there is a gap between the inflation rate and the 90-day bill rate providing a real rate of return to investors. Note the increase in the interest rate as inflation crept up from 2005 to 2008.

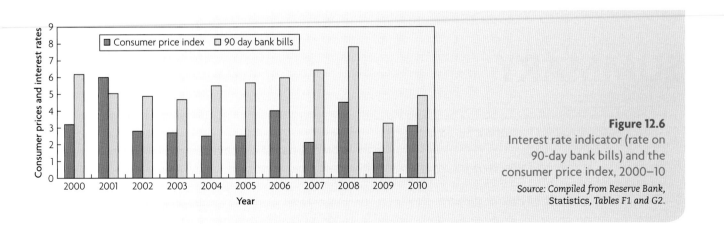

Figure 12.6
Interest rate indicator (rate on 90-day bank bills) and the consumer price index, 2000–10
Source: Compiled from Reserve Bank, Statistics, Tables F1 and G2.

THE IMPORTANCE OF LOW INFLATION

LINK TO BUSINESS

Sustained low inflation makes business and personal financial planning less complicated than when inflation is high and variable, and it generates lower levels of nominal interest rates.

Some of the effects of low inflation are:

- It is easier to forecast the repayments required for borrowings because changes in interest rates become less frequent and rates tend to settle at low levels. Thus the cash cost of repayments becomes less.
- The demand for borrowings is reduced because less emphasis is placed on buying existing assets for capital gain and more emphasis is placed on new income-generating investments.
- People are more likely to buy equity ownership rather than relying on debt finance, because the impact of taxation and inflation is lower on debt repayment costs.
- Investors are likely to take a long-term view, and hurdle rates of return for new investments are set at lower levels with longer payback periods. More investment projects are likely to be financed.
- Businesses may go direct to money markets for long-term finance by issuing their own debt securities.
- Interest-bearing assets become more attractive relative to inflation hedges like commodities. This is because commodities like gold do not pay a return to the holder. The return only comes about through increases in the price of the commodity.

Managers used to operating in an inflationary environment tend to be replaced by managers who are more comfortable in an environment where mistakes cannot be hidden, tougher cost controls are required, and detailed business plans are required to justify expansion plans.

QUESTIONS

1. What are the effects of low inflation on perceptions of:
   (a) individual borrowers?
   (b) business borrowers?
2. Explain the likely effect of low inflation on the rate of economic growth.

SUMMARY

1. This chapter identifies inflation as being 'a persistent increase in the general level of prices'. The key points are that inflation is ongoing and generalised throughout the economy.
2. Inflation has a significant impact on the various sectors in the economy: households, business and government. It has significant social, political and economic consequences, which is why maintenance of low inflation is a key objective of economic policy.
3. While it is difficult to identify any single cause of inflation, economists have identified a number of factors that are associated with high inflation. These include external factors, demand-pull and cost-push factors, government-induced inflation and inflationary expectations.

4. The most common way of measuring inflation is by price indices. Price indices can be used to compare price rises over time by adjusting market or current prices to 'real terms', thus removing the effect of inflation.

5. There are two major measures of inflation:
    (a) implicit price deflator index (IPDI) or GDP deflator
    (b) consumer price index (CPI).

6. In the 1990s Australia became a relatively low-inflation country among the advanced industrial economies and maintained this performance through most of the 2000s. The main sources of inflation during this period appear to have been governments seeking higher revenue through indirect taxes and charges, the duopolistic nature of consumer goods markets and the rising costs of health and education.

7. Australia has continued to have relatively low inflation rates in the 2000s, compared to rates in the 1970s and 1980s.

KEY TERMS

		demand-pull inflation	252	price indices	253
base period	254	GDP deflator (or implicit price		real value	254
consumer price index (CPI)	255	deflator index (IPDI))	255	stagflation	250
cost-push inflation	252	inflation	249		
deflation	249	nominal value	254		

REVISION QUESTIONS

1. Define and explain inflation.
2. Discuss the impact of inflation on
    (a) government
    (b) business
    (c) households.
3. Why is inflation an important issue in economics?
4. Outline and explain Australia's recent inflation performance.
5. Why is it important to differentiate between long-term and short-term trends in inflation?
6. Explain how the CPI is constructed.
7. Explain how changes in exchange rates can affect the CPI.
8. Explain three causes of inflation.
9. Explain three consequences of inflation.
10. If the CPI rose from 100 to 105 and your wages rose by 10 per cent would you be better off? Explain.
11. Give two reasons for the low inflation rate experienced by Australia in the early 2000s.

APPLIED QUESTIONS AND EXERCISES
FOOD PRICE INFLATION IN CHINA

In China the price of food accounts for about one-third of the weight in the consumer price index (CPI). In 2010 food prices rose by 5.7 per cent in June and 6.8 per cent in July as a result of floods and natural disasters.

Overall the CPI rose by 3.3 per cent in the year to July. The CPI was expected to grow by 3.0 per cent over the rest of 2010. In 2009–10 average hourly wages in China grew by 13.5 per cent and farmers' incomes grew by about 9 per cent.

QUESTIONS

1. Compare the weighting for food in the CPI of Australia and China.
2. Which group in China benefits from rising food prices?
3. Describe the causes of inflation in China using the demand-pull and cost-push concepts.
4. Describe two effects of rising food prices on farmers in China.
5. Describe the effects of food price inflation on China's agricultural exports.

5

THE AUSTRALIAN FINANCIAL SYSTEM

Chapter **13**

Money and interest

LEARNING OBJECTIVES

After studying this chapter, you will be able to:

1. explain the nature and functions of money
2. explain the measures of money
3. describe the theoretical process of credit creation
4. explain the differences between the theory of credit creation and the limitations imposed by the real world of finance on the operation of the theory
5. explain the difference between the transaction and asset demand for money
6. explain the relationship between the supply of money and interest rates
7. explain the nature of interest rates and the links between interest rates in Australia and the rest of the world.

INTRODUCTION

The overall objective of this chapter is to explain the nature of money, the process of credit creation and the influences that affect interest rates. **Money** is important to most people. Once economies move beyond the subsistence level, money in some form or another becomes essential to 'oil the wheels of exchange'. An economy without money has to operate as a barter economy, whereby people exchange goods for goods in order to satisfy their needs and wants: I swap my bucket of milk for your bucket of eggs. The barter system of exchange can be clumsy and difficult for its participants.

money
a generally acceptable medium of exchange for goods and services

As part of the process of economic development, human beings have created systems of exchange using symbolic 'money', such as shells, stones or pigs. In order to be effective, whatever is used as money must have certain characteristics: it must be portable, it must be divisible, it must enjoy universal acceptance, and it must have a reasonably stable value in terms of other commodities. In periods of very high inflation, people tend to lose faith in the currency issued by the national government and frequently revert to barter trade.

Modern economic systems use highly sophisticated forms of money: they extend from the notes and coins and credit cards you carry in your wallet or purse to electronic pulses travelling via satellite that debit and credit the New York accounts of Australian-based banks. For example, it is possible for a person in Brisbane to buy a boomerang, using a credit card issued in Tokyo, at a shop that can be sure it will be paid by a bank in Sydney.

Since the early 20th century all governments have recognised the importance of managing the national currency and money supply. However, not all economists agree on the 'correct' definition of money or on the significance of the money supply for the economic performance of a country. Nevertheless, an understanding of money and the financial system is essential for anyone contemplating a career in business.

THE FUNCTIONS OF MONEY

The four **functions of money** are as a:

1. medium of exchange
2. measure of value
3. store of wealth
4. standard for deferred payments.

Let us look at each of these functions more closely.

functions of money
money performs the functions of a medium of exchange, measure of value, store of wealth and standard for deferred payments

MEDIUM OF EXCHANGE

Money makes it easier to exchange goods and services. Our society is based on specialisation by individuals and on exchange between these specialists. We could function without money, but it would be inconvenient and time-consuming for people to value their goods and services in terms of other people's goods and services and to work out appropriate rates of exchange. That's where money comes in. It is convenient and easy because it is a generally acceptable medium of exchange.

The term we use to describe your ability to make purchases is **liquidity**.

liquidity
a consumer's ability to make purchases

MEASURE OF VALUE

In Australia, goods and services are usually valued in money terms. For example, success in individual sports can be measured by the value of player payments and product endorsements. In a barter system (where a sheep might be worth 10 chickens, for example), goods are valued in terms of other goods. Barter is cumbersome; the owner of the sheep might not need chickens.

Money enables us to apply a standard, easily understood measure of value to all goods and services.

STORE OF WEALTH

Early in the 20th century people often kept their wealth in the form of notes under the bed or in a tin buried in the garden, because this was a good way of storing their wealth or purchasing power. Nowadays there is a wide range of financial assets that serve the same purpose: bank deposits, investment trusts, bank bills and so on.

Financial assets like bank deposits will retain their purchasing power over time, provided prices do not change. In contrast, most other assets (cars, for instance) tend to lose value over time.

This raises the interesting question of what money is worth. Money is worth what you can buy with it, that is to say, it is a matter of belief and confidence. If you have travelled overseas you will be aware that some currencies (e.g. United States dollars) are more acceptable than other currencies. This is the result of the degree of confidence in the purchasing power of the currency. The key factor that determines the value of money inside a country is the rate of **inflation** (see Chapter 12). In an inflationary period money is not a good store of value or wealth, because prices rise and money loses value because it buys less. In inflationary periods non-money assets (like houses or antiques) may increase in value faster than the general rate of price increase. In this situation, people may prefer to hold their wealth in non-money assets because money is simply not adequate as a store of value or wealth.

inflation
a situation of continuously rising prices or, to put it another way, continuous reductions in the value of currency

Thus the rate of price change can have a drastic effect on the usefulness of money as a store of wealth. People's attitudes towards saving and spending can be heavily influenced by price changes. When prices are rising rapidly and money is losing its value quickly, people will try to spend it as fast as they can because the purchasing power of money this year is greater than it will be next year. In the last few decades of the 20th century Australia was a high-inflation developed country which affected people's attitudes towards savings. However in the 21st century Australia has become a relatively low-inflation economy as Figure 13.1 indicates. This was the result of economic and industrial relations reform carried out in the 1980s and 1990s which improved the productivity and competitiveness of the economy.

STANDARD FOR DEFERRED PAYMENTS

This function of money enables the process of borrowing and lending to occur. It would be difficult to borrow a bucket of eggs in return for regular repayments of vegetables, but it could be done. By using money we can have a convenient form of credit. Credit or the provision of finance is crucial in our economic system: Australia has to borrow from the rest

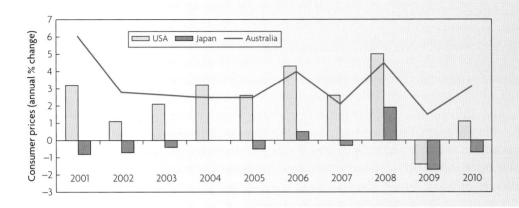

Figure 13.1
Inflation rates in Australia, United States and Japan 2001–10

Source: Compiled from Reserve Bank, Bulletin, various, Tables G1 and I2.

of the world to pay for the difference between what it earns from the rest of the world and what it has to pay for things like imports and interest on borrowings.

Governments and businesses borrow to finance budget deficits and investment projects. Individuals borrow to finance the purchase of consumer goods, houses and a host of other things. These arrangements involve credit and, in each case, the loan must be repaid at some point in the future.

Money provides a useful standard and medium for calculating and making repayments on loans.

INFLATION EFFECTS ON BORROWING AND LENDING

We have already mentioned the effect of inflation on the function of money as a store of wealth. Inflation is explained in Chapter 12, but here we will consider the effects of inflation on borrowing and lending in general.

The key point about inflation is that it reduces the purchasing power of money. We can illustrate some of the effects of inflation on the functions of money by considering the concepts of real and nominal values.

In economics, the nominal value of a collection of goods is its face value expressed in money terms. However, the 'real' value of the collection is the face value less an allowance for inflation.

For example, your income might rise by 10 per cent from one year to the next. However, if prices also rise by 10 per cent then you are no better off in 'real terms' because the increase in your nominal income has been offset by an increase in prices. However, if your income rose by 10 per cent and prices did not change, then you are better off in real terms because your income will buy more goods and services.

We have already mentioned how high rates of inflation can act as a disincentive to savings because people learn that it is better to borrow and spend now, and repay later with money that is worth less in real terms.

Many people and organisations sought to make gains from asset inflation bubbles of the 2000s by borrowing large amounts and hoping to make the repayments out of what they thought would be the ever-increasing values of the shares or other assets that had been purchased. Unfortunately for them and their financiers, most asset prices fell dramatically in 2008 causing many people to lose much of their wealth or indeed to become bankrupt.

During the 20th century governments and markets responded to high inflation rates by making arrangements which take account of the effects of inflation on 'money' values.

For example in Australia most Commonwealth social welfare payments are **indexed** to the **consumer price index (CPI)**. The CPI measures the rate of inflation as it affects consumers living in cities, which is where the surveys are carried out. Indexation means adjusting cash payments in line with changes in the index. This means that if the CPI rises by 10 per cent, welfare payments are increased by 10 per cent. Many financial instruments have 'floating' interest rates which adjust to changes in the inflation rate.

However, unanticipated changes in the inflation rate can still make some groups better off at the expense of others. Also the government's approach to adjusting values for inflation is not uniform. For example, inflation effects are excluded from income for income tax calculations in many areas, but not from calculations relating to the Higher Education Contribution Scheme.

Although levels of inflation in the 2000s were lower than in the 20th century, considerations such as those raised by this example are important for young people today who will be required to finance a large part of their income after they cease working. Taxpayer contributions to this post-retirement income are likely to shrink over the next 50 years, so careful thought must be given to long-term investments in terms of rates of return after inflation.

indexed
adjusting cash payments in line with changes in the CPI

consumer price index (CPI)
measures the rate of inflation as it affects consumers living in cities

LINK TO BUSINESS

INFLATION AND ECONOMIC WELFARE

In the 2000s inflation in Australia averaged about 3 per cent per year. Let us consider the effects of inflation in the 2000s on the economic welfare of three different people:

1. Rita worked as an editor in a publishing house that she part-owned. On average her income rose by 2 per cent a year. The company borrowed a substantial amount to purchase its headquarters. During the decade the value of the property doubled then collapsed to less than the value used in the loan agreement.
2. Bob was a retired accountant who owned a small office building and had a portfolio of shares. During the 2000s the value of his property and shares rose by 50 per cent, then collapsed in 2008. The average return on his investments was 3 per cent a year.
3. Shirley was a retired Commonwealth public servant. The taxpayer-funded pension she receives was fully indexed for inflation. She retired in 2001.

QUESTION
Explain how the economic welfare of these people was affected by inflation during the 2000s. Who did best and who worst during the decade?

FINANCIAL CRISIS IN ZIMBABWE

Zimbabwe is an outstanding example of hyperinflation. Although no reliable figures are available it has been estimated that the monthly inflation rate soared to well over 1000 per cent in 2008. This rate of inflation made normal business impossible because prices rose so rapidly. In 2008 an egg cost ZW$50 billion, shops would only cash cheques if the customer wrote twice the amount because costs would have risen by the time the cheque cleared. The maximum withdrawal at an ATM was ZW$100 billion. One British pound was worth ZW$1.2 trillion on 24 July 2008.

In 2009 the Zimbabwe currency was officially abandoned and foreign currencies like the United States dollar were used for most transactions.

LINK TO
INTERNATIONAL
ECONOMY

QUESTIONS

1. A lady left her purse with her pay in it and her lunch on a bus in Zimbabwe. The lunch was stolen but the purse was left behind. Explain why.
2. Why would the people of Zimbabwe prefer to use the United States dollar in transactions rather than the Zimbabwe dollar?

MEASURES OF MONEY

> **LEARNING OBJECTIVE 2**
> Explain the measures of money

Anything that is acceptable as a medium of exchange could be included in a definition of 'money'. Various countries use a wide range of measures of money supply which can change over time. Changes in regulations governing the activities of banks in Australia have made definitions such as M1 (currency plus funds in cheque accounts) less important, although they are still used in countries such as the United States.

M3

M3 is currently the most significant measure of 'the money supply' in Australia. It incorporates M1 plus all bank deposits and certificates of deposit issued by banks plus all deposits in other authorised deposit-taking institutions by the non-financial private sector. (This is to avoid double counting.)

Within M3 a significant measure of money is the **money base**. This comprises private sector holdings of notes and coins plus deposits of banks with the Reserve Bank of Australia, and Reserve Bank liabilities to the private non-bank sector. The significance of the money base is that these funds are core funds used by banks to support the growth of their lending. These funds are sometimes referred to as 'high-powered money'.

money base
private sector holdings of notes and coins plus deposits of banks with the RBA and RBA liabilities to the private non-bank sector

BROAD MONEY

The other main measure of money is **broad money**; it comprises M3, plus deposits lodged with non-bank financial institutions, less non-banks' holdings of currency and bank deposits to avoid double counting. In other words, broad money incorporates the public's holdings of cash, bank deposits and net deposits with non-bank financial institutions.

broad money
M3 plus deposits lodged with non-bank financial institutions, less non-banks' holdings of currency and bank deposits

CREDIT

A third measure of money which is significant for economic policy is credit (including securitisation) by financial intermediaries. It includes lending for housing, personal loans and business lending by those financial intermediaries whose deposit liabilities are included in broad money.

According to the basic theory of credit creation the growth of credit should reflect the rate of growth of deposits in financial institutions. However, the link between bank deposits and advances was broken in the 1980s. Nowadays banks do not necessarily depend on deposits to fund advances. If anything, banks tend to make advances and then seek liabilities, which may be deposits, to match the newly created assets. Growth in credit occurs in three areas:

1. house lending, which broadly follows the housing investment cycle
2. personal credit, which broadly reflects growth in private consumption
3. business credit, which reflects the short-term credit and the long-term investment requirements of business.

Figure 13.2 illustrates how the measures of money supply and credit tend to move together through the cycle. The impact of the GFC can be seen in the reduction in the growth rate of the monetary aggregates since 2008.

CHANGES IN THE MONEY SUPPLY

primary sources of money
the primary sources of money are the net effects of governmental and international transactions on the money supply inside Australia

The money supply in the Australian economy can be altered by a number of factors. The **primary sources of money** are the net effects of governmental and international transactions on the domestic economy. The secondary source is the effect of credit creation.

PRIMARY SOURCES OF MONEY
Governmental transactions

Government finances are usually either in surplus (where revenue is greater than spending) or in deficit (where spending exceeds revenue).

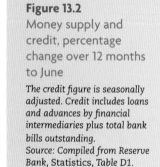

Figure 13.2
Money supply and credit, percentage change over 12 months to June

The credit figure is seasonally adjusted. Credit includes loans and advances by financial intermediaries plus total bank bills outstanding.
Source: Compiled from Reserve Bank, Statistics, Table D1.

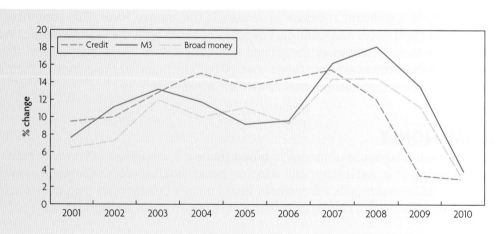

If we assume that the government has a budget deficit, this means it is spending more than it is collecting in revenue from the private sector. The government can choose to finance this deficit in a number of ways:

1. Issuing securities (IOUs like Treasury Notes) to the Reserve Bank and drawing cheques against the value of these securities. This is often called 'printing money' because effectively the government sector is spending more, but no other part of the economy is spending less. If the Reserve Bank sells these securities to the private sector, then the deficit is being 'funded' by a reduction in private-sector spending.
2. Borrowing from abroad and using the funds in Australia.

These two methods increase the money supply because the government sector is spending more and expanding the money supply, but the private sector is not reducing its spending.

There are three other methods of financing a deficit that do not add to the money supply:

1. Borrowing from the banking sector. If the government is able to borrow from banks (by issuing government securities to the banks), the banks' ability to lend is reduced because they have used some of their cash holdings to purchase the securities.
2. Increasing taxes to collect more revenue.
3. Issuing government securities to the non-bank public.

These measures reduce the private sector's holdings of money, and this reduction offsets to some extent the money injected into the economy as a result of the deficit.

International transactions
Fixed exchange rate

Prior to December 1983 Australia had a fixed exchange rate. A **fixed exchange rate** means that the rate is set by the government. With a fixed exchange rate, when Australians buy goods and services from overseas or when they invest or transfer funds overseas, they have to convert their holdings of Australian dollars to the appropriate foreign currency (often United States dollars). Usually they buy this foreign currency from a bank. These transactions effectively lower Australia's international reserves.

Similarly, when foreigners purchase Australian goods and services or invest in Australia, they must convert their currency into Australian dollars. This raises Australia's international reserves.

A balance of payments deficit means a loss from international reserves, while a balance of payments surplus means a gain.

Figure 13.3 overleaf shows how these primary sources of change in the money supply work.

fixed exchange rate
when the rate is set by the government

Floating exchange rate

Since December 1983 Australia has had, more or less, a **floating exchange rate** system (see Chapter 19), whereby the value of the Australian dollar in terms of other currencies can rise or fall depending on market conditions. A balance of payments deficit is likely to result in a declining Australian dollar because the volume of Australian dollars being offered for sale is greater than the value of Australian dollars being sought. In a floating system, foreign exchange transactions do not affect the domestic money supply.

The Reserve Bank, however, does intervene in the foreign exchange market sometimes to push the dollar up or down or to hold it steady, depending on the circumstances and government policy at the time. When the Reserve Bank intervenes, whether by buying or

floating exchange rate
the value of a currency in terms of other currencies is set by the market forces of demand and supply, and it can rise or fall depending on market conditions

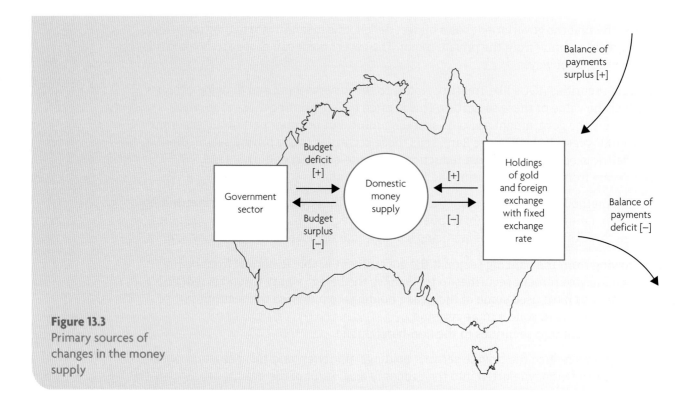

Figure 13.3
Primary sources of changes in the money supply

selling, the effect on the money supply is similar to the fixed exchange rate system except that the deals are usually done within Australia. That is, when the Reserve Bank buys Australian dollars and sells foreign currency to local banks, it reduces the money base held by banks. When it sells Australian dollars to local banks and buys foreign currency, it adds to the local banks' money base, thus increasing their ability to lend.

LEARNING OBJECTIVE 3

Describe the theoretical process of credit creation

SECONDARY SOURCE OF MONEY
Credit creation

The theory of credit creation explains the process by which banks can 'create money'. This is the **secondary source of money**. This theory explains one of the reasons why banks receive a lot of attention from economic policy makers.

A simple model

We will look at a model that shows in simplified form how banks create credit.

The model assumes that the only function performed by banks is taking in deposits and lending out part of those deposits. It deals only with changes in the level of deposits, reserves and loans as a result of the initial increase in deposits. The key term is '**credit multiplier**'. This is a technical term for the number of times an initial deposit can multiply in the process of credit creation.

The credit multiplier arises because banks must lend out a proportion of their deposits to earn enough income to pay expenses and to make a profit. They can lend a large percentage of their deposits because they know from past experience that only a relatively small proportion of depositors will want to withdraw their funds at any given time; besides, new deposits are being made all the time.

secondary source of money
increasing money supply through credit creation

credit multiplier
the number of times an initial deposit can multiply in the process of credit creation

The relationship between a bank's total deposits and the amount it keeps in liquid form is called the cash to deposits ratio or reserve asset ratio.

In Australia, banks must submit a liquidity management plan that describes their intentions about their reserve asset ratios to the Australian Prudential Regulation Authority, which is responsible for bank supervision.

EXAMPLE

We will illustrate the process of credit creation using a change in the level of deposits as the starting point. Let us make the following assumptions:

- The reserve asset ratio is 20 per cent.
- There is only one bank.
- There are no leakages from the system: all loaned funds are used to make purchases and the total proceeds of loans end up as deposits.
- There is an increase in deposits of $100.

Progressive changes to the bank's balance sheet are shown below:

ASSETS		LIABILITIES	
Reserves	20	Deposits	100
Available for lending	80		
Loans	0		
	100		100

If the bank makes a loan of $50, this will change the balance sheet as follows:

ASSETS		LIABILITIES	
Reserves	20	Deposits	100
Available for lending	30		
Loans	50		
	100		100

If the $50 is used to make a purchase, the seller has a cheque for $50 which is deposited in the bank. This will alter the balance sheet as follows:

ASSETS		LIABILITIES	
Reserves	30	Deposits	150
Available for lending	70		
Loans	50		
	150		150

continued ↘

continued

The bank manager has added 20 per cent of the extra funds ($10) to reserves, and the balance ($40) has been added to loanable funds. See if you can continue these calculations until the limits of the credit multiplier are reached. This will occur when the addition to the bank's balance sheet looks like this:

ASSETS		LIABILITIES	
Reserves	100	Deposits	500
Available for lending	0		
Loans	400		
	500		500

At this point, there are no funds available for lending, because the cash to deposits ratio is 20 per cent and the advances to deposits ratio is 80 per cent. New deposits are required to start the cycle again. This concept is known as **credit creation** and depends on the credit multiplier which is the reciprocal of the reserve asset ratio. In this example the bank manager keeps 20 per cent or one-fifth of deposits in cash. Consequently, when the bank reaches the position where there are no funds available for lending, 20 per cent of deposits are held in cash and 80 per cent has been loaned out, the limits of the process have been reached. Thus, if you know the reserve asset ratio and the increase in deposits, you can predict the final change in the level of deposits as a result of the credit creation process.

credit creation
the process by which bank deposits are created as a result of the lending ability of banks

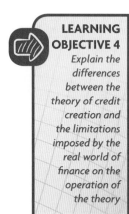

LEARNING OBJECTIVE 4
Explain the differences between the theory of credit creation and the limitations imposed by the real world of finance on the operation of the theory

Limits to the process of credit creation

The key assumptions in this model are that there are no losses and that the total proceeds of loans end up as deposits. In real life, new deposits are being made all the time and there may be losses to the system. For example the proceeds of a loan may be used for the following:

- To pay for imports. In this case, the funds are lost to the Australian banking system and overseas bank deposits rise as the overseas sellers receive payment from the Australian importer for their goods and place the funds in their own bank accounts.
- To satisfy a tax liability with the government. In this case the funds are also lost to the banking system. They enter the government's accounts with the Reserve Bank.

In addition, if the public chooses to hold a larger proportion of its assets in cash and keep a lower proportion in bank deposits, or if the bank decides to increase its desired reserve asset ratio, then this will reduce the bank's ability to create credit. Also, the Reserve Bank may choose to control bank advances by specifying the amount that banks may lend each week or month. Obviously this will limit the banks' ability to create credit.

The method of regulation used on banks can also affect the process of credit creation. For example, in the 1970s the Reserve Bank controlled bank advances by specifying the amount banks could lend on a weekly or monthly basis. This meant that the rate of increase in bank lending did not necessarily bear any relationship to the rate of growth of bank deposits.

In the 1980s the rate of growth of credit became disconnected from the rate of growth of bank deposits. The process of deregulation occurred over several years with the regulatory system being gradually dismantled. The statutory reserve deposit ratio was not removed until 1988. This was a requirement that banks lodge a percentage of deposits in a special account with the Reserve Bank. It had the effect of penalising banks for accepting deposits in Australia. Banks reacted to this penalty by pursuing other methods of providing finance to their customers such as borrowing overseas.

The result was that banks arranged the loan (asset), then sought a matching financial debt instrument (liability). This is the reverse of the credit creation process, whereby growth in liabilities (deposits) is used to finance growth in assets (loans).

Consequently, the rate of growth of bank lending was much faster than M3 as banks used non-deposit liabilities to fund their lending. Since the early 1990s the rates of growth in the monetary aggregates and credit have tended to adopt a closer relationship, as predicted by the theory of credit creation.

DEMAND FOR MONEY

The demand for money can be defined as the desire to hold money.

Transactions demand

People want to use money as a medium of exchange to carry out functions such as paying for their lunch and paying their bills. This is known as the **transactions demand for money** and it is closely related to the level of nominal GDP (see Chapter 9). At Easter and Christmas the transactions demand for money rises as people want cash to finance travel and gift giving, although the use of debit and credit cards is eroding demand for cash in general. The transactions demand for money tends not to be influenced by the level of interest rates.

Asset demand

The **asset demand for money** reflects peoples' choices as to whether to hold their wealth in the form of money or in financial assets such as shares, government securities or bank deposits. In making their decisions people assess the interest rates available, the level of risk associated with various assets and the economic outlook. In general, the higher the level of interest rates available on financial assets, the greater will be the demand for them and the lower will be the demand for cash money. In other words there is an inverse relationship between the asset demand for money and the rate of interest.

THE RELATIONSHIP BETWEEN MONEY SUPPLY AND THE RATE OF INTEREST

For the sake of simplicity we will assume that the money supply is exogenous, that is, it is set by the government and the monetary authorities. This is illustrated in Figure 13.4 overleaf where you can see that the money supply is the same regardless of the level of interest rates. In the real world, as we have seen, banks can create credit which has the effect of raising the money supply.

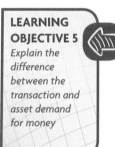

LEARNING OBJECTIVE 5
Explain the difference between the transaction and asset demand for money

transactions demand for money
the desire to use money for cash transactions such as buying an ice-cream

asset demand for money
people have to choose between holding money in the form of cash or financial assets such as bank accounts

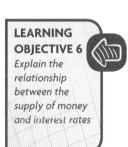

LEARNING OBJECTIVE 6
Explain the relationship between the supply of money and interest rates

The demand for money curve is also illustrated in Figure 13.4. In simple terms, the higher the level of interest rates, the less money will be demanded, as people prefer to swap their holdings of cash for financial assets because this will provide a better return than holding cash.

Figures 13.4 and 13.5 illustrate the effects of changes in the money supply. Equilibrium (point E^1 and E^2) in the money market occurs when the demand for money is equal to the supply of money.

Figure 13.4 illustrates the effect of an increase in the money supply from MS^1 to MS^2, which leads to a fall in the rate of interest (E^1 to E^2). This will make borrowing cheaper because there is a surplus of funds available. As it is less costly to borrow there is likely to be an expansion of spending on investment and consumption and thus aggregate demand will increase (see Chapter 10).

In Figure 13.5 a decrease in the money supply from MS^1 to MS^2 leads to an increase in the equilibrium rate of interest from E^1 to E^2. Higher interest rates are likely to lead to less borrowing and more saving thus reducing spending and aggregate demand.

In the real world the money supply is not exogenous and there are many interest rates. The purpose of Figures 13.4 and 13.5 is to illustrate in simple terms the relationship between the money supply and interest rates. This relationship is very important as we will see in the Link to Business later in this chapter.

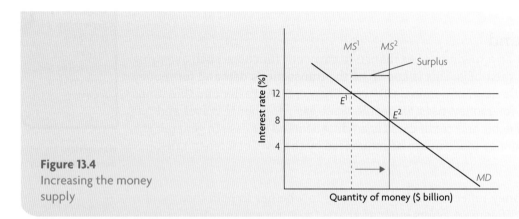

Figure 13.4
Increasing the money
supply

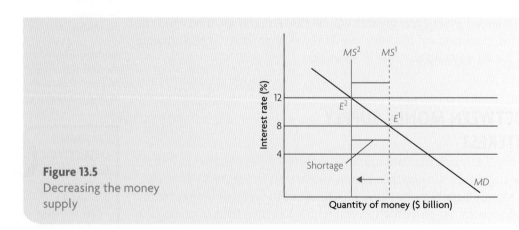

Figure 13.5
Decreasing the money
supply

INTEREST RATES

LEARNING OBJECTIVE 7
Explain the nature of interest rates and the links between interest rates in Australia and the rest of the world

Interest rates represent compensation to the lender for giving up 'liquidity', that is, for giving up the ability to purchase goods and services and the opportunity to make other investments.

Interest rates also represent the cost to the borrower of gaining the opportunity to make purchases or investments.

From the lender's point of view, we can define the interest rate (or yield) on a security (like a government bond, or a share or bank deposit) as the annual rate of return on the market price of the security that will be earned if the security is held to maturity.

This means that the yield on a security will rise if the interest rate rises (say, the interest rate on our bank deposits increases) or if the market price falls.

Some securities, like bank deposits, have a fixed dollar value and their yields can only rise if the interest rate rises. Others, like government bonds, are bought and sold on secondary markets, so their market price fluctuates. As the price changes, so does the yield.

Another way of looking at interest rates is to consider them as payment made for the use of funds expressed as a ratio between dollars paid per year and dollars borrowed.

There are different methods of calculating interest rates, some of which do not show the true effective cost to the borrower. Most credit contracts now require the lender to disclose the 'effective' rate of interest as opposed to the advertised rate.

Newspaper headlines often refer to interest rates going up or down. The community fascination with interest rates usually relates to rates payable on housing mortgages. However, a huge array of interest rates are offered and charged in the financial system and many groups, such as those depending on superannuation for their income, benefit from higher interest rates.

interest rates *compensation to the lender for giving up liquidity, expressed as the ratio between dollars of repayments per year and the amount borrowed*

FACTORS AFFECTING INTEREST RATES

Rates charged by lending institutions differ according to the nature of the loan or the borrower. Interest rates are affected by the following factors:

- The degree of risk involved. Loans to the Commonwealth Government are risk-free because the government has taxing powers and can rely on the credit extended by the Reserve Bank. On the other hand, a loan to a person with no assets and unreliable income is a high-risk loan. Interest rates reflect different 'risk premiums'.
- The maturity term. A long-term commitment usually requires higher interest rates than a short-term one.
- Expectations about future interest rates. If we expect interest rates to rise in the future, we would prefer to commit ourselves to borrowing now at the current, relatively lower, interest rates, rather than wait and take the risk of higher rates later on. This tends to increase rates as a kind of self-fulfilling prophecy, because relatively more loans will be demanded, thus forcing the price of money (interest rates) up.
- Degree of liquidity. Some assets are 'highly liquid': they can be converted into cash readily. Shares which can be bought and sold on the stock exchange are an example. Other assets, like houses, are 'illiquid': it can take a long time for these assets to be sold for cash (or converted into cash). A loan for the purchase of illiquid assets is likely to attract a higher interest rate than a loan for liquid assets.

- Administrative costs. This element reflects the cost of establishing and monitoring the performance of a loan. A loan repaid by automatic salary deduction is much less expensive to monitor than, say, a loan on a credit card to a transient individual, like an itinerant fruit picker who travels across several states over a year.
- Inflation. For example, lenders might require a 'real' return of about 5 per cent.

REAL AND NOMINAL INTEREST RATES

We have already mentioned the effects of inflation on the functions of money.

nominal interest rate
the face value paid to the lender, or by the borrower

The **nominal interest rate** is the face value rate paid to the lender, or by the borrower. The **real interest rate** is the nominal rate adjusted for the effects of expected inflation. The real rate takes into account the impact of inflation on purchasing power.

real interest rate
the nominal rate adjusted for the effects of expected inflation

For example, if you lend $100 to your bank for a year in return for $10 in interest, and the inflation rate was zero, then your real rate is 10 per cent. However, if the inflation rate is 10 per cent then your real rate would be zero. The $10 in interest you have received was simply compensation for the decline in your purchasing power. If the inflation rate is 15 per cent, then your real rate is negative—minus 5 per cent. If you include marginal income tax rates in this calculation, you can understand why some people consider that saving via bank deposits is not an effective method of storing the value of their wealth.

LINK TO BUSINESS

RECURRING FINANCIAL CRISES

The global financial crisis (GFC) which began in the United States in 2006 was the latest in a long line of international financial dramas.

In 1990 the collapse of a real estate price bubble left Japanese banks with loans secured against high property values which could not be realised when the property was sold. The Japanese Government did not intervene, in the hope that the banking system would correct itself. After eight years of stagnation the government began to inject capital into the banks, however the economy continued to stagnate losing a decade of economic growth and experiencing falling asset values.

In 1995 Mexico was unable to meet loan repayments which caused a panic among lenders and investors. As concern mounted about a withdrawal of loans to all developing countries, the United States Government intervened partly because 40 per cent of its exports were bought by developing countries and a collapse in demand would have caused an economic contraction. The United States arranged loan guarantees of USD 40 billion from the United States Treasury and the International Monetary Fund which calmed the markets and provided Mexico with time to improve its circumstances.

In 1997 Thailand was forced to devalue its currency when lenders refused to continue to provide short-term finance. Concern about all developing economies led to flights of funds from Malaysia, the Philippines, Indonesia and South Korea. Even Brazil and Russia were affected with Russia defaulting on its government bonds.

The standard response to these events which developed during the 1990s was to increase the money supply very quickly in order to lower borrowing costs and restore confidence.

The GFC followed the collapse of a housing price bubble in the United States in 2006 when house prices began to fall.

Massive intervention by the United States and other national governments was required to prevent the collapse of the global financial system. It involved transferring large amounts of private debt into public ownership and the injection of large amounts of money into economies via direct government payments to individuals and the commencement of building projects and the injection of funds via issuing securities (printing money) as governments used fiscal policy to offset declines in private spending.

QUESTIONS

1. Explain how increasing the money supply lowers borrowing costs.
2. Explain how increased confidence might have a positive effect on business in an economy suffering from a financial crisis.

RELATIONSHIP BETWEEN INTEREST RATES IN AUSTRALIA AND OVERSEAS

Money is an international commodity. The global financial market is probably the closest approximation of a perfect market to be found. Thus interest rates in Australia have to reflect the relationship between Australia's economic performance and that of the rest of the world.

Unfortunately, because Australia's record on inflation and international debt was relatively poor over the last few decades of the 20th century, nominal interest rates in Australia tended to be higher than those prevailing in many other countries.

The link between interest rates in Australia and interest rates overseas, particularly in the United States, comes about primarily through Australia's participation in international finance markets. Australia has a chronic balance of trade deficit and a need for investment in major projects which require financing by overseas interests. In order to encourage overseas financiers to continue to lend to Australia, real interest rates in Australia have to be attractive relative to other possible borrowers.

This means that interest rates in Australia are often higher than those available in the United States, reflecting the degree of risk in lending to Australia and the relative inflation rate in Australia compared to overseas. The interest rate data in Figure 13.6 from 2008 reflects the severe impact of the GFC in the United States and the attempt by the Federal Reserve to stimulate economic activity by keeping official interest rates at very low levels, in fact negative in real terms (after

LINK TO
INTERNATIONAL
ECONOMY

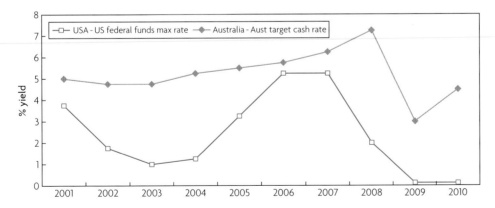

Figure 13.6

Official interest rates, United States and Australia, June, 2001–10

Source: Compiled from Reserve Bank, Statistics, Table F13.

continued ↘

continued

deducting the rate of inflation). In contrast the Reserve Bank had begun to increase the target cash rate in Australia.

QUESTIONS

1. Describe what would happen to interest rates in Australia if the United States increased interest rates by 5 percentage points.
2. Give two examples in the areas of car sales and sales of building materials of the likely effects in Australia if interest rates rose 5 percentage points in the United States.

SUMMARY

1. Money is a human invention to facilitate the exchange of goods and services. It performs the functions of:
   (a) medium of exchange
   (b) measure of value
   (c) store of wealth
   (d) standard for deferred payments.
2. Inflation affects both the value and functions of money.
3. The main measures of money are:
   (a) broad money
   (b) credit to the private sector by financial intermediaries.
4. The money supply is affected by the transactions of the government with the private sector and by international transactions. It is also affected by the credit-creating activities of banks.
5. The demand for money can be either for transactions or as an alternative to holding financial assets.
6. Interest rates are affected by both the demand for and supply of money. Interest rates in Australia are also heavily influenced by interest rates in other major countries because of Australia's heavy international indebtedness.

KEY TERMS

asset demand for money	277	floating exchange rate	273	money base	271
broad money	271	functions of money	267	nominal interest rate	280
consumer price index (CPI)	270	indexation	270	primary sources of money	272
credit creation	276	inflation	268	real interest rate	280
credit multiplier	274	interest rates	279	secondary source of money	274
fixed exchange rate	273	liquidity	267	transactions demand for money	277
		money	267		

REVIEW QUESTIONS

1. In your own words define the following terms:
   (a) money
   (b) symbolic money
   (c) medium of exchange
   (d) measure of value
   (e) store of value
   (f) standard for deferred payments
   (g) inflation
   (h) real terms.

2. Compare the usefulness of the following forms of money in terms of portability, divisibility and acceptability:
   (a) shells
   (b) cigarettes
   (c) debit cards.

3. In your own words define the following terms:
   (a) M3
   (b) money base
   (c) broad money
   (d) credit to the private sector by financial intermediaries.

4. Explain the difference between broad money and credit to the private sector by financial intermediaries.

5. In your own words define the following terms:
   (a) government budget deficit
   (b) public sector
   (c) private sector
   (d) balance of payments deficit.

6. Explain how a government budget surplus would affect the money supply in Australia.

7. Explain how Reserve Bank support for the Australian dollar would affect the money supply in Australia.

8. Draw up a balance sheet illustrating a situation according to the credit creation model, with $1000 in new deposits and a cash to deposits ratio of 10 per cent.

9. Illustrate the effects of three loans of $500.

10. Draw up a final balance sheet based on Question 8 when the limits of the credit creation process have been reached.

11. In your own words define the following terms:
    (a) cash to deposits ratio
    (b) advances to deposits ratio
    (c) loanable funds
    (d) credit multiplier
    (e) reserve assets ratio.

12. Briefly explain the process of credit creation.

13. Explain the limits to the process of credit creation.

14. In your own words define the following terms:
    (a) interest rate
    (b) yield
    (c) risk
    (d) liquidity
    (e) maturity term
    (f) real interest rate
    (g) nominal interest rate.

15. List the factors that influence the level of interest rates in Australia.

16. Explain why bank deposits may not be an effective means of storing your wealth in periods of high inflation.

APPLIED QUESTIONS AND EXERCISES
IMPACT OF THE GLOBAL FINANCIAL CRISIS

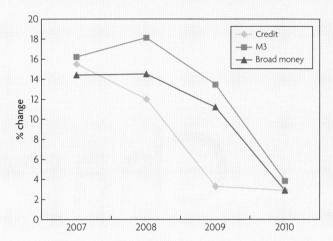

Figure 13.7
The impact of the GFC on attitudes to risk
Source: Reserve Bank, Statistics, *Table D1.*

Figure 13.7 illustrates the impact of the GFC on attitudes to risk.

QUESTIONS

1. Explain what has happened to the relationship between bank deposits and lending by banks.

2. Refer to Figures 13.4 and 13.5 on page 278 and give two reasons for the fall in official interest rates.

3. List two issues you would have to deal with if you were the CEO of a construction company in 2009.

THE CREDIT UNION

Imagine you are a lending officer for a credit union. You have three loan proposals to consider:

1. A member who is retired wants to borrow $50 000 for 10 years to establish a portfolio of shares in leading Australian companies.

2. A schoolteacher wants to borrow $10 000 for two years to finance a holiday.

3. A member who works part-time wants to borrow $5000 to buy a vehicle so he can become a sheep shearer.

QUESTIONS

1. What considerations would you take into account in deciding what interest rate to charge for these loans?

2. List the propositions from best to worst in terms of:
   (a) liquidity
   (b) ability to repay
   (c) administrative cost.

Chapter **14**

Financial institutions

LEARNING OBJECTIVES

After studying this chapter, you will be able to:

1. explain the functions performed by lenders and savers
2. explain the role of financial intermediaries
3. describe the main instruments of finance
4. explain the role of financial markets
5. explain the role and functions of the Reserve Bank
6. explain the role and functions of the Australian Prudential Regulation Authority
7. explain the role and functions of the Australian Securities and Investments Commission.

INTRODUCTION

The overall objective of this chapter is to explain the nature and role of the Australian financial system. The financial system includes banks, stock exchanges, superannuation funds, insurers, central banks and national regulators. These institutions provide a system for carrying out economic transactions and monetary policy and help to channel savings into investments. A resilient well-regulated financial system is essential for economic and financial stability in a world of increasing capital flows. We will examine the role of the Australian Prudential Regulation Authority in monitoring the performance of banks in particular and the role of the Reserve Bank of Australia in monitoring the stability of the financial system.

Before discussing the Australian financial system, there are some basic economic concepts with which you should be familiar.

SURPLUS AND DEFICIT UNITS

A **surplus unit** is an economic agent—for example an individual, household, company, country—that spends less than its current income. Thus it has surplus income available. Currently Singapore is an example of a surplus country because its national savings are so high that they exceed its domestic investment opportunities and so the surplus is used for investment overseas. Thus Singapore is making its excess savings available for use in other countries.

A **deficit unit** is an economic agent that spends more than it receives in current income. Thus it seeks to borrow money from surplus units to finance its excess spending. Countries like the United States and Australia are examples of deficit units because domestic savings are inadequate to fund domestic investment. Thus both countries need to use the savings of other countries to meet the shortfall between domestic savings and investment. When a Chinese company purchases shares in a mine in Australia it is helping to finance the gap between savings and investment in Australia.

In general, over an individual's life cycle, there are surpluses early in working life, then deficits while mortgages are paid and children raised, then surpluses later in life prior to retirement.

Financial intermediaries like banks facilitate the transfer of funds between surplus and deficit units. They provide a repository for the funds of surplus units and lend out parcels of funds to deficit units.

surplus unit
an economic agent that spends less than its current income

deficit unit
an economic agent that spends more than it receives in current income

asset
wealth which might take the form of bank deposits, shares, property, antiques and jewellery

ASSETS AND LIABILITIES

An **asset** is a form of wealth, whereas a **liability** is a burden. For example, if you are lucky enough to have money deposited in a bank, then that deposit is an asset to you because it is a store of your wealth. On the other hand if you have a loan from a bank, that represents a liability because you have to repay that loan.

It is interesting also to look at assets and liabilities from the bank's point of view. To the bank, your deposit is a liability because the bank has to be ready to repay it at some time. However, your loan represents an asset because it represents a stream of repayments to the bank.

When you are reading about financial assets and liabilities it is worth keeping in mind whose assets and liabilities are being discussed.

liability
a form of negative wealth where you owe something to someone else (e.g. a car loan, gambling debts, mobile phone bill)

DEFINING THE FINANCIAL SYSTEM

financial system
those institutions and arrangements that allow individuals and businesses to store savings, receive financial advice and assist in the settlement of financial transactions

The **financial system** consists of those institutions and arrangements that have developed to provide:[1]

- investment products for surplus economic units
- financial risk management products and services
- alternative funding sources for deficit economic units
- facilities for transferring funds from surplus to deficit economic units by creating new financial assets
- arrangements for trade in existing financial assets in secondary finance markets.

The Campbell Inquiry[2] summarised the functions of the financial system as:

- facilitating transactions
- enabling funds to be transferred between savers and borrowers
- assisting investors to balance risk, liquidity and returns.

Thus we can say that the financial system consists of financial institutions and financial instruments that are used to carry out the financing task. This chapter focuses on these institutions and instruments.

FINANCIAL INSTITUTIONS IN AUSTRALIA

Australia's standard classification of financial institutions categorises them on the basis of sources and uses of funds. There are five categories:

deposit-taking financial institutions
those that obtain most of their funds in the form of deposits from savers (e.g. banks and credit unions)

contractual savings institutions
(e.g. insurance companies) where a person makes periodic payments for life insurance on the basis of a contract that specifies if the person dies certain benefits will be paid to a nominated person

1. **Deposit-taking financial institutions** like banks and credit unions that obtain most of their funds in the form of deposits from savers.
2. **Contractual savings institutions** like insurance companies where a person makes periodic payments for life insurance on the basis of a contract that specifies if the person dies certain benefits will be paid to a nominated person.
3. Finance companies that raise funds by issuing securities and use the funds to make loans to other borrowers.
4. Money market corporations such as merchant banks that borrow short-term funds in large amounts to provide finance to businesses.
5. Unit trusts such as cash management trusts that gather money from the public and have the funds invested by a funds manager in assets specified in the trust deed—a legal document.

Key developments affecting financial institutions are:

- Increasing the role of regulators in response to market failures. In many countries legislation to increase the powers of regulators and to reduce freedom of action by financial institutions is under way in response to the global financial crisis (GFC).

- Globalisation of finance markets, which has meant that the Reserve Bank, for example, must take into account flows of funds into and out of Australia when setting interest rates and the role of offshore finance markets in funding financial institutions and capital investment in Australia.
- Increasing the focus on efficiency, for example on reducing cost to income ratios and taking advantage of economies of scale in areas such as risk pooling, staff training and computer systems.
- Strong competition for profitable market niches such as provision of services to wealthy individuals and for low-risk stable business such as home mortgage lending. As a result, profit margins tended to shrink in these niches during the 2000s.
- Centralisation and 'offshoring' of processing operations such as mortgage processing.

ROLE OF FINANCIAL INTERMEDIARIES

In order to understand the role of financial intermediaries it is important to be able to differentiate between direct and indirect financing.

Direct financing occurs when economic agents such as businesses and governments borrow by issuing their own securities such as shares or government bonds without help from a financial intermediary. The advantages of direct financing include lower costs.

Indirect financing occurs when finance is arranged through an intermediary. Borrowing money from a bank to purchase a house is an example of indirect financing. The advantages of indirect financing include the economies of scale in financial institutions, which are able to offer specialised skills and efficient systems for processing the array of documents involved in complex transactions like property purchases.

Financial intermediaries can be defined as:[3]

> institutions which accept funds from depositors and lend them to borrowers. They enable funds to flow smoothly and efficiently from those who wish to lend to those who wish to borrow. They reduce costs and risk to both groups by accepting and lending funds in amounts, for maturities and at times which lenders and borrowers prefer.

The major financial institutions in Australia are banks. Other organisations, such as merchant banks, finance companies, building societies and credit unions, share a smaller slice of the market.

The financial sector is one of the most dynamic parts of the economy. During the 1980s many controls that had been in place since World War II were removed from the financial sector, which dramatically increased the level of competition. This, combined with the rapid development of information technology, caused substantial changes in the structure and nature of services provided by the financial system. During the 1990s, the pace of change accelerated because of the impact of changing technology and the entry of many new players into the financial services arena.

The Wallis Report recommended that non-banking institutions be allowed to offer a wide range of services that were formerly the exclusive preserve of banks, provided that the strict capital requirements were met. One outcome of this was the new line of business for Australia Post in facilitating payments services in competition with the bank electronic bill payments services. In 2010 Australia Post was considering seeking a licence to establish a bank.

LEARNING OBJECTIVE 2
Explain the role of financial intermediaries

direct financing
when economic agents such as businesses and governments borrow by issuing their own securities such as shares or government bonds without help from a financial intermediary

indirect financing
when finance is arranged through an intermediary

financial intermediaries
institutions that accept funds from depositors and lend them to borrowers

BANKING: A BRIEF HISTORY

The first bank in Australia was established in 1817 as a result of support from the Governor of the colony. It was known as the Bank of New South Wales. Nowadays, it is known as Westpac Banking Corporation.

The history of banking in Australia is littered with bank failures and mergers; periods of increasing government intervention were followed by periods of deregulation. Banks have been important in financing development and booms as well as participating in busts.

Periods of strong economic development occurred in the 1830s, 1850s to 1880s, 1920s, 1950s, 1960s, 1980s and the 2000s. Most of this development was financed by overseas borrowing, facilitated by the banking system. Severe economic downturns occurred in the 1840s, 1890s, 1930s and late 1980s, usually as a result of downturns in commodity prices, excessive property speculation, and the withdrawal of funds by overseas investors. Australia narrowly avoided being severely impacted by the GFC in 2008–10 thanks to sound banking and regulatory practice and government intervention to support incomes in Australia (see Chapter 22).

For most of the 19th century, Australia had a deregulated banking sector, that is, banks were not subject to much government control. One of the results of the catastrophic depressions of the 1890s and 1930s was increased government intervention in the finance sector, which culminated in the Reserve Bank of Australia having virtual control over the operation of banks in the 1960s and 1970s. From the early 1980s to 2010, the activities of banks were deregulated to an increasing extent; the emphasis shifted from seeking to control operational aspects to ensuring the adequacy of the capital asset backing of banks and their risk-management systems.

One of the results of deregulation of the financial system was a decline in the market share of financing held by non-bank financial institutions as banks were able to out-compete their smaller rivals. This was also due to some NBFIs being converted to bank status.

BANKS

banks
as the major repositories of savings and operators of the payments system, Australian banks are licensed by the government (however, many organisations perform many of the same functions but do not call themselves 'banks')

Banks are different from other financial institutions. In order to call itself a 'bank', an organisation has to be a body corporate that has been granted authority to operate as a bank under the *Banking Act 1959* (Cwlth). In 1992 the federal government banned the use of the word 'bank' from the title of all businesses that do not possess a banking licence. Since 1 July 1998, banks are subject to supervision and regulation by the Australian Prudential Regulation Authority (APRA) along with the other authorised deposit-taking institutions.

Banks receive special attention from the authorities because they are the major depository of savings, and they play a central role in the payments mechanism in the economy. According to the Campbell Report, they should be at the zero end of the risk spectrum.

As Figure 14.1 shows, banks dominate the financial system in Australia, accounting for more than 50 per cent of total assets of financial institutions.

The market share held by banks increased over the period of deregulation from 1983 as a result of superior competitive ability unleashed by the process of deregulation and the general economic environment. Massive assets were accumulated in shares and property, along with other assets ranging from racehorses to paintings, all financed by debt. This boom was followed by a slump at the end of the 1980s, which saw a 'flight to quality' as people transferred funds from non-bank financial institutions to banks. The period from 1992 saw a recovery in terms of asset growth and profitability, but market share declined as superannuation and funds managers increased their market penetration. Figure 14.1 illustrates the increase in the market share of banks since 2007 as a result of a 'flight to safety' as people sought to preserve the value of their assets by placing them in government-guaranteed bank deposits.

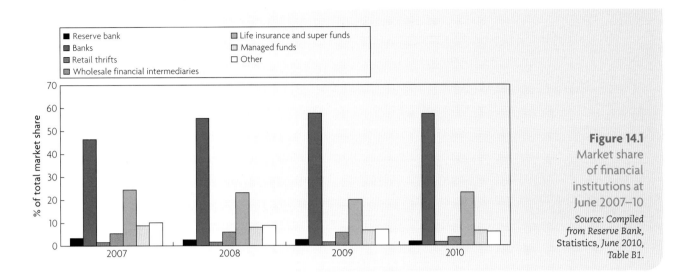

Figure 14.1
Market share
of financial
institutions at
June 2007–10

*Source: Compiled
from Reserve Bank,
Statistics, June 2010,
Table B1.*

The major activities of banks in Australia are:

- the operation of the payments system
- the acceptance of deposits and the creation of credit via financial assets by lending to businesses, households and individuals
- the facilitation of financing by assisting with the process of issuing bills of exchange (remember that an asset to a bank is a liability to a customer)
- generating income from fees and other activities such as specialist advice, organisation of international trade finance, risk management services, foreign currency dealing and leasing.

The payments system is like the bloodstream of modern society: it exchanges electronic signals and notes of promise for monetary value, just as the bloodstream exchanges oxygen for carbon dioxide. Any transaction that takes place without an exchange of cash uses the payments system.

Banks earn revenue from operating the payments system. They were in a position to acquire information about customers because it was almost impossible to operate in modern society without using a bank to access the payments system. This bank monopoly was removed in 1999.

Banks finance the creation of assets by accepting liabilities in the form of deposits and by other forms of fund raising, both in Australia and overseas. As Figure 14.2 overleaf illustrates, banks' major liabilities are deposits, bill acceptances and foreign currency borrowings. Their main assets are loans, advances and commercial bills held and receivable.

Essentially, banks cover the costs of their operations through the differential between what they pay for their liabilities (e.g. interest on deposits) and what they charge for their assets (e.g. interest on overdrafts). This is known as a **bank margin**. They also earn income from fees for facilitating financing via commercial bills, and by trading in foreign exchange. This income is called non-interest income or trading profits.

The main expenditures of banks are on staff and premises and on loans that are not repaid (bad debts).

Bad debts tend to rise when the economy goes into recession.

Banks provide a range of services to business including: transaction accounts, telephone and online services, payment services including facilitating online payments, credit cards and business finance to assist with cash flow and facilitate investment in assets to enable business growth.

bank margin
*the differential
between what a
bank pays for their
liabilities and charges
for their assets*

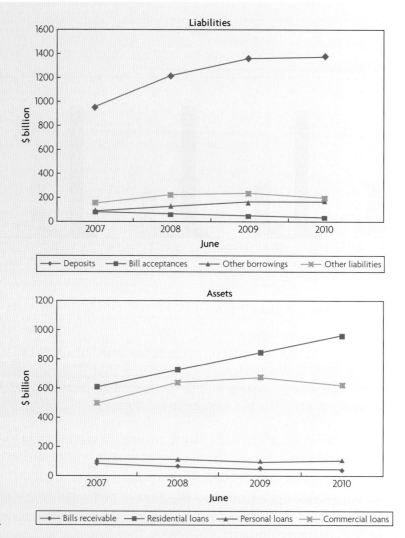

Figure 14.2

Banks: liabilities and assets

Source: Compiled from Reserve Bank, Statistics, June 2010, Tables B2 and B3.

LINK TO
BUSINESS

THE BASIC BANKING MODEL

The basic bank business model involves accepting deposits and lending those deposits out at an interest rate which is higher than that paid on deposits. For most banks there is a fundamental flaw in that there is a mismatch in the terms of deposits and loans. For example the bank does not have 30-year deposits to match the term of a 30-year mortgage. So it must manage the difference between its deposits and withdrawals (liquidity) to ensure that it can always meet requests for funds. Over the years there have been many occasions when banks in Australia and elsewhere have not been able to maintain their liquidity and have collapsed (see 'The banking collapse of 1893' later in this chapter).

Banks generate income from these sources:

• bank margin is the difference between interest earned on loans (assets) and interest paid on deposits or other borrowed funds (liabilities)
• fees charged to customers

- trading profits generated by banks trading in their own right or by facilitating customer transactions (e.g. foreign exchange transactions).

Banks usually generate net income before expenses of about 3 per cent of the value of their assets. The net income generated from the above activities is used to pay for:

- staff and premises
- other operating costs
- expensing and making provisions for bad loans
- taxation.

Of the activities undertaken by banks, trading activities are the most risky. One of the causes of the GFC was the downturn in the markets for derivatives based on the United States property market (see Chapter 15).

In 2010 the Commonwealth Bank compared its balance sheet with that of a United Kingdom and a United States bank.

The CBA had over 80 per cent of its assets in loans whereas the United Kingdom bank had only about 60 per cent and the United States bank had 50 per cent. In other words the United Kingdom and United States banks had 30 to 40 per cent of their assets in speculative trading positions. If the market turned down these banks would have many times their capital base exposed and would face the possibility of collapse.

QUESTIONS
1. Explain why bank regulators are interested in 'liquidity'.
2. Explain why banks make provision for bad loans.
3. What is the key difference between the CBA and the other two banks mentioned?

Overdrafts

Bank **overdraft** were the main source of business finance up to the 1990s. An overdraft involves an extension of a line of credit to a bank customer. The essential function of an overdraft is to cover seasonal and working capital requirements.

The arrangement enables the customer to write cheques up to an agreed limit. Deposits made to the account increase the credit balance or decrease the overdraft, while cheques drawn decrease the credit balance and increase the overdraft.

From the point of view of a business, an overdraft is ideal for meeting day-to-day peaks and troughs in a firm's cash flow. Overdraft arrangements are subject to various fees, as well as interest charges.

Commercial bills

Commercial bills are a common source of short-term business finance for up to 180 days. In simple terms, a party that requires finance issues a bill of exchange to an acceptor, in return for a discounted sum of money. The buyer of the bill pays to the holder of the bill the face value of the bill, less a discount that is calculated on the prevailing discount rate for bank bills and the number of days to maturity.

A commercial bill is a negotiable instrument, which means it can be bought and sold many times before it reaches maturity. The bill is retired or extinguished after the drawer repays the bill or 'rolls it over' (i.e. starts the whole process over again).

LEARNING OBJECTIVE 3
Describe the main instruments of finance

overdraft
an extension of a line of credit to a bank customer

commercial bills
issued to a lender by a borrower as evidence of a lender's debt and the borrower's asset, and can be sold to another party during the life of the debt

The advantage of a commercial bill, from the bank's point of view, is that it is potentially a liquid asset. It can be converted into cash at short notice, or the bank may sell the bill onto the market as soon as it has been drawn, thus freeing up cash to finance another bill.

The advantage of bill financing to a business usually lies in its relatively lower cost.

Interest charges on bills can change daily, reflecting market conditions. As well as interest costs, there are other charges to pay such as acceptance, facility and activation charges.

Asset finance

The purpose of asset finance is to enable businesses to fund vehicles or business plant and equipment without using working capital. Asset finance might take the form of a chattel mortgage, hire purchase or a lease arrangement. The nature of these arrangements could range from repayment of both interest and principal at the end of the term, to regular repayments of principal and interest. Interest rates may be floating, or fixed for a time then subject to review.

CHANGES TO BANK ACTIVITIES IN THE 2000s
The economics of banking

During the 2000s, the pace of change in the banking industry accelerated. The economics of banking altered dramatically with the rapid introduction of electronic commerce, which offered a much less costly alternative to the traditional network of branches as the core channel for distributing bank services. The introduction of automatic teller machines (ATMs), Electronic Funds Transfer at Point of Sale (EFTPOS), telephone banking and mobile bankers equipped with laptop computers enabled customers to conduct banking activities without ever entering a bank. Bank branches were converted into service centres and bank staff became more focused on selling products to customers.

Electronic commerce also enabled new players to enter the financial services market, for example mortgage originators like Aussie Home Loans and Australia Post payment services. These new players gained market share at the expense of banks prior to the GFC.

Not only did banks face competition in the provision of services, they also faced competition for deposits in the form of superannuation and other such funds. These pressures caused a decline in the average interest margin for banks and forced reductions in costs. As a result, employment in the major banks fell, the number of bank branches was reduced and massive investments in electronic banking took place. Also banks took steps to develop their own financial planning and asset management arms.

As the GFC struck Australia in 2008 the Australian Government guaranteed the deposits held in Australian banks, and banks' market share increased as people moved their funds into bank deposits and out of non-bank institutions (see Figure 14.2, p. 290).

The banking sector became more concentrated as the CBA took over Bankwest and Westpac took over the St George Bank.

Australian banks did not engage in the risky trading activities of many overseas banks in areas such as trading debt securities, insuring debt securities against default and funding trading companies with excessive amounts of leverage. However both ANZ and NAB had some small exposures to highly leveraged companies which went under. Australian banks are exposed to developments overseas because of their reliance on overseas funding and overseas debt markets.

Figure 14.3 illustrates the mismatch between Australian banks' overseas assets and liabilities.

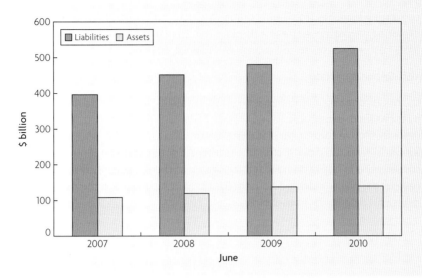

Figure 14.3
Banks'
non-resident
liabilities and
assets as at
June 2007–10
($ billion)

*Source: Reserve
Bank, Statistics,
Table B1.*

Internationalisation

Australian banks have sought to expand their overseas operations to provide a broader service to existing clients and to increase their size. This is seen as necessary to meet international competition. The National Australia Bank purchased four regional banks in Britain and Ireland, as well as the Bank of New Zealand and the Michigan National Corporation during the 1980s. Westpac also made a number of acquisitions, including the Challenge Bank and the Trust Bank, New Zealand. In the 2000s the ANZ Bank embarked on a strategy of expansion into Asia.

In 2010 Chinese mega banks accounted for three of the top seven global financial institutions. In May 2010 the Agricultural Bank of China (ABC) set up a representative office in Sydney. It joined the world's biggest lender by market value, the Industrial and Commercial Bank of China (IBC). At the time IBC was discussing a retail banking partnership with Westpac, while the China Development Bank had already established an agency arrangement with the ANZ. These Chinese banks joined a large number of foreign banks with operations in Australia.

Overall in 2010 about 40 foreign banks were authorised to operate in Australia.

Development of new products

New products offered by banks have affected every household in Australia. We have become accustomed to ATMs, EFTPOS, telephone and online banking. Similarly, new financial instruments—home equity loans, mortgage offset accounts, swaps, options, internet banking,

CHANGES IN THE NATURE OF BANKING

Major changes in the Australian banking industry in the decade since 2000 have included:

- exploiting economies of scale in back-office business processes
- improving the quality of lending through better use of systems to identify costs and risks
- reducing costs by reducing the size of workforces and increasing the use of information technology
- reducing the number of bank branches and increasing the use of electronic platforms to deliver services

LINK TO
BUSINESS

continued ↘

continued

- converting branches from being primarily places for transactions to service centres
- exploring new revenue streams through wealth management to earn income from fees, and using customer bases to sell a range of financial services.

Threats to banks include:

- the risk of ongoing international financial instability which would make offshore borrowing by banks more expensive
- more restrictive banking regulations
- a slowdown in the growth of credit as interest rates rise and people become more conservative in taking on new debt obligations. The flip side of this is the exposure banks have to the highly indebted household sector in Australia and the risks arising from bad debts and defaults by households.

QUESTIONS
1. Give two examples of how you or your family has been affected by the above changes.
2. Explain how you or your family would be affected by a rise of 2 per cent in interest rates in general.

cash management products—have increased the flexibility available to bank clients. In 2010 distribution of banking services via mobile phones commenced with most banks offering internet banking services via browser or applications.

NON-BANK FINANCIAL INSTITUTIONS (NBFIs)

Non-bank financial institutions (NBFIs) include finance companies, building societies, credit unions, cash management trusts, money market corporations and life insurance offices.

During the period of regulation after World War II, NBFIs assumed a more prominent role within the Australian financial system. From 1968 to 1982, the share of total deposits held by banks fell from nearly 80 per cent to about 55 per cent.

The most important reason for the growth of NBFIs, particularly during the 1960s and 1970s, was that these institutions were not subjected to Reserve Bank controls. Therefore they could manage their liquidity and interest rate policies without restrictions. They could offer higher rates for deposits than banks, provide a wider range of more attractive products, and accept higher-risk business.

NBFIs were distinguished from banks in several important respects. Most obviously, NBFIs were not banks and did not require banking licences; they did not have to comply with Reserve Bank controls and were not supervised by the Reserve Bank. The Reserve Bank also was not obligated to assist NBFIs in difficulty, as evidenced by the collapse of the Pyramid group of building societies in 1989. NBFIs also tend to provide a smaller range of services to specific client groups, as opposed to the more general approach of the bank sector.

In 1992 building societies and credit unions became regulated and supervised under the Australian Financial Institutions Commission (AFIC). This was the outcome of legislation passed by the states to place these financial institutions under a national coordinated system of prudential supervision similar to that of the banking industry.

In 1999 APRA took over responsibility from AFIC for the supervision of building societies, credit unions and friendly societies. The aim of APRA is to minimise the risk that deposit-taking institutions will be unable to meet their obligations to depositors. APRA has the power to intervene if this seems likely to occur.

APRA administers licensing conditions and develops prudential standards and requirements for institutions to adopt. It also has regular consultation with senior management and conducts onsite reviews.

There are several different types of non-bank financial institutions, each performing slightly different functions for different markets.

Retail thrifts

Retail thrifts, which include building societies and credit unions, offer deposit and loan services that essentially compete with banks. They are cooperatives owned by their members and thus are able to offer more personalised service. Their profit margins are probably lower than those of banks.

Building societies

The primary function of **building societies** is the provision of mortgage finance for owner-occupied housing.

The building society sector has been static for many years. In the 1970s there were about 200 building societies; in 2010 there were less than 15. Deregulation meant that banks became able to compete with building societies, and many building societies amalgamated or became banks. For example, the biggest building society of the 1980s became the St George Bank and is now part of Westpac.

Credit unions

Credit unions—or credit cooperatives—are financial institutions in which membership is restricted to individuals who share some common bond, generally similarity of employment. Credit unions are owned by their members and are typically operated on a non-profit basis.

Individual credit unions are generally small. In 2010 fewer than 120 credit unions operated within the Australian financial system, compared to more than 700 in the 1970s. The major source of credit union funds is deposits from members, and the majority of their lending is in the form of personal loans to members.

Wholesale financial intermediaries

Wholesale financial intermediaries include finance companies, money market corporations, mortgage companies and managed funds. These entities usually on-lend money loaned to them by corporations such as banks.

Finance companies

Finance companies were traditionally providers of personal credit to individuals, but now provide a diverse range of services to both consumers and business, such as leasing, factoring and wholesale financing. Traditionally finance companies will provide finance to high-risk borrowers with whom banks are unwilling to be associated. Most loans advanced to consumers are for the purchase of durable items, such as cars and television sets. During the GFC some of the major overseas-owned finance companies ceased operating in Australia.

Money-market corporations

Money-market corporations—or merchant banks—tend to be the most dynamic component of the Australian financial system.

retail thrifts *offer deposit and loan services that essentially compete with banks; include building societies and credit unions*

building societies *NBFIs whose primary function is the provision of mortgage finance for owner-occupied housing by accumulating the funds of members into loans for housing*

credit unions *NBFIs in which membership is restricted to individuals who share some common bond, generally similarity of employment*

wholesale financial intermediaries *include finance companies, money-market corporations, mortgage companies and managed funds, and usually on-lend money loaned to them by corporations such as banks*

finance companies *NBFIs that provide businesses and individuals with services such as personal credit, leasing, factoring and wholesale financing*

money-market corporations *NBFIs that almost exclusively service the corporate sector and operate in the short-term wholesale finance market*

Merchant banks almost exclusively service the financial needs of the corporate sector and operate in the short-term wholesale finance market. Usually the core business of merchant banks is the provision of specialist corporate advisory functions which earn a substantial income in fees. Merchant banks generally operate with large parcels of funds. Other areas of business include corporate advice and other fee-for-service activities, as well as foreign currency dealing.

Mortgage companies

mortgage companies
companies that trade in mortgages either by on-lending funds to borrowers for housing or by packaging mortgage loans for sale in the wholesale finance market

There are two types of **mortgage companies**: mortgage originators and securitisation vehicles.

The first group includes companies like Wizard and Aussie Home Loans, which provide home loans and are in competition with banks. Their business model involves raising large amounts of funds via the professional money market and arranging small loans to households in return for a fee. Thus they have the title of mortgage originator. It is important to note that the household's loan is provided in the professional money market by insurance companies, fund managers or sometimes banks. Mortgage originators can compete with banks because they have very little in the way of costs compared with banks.

The second group is called securitisation vehicles. These do not originate mortgages but rather package thousands of existing mortgages into large parcels for investment called mortgage-backed securities. The attraction of these parcels to big investors is that they are low risk and represent a stable income stream. Banks have been a ready source of these mortgages as they move them off their balance sheets to make room for new mortgage business that is competitive in the market place.

Mortgage companies lost significant market share during the GFC and the securitisation market shrank dramatically.

Managed funds

managed funds
these accumulate the funds of many individuals into large parcels for investment purposes

Entities like investment funds, public unit trusts, cash management trusts and superannuation funds are all examples of **managed funds**.

Superannuation funds collect contributions and in return promise benefits after retirement. Since 1987 it has been compulsory for employees in Australia to contribute a certain percentage of their salary to a superannuation fund. These funds are invested in a wide range of assets both in Australia and overseas.

Financial conglomerates

financial conglomerates
financial services organisations providing a full range of financial services to meet the needs of their customers

Many large financial institutions are now regarded as **financial conglomerates** or financial services organisations providing a full range of financial services to meet the needs of their customers. Examples include banks establishing funds management subsidiaries and offering life insurance. Life insurance companies have purchased bank subsidiaries. These conglomerates are difficult for governments to supervise effectively because they span different markets, but have interdependent and complex corporate structures.

LEARNING OBJECTIVE 4
Explain the role of financial markets

FINANCIAL MARKETS

Financial institutions interact with each other as well as with non-financial organisations. Much of this interaction takes place in financial markets.

Financial markets involve the purchase and sale of financial assets. They are networks of traders using telephones and computers to buy and sell assets such as shares, bonds, securities and foreign exchange.

One of the effects of deregulation of the financial system was the expansion of financial markets. The growth in diversity of financial markets has considerably extended the range of options available to investors and savers. There are retail markets and wholesale capital and money markets. A feature of financial market development has been the provision of more specialised products and services to specific groups of investors.

As you know, a market is any situation where people buy and sell items—fruit, trash and treasure, or money. There are three main financial markets. The money market and the foreign exchange market are networks of traders working via telephones and linked to each other by computer networks and satellites. The stock market originally traded in a physical location—the stock exchange—but now this market also uses telephones and computer screens and much trading is conducted by computers pre-programmed to buy or sell according to prescribed conditions. Conceptually we can divide the two functions of finance markets into a primary and a secondary role.

The **primary market** is where new issues of government bonds or shares, for example, are purchased for the first time. Usually traders purchase them and then 'on-sell' them into secondary markets. A **secondary market** involves traders buying and selling these bonds and shares. As a rule, the volume of trading in secondary markets is much bigger than in primary markets.

financial markets
networks of traders using telephones and computers to buy and sell assets such as shares, bonds, securities and foreign exchange

primary market
where new issues of government bonds or shares, for example, are purchased for the first time

secondary market
where traders buy and sell shares that were originally issued in the primary market

GOVERNANCE OF THE FINANCE SECTOR IN AUSTRALIA

In 1996 the Wallis Committee was established to make recommendations on 'the nature of the regulatory arrangements that will best ensure an efficient, responsive, competitive and flexible financial system to underpin stronger economic performance, consistent with financial stability, prudence, integrity and fairness'.[4]

The Australian Government accepted the findings of the report and implemented a new structure in 1998, which regulated by function rather than by type of financial institution. The new structure has the following key features:

- The Reserve Bank has the functions of monetary policy, systemic stability, regulation of the payments system and other central banking responsibilities.
- APRA conducts **prudential supervision** and **prudential regulation**. Prudential supervision and regulation are aimed at minimising the impact on consumers of the effects of market failure.
- The Australian Securities and Investments Commission is responsible for market integrity, consumer protection in the finance area and corporations law.
- The Australian Competition and Consumer Commission has a limited role in dealing with the competition issues in the finance industry.
- The Reserve Bank, APRA, ASIC and the Australian Treasury form the Council of Financial Regulators to advise governments on the adequacy of Australia's financial regulatory arrangements.
- In addition there are pressures for banks to improve and assess risk-management processes as new global standards are formulated.

prudential supervision
prudential supervision involves checking that the regulations are being observed

prudential regulation
involves the creation of rules for financial institutions aimed at minimising the risk of market failure

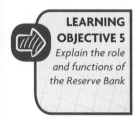

THE RESERVE BANK OF AUSTRALIA

All advanced financial systems have a **central bank** at the apex. In Australia this is the **Reserve Bank of Australia (RBA)**. Functions performed by the Reserve Bank include:

- monetary policy
- ensuring the stability of the finance and payments systems
- banker to banks
- banker to governments
- custodian of Australia's international reserves of foreign currency
- control of the note issue.

central bank
the bank at the top of a financial system, responsible for conducting monetary policy and ensuring the stability of the payments system

The Reserve Bank was established in 1959 by the *Reserve Bank Act 1959* (Cwlth). Before 1959, central banking functions were performed by the Commonwealth Bank. Central banking in Australia developed from the collapse of the banking system and the hardship associated with the depression of the 1890s.

The Act states that it is the duty of the Bank Board to exercise its powers so as to contribute to the:

Reserve Bank of Australia (RBA)
Australia's central bank, responsible for monetary policy and financial system stability

- stability of the currency of Australia
- maintenance of full employment in Australia
- economic prosperity and welfare of the people of Australia.

The Act is augmented by a 'Statement on the Conduct of Monetary Policy' which records the common understanding of the Governor of the Reserve Bank and the government on key aspects of monetary and central banking policy. In September 2010 a revised statement was issued which contained a significant change. This confirmed the responsibility of the Reserve Bank for managing the stability of the financial system. The text reads: 'Without compromising the price stability objective, the Reserve Bank seeks to use its powers where appropriate to promote the stability of the Australian financial system . . .' Thus the role of the Reserve Bank has effectively been extended by agreement with the government of the day to enable it to play an active role in dealing with threats to the economy arising from innovations in credit markets which may promote excessive credit growth and asset price bubbles.

Reserve Bank operations are directed by a 10-member board, the chair of which is also the governor and general manager of the bank. The Reserve Bank Act outlines the relationship between the bank and the Commonwealth Government and specifies that, in the event of a dispute between the two bodies, the view of the government will prevail.

Prior to 1998 the two major functions of the Reserve Bank were the conduct of monetary policy and the prudential supervision of banks. Monetary policy was aimed at assisting the achievement of goals in the area of macroeconomic policy while prudential supervision was aimed at the protection of depositors' funds. In July 1998 responsibility for the prudential supervision of banks was transferred to APRA.

FUNCTIONS
Monetary policy

Monetary policy is conducted through the use of open market operations, which involves the Reserve Bank buying and selling Commonwealth Securities on the secondary market to alter financial conditions, so as to support its stated target for the cash rate. We will look at monetary policy in Chapter 23.

System stability

The Reserve Bank of Australia focuses on potential risks to the stability of the financial system with the aim of avoiding situations where a shock to the financial system may threaten the stability of the national economy. The Reserve Bank is the only institution that can provide emergency cash support to the financial system. Its role is complementary to APRA's role in supervising individual financial institutions.

In mid 2004 the Reserve Bank published its first examination of the stability of the Australian financial system. It described Australia's banks as being profitable, carrying few bad debts and holding capital considerably in excess of their minimum regulatory requirements. It noted that the shift in bank lending away from business towards households had reduced the overall level of risk for banks.

The payments system

The **payments system** is the means by which debts are settled between economic agents. In Australia, while cash is the most important payment instrument, non-cash payment instruments include cheques, EFTPOS, direct debits and credits, and credit cards. All non-cash transactions use the payments system. Cash transactions involve direct payments between the giver and the receiver and thus do not involve the payments system.

payments system
the means by which debts are settled between economic agents, facilitated in Australia by banks

In 1998 the Reserve Bank was given responsibility for the Payments System Board (PSB), which has the aim of increasing the efficiency of the Australian payments system without compromising its integrity. Some of the aims of the PSB are to contribute to:

- controlling risk in the financial system
- promoting the efficiency of the payments system
- promoting competition in the market for payments services consistent with the overall stability of the financial system.

Banker to banks

All banks that operate in more than one state in Australia are required to conduct various accounts with the Reserve Bank. The most important of these accounts is the Exchange Settlement Account, which is used by banks to settle each day the net amounts owing among themselves as a result of their customers' transactions.

Banker to government

The Reserve Bank conducts all accounts for the Commonwealth Government. All receipts to and payments by the Commonwealth pass through the Reserve Bank.

The bank also provides the finance to cover any shortfalls in revenue. For example, the Commonwealth Government may run a deficit budget, where its expenditure exceeds its revenue. The Reserve Bank lends the government the funds necessary to cover the shortfall. In return, the government issues debt securities, like Treasury Notes to the Reserve Bank, which the bank can use in its conduct of monetary policy.

Changes in the Reserve Bank's balance sheet can have effects on the balance sheets of other banks, which then affects the banks' ability to create credit. For example, a government purchase financed by the Reserve Bank results in the Reserve Bank losing funds and the banks gaining funds. On the other hand, sales tax collections have the reverse impact.

Custodian of Australia's international reserves

international reserves

consist of Australia's holdings of foreign currency and gold

The central bank has been responsible for managing Australia's **international reserves** since World War II.

In June 2010, gold and foreign exchange reserves were A$43.7 billion. The Reserve Bank uses these reserves in its operations to influence the exchange rate. In 2009 the Reserve Bank sold Australian dollars because they were increasing in value against other currencies. Figure 14.4 illustrates the cycle of Reserve Bank sales and purchases of foreign exchange and total official reserve assets.

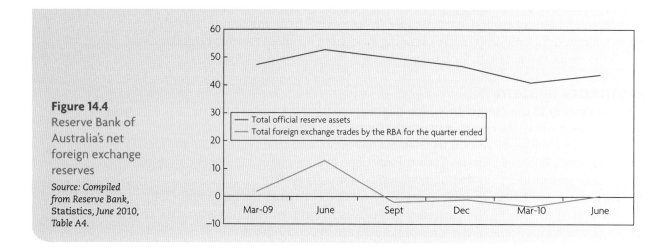

Figure 14.4
Reserve Bank of Australia's net foreign exchange reserves

Source: Compiled from Reserve Bank, Statistics, June 2010, Table A4.

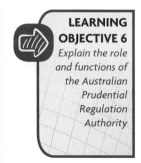

LEARNING OBJECTIVE 6
Explain the role and functions of the Australian Prudential Regulation Authority

AUSTRALIAN PRUDENTIAL REGULATION AUTHORITY (APRA)

Australian Prudential Regulation Authority (APRA)
the prudential regulator for banks, life and general insurance companies, superannuation funds, building societies, credit unions and friendly societies

Established in 1998, the **Australian Prudential Regulation Authority (APRA)** supervises authorised deposit-taking institutions (ADIs) and has responsibility for the stability of the financial system. This means it is the prudential regulator for banks, life and general insurance companies, superannuation funds, building societies, credit unions and friendly societies. All ADIs must hold a licence issued by APRA to operate in Australia. APRA has developed a comprehensive framework of prudential standards and guidelines to promote sound financial and risk management and good governance, to provide for financial safety and protect customers from market failure.

APRA responds to the recommendations of the Basel Committee of Banking Supervision, established under the auspices of the Bank for International Settlements—the body charged with establishing an international framework setting the minimum level of capital that banks should hold.

APRA also conducts stress tests which involve testing bank balance sheets to see how much financial pressure they can withstand in a simulated crisis. Stress testing seems likely to become a regular activity in Australia, Europe, the United States and India in the future.

PRUDENTIAL REQUIREMENTS

APRA's prudential standards, which apply to all ADIs, address solvency and capital adequacy, corporate governance, asset quality and concentration, liquidity and liability valuations.

From a customers' perspective the main prudential requirements for authorised deposit-taking institutions are the capital adequacy and liquidity requirements.

Regulations were implemented from 2008 following the recommendations of the Basel Committee. The Basel II accords have the aims of making the allocation of capital more sensitive to risk, separating operational risk from credit risk and aligning economic and regulatory risk more closely. It uses a 'three pillars approach' with the pillars being minimum capital requirements, reviews by the supervising authority, and market discipline.

The minimum capital requirements deal with the three major risk areas for banks: credit risk, operational risk and market risk.

Banks can adopt two approaches. They can adopt a standardised approach using specific risk weights for different degrees of credit risk or they can develop their own system which is appropriate for their particular risk profile. If a bank develops its own system it may have a lower capital requirement and hence have the scope for increased levels of lending and profit. If an Australian bank adopts the standardised approach it has to set aside a minimum of 8 per cent of its risk-weighted assets as capital.

CAPITAL ADEQUACY REQUIREMENT (CAR)

An example of a capital adequacy requirement is set out below.

Let us assume that for 'our bank' the **capital adequacy requirement (CAR)** is expressed as a ratio which means that the bank must, as a minimum, hold capital equal to 8 per cent of the value of its assets, which have been adjusted for credit and market risk. The weights reflect the risk associated with each type of asset. The weightings below are a simplified version of the actual weights used by APRA in 2010.

capital adequacy requirement (CAR) *banks are required to hold a certain amount of capital, usually expressed as a ratio, against credit and market risk*

Capital is the accumulated wealth of the business. For banks, capital includes the value of shares, reserves, retained earnings and other types of capital assets including top-rated corporate bonds and government securities. The risk weightings applied to the assets of the banks in calculating how much capital they must hold are based essentially on the collateral or security of the assets.

- On cash and on Commonwealth, state and territory government securities with the highest credit grade rating, the risk weights are zero, meaning that 'our bank' does not need to hold capital against these assets.
- On lending to local governments and non-commercial public sector entities in Australia and overseas with the highest credit grading, the weighting is 20 per cent. Thus 'our bank' must hold capital equal to 20 per cent of 8 per cent of the value of these assets.
- On mortgages secured by residential real estate, the weighting depends on the **loan to valuation ratio** (LVR) which is the relationship between the loan and the valuation of the property. If the property is valued at $1 million and the loan is $800 000 then the LVR is 80. The weighting also depends on whether the lender is covered by mortgage insurance. If the lender is covered for losses of up to 40 per cent of the higher of the original loan or the outstanding value of the loan then the risk weighting is 35 per cent. However if the loan is for $900 000 then the LVR is 90 and the risk weighting is 50. If mortgage insurance is taken out then the risk weighting drops to 35. The mortgage insurance has the effect of reducing the risk of loss to the bank thus the risk weighting is lower. This covers mortgages for owner-occupied housing and for rental housing. See Table 14.1 overleaf.

loan to valuation ratio *ratio of the amount of the loan to the valuation of the property*

Table 14.1   **Risk weightings for mortgages secured against residential real estate**

LOAN TO VALUATION RATIO	RISK WEIGHT (NO MORTGAGE INSURANCE)	RISK WEIGHT (AT LEAST 40% OF THE MORTGAGE INSURED)
0 to 80	35	35
80.01 to 90	50	35
90.01 to 100	75	50

- On all other bank assets, the risk weighting is 100 per cent. This includes loans to companies, loans secured by mortgage over commercial property, consumer loans and the debt of all commercial government enterprises, not carrying a formal government guarantee. Note that loans to companies—even top companies like BHP Billiton—and loans secured by commercial mortgages have a larger weight than loans on residential mortgages. 'Our bank' needs the full 8 per cent of capital against '100 per cent items'. Assets of this type are not as attractive to banks as, say, lending for residential mortgages.
- On exposures to equities the capital adequacy requirement ranges from 300 to 400 per cent and for margin lending secured against listed shares the capital adequacy requirement is 20 per cent.

Since the beginning of the 21st century banks have been required to establish their own internal liquidity management policies and systems. The significance of this is that the management and the board of financial institutions are recognised as being primarily responsible for the prudent management of the institution rather than the regulator.

EXAMPLE

'Our bank', with $100 million worth of loans (the structure of which is set out in Table 14.2), would have to maintain capital to the value of $3.84 million to support the loans.

In this example the bank has residential mortgages of $40 million against which it has to hold 35 per cent of 8 per cent as capital. So 8 per cent of 40 million is $3.2 million and 35 per cent of 3.2 million is $1.12 million.

Table 14.2   **Calculation of capital adequacy ratio**

TYPE OF LOAN	$m	CAR (% OF 8%)	$m
Commonwealth Government securities	10	0	0
Loans to local government	20	20	0.32
Residential mortgages (LVR less than 80)	40	35	1.12
Commercial loans	30	100	2.40
	100		3.84

CAPITAL ADEQUACY RATIO AND THE COST OF FINANCE

There is a connection between the requirements of the capital adequacy requirement and the interest and fees charged by banks for loans.

For example, if you owned a small business and you were looking for finance to expand your business, you would have to consider which of the different forms of financing are suitable for your requirements and how the security you offer for the loan will affect the cost. Consider the main forms of finance:

- Overdraft: for a business with cyclical cash flows; carries a fixed rate of interest.
- Commercial bills: to cover periods of temporary shortages of cash; carries a floating interest rate.
- A mortgage or lease arrangement: for business asset finance requirements; might carry a fixed rate of interest, reviewed periodically.

The nature of the security could be:

- mortgage secured against residential real estate, which has a CAR of 35 per cent
- mortgage secured against commercial real estate, which has a CAR of 100 per cent

QUESTIONS

What combination of financing would you choose, if you were in the following circumstances?

1. You operate a milk bar at a tourist resort, and you need to carry more stock.
2. You operate a factory making water pipes, and you want to buy more efficient machines.
3. You operate a school and you want to build some new classrooms, but you expect interest rates to fall; you want to be able to benefit from that, but also have some predictability about the cash flow required to repay the loan.

LINK TO BUSINESS

Changes at the international level

In 2010 the Basel Committee released proposals to increase the capital requirements of banks in order to strengthen global capital and liquidity regulations with the objective of improving the banking system's ability to act as a shock absorber rather than a transmitter of shocks to the real economy. During the negotiations regarding implementation, Australian banks were exempted from a requirement that they keep a minimum level of capital in the form of government bonds against total assets to meet 30 days of cash withdrawals. This was because Australian Government debt was so low that there were not enough government bonds in circulation to cover the requirement.

Also, the four major Australian banks were covered by legislation in the United States because they are listed on the United States stock exchange. The Dodd Frank Bill, legislation passed in 2010 in response to the GFC, gave regulators the power to seize and break up large financial institutions, created a new consumer protection bureau, and introduced greater transparency into derivative markets (see Chapter 15.)

INSURANCE COMPANIES AND FRIENDLY SOCIETIES

The aim of APRA is to minimise the risk that insurers and friendly societies will be unable to meet their obligations as a result of financial weakness. It has the power to intervene if such a situation looks likely to arise.

ISLAMIC BANKING WITHOUT INTEREST

LINK TO
INTERNATIONAL
ECONOMY

Islamic banks operate on a different basis to banks in the European model.

The Islamic concept of banking, which began in 1973 with the First Dubai Islamic Bank of Bahrain, is little known outside the world of Islam. It has been estimated that in 2010 about US$300–500 billion was held inside the international Islamic banking system in the more than 100 banks scattered through countries such as Saudi Arabia, Jordan, Pakistan, Malaysia, the Philippines and Indonesia and that this market was growing at 15–20 per cent per year.

The principle behind Islamic banking is that financial activities must be in keeping with Sharia, the ethical code derived from the Koran. This means that many of the fundamental concepts of Western banking are not acceptable. For example, the collection of interest is banned because it is regarded as sinful. Also, activities supporting industries associated with alcohol, tobacco, gambling and armaments are not permitted.

In order to ensure that this code is followed, Islamic banks are co-governed by religious leaders. This takes the form of Sharia supervisory boards comprised of Islamic scholars. This is a stark contrast to Western banks, where management is mainly based on financial knowledge and ability. One of the problems for Islamic banking is the varying interpretation of the Sharia and the effect this has on different accounting treatment of lending by different banks.

How do Islamic banks pay for their costs and make a profit without charging interest? The answer is through profit-sharing, fees and commissions. There is an acceptance of payment for services rendered, and the providers of funds earn a profit on their investment as opposed to interest on their funds. Profits earned from the use to which borrowed money is put are shared between the provider of the funds and the borrower. The ratio varies in different situations: the most common is 80 per cent for the provider and 20 per cent for the borrower.

QUESTION

Given the globalisation of finance markets and the activities of the Basel Committee of Supervisors, what issues can you foresee arising in the future for Islamic banking?

SUPERANNUATION FUNDS

The aim of APRA is to ensure as far as possible that fund trustees manage superannuation funds prudently and in the long-term interests of the members. This is pursued through licensing of operators and requiring trustees to have appropriate investment management strategies and governance standards.

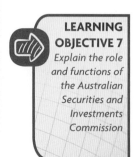

**LEARNING
OBJECTIVE 7**
*Explain the role
and functions of
the Australian
Securities and
Investments
Commission*

AUSTRALIAN SECURITIES AND INVESTMENTS COMMISSION (ASIC)

The key principles underlying the role of the **Australian Securities and Investments Commission (ASIC)** are market integrity and consumer protection. Market integrity involves promoting market development by securing confidence and protecting participants from fraud and other unfair practices. Consumer protection aims to ensure that retail investors have adequate information, are treated fairly and have adequate avenues for redress.

The role of ASIC came under review in 2010 following the collapse of several finance sector companies during the GFC.

AUSTRALIAN COMPETITION AND CONSUMER COMMISSION (ACCC)

The main role of the Australian Competition and Consumer Commission (ACCC) is in enforcing the *Competition and Consumer Act 2010* (Cwlth) in relation to financial institutions, in particular anti-competitive trading practices. In 2008–09 the ACCC approved the takeovers of Bankwest by the CBA and of the St George Bank by Westpac. We discussed the role of the ACCC in Chapter 7.

SUMMARY

1. The financial system consists of lenders and borrowers and the financial institutions that facilitate transfers between them. The claims and entitlements of lenders and borrowers are known as assets and liabilities.
2. The stability of the financial system is a key element in maintaining a stable economy. In Australia the financial system has undergone many periods of instability, the latest being during the GFC between 2007 and 2010.
3. There are five categories of financial institution in Australia:
   (a) deposit takers
   (b) contractual savings institutions
   (c) finance companies
   (d) money market corporations
   (e) unit trusts.
4. Financial intermediaries facilitate indirect financing.
5. Banks dominate the Australian financial system and are subject to regulation and supervision by the Australian Prudential Regulation Authority (APRA). Most other financial intermediaries are also subject to some supervision and regulation.
6. The functions of the Reserve Bank include:
   (a) conduct of monetary policy
   (b) system stability
   (c) the payments system.
7. The functions of APRA include the prudential regulation of banks, life and general insurance companies, superannuation funds, building societies, credit unions and friendly societies.
8. The Australian Securities and Investments Commission aims to ensure finance market stability and consumer protection.

REFERENCES

1. R. Crane, I. Fraser and A. Martin, *Financial Institutions, Markets and Instruments*, 5th edn, LBC Information Services, Sydney, 2000, p. 1.
2. M.G. Porter, *Report of the Committee of Inquiry into the Australian Financial System*, Parliamentary Paper 208/1981, September, Department of the Parliamentary Library, Canberra, 1982 (Campbell Report).
3. B.W. Fraser, 'Aspects of the Reserve Bank's Supervisory Function', address to the annual conference of the Australian Association of Permanent Building Societies, Sydney, 19 April 1990.
4. *Financial System Inquiry Final Report Overview*, AGPS, Canberra, 1997 (Wallis Report), Terms of Reference.

REVIEW QUESTIONS

1. In your own words, define the following terms:
   (a) surplus unit
   (b) deficit unit
   (c) financial intermediary
   (d) asset
   (e) liability
   (f) financial sector.
2. Explain the differences between assets and liabilities from your point of view and from your bank's point of view.
3. List the key functions carried out by the financial system.
4. Explain the functions of financial intermediaries.
5. In your own words define the following terms:
   (a) banks
   (b) building societies
   (c) credit unions
   (d) finance companies
   (e) money-market corporations
   (f) financial markets
   (g) mortgage companies
   (h) managed funds
   (i) financial conglomerates.
6. Explain the effects of deregulation on banks' market share.
7. Explain the effects of the GFC on non-bank financial intermediaries.
8. Describe some of the major changes that have occurred in the Australian financial system in the 2000s.
9. In your own words define the following terms:
   (a) system stability
   (b) the payments system
   (c) Australian Prudential Regulation Authority
   (d) authorised deposit-taking institutions
   (e) capital adequacy requirement
   (f) prudential supervision.
10. Why do virtually all developed countries have a central bank at the apex of their financial system?
11. 'The Australian Prudential Regulation Authority guarantees that no bank will ever go out of business.' Discuss this statement, indicating whether or not you agree with it and giving reasons for your answer.
12. Explain the role of financial intermediaries in the Australian economy.
13. Why do some economic agents use financial intermediaries rather than dealing directly with each other? Give examples to support your answer.
14. What distinguishes banks from non-bank financial intermediaries?
15. Classify the following as assets or liabilities from a bank's perspective:
   (a) deposits
   (b) credit card advances
   (c) overdrafts
   (d) cheque account balances
   (e) unused lines of credit on credit cards.
16. Outline the two main functions of the:
   (a) Reserve Bank of Australia
   (b) Australian Prudential Regulation Authority
   (c) Australian Securities and Investments Commission
   (d) Payments System Board.

17. Explain the nature and purposes of the following:
   (a) capital adequacy requirement
   (b) prudential supervision
   (c) liquidity requirements.

APPLIED QUESTIONS AND EXERCISES
THE BANKING COLLAPSE OF 1893

Most people who operate in a modern economy find it necessary to use a bank to facilitate transactions. When a bank collapses it can take all the funds of its depositors with it. The deregulation of the Australian finance system continued up to 2008. This makes the bank customer responsible for deciding on the safety of a bank, because there will be no government guarantees for depositors if a bank collapses. Given this situation, it is worth considering the history of the major banking collapse that occurred more than 100 years ago.

On 6 April 1893 the then largest bank in Victoria, the Commercial Bank of Australia (CBA), closed its doors and suspended repayments to depositors. This action precipitated a run on all banks. Over the next five weeks, 12 of the 28 banks operating in Australia also closed their doors.

Eventually, most banks reopened in a 'reconstructed' form. Reconstruction meant that term deposits were converted to preference shares which, years later, could be bought and sold and paid dividends. Depositors with the CBA waited between five and 29 years for their money. The volume of money, M3, fell by 40 per cent in 1893.

The effects of this calamity are hard to imagine today.

In the 1890s there was very little superannuation, sick pay or social welfare. The disaster was concentrated in Melbourne, where many new banks had started during the gold rush. The position of Sydney was relatively strong because of the dominance of the long-established Bank of New South Wales and the Commercial Banking Company of Sydney. In Victoria the population fell during the 1890s and did not start growing again until 1906. Real estate values fell and banks had to wait 10 to 15 years, 50 years in some cases, for the price of mortgaged assets to reach a level where they could be sold without sustaining large losses. Office building in Melbourne was almost non-existent until the 1950s.

How could such a calamity come about? In 1851 there were only seven banks, operating 12 branches across the country, with combined assets of 5 million pounds. By 1888 there were 28 banks with 1404 branches and combined assets within Australia of about 50 million pounds. They provided a range of services suitable for a rapidly growing commercial economy which was heavily involved in international trade.

There were many similarities between the 1880s and the 1980s in Australia and some Asian economies in the 1990s. The level of competition between banks was fierce, with high interest rates and gimmicks being used to attract deposits. This competition for deposits extended to London. Overseas borrowing was required to offset a poor balance of payments.

Much of the lending was for the purchase of, or against the security of, real estate. This lending financed a land boom, which reached its peak in 1887–88 when the price of suburban land in Melbourne increased by several hundred per cent.

Banks developed structural weaknesses such as:
- Their level of liquidity ran down during the decade, particularly in Britain, where increased deposit liabilities were not matched by increases in liquid assets.
- In the competitive scramble for business the degree of risk in bank lending rose dramatically.
- The volume of business overwhelmed banks' reporting systems. Some head offices did not know what was happening at branch level. Reserves were allowed to run down.

As property and share prices crashed, large numbers of borrowers were unable to repay their loans. Banks were left holding titles to property with a value far less than when taken as security for loans. Banks' income from loans fell, and if they sold property they would have large capital losses. A wholesale collapse of building societies in the early 1890s, and the collapse of the Federal Bank in January 1893, led to the run on the Commercial Bank.

Source: Adapted from D. Merrett, 'The Boom, Bust and Banking Collapse of 100 Years Ago', Business Review Weekly, 14 January 1988, pp. 87–90.

QUESTIONS

1. List the causes of the collapse of the banking system in 1893.
2. Could such a collapse happen today? Give reasons for your answer.
3. What qualities should you look for in the bank that holds your funds?

APRA STRESS TESTS BANKS

In 2003, 2005 and 2008 APRA conducted stress tests on the Australian banks. These are simulations of the impacts of a series of hypothetical events. The main assumptions used by APRA were:
- a sudden 3 per cent contraction in real GDP followed by a sharp recovery
- a rise in unemployment to 11 per cent
- a fall in housing prices of 11 per cent
- a fall in commercial property prices of 45 per cent.

The findings during the GFC were:
- none of the banks would have failed
- none of the banks would have breached the minimum capital adequacy ratio of the Basel II framework.

These results were much better than the outcomes of similar tests in other countries.

QUESTIONS

1. Describe the functions of APRA.
2. Why would APRA want to conduct stress tests on Australian banks?
3. How would a rise in unemployment and a fall in house prices affect banks?
4. Define capital adequacy ratio and the Basel II framework.
5. Explain why these are relevant to banks in Australia.
6. Explain how these tests might affect interest rates charged by banks in Australia.
7. If the tests had shown that some banks would have collapsed under the assumptions, explain the impacts on the ability of the Australian banks to raise funds in overseas markets.

Chapter **15**

Financial regulation: Australian and global trends

LEARNING OBJECTIVES

After studying this chapter, you will be able to:

1. explain the reasons for deregulation in general
2. explain the reasons for deregulation of the financial system in particular
3. describe the effects of deregulation of the financial system
4. explain the effects of deregulation on the conduct of monetary policy by the Reserve Bank
5. describe the findings of the Wallis Committee on the case for regulation of financial markets
6. explain the reasons for and impact of the GFC which commenced in 2007
7. summarise the regulatory reaction to the GFC.

INTRODUCTION

deregulation

the removal of regulations, usually government regulations, that restrict certain types of activities in the market

Until the 1980s, many areas of private business activity in Australia were highly regulated; during the 1980s they were partially deregulated. **Deregulation** is the removal of regulations, usually government regulations that restrict certain types of activities in the market. Advocates of deregulation argue that regulation in effect protects existing firms in an industry from competitors. The result is that these firms tend to be less efficient and innovative and to operate at higher costs than would be the case in a more competitive environment.

In the 2000s corporate irregularities and corporate failures led to a form of reregulation in order to reduce the risks of market failure. The aim of this chapter is to focus on deregulation and reregulation of the financial system and the global financial crisis (GFC) as case studies of deregulation in general and its aftermath.

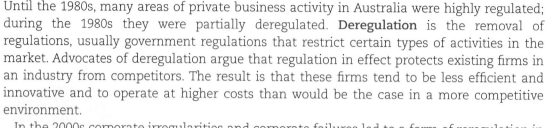

LEARNING OBJECTIVE 1

Explain the reasons for deregulation in general

The aim of deregulation is usually to increase efficiency by imposing competition and removing regulations that distort economic activity.[1] In a broad sense, deregulation is an attempt to make the economy more like a perfect market—that is, to increase the degree of competition so that consumers are more likely to be able to buy higher quality goods at competitive prices. Financial deregulation was designed to enhance competition, creating a more efficient financial system that would benefit individual investors and savers, and the economy as a whole, by forcing the development of a more efficient system of intermediation that would help to promote economic growth.

Deregulation of the financial system did have the effect of increasing the degree of competition. At the beginning of the 1970s banks were subject to Reserve Bank controls on how much they could lend, to whom they could lend, the interest rates they could offer and charge, and the terms they could offer.

Non-bank financial institutions were not subject to these controls and thus building societies, credit unions, merchant banks and finance companies were able to grow rapidly. By the beginning of the 1990s, when none of the Reserve Bank controls applied to banks, building societies and credit unions had only just become subject to national supervision.

By the end of the 1990s there was much greater competition in the financial marketplace. The major banks competed with each other, as well as with foreign-owned banks, with smaller, new locally-owned niche banks, and with other providers of financial services, such as mortgage originators serving mainly the house mortgage market.

In the 2000s the impact of the GFC and the government guarantee provided to Australian banks led to a flight of business away from non-bank financial intermediaries. Also the banking sector was consolidated with the larger banks, the Commonwealth Bank and Westpac taking over the smaller banks, Bankwest and the St George Bank respectively.

THE HISTORY OF REGULATION

regulation

involves the creation of rules for the conduct of business activities under the umbrella of legislation

The history of **regulation** of the finance sector can be traced back to the aftermath of the banking collapse during the 1890s. The social effects of the collapse and the general economic depression were so severe that the political reaction included the establishment of Australia's unique industrial relations system, and a desire to regulate the private banking system, if not replace it completely with government-owned banks.

Following the foundation of the Federation of Australia in 1901, a series of moves towards an increasing degree of control of the banking system took place, culminating in the attempt to nationalise the banking system in 1948.

In 1910 the Commonwealth Government began to produce notes and coins which replaced gold and the currency issued by banks and by the British and Queensland Governments.

CENTRAL BANK

In 1911 the Commonwealth Bank of Australia was established. It undertook commercial and savings bank business and was guaranteed by the government. Its functions were widened to support government intervention in the economy during World War I. In 1924 the Commonwealth Bank took over the note issue from the Commonwealth Treasury. By 1930 it had complete authority over gold holdings and Australia's international reserves. In 1931 it became responsible for setting the exchange rate of the Australian pound.

Other central banking functions were added during the 1930s. When World War II began, the Commonwealth Bank was given substantial emergency powers:

- the issue of bank licences
- control over bank lending policy and interest rates
- lodgment of surplus funds held by trading banks in special accounts held with the bank.

These powers were made permanent in the Banking Act of 1945.

In 1948 the Labor Government attempted to nationalise the privately-owned banks, but the move was declared unconstitutional and the government was defeated at the polls.

The *Banking Act 1959* (Cwlth) removed central banking powers from the Commonwealth Bank and created the Reserve Bank of Australia, in response to criticism that it was unfair for the central bank to compete with the privately-owned banks.

In 1974 the *Financial Corporations Act 1974* (Cwlth) was passed, enabling the Reserve Bank to collect information about non-bank financial intermediaries. Part IV of the Act, which was never proclaimed, gave the Reserve Bank the same powers over non-banks as it had over banks.

THE ARGUMENT FOR DEREGULATION

In 1979 the Campbell Committee of Inquiry began.[2] It was the first inquiry into the Australian financial system since the 1936 Napier Royal Commission.

The Campbell Committee presented a series of reasons for recommending deregulation, putting forward the view that the regulation of the banking sector had made the Australian financial system inefficient in an economic sense. Too many resources were being used for the level of service being provided. As a result, Australian industry was at a disadvantage in the international marketplace because the costs of financial services were high relative to its competitors.

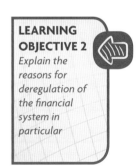

LEARNING OBJECTIVE 2
Explain the reasons for deregulation of the financial system in particular

Economic costs

The Campbell Committee pointed out that regulation of the banking sector caused fragmentation of the financial system by encouraging the growth of non-bank financial institutions able to operate without much regulation. Since banks were not allowed to compete on interest rates, they sought to compete on service. This created over-servicing: branches proliferated, the range of products widened to include all sorts of special accounts, and the system was over-used because there was no rational pricing of services.

Hardships for high-risk borrowers

Regulation forced many small businesses to use the non-banking sector for their financing needs when they could have been better served by the banking system.

In the area of housing, controls on interest rates meant that banks could not compete with building societies for funds. Consequently, there was a smaller pool of savings available with banks to finance housing purchases. The banks were forced to ration credit—usually by lending only to the most secure borrowers. Thus, while one of the objectives of controlling interest rates was to help low-income earners, the outcome was to provide assistance to high-income earners who were a better risk. Low-income earners were forced into the non-bank sector, and as a result paid higher interest rates on their housing mortgages.

Less innovation

Another serious effect of regulation was to slow down innovation in financial instruments because regulation had the effect of removing competitive pressures from banks.

MOVES TO DEREGULATE

During the 1980s, regulation of day-to-day operations in the financial system was replaced by a system of prudential supervision. Deregulation involved removing many of the controls on banks. The Australian dollar was floated, interest rate ceilings were removed and most housing mortgage rates deregulated. This caused dramatic changes in the financial system.

In summary, the deregulation process may be attributed to two main forces:

- A breakdown of the old system of direct regulation as governments realised that the highly regulated Australian economy was unable to adapt to changing economic and institutional circumstances, and that changes were required to arrest the long-term decline in Australia's living standards compared to the rest of the world.
- Growing internationalisation of finance and the emergence of an intellectual climate in favour of greater reliance on markets and less government involvement.

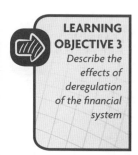

LEARNING OBJECTIVE 3
Describe the effects of deregulation of the financial system

BENEFITS OF DEREGULATION

Deregulation of the Australian financial system brought both costs and benefits. The benefits include:

- increased competition
- product innovation
- more flexibility in interest rates and a closer relationship between risk and interest rates
- increased flexibility in the banking system, leading to reduced margins between lending and deposit rates.

spread
the difference between the interest rate margins that banks offer customers for their deposits and the rates that banks charge borrowers

INCREASED COMPETITION

Deregulation increased freedom of entry into banking, which resulted in greater competition. This extra competition produced most of the benefits of deregulation.

The clearest evidence of competition after deregulation was in the markets for foreign exchange and domestic financial products at the wholesale level, where the **spreads** became low by world standards. This means that the difference between the interest rate margins that banks offer customers for their deposits and the rates that banks charge borrowers is low compared to banks in other countries. Also, banks now offer a much greater choice of products, providing benefits for the customer.

PRODUCT INNOVATION

The most visible benefit of deregulation brought on by greater competition was product innovation. A vast increase in the products offered by the banks occurred in the 1980s. These can be grouped under four broad categories:

- new technology
- new financial packages
- new products
- other financial services.

New technology

- Automatic teller machines (ATMs) first became widely available in 1980, having been introduced to Australia by a credit union.
- **Electronic Funds Transfer at Point of Sale (EFTPOS)** was introduced in 1985. Australians have been enthusiastic users of this service and market penetration here is now among the highest in the world.
- Smart Cards are cards that have a microelectronic chip embedded in the plastic rather than a simple magnetic strip. More information can be loaded onto these cards, thus making possible more complicated transactions than simple cash withdrawals. In the future, cards might be able to recognise your voice, your eye, your ear or your fingerprint.
- Better computer systems in banks allowed selective use of automatic sweep accounts. These enable funds over an agreed balance to be transferred to higher-yielding deposit facilities like cash management funds.
- Advances in data processing and telecommunications enabled banks to offer home banking (for personal customers) and cash management systems (for corporate customers). These allow customers to undertake banking activities from their homes or offices.
- In 1987 the large banks introduced the **Bank Interchange Transfer System (BITS)**, an inter-bank electronic funds transfer mechanism for high-value transactions.
- Banks have offered electronic data interchange services to corporate customers since 1988. These services link companies, their customers and their bank so that, on completion of a payment, remittance details are automatically sent to the receiver and payment confirmation and audit details to the sender.

Electronic Funds Transfer at Point of Sale (EFTPOS)
a system that allows purchases to be funded directly from a bank account via a computer link

Bank Interchange Transfer System (BITS)
an inter-bank electronic funds transfer mechanism for high-value transactions

New financial packages

These packages, such as low-start home loans, used existing technology. Bill payments can be made over the telephone, by direct debit or via internet banking. Specialised rural and small business centres were established by many banks on a regional basis.

These two waves of innovation were not directly related to the process of financial deregulation. However, measures taken to increase competition in the system probably caused banks to embrace new technology and develop products more swiftly.

New products made possible by deregulation

These included interest-paying chequebook facilities and a wider range of term deposit facilities and fixed-rate home loans.

Other financial services

New products were offered by bank branches on behalf of affiliated parts of the corporate group. During the 1990s and 2000s, insurance, superannuation, approved deposit funds and other managed funds products became more important, partly because governments encouraged them. Thus deregulation widened the range of banking products available to customers and banking services became available more or less 24 hours a day.

INTEREST RATES

Another beneficial aspect of deregulation was in the field of interest rates. Deregulation meant that customers (savers) enjoyed a better return on their savings due to higher average interest rates (but remember that other factors, including monetary policy, affect the level of interest rates).

Large business borrowers enjoyed falling interest rate margins (the difference between the savings and lending rates).

INCREASED EFFICIENCY

Deregulation was beneficial to banks in that they were able to increase efficiency and to win back market share from non-bank intermediaries during the 1980s. Prior to deregulation, NBFIs had an artificially competitive edge over banks, because Reserve Bank controls had no impact on their activities. Consumers were unable to benefit, as outlined above, because the banks were able to offer the benefits derived from economies of scale.

However, in the 1990s and 2000s new competitors, such as home lending and bill-payment services, appeared in what had been comfortable niches for banks. Banks responded to this changing environment by pursuing strategies of cost-cutting. They reduced their staff numbers, improved their business processes, increased investment in information technology, and diverted more resources to market segmentation.

From an international perspective, the reforms gave Australia a flexible and effective financial system which contributed to growth and made Australia attractive to international investors.

BANKS RESPOND TO THE CHANGING ENVIRONMENT

LINK TO
BUSINESS

In the 2000s retail financial services became very important for banks. Wealth management had been the fastest growing segment of the sector and was expected to grow further as the baby boomer generation increased savings prior to retirement. Banks were able to use their broad customer base and distribution networks to provide a range of financial services.

Issues for banks included:

- pressures to reduce costs to meet competition from new entrants to retail finance such as internet banks, supermarkets and payments service providers like Australia Post
- pressures to outsource in an effort to improve service quality, for example using software developers based in India

- trying to direct customers towards becoming multiproduct holders using customer relationship management technology and branch staff to cross-sell products
- how to use market segmentation techniques to identify high-value customers and provide benefits like personal banking, customised products, flexible fee structures and negotiable interest rates
- the impact of the GFC was to drive customers towards the banks and their share of deposits and the housing mortgage market increased markedly while lending to business became relatively less important (see Chapter 14)
- the ANZ Bank decided to pursue a growth strategy based on becoming a major bank in the Asian region because of relatively low growth prospects in Australia.

QUESTIONS

1. What role did deregulation play in forcing banks to focus on retail financial services?
2. List two advantages and two disadvantages facing banks in pursuing the retail finance sector.

COSTS OF DEREGULATION

No economic policy can produce only winners or only losers. On the other side of the balance sheet, there were costs resulting from deregulation of the Australian financial system:

- customers' lack of knowledge
- higher costs for some customers
- growth in bad debts.

CUSTOMERS' LACK OF KNOWLEDGE

Although deregulation had expanded the range of financial services, it soon became apparent that customers did not know enough about the interest rates to be paid and received, the fees and costs, and the risks of certain forms of borrowing, such as the **foreign exchange risk** associated with currency loans. Foreign exchange risk for borrowers of foreign currency means that falls in the value of the local currency will mean that more local currency is required to purchase the foreign currency needed to repay the loan.

In particular, the lack of information about foreign currency loans placed many customers and their guarantors in difficulties due to adverse movements in exchange rates. The 1991 Martin Committee[3] found that foreign currency borrowing caused big losses to primary producers, professionals, property investors and developers. Although these borrowers were mostly astute business people, they failed to understand the foreign exchange risk and had little capacity to manage the risk.

Changes to the financial system introduced from 1999 placed an even greater burden on bank customers to understand the nature and costs of bank products, as well as assess the stability and risk associated with the different banks.

HIGHER COSTS FOR SOME CUSTOMERS

Another cost of deregulation was that customers had to pay for some services that used to be 'free'. These 'free' services were previously paid for by higher charges on other services or by lower returns to depositors; in other words, banks **cross-subsidised** some of their products.

foreign exchange risk
the risk that borrowers of foreign currency may face falls in the value of local currency, requiring more local currency to purchase the foreign currency needed to repay the loan

cross-subsidisation
subsidising the delivery costs of free or low-cost products through higher charges on other products

As banks discontinued this practice, small customers in particular felt the disadvantage of losing cross-subsidies and having to meet the real cost of banking services.

Thus, full marginal cost pricing of financial services, or 'user pays', which deregulation was supposed to produce, meant higher costs for many groups of customers.

GROWTH IN BAD DEBTS

When banks were regulated, credit was rationed and so only the lower-risk customers got loans. Groups such as farmers and small business people were particularly disadvantaged by this situation. They were usually shunted away from banks into finance companies or merchant banks.

The move away from credit rationing as a process of deregulation widened the range of customers being funded by banks and highlighted the lack of risk assessment skills in banks. However, this lowering of bank asset quality, combined with a severe recession, produced a dramatic growth in bad debts owed to the banks at the beginning of the 1990s.

Rationalisation of bank branch networks

Banks were forced by the pressure of competition to reduce costs. Bank branch networks represent very high costs compared to other methods of delivering bank services. Consequently, unprofitable branches were closed. This had the effect of reducing services and employment in country towns in particular. **Bank concentration** involves consolidating delivery points in large regional centres.

bank concentration
consolidating delivery points for banking services in large regional centres

SUPPORT FOR DEREGULATION

The 1991 Martin Committee, which was established to review deregulation in the 1980s, concluded that there should be no winding back of the deregulation that had occurred. It recommended a role for government in ensuring:

- that markets work efficiently and competitively
- that the financial system remains safe and sound
- there is an adequate flow of information to consumers
- the prevention of monopoly control
- there is an appropriate system of prudential control.

In summary, financial deregulation created major structural changes in the Australian economy. The stresses imposed on the banks by the recession of the early 1990s and failures of high profile financial institutions led to an approach to regulation focused on ensuring that institutions have appropriate risk management policies and processes in place.

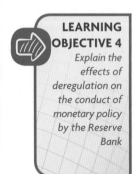

LEARNING OBJECTIVE 4
Explain the effects of deregulation on the conduct of monetary policy by the Reserve Bank

EFFECTS OF DEREGULATION ON MONETARY POLICY

From 1941 to about 1983, as we have seen, the activities of banks in Australia were regulated, first by the Commonwealth Bank and then by the Reserve Bank. (A detailed discussion of monetary policy is included in Chapter 23.)

MONETARY POLICY CONTROLS

Forms of regulation included monetary policy controls such as:

- reserve asset ratios, like the statutory reserve deposit ratios and other liquidity ratios. These were designed to ensure minimum liquid asset ratios to protect depositors, and also provided the opportunity to manipulate banks' ability to create credit
- interest rate controls, which determined bank deposit and loan rates, thus effectively determining profitability
- quantitative controls, used to determine the volume of bank lending that could be carried out
- qualitative controls, directing banks to lend, or not to lend, to particular sectors of the economy
- exchange rate controls
- foreign exchange controls, which could be used to prevent flows of capital into and out of Australia.

OPEN MARKET OPERATIONS

The process of deregulation has meant the removal of most of these controls. Consequently, monetary policy today consists mainly of targeting the cash rate in very short-term money markets. This is covered in detail in Chapter 23.

By influencing the cash rate the Reserve Bank aims to influence the availability of credit and interest rates (the price of credit) indirectly, by buying and selling government securities from and to other financial institutions that participate in the secondary market for government debt (see Chapter 14).

SLOWING THE CHINESE ECONOMY

China has a highly regulated financial system. In 2010 the Chinese Government became concerned about the rising inflation rate, in particular house prices.

The government adopted various measures to slow the rate of inflation. These included increasing the reserve asset ratios of banks to reduce their ability to lend and create credit, tightening of controls over the quantity of bank lending and the industries that banks could lend to, and higher capital adequacy ratios for loans to particular industries.

LINK TO
INTERNATIONAL
ECONOMY

QUESTIONS

1. Explain the difference between a regulated and a deregulated financial system.
2. Explain the meaning of:
   (a) credit creation
   (b) capital adequacy ratios
   (c) reserve asset ratios.
3. Explain how an Australian government with a more deregulated environment would have approached this problem.

THE POST-DEREGULATION PERIOD AND THE GLOBAL FINANCIAL CRISIS

During the 1980s, deregulation, combined with developments in technology and globalisation, produced major changes to the Australian financial system. The impact of the major recession at the beginning of the 1990s and the stresses imposed on the banking system led to significant extensions of the regulatory framework, so that by the late 1990s some market participants were complaining about 'reregulation'.

During the 1990s banks became subject to liquidity and asset ratio controls by the Reserve Bank, as well as to reviews of risk management systems, restrictions on involvement in funds management and reporting requirements on asset quality. In all, there were four agencies with the responsibility of overseeing banks and non-bank financial institutions.

These agencies played an important role in Australia's experience of the GFC.

The Wallis Committee[4] highlighted the point that while regulation imposes costs on the community and the economy there is a need to balance these costs against the costs of market failure (see Chapter 7). Market failure comes about when decisions taken by individuals or firms in the market do not result in an efficient allocation of resources.

Wallis found that there is a case for regulation of all economic markets for the following purposes:

- general market regulation to ensure that markets work efficiently and competitively so that the social benefits of interventions exceed the social costs in the form of higher costs of doing business
- regulation to prescribe certain standards or qualities of service
- regulation that is intended to achieve social objectives.

Wallis argued that regulation is warranted in finance markets to ensure that participants act with integrity and consumers are protected. However, the assurance provided by prudential regulation should not extend to a government guarantee of any financial promises.

The Wallis Report led to a new regulatory structure for the Australian financial system, which is described in Chapter 14. This structure was put to the test during the GFC.

LEARNING OBJECTIVE 5
Describe the findings of the Wallis Committee on the case for regulation of financial markets

THE GLOBAL FINANCIAL CRISIS

LEARNING OBJECTIVE 6
Explain the reasons for and impact of the global financial crises which commenced in 2007

As noted in Chapter 9 the GFC was one of many financial crises arising from excessive use of credit to finance high-risk lending. The standard response to such crises involved flooding the financial markets with money very quickly in order to lower borrowing costs and to restore confidence. The response to the GFC followed this standard pattern but was more extensive and involved the United States and most developed economies using monetary and fiscal policy and the effective nationalisation of many companies to offset the effects of a dramatic loss of confidence in the financial system. By 2010 it was becoming clear that the massive increase in government spending and intervention in the economy had managed to defer the effects of what had been described as the worst financial crisis since the Great Depression of the 1930s. However in many developed economies other than Australia it was not obvious that confidence among consumers had grown to the point that private sector enterprises could confidently invest in new inventories and new production capacity.

The nature of the GFC

The GFC resulted from the collapse of a housing **bubble** with rapidly rising prices, particularly in the United States and Europe which peaked in 2006. The collapse caused the value of securities built on real estate prices to crash thus causing great damage to many financial institutions across the world. The nature of the GFC can be traced back to some of the peculiarities of the United States financial system.

Background to the GFC

The following points highlight the key issues underlying the GFC:

- As the United States financial system was deregulated financial innovations included **securitisation**, **adjustable rate mortgages**, **non-recourse lending** and **sub-prime mortgages**. Securitisation involves the creation of packages of mortgages into securities that are onsold to investors. Securitisation enables the asset and the attached risk to be transferred from the institution that originated the mortgages to investors. Sub-prime mortgages are issued to people who are poor credit risks. These loans were sometimes referred to as **'ninja' loans** because the borrower had 'no income, no job and no assets'—obviously a poor credit risk. These loans often involved low up front interest rates which were adjusted upward after a set period of time. The risks for the mortgage originator from sub-prime mortgages can be transferred to others via securitisation. In the United States mortgage lending is on a non-recourse basis, which means that if a borrower cannot meet their repayments they can simply leave the keys with the bank and walk out of the house. Selling the house to recover the loan becomes the bank's problem: there is no obligation on the borrower to repay the loan. (Note that in Australia the borrower is liable to repay the loan.)

- The financial instruments developed to securitise mortgages were known as **mortgage backed securities (MBS)** and **collateralised debt obligations (CDO)**. These instruments derived their value from mortgage repayments and housing prices. Some were so complex that ratings agencies relied on information provided by the originators of the securities and their faith in their financial models to give these securities **triple A ratings**. Given the triple A ratings, many financial institutions and other investors from all over the world (including some from Australia) purchased these securities thus acquiring an exposure to the United States property market.

- In the United States in particular many home owners took advantage of the rising price of their house to acquire further debt in the form of **home equity loans**. This debt was used to fund the purchase of cars, holidays, personal expenses and various other lifestyle assets. United States household debt as a percentage of annual disposable personal income was 127 per cent in 2007 compared to 77 per cent in 1990.

- Finance industry and welfare lobbyists had waged long and successful campaigns for deregulation of the finance sector and access to housing finance for low-income earners.

- From 2000 to 2004 the Federal Reserve (the United States central bank) target rate for funds was reduced from 6.5 per cent to 1 per cent. From 2004 to 2006 the target rate was increased substantially to 5.25 per cent. This caused sharp increases in the interest rate resets for adjustable rate mortgages leading to an increase in loan defaults and contributing to the rapid decline in United States housing prices and financial asset prices in 2007–08.

- There was extensive 'predatory lending' which included behaviour ranging from unethical to outright fraud (e.g. ninja loans).

bubble
rapid inflation in the price of assets like housing or commodities such as gold and shares in particular industry sectors. The dotcom bubble of the early 2000s involved a massive inflation of shares in companies in the information technology sector

securitisation
the collecting of assets like mortgages into a pool to create a new financial security, the value of which is backed by the assets and cash flows deriving from the underlying mortgages. It is a method used by many financial institutions to pass the risk embedded in their lending portfolio on to those who purchase the securitised assets

adjustable rate mortgage
mortgages with a low initial rate of interest where the interest rate is reset after a period of time usually at a higher rate, with a link to some indicator rate like the 10-year government bond rate

non-recourse lending
where there is no recourse to the borrower if he or she is unable to continue to service the loan. The lender takes possession of the property and the borrower walks away with no obligation

sub-prime mortgage
the most risky form of mortgage lending to people with a history of not being able to make loan repayments on a consistent basis

- Much of the process of securitisation was carried out via what has become known as the **'shadow banking' sector** which consists of unregulated financial institutions, often set up or supported by regulated banks as a way of bypassing the regulations. By 2007 estimates suggested the shadow banking system might be as big as the regulated banking system and failures in the shadow system could threaten the viability of regulated institutions.

Course of the GFC

- As a result of the collapse in house prices in the United States major global financial institutions reported significant losses from 2007.
- The unregulated shadow banking system did not have the financial reserves to absorb the large defaults and losses on mortgage backed securities.
- Doubts about the stability of banks reduced their ability to borrow and lend thus slowing economic activity and causing rising unemployment.
- Governments responded by:
  - conducting quantitative easing via open market operations to increase the money supply (see Chapter 23)
  - bailing out key financial institutions and companies and providing guarantees to potential lenders. Examples of bail-outs included the American Insurance Group, the largest insurance company in the world, and American icon the General Motors Corporation
  - carrying out massive fiscal stimulus programs involving large budget deficits to offset the reduction in private sector spending (see Chapter 22).
- Between June 2007 and November 2008 United States citizens lost about a quarter of their net collective wealth and housing prices dropped by 20 per cent. Such large losses inevitably impacted on private consumption expenditure and investment.
- The United States crisis rapidly spread to Europe with bank failures and concerns about sovereign debt sparking runs on currencies, particularly for countries with chronic fiscal deficits and extensive offshore borrowings by government. Several European countries undertook severe measures to reduce their government liabilities by increasing taxes and charges and increasing the retirement age pension qualification.

Regulatory response

In 2010 both houses of the United States Congress passed regulatory reform legislation. Key points included:

- increased transparency in markets for complex financial instruments
- creation of a federal regulator to provide protection for consumers of financial products like mortgages
- establishment of a council of regulators to monitor the development of **systemic risks**
- authorised regulators to impose restrictions on large finance companies and to liquidate failing companies with no costs for taxpayers
- companies required to have executive salaries set by independent directors

- companies selling complex securities, in particular mortgage-backed securities, required to retain a portion of the embedded risk
- investors allowed to sue ratings agencies.

Australian banks had very little direct exposure to the GFC, although some bank clients failed in the aftermath of the peak of the crisis in 2008–09. During the GFC the Australian Prudential Regulation Authority (APRA) conducted stress tests (see Chapter 14) on the Australian banks, assuming a sharp contraction in GDP, a rise in unemployment of 11 per cent, a fall in house prices of 25 per cent and in commercial property prices of 45 per cent. It found that none of the banks would have failed or breached the Basel rules on capital adequacy. Also during the GFC the Australian Government guaranteed the deposits of all Australian banks in order to prevent them from failing as a result of a run on their deposits.

In 2010 at the request of the **Group of 20**, the Basel committee agreed on a new wave of regulatory reforms, known as 'Basel III' involving higher capital adequacy and liquidity ratios, and restrictions on the amount of leverage banks could absorb, to be implemented from 2013. These reforms would require banks to raise more capital and hold more liquidity, thus raising their costs and reducing their ability to make profits.

In 2010, Australian banks already met many of the proposed requirements. During that year APRA and the Reserve Bank convinced the Basel committee to allow some variations in national jurisdictions which would effectively recognise the sound regulation and practices of the Australian banking system.

systemic risk
the risk of failure of an entire system, such as a national financial system, resulting from the failure of a key component such as a large bank becoming unable to meet its financial obligations to other banks

LEARNING OBJECTIVE 7
Summarise the regulatory reaction to the GFC

Group of 20
established in 1999 in the wake of the Asian financial crisis the G20 includes all major developed and developing nations and aims to promote financial stability and sustainable economic growth and development

REGULATION AND BANKS

In the period prior to the GFC Australian banks had to deal with a range of regulatory and governance issues aimed at addressing market failure:

- the new Basel global capital adequacy rules, which bind Australian banks, required them to be assessed on operational risk as well as capital adequacy risk
- a new *Financial Services Reform Act 2001* (Cwlth), which established a common licensing regime for financial product advice to ensure that financial advisers were properly trained and complaints were handled appropriately
- new accounting standards that require increased disclosure
- higher standards for corporate governance.

QUESTIONS
1. Define market failure.
2. List two of the outcomes that were being sought by the above measures.
3. Should the government guarantee the performance of all promises by financial service providers?

LINK TO BUSINESS

SUMMARY

1. The key objective of deregulation is to improve economic performance and thus the economic welfare of the country.
2. Most commentators seem to conclude that the benefits of deregulation outweigh the costs. The two reports commissioned to review the process have supported the process of deregulation.
3. One of the key effects of deregulation has been a reduction in the number of monetary policy instruments available to the Reserve Bank to only one—targeting the overnight cash rate.
4. The Wallis Report found that there was a case for regulation to reduce the risk of market failure.
5. In the 1990s a new regulatory regime was established which focused on market behaviour and consumer protection.
6. The GFC exposed deficiencies in regulatory regimes in the United States and Europe in particular, leading to the near collapse of the global financial system.
7. While some institutions collapsed damaging individual investors, the Australian financial system emerged from the GFC in healthy condition.
8. New global banking regulations will come into force from 2013.

KEY TERMS

adjustable rate mortgage	319	deregulation	310	ninja loans	320
bank concentration	316	Electronic Funds Transfer at Point		regulation	310
Bank Interchange Transfer System		of Sale (EFTPOS)	313	securitisation	319
(BITS)	313	foreign exchange risk	315	shadow banking	320
bubble	319	Group of 20	321	spread	312
collateralised debt obligation	315	home equity loan	320	sub-prime mortgage	319
cross-subsidisation	315	mortgage backed security	320	systemic risk	321
		non-recourse lending	319	triple A rating	320

REFERENCES

1. *The Penguin Macquarie Dictionary of Economics & Finance*, Ringwood, Vic, 1988.
2. *Australian Financial System: Final Report of the Committee of Inquiry*, AGPS, Canberra, 1981 (Campbell Committee Final Report).
3. House of Representatives Standing Committee on Finance and Public Administration, *A Pocket Full of Change: Banking and Deregulation*, AGPS, Canberra, 1991 (Martin Committee).
4. *Financial Systems Inquiry Final Report Overview*, AGPS, Canberra, 1997 (Wallis Report).

REVIEW QUESTIONS

1. In your own words define the following terms:
   (a) deregulation
   (b) perfect market.
2. List the costs of regulation as indicated by the Campbell Committee of Inquiry.
3. Explain the reasons behind the decision to deregulate the financial sector in the early 1980s.
4. In your own words define the following terms:
   (a) foreign currency loan
   (b) cross-subsidisation
   (c) credit rationing.
5. Describe some of the costs of deregulation.
6. Briefly describe the effect of deregulation on the implementation of monetary policy.
7. Explain the differences between regulation and deregulation.
8. What are the objectives of deregulation?
9. List the costs and benefits of deregulation.
10. What do you think is the appropriate role of government in financial markets?
11. List the causes of the GFC.
12. Explain two effects of the GFC in the United States.
13. Explain one effect of the GFC in Europe.
14. Explain how the GFC affected Australia.
15. List the responses to the GFC in the United States and through the G20.

APPLIED QUESTIONS AND EXERCISES
COMPETITION IN CONSUMER FINANCE

In the 2000s the Australian credit card market was like a battleground with companies competing on the basis of price, loyalty rewards and innovation.

Non-banks like the global giant GE Capital established alliances with large retailers like Coles Myer. Some banks reopened branches. For example, the Bank of Queensland opened 'owner-managed branches', offering the full range of banking services supported by internet banking, phone banking and ATMs, and a manager who has the authority to make decisions on the spot, subject to the bank's credit control procedures.

QUESTIONS

1. Why would a global giant like GE Capital form an alliance with Coles Myer?
2. Why would the Bank of Queensland open owner-managed branches?
3. What advantages would these players have over small institutions like credit unions?

GLOBAL REGULATORY SUPERVISION

The framework of regulatory supervision in Australia consists of the Reserve Bank, the Australian Prudential Regulation Authority, the Australian Securities and Investments Commission and the Australian Competition and Consumer Commission. The role of these institutions was important during the GFC.

In 2010 there were concerns that the new Basel III agreement, led by the G20 to tighten the supervision of financial institutions by imposing higher capital and liquidity requirements, would cause unintended consequences.

QUESTIONS

1. Summarise the impact of the GFC on Australia.
2. Briefly explain the background to the proposed tighter global regime.
3. Explain two of the possible unintended consequences for Australian banks.

SYSTEMIC RISK

Systemic risk is the risk of failure of an entire system such as a national economy or a financial system. Such a failure may arise from internal or external events when a component may fail because it is put under stresses greater than it can cope with. Banks are independent organisations that compete with each other but they also depend on each other. For example they rely on each other to honour transactions made by their customers. In a system like Australia where there are only four main banks, failure of one may have a critical effect on the ability of the others to survive. For example if, during the GFC, foreign lenders had become unwilling to finance the borrowing needs of Australian banks they might have collapsed.

QUESTIONS

1. Explain the linkages between Australian banks and the reasons why they need to borrow offshore (you may need to refer to Chapter 14).
2. Explain the action taken by the Australian Government to prevent a run on the Australian banks.

6

WEALTH
CREATION

Chapter **16**

Wealth creation

LEARNING OBJECTIVES

After studying this chapter, you should be able to:

1. identify different investment objectives
2. identify the general and specific risks associated with different asset classes
3. explain the differences between the different classes of assets
4. explain the principles of diversification
5. explain the difference between simple and compound interest
6. explain the reasons for compulsory superannuation in Australia
7. give examples of the impact of different assumptions on forecasts of final superannuation lump sums.

INTRODUCTION

The reasons for writing this book include enabling you to apply the principles of economics to your business and personal lives. This chapter provides some basic information about the process of wealth creation in Australia.

According to the *Oxford Reference Encyclopaedia*, **wealth** in economics represents:

> the stock of assets accumulated by individuals, households, businesses, or nations. These assets can be physical possessions (e.g. land or buildings), financial assets (bank accounts or securities), 'human capital' (people's skills and talents) or natural resources (mineral deposits). Wealth may be accumulated by saving out of current income or it may be inherited. Wealth, in turn, can create income.[1]

wealth
an individual, household, business or nation's accumulation of assets

Your own **wealth creation** can be defined as increasing the value of your net assets and protecting this value against the effects of both inflation and taxation. Assets might include land, houses and other forms of real estate property, shares, bonds, bank and other forms of deposits, paintings, antiques, jewellery and superannuation contributions. If you own your own business then the value of the assets of the business is part of your wealth portfolio. Your net assets are the total value of your assets less any debts you are liable to repay.

wealth creation
increasing the value of your assets and protecting against the effects of both inflation and taxation

Wealth can take various forms including your personal property such as your home or car, the money savings that you hold in the bank and income-producing assets you might own like rental accommodation, shares and other financial assets.

Unless you have inherited substantial assets from your relatives, in order to create personal wealth you have to be willing to save some of your income or to put it another way, to reduce your consumption expenditure below your level of current income. This scenario applies whether you finance your wealth creation strategy from savings or through debt. You will usually have to repay your loans out of your current income.

It is worth noting that many religions and political ideologies are opposed to the concept of wealth creation and accumulation, particularly by individuals. However, in Australia the resources available to governments to provide for individuals are limited and consequently a large proportion of the population is interested in wealth creation as a way of improving living standards now as well as providing for themselves as they get older.

A BRIEF HISTORY OF WEALTH CREATION

Historians like Catherwood[2] trace the beginnings of wealth accumulation in modern Europe to the development of what was called the Protestant Ethic whereby the accumulation of wealth by hard work was regarded as a pathway to heaven. For example, the diligent efforts of merchant classes that arose in western Europe during the 16th century involved habits of work ethic, savings and wealth creation based to a great extent on their religious beliefs. This can be contrasted with Christian monks who took a vow of poverty.

The communist view of wealth creation was based on the *Communist Manifesto* first published in 1848 in London by Karl Marx and Frederick Engels. Wealth, said the manifesto, has been concentrated into the hands of 'industrial millionaires', and it was only a matter of time before the working classes of the world, realising their common goals, would unite to overthrow the capitalists and redistribute the wealth.

The ideal of communism is a classless society in which all property is owned by the community as a whole and where all people enjoy equal social and economic status. Individuals should give according to their ability and receive according to their needs.

In practice, as Professor Walder[3] of Stanford University has noted, command economies gave communist-era bureaucratic elites administrative control and material privilege, but severely restricted money income and private wealth.

CURRENT APPROACHES TO WEALTH CREATION

In Chapter 3 we discussed disposable income as part of real income and as a main condition of demand at the microeconomic level. Personal consumption expenditure is also discussed in Chapter 9 and the issue of making choices is reviewed in Chapter 1. Disposable income is that which is available to consumers to use according to their personal choice. A person can choose to spend all their income on consumption or to save part of their income using a financial institution. For a discussion of the role of financial institutions in Australia see Chapter 14.

One of the challenges facing young people in Australia is managing their personal finances and the creation and accumulation of personal wealth. For those who attend university there is a need to pay their Higher Education Contribution Scheme (HECS) debt as well as developing a financial plan that will enable them to achieve their goals as well as fund their retirement. This is sometimes referred to as life cycle financial planning. In the past the usual life cycle involved people borrowing to fund the purchase of real estate. In this cycle, it is not until between 45 and 64 years of age that people's disposable income reaches a peak because by then they are at the peak of their earning power and are relatively debt-free.

Various surveys of the disposable income or spending power per week of people at different stages of their life cycle have shown a similar pattern. Note that this spending power can also be harnessed to fund savings which can be used to acquire different types of assets. The group with the highest proportion of disposable income to total income is young couples with no children. Those with the least spending power are single people over the age of 65.

In Australia the main source of income for most people is wages and salaries paid in return for their labour. Other sources of income include:

- profits earned by self-employed small-business people
- dividends earned from share holdings
- rent earned from property
- interest earned from financial assets
- income derived from superannuation funds
- government transfer payments such as pensions, family allowances and unemployment benefits.

FINANCIAL INVESTMENT OBJECTIVES AND STRATEGY

LEARNING OBJECTIVE 1
Identify different investment objectives

In the early chapters we defined investment in the economic sense, meaning investment in capital such as technology, factories and machinery. In this chapter we refer to **financial investment** as that activity conducted by individuals, funded by savings primarily to increase their wealth.

When deciding on a financial investment strategy, some people hand their funds over to an intermediary like a financial planner to invest and manage their funds. This is called a **managed investment**

Financial planners/advisers provide services such as preparation of investment plans to suit your profile and carrying out the investment plan on your behalf. In Australia, the activities of financial advisers are regulated (see Chapter 14).

Other people prefer to undertake the task of developing and executing a financial investment strategy themselves. This is called **direct investment**.

Most people have very little ability to increase their income levels in the short run but they do have the ability to control their expenditure. The ratio of consumption expenditure to income determines the amount of money you can save for wealth-creation purposes.

As people move through the different phases of life their **investment objectives** change. For example, creating the basis of a superannuation fund in your 20s might enable a more comfortable retirement than someone who starts saving for superannuation purposes in their 40s, because of the time elapsed and compounding returns that we will discuss later.

If your time frame is short (one to three years) protecting the value of your capital may be of primary importance so you would invest in lower-risk investments such as cash and fixed income securities. If your time horizon is more long term you may be more interested in higher risk but potentially higher yielding forms of investment such as property and shares.

Examples of time frames for different savings purposes might be:

- up to two years: new car
- two to five years: travelling overseas
- more than five years: purchasing a house.

An important task when implementing a savings plan is to monitor the use of credit cards and mobile phone services with great care as these are heavily promoted as lifestyle products and are paid for after the event. Because the consumption of the service is not visibly connected to the payment, it is easy to run up significant debts which become hard to repay as they tend to accumulate rapidly.

financial investment
activity conducted by individuals, funded by saving primarily to increase their individual wealth

managed investment
an investment handled by a financial intermediary

financial planner/ adviser
provides services such as the preparation and management of investment plans to suit an individual

direct investment
when an individual undertakes the task of developing and executing their own financial investment strategy

investment objectives
the purpose for which you are saving money

rate of return
ratio of dollars gained or lost relative to the cost of the investment

RISKS AND THE RATE OF RETURN

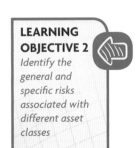

LEARNING OBJECTIVE 2
Identify the general and specific risks associated with different asset classes

The **rate of return** or return on investment is the ratio of money gained or lost on an investment relative to the dollars that were invested. Thus if your rate of return on your

$100 savings account is 10 per cent per annum then your account will receive 10 per cent in interest each year.

When you are making investment decisions it is important to identify your investment objectives and the level of **risk** relative to the rate of return that you are prepared to accept. Factors you should take into account include:

risk
the chance of bad consequences

liquidity of the asset
the ability to convert the asset into cash

- The **liquidity of the asset**. This means the ability to convert the asset into cash. For example, you can sell shares on any business day providing someone wants to buy them. On the other hand it may take many months to sell a house if the market is slow. Thus, if you think you may need cash quickly at some point in the future it is not a good idea to invest all your cash in a house as you run the risk of not having cash when you need it.
- The time frame over which you are expecting a return.
- Your need for a regular income from your investments as opposed to long-term capital growth.
- Your level of comfort with volatility in returns or capital values.

risk mitigation
the steps you might take to reduce the impact should particular risks actually happen

An important part of your strategy should be **risk mitigation** which includes the steps you might take to offset risks where possible. For example a self-funded retiree might always try to keep a large amount of cash in their bank account as a buffer against unexpected expenses.

GENERAL RISKS

general risk
the possible variations in returns, the potential to suffer losses in the value of your capital sum, or the possibility that you will not meet your investment goals

General risk can be defined as the possible variations in returns, the potential to suffer losses in the value of your capital sum, or the possibility that you will not meet your investment goals.

All investments have inherent risks arising from the trade-off between risk and returns, that is, usually the higher the potential level of return on an investment, the greater the risk in the form of variability of returns or capital values. Generally the longer the time frame the more risk you can afford in your investments.

There are also risks in the form of delays in repayment; indeed with some forms of investment there is no guarantee that you will receive income or be able to recover your initial investment.

systematic risk
risks associated with movements in the whole market

unsystematic risk
movements arising in particular industries or individual companies

There are also risks arising from the volatility of the general business environment including inflation, changes in interest rates and political or economic instability in Australia and overseas. **Systematic risk** is the risk associated with returns in the total market. This can be compared to **unsystematic risk** which is the risk associated with a particular industry or company and not necessarily related to the fortunes of the whole market. You can guard against unsystematic risk by diversifying your portfolio of assets but as the global financial crisis (GFC) showed, you cannot guard against systematic risk (see Chapter 15). There are also changes in the business legal and industrial relations environment which have the potential to have a negative effect on your assets. They are discussed in various chapters in this book, and are listed in the glossary.

There are also risks to your life and health as well as any property you might own. Strategies to address these risks could include life, income protection and property insurance.

ASSET CLASSES

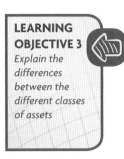

LEARNING OBJECTIVE 3
Explain the differences between the different classes of assets

There are four major **asset classes** or types that could form part of a typical investment portfolio. These are:

- cash or short-term money market securities
- fixed income securities, or government bonds that are long-term, interest-bearing securities
- property
- shares (also known as equities).

CASH

Cash refers to notes and coins as well as investments in assets such as short-term money market instruments (less than 365 days). These investments include bank-accepted or endorsed bank bills, high-rating corporate securities and Commonwealth or semi-government debt. Cash assets usually offer a secure but variable income stream with low capital volatility. Returns vary according to changes in short-term interest rates.

FIXED INCOME SECURITIES

A **fixed income security** is a type of loan whereby the lender makes the funds available in return for a legal debt instrument. Fixed income securities represent an obligation by the issuer (borrower) to repay a loan in the future plus interest.

Traditionally, fixed income securities have:

- A maturity, that is, a date on which the funds are to be repaid to the lender. This is the lifetime of the security and can range from one year to 30 years.
- A stream of coupons, that is, each fixed income security has a guarantee of a certain number of defined payments to the lender during the life of the security. Each of these coupons represents a payment.
- A yield, which is the dollar value of the repayments divided by the price of the security.

Fixed income securities are issued by government and semi-government authorities, statutory bodies and corporations or may be backed by pools of assets like mortgages. The lender or investor receives interest in the form of regular coupon payments plus repayment of capital (the amount invested) at the maturity date. Often the interest rate to be offered on a fixed income security will be influenced by the rating it receives from a **credit rating agency**. These agencies assign credit ratings for the issuers of the debt and the securities being issued. The ratings are supposed to indicate the creditworthiness of the issuer (ability to repay) and the quality of the debt security. Obviously the higher the credit rating, the lower the interest rate that has to be offered. Credit ratings agencies fell into disrepute during the GFC as many securities that had been rated triple A turned out to be worthless. Credit ratings agencies are subject to a range of criticisms including concerns about conflicts of interest given that the agencies' fees are paid by the clients being rated.

asset classes
the four major types of assets that could form part of a typical investment (cash or short-term money market securities, fixed-income securities or bonds, properties, and shares)

cash
notes, coins and investments in assets such as short-term money market instruments

fixed income security
type of loan whereby the lender makes the funds available in return for a legal debt instrument

credit rating agencies
agencies that rate the financial soundness of companies issuing financial securities

The capital value of fixed income securities will change over time due to fluctuations in market interest rates. A rise in market interest rates generally reduces the capital value of fixed income securities and a fall in market interest rates generally increases the capital value of fixed income securities. (For an explanation of this process see Chapter 23.)

PROPERTY

property
real estate (e.g. houses, apartments, factories, office buildings)

Property is usually used as an asset to provide capital growth as well as rental income. Different categories of property include:

- office blocks
- retail (shopping centres)
- industrial (factories and warehouses)
- residential (apartments and houses)
- tourism (hotels and resorts)
- rural (large farms).

The primary objective of owning property is to generate an income stream in the form of rent. The secondary objective is to have the opportunity to benefit from growth in the capital value of the asset.

SHARES

shares (equities)
represent a unit or part ownership of a company and entitle an investor to a proportion of the company's profits in the form of dividends

Shares (also known as equities) represent a unit or part ownership of a company. A share entitles an investor to a proportion of the company's profits in the form of dividends. Shares also carry the potential for capital growth over time. Capital growth can arise from increasing the size of the business, from takeovers, or from improvements in competitive positioning (which leads to the potential for higher profits). When this potential is represented in a rising share price, it signals an opportunity for capital gain to an owner of the shares. See Chapter 25 for a discussion of the causes of economic growth.

LEARNING OBJECTIVE 4
Explain the principles of diversification

DIVERSIFICATION

diversification
spreading investments across a range of asset classes

One of the basic principles of investment is **diversification**, which means spreading your investments across a range of asset classes (e.g. bonds, shares and property) rather than 'putting all your eggs in the one basket'. Diversification has the following benefits:

- It reduces your dependence on the performance of any particular asset class.
- It reduces the level of risk to your portfolio as positive performance in some asset classes can offset periods of weakness in others.
- When undertaken within asset classes, it spreads your risks more widely.

Because Australia has a market economy the value of different assets and the returns they generate can vary widely depending on the phase of the business cycle. For example, when the economy is expanding, businesses are able to produce more from a given stock of capital equipment, which will tend to generate higher profit levels and the potential for higher dividends. These expectations will tend to drive the price of shares to higher levels.

As the economy expands, the value of assets like factories and warehouses will also tend to rise. The reverse scenario occurs when the economy is contracting. See Chapter 8 for a discussion of the business cycle.

SPECIFIC RISKS ASSOCIATED WITH DIFFERENT ASSET CLASSES

There are particular risks associated with specific asset classes. (This is shown graphically in Figure 16.1 on page 335.)

CASH

Cash carries a low risk of losing your original investment; however, there is no potential for capital growth.

FIXED INCOME

Fixed income investments generally represent a higher risk than cash because the price of a fixed interest security will vary with movements in market interest rates and time to maturity (See Chapter 23).

Fixed income securities are also exposed to the credit risk of the issuer. This means that if the issuing enterprise collapses, then its debts may not be repaid in a timely fashion or maybe, not at all.

PROPERTY

Property investments are potentially higher risk than fixed income securities but lower than shares. The risk level can vary between high for property development to lower for established properties depending on the circumstances. Different types of property also tend to have unique mini business cycles which are different to the cycles tracked by other asset classes such as shares.

In Australia the demand for property can be heavily affected by a concept called **negative gearing** which enables people who borrow to invest in property to deduct losses caused by rental income not covering the costs of property ownership, from total income for tax purposes (see Chapter 22).

SHARES

It is often stated that historically, shares have performed better over the long term than most other kinds of investments;[4] however, share prices change constantly and can generate losses over the short to medium term. Also historical performance of a particular share is no guarantee of future performance.

negative gearing
using borrowed money to invest in assets like property and shares in the hope that the returns from the investment will be greater than the costs of interest and loan repayments. In Australia investors can deduct the net losses arising from the costs of owning negatively geared assets, including the interest costs of their loan, from their total income for tax purposes. Australia is unusual among advanced economies because there is no limit on the amount that can be claimed as a loss for tax purposes on negative gearing arrangements

THE SHARE MARKET

tangible assets
*assets that have a
physical existence
like buildings*

intangible assets
*non-physical assets
like know-how*

**intellectual
property**
*knowledge
embedded in the
workforce*

shareholder equity
*value of the assets of
the business after all
debts have been paid*

leverage
*borrowing to invest
in assets that are
expected to produce
a rate of return
greater than the cost
of the borrowing*

margin loan
*loan secured against
a holding of shares*

**loan to valuation
ratio**
*the value of the loan
compared to the
value of the whole
shareholding*

**algorithmic
computerised share
trading**
*where computers
trade directly with
each other*

Many people are exposed to the share market either as direct investors or via their superannuation fund. Any growth oriented portfolio will include a high proportion of shares. Share prices reflect a number of aspects.

The fundamental aspect is the value of the company. In its accounts a company listed on the stock exchange has to describe the value of its assets. Assets are the economic resources of the company that are valued at what they could be sold for and thus converted into cash. The balance sheet records the monetary value of the assets owned by the firm. **Tangible assets** have a physical existence and include items like buildings, machinery and stocks, while **intangible assets** are non-physical and include items like trademarks, patents and **intellectual property** and financial assets like debts owing to the firm. Intellectual property includes the sum of knowledge of the business and organisational know how of the workforce.

Shareholder equity or risk capital is the value of the assets of a business after all liabilities have been paid. If debts are greater than assets then there is no shareholder equity left because the value of the business is zero.

Leverage usually involves borrowing to invest in projects or assets that are expected to produce gains. Financial institutions, like banks, use leverage to multiply their asset base through lending. One danger with leverage is that it also multiplies losses. The aim of leverage is to generate a rate of return greater than the cost of the interest on the borrowing. If a company is heavily leveraged and becomes unable to pay its debts it is said to be insolvent and shareholder equity will be zero.

Individuals can also leverage their investment in shares by taking out a **margin loan**. A margin loan involves borrowing funds secured against shares and other assets including cash and using those funds to invest in shares. Interest must be paid on the loan and it is repayable at short notice if the conditions of the loan are breached. The maximum that can be borrowed is determined by the **loan to valuation ratio** which means that the loan cannot exceed a maximum percentage of the value of the total portfolio. If shares rise in value a margin loan will generate returns beyond those which would have been achieved through personal investments. However if shares fall in value the losses are magnified as the value of the portfolio falls and a proportion of the loan has to be repaid. During the GFC many people lost their homes or retirement savings because the value of their shares shrank to the point that the shares were worth less than the amount of the loan and repayment required selling other assets.

A new phenomenon in Australia is **algorithmic computerised share trading**. This is where shares are traded between computers with no human intervention. In the United States up to 70 per cent of trades are conducted between computers programmed to react to a range of factors ranging from complex event scenarios to simple measures of the movement or momentum of stock markets. It raises the issue of whether any judgment is being exercised in the setting of a share price or whether the price is simply the outcome of duelling computers responding to programmed instructions.

QUESTIONS

In your answers, refer to issues such as wealth creation, investment objectives, risk and returns.

1. Explain the concept of shareholder equity.
2. Explain the concept of leverage and the risks involved.
3. What is the objective of taking out a margin loan?
4. List two risks associated with a margin loan.

INTERNATIONAL INVESTMENTS

Many people invest in assets, usually in the form of shares or government securities held in another country. The difference between foreign direct investment and portfolio investment overseas is covered in Chapter 18.

Risks associated with international investments include:

- Differences between countries relating to accounting, auditing, financial reporting, government regulations, securities exchanges and transactional procedures.
- Foreign markets may have different levels of liquidity, pricing, availability, settlement and clearance procedures.
- Actions of foreign governments, exchange controls, defaults on government securities, political and social instability which can prevent investors from extracting their funds.
- Currency risk arising from the fact that international assets are usually priced in the currency of their home country. Consequently changes in exchange rates will affect the value of assets denominated in foreign currencies and this will affect the returns when converted to Australian dollars. See Chapter 18 for a discussion of the effects of changes in exchange rates.

The risk and return chart in Figure 16.1 provides a general idea of where the various asset classes sit on the risk return spectrum.

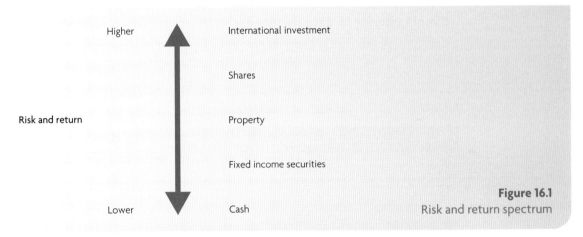

Figure 16.1
Risk and return spectrum

THE NIGERIAN SHUFFLE

Assume you receive a desperate email from Nigeria requesting details of your bank account and a promise of a deposit of A$2000 in your account so that 26 million euros from the estate of a general can be transferred secretly from Nigeria to Australia. In return you get to keep 1 million euros and you receive Nigerian Government bonds to the value of 10 million euros.

Just as you are about to send your bank details your partner suggests you rethink your decision. As you discuss the situation you begin to consider the following risk and return issues:

- how your bank account details might be used
- the risks involved in international transactions
- the long-term value of Nigerian Government bonds.

QUESTION
Briefly describe the conclusions you come to after your discussion.

LINK TO
INTERNATIONAL
ECONOMY

TAXATION

The Australian taxation system is extremely complex. Investment returns are subject to federal taxes on income and capital gains. Purchases of investments are subject to state taxes such as stamp duties and land taxes. It is important that you understand how taxes affect your particular circumstances when making decisions aimed at wealth creation.

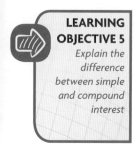

LEARNING OBJECTIVE 5

Explain the difference between simple and compound interest

SUPERANNUATION IN AUSTRALIA

The following sections deal with superannuation, which is a compulsory form of wealth creation in Australia. In order to understand the principles of wealth accumulation underlying superannuation we first discuss simple and compound interest. Then we consider superannuation arrangements in Australia and some of the key issues. All working people in Australia have to contribute to a superannuation fund.

COMPOUND AND SIMPLE INTEREST

simple (or flat rate) interest
interest rates calculated on the initial sum deposited or borrowed

It is important to understand the two basic methods of calculating interest because one day you may be a saver or a borrower or both at the same time.

Simple interest or flat rate interest rates are calculated on the initial sum deposited or borrowed. For example, let us say you deposit $100 at 5 per cent simple interest for five years. Table 16.1 illustrates the effects of this form of interest.

Table 16.1   **Example of simple interest**

YEAR	DEPOSIT	INTEREST RATE (%)	DOLLARS EARNED	TOTAL
1	$100	5	$5	
2	$100	5	$5	
3	$100	5	$5	
4	$100	5	$5	
5	$100	5	$5	
			Total $25	$125

compound interest
interest that is calculated on the initial deposit but also takes into account interest that is reinvested

Compound interest is calculated on the initial deposit but also takes into account interest that is reinvested. That is to say you can earn interest on your interest, as shown in Table 16.2.

You can see the difference between the outcomes for a 5 per cent simple interest deposit and a 5 per cent compound interest deposit. At the end of five years there is a 2 per cent or $2.63 gap.

The impact is the same if you are a borrower. Imagine the effects on your loan repayments if the amount above was a $100 000 loan rather than a $100 deposit.

That is why it is important to clearly understand the terms of any loan contract before you sign. In many Australian states, lenders are required to disclose the total amount of interest

Table 16.2   **Example of compound interest**

YEAR	DEPOSIT	INTEREST RATE (%)	DOLLARS EARNED	TOTAL
1	$100	5	$5	
2	$105	5	$10.25	
3	$110.25	5	$15.76	
4	$115.76	5	$21.15	
5	$121.15	5	$27.63	
				$127.63

payable on loan contracts prior to completion of the contract and there are upper limits on the rate of interest that can be charged on loans.

SUPERANNUATION

In Australia, **superannuation** schemes are marketed on the basis of compounding as illustrated in the previous section. Essentially the idea of superannuation is to save a proportion of your income over a long period of time with no withdrawals. Thus you are earning returns compounded by the inclusion of previous returns on your investment funds. Australian superannuation funds usually invest in the types of assets referred to earlier in the chapter.

In the 1980s trade unions in Australia agreed to reduce their wage claims in return for government legislation that required employers to contribute to superannuation for each employee. In the mid 2000s employers were required to contribute the equivalent of 9 per cent of each employee's salary to a superannuation fund. Employee contributions vary from industry to industry.

The reason for compulsory superannuation for all employees is the ageing of the Australian population. For example, between 2002 and 2012 the most rapidly growing age group is people aged between 60 and 64. This means that the proportion of the population paying taxes to support pension payments to older people is going to shrink. Compulsory superannuation is a form of forced savings to enable the proportion of people depending on tax-financed pensions to decline and the proportion of self-funded retirees to increase. The aim is for the government-funded pension to be limited to providing a safety net at a basic level of income to a relatively small proportion of the population. Some commentators describe the approach as the privatisation of old age because the risks involved in saving for retirement are mostly borne by the individual.

In this context, financial planners tend to have an arbitrary target for the amount of lump sum required to generate an income stream of 60 to 65 per cent of final salary. It is thought that this will generate a reasonable standard of living for the retiree.

The lump sum, which is the total outcome of savings over 30 to 40 years, depends on a number of factors which are difficult to predict. Two examples of how this prediction can be made are set out in Table 16.3 overleaf.

LEARNING OBJECTIVE 6
Explain the reasons for compulsory superannuation in Australia

superannuation
requires people to save a proportion of their income over a long period of time with no withdrawals

LEARNING OBJECTIVE 7
Give examples of the impact of different assumptions on forecasts of final superannuation lump sums

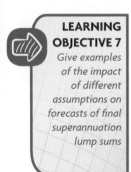

Table 16.3   **Example of final superannuation lump sums**

ASSOCIATION OF SUPERANNUATION FUNDS OF AUSTRALIA	**HONG KONG & SHANGHAI BANKING COMPANY**
Lump sum from 9 per cent of salary	Lump sum from 9 per cent of salary
contributions after:	contributions after:
30 years $167 000	30 years $287 630
40 years $267 508	40 years $523 262
ASSUMPTIONS	
Average ordinary time earnings of $45 000	Total average adult earnings of $51 000 including overtime
Fund earnings of 7 per cent per year after fees and taxes	Fund earnings of 7 per cent per year after fees and taxes
Inflation of 2.5 per cent	Inflation of 2.5 per cent
Real salary growth of zero per year	Real salary growth of 1.25 per cent per year

You can see from the above that differing assumptions regarding salary growth and average salaries produce dramatically different results even when the other basic assumptions are the same.

When considering superannuation plans you need to take your own circumstances into account. For example, many people do not work continuously from age 20 to age 60. Thus, calculations using this assumption may not be appropriate for your situation.

ISSUES AFFECTING SUPERANNUATION IN AUSTRALIA

There are several important issues affecting attitudes towards superannuation. For example, the attraction of saving via superannuation in Australia is reduced by the rate of taxation applied by the federal government and the level of fees applied by superannuation fund managers. A study using APRA statistics by the Australian Broadcasting Commission[5] in 2010 found that net annual compound return from 1997 was 3 per cent per annum. This rate of return barely exceeded the inflation rate of 2.8 per cent over the period and can be compared to the return on 10-year Australian treasury bonds which averaged 5.75 per cent. The main factors contributing to such a low rate of return were the 15 per cent tax on contributions to superannuation and the fees charged by those who manage the funds.

Broadly speaking if a superannuation investment is earning 6 per cent per annum then 2 per cent is taken by tax and 2 per cent by fees. Thus the investor's funds are compounding only at 2 per cent per annum.

This situation and the highly volatile stock market explains the disillusionment with superannuation that had set in by the late 2000s, with many people reacting to negative returns on superannuation resulting from the GFC by turning to do-it-yourself superannuation or seeking to develop wealth portfolios of shares and property without involving intermediaries such as funds managers.

Figure 16.2 illustrates the rate of return to different categories of superannuation funds in the 2005–10 period. You can see that corporate and retail funds were the worst affected by the GFC although all categories of funds suffered negative returns.

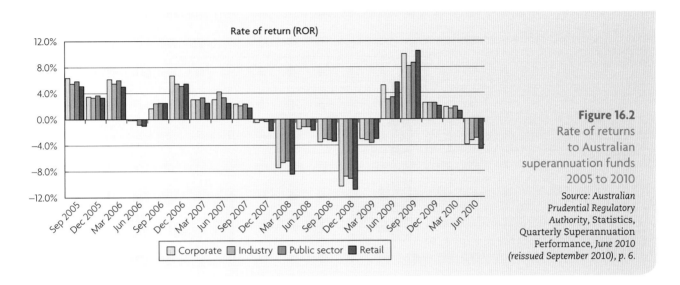

Figure 16.2
Rate of returns
to Australian
superannuation funds
2005 to 2010

*Source: Australian
Prudential Regulatory
Authority, Statistics,
Quarterly Superannuation
Performance, June 2010
(reissued September 2010), p. 6.*

In 2010 the Super System Review[6] (commonly known as the Cooper Review) was published which focused on management, efficiency and the structure of the superannuation industry. It found that over 80 per cent of Australians do not actively choose a superannuation fund when they commence employment, and the outcomes, in terms of their lump sum or pension, are highly variable depending on the costs, complexity of the products, commissions taken by financial planners and the investment options provided.

The Cooper Review recommended that, where employees do not make a choice of superannuation fund, they are offered a standard fund which complies with a set of standards known as 'Mysuper'.

To comply with these standards the fund must have:

- low fees
- a single diversified investment option
- no commissions
- simple insurance coverage
- access to basic financial advice
- electronic communications to minimise costs.

According to the review, the vast majority of workers would take the default option of the 'Mysuper' type fund which would result in them accumulating significantly higher benefits over their working life.

The high level of risk embodied in the asset allocation of super funds in Australia has been raised by many commentators. Figure 16.3 overleaf illustrates asset allocation by pension funds in Australia, the United States and Japan. You can see different attitudes to risk embodied in the allocations between shares (high risk) and other categories with the asset allocation by Japanese pension funds being the most conservative and the Australians being the most risky. This raises the question of whether Australian superannuation funds should adjust their asset allocation models to reduce the overall risk profile with a bigger percentage of funds allocated to fixed interest securities.

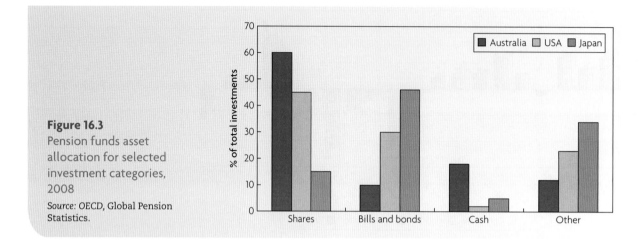

Figure 16.3
Pension funds asset allocation for selected investment categories, 2008

Source: OECD, Global Pension Statistics.

SUMMARY

1. The key issues in personal financial investment and wealth creation are to establish personal objectives and to understand the different categories of assets and the risks associated with each asset class.
2. Investment objectives will vary with your personal circumstances and the phase of your life cycle.
3. There are four basic classes of assets:
    (a) cash
    (b) fixed income securities
    (c) property
    (d) shares.
4. Apart from cash all asset classes involve a degree of risk. Usually the higher the potential return, the greater the level of risk.
5. In general shares carry the highest risk and cash the lowest risk.
6. International investments can be very risky.
7. Risks include returns not meeting expectations and variations in the capital value of assets. High-risk investments can involve total loss of capital.
8. Simple rates of interest and compound rates of interest produce quite different outcomes.
9. Superannuation is based on the compounding effect of investments over a long period of time.
10. There are several disincentives to superannuation as a form of wealth creation in Australia some of which were addressed by the Super System Review.

REFERENCES

1. *Oxford Reference Encyclopaedia*, Oxford University Press, Oxford, United Kingdom, 1998.
2. Fred Catherwood, *The Creation of Wealth: Recovering a Christian Understanding of Money, Work and Ethics*, Good News Publishers/Crossway Books, Wheaton, Illinois, 2002.
3. A.G. Walder, *Politics and Property in Transitional Economies: A Theory of Elite Opportunity*, Asia/Pacific Research Centre Institute for International Studies, Stanford University, Palo Alto CA, United States, April 2003.
4. Russell Investments, press release on research conducted for the Australian Stock Exchange, May 2010, <www.russell.com/AU/press/press-releases/may-2010/26-asx-lo>, accessed 20 September 2010.
5. Stephen Long, 'A super scandal', Australian Broadcasting Commission, <www.abc.net.au/news/stories/2010/08/05/2974671.htm.>, accessed 20 September 2010.
6. Review into the Governance, Efficiency, Structure and Operation of Australia's Superannuation System, 30 June 2010, <www.supersystemreview.gov.au>, accessed 20 September 2010 (Cooper Review).

REVIEW QUESTIONS

1. Explain two of the differences between cash and fixed income securities.
2. Explain the difference between rent and dividends.
3. What is your time horizon for investment? Give reasons for your answer.
4. Describe the effect of a large increase in interest rates on the economic cycle and on the value of shares and housing.
5. How would you react to a financial adviser who offered you a 'risk-free investment with above-market rates of return'?
6. Compare the risks involved in buying shares as opposed to purchasing a property.
7. Calculate the return from $100 invested for two years at 10 per cent simple and 10 per cent compound rate of interest.
8. Briefly describe the concept of superannuation.
9. Give an example of the importance of assumptions in calculating final superannuation lump sum payouts.
10. Give a reason for governments imposing taxes on superannuation contributions and payouts.
11. Assume you win $500 000 in a lottery. Explain the difference between managed and direct investments.
12. Explain the concept of 'compound interest'.
13. Define your savings goals and describe the level of risk you are willing to accept.
14. Describe how you would allocate your funds to different asset classes in order to achieve your objectives and take account of your risk preferences.
15. Explain the key issues in regard to superannuation for Australian workers.

APPLIED QUESTIONS AND EXERCISES
DEVELOPING A FINANCIAL INVESTMENT PLAN

Various reports have shown that:

- 37 per cent of people between 16 and 34 years of age save more than $250 per month
- between 23 and 50 per cent of all Australians save less than $50 per week
- only half of people under 20 save anything at all

- 10 per cent of average household income is saved
- 16- to 34-year-olds paid 18 per cent of their income in billed expenses compared to 26 per cent for other Australians. They also spent more on entertainment (15 per cent) compared to older Australians (10 per cent)
- the main obstacles to saving are:
  - low incomes
  - taxes
  - interest rates
  - bills for items like rent, mobile phones and credit cards.

Various comments were made on this data:

- Some young people were in a significant debt crisis with mobile phone and credit card debt being major causes.
- Some young people had lower spending commitments and were clearly allocating some savings towards housing deposits, retirement, health care and education.

QUESTIONS

Review your personal circumstances.

1. Do you have financial goals? If so, what are they?
2. What is your current consumption to income ratio?
3. What do you have to do to achieve your goals in terms of:
   (a) changing spending patterns
   (b) identifying asset classes that suit your profile.

NEGATIVE GEARING

On its website the Australian Securities and Investment Commission (ASIC) discusses the topic of borrowing money and negative gearing. It recommends that a good investment must sooner or later show a profit, not a loss, and should also provide a reliable and rising income. It says that choosing a good investment takes time, knowledge and experience. People who negatively gear their investment are taking risks, for example you can only negatively gear an investment if you have money left over after paying your regular expenses to cover the losses associated with negative gearing. Also you need to understand that you are using today's money to fund the losses in the hope that you will recover your losses and make a profit at some point in the future. ASIC recommends that if you do want to negatively gear investments then you should borrow conservatively so you can meet future cost increases such as those arising from higher interest rates and that you maintain a regular income so you can cover the borrowing costs.

Source: Australian Securities and Investment Commission, <www.fido.gov. au/fido/fido.nsf/by headline/Borrowing+money+and+negative+gearing? openDocument>, accessed 18 October 2010.

QUESTIONS

You will also need to refer to Chapter 14 to answer these questions.

1. Explain the role of ASIC.
2. Explain the meaning of negative gearing and the risks involved.
3. List two risks arising from investing in shares and property.
4. Explain your investment objectives and timelines that would be involved in a decision to negatively gear an investment.
5. Consider your personal income and identify how much money you can afford to lose each month on a negatively geared investment.

DECISIONS ON STRATEGY

In developing your wealth creation strategy, you have to consider factors such as whether to directly manage your portfolio or to use a funds manager and whether to use debt to finance accumulation of assets or savings.

QUESTIONS

1. What factors would you take into account in making the decision to use:
   (a) a funds manager
   (b) debt to accumulate wealth?
2. Describe two risks associated with your approach.

APPENDIX TO CHAPTER 16: FINANCIAL MODELLING TECHNIQUES FOR BUSINESS AND PERSONAL DECISIONS

Financial modelling is the task of building a financial model, a tool designed to forecast the performance of a business, project or any other form of financial investment.

Financial modelling with various degrees of complexity can be used in decision making by government organisations, private firms or individuals.

In the Appendix to Chapter 6 we discussed a couple of such financial tools: break-even analysis and contribution margin analysis.

In this appendix we will overview several other similar financial models:

- net present value (NPV) and discounted cash flows
- yield curves
- analysis of segmental performance and profit variance
- value-at-risk (VaR)
- credit scorecards.

THE NET PRESENT VALUE (NPV) AND DISCOUNTED CASH FLOWS

Following the discussion in this chapter about compound interest we can now understand the concept of the time value of money. $1000 today is always preferred by anyone to $1000 in two years time, because of the interest factor.

The present value is the value now of a given amount to be invested or received in the future assuming compound interest.

The present value is based on three variables: (1) the dollar amount to be received (future amount), (2) the length of time until the amount is received (number of periods), and (3) the interest rate (the discount rate).

The process of determining the present value is referred to as discounting the future amount.

To illustrate the present value concept, assume that you are willing to have $1000 in a couple of years' time. The question is what amount would you need to invest today that will yield $1000 in two years if you want a 10 per cent rate of return per annum on your money. The calculation of this amount is shown in Figure 16.4 overleaf.

Another method that may be used to calculate the future value of a single amount involves the use of tables which show the present value of 1 for n periods. The future value is multiplied by the present value factor specified at the intersection of the number of periods and the discount rate. In our example, the present value factor for two periods at a discount rate of 10 per cent is 0.82645, which equals the $826.45 ($1000 × 0.82645) calculated in Figure 16.4.

Ultimately, the value of all financial investments is determined by the value of cash flows received and paid.

The decision to make long-term investments is best evaluated using discounting techniques that recognise the time value of money, i.e. the present value of the cash flows

Figure 16.4

Present value
calculation $1000
discounted at
10 per cent

- Present value (PV) = Future value (FV)/$(1+i)^n$
- PV = $1000/$(1+10\%)^2$
- PV = $1000/(1.10 × 1.10)
- PV = $826.45

involved in a capital investment. Under the net present value (NPV) method, cash flows are discounted to their present value and then compared with the capital outlay required by the investment.

Some typical cash outflows and inflows related to equipment purchase and replacement include:

- cash outflows: initial investment; repairs and maintenance; increased operating costs; overhaul of equipment
- cash inflows: sale of old equipment; increased cash received from customers; reduced cash outflows.

Capital budgeting techniques that take into account both the time value of money and the estimated total cash flows from an investment are called discounted cash flow techniques.

The interest rate to be used in discounting the future cash inflow is the required minimum rate of return. A proposal is acceptable when net present value is zero or positive. At either of those values, the rate of return on the investment equals or exceeds the required rate of return. When net present value is negative, the project is unacceptable. Figure 16.5 shows the net present value decision criteria.

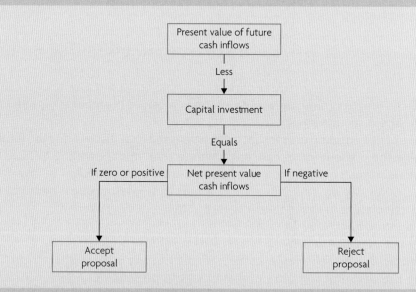

Figure 16.5

Net present value
decision criteria

*Source: Carlon et al,
Accounting Business
Skills, 3rd edn, John
Wiley Australia, 2009.*

Discounted cash flow analysis is widely used in investment finance, real estate development and corporate financial management.

YIELD CURVES

In finance the yield curve is the relation between the interest rate (or cost of borrowing) and the time to maturity of the debt for a given borrower in a given currency.

yield curve
the relation between the interest rate (or cost of borrowing) and the time to maturity of the debt for a given borrower in a given currency

The yield curve (also known as the 'term structure' of interest rates) is a graph that plots the yields of similar-quality bonds against their maturities, ranging from shortest to longest.

The most frequently reported yield curve compares the three-month, two-year, five-year and 30-year United States Treasury debt. This yield curve is used as a benchmark for other debt in the market, such as mortgage rates or bank lending rates. The curve is also used to predict changes in economic output and growth.

The yield curve shows the various yields that are currently being offered on bonds of different maturities. It enables investors at a quick glance to compare the yields offered by short-term, medium-term and long-term bonds.

The shape of the yield curve is closely scrutinised because it helps to give an idea of future interest rate change and economic activity. There are three main types of yield curve shapes: normal, inverted and flat (or humped). A normal yield curve is one in which longer maturity bonds have a higher yield compared to shorter-term bonds due to the risks associated with time. An inverted yield curve is one in which the shorter-term yields are higher than the longer-term yields, which can be a sign of upcoming recession. A flat (or humped) yield curve is one in which the shorter-term and longer-term yields are very close to each other, which is also a predictor of an economic transition. The slope of the yield curve is also seen as important: the greater the slope, the greater the gap between short-term and long-term rates.

If short-term yields are lower than long-term yields (the line is sloping upwards), then the curve is referred to as a positive (or 'normal') yield curve. Below you'll find an example of a normal yield curve.

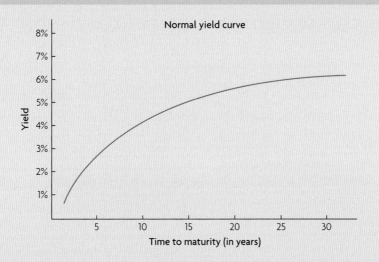

Figure 16.6
Normal yield curve

THE RISK OF CONSERVATIVE INVESTMENT

Australian Budget changes to superannuation have generated a subtle shift in the yield curve, which has suddenly turned normal.

This shows how thinking is changing for investors and for providers of retirement income products, from term deposits to long-term fixed income investments such as annuities and bond funds.

Over 1994–2010, the yield curve has been inverted or flat; now it has turned normal and it is in fact at its steepest since 1994. Having a normal curve matters to people heading to retirement, who would generally be looking for some certainty of income over a longer period, or a guaranteed base level to cover living expenses or to maintain their lifestyle.

Once upon a time, before the global financial crisis, the most popular retirement income product was an allocated pension, whose value would likely rise with the market, in preference to an annuity, or capital guaranteed, fixed-rate security or government bond fund. Retirees hated the idea of missing out on market gains when long-term interest rates were low.

With the GFC, the wisdom of locking much of your retirement income in the volatile share market is under doubt. The crash has wiped up to half the value from many account-based pensions and super funds—wealth that was supposed to last 20 to 25 years, or about as long as the rest of your life.

In the wake of the depredations of the GFC on investment returns, market risk and longevity risk have, naturally, been pushed to the front of the risk queue.

But as markets slowly recover from a tough few years, a risk little noticed before might be more of a problem: the risk of conservatism.

Financial experts show that many people mistakenly believe that market volatility is the only investment risk during retirement. In fact the biggest risk is the potential that a retiree will outlive their savings.

The experts' advice is that the only way to avoid running out of money in retirement is to have a post-retirement asset mix that can generate strong and steady cashflows.

ANALYSIS OF SEGMENTAL PERFORMANCE AND PROFIT VARIANCE

When entities have significant operations in different industries or groups of related products that have different risks and returns, they are required to report segmental data, i.e. information about the financial performance and position of each reportable segment.

For example, Woolworths Ltd provides information about its business segments: supermarkets (including retail liquor and petrol outlets), general merchandise, consumer electronics, hotels and wholesale operations. The disclosures include sales revenue, other revenue, result (revenue less expenses), assets, liabilities, depreciation and amortisation, other non-cash expenses, and acquisition of non-current assets for each segment.

On the other hand, Foster's Group provides disclosures about its geographic segments: Australia; Asia and Pacific; Europe; and the Americas, and business segments: Australian beer; international beer; and wine.

Analysis of segmental performance assists in determining the success or failure of the divisional manager as well as the division itself. Divisional performance measures are concerned with the contribution of the division to profit and quality and whether the division meets the overall goals of the company.

Many analysts and other users of financial statements consider the segment disclosures to be among the most important information in the financial statements. Without the segment disclosures, comparing diversified entities becomes very difficult.

Most models that measure performance in the private sector are tied to profits—for example, profit percentage (profit divided by sales), return on investment (profit divided by initial investment), or residual income (profit minus a deduction for capital costs). Profits are seldom a viable measure at the cost centre level, however. Rather, performance is most often measured by comparing actual costs against a budget. A *variance* is defined as the difference between the amount budgeted for a particular activity and the actual cost of carrying out that activity during a given period. Variances may be positive (under budget) or negative (over budget).

Differences between actual profit and budgeted profit are affected by three basic items: sales price, sales volume, and costs. In a multi-product firm, if all products are not equally profitable, profit is also affected by the mix of products sold. If actual profit is greater than budgeted profit, the total profit variance is favourable and credited; otherwise, it is unfavourable and debited.

VALUE-AT-RISK (VaR)

Value-at-risk (VaR) is the maximum loss that will occur within a given period of time and with a given probability.

For example, if a portfolio of stocks has a one-day 5 per cent VaR of $1 million, there is a 0.05 probability that the portfolio will fall in value by more than $1 million over a one day period, assuming markets are normal and there is no trading in the portfolio. Informally, a loss of $1 million or more on this portfolio is expected on one day in 20. A loss which exceeds the VaR threshold is termed a VaR break.

Value-at-risk has become the standard measure of market risk in financial institutions such as banks. The main reason for its popularity is that it shows the total risk of a portfolio in a single number. Internally, banks use VaR as a risk management tool by setting VaR limits for individual activities. Externally, regulators impose capital requirements on banks based on their VaR values.

CREDIT SCORECARDS

Credit scorecards are mathematical models which attempt to provide a quantitative measurement of the likelihood that a customer will display a defined behaviour (e.g. loan default) with respect to their current or proposed credit position with a lender.

Credit scoring typically uses observations or data from clients who defaulted on their loans plus observations on a large number of clients who have not defaulted. Statistically, estimation techniques such as logistic regression or probit are used to create estimates of the probability of default for observations based on this historical data. This model can be used to predict probability of default for new clients using the same observation characteristics (e.g. age, income, house owner). The default probabilities are then scaled to a 'credit score'. This score ranks clients by riskiness without explicitly identifying their probability of default.

7

AUSTRALIA IN THE INTERNATIONAL ECONOMY

Chapter 17

Australia's international trade and investment

LEARNING OBJECTIVES

After studying this chapter, you will be able to:

1. outline the reasons for international trade
2. explain the main theories of international trade
3. outline the main changes in the patterns of Australia's international trade
4. identify the main changes in the patterns of Australia's international investment.

INTRODUCTION

For a small country like Australia, the overseas sector provides a vital connection between the domestic economy and the global economy. Trade between nations is an important component of relations between the national economies of the world.

As with all other economic activities, international trade is very much related to the economic problem. The world is characterised by an uneven distribution of economic resources. For example, Australia is well endowed with every type of mineral resource except oil. Saudi Arabia has few mineral resources but it does have plenty of oil.

Resources are scarce relative to the unlimited wants of society and the mobility of such resources between nations is, for various reasons, restricted. Therefore it makes good economic sense for nations to engage in:

- exporting those items and productive resources of which they have a surplus
- importing those items and productive resources for which there is internal demand.

This chapter deals also with a few features of Australia's foreign direct investment (FDI). Since the arrival of European settlers, Australia has relied heavily on foreign investment to fund higher levels of investment than domestic saving alone would allow and to promote faster economic growth and higher living standards.

It is well known that Australia's international trade and foreign investment activities are interlinked and their intensification is a relevant feature of the process of progressive globalisation of the Australian economy.

REASONS FOR TRADE

LEARNING OBJECTIVE 1
Outline the reasons for international trade

International trade can be broadly defined as the exchange of goods and services between two interested parties, located within different national boundaries. Let's examine the main reasons for international trade.

THE BENEFITS OF EXPORTING GOODS AND SERVICES

The Link to International Economy on page 359 shows that the expansion of a high-tech sector of the Australian economy has been very much based on export markets, and illustrates the benefits of exporting on a global scale. An astute organisation such as Cochlear Limited is constantly searching for ways of increasing the size of the market for its product, because the potential in Australia is limited and export markets provide an obvious opportunity to expand the scale of the business.

Managers know that higher sales generate larger profits. At a national level the other benefits of large-scale exporting of goods and services include:

- Increased employment, generated by higher output and orders to Australian subcontractors. (For instance, 4000 to 5000 new operations like Cochlear Limited or GBC Scientific Equipment could significantly reduce the level of unemployment in Australia.)

international trade
the exchange of goods and services between two interested parties, located within different national boundaries

- Export-oriented industries will grow in size, encouraging specialisation of tasks, mass-production techniques and economies of scale.
- Firms within export industries, being more profitable, will have the opportunity of diverting greater funds into the development of existing land, plant and machinery.

REASONS FOR IMPORTS

Goods are imported by nations for various reasons:

- The goods cannot be produced within the country. If a nation does not possess either the resources or technology necessary to produce a certain commodity, and there is a strong demand for it, the nation may import all of its requirements. In Australia, we import cocoa, rubber, commercial aircraft and satellites for these reasons.
- The goods can be produced, but not in sufficient quantities to satisfy internal demand. Such is the case with crude oil, where imports cover about 30 to 40 per cent of our domestic requirements.
- The goods are available more cheaply from overseas, or are of superior quality. For instance, we import about 70 per cent of our machinery and equipment, as well as a large proportion of our domestic requirements of motor cars and electronic goods, because they are available at competitive prices and quality levels from overseas.

THE BENEFITS OF IMPORTING GOODS AND SERVICES

It is often argued that imports lead to loss of employment in Australia, but this applies only where equivalent goods could be produced domestically. In fact, there are strong reasons to believe that imports provide great benefits to Australians:

- The quantity (and often the quality) of goods and services flowing onto the domestic market is enhanced, thereby providing for the wants of firms and consumers which domestic producers cannot satisfy.
- Imports of capital goods, production materials and technologies help to increase the efficiency and variety of output by domestic suppliers.
- Many domestic products could not be produced without the inclusion of imported intermediate goods and services.
- The competition provided by imports may force local suppliers to improve their production techniques and pricing.
- Overall, imports allow us to consume a more diverse range of goods and thereby raise our standard of living.

LEARNING OBJECTIVE 2

Explain the main theories of international trade

THEORIES OF INTERNATIONAL TRADE

There are many theories that attempt to explain international trade patterns, what the gains are from trade and how they are divided among trading countries. Two major concepts of the international trade theory are absolute advantage and comparative advantage.

THEORY OF ABSOLUTE ADVANTAGE

The theory of **absolute advantage**, developed by Adam Smith in 1776, is the basic explanation for patterns of international trade. Saudi Arabia exports petroleum to Japan. Australia exports beef to South Korea. The United States exports aircraft to Australia. These examples illustrate the principle of absolute advantage, whereby the exporting country has superiority in the availability and cost of certain goods.

Absolute advantage may come about because of such factors as climate, quality of land, and natural resource endowments; or because of differences in labour, capital, technology and entrepreneurship.

Some nations have oil, but most do not: this is a case of absolute advantage because of physical availability. A developing country located close to the equator (e.g. Papua New Guinea) can produce coffee efficiently because of its suitable climate and low labour costs. Australia can import and consume cocoa at much less cost than if it tried to produce coffee in Queensland.

Acquired advantages, as in the case of aircraft in the United States and beef in Australia, can be the result of specialisation and large-scale production.

absolute advantage
the ability of a country to produce a good using fewer resources than another country

EXAMPLE

The concept of absolute advantage can be illustrated with a simple example of two countries and two products. To simplify the example further, we will use units of resource input (land, labour and capital) for comparison, rather than money.

The hypothetical example in Table 17.1 compares the output resulting from the use of 100 units of resources. Clearly, Australia has an absolute advantage in the production of beef, since it can produce 8 tonnes of beef per resource unit, as compared to 4 tonnes in Japan.

Table 17.1   **Alternate output possibilities from 100 units of resources**

	BEEF (TONNES)	TV SETS (UNITS)
Australia	800	200
Japan	400	1000

However, Japan can produce eight more TV sets per resource unit than Australia, which indicates that Japan has an absolute advantage in the production of TV sets.

THEORY OF COMPARATIVE ADVANTAGE

The theory of **comparative advantage** derives from the theory of absolute advantage, and was initially developed by D. Ricardo[1] in 1817. In simple terms, one country is said to have a comparative advantage over another in the production of a certain commodity if its opportunity cost of producing that commodity is lower.

comparative advantage
the ability of a country to produce a good at a lower opportunity cost than another country

EXAMPLE

We will explore this concept using another hypothetical example, with Australia and the United Kingdom as the two countries and cheese and cloth as the two products. Assume that with 100 units of resources the two countries can produce the alternative quantities of goods shown in Table 17.2. According to this information, Australia is more efficient in producing both cheese and cloth.

Table 17.2   **Alternative production possibilities**

	CHEESE (1000 KG)	CLOTH (1000 M)
Australia	200	160
United Kingdom	80	120

The comparative efficiency of Australia and the United Kingdom is measured by the opportunity cost of producing each good. The opportunity cost of any product is what has to be sacrificed in order to obtain it, as shown in Table 17.3.

Table 17.3   **Opportunity cost and comparative advantage**

OPPORTUNITY COST		
PRODUCTION	AUSTRALIA	UNITED KINGDOM
1.00 kg cheese	0.80 m cloth	1.50 m cloth
1.00 m cloth	1.25 kg cheese	0.67 kg cheese

In this example, Australia has an absolute advantage over the United Kingdom in the production of both products.

- In the case of cheese, Australia can produce 200 tonnes with the same resources, compared to 80 tonnes in the United Kingdom.
- In the case of cloth, Australia can produce 160 000 metres, as compared to 120 000 metres in the United Kingdom. Thus, Australia's absolute advantage in cheese is 20 to 8, and in cloth it is 16 to 12.

On a relative basis, Australia's comparative advantage is greatest in cheese:

200:80 = 2.5 to 1, versus 160:120 = 1.33 to 1

The United Kingdom's comparative disadvantage is least in cloth:

120:160 = 1 to 1.33, versus 80:200 = 1 to 2.5 for cheese

Trade under constant opportunity costs

When trade takes place, according to our example, Australia will specialise in cheese, which it then trades for cloth. Conversely, the United Kingdom will trade cloth for cheese. The opportunity for trade creates a single market for the two countries. If we ignore transport costs and tariffs, a single price for cloth and cheese will emerge, somewhere between the internal price ratios—that is, the national prices before trade occurred.

The exchange price for a metre of cloth would have to be less than 1.25 kilograms of cheese, the opportunity cost for Australia, and higher than 0.67 kilograms of cheese, the opportunity cost for the United Kingdom. Otherwise, there would be no incentive for the two countries to develop trade relations. Let us assume that the trade price between Australia and the United Kingdom is set at 1 kilogram of cheese for 1 metre of cloth.

This exchange rate benefits Australia (because the opportunity cost of 1 metre of cloth produced domestically is 1.25 kilograms of cheese). At the same time it benefits the United Kingdom: by giving up 1 metre of cloth, it could produce domestically only 0.67 kilograms of cheese, while through trade it can procure 1 kilogram of cheese.

According to the theory of comparative advantage, Australia will specialise in the production of cheese and the United Kingdom will specialise in the production of cloth. This will be more efficient and will conserve resources. Both countries will gain through trading with each other.

Factor endowments

Ricardo's theory of comparative advantage simply assumes that different countries have different opportunity costs, but it makes no attempt to explain the reasons for these differences. Later economists (such as Heckscher[2] and Ohlin[3]) developed the concept and argued over alternative explanations.

The factors of production—land, labour and capital—enable production to take place. A country's share of factors of production is referred to as its **factor endowment**.

factor endowment
a country's share of factors of production

It is generally agreed that variations in comparative costs exist because both the quality and the quantity of the factors of production are unequally distributed between countries. Most countries possess some factors in greater abundance than others. A nation will be the most efficient producer of those goods that make intensive use of the abundant factors, which are relatively cheap. Therefore, the opportunity cost of forgoing production in other goods will be lower than the opportunity cost of forgoing production of goods that make intensive use of the abundant factors.

This theory explains the pattern of Australian trade with Japan. Australia specialises in producing and exporting primary products (grain, beef, minerals), which make use of our abundant factors (land and natural resources). Japan specialises in producing and exporting manufactured goods, which use its abundant factors (capital and labour) intensively.

LIMITATIONS OF THE TRADE THEORY

Although specialisation by countries can increase production, the concept is highly theoretical and merely indicates some reasons why certain countries have specialised in the production of certain goods.

The theory of comparative advantage in international trade does not take into account a number of considerations, such as:

- the difficulty in moving resources, especially the labour force, into the desired industries
- fluctuations in demand, or the collapse of a market in a country's product, in a situation of international recession or unfair (subsidised) competition
- artificial limitations, such as import restrictions, placed on a product by overseas countries
- other political restraints.

LEARNING
OBJECTIVE 3
Outline the
main changes in
the patterns of
Australia's
international
trade

PATTERNS OF AUSTRALIA'S INTERNATIONAL TRADE

We will discuss below a number of developments in Australia's international trade in goods and services with the rest of the world, which can illustrate the significance of the international trade sector for Australia's economy, as well as Australia's trade performance in a global context.

AUSTRALIA'S SHARE OF GLOBAL TRADE

We learnt in Chapter 9 that Australia was in 2009 the world's 13th largest economy with around 1.6 per cent of the global GDP. We also discussed the position of the external sector in Australia's GDP by its main components.

World Trade Organization (WTO) statistics indicate that in 2009 Australia's merchandise exports amounted to around US$154 billion, which placed Australia in the 23rd place among world exporting countries, with a share of 1.2 per cent of global merchandise exports. In the same year, Australia held the 19th ranking with a share of 1.3 per cent among the world's importing countries. Australia's share in the value of world merchandise exports since World War II has generally trended downwards. For instance, in 1950 Australia had a share of world exports of around 2.9 per cent, which has subsequently declined, fluctuating at about 1.0 to 1.3 per cent after 1977. Australian services in the last years of the 2000s have also accounted for around 1.3 per cent of the global services trade.

Therefore, a primary observation is that Australian exports' share of global exports is lower than Australia's share of world GDP, which would suggest that, irrespective of the technical differences in their valuation method (with GDP, unlike exports, being a value-added concept), Australian exports seem to perform at a lower level than the Australian production of goods and services.

The declining share for Australia in global exports (with a more recent stabilisation trend) would also suggest that the overall value of Australian exports has grown more slowly than the value of world trade over the last four or five decades. Various experts have identified as a main reason for this decline the continuous dominance of Australian exports by primary products, the prices of which have experienced a long-term downward trend.

EXPORTS AS A PERCENTAGE OF GDP

Although there is no single measure of the importance of international trade to the domestic economy, economists generally refer to 'exports/GDP ratio', as a measure of the contribution of exports to the domestic output of goods and services.

Table 17.4 reveals that, in line with global trends, Australia's exports of goods and services have represented an increasing share of GDP. But this share is still lower than that of Western economies of comparable size (e.g. Canada, Sweden, New Zealand) or than that of fast-growing East Asian economies.

One should note that, despite trading internationally relatively small shares of their GDP, the very large economies of the United States and Japan still participate actively in the process of globalisation, accounting for large shares of global exports and global investment flows.

Table 17.4   **Exports of goods and services as a percentage of GDP, selected countries, 1970, 1995 and 2008**

COUNTRY	1970	1995	2008
Australia	14	18	21
United States	6	11	12[1]
Canada	22		35[1]
Japan	11	9	18[1]
Sweden	24	40	54
New Zealand	23	29	29[1]
Singapore	102	–	234
Malaysia	42	94	110[1]
China	3	23	37
India	11	11	23
Thailand	15	42	77

Note: [1] = 2007.
Source: Compiled from World Bank, World Development Indicators, 2003 and 2010.

PRODUCT COMPOSITION OF AUSTRALIAN MERCHANDISE TRADE

According to Department of Foreign Affairs and Trade (DFAT) data, in 2009 Australia's export value fell by 9.8 per cent to A$249.9 billion. However export volume rose 0.6 per cent in 2009, making Australia one of only three OECD economies to record export volume growth in 2009 (the others being Iceland and New Zealand).

It is well known that Australia has traditionally rated very highly in terms of its share of the world's natural resources and in their utilisation. Australia has around 20 per cent of the world's bauxite and lead resources and around 10 per cent of world's iron reserves, as well as substantial resources of wool, wheat, meat, coal, mineral sands, gold, zinc, lead, copper and diamonds. Table 17.5 presents the composition of Australia's exports in 1995 and 2008.

Table 17.5   **Comparative composition of merchandise trade, selected economies, by main sectors, 1995 and 2008**

ECONOMY	RURAL PRODUCTS[1] (% OF TOTAL)		FUELS AND MINERALS[2] (% OF TOTAL)		MANUFACTURES[3] (% OF TOTAL)		MACHINERY AND TRANSPORT EQUIPMENT[4] (% OF TOTAL)	
(COLUMN 1)	(COLUMN 2)		(COLUMN 3)		(COLUMN 4)		(COLUMN 5)	
	1995	2008	1995	2008	1995	2008	1995	2008
Australia	30	14	37	61	30	20	13	7
Brazil	34	32	6	13	54	45	19	21

continued ↘

continued

ECONOMY	RURAL PRODUCTS[1] (% OF TOTAL)		FUELS AND MINERALS[2] (% OF TOTAL)		MANUFACTURES[3] (% OF TOTAL)		MACHINERY AND TRANSPORT EQUIPMENT[4] (% OF TOTAL)	
(COLUMN 1)	(COLUMN 2)		(COLUMN 3)		(COLUMN 4)		(COLUMN 5)	
	1995	2008	1995	2008	1995	2008	1995	2008
Canada	17	14	18	34	63	47	38	25
Denmark	27	19	6	13	60	66	26	27
Germany	6	6	2	4	87	82	49	49
Malaysia	16	14	13	20	75	74	55	43
New Zealand	64	62	21	16	29	23	9	9
Sweden	8	8	8	11	94	89	45	42
United Kingdom	9	7	7	14	81	70	43	32
WORLD	12	10	10	14	76	70	38	33

Note: Components may not sum to 100 per cent because of unclassified trade. Exports of gold are excluded.
[1]Agricultural products include, with a few exclusions, SITC sections 1 (food and live animals), 2 (crude materials, excl. fuels), and 4 (animal and vegetable oil and fats), plus division 22 (oil seeds, nuts, and kernels).
[2]Minerals include fuels (SITC section 3) and ores and metals (SITC divisions 22, 67 and 68).
[3]Manufactures include SITC sections 5 (chemicals), 6 (basic manufactures), 7 (machinery and transport equipment), and 8 (miscellaneous manufactures), excluding division 68 (non-ferrous metals).
[4]This is SITC section 7, included also above in manufactures, as recorded by the WTO.

Source: Adapted from World Bank, World Development Indicators 2010, Table 4.4, and WTO, Statistics Database, <http://stat.wto.org/Home/WSDBHome.aspx?Language=>, accessed 25 August 2010.

Several important trends emerge from Table 17.5:

- The decline of the manufacturing sector in the composition of merchandise trade is a world trend, as well as for all economies in the sample group, except for Denmark.
- However, Australian manufacturing has never reached a 'critical mass' and its share is the lowest among the nine economies in the sample group, including resource-rich economies such as those of Canada, Brazil and Malaysia. It is also three and a half times lower than the corresponding share of manufacturing in global exports. This is also a reflection of Australia's strong endowment with natural resources, as well as of the strength of global minerals prices (e.g. iron ore and coal) in 2008.
- No economy in the sample group has such a high dependence on merchandise exports in the primary sector as Australia (75 per cent in 2008).
- 'Machinery and transport equipment', which has traditionally been the backbone of the manufacturing sector in all advanced economies, has the lowest representation in the composition of merchandise exports in Australia, and its Australian share is almost five times lower than the corresponding global share.

elaborately transformed manufactures (ETMs) *identified by the ABS as finished, or value-added, goods*

The Australian Bureau of Statistics (ABS) has noted for many years since the mid 1980s a positive trend in Australia's manufactures exports in the expansion of **elaborately transformed manufactures (ETMs)**, including engineering products such as cars and transport equipment, computers, power generators and telecommunications, at a higher rate than that of **simply transformed manufactures (STMs)**, which require less processing and include goods such as basic chemicals semi-manufactures and metals.

Recent statistics (see Table 17.6) seem to indicate a reversal of that favourable trend.

simply transformed manufactures (STMs) *the opposite of ETMs, these are goods with a low level of processing, for example bauxite and cotton fabric*

Table 17.6   **Australian manufactures exports: Simply transformed (STM) versus elaborately transformed (ETM), percentage share of total Australian merchandise exports and trend growth, annual averages for selected periods**

| | MANUFACTURES AS A % OF MERCHANDISE EXPORTS | | | TREND GROWTH (% P.A.) | |
	1984–86	1991–93	2007–09	1984–93	2004–09
STM	8.0	9.8	7.5	12.6	6.0
ETM	11.4	18.7	15.0	17.5	3.3
Total manufactures	19.4	28.5	22.6	15.6	4.2

Source: Adapted from DFAT, Exports of primary and manufactured products Australia 1993; DFAT, Composition of Trade 2009.

It comes as no surprise that in 2009 Australia's top 10 commodities were all primary products (e.g. coal, iron ore and concentrates, gold, natural gas, crude petroleum etc), except for one STM (aluminium).

Australia's leading STM exports over 2007–09 with average annual values in the A$1–3 billion range included: medicaments (including veterinary); passenger motor vehicles; medical instruments; measuring and analysing instruments; telecom equipment and parts.

A number of Australian ETM exporters like Cochlear Limited have become major international players in their industries (see Link to International Economy below).

EXPORT ACHIEVERS—COCHLEAR LIMITED

Cochlear Limited is one of Australia's leading biotechnology organisations and is the global leader in the cochlear implant industry with more than 100 000 children and adults around the world having one of its cochlear or bone conduction implants.

The so-called 'cochlear' implant, or 'the bionic ear' was the brain child of Professor Graeme Clark of Melbourne University. Professor Clark's team realised very soon that to reach a larger market, their innovative product required a company's financial resources. In 1979, Nucleus, a group of medical equipment manufacturers, became interested in the commercial potential of Professor Clark's work.

A survey performed by Nucleus discovered that the Australian market was too small, and to achieve commercial success the product needed export markets. By 1988 sales figures indicated that nearly 90 per cent of Cochlear's profits were from export sales.

At that stage, Cochlear realised that it needed assistance from a company with a higher degree of experience in dealing with export markets. In 1988, Cochlear became part of the medical

LINK TO INTERNATIONAL ECONOMY

continued ↘

continued

division of Pacific Dunlop. The Cochlear subsidiary of Pacific Dunlop was successfully listed on the Australian stock exchange in 1995, creating Cochlear Limited.

The main manufacturing base (where the company's 'Nucleus Freedom' range is produced) is located in Sydney. Its range of 'Baha' bone anchored implants is manufactured in Göteborg in Sweden.

Regional and global growth of this leading Australian multinational organisation has been outstanding by any sort of standards.

* Cochlear's global sales have increased 5.6 times from 1999 to 2009 to reach A$712 million in FY 2009, accounting for 65–70 per cent of the world market for Cochlear implants.
* Group sales in physical units have been expanded from less than 3000 in 1996 to over 9000 in 2003, and 18 853 in FY 2009.
* Cochlear's number of employees has increased from 334 in 1996 to 1888 in 2009 (of whom around 1000 are in Australia).
* R&D expenses in FY 2009 went up by 21 per cent to $96.7 million, accounting for around 14 per cent of Cochlear's total revenue.
* The company's share price has increased from an initial issue price of $2.50 in December 1995 to $57.7 per share by the end of FY 2009.

Despite the global financial crisis, Cochlear's sales in FY 2009 were up 23 per cent, representing 10 per cent growth in constant currency (i.e. local currency).

Cochlear's global sales in FY 2009 in some 100 countries were distributed as follows:

REGION	$A MILLION	% SHARE
Europe	319	44.8
Americas	300	42.1
Asia-Pacific	93	13.1

In 2010, Cochlear Limited moved to a new, purpose-built, $128 million global headquarters, manufacturing and research facility on the Macquarie University Campus, North Ryde, Sydney.

Cochlear's new facility underpins the company's commitment to continue investing in Australian-based research, development and manufacturing and is expected to create synergy for what is essentially a knowledge-based business.

Cochlear's future success will depend both on its ability to stay at the cutting edge of technology as well as its ability to meet customer demand in a time-critical manner through its international logistics network.

DFAT statistics indicate that over 2004–09, Australian exports of primary products have increased at higher trend growth rates (around 15% per annum) than manufactures (around 6% per annum). This was common in all major components of primary products: fuels (over 17% per annum), minerals (almost 13% per annum) and processed food (around 12% per annum).

A slowing Australian economy, due to the GFC, has also impacted Australia's merchandise imports value, which fell in 2009 around 10 per cent to A$257 billion (with import volumes falling 7.8%).

The good side of the reduced domestic consumption and investment was that imports fell faster than exports with the trade deficit improving by A$2.3 billion to A$7.1 billion.

One should note that the composition of Australia's merchandise imports is very much different from that of exports.

Australian merchandise imports have traditionally been dominated by manufactures, which accounted in 2009 for almost three-quarters of Australian total imports, with ETMs alone representing around 70 per cent. (In many previous years, manufactured goods have exceeded 80 per cent of Australian merchandise imports.)

Consequently, the list of Australia's top 10 import commodities in recent years includes, along with a few high-volume/value commodities such as crude oil, refined petroleum and gold, a number of ETMs with import values in excess of $A1 billion such as: passenger motor vehicles (A$15–17 billion); medicaments (A$7–8 billion); telecom equipment and parts (around A$7 billion); computers (just under A$6 billion); goods vehicles (A$4.5–6.5 billion); pumps and parts (A$2–3.5 billion); monitors, projectors and TVs (around A$3 billion).

TERMS OF TRADE

Changes in trade values are the result of changes in physical volumes and also in prices. Therefore, international prices have an important impact on Australia's performance in international trade.

International trade statistics have shown a long-term downward trend in the relative prices of most primary products compared to those of manufactured products, which has disadvantaged Australia. However, especially after 1995, there has been a reverse in trends favouring primary products and, consequently, Australia's merchandise trade (Table 17.7).

Table 17.7   **World unit value indices for total merchandise and by main sectors, 1995, 2000, 2008 (2000 = 100)**

	WORLD UNIT VALUE INDICES (2000 = 100)		
	1995	2000	2008
Total merchandise	112	100	168
Agricultural products	125	100	178
Fuels and mining products	74	100	325
Manufactures	116	100	140

Source: Adapted from WTO, International Trade Statistics, 2009 and 2006.

Economists have attempted to measure the directions of the gains a country enjoys from its foreign trade, by calculating changes in the so-called **terms of trade**. The terms of trade index measures the relationship between the prices a country gets from its exports and the prices it pays for its imports. It is expressed as a ratio of export prices to import prices, that is:

Terms of trade index = Export price index/Import price index × 100

terms of trade
ratio of the price index of a nation's exports of goods and services to the price index of the nation's imports of goods and services

An improvement in a country's terms of trade requires that the price of its exports rises relative to the prices of its imports over the given time period. A smaller number of export goods sold abroad is required to obtain a given number of imports. On the other hand, a deterioration in a country's terms of trade is due to a rise in its import prices relative to its export prices over a time period.

The World Bank publishes each year a net barter terms of trade index, which is calculated as the percentage ratio of the export unit value indexes to the import unit value indexes. Figure 17.1 illustrates World Bank net barter terms of trade indices (NBTTI) for Australia between 1980 and 2008, measured relative to the base year 2000.

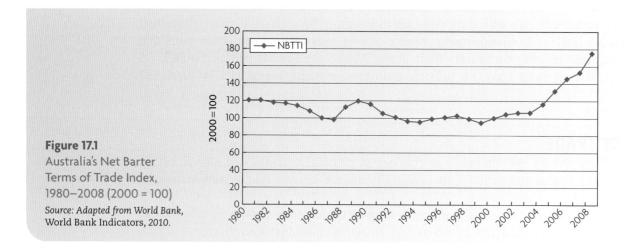

Figure 17.1

Australia's Net Barter Terms of Trade Index, 1980–2008 (2000 = 100)

Source: Adapted from World Bank, World Bank Indicators, 2010.

It appears that Australia's NBTTI, with small temporary fluctuations, declined by about 20 percentage points between 1980 (120) and 2000 (100), registering afterwards a steady rise to reach a level of 174.6 in 2008, the best performance among OECD members.

By comparison, Australia's NBTTI was higher than that of New Zealand (126), United Kingdom (105), and that of strong exporters of manufactures like Germany (100), United States (92), Republic of Korea (92) and Japan (62). Australia was outranked on this indicator only by a dozen or so exporters of commodities, especially crude oil exporting countries, such as Brunei (253), Venezuela (249), Qatar (249), Algeria (239), Nigeria (210), Libya (205), and Iran (175.3).

According to DFAT, Australia's terms of trade in 2009 decreased by 8.2 per cent from their peak in 2008. The fall in the terms of trade was mainly the result of a 10.1 per cent fall in export prices, due to falling world commodity prices for many resources and energy exports. A future long-term strength in commodity prices would certainly be a most favourable scenario for Australia's international trade and economy as a whole.

Direction of Australia's merchandise trade

The second half of the 20th century was marked by the redirection of Australian exports away from traditional markets in the United Kingdom towards Japan and other East Asian countries (Republic of Korea, Taiwan, Hong Kong, China and **ASEAN** countries). The main reasons for this change of direction were the rapid growth of the Japanese economy and of the newly industrialising countries in East Asia, as well as the United Kingdom's entry into the European Community (now the European Union), which cut off access for Australian rural products to the United Kingdom and other European markets.

Table 17.8 shows that Asia's share of Australian merchandise exports over 1989–2009 increased from around 57 per cent to around 75 per cent. (One should note within Asia, the fast expansion of East Asia, including Japan, as the main regional destination for Australian

ASEAN (Association of South-East Asian Nations) *a regional organisation formed in 1967 to promote regional stability*

exports, with a share which has increased from only 18 per cent in the first half of the 1950s to some 51 per cent in 1989 and to almost 64 per cent in 2009.) Actually, in late 2000, the list of Australia's top 15 export markets included 10 Asian economies (e.g. China, Japan, Republic of Korea, India, Taiwan, Singapore, Thailand, Indonesia, Malaysia and Hong Kong SAR of China).

Table 17.8 **Geographic distribution of Australia's merchandise exports and imports, total (A$ billion) and per cent by main region, 1989 and 2009**

	MERCHANDISE EXPORTS		MERCHANDISE IMPORTS	
	1989	2009	1989	2009
World (A$ billion)	47.0	196.3	51.7	256.9
	OUT OF WHICH (% OF TOTAL)		OUT OF WHICH (% OF TOTAL)	
Asia	56.8	75.0	41.1	50.2
Europe	18.9	9.5	26.9	22.6
Americas	13.4	6.8	26.7	15.5
Oceania	8.1	5.3	4.7	5.7
Africa	1.5	1.4	0.4	0.6
Other	1.3	2.0	0.2	5.4

Source: Adapted from DFAT, Composition of Trade, Australia, 1993 and 2009.

The Middle East, as a sub-component of Asia, has maintained a relatively stable market share over the 20-year period at around 3.5 per cent of Australian merchandise exports.

At the same time, Europe's share of Australian exports over the same 20-year period has halved from 19 per cent to less than 10 per cent. (One has to note that, within Europe, the European Union has registered, despite its progressive enlargement, a long-term decline in market share, from 63 per cent in the first half of the 1950s to some 22 per cent in 1989 and to less than 9 per cent in 2009.)

Within the Americas, a major decline in market share has been recorded by the United States from around 11 per cent in 1989 to less than 5 per cent in 2009, despite the Free Trade Agreement (FTA) signed with Australia in 2005. (Read more about Australia's FTA's in Chapter 24 dealing with Australia's external policy.)

In relation to the most significant trends in the direction of Australian imports over the 20-year period one can note:

- The decline of Europe and the Americas as sources of imports (Table 17.8). Within Europe, the European Union has increased share from around 14 per cent to just under 20 per cent over the period, mainly due to its enlargement. However, one should consider that the predecessor of the European Union in the mid 1950s held around 60 per cent of Australia's merchandise imports.
- Overall, the European Union (27) and the United States have a larger share as a source of imports than as export markets for Australia.
- Asia has increased market share by about 10 percentage points. (However, Asia has less importance for Australia as a source of imports than as a regional export market.)

Australia's list of top individual import sources in the late 2000s included six Asian economies (China, Japan, Singapore, Thailand, Malaysia, Republic of Korea), United States, two European Union member economies (Germany and the United Kingdom) and New Zealand.

TRADE IN SERVICES

Reflecting the growing role of services in so-called post-industrial societies, Australia's trade in services has grown strongly since the opening of the economy to international competition in the early 1980s. Services are grouped as transport services, travel services, and other services (financial, insurance, education, construction, telecommunications, computing and entertainment).

According to World Trade Organization (WTO) data, Australia's share of world services exports has varied over the last two decades or so between 1.2–1.4 per cent, being slightly higher than Australia's share in the global merchandise trade.

DFAT statistics indicate that in 2009, exports of services represented around 21 per cent of the value of Australia's exports of goods and services, down from 23 per cent in 1996. Over 2004–09, Australian services exports have increased at a five-year trend rate of 7.5 per cent per annum, which was higher than that recorded by Australian manufactures (4.2 per cent), but lower than that registered by Australian exports of minerals and fuels (21.8 per cent). The differences in growth rates between the three categories of exports are in the main a reflection of international prices as discussed in the previous section on terms of trade.

At the same time, Australian imports of services over 2004–09 have increased at a trend rate of 8.6 per cent per annum, which was higher than the corresponding rate for goods (6.6% p.a.).

As a rule of thumb, Australian services trade is in closer balance than Australian merchandise trade.

A few comments about Australia's composition of services exports:

- Table 17.9 shows that Australia's number one category of services exports is travel services, and their share at around 56 per cent in 2008 has increased by some

Table 17.9   **Comparative composition of services exports for Australia, the Euro area and the world, 1995, 2008, by main category (US$ billion and per cent of total)**

	AUSTRALIA		EURO AREA		WORLD	
	1995	2008	1995	2008	1995	2008
Total services value (US$ billion)	16.1	44.5	422.6	1225.7	1211.4	3799.2
SERVICE CATEGORY	% OF TOTAL EXPORTS		% OF TOTAL EXPORTS		% OF TOTAL EXPORTS	
Transport	29.3	17.8	25.6	23.6	26.9	24.3
Travel	50.6	56.3	31.5	24.1	32.5	26.3
Insurance and financial services	5.4	3.4	5.6	5.4	6.0	7.8
Computer, information, communications, and others	14.8	22.5	37.6	46.9	35.3	41.7

Source: Adapted from World Bank, World Development Indicators 2010.

6 percentage points compared to 1995. This level is much higher than the corresponding shares for the Euro area and the world as a whole, where travel has recorded over the 12-year period a downward trend. A strong component of Australian travel exports is education-related travel services. DFAT statistics show that exports of travel services have risen over 2004–09 by an average of 9.9 per cent per annum (compared to only 7.5% p.a. for total services exports).

- Australia's transport services recorded an under-average growth over the period and consequently their share in Australia's total exports of services declined to under 18 per cent in 2008.This trend is in line with international trends, but somewhat more pronounced. The lower growth in this sector reflects increased competition and lower rates on air routes and a reduction in Australian shipping operations.
- Australia has a below world-average position in financial and insurance services exports which have declined in share against the global trends.
- Finally, the last category of computer and information services, communications and other commercial services is where Australia rather surprisingly appears to have the worst competitive position. It has a 27 per cent share of its total service exports, which is some 16 percentage points below the corresponding share recorded by the Euro area, and 10 percentage points under the world average share.

In relation to the composition of Australia's services imports (Table 17.10):

- Travel services show an upward trend over 1995–2008, which is out of line with international trends.
- Australia's transport services have recorded a decline in the share of total imports services which is comparable with international trends.
- Australia's share of financial and insurance services imports in its total services imports is three times lower than the corresponding global share.
- Finally, the last category of computer and information services, communications and other commercial services has shown an upward growth trend in market share in line with global trends but at a lower rate than the rest of the world.

Table 17.10   **Comparative composition of services imports for Australia, the Euro area and the world, 1995, 2008, by main category (US$ billion and per cent of total)**

	AUSTRALIA		EURO AREA		WORLD	
	1995	2008	1995	2008	1995	2008
Total services value (US$ billion)	17.0	47.6	421.7	1114.7	1219.1	3440.4
SERVICE CATEGORY	% OF TOTAL IMPORTS		% OF TOTAL IMPORTS		% OF TOTAL IMPORTS	
Transport	37	31	25	26	31	29
Travel	30	39	32	26	31	25
Insurance and financial services	7	3	5	4	6	9
Computer, information, communications and others	26	27	38	43	32	37

Source: Adapted from World Bank, World Development Indicators 2010.

Direction of trade services

In relation to Australia's geographic distribution of services trade, Table 17.11 presents Australia's principal export markets and import sources in 2009 compared to FY 1989.

Table 17.11   **Australia's top 10 services export markets and services import sources, 2009, 1989*, per cent of total**

AUSTRALIA'S TOP 10 SERVICES EXPORT MARKETS (% OF TOTAL)			AUSTRALIA'S TOP 10 SERVICES IMPORTS SOURCES (% OF TOTAL)		
ECONOMY	2009	1989*	ECONOMY	2009	1989*
United States	10.6	14.6	United States	18.7	21.1
China	10.3	1.8	United Kingdom	9.1	18.4
United Kingdom	8.0	13.2	Singapore	6.5	5.1
India	7.0	–	New Zealand	5.4	5.5
New Zealand	6.1	11.0	Thailand	4.2	2.0
Singapore	5.5	2.7	Japan	4.0	7.4
Japan	4.1	15.2	Hong Kong SAR	3.5	4.8
Republic Of Korea	3.4	0.9	China	2.7	0.8
Hong Kong SAR	3.2	3.2	Indonesia	2.7	1.3
Malaysia	3.1	3.1	Switzerland	2.3	1.1

*Note: *Financial year 1988–89.*

Source: Adapted from DFAT, Composition of Trade Australia 2009; *DFAT,* Trade in Services Australia 1997–98.

A few interesting developments to be noted in relation to the changes in the direction of Australia's services exports:

- Seven of Australia's top 10 export markets in services are located in Asia: China, India, Singapore, Japan, Republic of Korea, Hong Kong and Malaysia.
- In 2009, the United States continued to lead the list of Australia's export markets, but with a major decline in market share compared to the late 1980s.
- In the same year, China was Australia's second largest services export market, with Australian exports increasing 16.4 per cent per annum over 2004–09.
- DFAT statistics show that, while in the late 1980s Australia had almost no services exports to India, over 2004–09, India was Australia's top growth market (around 35 per cent per annum). A major component in Australia's services exports to India was education, with India representing the second country of origin for student enrolments in Australia next to China.
- Other Asian markets identified by DFAT as markets with strong growth for Australian services exports over 2004–09 include Vietnam (30.7% p.a.) and the Philippines (23.6% p.a.).
- The United Kingdom and New Zealand have lost significant market share over the two decades, mainly due to the strong growth in demand for Australian services exports from developing Asian markets.

In relation to the changes in the direction of Australia's services imports, one should note the following:

- The United States and the United Kingdom continue to lead the list of Australia's leading sources of imports of services with a joint share of around 28 per cent of total (down from 39.5 per cent in the late 1980s).
- The top 10 sources for Australia's imports of services include six Asian economies: Singapore, Thailand, Japan, Hong Kong, China and Indonesia.
- According to DFAT statistics, the economies which have shown the highest growth among Australia's sources of services imports over 2004–09 include: Thailand (24.7% p.a.), India (22% p.a.), Ireland (20.4% p.a.), Papua New Guinea (16.2% p.a.) and Vietnam (12.7% p.a.).

PATTERNS OF AUSTRALIA'S INTERNATIONAL INVESTMENT

LEARNING OBJECTIVE 4
Identify the main changes in the patterns of Australia's international investment.

FORMS OF INTERNATIONAL INVESTMENT

Australia has traditionally been an importer of capital, partly reflecting our rapid population growth (with a solid migration component) and the consequent need to provide social and economic infrastructure.

As a relatively small economy, Australia has managed to attract more foreign investment than it was able to generate overseas.

ABS data (cat. no. 5352) indicates that in 2009, the level of foreign investment in Australia amounted to around A$1900 billion. Given its sophisticated financial infrastructure, Australia is present in all major forms of financial investment. At the end of 2009, portfolio investment accounted for around 58 per cent of all foreign investment in Australia, followed by direct investment (23%), financial derivatives (e.g. futures, options, swaps) at around 4 per cent and other investment liabilities (15%).

According to the OECD, '**foreign direct investment (FDI)** is a category of investment that reflects the objective of establishing a lasting interest by a resident enterprise in one economy (direct investor) in an enterprise (direct investment enterprise) that is resident in an economy other than that of the direct investor.'[4]

A foreign direct investment relationship is established when an investor, who is a resident in one economy, holds 10 per cent or more of the ordinary shares or voting stock of an enterprise (direct investment enterprise) in another economy. The **portfolio investment** category covers investment in equity where the investor holds less than 10 per cent of the ordinary shares or voting stock of an enterprise and investment in debt securities. Foreign direct investment is one component of the overall inflow of foreign capital into Australia, which is widely recognised as having benefits not shared by other forms of capital inflow. Foreign direct investment is typically accompanied by the transfer of technology, improved management techniques, intellectual property rights and other forms of intangible capital, all of which may yield productivity gains and spillover benefits, apart from the contribution to the expansion of the domestic capital stock. UNCTAD data shows that foreign direct

foreign direct investment (FDI)
a category of investment that reflects the objective of establishing a lasting interest (more than 10 per cent of ordinary shares) by a resident enterprise in one economy (direct investor) in an enterprise (direct investment enterprise) that is resident in an economy other than that of the direct investor

investment inflows accounted for around 17 per cent of Australia's gross fixed capital formation, which was twice as much as the average for 1995–2005.

Foreign direct investment can generate employment (e.g. in the case of 'green field investment') and exports of goods and services. Foreign direct investment is typically more long term, and therefore more stable, than other forms of foreign investment, such as portfolio investment, which is generally regarded as short-term money parking.

Whereas portfolio investment in equity and debt securities can be very quickly reversed (as happened in the East Asian financial crisis of 1997–98), direct investment gives foreign investors a more substantial stake in the relevant assets, and more commitment and involvement in the day-to-day management of the assets. Foreign direct investment is often accompanied by a substantial level of reinvestment of retained earnings in the host economy. For instance, in Australia since the late 1980s, retained earnings on average accounted for around 35 per cent of foreign direct investment in Australia.

In this text, we focus on foreign direct investment (FDI), because of its obvious benefits to the domestic economy and its intimate relationship with international trade.

It is important to distinguish between the flow of FDI and the stock of FDI. **FDI flows** refer to the movements of FDI during a given period, usually a year. Outflows of FDI represent the flow of FDI out of the country, while FDI inflows refer to the flow of FDI into the country.

FDI stock (outward and inward) presents a static picture of a given moment in time of the accumulated value of foreign-owned assets over the years.

Table 17.12 indicates that the share of Australian FDI inflows in global flows has been steadily decreasing since the 1970s, while the share of Australian FDI outflows, after a strong expansion in the 1980s, dropped threefold in the 1990s and has remained steady since.

Table 17.12   **Average annual Australian FDI flows (US$ million), percentage share of global FDI flows and Australian FDI outflows/Australian FDI inflows ratio, 1970–2009**

PERIOD	AUSTRALIAN FDI INFLOWS (ANNUAL AVERAGE)		AUSTRALIAN FDI OUTFLOWS (ANNUAL AVERAGE)		AUSTRALIAN FDI OUTFLOWS AS A PER CENT OF FDI INFLOWS
	US$ MILLION	% OF GLOBAL	US$ MILLION	% OF GLOBAL	FDI INFLOWS = 100
1970–79	1037	4.3	212	0.7	20.4
1980–89	3708	4.0	2295	2.5	61.9
1990–99	6245	1.6	3195	0.8	51.2
2000–09	16534	1.5	11472	1.0	69.4

One should note that Australian foreign direct investment abroad has been growing faster on average than foreign direct investment in Australia, such that Australia has in recent years seen periods in which it was a net exporter of direct investment capital (e.g. 1996, 2001, 2007).

As a result, the ratio between Australian FDI outflows and Australian FDI inflows has shown more than a threefold increase from some 20 per cent in the 1970s to around 70 per cent over 2000–09.

FDI IN AUSTRALIA

The volume of overseas capital and the industries into which it went were most often determined throughout Australian history by the preferences of overseas investors.

Australian FDI inflows in recent decades have generally followed global trends, with an increase in the services area and a decline in the manufacturing sector. Investment in the mining sector, in general more relevant to the Australian economy than to other economies, has followed global commodity prices and has been quite strong over the decade to 2009.

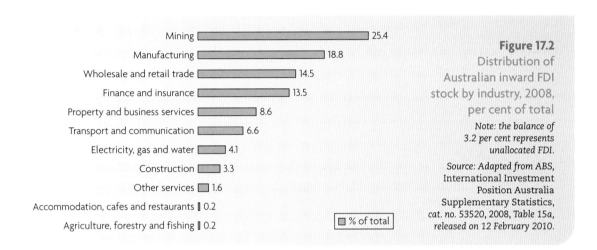

Figure 17.2
Distribution of
Australian inward FDI
stock by industry, 2008,
per cent of total

*Note: the balance of
3.2 per cent represents
unallocated FDI.*

*Source: Adapted from ABS,
International Investment
Position Australia
Supplementary Statistics,
cat. no. 53520, 2008, Table 15a,
released on 12 February 2010.*

ABS data indicates that foreign direct investment in mining is not only the largest, but also one of the fastest-growing destinations for inward FDI (next to construction, which would have also benefited from the mining boom).

Manufacturing has continued the long-term decline in attracting FDI. In 1992 the share of manufacturing in Australian inward FDI was some 30 per cent, while the corresponding ratio in the late 1950s was 77 per cent.

Statistics from the International Trade Centre UNCTAD/WTO have identified a number of Australian services sectors, apart from construction, which have enjoyed an above-average growth of inward FDI flows in the second half of 2000: 'Electricity, gas and water', 'Business services' and 'Other services'.

Australian agriculture is notorious for a very low level of foreign FDI, and a very high ratio of Australian ownership.

Sources of Australian FDI

The United Kingdom has traditionally been the leading source of Australia's inward FDI, accounting in the late 1940s for 79 per cent of all inflows. Between 1947–48 and 1970–71, overall 44 per cent of FDI inflows into Australia came from the United Kingdom, 39 per cent from the United States and Canada and only 17 per cent from other countries.

Table 17.13 overleaf shows that over the last 15 years or so, the United States took over as Australia's leading source of direct investment followed by the United Kingdom and Japan.

Table 17.13   **Australia's main sources of foreign direct investment stock, per cent share, 1992, 2009**

	1992	2009
United States	30	23
United Kingdom	24	15
Japan	14	10
European Union (excluding the United Kingdom)	8	19
East Asia	1	9
New Zealand	4	1
Other	19	23

UNCTAD contended that the decline in the importance of the United Kingdom is due to several factors, including the orientation of its investments to other European countries (e.g. following the United Kingdom accession to the European Communities in 1973) and the rise in investment by United States transnational corporations in the post World War II era.

Other major individual holders of FDI stock in Australia in 2009 included other European Union economies (such as Netherlands, Germany, France, and Belgium).

Japan has lost market share since 1992, in line with its decline among major global investors.

East Asia has made a major gain in market share among Australian sources of FDI. China has increased its FDI stock in Australia from only A$293 million in 1997 to over A$9.0 billion in 2009 (e.g. 2.5% of total). ASEAN has lost some market share in the 2000s, but it is still holding around A$21 billion (just under 5 per cent of total Australian inward FDI stock). The largest ASEAN investor in Australia was Singapore (around A$16 billion), which concluded a free trade agreement with Australia in 2003.

New Zealand lost market share in Australia's inward FDI, with a stock of around A$6 billion, almost unchanged from 2001.

Other major sources of inward FDI stock for Australia are developed countries outside the European Union such as Switzerland (A$17.5 billion in 2009), and Canada (around A$11 billion).

In its annual *World Investment Report 2010*, UNCTAD identified a number of 1991 affiliates of foreign transnational corporations located in Australia in 2006. This would account for only 0.25 per cent of the global number of affiliates of TNCs of 794 894.

AUSTRALIAN DIRECT INVESTMENT OVERSEAS

UNCTAD's *World Investment Report 2010* shows that at the end of 2009, Australia held a total amount of around US$344 billion direct investment stock in other countries. This was an Australian record 1.8 per cent of the global outward FDI stock. The increasing tendency for Australian firms to invest abroad has added another dimension to the contribution that FDI makes to Australia's economic growth. Actually, the value of Australia's outward FDI stock accounted in 2009 for around 35 per cent of Australia's GDP in that year. This is a comparable level to the average for developed economies in 2009 (around 41%) and slightly above the world average (33%).

FOREIGN-OWNED ENTERPRISES (FOEs) IN AUSTRALIA

LINK TO BUSINESS

Apart from foreign affiliates which are wholly-owned subsidiaries of TNCs from various countries, there is a larger number of joint ventures, located in Australia, with foreign participation.

A 2004 survey by ABS based on a sample of about 20 000 management units selected from the ABS Business Register has identified a number of 7684 majority foreign-owned enterprises (FOEs) representing about 1 per cent of all Australian businesses in 2000–01.

In that year, foreign-owned enterprises employed 783 300 workers (12% of all private sector employees) and contributed 25 per cent of all capital formation and 21 per cent of total value added in Australia.

Overall, United States-owned businesses made a greater contribution to the Australian economy than businesses owned by residents of any other foreign country. They led in all indicators, except operating profit, where United Kingdom-owned businesses contributed the largest amount ($9602 million).

A few survey findings by major industries:

- In mining, some 48 per cent of all mining industry assets were owned by FOEs, which employed 28 per cent of the workforce and produced 45 per cent of industry value added.
- The manufacturing industry's FOEs employed 23 per cent of all employees and contributed 34 per cent of industry value added.
- In a number of service industries, SOEs made a significant contribution to the total value added in the respective industries: wholesale trade (31%), electricity, gas and water (21%), property and business services (18%) and transport, storage and communication industries (13%).

ABS data shows that Australian outward FDI accounts for around 30 per cent of total Australian investment overseas, while portfolio investment abroad represents only around 38 per cent (much lower than the share of portfolio investment in Australia).

Outward FDI enables Australian firms to:

- become more efficient and competitive in global markets
- secure resources, expertise and technology
- expand their businesses beyond the potential constraints of a limited size domestic market
- benefit from a multiplier effect on the domestic economy from the stimulus to the demand for goods and services provided by component and other input suppliers.

SECTORAL COMPOSITION OF OUTWARD FDI STOCK

When it comes to the sectoral distribution of Australian outward FDI, Table 17.14 overleaf based on ABS data (cat. no. 53520, 2009) indicates that manufacturing, finance and insurance are the industries which have attracted the largest amounts of investment from Australian investors overseas, with a cumulative share of 80 per cent of total outward FDI stock.

At the same time, the same ABS data suggests that over 2001–07, the fastest-growing areas of overseas investment for Australian companies have been: property and business services, other services, electricity, gas and water, mining, finance and insurance, which shows the preponderance of service industries.

Table 17.14   **Sectoral distribution of Australia's outward FDI (A$ million, per cent share) in 2007 and per cent change growth over 2001–07**

ALL INDUSTRIES	A$ MILLION	% TOTAL	% CHANGE 2001–07
	323.6	100	51
Manufacturing	142.9	44.2	13
Finance and insurance	116.5	36	143
Mining	25.5	7.9	187
Property and business services	10.7	3.3	645
Transport and communication	8.3	2.6	−47
Wholesale and retail trade	6.1	1.9	10
Other services	4.7	1.4	236
Construction	4.5	1.4	−20
Electricity, gas and water	3.6	1.1	211

Source: Adapted from ABS, International Investment Position, Australia: Supplementary Statistics, cat. no. 53520, 2009.

DIRECTION OF AUSTRALIA'S OUTWARD FDI

The geographic destinations for Australia's FDI abroad changed considerably over the last 30 years or so. In 1980, around 60 per cent of FDI stocks were held in Australia's neighbouring region, including the ASEAN countries, Hong Kong, New Zealand and Papua New Guinea.

However, over the 1980s, Australia's FDI outflows were diverted from ASEAN countries to other places, first of all the United Kingdom, the United States and to a lesser extent New Zealand.

In the 2000s, the United States became by far the main destination for Australian direct investors, attracting close to 50 per cent of Australia's outward FDI stock (Table 17.15).

Table 17.15   **Australian outward FDI stock, total values and per cent share, by main geographic destinations, 1992, 2000, 2009**

	AUSTRALIAN OUTWARD FDI		
	1992	2000	2009
Total value A$ billion	A$50.2 billion	A$150.2 billion	A$344.6 billion
DESTINATIONS	OUT OF WHICH (% OF TOTAL)		
United States	28	46	47
United Kingdom	27	22	19
New Zealand	13	10	12
European Union (except United Kingdom)	4	3	9

continued ↘

DESTINATIONS	OUT OF WHICH (% OF TOTAL)		
East Asia	15	6	9
Other	13	13	4

Source: Adapted from ABS, International Investment Position, Australia: Supplementary Statistics, *cat. no. 53520, 2010;* UNCTAD 2005, World Investment Directory Country Profile: Australia.

Gionea[5] suggested that the substantial decline since 1980 in the ASEAN/East Asian share of Australian outward FDI and the associated substantial increase in the shares hosted by the United States, United Kingdom, and New Zealand, may be due to a number of factors. On one hand Australian investors may have had:

- a more accurate perception of the risks associated with direct investment in the ASEAN region, especially after the bad experiences of some companies in this area
- a better appreciation of the impediments to investing in East Asia (such as some restrictions on foreign investment, poor quality business infrastructure, poor enforcement of intellectual property rights).

On the other hand, the United Kingdom, the United States and New Zealand may have seemed more attractive to Australian companies because of factors such as:

- historical ties, common language, cultural and commercial familiarity
- the anticipation of further regional trade integration in Europe and North America and the closer economic relations between Australia and New Zealand
- an advanced business infrastructure with fewer impediments to Australian direct investment activity than in the ASEAN region.

DFAT's East Asian Analytical Unit advanced the argument that Australian investors were not familiar with the opportunities of the Asia-Pacific region and also tended to be 'risk averse'.

UNCTAD contended that the parent companies of foreign affiliates in Australia have sometimes discouraged their affiliates' investments in Asia, preferring to channel investment through their existing Asian affiliates.

However, ASEAN countries and East Asia as a whole increased their share in the 2000s and may soon regain their top positions among destinations for Australian FDI outflows.

CONCLUSION

Australia's external sector (international trade and investment) is a growing sector of the Australian economy, in line with the trends prevailing in the global economy.

The fluctuations of Australian trade and investment flow values and shares can be explained by a number of developments in the Australian and the global economy, having to a certain extent a cyclical nature.

Certainly, the expansion of various international business activities of Australian firms is the result of good planning and promotion of their products and services on an international scale, but also of a more liberal global framework and of steady assistance provided by the Australian Government to various Australian industries. These matters will be discussed in more detail in Chapters 20 and 24, dealing with structural changes and micro-reform in the Australian economy and with government external policies.

SUMMARY

1. International trade is an important influence on the level of domestic economic activity and is a means of providing goods that Australia cannot produce at all, and goods that Australia cannot produce as efficiently as another country can.
2. Trade involves international specialisation, which is explained by the theories of absolute and comparative advantage.
3. As the Australian economy has developed, both the composition and direction of trade have changed: there is less dependence on rural products as part of total exports, less trade with the United Kingdom, and expanded trade with Japan and other East Asian countries. The mix of Australian exports has more recently swung to services exports (especially tourism), with primary products continuing a major role in Australia's total exports.
4. Australia's merchandise trade is dominated by Asian partner countries, while services trade is dominated by developed economies, with Asian economies playing an increasing role.
5. Australia has expanded its foreign investment flows, especially after the deregulation of the financial system in the 1980s. Australia's FDI flows in both directions are dominated by developed economies. However, economies in ASEAN, other East Asian economies and increasingly India, have a growing role in Australian FDI activities.
6. The sectoral composition of Australian FDI activities shows the preponderance of services sectors, in line with global trends.

KEY TERMS

absolute advantage	353	factor endowment	355	portfolio investment	368
ASEAN—Association of South-East Asian Nations	362	FDI flows (outflows and inflows)	368	simply transformed manufactures (STMS)	359
comparative advantage	353	FDI stock (outward and inward)	368	terms of trade	361
elaborately transformed manufactures (ETMs)	358	foreign direct investment (FDI)	367		
		international trade	351		

REFERENCES

1. David Ricardo (1772–1823). His most important work was *The Principles of Political Economy and Taxation*, 1817, which dominated English classical economics for the next 50 years.
2. Eli Heckscher, the noted Swedish economic historian, developed the core idea of this concept in an article published in 1919. The article was later reprinted in *Readings in the Theory of International Trade* (1949).
3. Bertil Ohlin, professor at Stockholm and later a Nobel Laureate, developed and publicised Heckscher's idea on factor endowments in the 1930s.
4. OECD, *Benchmark definition of foreign direct investment*, 4th edn, OECD, Paris, April 2008, <www.oecd.org/dataoecd/56/1/2487495.pdf>, accessed 17 November 2010.
5. J. Gionea, *International Trade and Investment— An Asia-Pacific Perspective*, McGraw-Hill, Sydney, Australia, 2005, p.122.

REVIEW QUESTIONS

1. Explain the difference between comparative and absolute advantage.
2. How do factor endowments help to explain trading arrangements?
3. What are the major limitations of the trade theory?
4. Outline two or three indicators which illustrate the importance of international trade to the Australian economy.
5. Outline the major changes in the product composition of Australian exports over the last two decades or so.
6. What are the major trends in Australia's direction of merchandise exports?
7. Outline the main changes in Australia's composition of trade in services.
8. Outline a couple of differences between Australia's geographic distribution of merchandise trade and that in services trade. Discuss the reasons.

9. Outline the main changes in the sectoral distribution of Australia's outward FDI and inward FDI.
10. Identify the main changes in the direction of Australia's inward and outward FDI.

APPLIED QUESTIONS AND EXERCISES

1. Assume that with a given number of resources Germany can produce 300 units of cars and 125 units of spectrophotometers, while Australia can produce 200 units of cars and 100 units of spectrophotometers. Calculate the opportunity cost of producing cars and spectrophotometers in each country.

2. From the production possibility schedule given in Question 1, in which goods (if any) does:
   (a) Germany have an absolute advantage?
   (b) Germany have a comparative advantage?
   (c) Australia have an absolute advantage?
   (d) Australia have a comparative advantage?

3. The table below presents Australian merchandise exports and imports by selected categories, in 2008:

PRODUCT CATEGORY	EXPORTS (US$ MILLION)	IMPORTS (US$ MILLION)	NET EXPORTS (US$ MILLION)
Mineral ores	34 547	434	34 112
Cereals	4378	173	4204
Motor vehicles	4194	22 985	−18 791
Electrical, electronic equipment	2609	18 757	−16 148
Toys, games, sports items	285	2272	−1988
Aircraft, spacecraft and parts thereof	851	3530	−2680
Iron and steel	1879	3039	−1160
Sugars and sugar confectionery	167	177	−10
Meat, fish and seafood preparations	150	539	−388
Vegetable, fruit, nut, etc. food preparations	202	688	−485

   (a) Which of these product categories appear to be consistent with the Heckscher-Ohlin theory and which appear to be inconsistent? Explain.
   (b) Outline a few possible reasons for inconsistencies with the Heckscher-Ohlin theory.

4. Extract data about Australia's merchandise exports and imports over the last 10 years from the WTO trade database at <http://stat.wto.org/StatisticalProgram/WSDBStatProgramHome.aspx?Language=E>.
   Compare the changes in the total values for Australia's exports and imports. Why do the export figures tend to be more variable than the import figures? Discuss.

5. 'DFAT announced that Australia's merchandise import value fell in 2009 by around 10 per cent to A$257 billion (with import volumes falling 7.8 per cent)'. What does it mean?

6. According to UNCTAD data, in 2008, FDI flows accounted for over 15 per cent of gross fixed capital formation (GFCF) in Australia, but for only around 2 per cent in Iran and Japan. In your opinion what can be the reason(s) for such differences in the FDI inflows/GFCF ratio between Australia, Japan and Iran.

7. Considering the case of Cochlear Limited, outline the contribution of this firm to the Australian economy. (Think of both exports and investment overseas.)

8. World Bank data shows that the net barter terms of trade index (NBTTI) for Australia over 2000–08 has progressively increased to reach 175, while the same indicator has declined for Japan to 62 (2000=100). Explain the reason for such different evolution of the NBTTI.

9. We have learnt in this chapter that Australia's merchandise trade is dominated by Asian developing economies (e.g. China, India, Singapore, Thailand, Indonesia), while Australia's FDI is dominated by developed economies (e.g. United States, United Kingdom, other European Union economies). In your opinion, what is the reason for this situation?

Chapter 18

The balance of payments

LEARNING OBJECTIVES

After studying this chapter, you will be able to:

1. define the balance of payments and outline the balance of payments structure

2. describe all the items that make up the current account of the balance of payments, and explain the reasons for Australia's deficit on the current account

3. explain what is meant by the capital and financial account in the balance of payments

4. explain the double-entry bookkeeping system of measuring balances of payments and illustrate with examples the way double-entry bookkeeping operates

5. describe how a country accumulates foreign debt, and discuss the size and significance of Australia's foreign debt.

INTRODUCTION

In Chapter 17 we analysed the international real trade flows (i.e. the movements of goods, services and financial assets) that occur between Australia's domestic economy and the rest of the world.

In this chapter, we will examine the monetary aspects of international trade by considering the nature and significance of a country's balance of payments. We will also explain a number of issues related to Australia's foreign debt.

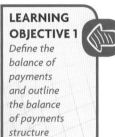

LEARNING OBJECTIVE 1
Define the balance of payments and outline the balance of payments structure

BALANCE OF PAYMENTS

The **balance of payments** is a record of the economic transactions between Australian individuals, businesses and governments, and their counterparts in other nations throughout the world for a given period of time.

Table 18.1 overleaf presents Australia's balance of payments in 2009–10 according to the new format compiled by the Australian Bureau of Statistics (ABS) from September 2009, on the basis of the sixth edition of the International Monetary Fund's *Balance of Payments and International Investment Position Manual* (BPM6).

The balance of payments accounts use a double-entry bookkeeping system, where every recorded transaction is represented by two entries (debit/credit) with equal values. This is discussed further below.

Even though the entire balance of payments, by definition, must balance numerically, it does not necessarily hold that any single account or subaccount of the statement must balance. For instance, goods credits (exports) may or may not be in balance with goods debits (imports). Double-entry accounting assumes only that the total of all the entries on the left-hand side of the statement matches the total of the entries on the right-hand side. (Examples are presented later in Table 18.3, p. 387.)

balance of payments
a record of the economic transactions between Australian individuals, businesses and governments, and their counterparts in other nations throughout the world for a given period of time

BALANCE OF PAYMENTS STRUCTURE

The standard components of the balance of payments are two main groups of accounts: the current account, and the capital and financial account.

The current account

The **current account** shows flows of goods, services, primary income and secondary income between residents and non-residents. When total payments for imports, primary income and secondary income (debits) exceed total receipts for the same items (credits), we have a current account deficit.

The capital and financial account

The capital and financial account is mainly concerned with the country's transactions in monetary and ownership claims. This account provides us with the data on capital flows in and out of Australia, and on Australia's transactions with the rest of the world in foreign financial assets and liabilities.

LEARNING OBJECTIVE 2
Describe all the items that make up the current account of the balance of payments, and explain the reasons for Australia's deficit on the current account

current account
measures exports and imports of goods and services, a country's income earned by and from the rest of the world, and current transfers

Table 18.1   Australia's balance of payments, 2009–10, A$ million

ACCOUNT/ITEM	CALCULATION	2009–10 (A$ MILLION)
(1) **Current account**	[(3) + (4) + (5) + (6)]	−56 103
(2) Goods and services	[(3) + (4)]	−5 965
(a) credits	[(3a) + (4a)]	254 004
(b) debits	[(3b) + (4b)]	−259 969
(3) Goods	[(3a) + (3b)]	−4 561
(a) credits		201 458
(b) debits		−206 019
(4) Services	[(4a) + (4b)]	−1 404
(a) credits		52 546
(b) debits		−53 950
(5) Primary income	[(5a) + (5b)]	−49 224
(a) credits		35 901
(b) debits		−85 124
(6) Secondary income	[(6a) + (6b)]	−914
(a) credits		6 380
(b) debits		−7 294
(7) **Capital and financial account**	[(8) + (11)]	56 613
(8) Capital account	[(9) + (10)]	−132
(9) Acquisitions/disposals of non-produced non-financial assets	[(9a) + (9b)]	14
(a) credits		4
(b) debits		10
(10) Capital transfers	[(10a) + (10b)]	−146
(a) credits		0
(b) debits		−146
(11) Financial account	[(12) + (13) + (14) + (15) + (16)]	56 745
(12) Direct investment	[(12a) + (12b)]	17 398
(a) Assets		−17 550
(b) Liabilities		34 948
(13) Portfolio investment	[(13a) + (13b)]	68 112
(a) Assets		−92 470
(b) Liabilities		160 582
(14) Financial derivatives	[(14a) + (14b)]	−5 951
(a) Assets		37 651
(b) Liabilities		−43 602
(15) Other investment	[(15a) + (15b)]	−28 743
(a) Assets		−20 009
(b) Liabilities		−8 734
(16) Reserve assets		5 929
(17) Net errors and omissions[a]	[(1) − (7)]	−510

(a) This item will have an opposite sign to the numerical overstatement or understatement.
Source: Adapted from Australian Bureau of Statistics, Balance of Payments and International Investment Position, Australia, cat. no. 5302.051, 2010.

The capital account records capital transfers (such as migrants' transfers and debt forgiveness) and the acquisition/disposal of non-produced, non-financial assets (such as sales of embassy land or copyrights) between residents and non-residents.

The financial account records transactions in financial assets and liabilities (such as shares, bonds and loans) between residents and non-residents.

Conventions for plus and minus

Current account entries for most items in the list of standard components show gross debits and credits. Most capital and financial account entries are made on a net basis; that is, each component is shown only as a credit or a debit.

Australia uses in its balance of payments the sign convention recommended by the International Monetary Fund. The principle is that for all transactions in assets—real or financial—a positive figure (credit) represents a decrease in holdings, and a negative figure (debit) represents an increase. In contrast, for liabilities, a positive figure is used to show an increase, and a negative figure shows a decrease (see Table 18.2). A definition of assets and liabilities is presented in Chapter 14.

Table 18.2   **Sign conventions in the balance of payments**

	DEBIT	CREDIT
Assets (real/financial)	+	−
Liabilities	−	+

+ = increase; − = decrease

This sign convention means, for example, that exports (which reduce real assets) are shown as positive entries; while the receipts of foreign exchange in payment (which increase financial assets) are shown as debit entries with a minus sign. Similarly, borrowing from abroad increases Australia's debt liabilities, so this side of the transaction is shown as a positive entry; while the foreign exchange proceeds of the borrowing increase assets, so this side of the transaction is shown as a negative entry.

A close examination of the balance of payments will give us a better understanding of the issues encountered by Australia in the global economy.

COMPONENTS OF THE CURRENT ACCOUNT

GOODS

Figures for 2009–10 are presented in row 3 of Table 18.1.

Goods include: rural goods; non-rural goods; goods procured in ports; and non-monetary gold (e.g. gold that is not held as a reserve asset).

The difference between the value of exports free-on-board (f.o.b.) and the value of imports is termed the **balance on goods**.

Note that in keeping with BPM6 convention, balance of payments credit entries are shown with an implied positive sign and debit items (representing money leaving Australia) are shown as negative entries.

If credits for exports exceed debits for imports, as in Table 18.1 (p. 378), there is a surplus in the balance on goods. Between 1979–80 and 2009–10, Australia recorded surpluses in goods trade in 1983–84, 1987–88, 1990–91, 1991–92, 1992–93, 1996–97 and 2009–10.

If debits for imports exceed credits for exports, there is a deficit in the balance on goods. Over the same 30-year period, Australia recorded deficits in goods trade in 23 years.

SERVICES

The services component of the current account is presented in row 4 of Table 18.1. It includes:

- services credits: money paid by foreigners to Australian exporters of services
- services debits: money paid to foreign suppliers of services by Australian residents.

The following categories of service transactions are included in this component:

- transport: includes transport of freight and passengers by all modes of transport (sea, air, land)
- travel: includes expenditure on goods and services (other than fares) by international travellers for education and other purposes, for trips of less than one year's duration
- other services: communications, construction, insurance, financial, computer information, personal, cultural, recreational and government services, royalties and licence fees, and other business services.

The 2009 format also includes:

- maintenance and repair services
- manufacturing services on physical inputs owned by others.

Traditionally, Australia has experienced a continuing negative balance in services trade, mainly due to net deficits in transport and insurance. However, the gap between debits and credits has steadily diminished and in the 2000s Australia managed a number of six annual surpluses varying between A$122 million (FY 2006) and A$1800 million (FY 2003). Deficits in the 2000s varied between A$400 million and A$2300 million.

GOODS AND SERVICES

The balance on goods and services is the total of the figures for goods and services items, row 2. During the period from 1979–80 to 2009–10 this item recorded a deficit in most years; the exceptions were the six annual services trade surpluses in the financial years 1980, 1992, 1997, 2001, 2002 and 2009.

PRIMARY INCOME

The primary income account shows primary income flows between resident and non-resident institutional units.

Two types of primary income are distinguished:

- compensation of employees is income for the contribution of labour inputs to the production process (e.g. wages, salaries and other benefits paid to border, seasonal and other non-resident workers, such as local staff of embassies)
- income associated with the ownership of financial and other non-produced assets (e.g. investment income and property income).

Investment income, which is by far the major category of income, consists of direct investment income, portfolio investment income, and other investment income (e.g. interest on loans).

Australian residents who have invested money in governments or businesses overseas receive interest, dividends and royalties. These remittances enter Australia and are shown as credits within the income section, row 5(a). Similarly, payments that Australians make to non-residents are recorded as debits, row 5(b).

The net income figure (–$49.2 billion) displayed in row 5 reflects a common result for the Australian balance of payments. Significantly bigger debits here represent interest payments on foreign borrowing, but in recent years dividends paid to foreign owners of Australian shares have increased markedly.

SECONDARY INCOME

The secondary income account shows current transfers between residents and non-residents. Secondary income (previously called 'current transfers') covers payment of money that is not likely to involve any return or remittance in the future. This occurs in two areas:

- general government transfers: for example current international cooperation between different governments, payments of current taxes on income and wealth
- transfers in other sectors: for example workers' remittances and other transfers such as claims on non-life insurance.

Secondary income is not a big item, with Australia showing alternative deficits and surpluses. In 2002–03, current transfers (row 6) recorded a deficit of $914 million.

THE BALANCE ON CURRENT ACCOUNT

In essence, the current account is a record of transactions between Australian residents and non-residents in goods, services, income and current transfers. The current account total in row 1 of Table 18.1 is a substantial negative value (–$56.1 billion).

The balance on the current account is the difference between the sum of credits and the sum of debits for the four categories of transactions. Therefore, it is much more than just trade. In fact, as Figure 18.1 overleaf illustrates, the crux of the problem of our current account deficit is represented not by the balance of trade, but by the net income deficit.

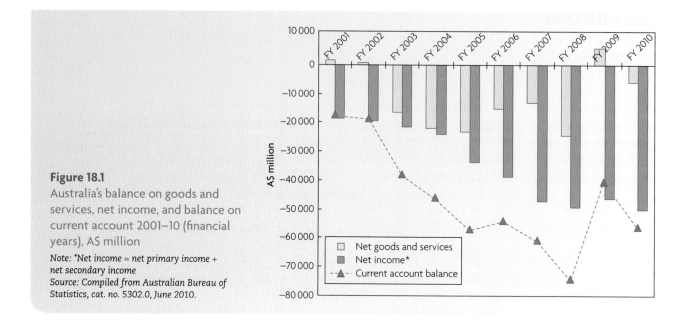

Figure 18.1

Australia's balance on goods and services, net income, and balance on current account 2001–10 (financial years), A$ million

Note: *Net income = net primary income + net secondary income
Source: Compiled from Australian Bureau of Statistics, cat. no. 5302.0, June 2010.

The current account balance becomes, in effect, an indicator of our performance in the world economy. According to Organisation for Economic Cooperation and Development (OECD) data, Australia's current account deficit measured as a proportion of GDP has varied in recent years between a low of –2.0 per cent in 2001 and a high of –6.1 per cent in 2007. Over 2007–09, Australia's current account deficit as a proportion of GDP averaged –4.9 per cent. By comparison, only five OECD members recorded over the three-year period higher negative shares of the current account in GDP: New Zealand (–6.5 per cent), Spain (–8.4 per cent), Portugal (–10.5 per cent), Iceland (–12.7 per cent) and Greece (–13.4 per cent).

The well-publicised United States current account deficit accounted for –4.3 per cent of GDP, while 12 member economies of OECD managed positive ratios, including Norway (15.5 per cent), Sweden (8.3 per cent), Luxembourg (6.9 per cent), Germany (6.5 per cent), Switzerland (6.4 per cent) and the Netherlands (6.3 per cent).

The overall sign (plus or minus) and the magnitude of the balance are significant. They play a role in determining trends in interest rates in the financial sector and the value of the Australian dollar in exchange markets. A number of related external policy issues and solutions to the problem of the current account deficit are discussed in Chapter 24.

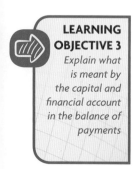

LEARNING OBJECTIVE 3

Explain what is meant by the capital and financial account in the balance of payments

THE CAPITAL AND FINANCIAL ACCOUNT

The capital and financial account, as its name implies, has two major components—the capital account and the financial account. It shows transactions in foreign financial assets and liabilities. Assets represent claims on non-residents, and liabilities represent indebtedness to non-residents.

CAPITAL ACCOUNT

The major components of the **capital account** are *capital transfers* and *acquisition/disposal of non-produced, non-financial assets*.

Capital transfers include two components:

- general government, subdivided into debt forgiveness and other
- other sectors (migrants' transfers, debt forgiveness and other).

The component called acquisition disposal of non-produced, non-financial assets (e.g. sales of embassy land or copyrights) is generally very small (less than $0.1 billion per year).

capital account comprises primarily capital transfers, including certain aid flows and transfers of migrants' wealth, and entries for the acquisition (less disposal) of non-produced, non-financial assets such as patents and copyrights

FINANCIAL ACCOUNT

The **financial account** has five components: *direct investment, portfolio investment, financial derivatives, other investment* and *reserve assets*.

financial account covers the direct investment, portfolio investment, other investment and reserve assets categories

Direct investment

A direct investment relationship is established when there is a 10 per cent or more equity holding in an enterprise (a direct investment enterprise) by a foreign investor (a direct investor). For this category there are directional distinctions: *abroad* or *in Australia*.

Australian direct investment abroad (Table 18.1, row 12(a), p. 378) was of minor importance before 1983, after which exchange controls were abolished and Australian companies (e.g. BHP, IXL, TNT, Boral, ANZ) started establishing branches overseas. As discussed in Chapter 17, at the end of FY 2009, Australian direct investment abroad reached a total of $344.6 billion being concentrated overwhelmingly in the United Kingdom and the United States, and to a lesser extent in New Zealand.

Direct investment in Australia (Table 18.1, row 12(b)) occurs when an overseas company:

- establishes a branch or subsidiary of its own operations in Australia: for example, Ford United States set up Ford Australia
- acquires ownership of 10 per cent or more of the ordinary shares of an Australian company: for example, General Motors (United States) acquires Holden Carriages (South Australia) and GM-H is born
- reinvests any undistributed income which it has earned on direct investment already undertaken in the source country.

All the branches of multinational corporations in Australia (e.g. Kelloggs, Shell, General Electric, Siemens, the car manufacturers) are the result of direct investment by those firms in subsidiary companies for the domestic production of their goods. In some cases the purpose is to avoid the tariffs that would be placed on their goods if imported from the parent company. Direct investment brings long-term benefits of foreign technology and new business and employment opportunities to the domestic economy, and new markets for domestic suppliers of their inputs.

Australia has been a traditional destination for foreign direct investment due mainly to its political and economic stability. The major foreign investors in Australia are the United Kingdom, the United States and Japan (see Table 17.13 in Chapter 17, p. 370).

Portfolio investment

Portfolio investment (Table 18.1, row 13, p. 378) covers transactions in equity securities (up to 10 per cent of shares equity of domestic companies) and debt securities (e.g. bonds and notes, money-market instruments).

This is a useful source of finance for firms undertaking expansion if there is a shortage of domestic capital due to the low level of savings. Otherwise, it has minimal direct benefit to the economy, and only results in increased foreign ownership of Australian firms.

As suggested by Table 18.1, in dollar terms, portfolio investment tends to represent in any individual year a higher net financial inflow for Australia than foreign direct investment (e.g. A$68 billion in 2009–10, which was four times more than net FDI inflows). However, portfolio investment is short term and speculative, so it tends to be more disruptive for the Australian economy than direct investment.

Financial derivatives

Financial derivatives (Table 18.1, row 14) such as swaps, forward rate agreements and forward foreign exchange agreements are financial instruments that are linked to a specific financial instrument or indicator (foreign currencies, government bonds, share price indexes, interest rates), or to a particular commodity (e.g. gold or sugar). They provide a hedge for market financial risk in a form that can be traded or otherwise offset in the market. In 2009–10, the value of financial derivatives (net) was around A$6 billion which was around A$2.3 billion higher than in the previous year.

Other investments

Other investment (Table 18.1, row 15) covers short- and long-term trade credits, loans, currency and deposits, and other accounts receivable and payable. (Transactions covered under direct investment are excluded.) Net inflows increased in 2009–10 by around A$18 billion to reach A$28 billion.

Reserve assets

Reserve assets cover transactions in those assets that are considered by the monetary authorities of an economy (e.g. the Reserve Bank) to be available for use in meeting balance of payments and other needs. Such items include monetary gold, reserve position in the International Monetary Fund and foreign exchange. As shown in Table 18.1, row (16), in 2009–10, Australia's reserve assets increased by around A$6 billion.

NET ERRORS AND OMISSIONS

Given the double-entry system, under which any international transaction gives rise to two offsetting entries in the balance of payments, the current account balance in Table 18.1, row 1, and the (net) capital and financial account, row 7, should always add up to zero.

The net capital and financial account, row 7, is the sum of all the net inflows. In theory, with a floating exchange rate, this should be equal to the deficit on the current account, because all outflows of money must be balanced by equivalent inflows (see examples below). In practice, however, when all actual entries are totalled, the resulting balance almost inevitably shows a net credit or a net debit.

For instance, in Table 18.1 we have an imbalance of $510 million. That balance is the result of errors and omissions in the compilation of data. Therefore, the statisticians insert an item for *Net errors and omissions*, row 17, covering statistical errors and omissions. This item is intended as an offset to the overstatement or understatement of the recorded components. Thus, if, as in Table 18.1, the balance of those components is a debit, the item for net errors and omissions will be shown as a credit of equal value, and vice versa.

double-entry bookkeeping
a system where each transaction is recorded as two offsetting entries

It is important to note that the overall balance of payments account is in complete balance but only in an accounting sense.

The deficit shown in the balance on *current account* (–$56 103 million) is offset exactly by the surplus ($56 103 million) occurring in the *capital and financial account* (inclusive of the *net errors and omissions* item), with the result that the balance of payments is equal to zero.

In other words, the huge deficits we have been running on the current account are paid for by capital and financial inflow—by overseas borrowings by governments, firms and individuals.

LEARNING OBJECTIVE 4
Explain the double-entry bookkeeping system of measuring balances of payments and illustrate with examples the way the double-entry bookkeeping operates

THE DOUBLE-ENTRY SYSTEM OF THE BALANCE OF PAYMENTS

The balance of payments accounts are based on what accountants term **double-entry bookkeeping**. Each transaction appears twice, once as a credit and once as a debit.

This principle is illustrated in Table 18.3 (p. 387), which is a hypothetical balance of payments for Australia. It lists seven transactions, worked out step by step.

TRANSACTION 1

An Australian exporter exports beef to Japan valued at $10 million and receives payment in the same period. The entries in the balance of payments are:

- credit $10 million: the export of merchandise is recorded as a credit, by convention (decrease in holdings of real assets)
- debit $10 million: the receipt for those exports is an increase in trading bank holdings of foreign currency assets (considered as a debit, by convention).

TRANSACTION 2

An Australian importer purchases computer hardware from the United States valued at $5 million, but has been granted a two-year credit for payment. The entries in the balance of payments are:

- debit $5 million: imports are debited, as they represent an increase in holdings of real assets
- credit $5 million: the extension of two-year credit (regarded as long term) represents an increase in liabilities of the importer and so is credited under 'other investment (long-term trade credits)'.

TRANSACTION 3

General Motors declares a profit of $1 million and decides to reinvest it in Australian operations. The entries in the balance of payments are:

- debit $1 million: recorded under the primary income component of the current account as a debit, because we have an increase in holdings of financial assets
- credit $1 million: the reinvestment of earnings is recorded as a direct investment by foreigners in Australian domestic enterprises (e.g. increase in liabilities).

TRANSACTION 4

The Australian Government gives $7 million of food aid for Somalia relief. The entries in the balance of payments are:

- credit $7 million: the donation reduces Australia's real assets (treated by convention as an export although paid for by the Australian Government)
- debit $7 million: there is no quid pro quo for the donation. The offsetting entry, by convention, must be a secondary income debit.

TRANSACTION 5

An Australian company borrows $15 million from abroad over one year. The entries in the balance of payments are:

- credit $15 million: Australia acquires increased foreign liabilities, recorded under other short-term investment (e.g. loans)
- debit $15 million: simultaneously, Australian banks' foreign currency balances rise by the same amount.

TRANSACTION 6

Optus takes delivery of a satellite manufactured in the United States and valued at $50 million. It is delivered to a site in South America, from where it is launched by an international consortium. Transportation and launch costs total $25 million, the launch rocket costs $15 million, and insurance paid to a foreign insurer adds another $15 million. All costs have been paid in previous periods. The entries in the balance of payments are:

- debit $105 million: the satellite is regarded as an import of goods (although is not delivered into Australia's territory) and is shown as a debit under goods. The other costs ($55 million) relate to the provision of services by non-residents and are shown as a service debit
- credit $105 million: the extinguishing of prepayments is a credit because they are a decrease in foreign currency assets under 'other investment'.

TRANSACTION 7

The Australian Government repays a loan of $50 million previously borrowed on international capital markets. The entries in the balance of payments are:

- credit $50 million: a negative amount is recorded under portfolio investment in Australia to reflect the repayment of a previous liability. Therefore liabilities decrease
- debit $50 million: shown as a reduction in assets of the Reserve Bank.

This, together with the borrowings components of portfolio investment, represents debt finance, in the form of loans to Australian enterprises (private and public) from overseas. The borrowings of Australian enterprises and governments add to the country's foreign debt, which is discussed later in this chapter.

Table 18.3   **Hypothetical balance of payments**

ITEM	DEBITS	CREDITS
Current account	−118	17
(a) Goods	−55	17
Beef exports to Japan (1)[a]		10
Hardware imports from the United States (2)	−5	
Food exports to Somalia (4)		7
Satellite import from the United States (5)	−50	
(b) Services	−55	
Import of services (5)	−55	
(c) Primary Income	−1	
GM income (3)	−1	
(d) Secondary income	−7	
Donation to Somalia (4)	−7	
Capital and financial account	−75	176
Capital account		
Capital transfers		
Net acquisition/disposal of non-produced, non-financial assets		
Financial account	−75	176
(a) Direct investment		1
Abroad		
In Australia (3)		1
(b) Portfolio investment		50
Government loan repayment (7)		50

continued ↘

continued

ITEM	DEBITS	CREDITS
(c) Other investment	−25	125
Long-term trade credits and loans (2)		5
Short-term trade credits and loans (5)		15
Foreign currency holdings (1) (5)	−25	105
(d) Reserve assets	−50	
Reduction in foreign exchange (7)	−50	
Total	**−193**	**193**

(a) The number in brackets represents the number of the balance of payments double-entry transaction.

LEARNING OBJECTIVE 5

Describe how a country accumulates foreign debt, and discuss the size and significance of Australia's foreign debt

foreign (external) debt

the total amount of money Australian residents have borrowed from overseas residents

THE FOREIGN DEBT

As a result of the inflow of debt finance, year after year, Australia has accumulated a large **foreign debt**. Foreign debt is referred to also as external debt. Foreign debt is distinguished from other kinds of foreign investment capital inflow such as foreign ownership, because it carries with it the obligation to pay interest or to repay principal.

One way of looking at debt is simply to add up all non-equity liabilities. This is *gross foreign debt*, which is basically the total amount borrowed from non-residents. It includes the accumulated external debts of private business firms, public enterprises, and the Commonwealth and state governments. Up until the 1980s in Australia, borrowing from foreigners represented less than 10 per cent of GDP. By 1985–86, Australia's gross external debt rose rapidly to nearly 40 per cent of GDP. Gross foreign debt by the end of June 2002 was $523.6 billion, representing around three-quarters of Australia's GDP. At the end of fiscal year 2010, Australia's gross foreign debt reached almost A$1194 billion, which was in excess of 90 per cent of Australia's GDP in the same year.

This dramatic rise occurred for four main reasons:

- Following the deregulation of the financial system, the growth in demand for funds far outpaced growth in Australian savings, and overseas interest rates were lower than Australia's.
- Federal and state governments borrowed heavily in the early 1980s, in response to an expected mineral boom.
- The Australian dollar experienced periods of massive depreciation during 1985, 1986, 1997, 1998, and over 2000 to 2002. (We will examine the impact of exchange rate changes in Chapter 19. At this stage, we should note that a fall in the value of the Australian dollar means that Australia has to pay back more dollars for every United States dollar, euro, Swiss franc, Japanese yen, or other currency borrowed from overseas.)
- As discussed above, Australia has traditionally run large current account deficits, and overseas borrowing has been needed to finance shortfalls.

Australia's foreign debt has a number of characteristics:

- The share of the public sector in Australia's gross foreign debt has recorded a significant decline in recent years from around 32 per cent in 1997 to only around 16 per cent in FY2010 (and as low as about 13 per cent in FY 2002). It is this low level of public debt that distinguishes Australia from developing country debtors.
- Over the past couple of decades, the maturity structure of debt trended towards shorter loan periods.
- The currency denomination of debt has also shifted over the past couple of decades to a greater proportion of Australian denominated liabilities. This fact has diminished the significance of the impact of exchange rate movements on the level of Australian debt.
- In relation to the composition of Australian foreign debt by country it appears that in the 2000s the most important creditor countries for Australia in terms of total debt were Japan, the United States and the United Kingdom.

NET FOREIGN DEBT

We noted before that in recent years the gross foreign debt has exceeded 90 per cent of GDP. However, a more significant figure is the net foreign debt, which is equal to gross foreign debt minus lending by residents of Australia to non-residents, including reserve assets.

Australia's net foreign debt reached A$329.7 billion in 2001–02, or about 47 per cent of GDP, up from only A$6.8 billion in 1980, before the floating of the Australian dollar and the deregulation of Australia's financial system.

ABS historical data indicates that Australia's net foreign debt has increased to around A$672 billion in the financial year 2010, or around 55 per cent of GDP.

The public share of foreign debt in Australia is extremely small. Over 2001–10 it accounted in most years for a share between 1 and 5 per cent of total net foreign debt. In financial year 2007 it had even a negative share (–3 per cent). In 2009–10, the public sector's share of net foreign debt increased to around 16 per cent, or about A$108.6 billion. By comparison, the share of the public sector in Australia's net foreign debt in financial year 1997 was 31.3 per cent.

Over the same 10-year period, net foreign debt levels of the private sector (e.g. financial corporations and private non-financial corporations) almost doubled from A$294 billion to A$563 billion, but its share in total net foreign debt declined from 98 per cent in financial year 2001 to 84 per cent in financial year 2010 (see Figure 18.2 overleaf).

Interest payments on foreign borrowings tended to stabilise in the 1990s, largely as a result of the fall in interest rates. During 2000–01, the ratio of net investment income payable (net foreign debt plus net foreign equity) on our foreign debt to the value of exports of goods and services reached about 12.7 per cent. This was down from about 21 per cent in 1989–90, reflecting falls in interest rates and strong export volumes. In 2008–09 Australia's debt servicing ratio accounted for around 10.5 per cent.

In other words, we have to spend about 10.5 per cent of the value of our exports of goods and services on servicing our net foreign liabilities. Again, this is a relatively small share compared to high-debt developing countries.

IN CONCLUSION

Our foreign debt problems are inseparable from the whole economic policy mix and, in particular, our failure to achieve higher savings levels in Australia. Since 1959–60, there have been only three years where domestic savings exceeded investment.

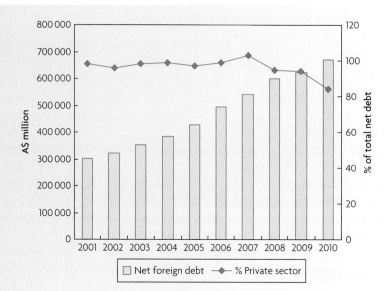

Figure 18.2

Australia's net foreign debt (A$ billion), and percentage share of private sector debt, 2001–10 (end of June)

Source: Adapted from Australian Bureau of Statistics, Balance of Payments and International Investment Position, cat. no. 5302.0, 2010.

The ratio of national net saving to GDP declined from around 16 per cent in FY 1961 to around 5 per cent in FY 1999. Over the following decade the same ratio increased by about three percentage points to reach 7.9 per cent in FY 2009.

To reduce our dependence on foreign savings, Australia will have to improve its economic fundamentals:

- keep wage increases, inflation and interest rates near—and preferably below—the rates enjoyed by our major trading partners
- encourage more investment in export-expanding and import-replacing industries (there is more on measures to encourage capital and financial inflows in Chapter 24)
- encourage domestic saving (further than done by recent budgets)
- further improve the productivity of our workplaces, transport and shipping facilities and management in order to boost exports and make imports less competitive and attractive.

CURRENT ACCOUNT DEFICIT: SHOULD WE WORRY?

LINK TO
INTERNATIONAL
ECONOMY

As Figure 18.1 (p. 382) shows, Australia's current account deficit (CAD) has varied in recent years between −A$17 billion and −A$56 billion, or close to 6 per cent of the value of Australia's GDP. At first glance, it does not look good. As a rule of thumb, a growing CAD should put downward pressure on the Australian dollar and may also require some measures to attract foreign investment. A lower dollar encourages exports, but it makes imports more expensive. When economic activity is strong, imports tend to accelerate and their increased prices in Australian dollars translate into higher inflation.

For simplicity, we can regard the CAD as having two parts—the balance on goods and services and the net income deficit. As explained above, the balance on goods and services has been up and down between deficit and surplus but mostly in deficit.

The second part of the CAD that creates the deficit is the net income deficit, which has been mainly driven by interest repayments on foreign debt.

CAD is serviced by the income generated by the nation's exports. In this respect, Australia's CAD is different to that of developing countries like Turkey or Mali, which have similar CAD to GDP ratios to ours. Australia has balanced services trade exchanges and has a reasonable deficit on trade in goods and as a result it can service its CAD reasonably well. As discussed above, around 90 per cent of Australia's net foreign debt belongs to the private sector and the management of Australian companies is responsible for it. The government's foreign debt is also managed responsibly. Mali and Turkey do not have the same potential to service their debts.

CAD is, in a way, like a house mortgage. The size of the mortgage is irrelevant as long as you have a regular source of income high enough to cover the repayments on it.

On the other hand, Australia's CAD of recent years is different from that of the late 1980s. Then the big import bills were leading to big CAD, high inflation and spiralling interest rates. During the Coalition Government's period in power the Australian Government produced a number of Budget surpluses in eight years or so, unemployment went below 6 per cent, inflation was relatively low and there was not so much pressure for higher interest rates.

The global financial crisis (GFC) changed the scenario, with the federal Budget again in deficit, but the deficit is manageable and we are promised that the Budget will get back into surplus by 2013.

One issue of concern is the destination of foreign debt in Australia. In recent years, the banks and other lenders have lent a net $82 billion to business and $345 billion to households. We are borrowing overseas not to invest so much as to drive up housing prices and consumer spending.

It would be much better to follow the example of newly industrialising economies such as Singapore and South Korea which ran up huge current account deficits in the early years of their development, and invested borrowed money in export-oriented projects that then produced large current account surpluses.

Let's be prudential on borrowing and let's spend borrowed money in productive sectors which can then increase the welfare of all Australians.

SUMMARY

1. The balance of payments is a record of the economic transactions between Australian individuals, businesses and governments, and their counterparts in other nations.
2. The balance of payments accounts utilise a double-entry bookkeeping system, in which each international transaction is recorded as two offsetting entries. The entire balance of payments, by definition, must balance numerically.
3. The current account of the balance of payments includes:
    (a) net goods trade (physical goods)
    (b) net services trade (e.g. balance of payments and receipts on trade in services such as tourism and transport)
    (c) net primary income (e.g. interest payments, royalties and profits of overseas companies)
    (d) net secondary income (e.g. pensions and other money remittances, foreign aid).
4. The capital and financial account shows transactions in foreign financial assets and liabilities. It is the mirror of the current account. That is, the current account equals the capital and financial account (inclusive of net errors and omissions), the amounts for the two accounts having opposite signs.
5. The accumulated external debts of private business firms, public enterprises, and the federal and state governments' current account deficit gives the nation's gross foreign debt. If we deduct from the gross foreign debt the nation's foreign

assets lending overseas, we get the nation's net foreign debt. In the 2000s, Australia's net foreign debt has been over 90 per cent private, and under 10 per cent public.

6. Servicing of Australia's debt takes about 10.5 per cent of the value of Australia's exports of goods and services. The major cause for the growing foreign debt in Australia is the lack of domestic capital and the corresponding reliance on foreign capital. To reduce its dependence on foreign savings, Australia will have to improve its economic fundamentals, including an increased amount of domestic savings.

KEY TERMS

balance of payments	377	current account	381
balance on goods	380	double-entry bookkeeping	385
capital account	383	financial account	383
		foreign (external) debt	388

REVISION QUESTIONS

1. What is the balance of payments?
2. How does the double-entry accounting system work?
3. What is meant by the current account of the balance of payments? Discuss the components of Australia's current account, and indicate why the balance is usually a deficit.
4. What are the principal sections in Australia's balance of payments after September 1997 and what are the principal 'balances' to be found in it?
5. What is the main reason for Australia's traditional current account deficit?
6. What are the major factors which have tended to dominate the pattern of Australia's balance of payments over the last two decades?
7. How is Australia's current account deficit presently funded?
8. What are the components of Australia's capital account of the balance of payments?
9. Outline the main components of Australia's financial account and give a few examples of transactions for each component.
10. What is the difference between direct investment and portfolio investment? Give examples.
11. What is the gross foreign debt?
12. What is the net foreign debt?
13. How can we reduce our dependence on foreign borrowings and equity?
14. Explain the statement: 'Australia's CAD is different to that of developing countries like Turkey or Mali.'

APPLIED QUESTIONS AND EXERCISES

1. Look at ABS figures for real GDP growth and trade balance since 1980s. In which phase of the business cycle does Australia tend to have a positive balance of trade? Why?

2. 'CAD is, in a way, like a house mortgage.' Do you agree with this statement? Explain.

3. Bucksland is an economy with a floating currency. Consider the data in Table 18.4 on Bucksland's current account on the balance of payments in the year 2010.

Table 18.4: Bucksland's current account on balance of payments, 2010

ITEM	B$ MILLION
Exports of goods	500
Imports of goods	400
Service exports	250
Service imports	400
Primary income credits	200
Primary income debits	360
Secondary income (net)	–140
Current account balance	?

Calculate the following:
(a) balance on goods
(b) balance on goods and services
(c) balance on current account.

4. Assuming that the current account result in Question 1 represented the continuation of a consistent trend over the last three to four years and all other things being equal, what is the likely direction of the Bucksland dollar in 2011?
(a) an appreciation
(b) a depreciation
(c) no change.

5. When there is a growing current account deficit the government may:
   (a) raise the exchange rate
   (b) encourage imports
   (c) encourage capital outflow
   (d) encourage capital inflow.
6. In relation to the transactions in the table below, which section of Australia's balance of payments is affected: goods, services, primary income or secondary income? Will these transactions be recorded as a debit (D) or credit (C)? Explain.

ECONOMIC TRANSACTION	CURRENT ACCOUNT SECTION	CURRENT ACCOUNT ENTRY (D/C)
(a) An Australian exporter hires a foreign shipping company for transporting wheat to an overseas destination.		
(b) There is a robust increase in the number of foreign students enrolled in Australian universities.		
(c) Toyota-Australia reinvests a profit of $20 million in Australia.		
(d) The Australian Government provides $5 million of food aid to Indonesia.		
(e) Qantas purchases a new Boeing jumbo jet.		
(f) Pensions paid to Australians living in Italy.		
(g) Interest paid on a loan from the United Kingdom.		

Chapter 19

The exchange rate

LEARNING OBJECTIVES

After studying this chapter, you will be able to:

1. understand what the exchange rates are and the effects of currency fluctuations on the Australian economy
2. explain the fundamental factors that determine exchange rates
3. outline the effects of exchange rate changes on the balance of payments
4. describe the major factors influencing the demand for and the supply of Australian dollars.

INTRODUCTION

In this chapter, we will examine the factors that contribute to the value of the Australian dollar and the effects of the Australian dollar fluctuations on various sectors of the Australian economy.

We will also explain how international payments for goods and services are made and examine the effects of exchange rate changes on the balance of payments.

In the final section, we will understand the impact of changes in export/import prices on the current account, the exchange rate and the economy as a whole.

EXCHANGE RATES

> **LEARNING OBJECTIVE 1**
> Understand what the exchange rates are and the effects of currency fluctuations on the Australian economy

The external sector of any economy could not exist without a foreign exchange market, where one money is sold and is paid for with another money. The price that is paid in one currency for a unit of another currency is called the foreign exchange rate (or the rate of exchange). The type of exchange rate adopted by a country has a significant impact on the internal and external sectors of the economy.

International trade transactions, involving the exchange of goods, services or capital for money, are more complicated because the currency of one nation is incompatible with that of the other.

When Australian producers sell goods overseas, they want to be paid in Australian dollars so that they can pay the wages of their employees and settle debts arising from the use of materials in the production process. The same applies to Japanese manufacturers who sell goods to Australia. They want to be paid in Japanese yen so that they may settle their debt at their end. Similarly, Italian suppliers want payment in their national currency (euros).

How then is this problem resolved? Businesspeople do not have to carry supplies of all the currencies in the world. It would be much too messy and unprofitable, because there would be vast sums of money lying idle. Instead, the banking system in each country comes to the rescue (see the following Link to Business).

CALCULATING THE EXCHANGE RATE

The **exchange rate** for any currency is the price at which it can be traded for other currencies. It is determined by the international supply of—and demand for—the currency on foreign exchange markets. For example:

> **exchange rate**
> *the price of one currency in terms of another currency*

$$A\$1 = US\$0.75 \text{ or conversely } US\$ = 1 \div 0.75 = A\$1.33$$

If the exchange rate falls (depreciates), a given amount of Australian dollars buys less of other currencies; if the exchange rate rises (appreciates), that amount buys more of other currencies.

It is possible for the exchange rate of the Australian dollar to fall against some currencies and rise or remain stable against others. This is why the Reserve Bank publishes daily a trade-weighted index (TWI). The TWI refers to an index of the value of the Australian dollar against a 'basket' of currencies of our major trading partners. The weights in the TWI are

INTERNATIONAL METHODS OF PAYMENT

LINK TO
BUSINESS

Figure 19.1 provides a simple outline of the payment procedures when commodities are exported from Australia to Japan under a contract priced in US dollars.

The individuals or firms use the currency of their own country, and the banks exchange this for US dollars. This keeps the foreign currency holding within the banking system or in the hands of those licensed to deal in the buying and selling of foreign currencies. Some of these foreign currency holdings are held by the central bank, namely the Reserve Bank of Australia, as part of international reserves.

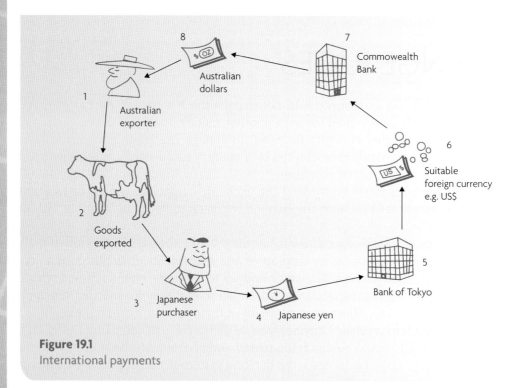

Figure 19.1
International payments

We have to emphasise that it is not necessary to physically transport the money from Japan to Australia. The transaction is performed by simply making adjustments to the bank accounts of the players involved. The Japanese bank debits the account of the Japanese importer with yen equivalent to the US dollar value of the contract, and the Australian bank credits the account of the Australian exporter with Australian dollars equivalent to the US dollar value of the contract.

calculated on an annual basis. There are 21 currencies included in the index for 2010–11. The regions associated with the 21 currencies account for 93 per cent of Australia's merchandise trade. The leading 10 currencies in Australia's TWI for 2010–11 as from 1 October 2010 are presented in Table 19.1.

In Figure 19.2, upward movements represent an appreciation of the Australian dollar against other currencies (US dollar, Japanese yen, TWI), while downward movements indicate a depreciation of the Australian dollar. It appears that the US dollar/Australian

Table 19.1   Weights in Australia's trade weighted index (TWI), per cent of total, 2010–11, and 2009–10

CURRENCY	2010–11 (%)	2009–10 (%)
Chinese renminbi	22.54	18.56
Japanese yen	14.94	17.12
European euro	9.92	10.44
United States dollar	8.54	8.98
South Korean won	6.41	6.26
Indian rupee	4.91	4.26
Thai baht	4.67	3.82
Singapore dollar	4.34	4.61
New Zealand dollar	4.09	3.79
United Kingdom pound sterling	3.53	4.99
Total 10 currencies	83.88	82.84

Source: Adapted from <www.rba.gov.au/media-releases/2010/mr-10-22.html>, accessed 7 October 2010.

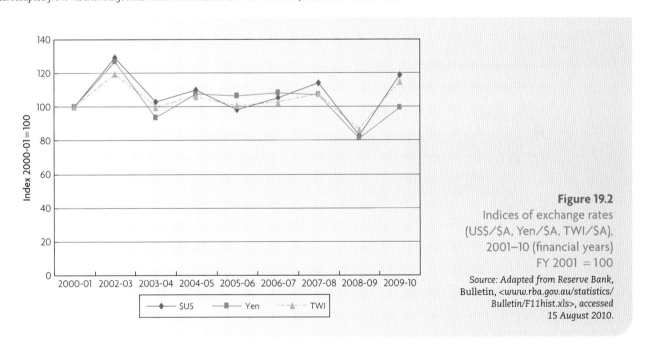

Figure 19.2
Indices of exchange rates (US$/$A, Yen/$A, TWI/$A), 2001–10 (financial years)
FY 2001 = 100

Source: Adapted from Reserve Bank, Bulletin, <www.rba.gov.au/statistics/Bulletin/F11hist.xls>, accessed 15 August 2010.

dollar exchange rate is the most responsive to changes in the business environment and records the most ample fluctuations.

For much of the 1980s, the TWI tracked commodity prices closely. The trend changed in the early 1990s, when the Australian dollar remained around 77 to 80 US cents, despite downward trends in commodity prices. Our high interest rates appeared to be pushing up the demand for the Australian dollar and holding up its price. Following the East Asian financial crisis and the slowdown in the world economy in 2001–02, the TWI again generally tracked commodity prices quite closely. During the global financial crisis, all three exchange rates showed a comparable downturn, but during the recovery, the US dollar/Australian dollar, Australia's main currency 'pair' in international transactions, has been the one to rebound most. We will explain more below.

ROLE OF THE BANKING SYSTEM IN CURRENCY CONVERSION

The banking system facilitates the conversion of currencies, which is so vital to international trade. Most of our major trading banks are large business corporations. They hold licences allowing them to operate as foreign currency (or exchange) dealers. When combined, their foreign currency departments and branches form a worldwide network of operations which constitutes the foreign exchange market (sometimes abbreviated to forex or FX). This network of operations is so extensive that it is possible to buy and sell currencies on a 24-hour basis.

THE EFFECTS OF CURRENCY DEPRECIATION

currency depreciation
the downward valuation of a nation's currency against a foreign currency

Suppose that the exchange rate of the Australian dollar alters from its position in our example, A$1 = US$0.75, to A$1 = US$0.60. This downward valuation of the Australian dollar against the US dollar is called **currency depreciation**. (However, since exchange rates are relative relationships, this would mean that the US dollar has increased in value against the Australian dollar, i.e. US$1 = 1 ÷ 0.60 = A$1.66.)

Impact on exports and economic activity

As Table 19.2 shows, the Australian dollar depreciation is positive for Australian exports. If the price is set in US dollars, the Australian exporter receives more Australian currency for the same volume of exports (+25 per cent).

Table 19.2   **Impact of Australian dollar depreciation**

COMMODITY/ EXPORT PRICE	EXCHANGE RATE (E/R)	AUSTRALIAN EXPORTER RECEIVES	COMMODITY/ IMPORT PRICE	EXCHANGE RATE (E/R)	AUSTRALIAN IMPORTER PAYS
Beef (US$1000/tonne)	A$1 = US$0.75	A$1333	Computer (US$1500/unit)	A$1 = US$0.75	A$2000
	A$1 = US$0.60	A$1666		A$1 = US$0.60	A$2500
	E/R effect	(+25%)		E/R effect	(+25%)

After the depreciation, an exporter of beef at a price of US$1000 per tonne receives $A333 more for each tonne, with no change in export price.

As for export prices set in Australian dollars, they become cheaper and more attractive to foreign buyers (e.g. for 1 tonne of beef at A$1000 the foreign importer will now pay only US$600, instead of US$750 per tonne).

Obviously, Australian suppliers will be encouraged to expand output for export markets, which will increase Australian aggregate demand, with positive effects on investment and employment.

At the same time, Australia becomes relatively more attractive to overseas visitors (because they have to spend less foreign currency for the same amount of goods and services purchased in Australia).

Impact on imports and consumer demand

The depreciation in the value of the Australian dollar against the United States currency makes imported goods more expensive to purchase. In our example, the imported computer price expressed in Australian currency increased from A$2000 to A$2500 after the depreciation occurred. This increase in relative prices will apply to all imported items, with the possible result being a reduction in demand for such commodities.

This is obviously a positive outcome for the economy. However, the demand for some imported items (such as parts for cars and machinery, aircraft and industrial chemicals) is highly inelastic. In other words, such imports will continue with little regard to price changes. Therefore, the slightest depreciation in the Australian currency will be translated into an increase in the rate of inflation within the domestic economy.

Another effect of the weaker Australian dollar is that it costs Australians more to travel overseas. For instance, in our example, a trip to the United States becomes 25 per cent more expensive for all goods and services priced in US dollars.

THE EFFECTS OF CURRENCY APPRECIATION

Currency appreciation occurs when the value of our currency moves upwards from the initial exchange rate. For instance, if it moves from $A1 = US$0.75 to $A1 = US$0.90, the Australian dollar has appreciated against the US dollar. (Conversely, the US dollar has depreciated against the Australian dollar.)

currency appreciation
when the value of a nation's currency moves upwards from the initial exchange rate

Impact on exports and economic activity

As shown in Table 19.3, after an appreciation, the income in Australian dollars for Australian exporters goes down. If they want to redress their profitability, Australian exporters will have to increase their prices in foreign currency, which will diminish their competitiveness against other foreign competitors. Demand for Australian exports will slow down, which will have an adverse effect on the export-oriented sectors of the Australian economy (including service industries such as tourism).

Table 19.3   **Impact of Australian dollar appreciation**

COMMODITY/ EXPORT PRICE	EXCHANGE RATE (E/R)	AUSTRALIAN EXPORTER RECEIVES	COMMODITY/ IMPORT PRICE	EXCHANGE RATE (E/R)	AUSTRALIAN IMPORTER PAYS
Beef (US$1000/tonne)	A$1 = US$0.75	A$1333	Computer (US$1500/unit)	A$1 = US$0.75	A$2000
	A$1 = US$0.90	A$1111		A$1 = US$0.90	A$1600
	E/R effect	(–17%)		E/R effect	(–20%)

Impact on imports and consumer demand

An appreciation of the Australian dollar increases the amount of foreign currency it will buy and reduces the price in Australian dollars of imported commodities, making them more attractive to Australian consumers. Since all imported items are cheaper, much domestic demand will be channelled towards them.

The effect of this stronger import demand depends on the state of the economy. If less than full employment exists, the diversion of demand will not be good news for the economy.

Imports will be purchased at the opportunity cost of locally produced goods. This of course implies that potential employment will be lost.

HOW DOES THE AUSTRALIAN DOLLAR INFLUENCE AUSTRALIAN MANUFACTURING?

LINK TO INTERNATIONAL ECONOMY

In the context of the Asian financial crisis, the Australian dollar suffered an important depreciation against a number of major currencies. For instance, over May 1997 (the fall of the Thai baht) and March 1999, the Australian dollar went down 17.3 per cent against the US dollar, 14.6 per cent against the Japanese yen and 15.9 per cent against the UK pound.

However, the weakness of the Australian dollar against the US dollar (the leading international currency) had not been mirrored in the exchange rate of many Asian currencies (e.g. the Indonesian rupiah, the Malaysian ringgit and the South Korean won), which had fallen even further against the US dollar, and consequently in relation to the Australian dollar. Over the same period, for example, the Indonesian rupiah depreciated by 66 per cent against the Australian dollar and the Malaysian ringgit by 20 per cent.

The effects on Australian manufacturing of this mixed situation of the dollar varied quite sharply, depending on what part of the world they were dealing with, in which currency, and whether the inputs and components were imported or locally manufactured.

The Australian manufacturers exporting to developing East Asia received a double hit: the East Asian market contracted because of the financial crisis, while Australian exports lost in competitiveness against the locally-produced manufactures.

Manufacturers exporting to the United States, Japan or the United Kingdom generally were not too disadvantaged, providing they were not relying on inputs that were imported at an inflated cost. Also on the positive side, local manufactures became more competitive against manufactures imported from industrial countries.

The relative strength of the Australian dollar against many Asian currencies has generated an increase in import competition for manufacturers from Asian imports, creating a downward pressure on prices and sales volumes of locally produced goods.

According to Heather Ridout, then director of public policy for the Metal Trades Industry Association: 'A decade ago, only two out of ten manufacturers were subject to import competition. Now it is nine out of ten.'

The situation changed in 2003 when the Australian dollar started to appreciate again. Over March 1999 to October 2003, the Australian dollar appreciated by around 12 per cent against the US dollar and 'US-linked' currencies such as those of China, Malaysia and Hong Kong, by almost 15 per cent against the New Taiwan dollar, by over 6 per cent against the UK pound and by over 3 per cent against the euro.

An unfavourable situation for Australian manufacturing was generated by the appreciation of the Australian dollar in 2010.

As already discussed, the rule of thumb is that a stronger currency makes exports less competitive, while making imports cheaper and more attractive to domestic consumers. However, one should not be too rigid in this assessment. Let's not forget that about three-quarters of Australia's capital goods and intermediate goods are not sourced locally, but imported by Australian manufacturers, mainly from the United States, Western Europe and Japan. The lower cost of re-equipping plants and of materials and components used in manufacture will improve profit margins. Indirectly, some exporters of manufactures will still benefit from the stronger Australian dollar through lower production costs and export prices. One can argue that a stronger Australian dollar will reduce the costs for primary producers as well, as they can buy lower-priced imported machinery and other manufactured goods (e.g. chemical fertilisers and herbicides).

The impact of the appreciation of the Australian dollar on imports also varies according to the price elasticity of demand. If the import has a low elasticity of demand (such as essential machinery), an appreciation will not have a significant effect on it. But if the commodity is price-elastic (such as luxury cars), then an appreciation could produce a strong surge in demand.

On the other hand, cheaper imports may provide some respite from the ever-rising general price level within the economy. (There may even be some downward pressure on the inflation rate.)

The net impact of the GFC on Australian manufacturing was that the value of manufacturing production in the worst year (2008–09) still managed to increase by around A$23 billion compared to the previous year.

But in the long run, a persistently high Australian dollar is expected to affect Australian manufacturing and will most likely cause further structural change in the Australian economy (see Chapter 20).

DETERMINATION OF THE AUSTRALIAN EXCHANGE RATE

We may want to learn what forces are responsible for a certain exchange rate of the Australian dollar and for its movements. In other words, we may look for an answer to the question: how is Australia's exchange rate determined? Prior to 1983 there was a regulated system, with **fixed exchange rates**, determined by the government. The main phases of Australia's regulated system were:

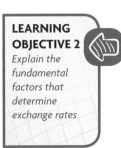

LEARNING OBJECTIVE 2
Explain the fundamental factors that determine exchange rates

- Prior to December 1971: The value of the Australian dollar was pegged to the value of the pound sterling.
- December 1971 to September 1974: The value of the Australian dollar was pegged to the value of the US dollar, following mounting balance of payments figures experienced by the UK economy in the late 1960s, resulting in undesirable pressures on the Australian dollar.
- September 1974 to November 1976: The value of the Australian dollar was pegged to a trade-weighted index (TWI) based on a basket of currencies belonging to the major nations with which we trade. The yen and the US dollar had the greatest weighting in the index, since Japan and the United States together accounted for more than 40 per cent of Australia's trade.
- November 1976 to December 1983: During this time Australia adopted what is known as a **managed float**. The value of the Australian dollar was not freely floating in the marketplace, nor was it fixed by the authorities. It was a combination of the two. The value of the Australian dollar was based on a TWI compiled from a basket of currencies, but additional fluctuations were incorporated by the Australian authorities when economic conditions required them. For instance, the Australian dollar was devalued by 10 per cent in March 1983.

fixed exchange rates
exchange rates for which the values are determined by government decision

managed float
the system where the central bank (RBA) intervenes and adjusts the TWI-based value of the domestic currency when economic conditions require it

Effects of the managed float on the money supply

As with any government price-fixing scheme, there was a tendency for the fixed rate of exchange to strip the foreign exchange market of its rationing function. Rates of exchange kept too low usually coincided with a balance of payments surplus. On a daily basis, this meant that the banks operating in the foreign exchange market would have to sell surplus amounts of foreign currencies to the Reserve Bank in exchange for Australian dollars, which became a direct injection of funds into the domestic money supply.

Conversely, as rates of exchange were kept artificially high, this meant that the balance of payments was in deficit. Foreign currencies required to facilitate trade would be purchased from the Reserve Bank in exchange for Australian dollars. In this case, the transfer of Australian dollars out of the hands of the banks meant that liquid funds had been leaked from the domestic money supply.

The impact of imbalances in the balance of payments on the money supply is summarised in Table 19.4.

Table 19.4   **Relationship between fixed exchange rates, balance of payments and money supply**

EXCHANGE RATE OF $A	BALANCE OF PAYMENTS EFFECT	MONEY SUPPLY VOLUME
Under equilibrium	Surplus	Up
Above equilibrium	Deficit	Down

Since interest rates throughout the economy are determined within the financial or money market, such changes in the money supply will have a destabilising effect. Under this type of fixed (or managed) exchange rate system, it is clear that the external performance of the economy is a major factor influencing the level and variability of domestic interest rates.

One should emphasise that, while discretionary changes were made to the value of the Australian dollar in these fixed (managed) regimes in response to developing pressures, it was extremely difficult to calibrate the adjustments either rapidly enough or accurately enough to provide an effective buffer against the shocks.

The floating exchange rate system

The Hawke Government decided to act against the destabilising effect of the managed Australian dollar, and in December 1983 it introduced a freely operating **floating exchange rate** system. From this time, the exchange rate responded to the forces of demand and supply in the foreign exchange market. At the same time, most other exchange controls were removed.

Experts appreciate that the floating exchange rate regime that has been in place since 1983 is widely accepted as having been beneficial for Australia. Such a regime is particularly well suited for the Australian economy, given it is relatively small, reasonably open and subject to sizeable shifts in its **terms of trade**. The floating exchange rate has acted as a buffer to external shocks, particularly shifts in the terms of trade, allowing the economy to absorb them without generating the large inflationary or deflationary pressures that tended to result under the previous fixed exchange rate regimes.

Further, the floating exchange rate has contributed to the reduction in volatility of output that has occurred over the past two decades.

With the floating of the exchange rate, Australia's interconnections with overseas capital markets were globalised.

FACTORS DETERMINING THE DEMAND FOR AND SUPPLY OF AUSTRALIAN CURRENCY

We can view the foreign exchange market in the same light as a commodity market. We know that in any market, free of government intervention, price eventually rests at a point that will clear the market.

floating exchange rate *exchange rates for which the values are determined by the unimpeded forces of supply and demand*

terms of trade *the ratio of the price index of a nation's exports of goods and services to the price index of the nation's imports of goods and services*

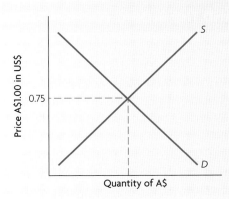

Figure 19.3
Supply and demand
for Australian dollars

Figure 19.3 represents the supply and demand for Australian dollars in exchange for US dollars in the foreign exchange market. The equilibrium price is set at US$0.75. (Therefore the exchange rate of the Australian dollar settled at A$1 = US$0.75; that is, our Australian dollar will buy 75 US cents.) At this price the supply of and demand for Australian dollars are equal.

The demand curve in Figure 19.3 is the demand for the Australian dollar by holders of US dollars. These include:

- Australian exporters of goods and services who have been paid in US dollars.
- Foreign investors wanting to purchase Australian dollars by payment in US dollars for either direct or portfolio investment in Australia (capital inflow).
- Speculators hoping to make a net gain on an Australian dollar appreciation or a depreciation in the US dollar.
- The Reserve Bank wanting to purchase Australian dollars with US dollars in order to force its value up against the US dollar.
- Tourists with US dollar funds requiring Australian dollars to spend in Australia.

The supply curve is the supply of Australian dollars by people who want to exchange them for US dollars. These include:

- Australian importers wanting to purchase US dollars to pay for foreign goods and services.
- Australian investors wishing to purchase US dollars to invest overseas (capital outflow).
- Speculators hoping to make a net gain on an appreciation of the US dollar or a depreciation of the Australian dollar against the US dollar.
- The Reserve Bank wanting to purchase US dollars to make payments on overseas debts or sell Australian dollars for US dollars in order to force down the value of the Australian dollar.
- Australians requiring US dollars for travel overseas.

The US dollar is the most important foreign currency for Australia's international business transactions. It is estimated that around 70 per cent of trade transactions between Australia and the rest of the world are settled in US dollars.

THE AUSSIE DOLLAR AND THE GLOBAL FOREIGN EXCHANGE MARKET

The Bank for International Settlements (BIS) based in Basel in Switzerland conducts every three years during the month of April a Survey of Foreign Exchange and Derivatives Market Activity. The objective of the survey is to provide the most comprehensive and internationally consistent information on the size and structure of global foreign exchange markets.

The 2010 triennial survey, in which 53 central banks and monetary authorities participated, found, among other things, that:

- Global foreign exchange market turnover was 20 per cent higher in April 2010 than in April 2007, with average daily turnover of $4 trillion compared to $3.3 trillion.
- The US dollar continued its slow decline from 89.9 per cent of global foreign exchange turnover in April 2001 to 84.9 per cent in April 2010 (out of 200%; this is because two currencies are involved in each transaction, the sum of the percentage shares of individual currencies totals 200% instead of 100%).
- The euro and the Japanese yen gained market share relative to April 2007.
- Among the 10 most actively traded currencies, the Australian and Canadian dollars both increased market share. The Australian dollar (Figure 19.4) increased its share in the global foreign exchange turnover from 3.0 per cent in 1998 to 7.6 per cent in April 2010, next to the US dollar (84.9%), the euro (39.1%), the Japanese yen (19%) and the British pound (12.9%). The New Zealand dollar experienced a slight drop in share over the most recent three-year period, but still gained position in the global foreign exchange turnover over the longer term.

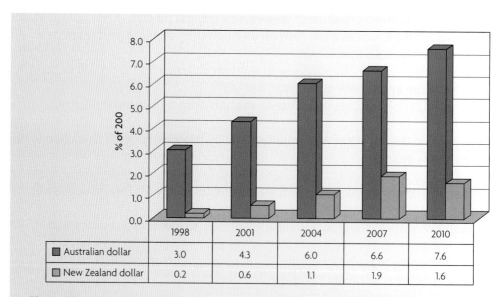

	1998	2001	2004	2007	2010
■ Australian dollar	3.0	4.3	6.0	6.6	7.6
□ New Zealand dollar	0.2	0.6	1.1	1.9	1.6

Figure 19.4

Shares of Australian dollar and New Zealand dollar in average April daily turnover of global foreign exchange, 1998, 2001, 2004, 2007, 2010 (%)

Source: Adapted from <www.bis.org/publ/rpfx10_tables.xls>, accessed 7 October 2010.

- In April 2010, Australia held seventh position among the world's major foreign exchange centres, with a daily turnover of US$192.1 billion (3.8% of global turnover), next to the following leading six foreign exchange centres: the United Kingdom (36.7%), the United States (18%), Japan (6%), Singapore (5%), Switzerland (5%) and Hong Kong SAR (5%).

As you are aware, the Australian dollar is traded vigorously throughout each business day. Since it was floated in December 1983, its value in terms of other currencies has been quite erratic, and its daily trading levels, for instance, over September 2008 and September 2010, have varied between a low of about $A143.6 billion in July 2009 and a high of $A230.4 billion in August 2010.

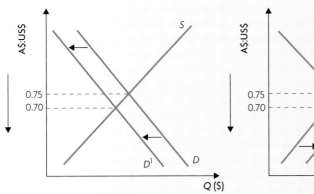

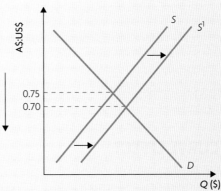

The *demand* for A$ has decreased (or shifted to the left). This may be due to:

- a decrease in the volume and value of exports leaving our shores
- a decrease in the flow of capital investment into the country
- a decrease in the number of A$ purchased by speculators because they expect it to fall in value
- a fall in the number of A$ purchased by the Reserve Bank
- a reduction in the number of A$ required by tourists visiting Australia.

The *supply* of A$ has increased (or shifted to the right). This may be due to:

- an increase in the volume and value of imports landed in Australia
- an increase in the flow of capital investment out of the country
- an increase in the number of A$ surrendered by speculators who expect it to fall in value
- a rise in the number of A$ being sold off by the Reserve Bank
- an increase in the amounts of foreign currencies required by Australian tourists going abroad.

Figure 19.5
The market for Australian dollars

LINKS BETWEEN THE EXCHANGE RATES AND THE BALANCE OF PAYMENTS

Economic analysis indicates that there is an important link between the balance of payments and the quantity of Australian dollars demanded or supplied. At any given level of the equilibrium price for the Australian dollar, the quantity of Australian dollars supplied to the market matches that taken off the market. As emphasised in Table 19.5 overleaf, the demand for Australian dollars comprises the total of all the credit components of our balance of payments. The supply of Australian dollars comprises the total of all debit components.

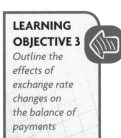

LEARNING OBJECTIVE 3
Outline the effects of exchange rate changes on the balance of payments

Table 19.5   **Australian dollar market: Major components of supply and demand**

SUPPLY OF AUSTRALIAN DOLLARS		DEMAND FOR AUSTRALIAN DOLLARS
Comprises all balance of payment **debit entries** e.g.		Comprises all balance of payment **credit entries** e.g.
Imports (goods)	=	Exports (goods)
Imports (services)		Exports (services)
Australian foreign investment abroad		Foreign investment in Australia

The effect of a floating exchange rate depends on the direction in which it moves. A wildly fluctuating exchange rate in the short term causes uncertainty and caution among money-market dealers, and can make foreign investors reluctant to risk their funds, thus reducing capital inflow. A depreciation can affect the balance of payments in several ways:

- the J-curve effect on the balance of trade
- effect on receipts for exports
- effect on domestic prices
- effect on foreign debt.

THE J-CURVE EFFECT

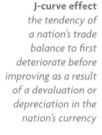

J-curve effect
the tendency of a nation's trade balance to first deteriorate before improving as a result of a devaluation or depreciation in the nation's currency

According to the **J-curve effect**, a depreciation has the immediate effect of raising the Australian dollar price of imports and lowering the price of exports to overseas buyers. The short-term effect on the balance of trade will be an increase in the deficit. But in the medium to long term, if the demand for imports and exports is reasonably price-elastic, the lower price for our exports will make them more competitive and encourage overseas buyers to increase their purchases; and the higher price for imports will discourage domestic consumers from buying them and cause them to turn to Australian products.

The result then should be a reduction (i.e. an improvement) in the balance of trade. All this is simply saying that when the depreciation occurs, the balance of trade will get worse before it gets better. This is known as the J-curve effect, illustrated in Figure 19.6.

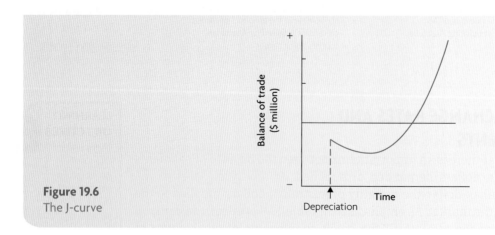

Figure 19.6
The J-curve

The J-curve analysis was first used in the United Kingdom in the mid 1960s and later in the United States and other countries. During the 1987 Australian federal election campaign, the then Treasurer, Paul Keating, claimed that the J-curve effect was at work and that the 'big gaps in the trade accounts have begun to close'.

The reality was different and still is different over 20 years later. The reasons we did not see the great structural transformation suggested by the J-curve proponents are threefold:

- Australia's narrow industrial base and the lack of a wide range of interdependent industries (as in the United States)
- Australia's dependence on imported machinery, equipment and producers' inputs—depreciation of the Australian dollar caused steep rises in the cost of these items
- Australia's higher interest rates and wage costs, relative to our competitors.

Experience suggests that further depreciation of the Australian dollar will not guarantee significant structural change and overall can be quite damaging to the manufacturing sector (see Link to International Economy, p. 400).

Effect on receipts for exports

A depreciation has the beneficial effect of immediately increasing the receipts for exports which have been negotiated in foreign currencies, and this helps to counteract the effect of lower prices for exports that have been paid for with Australian dollars. So, on the whole, exporters tend to benefit from a depreciation.

Effect on domestic prices

Higher import prices caused by the depreciation may be passed on in higher wages (through wage indexation to the consumer price index, which includes import prices). In this case, the costs for export producers will rise, and they may have to pass on the higher wages in inflated prices. In the long term, this could counteract the beneficial effect of the depreciation on the competitiveness of our exports.

As a higher inflation rate has other harmful effects on the economy, the inflationary impact on domestic prices is regarded as the most undesirable effect of depreciation.

Effect on foreign debt

As well as increasing the value of our foreign debt, a depreciating exchange rate adds to the Australian dollar cost of interest charges on overseas borrowings. Thus, it worsens the current account deficit in the short term and adds to the downward slope of the J-curve.

An appreciation of the exchange rate has the opposite effect to a depreciation. An appreciation is beneficial in counteracting domestic inflation and curtailing the size of the foreign debt. But it could cause a widening of the current account deficit in the medium to long term—the J-curve in reverse.

In the final section of this chapter we will overview the major factors which influence the demand for and the supply of Australian dollars.

FACTORS AFFECTING THE DEMAND FOR AUSTRALIAN DOLLARS

(1) THE DEMAND FOR AUSTRALIAN EXPORTS

When Australian goods and services are bought by overseas consumers, Australian exporters being paid in foreign currencies (mainly US dollars) need to convert their foreign currency proceeds into Australian dollars. This is because most of Australian exporters' costs (e.g. salaries for their employees, payments to Australian suppliers, bank repayments, government taxes) have to be paid in Australian dollars. Therefore, any increase in the demand for Australian exports should increase the demand for Australian dollars and the value of the Australian dollar.

In graphical terms, the demand curve of the Australian dollar will shift to the right, which will increase both its price and quantity demanded on the foreign exchange market.

The reverse happens when the demand for Australian exports declines. For instance, the events in the United States on 11 September 2001 reduced the number of tourists coming to Australia, and consequently, the demand for Australian dollars.

(2) CHANGES IN WORLD ECONOMIC CONDITIONS

The Australian dollar is used by international investors and currency traders as a proxy for commodity prices and world growth. What this means is that if prospects for global economic growth are good and commodity prices rise internationally, currency traders and investors purchase Australian dollars. However, the economic recession in 2001–02 reduced the demand for Australian commodities from our major trading partners with the Australian dollar reaching lows of $US0.48 in March 2001, and $US0.49 in September 2001. In periods of crisis, investors and currency traders tend to sell Australian dollars and purchase currencies and/or securities nominated in currencies perceived as 'safer' (e.g. the US dollar, the euro).

(3) RELATIVE INTEREST RATES AND CAPITAL INFLOW

Foreign investors wishing to invest in Australia must exchange their own currency for Australian dollars. A number of factors may influence their investment decisions. For example, if Australian interest rates are relatively higher compared with overseas interest rates this will increase capital inflow (especially portfolio investment) and the demand for Australian dollars. Table 19.6 indicates that Australia's benchmark interest rate (RBA's cash rate) in October 2010 was higher than comparative interest rates in all major economies.

The interest rate differential generated an increase in demand for Australian dollars (D^1 in Figure 19.7), with an increase in the equilibrium exchange rate to E^1. At the same time, Australian investors and businesses would be likely to keep their surplus funds in banks and instruments in Australia, rather than in the United States or other major economies with the lower rate of return. With fewer Australian dollars being placed overseas, there would be a reduction in the supply of Australian dollars in the foreign exchange market (S^1 in Figure 19.7) and the Australian dollar will be further pushed up to E^2.

The higher interest rates in Australia were a major factor in the appreciation of the Australian dollar in the fourth term of 2010, with the Australian dollar reaching parity with the US dollar on 23 December 2010.

Table 19.6   **Comparative benchmark interest rates in Australia and other selected economies, October 2010, per cent**

ECONOMY	BENCHMARK INTEREST RATE (%)
Australia	4.50
New Zealand	3.00
Euro area	1.00
United Kingdom	0.50
United States	0.25
Switzerland	0.25
Japan	0.10

Source: Trading Economics, <www.tradingeconomics.com>, accessed 10 October 2010.

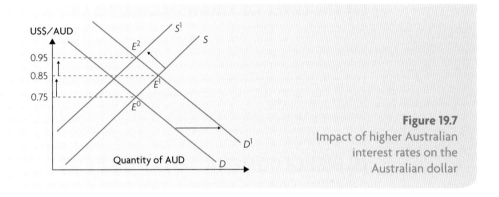

Figure 19.7
Impact of higher Australian interest rates on the Australian dollar

The expectation of higher levels of domestic economic growth will also influence the size of the capital inflow and increase the demand for Australian dollars, causing a currency appreciation. On the other hand, a decline in the level of capital inflow may cause a fall in the demand for Australian dollars, resulting in a currency depreciation.

(4) SPECULATION

Speculation occurs when currencies are bought and sold by foreign investors for the purpose of making a profit. If currency speculators expect the value of the Australian dollar to increase in the future ('bull speculators'), they may sell other currencies and buy Australian dollars. This would increase the demand for Australian dollars and put upward pressure on the exchange rate.

Interestingly, it is estimated that around 98 per cent of all global foreign exchange transactions are for speculative purposes only.

(5) LOWER INFLATION AND INTERNATIONAL COMPETITIVENESS

To be competitive in the global market, Australia's goods and services must be as cheap as or cheaper than those of its international competitors. If Australia's inflation rates and costs are higher than those of its overseas competitors, Australian goods will be more expensive and less competitive internationally. High Australian inflation rates will cause a loss of export markets, reduce demand for Australian dollars, and force a depreciation of the Australian dollar.

On the other hand, lower rates of inflation typically increase the demand for Australian exports, and appreciate the value of the Australian dollar.

FACTORS AFFECTING THE SUPPLY OF AUSTRALIAN DOLLARS

(1) DEMAND FOR IMPORTS

Just as foreigners must pay for Australian exports with Australian dollars, Australian importers must pay overseas producers foreign currency for imported goods. If Australian demand for imported goods and services increases, so does the supply of Australian dollars. The increase in supply of Australian dollars puts downward pressure on the value of the Australian dollar.

(2) THE LEVEL OF FINANCIAL FLOWS OUT OF AUSTRALIA

An increase in financial outflows can occur as a result of higher interest repayments on overseas loans (primary income) or increased demand for foreign assets, such as company shares, bonds and real estate by Australian residents.

This means that investors need to sell Australian dollars (increasing supply) in the forex markets to obtain other countries' currencies. The increase in the supply of Australian dollars could cause a decrease (depreciation) in the value of the Australian dollar.

(3) HIGHER DOMESTIC INFLATION RATES

If there were high rates of inflation in Australia, imported goods and services would be cheaper relative to domestically produced products. As consumers subsequently purchase increasing amounts of imported goods and services, the supply of Australian dollars in the forex market would increase, causing a decrease or depreciation in the value of the Australian dollar.

(4) SPECULATION

If speculators lose confidence in the economy and feel that future values of the Australian dollar will be lower than present levels, they will sell the Australian dollar ('bear speculators'). Ceteris paribus, a depreciation of the Australian exchange rate will occur. This is because when speculators sell Australian currency to avoid future losses, the supply of dollars increases, putting downward pressure on the exchange rate.

(5) CURRENT ACCOUNT DEFICIT

Australia's chronic current account deficit offers a strong intuitive explanation of movements in the exchange rate in certain circumstances. All other things being equal, episodes of weaknesses in the Australian dollar can be explained by the growing current account deficit (which basically means an increased supply of Australian dollars on the foreign exchange market with a depressing impact on its value). However, as in the real economy all other things (e.g. interest rates) do not stay the same, the net impact of various factors can contribute to a strong Australian dollar.

ON *REVIENT TOUJOURS*, OR CURRENCY WARS REVISITED

LINK TO INTERNATIONAL ECONOMY

One well-documented feature of the Great Depression of the 1930s was the trade wars between the big economic powers, including the introduction of high tariff barriers and competitive currency devaluations. Historical accounts indict the devaluations of the 1930s for worsening the Great Depression.

The Bretton Woods system, established after World War II to serve the process of trade liberalisation, established that devaluations were not to be used for competitive purposes, and a country could not devalue the currency by more than 10 per cent without IMF approval.

A major 51 per cent decline in the exchange rate value of the US dollar took place from 1985 to 1987. However this was the result engineered through the 1985 Plaza Accord between France, West Germany, Japan, the United States and the United Kingdom to depreciate the US dollar and to rebalance the world economy.

In 2010, 25 years after the Plaza Accord, the currency situation was different, because, according to a *Financial Times* count, some 25 countries have unilaterally intervened or planned intervention in the foreign exchange market in order to gain a trade advantage.

The 2010 'currency wars' seem to be an extension of the global financial crisis, but can very well reignite and prolong the crisis for some years to come.

A prominent currency dispute is that between the United States and China. The United States has accused China for many years of refusing to allow its renminbi to rise quickly, allegedly distorting trade flows. The United States Administration announced plans for 'quantitative easing' (in effect, printing dollars) and introduced legislation meant to treat the Chinese management of the renminbi as an export subsidy requiring United States countervailing duties against Chinese exports. The Chinese claimed that the biggest distortion was deriving from the rich economies' failed economic policies. China does not want to make the mistake Japan made in 1985 in accepting the Plaza Accord, which led to a soaring yen, from which Japan has yet to recover.

Actually, Japan has suffered the greatest damage from recent cheap currencies policies in the major economies of the world, as investors and speculators have shifted from dollar and euro-denominated investments to the yen, driving up the yen's exchange rate to record levels. In response, in October 2010, Japan unilaterally intervened in currency markets to drive down the exchange rate of the yen by selling an estimated 1 trillion yen (worth some US$20 billion), which was a breach of a tacit agreement among the established industrial powers to avoid unilateral currency moves.

Given that the exchange rate between the Chinese and American currencies moved very little, other emerging markets in South East Asia and Latin America had to bear the brunt as the US dollar adjusted elsewhere. Countries like Brazil, Mexico, Indonesia, Thailand—as well as developed but fast-growing economies such as Australia and South Korea—faced unpleasantly large appreciation pressures. These have placed a heavy burden on their export and import-competing sectors, principally agriculture and manufacturing.

Certainly, the global economy needs a new Plaza Agreement. However, there are no signs that a genuine G20 deal could replicate anywhere near the G5 arrangement of 25 years ago. Notwithstanding that, *Financial Times* analysts have already advanced a suggestion about the location of any new major international currency deal: 'given where power now resides, the Plaza is no longer the appropriate place for talks. The 93rd floor of the Park Hyatt Shanghai, the world's tallest hotel, would be much more fitting.'

SUMMARY

1. International trade has a monetary aspect because trade between nations requires the exchange of one nation's currency for that of another. A nation's exports of goods, services and financial obligations give rise to a demand for its currency and a supply of foreign currency in the foreign exchange market.

2. The exchange rates appreciate when the price of the Australian dollar goes up and depreciate when the price falls.

3. The Asian financial crisis of the late 1990s generally caused a depreciation of the Australian dollar in relation to the US dollar, Western European currencies and the Japanese yen. At the same time, the Australian dollar appreciated in relation to most East Asian currencies, which has caused a temporary shift of Australian exports from developing East Asian countries to industrialised economies in Western Europe and North America. During the recent global financial crisis, the Australian dollar has depreciated first, helping exports, but has appreciated again with economic recovery on the back of higher interest rates and demand from Asia for Australian commodities.

4. The major factors influencing the demand for Australian dollars are: demand for Australian exports; prospects for world economic growth; relative interest rates and financial inflows; 'bull' speculators; level of inflation; and international competitiveness.

5. The major factors influencing the supply of Australian dollars are: demand for imports; level of Australian financial outflows; higher relative inflation; 'bear' speculators; and chronic current account deficit.

KEY TERMS

currency appreciation	399	floating exchange rate	402
currency depreciation	398	J-curve effect	406
exchange rate	395	managed float	401
fixed exchange rates	401	terms of trade	402

REFERENCES

1. The Organisation for Economic Cooperation and Development (OECD) was founded in 1961. Its Paris headquarters provides a forum where its 33 industrialised member nations—as at September 2010—(including Australia) can share information on their domestic economies and consult on approaches to international economic issues.

REVIEW QUESTIONS

1. Outline the stages of change in Australia's exchange rate determination method.

2. Explain why domestic money supply is unaffected under a floating exchange rate.

3. Outline the relationship between the exchange rate and the current account balance.

4. Explain the operation of the J-curve effect.

5. Summarise the major factors which influence the demand for Australian dollars.

6. Outline the major factors for the supply of Australian dollars.

APPLIED QUESTIONS AND EXERCISES

1. In an export sale from Australia to Japan with payment in US dollars, in which currency is the final payment to the Australian exporter made? Why?

2. 'At present it is estimated that about 70 per cent of export contracts and 50 per cent of import contracts are written in US dollar terms. Given these proportions and the general improvement in the Australian exchange rate against the US dollar ... it is reasonable to conclude that only some of the growth in the terms of trade in recent years is attributable to the rising exchange rate.' Do you agree with this statement? Why or why not?

3. In which item of Australia's balance of payments are the RBA's foreign currency holdings recorded?

4. According to RBA monthly data, during 2003 the Australian dollar appreciated against the US dollar from US$0.5884 in January to US$0.7046 in October. Over the same period, Australia's target cash rate was steady at 4.75 per cent per annum. At the same time, the RBA provided the following information about overseas

official interest rates in other industrialised economies (Table 19.7):

Table 19.7: Official interest rates in industrialised countries, 2003

ECONOMY	JANUARY 2003 (% P.A.)	JUNE 2003 (% P.A.)	OCTOBER 2003 (% P.A.)
United States	1.25	1.00	1.00
Canada	2.75	3.25	2.75
United Kingdom	4.00	3.75	3.50
Euro area	2.75	2.00	2.00
Japan	0.00	0.00	0.00

The RBA also indicated that the monthly index of commodity prices in US dollars, after a slight decline in the first quarter of 2003, steadily increased from 106.5 in April 2003 to 115.2 in October 2003 (with a base year of 2001–02 = 100). Examining the above developments, discuss the main demand/supply factors that may explain the appreciation of the Australian dollar against the US dollar during 2003.

5. Discuss the likely effects of the depreciation of the Japanese yen on Australia's economy (e.g. Australia–Japan trade in goods and services, foreign direct investment).

6. Over the 12 months to the 6 February 2002, the exchange rates of six economies against the US dollar recorded the following fluctuations (Table 19.8):

Table 19.8: Movements against the US$ (6 February 2001–6 February 2002)

NATIONAL CURRENCY	+/–% CHANGE
Australia dollar	–7.1
Japan yen	–13.4
Malaysia ringgit	0.0
Hong Kong dollar	0.0
Singapore dollar	–4.4
China renminbi	1.1

All other things being equal, what are the likely effects of the above currency movements on the following international business transactions, assuming that all transactions involved have taken place in US dollars? For each question, insert one of the following in the table below:

(+) for increase
(–) for decrease or
(=) for no change.

INTERNATIONAL BUSINESS INDICATORS	CHANGE + / – / =
(a) Australian exports to Japan	
(b) United States exports to Australia and Japan	
(c) Australian dollar returns from old Australian direct investment in Malaysia	
(d) Car parts exports from Japan to Malaysia and Singapore	
(e) New United States investment in Malaysia and Hong Kong	
(f) Numbers of Japanese tourists to Malaysia	
(g) Enrolments of Chinese students in Australian universities	
(h) The ringgit size of Malaysia's foreign debt denominated in yen	
(i) Exports from Malaysia to Hong Kong	
(j) Malaysian exports to Japan and Australia	

7. Assuming ceteris paribus, how will the following developments in the world economy impact on Australia's terms of trade? Circle **F** for favourable and **U** for unfavourable.

ECONOMIC DEVELOPMENTS	TERMS OF TRADE (F/U)
(a) A drought in North America causes a worldwide grain shortage.	F/U
(b) A major increase in the crude oil price increases the price of manufactured goods worldwide.	F/U

continued ↘

continued

ECONOMIC DEVELOPMENTS	TERMS OF TRADE (F/U)
(c) A recession in Japan, Western Europe and the United States.	F/U
(d) The United States and the European Union escalate their export subsidy war in the farm sector.	F/U
(e) Strong growth in the United States strengthens the US dollar.	F/U
(f) Following the Asian financial crisis, the Australian dollar appreciates against most East Asian currencies.	F/U

8. Using RBA data over the last six months, examine the position of the Australian dollar against the euro and assess the likely short-term future of Australia's trade in manufactures with Western European countries.
9. Outline two major effects on Australian manufacturing from the depreciation of most East Asian currencies.
10. True or False questions:
   (a) The forex market is used by Australian firms for the purchase of foreign currencies to pay for imports of goods and services and for physical and financial assets overseas. True or False?
   (b) Japanese tourists in Australia generate a supply of Australian dollars. True or False?
   (c) The trade weighted index measures the Australian dollar against Australia's main trading partners. True or False?
   (d) Relatively higher Australian interest rates contribute to a greater supply of Australian dollars. True or False?
   (e) A higher inflation rate in Australia compared to that of partner economies will stimulate Australian exports. True or False?
   (f) 'Bull' speculators will sell the Australian dollar when they expect a deterioration of Australian economic conditions. True or False?
   (g) When business confidence in the Australian economy declines, the increased financial outflows will increase the value of the Australian dollar compared to other currencies. True or False?
   (h) The Australian dollar was floated during the Asian financial crisis of 1998. True or False?
   (i) According to the J-curve effect, a depreciation has the immediate effect of raising the Australian dollar price of imports and lowering the price of exports to overseas buyers. True or False?
   (j) In April 2010, the Australian dollar was the fifth most traded currency in the global economy. True or False?

8

ECONOMIC POLICIES

Chapter 20

Structural change

LEARNING OBJECTIVES

After studying this chapter, you will be able to:

1. define the meaning of structural change and related concepts such as microeconomic policy, structural reforms and non-structural reforms
2. explain the reasons for the process of structural change in Australia and around the world
3. review the process of structural change occurring in the Australian economy since the early 1970s
4. examine the main changes undertaken in Australian manufacturing and the prospects for this economic sector
5. examine microeconomic reform in the telecommunications sector
6. outline the performance of government business enterprises in the context of the process of corporatisation and privatisation.

INTRODUCTION

In an increasingly interdependent world, the walls (represented by barriers such as import tariffs, quotas, standards and capital controls) that historically have separated national economies are being broken down, so national economies are merging into a single, global economy. Developments in telecommunications, computers and transport have slashed the cost and increased the ease and speed with which information, people and goods can move between countries.

The process of globalisation is far from complete, and structural changes in individual national economies vary in timing, speed and magnitude. Australia, like most developed economies, has reacted to the globalisation of international markets by deregulating various industries, abandoning foreign-exchange controls and other controls, and floating its currency.

During the 1980s and early 1990s, structural or microeconomic reform as a policy issue increased steadily in importance in Australia, to the extent that it is now regarded as the major long-term issue facing the country. It is considered that the performance of the Australian economy is lacking, and that the poor performance of many individual industries and markets has contributed to this.

This chapter will examine the main structural changes that have occurred in Australia during the last two decades, the reasons for such changes, and the prospects of structural reform in the Australian economy, with emphasis on the manufacturing sector.

STRUCTURAL CHANGE AND RELATED CONCEPTS

LEARNING OBJECTIVE 1
Define the meaning of structural change and related concepts such as microeconomic policy, structural reforms and non-structural reforms

Economic history, especially after World War II, shows that nations tend to develop through an initial expansion in manufacturing relative to primary industries, followed by an increase in the size of the service sector compared with both the primary and the manufacturing sectors.

The broad transition in the structure of production in various countries is illustrated in Table 20.1 overleaf.

Obviously, economic transformation throughout the world is more complex than this broad picture, with changes occurring within each sector and a higher level of specialisation contributing to a growing intra-industry trade, that is, trade in the same industry (e.g. Australia exports cars and car components and imports the same).

Structural change involves a shift in the pattern of production in the economy resulting in an improvement in the overall level of output and productivity. Structural change is producing sunrise industries (new, expanding industries) in the areas of electronics, computers, medicine and biology, as well as new service industries, especially in connection with finance, communication, recreation and community services.

Structural change also includes the decline of industries that are inappropriate and by world standards inefficient—these are known as sunset industries (old, declining industries). Overall, structural change should mean a more effective and more productive workforce. Structural change can be market-induced, caused by changes in consumption patterns,

structural change
when a shift in the pattern of production in the economy results in an improvement in the overall level of output and productivity

Table 20.1   **Structure of production in selected countries, 1965 and 2008 (%) GDP[a] distribution by sector**

COUNTRY	US$ BILLION		AGRICULTURE		INDUSTRY		MANUFACTURING[b]		SERVICES ETC.	
	1965	2008	1965	2008	1965	2008	1965	2008	1965	2008
Australia	24	1015	9	4	39	29	26	10	51	68
Japan	91	4911	10	1	44	29	34	21	46	69
Denmark	10	341	9	1	36	26	23	15	55	73
Austria	10	413	9	2	46	31	33	20	45	67
Finland	8	277	16	3	37	32	23	24	47	65
China[c]	202	4326	30	11	49	49	41	34	21	40
Hong Kong	2	215	2	0	40	8	24	3	58	92
Singapore	1	182	3	0	24	28	15	21	74	72
Republic of Korea	3	929	38	3	25	37	18	28	37	60

(a) GDP and its components are at purchaser values, unless stated otherwise.
(b) Because manufacturing is generally the most dynamic part of the industrial sector, its share of GDP is shown separately.
(c) GDP is calculated at producer prices.

Source: Compiled from World Bank, World Development Report, 1992 and 2010.

technological changes or demographic factors; or government-induced, caused by industry regulations in the areas of import protection, export assistance, and training and retraining of the workforce.

structural policy (microeconomic policy)
includes those measures taken at the microeconomic level to make the economy perform better in terms of creating real income from the available inputs

Structural policy—or microeconomic policy, as it is also called—includes those measures taken at the microeconomic level to make the economy perform better in terms of creating real income from the available inputs. Improving the efficiency of the economy will enable it to grow faster than it would otherwise. The ultimate aim of structural change is to improve living standards in Australia.

Microeconomic policy can act as a useful supplement to traditional macroeconomic policies (as explained throughout Part 8) by removing impediments to the mobility of resources and fostering genuine efficiency and international competitiveness of Australian exports.

STRUCTURAL REFORMS

Among economists there is a fair degree of agreement as to what microeconomic reform might consist of, in terms of achieving better pricing and investment decisions and more efficient production. There is less agreement about the framework within which these might be achieved. In this respect, a distinction is made between structural and non-structural reforms.

structural reforms
those changes to the environment of decision making that induce decisions leading to greater efficiency

According to Peter Forsyth,[1] **structural reforms** are those changes to the environment of decision making that induce decisions leading to greater efficiency.

There are two broad types of structural reform:

• changes to the regulatory or competitive environment external to the firm
• changes to incentives within the enterprise.

Changes to the regulatory environment

Changes to the regulatory environment include changes to:

- the amount of competition allowed in a market
- levels of tariffs and quotas
- regulation of prices or rates of return
- what is not allowed under competition policy
- Commonwealth–state relationships.

For example, increased competition for Telstra has increased pressure for it to work and price efficiently, and lower tariffs induce domestic producers to produce and sell more efficiently or yield their market to imports.

Changes to incentives

Changes to the incentives within enterprises come about through privatisation, or genuine corporatisation, whereby managerial rewards are dependent on actual measured performance. Incentive changes make the firm behave differently of its own accord, for example to lessen costs and/or to raise its prices and profits.

The advantage of structural reforms is that, if they are appropriately designed, they automatically provide pressure for efficiency once in place. Governments do not need to undertake continual reforms.

NON-STRUCTURAL REFORMS

Non-structural reforms are those that do not alter the decision-making environment or incentives.

There are many examples, such as efficiency drives in the railways or water authorities, plans to reduce manning levels on ships or the waterfront, industry plans for motor vehicles and textiles (there are structural elements in these), and changes to road funding and charging formulas. These can all be genuine reforms that increase efficiency; but they do not provide sustained pressure or incentives for efficiency. The reforms tend not to last long. Non-structural reforms can be easier to impose than structural reforms, because they do not expose firms and their workforces to the unpredictability of a new environment.

non-structural reforms
those that do not alter the decision-making environment or incentives

REASONS FOR STRUCTURAL CHANGES

LEARNING OBJECTIVE 2
Explain the reasons for the process of structural change in Australia and around the world

Among the main reasons establishing the need for structural change we can mention:

- technological change
- overall economic performance
- information and analysis
- international factors.

TECHNOLOGICAL CHANGE

technological change
the introduction of new technologies, resulting in changes to production techniques and the development of new products

Technological change results in new ways of making things and the development of new products.

Such change can alter the nature of an industry, making it difficult to maintain either large or small productive units, and breaking down the differences between industries. Two (now closely related) industries where technological change has taken place are banking and telecommunications. It has been difficult to maintain the old regulatory structure in the presence of new technology. The response has been full or partial deregulation in Australia, as in the United States, the United Kingdom and New Zealand. Advances in transport and communications have enhanced the efficiency of international markets, reduced consumer prices and increased international competition.

The introduction of new technology puts out of work those whose skills, training, education and previous experience have been made irrelevant, contributing to so-called 'structural unemployment'.

At the same time, new technology threatens businesses: technology is often expensive and it causes traditional areas of production to become obsolete as fashions and substitutes evolve. Consequently, firms and industries that fail or are unable to adapt and make structural changes can collapse, often causing severe hardship for towns and local communities.

Of course, the introduction of technology may have a positive impact on employment in other areas.

OVERALL ECONOMIC PERFORMANCE

Another reason for structural reform is change in overall economic performance. There is no doubt that Australia showed an improved economic performance after the recession of 1990 to 1992, achieving relatively high economic growth combined with low inflation.

As discussed in previous chapters, the Australian economy has shown more resilience than other major economies in the context of the global financial crisis.

Nonetheless, a comparative analysis of Australia's performance indicates that several areas require further improvement. Let's illustrate with a few economic indicators.

GDP per head

In 2009, Australia was ranked 12th among the IMF's 33 advanced economies in terms of the level of real GDP per head, down from the third ranking in the world in the early 1950s.

Previous OECD data indicated that during the period 1965 to 1990, Australia's GDP per head increased at an annual average rate of 1.9 per cent per annum, while the corresponding rate for the OECD as a group was 2.4 per cent.

The main causes of the widening gap between Australia and the United States were a relatively poor productivity performance through the 1950s and 1960s, indeed, one of the worst in the OECD, and a relatively poor participation to the workforce performance in the 1970s and 1980s.

However, Table 20.2 suggests that the growth in Australia's GDP per head from 1990 to 2009 has outpaced that of the major industrialised countries mainly through improved productivity growth and reasonable participation growth.

Labour productivity

Another aspect of Australia's poor economic performance over the last few decades is the slow growth in labour productivity. Table 20.3 presents comparative labour productivity indicators in selected OECD countries.

Table 20.2   **Comparative GDP per head level (2009) and GDP per head growth trend rates, selected advanced economies, 1980–89, 1990–99, 2000–09 (per cent per annum)**

ECONOMY	GDP PER HEAD (US DOLLARS)	GROWTH TREND RATES (% P.A.)		
		1980–89	1990–99	2000–09
Australia	45 587	1.9	2.6	1.8
Canada	39 669	2.2	1.8	1.1
Denmark	56 115	2.6	2.3	0.8
France	42 747	1.7	1.3	0.8
Germany	40 875	2.0	1.3	1.0
Japan	39 731	3.1	0.8	1.0
New Zealand	27 259	1.2	1.9	1.3
United Kingdom	35 334	3.1	2.4	1.4
United States	46 381	2.7	2.2	1.1

Source: Adapted from IMF data in Economic Outlook, April 2010, <www.imf.org/external/pubs/ft/weo/2010/01/weodata/index.aspx>, accessed 11 November 2010.

In the OECD Productivity Database, labour productivity has only one definition: labour productivity per hour. This is calculated as gross domestic product per hour worked. GDP refers to real GDP in US dollars, constant purchasing power parities (PPPs).

Table 20.3(A) presents 'levels' of productivity related to the United States (US = 100). Despite recent increases in productivity in Australia, its level in 2008 (US$44.5/hour worked) was only

Table 20.3   **Comparative labour productivity indicators, GDP per hour worked and annual labour productivity growth**

	A. GDP (PPP)[1] PER HOUR WORKED		B. LABOUR PRODUCTIVITY AVERAGE ANNUAL % RATE CHANGES	
	US $/HOUR	AS A % OF US (US = 100)	2000–04 (% P.A.)	2005–08 (% P.A.)
Australia	44.5	80.5	1.6	0.9
Canada	43.2	78.2	1.2	1.2
Denmark	43.6	78.8	1.3	1.0
France	53.2	96.2	1.9	−0.5
Germany	50.5	91.4	1.5	0.8
Japan	38.3	69.3	2.3	1.3
New Zealand	30.5	55.1	2.4	1.5
United Kingdom	44.9	81.2	2.4	1.5
Euro zone	46.5	84	1.3	1.0
United States	55.3	100	2.7	1.6

[1]*PPP is purchasing power parity; an international dollar has the same purchasing power over GDP as US$X.*

Source: Adapted from OECD. Statistics, <http://stats.oecd.org/Index.aspx?DataSetCode=PDYGTH>, data extracted 30 July 2010.

80.5 per cent of that of the United States, and lower than that of advanced economies such as France, Germany, the United Kingdom, and of the Euro zone as a whole.

In 2008, Australia's overall rank for this indicator, among OECD member countries, was 13th.

Table 20.3(B) presents average annual rates of change of labour productivity over two recent periods, with Australia showing a modest performance, especially in the second period. The OECD database shows that Australia's rank among some 32 OECD member countries for this indicator was 18th over 2000–04 and only 27th over 2005–08.

It is believed that structural change and microeconomic reform in the Australian economy will enable ongoing efficiencies to be introduced, both to bridge the existing gaps and to match further advances in world best practice. Improved productivity is a major objective of microeconomic reform because, as we know, productivity increases represent the main source of continued rises in living standards.

External sector performance

As explained in Part 7 and later in Chapter 24, another aspect of Australia's poor economic performance over the last two decades is its difficulties in the international business sector.

Australia has traditionally relied on export markets for primary products (minerals and farm products), which are inelastic in both price and income. They experience large fluctuations in price in response to changes in demand and supply. Also, Australia's export mix is dominated by resource-processing industries, which are themselves influenced by fluctuating commodity prices.

At the same time, Australia's imports are dominated by manufactured goods (especially machinery and equipment), whose prices are generally trending upwards. The unstable balance of merchandise trade, combined with steady deficits in net primary income (mainly interest paid on foreign investment), result in worsening current account deficits and growing foreign debt (for details see Chapter 18).

In 2007, Australia's current account deficit (CAD) accounted for a record 6.1 per cent of GDP, which was a higher ratio than that for the much-debated United States deficit and smaller than that of only three other OECD members (Greece, Iceland and Spain).

It is generally acknowledged that the main contributor to the chronic deficit of our current account is the net primary income deficit. It reflects the poor savings levels in our economy and a continuous need for foreign investment, resulting in a fast growth of foreign ownership of Australian industries and increasing indebtedness to foreign lenders.

Microeconomic reform is expected to complement macroeconomic policies (e.g. fiscal, monetary, income and external policies) in encouraging a higher level of savings in Australia and in making the Australian economy more competitive internationally.

Australia's national competitiveness rankings

A thorough analysis of Australia's competitiveness on a global scale is carried out by the World Economic Forum (WEF) in its annual *Global Competitiveness Report* (GCR). The fundamental objective of the GCR is to evaluate the economic competitiveness of a large sample of countries (133 in 2009–10).

The first report was released in 1979. The 2009–10 report covers 133 major and emerging economies.

The *Global Competitiveness Report*'s competitiveness ranking is based on the global competitiveness index (GCI), developed for the World Economic Forum by Sala-i-Martin and introduced in 2004.

The report contains a detailed profile for each of the 133 economies featured in the study, providing a comprehensive summary of the overall position in the rankings as well as the most prominent competitive advantages and disadvantages of each country/economy based on the analysis used in computing the rankings. Also included is an extensive section of data tables with global rankings for over 110 indicators.

According to the report, in 2009–10, the leading economy in the world on the overall CGI was Switzerland. Australia was ranked overall 15th in the world ahead of France and Austria, up from 18 in 2008–09. (Note that in 2003, in the previous index format, Australia was ranked 10th in the world ahead of advanced economies such as those of Japan, Germany and the United Kingdom.)

The 2009–10 GCI is subdivided into three sub-indexes and 12 pillars of competitiveness, providing a comprehensive picture of the competitiveness landscape in countries around the world at all stages of development.

The three CGI sub-indexes, corresponding to progressive levels of development, include:

a) basic requirements
b) efficiency enhancers
c) innovation and sophistication factors.

Table 20.4   **Global Competitiveness Index 2009–10: Summary of Australia's overall performance and in the main sub-indexes and pillars compared to the top country performance in each category**

OVERALL CGI/SUB-INDEXES/ PILLARS	AUSTRALIA'S CGI PERFORMANCE		THE LEADING INTERNATIONAL PERFORMANCE ON THE CGI	
	RANK	SCORE	COUNTRY	SCORE
Overall CGI	15	5.15	Switzerland	5.60
A. Basic requirements	14	5.63	Finland	6.04
1. Institutions	12	5.60	Singapore	5.99
2. Infrastructure	25	5.19	Germany	6.59
3. Macroeconomic stability	18	5.56	Brunei Darussalam	6.64
4. Health and primary education	16	6.18	Finland	6.46
B. Efficiency enhancers	9	5.29	United States	5.66
5. Higher education and training	14	5.33	Finland	5.97
6. Goods market efficiency	9	5.20	Singapore	5.77
7. Labour market efficiency	9	5.20	Singapore	5.91
8. Financial market sophistication	4	5.51	Hong Kong SAR	5.95
9. Technological readiness	20	5.39	Sweden	6.15
10. Market size	19	5.10	United States	6.93
C. Innovation and sophistication	21	4.61	United States	5.71
11. Business sophistication	26	4.79	Japan	5.89
12. Innovation	205.60	4.43	United States	5.77

Source: Adapted from the Global Competitiveness Report 2009–10 © 2009 World Economic Forum, *Tables 4–8, pp. 13–20.*

According to the GCI, in the first stage of development (Table 20.4, sub-index A and pillars 1 to 4), the economy is *factor-driven* and countries compete based on their factor endowments: primarily unskilled labour and natural resources. Maintaining competitiveness at this stage of development requires primarily well-functioning public and private institutions (pillar 1), well-developed infrastructure (pillar 2), a stable macroeconomic framework (pillar 3), and a healthy and literate workforce (pillar 4).

In the next stage of development (sub-index B), countries move into the *efficiency-driven* stage of development, when they must begin to develop more efficient production processes and increase product quality. In this stage, competitiveness is increasingly driven by higher education and training (pillar 5), efficient goods markets (pillar 6), well-functioning labour markets (pillar 7), sophisticated financial markets (pillar 8), a large domestic and/or foreign market (pillar 10), and the ability to harness the benefits of existing technologies (pillar 9).

In the third stage of development (sub-index C), companies must compete through innovation (pillar 12), producing new and different goods using the most sophisticated production processes (pillar 11).

The concept of stages of development is integrated into the index by attributing higher relative weights to those pillars that are relatively more relevant for a country given its particular stage of development.

Table 20.4 summarises Australia's position (e.g. ranks and scores) in all three sub-indexes and 12 pillars, and for a comparison with the best international practice, it identifies the leading economy and score in each category. One has to note that for those economies, like Australia, ranked from 11 through 50 in the overall GCI, variables ranked higher than the economy's own rank (15, in the case of Australia) are considered to be advantages. Any variables ranked equal to or lower than the economy's overall rank are considered to be disadvantages.

Therefore, Table 20.4 suggests that the prominent competitive advantages of the Australian economy are factors such as: financial market sophistication, good market efficiency, labour market efficiency, institutions.

The *Global Competitiveness Report* notes that Australia's slight improvement on the 2009–10 GCI ranking (by three places) is mainly due to a notable improvement in the macroeconomic environment (18th, up 10 places), including the balancing of the Budget and a reduction in public debt to 14 per cent of GDP—the second lowest in the OECD next to Luxembourg.

The report also notes Australia's improved position in the financial markets pillar (by two places, 4th worldwide), with its score decreasing less than that of other large economies. A positive feature is that the trustworthiness of, and confidence in, Australia's banking system remained essentially intact.

According to the WEF report, Australia remains a prime location for doing business with efficient goods markets and flexible labour markets (both ranked 9th), and excellent public and private institutions (12th on average, with private institutions faring better than the public ones).

One should note that under the higher education and training pillar, Australia is ranked 14th worldwide, which is just above the bottom line set by the report for competitive advantages.

As we can see from Table 20.5 (p. 428), Australia's main competitive disadvantages appear to be: business sophistication, infrastructure, innovation and technological readiness, and market size.

To progress even further, the report suggests that the country will need to improve on several measures of business sophistication (26th) and strengthen its innovation capacity (20th). Most importantly, there is a need to upgrade infrastructure (25th), particularly ports, so important to a leading bulk commodity supplier like Australia.

INFORMATION AND ANALYSIS

A third reason for structural change is better information and analysis. Regulation and public ownership have been subjected to much more scrutiny in the past two decades than they were previously.

Economists have estimated the costs of distortions to various markets through over-regulation. Australia's tariff protection and various industries—motor vehicle, telecommunications, transport, agriculture—have been subjected to exhaustive analysis and the benefits of deregulation were documented by the Industry Commission. In 1996 the Industry Commission merged with the Bureau of Industry Economics and the Economic Planning Advisory Commission to form the Productivity Commission.

Increased public awareness of the costs of regulation has made government more critical of regulation generally.

INTERNATIONAL FACTORS

In looking at the reasons for microeconomic reform, it is important to recognise the international dimension. OECD analysis indicates that the most successful OECD member countries in the 1990s were small economies that implemented microeconomic reforms: Australia, New Zealand, Ireland, the Netherlands and Norway. Australia is not the only country pursuing reform. In contrast, the worst relative performers in the 1990s were big economies—Japan, Germany and France—which fell behind because they did not implement such reforms.

The experience of one country is often extrapolated to others. In some cases, information gained about the impact of certain policies is relevant for another country. Or perhaps governments wish to be seen to be doing something, and thus adopt a policy that has been popular or successful elsewhere.

STRUCTURAL CHANGE IN AUSTRALIA: THE RECENT EXPERIENCE

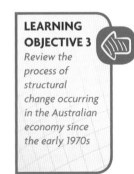

LEARNING OBJECTIVE 3
Review the process of structural change occurring in the Australian economy since the early 1970s

Prior to the 1980s, the industrial and regulatory structure of the Australian economy had remained little-changed for a long time—at least since the end of World War II.

PROTECTION

Since the earliest days of white settlement, Australia has had a long tradition of government intervention and regulation in the economy, which was intensified with the state enterprise boom of the 1920s and 1930s. Australia has small and geographically dispersed local markets and high wage and infrastructure costs. To compensate for this, federal and state governments provided a wide range of assistance to industry, ranging from tariff protection, bounties, preferential purchase of Australian-made products, import embargoes and quotas, subsidies, through to export grants and credits and anti-dumping legislation.

This highly protectionist approach to industry policy was based on a belief that we should shelter our 'infant industries' from overseas competition and assist exporters. It is estimated that in the 1960s about 70 per cent of manufacturing jobs depended on high levels of protection.

Disadvantages of protection

Although this protectionist strategy helped establish basic manufacturing industries, it had a number of long-term disadvantages:

- Protected from international competition, Australian companies in import-replacement industries faced little pressure to adopt world-best practice and to develop export markets.
- Protection encouraged foreign takeover of key sectors of Australian manufacturing, such as the automotive industry and food processing. In this way, multinational companies bypassed our protection walls and in recent years have become major recipients of government assistance to manufacturing.
- Little incentive was provided to improve the efficiency of input-providing industries and infrastructure, so that manufacturers paid higher prices for their electricity, telecommunications and transport than their overseas competitors.
- Protection added to the cost of key inputs (for example machinery and equipment, components), making it harder for Australian firms to compete against imports and on world markets.

Protection became a kind of regressive tax on the consumer. For example, it added about $5000 to the price of the average new car and meant that low-income families paid high prices for necessities such as food, clothing and footwear. There were some efforts at regulatory change before 1980, such as the interstate freight deregulation of the mid 1950s and the one-off tariff cut of 25 per cent in 1974, but they remained isolated examples.

As circumstances dictated, other reforms were undertaken, though they were not part of any general pattern. For instance, some states relaxed regulation of road freight at different stages before 1980, but at the same time they were tightening regulation of other industries.

By the 1970s, however, a more critical attitude had developed. The Industries Assistance Commission (replacing the old Tariff Board) for the first time attempted to quantify the effects of our heavy protection and its impact on different groups in the community.

In the 1980s, microeconomic reform had become an important part of the federal government's policy arsenal. It aimed to improve productivity, international competitiveness, economic efficiency, and long-run economic growth.

effective rate of assistance
is 'a measure of the net assistance to an industry divided by its unassisted value added'—that is, the net assistance to an industry relative to its contribution to the economy

One common measure of assistance to industry is the **effective rate of assistance** ('a measure of the net assistance to an industry divided by its unassisted value added'—that is, the net assistance to an industry relative to its contribution to the economy).

The Productivity Commission estimated that in 2006–07 the highest effective rates of assistance were provided to four Australian industries: dairy farming (15.1%), textiles, clothing, footwear and leather (13.5%) and fisheries (12.7%), and automotive industry (12.2%).

The levels of assistance to the Australian automotive industry have, however, declined since 1985, when the automotive industry, for instance, was protected by tariffs of 57.5 per cent and import quotas, and when the effective rate of assistance to the industry was about 140 per cent (more about protection to the automotive industry in Link to International Economy, p. 438).

Analysts like the Economist Intelligence Unit appreciated that the pace of economic reform in Australia has been slowing: 'the two major political parties, both of which have undertaken major reforms of various types over the past two decades, have responded to "reform fatigue" by softening their approach'.[4]

MICROECONOMIC REFORM

There are three major objectives of microeconomic reform:

- to raise the supply potential of the economy, leading to higher economic growth, domestic demand and living standards
- to reduce interference with price signals in the labour and product markets, enhancing economic efficiency, competition and reducing inflationary pressure
- to stabilise external debt and increase the efficiency with which the capital stock is used, reducing demand on domestic saving without reducing living standards.

Microeconomic reform in Australia has been taking place in a wide range of areas, such as:

- competition policy
- communication services
- government business enterprises
- taxation reform
- labour market
- financial system (explained in Chapter 15)
- industry assistance.

AUSTRALIAN MANUFACTURING DECLINE: REASONS AND IMPLICATIONS

LEARNING OBJECTIVE 4
Examine the main changes undertaken in Australian manufacturing and the prospects for this economic sector

According to *Trends in Australian Manufacturing*, a research paper published by the Australian Productivity Commission in August 2003, Australia's manufacturing output quadrupled since the mid 1950s, with the fastest-growing activities being those with links to Australia's natural endowments and high-tech goods with higher skill levels and research and development intensities. However, manufacturing growth could not match that of services growth. For instance, manufacturing accounted for one in four dollars of national output in the 1960s, but only one in eight by the turn of the century.

The above research paper has identified several causes and implications related to the relative decline in Australia's manufacturing:

- On the output side, the relative decline of manufacturing mainly reflects Australians' preferences for more services as incomes rise. Import competition from lower-wage developing economies has only been a small contributor.
- On the employment side, the decline is testimony to strong labour productivity growth.
- Some services activities once categorised as part of manufacturing have been outsourced, though this effect is relatively modest.
- The impacts of structural change on unemployment have generally been moderate, though the effects have been bigger for some less competitive industries and regions.

- Continuing rises in 'intra-industry trade'—exports and imports of similar products—suggest that Australian manufacturing can develop capabilities within most areas.
- Regional dependence on manufacturing has fallen.

According to ABS data, in 2008–09 the Australian manufacturing sector employed around 1 million workers and contributed to Australia's GDP with a gross value added of around $105.1 billion. In 2008–09 manufacturing was one of the hardest-hit sectors of the Australian economy. On a financial year basis, in 2008–09 the manufacturing sector lost around 31 000 jobs and some $2.5 billion in production value. Other sources indicate that over the period September 2008–September 2009 the sector lost around 80 000 jobs.

Table 20.5 illustrates the relative positions of various industry subdivisions in the manufacturing sector's total production and employment in 2008–09 compared to 2001–02.

Table 20.5   **The Australian manufacturing sector: Changes in the share of total manufacturing production and employment, by main manufacturing industry, 2008–09 and 2001–02**

MANUFACTURING INDUSTRY	% SHARE OF MANUFACTURING PRODUCTION[a]		% SHARE OF MANUFACTURING EMPLOYMENT	
	2008–09	2001–02	2008–09	2001–02
Machinery and equipment	20	19.9	21.4	22
Food, beverages and tobacco	19	21.4	24.1	17.2
Metal products	20	23.4	19.4	15.3
Petroleum, coal, chemicals and associated products	12.7	13.7	10.3	10.5
Printing, publishing and recorded media	8	4.2	5	10.2
Non-metallic mineral products	5.2	5.5	4.2	4.5
Other manufacturing	4.5	2.5	3.9	6.8
Wood and paper products	7.4	6.7	7.0	6.3
Textile, clothing, footwear and leather	3.2	2.7	4.7	7.2
Total manufacturing	100	100	100	100

(a) As measured by industry gross value added.

Source: Adapted from ABS, Manufacturing, cat. no. 8225.0, 2002; ABS 81550DO002_200809 Australian Industry, 2008–09.

With regard to the performance of various manufacturing industries, Table 20.5 indicates that three sectors (machinery and equipment; food, beverages and tobacco; and metal products) still dominate the manufacturing sector. Their dominance has increased in terms of employment accounting in 2008–09 for almost 65 per cent of manufacturing employment (with a slightly lower share in terms of production value). The best performers among manufacturing industries, with positive production growth during the crisis were: food (3.2%), printing (8.2%), machinery and equipment (excepting transport equipment), basic chemicals. But, as other ABS data shows, their growth paled compared to that of the mining sector (48%), or services like private education and training (10.1%).

Media reports indicate that manufacturing has been under pressure for the past two decades and was overtaken as Australia's biggest employer by retail trade in 2001. Growth in the health sector meant it overtook manufacturing as the second-largest industry in 2006.

So where are the jobs of the future in Australia? Most certainly in services: retail trade, tourism, computer software, banking, telecommunications, construction and engineering, consulting, and education.

COMPETITION POLICY

The **Hilmer Report** of 1993 made extensive recommendations on the adoption of **competition policy** in Australia on a new scale.

The formation in November 1995 of the Australian Competition and Consumer Commission (ACCC), by the merger of the Trade Practices Commission and the Prices Surveillance Authority,

Hilmer Report
released in 1993, the report—formally The National Competition Policy Report, commissioned by the Prime Minister and undertaken by a committee chaired by Professor Fred Hilmer—argued for greater competition among government-owned entities and made extensive recommendations on the adoption of competition policy in Australia on a new scale

AN OVERVIEW OF THE NCP REFORMS

NCP reforms included general reforms and sector-specific reforms.

(a) General reforms

- Extension of the anti-competitive conduct provisions in the *Trade Practices Act* (TPA, now superseded by the *Competition and Consumer Act 2010*) to unincorporated enterprises and government businesses.
- Reforms to public monopolies and other government businesses.
- The introduction of a national regime to provide third-party access on reasonable terms and conditions to essential infrastructure services with natural monopoly characteristics.
- The introduction of a Legislation Review Program to assess whether regulatory restrictions on competition were in the public interest and, if not, what changes were required. The legislation covered by the program spanned a wide range of areas, including: the professions and occupations; statutory marketing of agricultural products; fishing and forestry; retail trading; transport; communications; insurance and superannuation; child care; gambling; and planning and development services.

(b) Sector-specific reforms

- Electricity: Various structural, governance, regulatory and pricing reforms to introduce greater competition into electricity generation and retailing and to establish a National Electricity Market in the eastern states.
- Gas: A similar suite of reforms to facilitate more competitive supply arrangements and to promote greater competition at the retail level.
- Road transport: Implementation of heavy vehicle charges and a uniform approach to regulating heavy vehicles to improve the efficiency of the road freight sector, enhance road safety and reduce the transactions costs of regulation.
- Water: Various reforms to achieve a more efficient and sustainable water sector including institutional, pricing and investment measures, and the implementation of arrangements that allow for the permanent trading of water allocations.

Source: Adapted from Productivity Commission (PC) Inquiry Report, No. 33, 28 February 2005, <www.pc.gov.au/__data/ assets/pdf_file/0016/46033/ncp.pdf>, accessed 15 July 2010.

LINK TO BUSINESS

was an important step in the implementation of the national competition policy (NCP) reform program agreed by the Council of Australian Governments (COAG) in April 1995. The NCP was underpinned by three intergovernmental agreements:

1. Competition Principles Agreement
2. Conduct Code Agreement
3. Agreement to Implement the National Competition Policy and Related Reforms (Implementation Agreement).

The NCP program, which ran from April 1995 until 2005, placed competition at the forefront as a means of securing productivity, economic growth and a broadly defined Australian national interest.

It is generally believed that national competition policy (NCP) delivered substantial benefits to the Australian community which, overall, greatly outweighed the costs.

It has:

- boosted Australia's GDP over the 1990s by 2.5 per cent, or $20 billion (note that this PC modelling did not pick up the effects of dynamic efficiency gains from more competitive markets so it is a conservative estimate)
- contributed to the productivity surge that underpinned 18 years of continuous economic growth, and associated strong growth in household incomes
- directly reduced the prices of goods and services such as electricity and milk
- stimulated business innovation, customer responsiveness and choice
- helped meet some environmental goals, including the more efficient use of water.

Benefits from NCP flowed to both low- and high-income earners, and to country as well as city Australia—though some households have been adversely affected by higher prices for particular services and some smaller regional communities have experienced employment reductions.

In February 2006, COAG agreed to pursue an ambitious new national reform agenda (NRA) as a successor program to the national competition policy.

The NRA is a new partnership between federal, state and territory governments, which includes:

- *Competition reform* to make the Australian economy more competitive and continue the successful reforms of the 1990s
- *Regulation reform* to reduce the red tape burden on Australian businesses
- *Human capital reform* to improve health, learning and work outcomes for all Australians.

The NRA is about all governments taking a long-term perspective and working together to resolve the big challenges in the coming decades, due to the ageing population and the increasing competitiveness of the global economy.

TELECOMMUNICATIONS SERVICES

LEARNING OBJECTIVE 5
Examine microeconomic reform in the telecommunications sector

In line with worldwide technological and economic trends, the telecommunications sector has been one of the fastest-growing industries in Australia. The expansion of the Australian telecommunications sector has been accompanied and supported by a continuous reform process. The market structure in this sector has evolved from the dominance of one monopoly (Post Master General's Department and later on Telecom) to a duopoly (Telecom/Telstra and Optus from 1992) and an extensive deregulated market after 1 July 1997, with removal of restrictions on the number of licensed operators and anti-competition mechanisms (replaced by general competition law under the oversight of the Australian Competition and Consumer Commission).

The opening up and liberalisation of the sector in 1997 dramatically changed the industry, encouraging competition, extensive investment in new technology and infrastructure, and improved services.

In 2008–09 some 175 licensed carriers were operating in Australia, providing a wide range of services and competitive prices for long distance and international calls, mobile services and broadband internet access.

Table 20.6 summarises a few changes in the performance of the Australian telecommunications industry over 1996–97 to 2008–09.

The table shows a strong increase in industry income production value (1.8 times over 12 years), with a gross profit before tax almost four times bigger.

Table 20.6   **Selected performance indicators of the Australian Telecommunications Industry 1996–97 and 2008–09**

MAIN INDICATORS	1996–97	2008–09
Number of licensed carriers	3	175
Employment June	79 654	54 000
Total income ($ million)	20 927	37 709
Income per person employed ($)	262 700	698 315
Operating profit before tax ($ million)	1473	5657
Industry value added ($ million)	12 234	19 139

Source: Adapted from ABS, Information Technology, Australia, 1998–99, cat. no. 8126.0; ABS, 81550DO002_200809 Australian Industry, 2008–09.

Income per person employed has increased 2.7 times, which shows increased productivity in the industry.

However, employment has experienced some short periods of strong growth (around 2000) with a long-term decline, due to a number of unfavourable circumstances:

- the Australian recession of the early 1990s
- the process of deregulation and privatisation in the telecommunications sector
- the impact of the global financial crisis (2008–09), with the industry losing some 6000 employees between 2006–07 and 2008–09.

Key trends in the telecommunications sector
Competition
- The telecommunications consultant BuddeCom estimates that Telstra still dominates the overall Australian telecommunications market with a massive 66 per cent market share of overall revenues in mid 2010. Optus' market share of overall telco service revenues has been fairly stagnant in recent years at just over 20 per cent.
- Four of the second-tier players: AAPT, Commander, Vodafone and Hutchison had in 2009 annual revenues exceeding the $1 billion mark. In 2009 Vodafone and Hutchison,

Australia's third and fourth largest mobile network operators, merged their operations as VHA, becoming a strong competitor to Optus.

- M2 acquired People Telecom in mid 2009 to create the largest firm without significant infrastructure assets, and further consolidation occurred over the period to 2011.
- Communication and media sector convergence.
- Network and device convergence is blurring the boundaries between communication and media services with communication companies offering content services directly to their broadband subscribers.

Shift to mobile services

- Since 2000, the number of connections for mobile telephones has exceeded fixed-line connections. In recent years, Australians continued to shift to mobile services with an estimated 24.22 million mobile services in operation at June 2009. (The number of fixed-line standard telephone services in Australia declined again in 2008–09 to reach 10.67 million.)
- Total mobile services revenue earned by the major mobile operators in the financial year to 2009 surged surprisingly despite difficult broader economic conditions in Australia. The industry as a whole earned around $14.3 billion in revenue from mobile services—a growth rate of nearly 10 per cent year-on-year. Figure 20.1 illustrates the estimates by lIBIS World of the increase in the mobile services' share in the total income of the industry to 40 per cent in 2008–09, going for the first time ahead of wired telecommunications.
- BuddeCom analysis shows that the main mobile players by revenue in 2009 were: Telstra (more than $6 billion), Optus (more than $4 billion); Vodafone Australia (just under $2.5 billion) and Hutchison (just over $1.5 billion). The new VHA entity would be only around 5 per cent behind Optus' income.
- Australian operators have more than 24 million mobile subscribers in 2011 as migration and business adoption continue to drive growth. Growth in the number

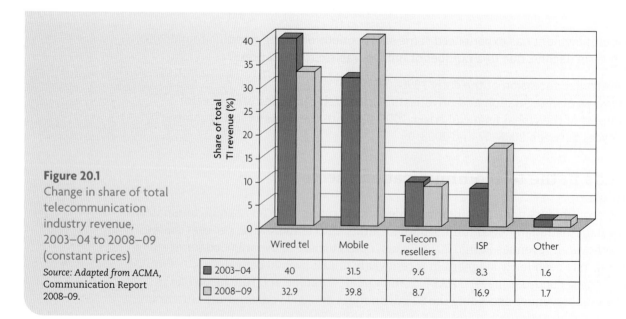

Figure 20.1

Change in share of total telecommunication industry revenue, 2003–04 to 2008–09 (constant prices)

Source: Adapted from ACMA, Communication Report 2008–09.

	Wired tel	Mobile	Telecom resellers	ISP	Other
2003–04	40	31.5	9.6	8.3	1.6
2008–09	32.9	39.8	8.7	16.9	1.7

of services was also boosted in Australia in 2009 by the effective use of economic stimulus. Telstra continues to dominate the market with more than 10 million subscribers. Optus has around 8 million subscribers and VHA has roughly 6 million subscribers.

Broadband

The total number of broadband subscribers reached 7.3 million by mid 2009, a 17 per cent increase over the previous 12 months. The business market has been quick to embrace broadband—by 2009 the vast majority of the business sector had made the transition. As business users gradually move to faster broadband access via ADSL2+ and, when it is built, services from the fibre-based national broadband network, businesses are increasingly embracing new broadband applications.

Prospects

The Australian Government announced on 7 April 2009 it would establish a new company to build and operate a new high speed National Broadband Network (NBN).

On 20 June 2010, the National Broadband Network Company and Telstra announced they had entered into an agreement on the rollout of the NBN. In support of that agreement the government will progress public policy reforms to support the transition to the NBN. (This might include the split between Telstra's wholesale and retail businesses to create a level playing field before the NBN roll-out.)

The extent to which new telephony services are developed will influence the pace of revenue growth.

The National Broadband Network Company is expected to build a nationwide high-speed network based on fibre-optic and wireless technologies. All of this will assist the industry to double its size to around $80 billion by 2020.

GOVERNMENT BUSINESS ENTERPRISES

LEARNING OBJECTIVE 6
Outline the performance of government business enterprises in the context of the process of corporatisation and privatisation

Government business enterprises (GBEs) play an important role in the Australian economy; however, despite their prominence it is difficult to quantify the overall significance of GBE activity. This is partly because there is no universally accepted way of defining the term 'GBE' and partly because comprehensive and up-to-date figures are difficult to obtain. According to the Australian National Audit Office (ANAO), in 1995–96 Commonwealth GBEs generated nearly $21 billion in revenue, provided dividends of $1.6 billion, controlled assets of approximately $41 billion and produced an average return on assets of 12.8 per cent. It is also reported that 'a number of GBEs play a central role in the economy and dominate certain strategic industries, including postal services and telecommunications'. The GBEs also provide other key inputs for the private sector. At federal level, these include railways, airports, and airlines; at state level, they include power, harbour management, and many other activities.

The **Government Businesses Advice Branch (GBAB)** provides advice to the Australian Government relating to its GBEs and other commercial entities.

Table 20.7 overleaf presents a list of major Australian GBEs in operation in 2010.

government business enterprises (GBEs)
government-owned enterprises

Table 20.7   **List of major Australian government business enterprises, areas of main activity, and total income in 2008–09 and 2007–08 ($ millions)**

GOVERNMENT ENTERPRISE	MAIN ACTIVITY	2008–09 $ MILLION	2007–08 $ MILLION
Australian Submarine Corporation (ASC)	Defence contractor	352	325
Australian Government Council (AGS)	Legal services to government	121	128
Australia Post	Postal services	4 852	4 807
Australian Rail Track Corporation Ltd (ARTC)	Interstate rail infrastructure	565	609
Defence Housing Australia (DHA)	Supply of housing and related services to ADF personnel and their families	278	265
Medibank Private Limited	Integrated private health insurance and health services	3 900	3 400

Source: Compiled from annual reports of various GBEs.

government businesses advice branch (GBAB) *provides advice to the Australian Government relating to its Government Business Enterprises (GBEs) and other commercial entities*

The annual reports of these GBEs indicate that, despite activity slowdown and in some cases a reduction in income and profit, the GBEs have managed to overcome the impact of the global and national downturn.

Among the commercial entities for which the GBAB provides advice to the government one can mention the following: Air Services Australia, Australian River Co., Australian Industry Development Corporation, Albury Wodonga Corporation, Export Finance and Insurance Corporation, Snowy Hydro Limited.

By providing a range of essential services to the business sector, GBEs influence business costs and the efficiency of private industry.

Australia's GBE sector has traditionally been larger than those of the United Kingdom, the United States, Japan and Sweden, but smaller than those of West European countries like Italy. During the 1990s the Australian Government implemented measures to improve the productivity and efficiency of GBEs. As part of this process, many GBEs were either corporatised or privatised.

Corporatisation

corporatisation *opening a government business enterprise (GBE) to elements of the private sector while the government maintains statutory ownership*

Corporatisation maintains the statutory ownership of a public enterprise but opens it to elements of the private sector. The process requires several steps: establishment of a corporate plan, removal of subsidies from other government departments, equalisation of tax, and corporate discipline as in the private sector.

GBEs which have been corporatised and subjected to the same cost structures as private enterprise have been obliged to improve their performance. Australia Post, which celebrated 200 years of existence in 2009, is one of the best-known and most successful cases of corporatisation (see Link to Business opposite).

AUSTRALIA POST AND THE GLOBAL ECONOMIC CRISIS

LINK TO
BUSINESS

Following a decade of consistent profit growth, Australia Post's financial results were hit heavily in the financial year 2008–09 by the global economic crisis and a slowing economy in Australia.

The corporation's profit before tax ($380.9 million) declined by 35.7 per cent from the previous year's record high of $592.2 million. However, Australia Post stated that its pre-tax profit was still a solid outcome, compared to many other international postal organisations that have reported substantial losses over the same period.

This result has ensured that Australia Post's cashflows continue to support capital investment in the postal network and the maintenance of the organisation's strategic business projects.

For instance, in 2010 Australia Post announced it will invest $20 million in training staff in growth areas such as parcels, logistics, retail and digital services over the following three years.

Despite the challenging trading conditions, all three core business portfolios of the corporation—letters and associated services, parcels and logistics, and agency services and retail merchandise—managed positive revenue growth in 2008–09, contributing to the corporation's overall annual revenue growth of $21.6 million (or 0.5 per cent).

- The letters and associated services portfolio achieved marginal revenue growth (0.7 per cent), mainly as a result of the 5 cent increase in the basic postage rate in September 2008. The volume of domestic letters declined from a peak of 5.2 billion last year to 4.9 billion this year. In particular, transactional mail lodgments from small businesses contracted sharply during the financial year.
- Agency services and retail merchandise was the strongest performing portfolio, with a revenue growth of 3.2 per cent. This growth was fuelled by the growing demand for in-person identity services and by the offering of a diverse range of retail products.
- Parcels and logistics achieved revenue growth of 2.5 per cent, well below the strong growth trend of previous years. Although the overall volume of parcels delivered by AP declined only marginally in 2008–09, the main downturn was suffered by the logistics business, which serves the business-to-business and business-to-consumer sectors.

In a difficult year, the corporation's return on revenue in 2008–09 declined to 7.6 per cent (from 11.9 per cent the previous year). An important factor for this decline was the impact of rising costs, especially the addition of approximately 200 000 delivery points to Australia's nationwide mail delivery network.

Based on the distribution of 75 per cent of the corporation's after-tax profit, ordinary dividends payable from the 2008–09 result were expected to total $184 million (down by $150.6 million), highlighting the impact of the volatile economic environment.

In the same year, the corporation met its obligation to provide the federal government with an additional $150 million dividend payment, related to earnings from both the 2008–09 financial year and previous years.

Privatisation

Privatisation, in contrast, changes the ownership of a public enterprise by selling it to the private sector. It is expected that private sector initiatives, enterprise and financial backing will improve the performance and efficiency of the former GBE.

GBEs sold during the 1990s under privatisation policy include: Qantas, the Commonwealth Bank, major city airports, Aerospace Technologies of Australia, Commonwealth Serum Laboratories Limited, and, as discussed in a previous section, Telstra (with the last tranche privatised in 2006).

privatisation
changing the ownership of a public enterprise by selling it to the private sector

Overall reforms to GBEs have resulted in lower costs for services provided. Surveyed prices for 58 major Commonwealth, state and territory enterprises fell by about 10 per cent in the first half of the 1990s.

TAXATION REFORM

In the period since World War II there have been several unsuccessful attempts at reforming the Australian tax system. Governments have tried to introduce a broad-based consumption tax to reduce the distortions caused by the 1930s wholesale sales tax, to allow marginal income tax rates to fall and, in some cases, to clean up the inefficient tax base of the states. After the election to government of the Liberal–National Coalition in 1996, it became apparent that its cautious reform agenda was inconsistent with the community's hopes for lower unemployment.

GST

goods and services tax (GST)
indirect tax at a rate of 10 per cent imposed on both goods and services, introduced in Australia on 1 July 2000

Before July 2000, it was mainly goods that were taxed via a system of wholesale and retail taxes, as opposed to services, which was traditionally a low-taxed area. As of 1 July 2000, the system changed to one where the sales tax net incorporated services as well as goods via the **goods and services tax (GST)**. The GST was introduced at a rate of 10 per cent and was accompanied by the abolition of the wholesale sales tax (WST) system and a cut in income taxes and some other taxes. There are a few exemptions to the GST (e.g. unprocessed food, health and medical care, education and exports). Specific excise taxes, however, continue to remain on beer and spirits, tobacco products and petroleum products.

The GST has had the effect of broadening the tax base and capturing consumption expenditures to a greater extent. The emphasis of the tax system has thus moved towards consumption and, to some degree, away from income.

Total tax revenue

OECD data shows that Australia's total tax revenue as a percentage of GDP increased from 26.6 per cent in 1975 to 29.3 per cent in 1990 and 31.5 per cent in 2000. However, by 2007, this indicator went down to 30.8 per cent, which was lower than the corresponding level for OECD Europe (38 per cent) and OECD as a whole (38 per cent), but higher than OECD America (26.8 per cent).

Corporate income tax

Australia's corporate income tax gradually declined from 49 per cent in 1988–89 to 39 per cent in 1995–96 and 30 per cent since 2000–01. At this level, in 2010, Australia was on a par with other OECD members such as Mexico, New Zealand, Spain and Germany. In the same year, only four OECD member countries had higher combined company income tax rates compared to Australia: Japan (39.5 per cent), US (39.2 per cent), France (34.4 per cent), Belgium (34 per cent). However, lower corporate rates were charged in economies such as the United Kingdom (28 per cent), Austria and Denmark (25 per cent), with the lowest corporate income tax being charged in Ireland (12.5 per cent).

The Henry Review

The Henry Tax Review, released by a team led by the Secretary to Treasury, Ken Henry, in May 2010 has been touted as the most comprehensive review of the tax system in the last 50 years.

The review recommended that existing taxes on resources should become a more effective means of raising revenue. The current system distorts investment and production decisions and it fails to collect a sufficient return for the Australian community as it does not respond to changes in profits made by the private sector.

The review contained 138 recommendations for tax reform with one of the centrepieces being a resource super profits tax of 40 per cent.

In its response the government rejected 20 of those in whole and a further six in part, leaving 118 recommendations (in whole or in part) that could possibly be implemented in the future.

The federal government used the release of the Henry Tax Review to announce a number of significant tax and superannuation changes in the lead-up to the release of the federal Budget in May 2010:

- company tax rate to fall to 28 per cent by 2014 (the Henry Review proposed 25 per cent)
- 40 per cent resource super profit tax to be in place from 2012
- instant write-off for small business assets to the value of $5000
- increase to employer superannuation contributions to 12 per cent by 2019.

Following negotiations between the government and the mining sector the resource super profits tax renamed 'Minerals Resources Rent Tax' (MRRT) has been capped at 30 per cent and it will apply only to iron ore and coal, which account for nearly 60 per cent of Australia's resource exports.

Details of the tax are still to be worked out before its introduction in 2012.

The Labor Government claimed that, despite revenue decline from MRRT, the federal Budget will still return to surplus by 2013.

Although the government announced in May 2010 the adoption of only three of the Henry Review's 138 recommendations, it is largely believed that the Henry Review will be a blueprint for taxation debate and reform for the next 25 years.

LABOUR MARKET REFORMS

For most of the 20th century Australia had a unique system of regulating industrial relations in the form of a highly centralised wage-fixing process. On the basis of public hearings involving unions, employer groups, government and other interested parties, the Australian Industrial Relations Commission (AIRC) and its predecessors were charged with determining pay and conditions for virtually all classes of employees. The Prices and Incomes Accord 1983, which operated between 1983 and 1996, was an agreement between the ACTU and the federal government on matters related to wages and incomes.

In the 1990s, Australia moved away from a centralised wage-fixing system towards an enterprise-based bargaining system. The process was accelerated by the federal *Workplace Relations Act 1996*.

This Act, as amended by the *Workplace Relations Amendment (WRA) Act 2005*, commonly known as 'Work Choices', was passed by the Howard Government in 2005. The WRA Act:

- dispensed with unfair dismissal laws for companies under a certain size
- removed the 'no disadvantage test', which had sought to ensure workers were not left disadvantaged by changes in legislation
- limited the powers of the Australian Industrial Relations Commission (e.g. required workers to submit their certified agreements directly to the Workplace Authority rather than going through the Australian Industrial Relations Commission).

'Work Choices' met massive opposition from the Australian Council of Trade Unions, which launched its 'Your Rights at Work' campaign opposing the changes.

'Work Choices' was also a major issue in the 2007 federal election, with the Labor Party vowing to abolish it. After assuming office, the Labor Government repealed the entirety of the *Workplace Relations Act 1996* and its subsequent amendments.

On 19 March 2008, a Bill was passed in the Australian Senate that prevented new Australian Work Agreements (AWAs) from being made, and set up provisions for workers to be transferred from AWAs into intermediate agreements. On 27 March 2008, the ban on new AWAs came into effect in Australia.

During the 2010 election campaign, Tony Abbot, the Leader of the Opposition, made it clear that the Liberal–National Coalition would not seek to reintroduce AWAs.

THE KEY FACTOR FOR FUTURE PROSPERITY

In conclusion, microeconomic reform, in conjunction with macroeconomic reform, has aimed to boost productivity and international competitiveness, encouraging investment, saving and profitability in the Australian economy, with a positive impact on standards of living.

Australian Government assistance to industry was estimated by the Australian Productivity Commission to have exceeded $15 billion in 2007. State and territory assistance programs, which are less transparent, would add a few billion on top of that.

Although strictly comparable estimates are not available, measured budgetary assistance for manufacturing appears to have roughly doubled in real terms since the 1960s, especially that tied to specific manufacturing industries (e.g. automotive, textile, clothing, footwear), without managing to fully compensate for the loss of tariff assistance in the same industries.

During the recent global financial crisis, Australia's economy has once again proven highly resilient in the face of major global pressures. However, the fiscal stimuli to achieve that have left a fiscal legacy that will present additional policy challenges in the years ahead.

Productivity Commission analysis shows that economic recovery needs support via a number of reforms that can reduce business costs and improve organisational flexibility and capability in order to bring additional productivity gains.

We have to agree that, in the final analysis, sustained productivity growth in the Australian economy is the key factor for the nation's prosperity into the future.

LINK TO INTERNATIONAL ECONOMY

TARIFF PROTECTION VERSUS INDUSTRY ASSISTANCE IN THE AUSTRALIAN AUTOMOTIVE SECTOR

The theory of economics tells us that an import tariff is a tax imposed by the government on imported goods with a similar effect as an indirect tax in that it provides the government with a source of revenue while increasing the price of the goods. You remember from Chapter 3 that high indirect taxes are damaging to both suppliers and buyers, while lower indirect taxes are a successful stimulant for the economy.

You also remember that production subsidies are a condition of supply with beneficial effects for both suppliers and consumers.

Tariff protection has been traditionally one of the most common devices used by the Australian Government to protect the local automotive industry, along with other devices such as: import quotas, tariff quotas, local content schemes. At the same time, the federal government has used a number of instruments and schemes to assist Australian automotive firms in their efforts in competing overseas (see the brief chronology in Table 20.8). It is acknowledged that the level of

Table 20.8   **Brief chronology of 25 years of automotive industry reform**

1985	Button plan	• A tariff quota replaced the 80/20 market sharing arrangement • The 85 per cent local content scheme was retained and the export facilitation scheme was extended and broadened • Rationalisation of the industry
1988	Mid-term review of the Button plan	• Abolition of import quotas • PMV tariff reduced to 45 per cent and scheduled to phase down to 35 per cent by 1992 • The local content scheme was replaced by a dual tariff arrangement, linking the tariff on components to the tariff on imported PMVs
March 1991	Economic statement from the federal government	• Continuation of the phased reduction of tariffs from 35 per cent in 1992 to 15 per cent in 2000 • Tariffs on car parts were to remain at 15 per cent until 2000
1997	Review of the Australian automotive sector	• Howard Government, under pressure from the car sector lobby, decided to freeze tariffs between 2000 and 2005 at the level of 15 per cent
1998	Announcement of ACIS	• Launch of the Automotive Competitiveness and Investment Scheme (ACIS) to commence operation on 1 January 2001
December 2002	Post-2005 package	• Prime Minister Howard announced the government's post-2005 package, to deliver $4.2 billion through the ACIS to the industry over 10 years, with all industry-specific support ceasing on 31 December 2015
1 January 2005	Tariff cut	• PMV tariff down from 15 per cent to 10 per cent
22 July 2008	Final report of automotive review	• Hon. Steve Bracks submits final report to Senator Kim Carr, Minister for Innovation, Industry, Science and Research
November 2008	The government's response to the Automotive Industry Review	The government launches 'A new car plan for a greener future' which includes, inter alia: • the Automotive Transformation Scheme (ATS), running from 2011 to 2020 and providing $3.4 billion to the industry • an expanded Green Car Innovation Fund of $1.3 billion brought forward to 2009 and running over 10 years • an Automotive Industry Structural Adjustment Program ($116.3 million in additional funding outside ATS) • an Automotive Supply Chain Development Program at a cost of $20 million over four years
1 January 2010		• The PMV tariff goes down to 5 per cent

continued ↘

continued

assistance to the Australian automotive industry is high compared with support for other domestic industry sectors in Australia. For instance, in 2006-07, motor vehicle and parts manufacturing received combined budgetary and tariff assistance of $1.3 billion, or nearly $4000 per vehicle manufactured domestically. However, the Australian Government has never been alone in the protection game, with nearly all major nations being known for providing assistance to many parts of their economies, including the automotive sector.

As with many other controversial trade policy issues, trade protection has its critics and supporters.

Tariff protection sounds like a bad thing not only for consumers, but also for manufacturers, miners, farmers and service providers using various types of vehicles in their operations. The car manufacturers themselves suffer the effects of tariff protection when importing car components from overseas. Budgetary assistance to the industry also affects other industries and consumers since tax revenue has to be raised or diverted from other uses.

Import tariff liberalisation ideas seeded over a long period in Australian academia at last conquered the minds of the Labor Government decision makers in the mid 1980s, when the late Senator Button launched his program of reforms of the Australian car sector, including a firm schedule of progressive tariff cuts. PMV declined from 45 per cent in 1988 to 25 per cent in 1996. The Coalition Government under John Howard in broad terms maintained the anti-protectionist stance with PMV tariffs reaching the 10 per cent level in 2005, with a target of a final reduction of 5 per cent in 2010, implemented by a new Labor Government according to the initial schedule.

The 2010 tariff reduction continues the structural adjustment process the industry has been undergoing since the mid 1980s. Taking into account Australia's current free trade agreements (e.g. United States and Thailand), the import-weighted tariff under the proposed transitional assistance arrangements is between 3 and 4 per cent from 2010.

However, Figure 20.2 brings in a finding which is not encouraging at all. The share of local car producers in the Australian automotive market declined from some 64 per cent in 1992 to less than 21 per cent in 2009, with a corresponding more than double increase in the share of imported PMV to around 79 per cent in 2009.

Have all car plans gone wrong? Does it mean that local automotive production is on the way out? Certainly, it is not and it should not be either. Figure 20.3 brings another angle to the picture. Despite the reduction by three times in market share, the value of local automotive production— except for the crisis year 2009—has remained quite stable (in dollar terms fluctuating in the band between A$7 to A$9 billion). Out of this value, Australian car components suppliers provided in excess of A$4 billion. The big point in favour of government assistance is that the automotive car industry has kept around 60 000 Australians employed in the car manufacturing industry and supplier chain. The automotive sector is also the user of inputs supplied by many other Australian industries, including high-tech operations, providing a major support for continuous technological progress in Australia.

HOW CAN THE APPARENT AUSTRALIAN CAR PRODUCTION PARADOX BE EXPLAINED?

Since the 1980s, the Australian automotive industry has become more open and efficient. It has responded to increased exposure to international competition through enhanced global integration and a more export-oriented focus. This has generated two positive developments illustrated in Figure 20.3. First, automotive exports have increased at a much higher rate than total domestic

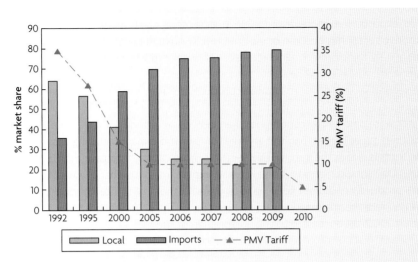

Figure 20.2
The Australian market for passenger motor vehicles (PMV),
1992–2009, per cent share of locally produced and imported
vehicles and per cent PMV import tariffs

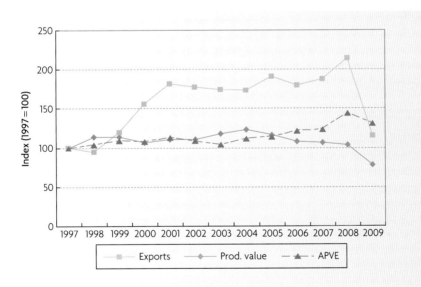

Figure 20.3
Comparative changes in total automotive production value, exports
and average production value (Index 1997 = 100)

Note: APVE = Average production value per employee.

continued ↘

continued

production, making up to a great extent for the loss of domestic market share of local producers. In 2008, exports were more than double in value compared to 1992 with a record $5.8 billion. The automotive sector has become one of the top 10 Australian export earners and the largest exporter of elaborately transformed manufactures, with total exports exceeding in value traditional exports such as wool, wheat and wine.

The second factor for the maintained production value is the increased sector productivity illustrated in Figure 20.3, with the average production value per employee (APVE). In 2008, this indicator was some 44 per cent higher than in 1992. At around $500 000 per employee, the APVE is about five times higher than the average for the whole manufacturing sector. (Certainly, a good reason for this is that the automotive sector is more capital-intensive than other manufacturing sectors.) One should mention, however, that experts maintain that the Australian automotive sector's productivity did not keep up with that of other major international automobile producers.

This is where the challenge lies for the success of the government's 'New car plan for a greener future' of 2008, the successor to the Button plan of the 1980s.

It is hoped that strong government assistance to the development of new 'green technologies' (with due observance of international assistance rules), combined with the R&D efforts of automotive companies, will further enhance the sector's development of environment-friendly cars with top performances, highly competitive internationally.

SUMMARY

1. Structural change involves a shift in the pattern of production in the economy, resulting in an improvement in the overall level of output and productivity. Structural change is not only an Australian phenomenon, but also a global development.
2. The main reasons for structural change are:
    (a) technological change
    (b) poor overall economic performance
    (c) better information and analysis
    (d) international influences.
3. Although Australia's historical policy of protection helped to establish basic manufacturing industries, it had a number of long-term negative effects, such as lack of competitiveness, low efficiency and higher prices.
4. Structural change or microeconomic reform policies were a major area of government policy in the 1980s and early 1990s. Microeconomic reform in Australia has taken place in a wide range of areas:
    (a) competition policy
    (b) financial sector
    (c) fiscal system
    (d) industry assistance
    (e) government business enterprises (GBEs)
    (f) labour market.
5. Microeconomic reform aims to boost productivity and export competitiveness and lead to a reduction in the current account deficit.
6. The Australian telecommunications and automotive sectors demonstrated that microeconomic reform can achieve good results for both business and consumers.

KEY TERMS

REFERENCES

1. Peter Forsyth (ed.), *Microeconomic Reform in Australia*, Allen & Unwin, Sydney, 1992, p. 12.
2. *The Economist*, 'The C-word strikes back', 1 June 1996, p. 76.
3. Ibid.
4. Economist Intelligence Unit, *Country Profile, Australia*, 2004, p. 17.
5. Organisation for Economic Cooperation and Development, <www.oecd.org/dataoecd/6/63/1962227.pdf>.

REVIEW QUESTIONS

1. What are the main reasons for structural change?
2. What is the impact of technological change on the economy?
3. Give examples of indicators that illustrate Australia's good economic performance over the last two decades.
4. How can better information and analysis contribute to structural change?
5. Is structural change in Australia influenced by developments in other countries? If yes, in what way?
6. What factors—internal and external—make the need for microeconomic reform obvious in Australia?
7. Outline several areas of recent microeconomic reform and their impact on overall economic activity. Illustrate with examples from the automotive and telecommunications sectors.
8. Outline a few reasons for the decline in manufacturing employment in Australia and other industrialised countries.
9. Which group of industries in Australia has traditionally favoured protection, and which group has been pressing for tariff reduction? Explain the reasons.
10. 'Sustained productivity growth is the key factor to increased Australian prosperity.' Do you agree with this statement? Why or why not?

APPLIED QUESTIONS AND EXERCISES

1. In relation to Table 20.1 (p. 418), outline the main changes in the structure of Australia's GDP during 1965 to 2008 and compare them to changes in other countries. Explain the reasons for the changes.

2. Demonstrate the effects of microeconomic reform on the external sector. Give examples in the manufacturing sector.
3. Explain how some microeconomic reforms can have a macroeconomic impact. Give an example to illustrate your answer.
4. 'Table 20.3 (p. 421) shows that GDP per hour worked in 2008 was US$30.5 in New Zealand and US$44.5 in Australia. It indicates that workers in Australia are around 50 per cent more productive than their counterparts in New Zealand.' Do you agree with this statement? Why or why not?
5. ABS data indicates that in 2008–09 employment in the Australian machinery and equipment industry increased by 8.3 per cent from the previous year, while production value over the same period declined by 4.8 per cent. What would be the possible reasons for this inverse development? Discuss.
6. Check ABS statistics on Australia's manufacturing sector in the most recent ABS release under cat. no. 8155.0:
   (a) What has happened to the value of production and total employment in the manufacturing sector since 2008–09?
   (b) Identify the manufacturing sectors which have recorded most growth in production value.
   (c) Identify the manufacturing sectors which have recorded most losses in employment.
   (d) Draw a few conclusions on the evolution of the Australian manufacturing sector.
7. Access the WTO statistics for trade in manufactures at <www.wto.org/english/res_e/statis_e/its2009_e/its09_merch_trade_product_e.htm>. Go to Table II.32 and Table II.33 which show exports/imports of manufactures of selected economies. Select three developed economies and three developing countries. Compare:
   (a) growth of exports in recent years
   (b) the share of manufactured exports in total exports
   (c) the ratio between exports and imports.
Draw up a brief report.

Chapter 21

Macroeconomic management in Australia

LEARNING OBJECTIVES

After studying this chapter, you will be able to:

1. explain the macroeconomic objectives of the federal government and the potential conflict between them
2. outline the government policy instruments for promoting stability and growth
3. explain the conflicting social and economic objectives
4. describe the major problems and limits—constitutional, institutional, practical and political—of economic management.

INTRODUCTION

In previous modules we have encountered government policies that affect individual components of the economy (consumers, firms, industries, markets). These are termed **microeconomic policies**. Policies that affect the aggregate level of economic activity (including total production, income, expenditure and employment) are called **macroeconomic policies**.

The distinction between micro and macro policies is not always clear: some microeconomic measures have macroeconomic implications, and vice versa.

We have discussed the general purposes or goals of government policies in three broad groups: **reallocation**, **redistribution** and **stabilisation**. Microeconomic policies are mainly concerned with reallocation and redistribution. Macroeconomic policy has twin goals of stability and growth. If these goals are achieved, the government has more scope to attain satisfactory reallocation and redistribution as well.

The goal of stabilisation is also referred to as economic management.

THE KEYNESIAN INFLUENCE ON ECONOMIC MANAGEMENT

The British economist J.M. Keynes, author of *General Theory of Employment, Interest and Money* (1936), overturned classical economics. He established a new school of economic theory on the causes of, and remedies for, fluctuations in the level of economic activity. Keynes pointed out for the first time that, where an economy was in equilibrium, it could experience such a low level of aggregate demand that there was mass unemployment. Keynes urged governments to try to raise aggregate demand to a level high enough to ensure full employment of resources. Keynes argued that two main weapons at the disposal of government to lift the level of aggregate demand are fiscal and monetary measures. (These are discussed in detail later in Chapters 22 and 23.)

THE 1945 WHITE PAPER

After the general acceptance of Keynes's theories before and during World War II, in 1945 the Australian Government published a White Paper on Full Employment. This argued that government should undertake a macroeconomic role in the management of the economy to promote the following objectives:

- full employment
- stability of the general price level
- economic growth
- external balance.

The government adopted the policy of the White Paper. It envisaged that appropriate measures would have to be used to fight unemployment and falling prices in some periods, and overfull employment (see overleaf) and rising prices in others.

microeconomic policies
government policies that affect individual components of the economy (consumers, firms, industries, markets)

macroeconomic policies
government policies that affect the aggregate level of economic activity (including total production, income, expenditure and employment)

reallocation of resources
when land, labour and capital are put to a different use. The government can determine reallocation through tax policies and incentives, subsidies and other forms of intervention

redistribution
intervention by the government to transfer income from high to low income earners through progressive income tax and cash transfer payments (social security)

stabilisation
pursuing economic growth under minimal business cycle fluctuations, providing more scope to attain satisfactory reallocation and redistribution (the two other goals of macroeconomic policies)

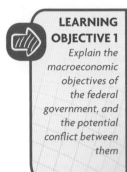

MACROECONOMIC OBJECTIVES OF THE FEDERAL GOVERNMENT

Current macroeconomic objectives of the federal government resemble those of the 1945 White Paper. We will look at them in more detail.

INTERNAL BALANCE

internal balance
stability of prices (a minimal rate of inflation), and stability of employment (a minimal rate of unemployment)

Internal balance is defined as **stability of prices** (a minimal rate of inflation), and **stability of employment** (a minimal rate of unemployment). A low and stable rate of inflation is desirable because it is fairer, it promotes economic efficiency, and it encourages savings.

Low inflation

stability of prices
a macroeconomic objective to achieve a minimal rate of inflation, through productivity improvements (mainly due to technological progress) and increased competition

Low inflation is a priority macroeconomic objective for the government, especially in the expansion and peak phases of the business cycle. After the output trough of 1991, the Australian economy has generally had a good performance in the area of inflation. The CPI was generally kept below 2 per cent per annum for the rest of the 1990s. Inflation generally exceeded the 2 per cent level in the 2000s, but not by much (see Chapter 12 for more details). Most experts agree that improvements in productivity, mainly due to technological progress and increased competition in goods (e.g. computers and motor cars) and services markets are the main factors behind the low inflation rates of the 1990s and the 2000s.

An accelerating inflation rate is not only politically undesirable for any government, it also results in an unplanned and inequitable redistribution of income among members of the society. Moreover, accelerating inflation can encourage investment in unproductive sectors (e.g. real estate) and reduce the purchasing power of savings. High levels of inflation make Australia less competitive on international markets.

More details on the effects of inflation are presented in Chapter 12.

Full employment

stability of employment
a macroeconomic objective to achieve a minimal rate of unemployment

full employment
a main macroeconomic objective geared towards a full employment zone or target, which allows for a relatively small proportion of unemployment

The **full employment** objective is geared towards a full employment zone or target which allows for a relatively small proportion of unemployment. Unemployment targets are also set at a level that complements the government's price stability objective. From a peak of about 11 per cent in 1993, Australia's unemployment rate was brought down to around 4.2 per cent in 2008. As discussed in Chapter 11, from an international perspective, Australia has a middle ranking among OECD members in terms of unemployment rates. As discussed before, the natural rate of unemployment or, as it is referred to in Australia, the Non-Accelerating Inflation Rate of Unemployment (NAIRU) can vary over time. In the late 1960s and 1970s the NAIRU was between 1 and 2 per cent, while in the late 2000s it was estimated to be around 5 per cent. Therefore, the NAIRU is that level of unemployment that can be achieved using expansionary macroeconomic policy, without causing inflation. Since the unemployment at the NAIRU is mainly structural unemployment, it follows that microeconomic policies are needed to reduce unemployment any further.

Let's remember also that under full employment, cyclical unemployment is absent.

When the actual unemployment figure is less than the targeted figure, the situation is called 'overfull employment'. Full employment has always been of major importance.

High levels of unemployment have many social costs, such as increases in crime rates, family break-ups and suicide rates. See Chapter 11 for more details.

In economic terms, high levels of unemployment imply that some economic resources are not utilised, which results in a lower standard of living. It is unrealistic to hope to achieve zero inflation or unemployment. There is little agreement about what is an acceptable rate of either, other than the lowest that can feasibly be maintained without too many undesirable side effects.

EXTERNAL BALANCE

External balance is an absence of substantial deficits on the current account of the balance of payments, and a relatively stable exchange rate.

external balance
an absence of substantial deficits on the current account of the balance of payments, and a relatively stable exchange rate

Current account deficit

Any current account deficit should be consistent with the required rate of financial capital inflow. Although a deficit on the current account of Australia's balance of payments is an accepted outcome in the Australian economic context, economists monitor the size of this deficit, especially as a ratio of GDP. A peak in the current account deficit was reached in 2007–08 (–$74.0 billion), representing around 6 per cent of Australia's GDP. However, as discussed in Chapter 18, the current account deficit is not necessarily a big issue, as long as the deficit is maintained within reasonable limits and the interest on the resulting foreign debt is serviced adequately from the export income.

Stable exchange rate

An external balance also encompasses a reasonably stable exchange rate at a level compatible with domestic economic welfare. The Australian dollar became reasonably strong after the low of 1993, but it recorded an all-time low against the US dollar in March 2001 (A$1 = US$0.4890). This was a result of lower demand for it following the East Asian financial crisis, combined with a weak situation in international commodity markets and relatively low interest rates in Australia.

A sharp increase in the exchange rate of the Australian dollar, as that in the late part of 2010, can become a hindrance to exporters and ultimately to economic growth.

ECONOMIC GROWTH

Economic growth is an increase in real GDP. Because it is the basis for improving standards of living in Australian society, it is a crucial objective of government.

Australia's recent economic growth performance as measured by real GDP growth was discussed in Chapter 9, and is further elaborated in Chapter 25. We emphasise here that the government's macroeconomic objective of economic growth does not mean a very high rate of economic growth to be implemented at any price. It has to be a sustainable rate of economic growth. A rate of growth that is relatively too high for the potential of the economy is called 'overheating'. The government tries to prevent overheating because of its consequences: it fuels inflation, increases demand for imports, and contributes to the deterioration of the current account balance. Australia's economy was overheated in the late 1980s, and possibly in the mid 1990s. In the phases of contraction and trough (e.g. 1982 to 1983, 1991 to 1993, and 2008 to 2009), the government has a priority objective in supporting higher rates of real GDP growth.

A negative aspect of Australia's economy is its low ratio of domestic saving and its corresponding dependence on overseas borrowings to finance much of its domestic investment, which over the years has generated high levels of foreign debt. Consequently, any acceleration in Australia's economic growth will be linked to those measures, which not only reduce our growing foreign debt, but also promote domestic saving. The main indicators related to Australia's macroeconomic objectives in selected years over 1996 to 2009 are presented in Table 21.1.

Table 21.1   **Main indicators related to Australia's macroeconomic objectives, in selected years over 1996–2009**

INDICATOR	1996	1997	1998	2001	2002	2005	2006	2007	2008	2009
Real GDP change (% p.a.)	4.0	3.9	5.1	2.1	4.0	3.1	2.6	4.2	2.3	0.8
Unemployment rate (% p.a.)	8.2	8.3	7.7	6.8	6.4	5.0	4.8	4.4	4.2	5.6
Consumer prices (% change p.a.)	2.6	0.3	0.9	4.4	3.0	2.7	3.5	2.3	4.4	1.8
Current account balance as a % of GDP	−3.3	−2.8	−4.7	−2.0	−3.6	−5.6	−5.2	−6.1	−4.4	−4.1
Exchange rate (A$1 = US$X)	0.783	0.742	0.628	0.517	0.543	0.762	0.753	0.837	0.835	0.780

Source: Adapted from OECD, Economic Outlook, November 2003 and May 2010.

The recession of the early 1990s was accompanied by high unemployment rates and relatively low inflation rates, which appears to be in line with Keynes's economics theory. However, the two next three-year periods of high to moderate economic growth seem to observe the theory only on the unemployment side with downward unemployment rates, while inflation was generally kept at reasonably low levels.

CONFLICT BETWEEN MACROECONOMIC OBJECTIVES

It is rare for a government to achieve all its macroeconomic objectives simultaneously. Therefore one of the main challenges for government is to prioritise its objectives. Many economic objectives are incompatible or mutually exclusive, and major conflicts between them must be considered.

Employment stability versus price stability

Economic history shows that the simultaneous achievement of these two objectives is almost impossible. During periods of high employment, labour shortages occur and workers push up their rates of pay. Employers are willing to pay higher labour costs because they realise that, during this period of high demand, these costs can be passed on in the form of higher prices. Inflationary expectations breed in this environment, leading to a further acceleration in inflation.

On the other hand, if unemployment rises, labour becomes more abundant and the pressure on wage rates declines. Employers are reluctant to absorb higher production costs as aggregate demand tapers off, while inflationary expectations decline. Higher unemployment usually leads to a lower rate of inflation.

Economic growth versus employment stability

Economic growth is an attractive goal because it brings about higher living standards. However, the objective of economic growth is not necessarily compatible with the objective of employment stability (minimal rate of unemployment).

As explained in Chapter 20, economic growth can result from technological changes: old skills become redundant as new technology demands new and different skills. Therefore, economic growth can be accompanied by structural unemployment, and lead to lower employment levels in the short term.

Employment stability versus external stability

Changes in internal economic conditions have implications for Australia's external viability. Conflicts occur between internal and external objectives. For example, if, as a result of full employment, our inflation rate exceeds that of our major overseas competitors, then Australia's export competitiveness and that of our import-competing industries can suffer.

A rising income and aggregate demand level in Australia (as experienced in 1988–89) can raise the level of our foreign debt through an increased level of imports, as well as producing pressure on the value of the Australian dollar. Conversely, if the federal government, as in 1989–90, targets a reduction in Australia's current account deficit, then the restrictive macroeconomic policies designed to reduce aggregate demand (and import demand) will increase Australia's unemployment rate.

WHY ECONOMIC STABILITY?

LINK TO BUSINESS

Let us examine the effects of economic instability on an individual entrepreneur.

Jasmine Smart, the owner of a software business, makes a number of assumptions in her business plan regarding the Australian demand for computer hardware and software (which is related to the economic growth for the whole economy and for various sectors). She sets a target for turnover and on this basis develops a price strategy. She assumes a certain level of interest rates and inflation. She plans her labour costs, and on this basis hires a certain number of staff. Most importantly, she sets the minimum level of profit margins that will cover her costs (including overheads) and will provide a net income in line with her effort, risk and expectations.

If, unexpectedly, the economy registers a sudden drop in activity, the demand for computer software and for Jasmine Smart's computer services will decline. As a consequence, the prices for computer software will weaken. Smart has to make a choice:

- to discount her products substantially and record a drop in turnover; among other things, this will reduce profitability per unit of product
- to maintain the listed prices more or less unchanged, and accumulate stocks and debt to the creditors, such as her suppliers and her bank.

In either case her net profit (if any) will be under pressure. If the situation continues, Jasmine Smart may be forced to close her business.

A substantial upward fluctuation for inflation is not good either. It erodes the business's profit margins, and also the disposable income of consumers. The resulting lower expenditure has a multiple regressive effect on business income.

Finally, an uncontrolled increase in the current account deficit is likely to put downward pressure on the Australian dollar. The price of imported computer hardware and software will increase, which will be a blow to Jasmine Smart's business.

We all need a stable economy.

QUESTIONS
1. Discuss the effects of too high economic growth on a small business.
2. What are the effects of inflation on a small business? Explain.

LEARNING OBJECTIVE 2

Outline the government policy instruments for promoting stability and growth

GOVERNMENT POLICY INSTRUMENTS FOR PROMOTING STABILITY AND GROWTH

The government's economic management policies are considered in detail in the subsequent chapters of this module. At this stage, we introduce the main instruments by which the government may try to achieve stability and growth: fiscal policy, monetary policy, external policy and incomes policy.

FISCAL (BUDGETARY) POLICY

Fiscal policy comprises decisions about the level and pattern of government outlays and receipts, and public debt management (Chapter 22).

At about Budget time each year (and sometimes more frequently) the federal government has to decide the 'stance' or 'setting' of fiscal policy during the new financial year.

- If it believes that domestic demand is growing too strongly (causing a build-up in inflationary pressure, or worsening the trade deficit by encouraging too many imports), the government attempts to slow demand by moving to a tighter (restrictive, contractionary) fiscal policy. It tightens fiscal policy by increasing taxation or cutting government spending (or some combination of both). So the tightening of fiscal policy usually results in a reduction in the size of the Budget deficit.
- Conversely, if the government believes that domestic demand is growing too slowly (causing unemployment to rise), it attempts to increase demand by moving to a looser (stimulatory, expansionary) stance of fiscal policy. The government loosens fiscal policy by reducing taxation or increasing government spending (or some combination), which usually results in a larger Budget deficit.

MONETARY POLICY

Monetary policy comprises measures to influence the growth of the money supply and the level of interest rates (Chapter 23).

The most important instrument to exercise a degree of control over the money supply is the market operations of the Reserve Bank. The government adopts a firm monetary policy at times of rapid economic growth and high (demand-pull) inflation by keeping a check on money supply growth and maintaining high interest rates. Conversely, it adopts an easy monetary policy, at times of high unemployment, to allow interest rates to fall and the money supply to grow, encouraging expansion of economic activity and employment.

The government's monetary policy is closely linked with its external policy, because of the relationship between interest rates and the exchange rate.

EXTERNAL POLICY

External policy comprises government decisions about the exchange rate, financial capital flows and other factors that affect the balance of payments in our transactions with the rest of the world (Chapter 24).

An unhealthy balance of payments and an unstable exchange rate have unfavourable effects on the domestic economy, which must be counteracted by appropriate macroeconomic policies, and these may be in conflict with those required for achieving internal stability. For instance, a huge current account deficit and a falling exchange rate require contractionary monetary and fiscal policies to raise interest rates and attract foreign capital inflows; but these will be a constraint on domestic economic management if there is a high level of unemployment, which requires expansionary policies.

INCOMES POLICY

Incomes policy comprises decisions that influence the rate of growth of incomes, particularly wages (Chapter 23).

The federal government's control over incomes is limited: the Constitution gives it no direct power in this area, and a referendum seeking that power was rejected in 1973. Therefore, the government must rely on indirect measures to influence wage growth.

Incomes policy was the Labor Government's favoured method of fighting inflation and unemployment, simultaneously, during the 1980s and early 1990s. The Howard Government's policy changed the emphasis from centralised wage negotiations (under the Accord) to a system of individual contracts and workplace agreements between employer and employees. The new system increased the potential for wages breakouts, especially in areas with labour shortages. After assuming office, the Labor Government repealed the entirety of the *Workplace Relations Act 1996* and its subsequent amendments.

Because the four arms of macroeconomic policy are interdependent, the government must try to ensure they are consistent with each other. Compromises must be made between conflicting goals (such as price stability and full employment), so such harmony of policies is difficult to achieve.

CONFLICTING SOCIAL AND ECONOMIC OBJECTIVES

LEARNING OBJECTIVE 3
Explain the conflicting social and economic objectives

Government decision makers must take into account conflicting macroeconomic objectives and possible lack of harmony of macroeconomic policies, as described above, and they must also recognise conflicting economic and social objectives.

- On one hand, the government must take action that it believes to be best for the economy, such as maximising economic growth and maintaining internal and external stability.
- On the other hand, many of the government's policies are based on humanitarian principles, such as foreign aid to low-income countries; or are desirable on the grounds of justice or equity, such as equity in income distribution, resource conservation, urban congestion, pollution, and other factors that affect the living standards of Australians.

EQUITABLE INCOME DISTRIBUTION

High economic growth often results in greater inequality of income distribution. Typically, high economic growth creates a scarcity in the supply of resources, and escalating inflation. As a result, income is redistributed away from people on fixed incomes, weak bargaining groups in the community, and others.

Often, in the process of economic growth, a 'dual economy' arises, where a particular sector of the economy benefits from growth at the expense of other sectors. It is the responsibility of government, through its taxation and expenditure policies, to ensure that the whole community has the chance to enjoy the benefits of Australia's economic growth.

Through its redistribution policy, government can ensure that the potential conflict between these objectives is minimised.

ENVIRONMENTAL PROTECTION

A growing area of community concern is the apparent conflict between economic growth and environmental protection; that is, the protection of non-renewable resources (e.g. minerals).

The fact is that market prices often fail to fully incorporate environmental costs. For example, the price of paper does not incorporate the full value of all natural resources used in its production, because it does not include the cost of some resources used up, such as the atmosphere, which are available to all for no charge. As a result, the production of paper, reflecting the inflated demand for paper caused by exaggerated waste in consumption, may be higher than optimal. Or, to put it in another way, the total costs to society may exceed the market price measured benefits. The exclusion of environmental costs means that paper manufacturers have no incentive to adopt alternative methods (e.g. more recycling) which could lower the cost to the environment.

The activities of the Green movement in Australia have focused attention on the pursuits of developers, miners, woodchippers, chemical companies, the uranium industry, and their effect on Australia's natural resources.

Economic development has been a major concern since the early 1990s, given our high unemployment levels. There is not necessarily a trade-off between environmental depletion and economic growth. Some companies have been required to restore environments that they have damaged. Reafforestation and redevelopment programs try to ensure sufficient resources for the future. The emphasis is now on sustainable economic development with concern for environmental factors. This includes measures for the expansion of the use of renewable forms of energy (e.g. solar, hydro, wind, tidal), energy efficiency measures and industrial/domestic waste minimisation measures, all which are meant to prolong the life expectancy of non-renewable resources (e.g. oil, gas, minerals) with obvious economic and social benefits for humankind.

LIVING STANDARDS

High economic growth may increase work stress, urban congestion, health problems and levels of pollution (see also Chapter 25). Clearly these are social problems, but they also have economic costs, such as absenteeism and low worker productivity, which lower our economic growth potential.

All these social costs are important in determining Australia's standard of living. Economic growth may make us all worse off, if these social considerations are neglected.

FOREIGN AID

Government foreign aid or official development assistance refers to all forms of concessional assistance provided to low-income countries to encourage economic development and welfare. It includes 'soft loans' (with favourable terms), emergency relief, grants, bilateral aid and multilateral aid. Budgetary restraints, especially in recessionary periods, may limit the amount of foreign aid. Official surveys indicate that while there is approval and support for foreign aid among the Australian public, there is stronger support for many alternative ways of spending public funds and for tax cuts. In competition with these other desirable ends, there is little support for additional spending on aid.

PROBLEMS OF ECONOMIC MANAGEMENT

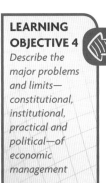

LEARNING OBJECTIVE 4
Describe the major problems and limits— constitutional, institutional, practical and political—of economic management

There are many factors in our economy which place limits on the extent and influence of government policies. These factors can be grouped into four types: constitutional, institutional, practical and political.

CONSTITUTIONAL LIMITS

The Constitution divides responsibilities between the Commonwealth (federal) and state governments, and defines the powers of the Commonwealth Government.

The Constitution prevents the federal government from exercising direct control over a range of matters outside the territories (the Australian Capital Territory and the Northern Territory). These exclusive powers of the states include law and order, prices and incomes, lands and national parks, companies, infrastructure, and public utilities.

However, the Commonwealth does manage to influence some of the activities over which it does not have constitutional control:

- by indirect influence
- by grants to the states
- by cooperation with the states.

INSTITUTIONAL LIMITS

The power of the government is limited and balanced by that of other organisations, such as trade unions, large corporations, and employers' associations. Furthermore, the public service itself may limit the effectiveness of government policies.

PRACTICAL LIMITS

Even where the government has legal power to implement a policy, it may face practical problems in trying to carry it out. One practical limit is the quality of information and statistics, and especially of forecasts on which economic and social policies are based. The government relies on information supplied to it by the Australian Bureau of Statistics and many departments and organisations. For instance, the estimated revenue from income tax in a Budget depends on the expected increase in the size of the labour force, and the rate of growth of wages and other incomes over the Budget year. If incomes grow less rapidly and unemployment is higher than was predicted, the Budget deficit can increase steeply.

A second practical limit is uncertainty about the reactions of the market sector to government Budget measures and other policies. For instance, the market sector was angered by indirect taxes in the 1993–94 Budget. Reactions to the introduction of the GST in 2000 represented another uncertainty.

The overseas sector imposes a third limit. The Australian Government has little power to control the exchange rate of the Australian dollar, overseas interest rates or investment plans of multinational companies.

POLITICAL LIMITS

Probably the greatest limit to the powers of the government is the election cycle, which obliges the government to face the voters every three years or so. This element of political uncertainty makes long-term planning almost impossible. That is why the government in office tends to implement certain changes in taxes or social security benefits cautiously, usually in the mid-term Budget, hoping that the voters will have accepted them before the next election.

MACROECONOMIC MANAGEMENT ISSUES IN CHINA

LINK TO INTERNATIONAL ECONOMY

With the economic reform initiated by its former leader Deng Xiaoping in the late 1970s, China started a phase of strong economic growth. The Chinese Government is aware that a high economic growth rate is paramount for an improvement in the living standards of the population. But this growth has been accompanied by complex macroeconomic difficulties, commensurate with the huge size of this nation.

One chronic problem of China's economy is the chronic weakness of central government finances. According to Asian Development Bank (ADB) data, the Chinese Government could not achieve its target of a balanced Budget by 2000, mainly because widespread abuses of the tax system had undermined revenues. In fact, in 2001 the Budget deficit reached a level of −2.5 per cent of GDP. It was only in 2007 that the Budget recorded a slight surplus (0.6 per cent of GDP), but the big fiscal effort to avoid the effects of the GFC brought China's Budget again in deficit in 2008 and 2009.

Table 21.2   **Indicators of China's macroeconomic performance, 2001–09 (selected years)**

	2001	2003	2005	2007	2008	2009
Real GDP change (% p.a.)	8.3	10.0	11.3	14.2	9.6	9.1
Consumer prices changes (% p.a.)	0.7	1.2	1.8	4.8	5.9	−0.7
Unemployment rate (% p.a.)	3.6	4.3	4.2	4.0	4.2	4.3
Current account balance (% of GDP)	1.3	2.8	7.1	10.6	9.6	6.0
Exchange rate (renminbi/US$1)	8.2771	8.2770	8.1943	7.6075	6.9487	6.8314
Foreign reserves (US$ billion)	218.7	412.2	825.6	1534.4	1953.3	2425.9
Overall Budget balance as a percentage of GDP	−2.5	−2.2	−1.2	0.6	−0.4	−2.2

Source: Adapted from Asian Development Bank, Key Indicators 2010.

The Budget deficit problem has forced the government to rely heavily on customs and excise charges and on taxes paid by state enterprises, more than half of which make a loss. As some 60 per cent of the government's revenue is drawn from the state sector, the poor performance of state-owned companies is an ongoing problem. A ratio between fiscal revenue and GDP of around 19 per cent, recorded in 2007, represented a slight improvement, but the picture for state-owned enterprises remains fairly bleak. For a number of years the privatisation of state-owned enterprises has been a major objective of the Chinese Government.

There is no question that urban unemployment—officially around 4 per cent, but in fact much higher—is a growing concern for the authorities, given that the large numbers of unemployed people represent a potential threat to social order in a country without a formal social security net.

But the government can be reasonably satisfied with having achieved broader macroeconomic targets. Retail price inflation fell to under 2 per cent over 2001–05, compared with a high (since the 1949 revolution) of more than 20 per cent in 1994. This was achieved without a contraction in economic growth, which varied at a high level of 10 to 14 per cent per annum over 2002–05, slowing down to around 9 per cent during the GFC.

In 2003, China's central bank moved to cool its overheated economy by raising the reserve requirement for banks and financial institutions from 6 to 7 per cent. A spokesperson for the People's Bank of China estimated that this would freeze some $30 billion worth of deposits in the banking system.

While China's massive export trade saw its official reserves soar to over US$2400 billion in 2009, the Chinese currency was allowed only a modest appreciation in a narrow band around 8.28 renminbi to the US dollar. Although an increasing number of economists are warning against an overheated economy, Chinese officials are refusing to take the pressure off by revaluing the currency, concerned that this could send the economy into a tailspin, similarly to Japan's experience when the yen was revalued under the 1985 Plaza Accord and the Japanese economy went into a prolonged recession. A much stronger renminbi would affect exports and would trigger enormous job losses.

Is China's economic performance of relevance to the Australian economy? Of course it is. China has become Australia's number one trade partner, taking over 21 per cent of Australia's total exports of goods, and providing about 18 per cent of Australia's merchandise imports. China is Australia's second market for exports of services and an increasingly important destination for Australian foreign investment. China has also provided foreign direct investment in recent years in several Australian industries, especially mining, agriculture, textiles and clothing.

China's economy is, undoubtedly, an important factor of stability for both the regional and the world economy.

QUESTIONS

1. What are the major macroeconomic objectives for the Chinese Government?
2. Is the potential conflict between high economic growth and inflation a real threat for China's economy? Explain.
3. Why is the Chinese Government reluctant to revalue the Chinese currency? Explain.

SUMMARY

1. Economic stability (management) is one of the major functions of the Australian Government. The major macroeconomic management objectives of the federal government, first defined in the 1945 White Paper on Full Employment, have remained substantially unchanged. They are:
   - (a) employment stability
   - (b) price stability
   - (c) economic growth
   - (d) external balance.

2. Many economic objectives are incompatible. Major conflicts that need to be considered include:
   - (a) employment stability versus price stability
   - (b) economic growth versus employment stability
   - (c) employment stability versus external stability.

3. The government uses several policy instruments to promote stability and growth: fiscal, monetary, external and incomes. Because the four arms of its macroeconomic policy are interdependent, the government must try to ensure that they are consistent with each other. However, the need for compromises on conflicting goals endangers policy consistency.

4. Many factors in our economy place limits on the extent and influence of government policies: constitutional; institutional (e.g. trade unions, big business); practical (e.g. quality of information and analysis, matters related to the overseas sector); and political.

KEY TERMS

external balance 447	macroeconomic policies 445	stabilisation 445
full employment 446	microeconomic policies 445	stability of employment 446
internal balance 446	reallocation of resources 445	stability of prices 446
	redistribution 445	

REVIEW QUESTIONS

1. What are the macroeconomic objectives of the federal government?
2. What are the main government policy instruments for promoting stability and growth?
3. What policy instruments can the government use if it believes that domestic demand is growing too strongly?
4. Give two examples of conflicts between macroeconomic objectives.
5. What are the practical limits on government economic management?
6. Explain the meaning of political limits in relation to government economic management.
7. Explain the meaning of internal stability.
8. Is there any relationship between internal stability and external stability?

APPLIED QUESTIONS AND EXERCISES

1. Using the statistical information in Table 21.1 (p. 448) and other relevant references about the situation of the Australian economy, outline the main macroeconomic objectives for the Australian Government in 2009.
2. Moves to achieve stable prices may cost jobs in the short term: why is this? Draw a diagram, using statistics on Australia's annual GDP growth, unemployment and inflation rates between 2007 and 2010. Explain if these indicators have behaved in accordance with Keynesian theory.
3. In relation to the Link to International Economy on page 454, outline similarities and/or differences in the issues for fiscal policy in China and Australia.
4. The theoretical wisdom is that when the Australian dollar falls, import prices rise and hence inflation rises too. Using the information in Table 21.1:

(a) Explain how rising import prices contribute in general to increasing inflation rates.

(b) Explain the relationship between the rising Australian dollar and consumer prices over 2006–09.

(c) Discuss the influence of the external sector (e.g. current account balance and exchange rate) on Australia's real GDP growth.

5. The table below shows some major macroeconomic indicators for Singapore from 1997 to 2003. In your opinion, what were the most important macroeconomic objectives for the Singapore Government in 2003?

	1997	1998	1999	2000	2001	2002	2003
Real GDP	8.6	−0.9	6.9	9.7	−1.9	2.2	1.1
CPI (% p.a.)	2.0	−0.3	0.1	1.3	1.0	−0.4	0.5
U/E rate (%)	1.8	3.2	3.5	3.1	3.3	4.4	4.7
CAB* US$ million	18 123	18 544	15 284	13 246	16 104	18 873	28 186
S$/1 US$	1.4848	1.6736	1.6950	1.7240	1.7917	1.7906	1.7422

Note: *Current Account Balance.*

Chapter 22

Fiscal policy

LEARNING OBJECTIVES

After studying this chapter, you will be able to:

1. explain what is meant by fiscal policy
2. broadly analyse the revenue and expenditure items in the federal Budget
3. explain the various Budget outcomes—surplus, deficit, balanced
4. distinguish between the domestic and overseas components and between cyclical and structural components of the federal Budget
5. explain how a federal Budget deficit can be financed
6. discuss the effects of federal Budget financing on Australia's economy
7. outline the strengths and weaknesses of fiscal policy in Australia.

INTRODUCTION

Fiscal policy involves the use of government expenditure and revenue to pursue macroeconomic policy objectives. Fiscal policy can be very effective in manipulating aggregate demand.

Fiscal policy can be defined as the **budgetary stance** of the central government of a country.

In Chapter 8 you studied the circular flow, which illustrates the dual role of government in the economy. Government taxation collections reduce income to the private sector, and its expenditure adds to aggregate demand. In Chapter 21 you read about the major macroeconomic objectives of the central government. These can be summarised as maximising the rate of growth of production and employment, while maintaining low inflation and a stable balance of payments.

Discretionary fiscal policy refers to those aspects of the Budget over which the government exercises control. It involves deliberate government action to change the level of spending in the economy by altering government spending and/or taxation.

You should understand that the central government has a significant influence on the level of spending, even if it does not use discretionary fiscal policy, because government spending constitutes a large proportion of total spending in the economy. For example, if private spending fell and government spending did not change, then total spending would fall. However, if the government used discretionary fiscal policy either to raise spending or to lower taxes to compensate for the fall in private spending, then total spending would not change. In 2009, in response to the global financial crisis (GFC) the government used discretionary fiscal policy in the form of a massive increase in government expenditure to offset the expected decline in private expenditure which would cause a large increase in unemployment.

fiscal policy
involves government expenditure and revenue to pursue macroeconomic policy objectives

budgetary stance
the current state of government fiscal policy (i.e. expansionary, contractionary or neutral)

WHAT IS FISCAL POLICY?

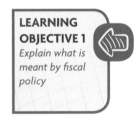

LEARNING OBJECTIVE 1
Explain what is meant by fiscal policy

Governments collect taxes, licences, rates and other levies to spend on goods and services on behalf of the country. The main areas of spending in Australia by the Federal Government are social security and welfare, health, education and defence.

To implement fiscal policy, the federal government makes decisions about how it raises revenue and how it distributes that revenue through its expenditure.

Proposals in these areas are announced each year in the federal government's Budget statements and in supplementary statements that the government may choose to make at other times.

A **budget** is a statement of intended income and expenditure, and fiscal policy covers those areas, so fiscal policy is sometimes also called **budgetary policy**. Budgets usually contain a statement about the outlook for the economy over the coming year.

It is important to note that the actual outcomes for government revenue and expenditure usually do not match budget forecasts. Revenue may be lower than expected if unemployment is higher than forecast and consequently income tax receipts are below forecast. When considering the impact of fiscal policy the actual outcomes should be contrasted with the intended outcomes.

budget
a statement of intended income and expenditure

budgetary policy
involves government expenditure and revenue to pursue macroeconomic policy objectives

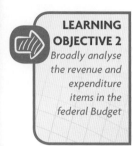

REVENUE AND SPENDING

Most central government spending is non-discretionary, in the sense that it is the outcome of prior commitments. For example, commitments to the purchase of military equipment, the payment of pensions and the funding of the health system are long-term and difficult to abandon. Similarly, most sources of taxation revenue are tied to the level of aggregate expenditure in the economy. For example, if total spending is rising then tax collections from income, from sales of goods and services and from sales of property and financial transactions will increase. The nature of the taxation system determines how rapidly government revenue will increase.

Nevertheless governments of different political persuasions will have different priorities in the way they levy the burden of taxation and the way they distribute the benefits of government spending, for example the way in which high income earners are dealt with varies between parties.

progressive taxation
as individual incomes rise, the percentage of income deducted as income tax rises

In Australia there is a **progressive taxation** of income: as individual incomes rise, the percentage of income deducted as income tax increases. Therefore a rise in incomes produces an even faster rise in income tax revenue for the government.

The main sources of revenue for the Australian Government are:

- taxes on income of individuals
- taxes on company profits and petroleum resource rent taxation
- excise and customs duties, which are taxes levied on the production of oil and gas products and on imports of certain products such as motor cars, textiles, clothing and footwear
- sales taxes
- taxes on deposits and withdrawals from superannuation funds.

The main areas of expenditure are:

- social security and welfare, including pensions and unemployment benefits
- health
- infrastructure, transport and energy
- defence
- education, mainly for schools.

balanced Budget
occurs when expenditure is equal to revenue

Note that all revenue from the Goods and Services Tax is allocated to state governments replacing payments made to states by the Commonwealth Government.

Figure 22.1 shows taxation and revenue for the 2010–11 federal Budget.

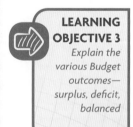

BUDGET OUTCOMES

Budgets may have long-term, medium-term and short-term goals. For the long term, a Budget may aim to influence the level of efficiency or the level of savings in the economy. In the medium term, the aim may be to reduce the Budget deficit as a percentage of GDP in order to assist with problems in the balance of payments. In the short run, the aim may be to reduce unemployment caused by external shocks.

When government expenditure exceeds tax revenue, the government is said to be running a Budget deficit. If government revenue exceeds expenditure, this is described as a Budget surplus. A **balanced Budget** occurs when expenditure is equal to revenue, which is an improbable event.

The charts below summarise Australian Government revenues and expenses for 2010–11 on an accrual basis. Total revenue for 2010–11 is expected to be $321.8 billion, an increase of 5.9 per cent on estimated revenue since the *Mid-Year Economic and Fiscal Outlook 2009–10*. Total expenses for 2010–11 are expected to be $354.6 billion, an increase of 2.8 per cent on estimated expenses since the *Mid-Year Economic and Fiscal Outlook 2009–10*.

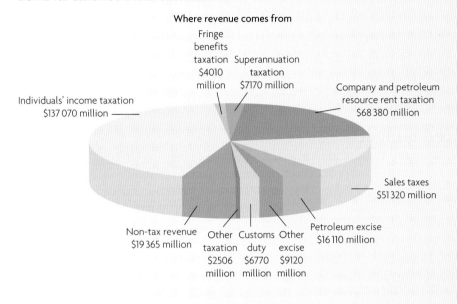

Where revenue comes from

Fringe benefits taxation $4010 million
Superannuation taxation $7170 million
Company and petroleum resource rent taxation $68 380 million
Individuals' income taxation $137 070 million
Sales taxes $51 320 million
Non-tax revenue $19 365 million
Other taxation $2506 million
Customs duty $6770 million
Other excise $9120 million
Petroleum excise $16 110 million

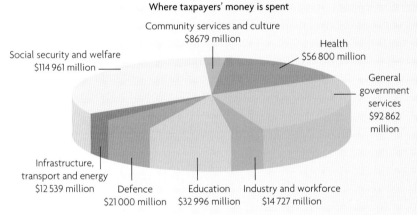

Where taxpayers' money is spent

Community services and culture $8679 million
Health $56 800 million
Social security and welfare $114 961 million
General government services $92 862 million
Infrastructure, transport and energy $12 539 million
Defence $21 000 million
Education $32 996 million
Industry and workforce $14 727 million

Figure 22.1
The nature and distribution of taxation and revenue in the 2010–11 federal Budget

Source: Australian Government taxation and spending, Australian Treasury, Budget, 2010–11, Appendix G.

The planned outcome of the central government's Budget is based, at least partly, on advice from economists and financial advisers in the Treasury and the central bank, and is a response to forecast changes in the economic cycle (Chapter 8). Given that most governments have macroeconomic objectives of minimising unemployment and inflation, the response to an expected downturn in private sector demand is likely to be either an increase in government spending or a reduction in tax levels. On the other hand, if there is concern that rapid growth in demand will lead to higher inflation, then fiscal policy is likely to move the Budget towards a surplus.

These possible outcomes and their effects are set out in Table 22.1 overleaf. Each outcome has significant consequences for the government's **economic management** and thus for the whole economy.

The third column in Table 22.1 reinforces the notion of the impact of the Budget on aggregate demand. In fact, the descriptions in that column require further discussion.

economic management
the use of the full range of policies, such as monetary and fiscal policy, to achieve economic objectives

Table 22.1   **Possible Budget outcomes and Budget stances**

OUTCOME ON THE ECONOMY	DESCRIPTION	BUDGET STANCE
Balanced Budget	Where expected revenue equals expected expenditure	Neutral
Budget contractionary surplus	Where expected revenue is higher than expected expenditure	Contractionary
Budget expansionary deficit	Where expected expenditure is higher than expected revenue	Expansionary

Balanced budget

No federal Budget is neutral in its effect. As we have shown, government Budget decisions affect the wider economy. However, that influence is reduced considerably by a balanced Budget.

To understand this, consider what equivalence of revenue and expenditure means. If total revenue remains unchanged, so must total expenditure. Note that both revenue and expenditure may change within their respective totals. Taxes may rise in one area and fall in another; expenditure may rise in one area and fall in another. The net effect on the Budget, though, is neutral.

This is also the case if revenue and expenditure rise or fall proportionately. There may in fact be a large increase in expenditure, but if there is a commensurate increase in revenue, then the Budget will balance.

But consider the impact of a large increase in expenditure on the community. There is an increased flow of funds to households and to business. An example of this occurred in the 2010–11 budget when a planned increase of $5 billion in health spending was offset by increased taxes on cigarettes and a reduction in spending on the Pharmaceutical Benefits Scheme. Essentially people using hospitals would benefit while smokers and pharmaceuticals companies met the costs.

Households benefit from government employment, pensions and income from government contracts, all of which may increase if Budget expenditure rises. Business benefits from government contracts and from the increased disposable income of households being spent on outputs from business.

So the impact of a large increase in government expenditure on the wider economy in the framework of a balanced Budget is by no means neutral. In fact, it is highly relevant to overall economic management, an issue that no government can overlook when considering expenditure changes.

Budget surplus

Budget surplus *occurs when expected revenue is higher than expected expenditure*

A **Budget surplus** causes a contraction in the economy as the government reduces net income flows. It arises from either or both:

- an increase in revenue
- a reduction in expenditure.

In this situation, aggregate demand falls. Moreover, because of the multiplier (Chapter 10), the fall is greater than the changes in revenue and/or expenditure. This is illustrated in Figure 22.2.

Gross national expenditure is the sum of spending on consumption, investment and government expenditure in a given period irrespective of whether the spending was on domestic products or imports. Figure 22.2 illustrates the effect of a reduction in government expenditure (G) on expenditure and income.

If a Budget surplus results from a reduction in government expenditure, then A^1 becomes A^2 and income falls from Y^1 to Y^2. The difference between A^1 and A^2 is the change in government

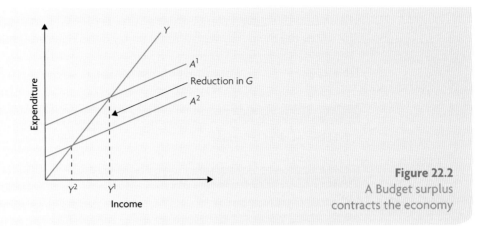

Figure 22.2
A Budget surplus
contracts the economy

expenditure, G. The reduced income represents a contraction in the economy and is greater than the reduction in G.

Budget deficit

A **Budget deficit** causes an expansion in the economy as the government increases net income flows. It arises from either or both of the following:

* a decrease in revenue
* an increase in expenditure.

Budget deficit
occurs when expected expenditure is higher than expected revenue

In this situation, aggregate demand rises. Again, because of the multiplier, the rise is greater than the changes in revenue and/or expenditure. This is illustrated in Figure 22.3.

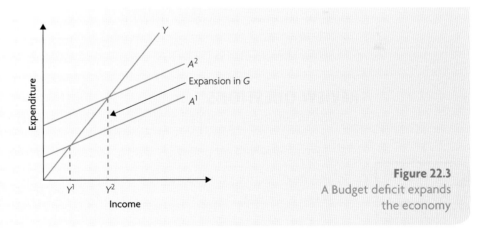

Figure 22.3
A Budget deficit expands
the economy

Income is again graphed against expenditure. If a Budget deficit results from an increase in government expenditure, then A^1 becomes A^2 and income rises from Y^1 to Y^2. The difference between A^1 and A^2 is the change in government expenditure, G. The increased income represents an expansion in the economy and is greater than the increase in G.

This last outcome deserves close attention because of its specific impact on the economy. It represents by far the most common situation for the Australian economy in that prior to the 21st century federal governments usually ran Budget deficits. In response to the GFC the federal government spent about $48 billion dollars on stimulus programs, including temporary tax cuts and the Building the Education Revolution and the Home Insulation programs. This resulted in a shift in the budget stance from a surplus of $19 billion to a deficit of $29 billion. Table 22.2 illustrates the means by which fiscal policy decisions can impact on aggregate demand.

Table 22.2   **The impact of contractionary and expansionary fiscal policy on aggregate demand**

IMPACTS ON AGGREGATE DEMAND			
Problem—risk of inflation		**Problem—risk of unemployment**	
Excess aggregate demand leading to inflation		Decline in aggregate demand leading to unemployment	
POSSIBLE ECONOMIC POLICY RESPONSES			
Contractionary fiscal policy		Expansionary fiscal policy	
IMPACTS ON INDIVIDUALS AND BUSINESSES			
Increase in income taxes	After tax, incomes fall and spending falls	After tax, incomes rise and spending rises	Reduction in income taxes
IMPACTS ON PUBLIC SERVANTS			
Reduced government spending	Salaries or numbers of public servants could be cut thus spending falls	Salaries or numbers of public servants could be raised thus spending rises	Increased government spending
IMPACTS ON RECIPIENTS OF GOVERNMENT BENEFIT PAYMENTS			
Pensions, unemployment benefits and social security could be cut thus spending will fall		Pensions, unemployment benefits and social security could be raised thus spending will rise	
IMPACTS OF CHANGES IN GOVERNMENT CAPITAL EXPENDITURE			
Spending on roads, rail and hospitals could be deferred thus government spending will fall, then private spending will fall as revenues and payrolls of construction companies and suppliers fall		Spending on roads, rail and hospitals could be brought forward thus government spending will rise, then private spending will rise as revenues and payrolls of construction companies and suppliers rise	

REVIEW QUESTIONS

1. Contractionary fiscal policy is likely to lead to an increase in the price of shares of construction companies. True or False?
2. Expansionary fiscal policy is likely to lead to an increase in retail sales. True or False?

In the next section, we look at the components of the Budget deficit. We then go on to discuss how a deficit is financed and the impact of each method on the domestic economy.

LEARNING OBJECTIVE 4
Distinguish between the domestic and overseas components and between cyclical and structural components of the federal Budget

COMPONENTS OF THE BUDGET OUTCOME

The actual outcome of the government's revenue and expenditure in any given period is rarely that forecast in its Budget. The main reason for this is unexpected changes in aggregate demand in the economy, which have an impact on government spending and tax revenue. In order to understand this, we have to differentiate between discretionary and non-discretionary fiscal policy. These terms can also be described respectively as structural and cyclical components of the Budget deficit.

Discretionary fiscal policy, or the structural component of the Budget deficit, refers to those aspects of spending and taxation in the Budget over which the government exercises control. This is where the government deliberately changes revenue or expenditure.

Non-discretionary fiscal policy, or the cyclical component of the Budget deficit, refers to those aspects of the Budget that come into play to offset fluctuations in the business cycle (see Chapter 11 for a complete discussion of economic fluctuations).

These counter forces in the Budget are known as **automatic stabilisers** because they are built into the economy and come into effect automatically as the business cycle expands and contracts without requiring explicit action by economic policy makers.

EXPANSION

Let us consider what happens when the economic cycle is in an expansionary phase. With progressive income taxation (as in Australia), the higher the income, the higher the rate of tax. If incomes increase with demand-pull inflation, income earners can expect to be paying a larger percentage of their income in tax. In other words, progressive income tax moderates the benefit of the rise in income to the individual by transferring a rising proportion of it to the government. This is known as **fiscal drag**.

CONTRACTION

In a contracting business cycle, rising unemployment brings other automatic stabilisers into play. One mechanism is unemployment benefits. Aggregate demand is propped up to some extent when unemployment occurs, because the wages lost when an employee loses a job are partly replaced by unemployment benefits. This represents disposable income that can be used for consumption spending.

Note that both stabilisers in the examples—progressive income tax and unemployment benefits—must be part of government policy. However, once those policies are in place, they operate automatically to lessen the impact of changes in the economic cycle.

Table 22.3 illustrates how the automatic stabilisers operate to counteract the effects on aggregate demand of changes in the business cycle and the effects on government finances.

discretionary fiscal policy, or the structural component of the Budget deficit
those aspects of spending and taxation in the Budget over which the government exercises control

non-discretionary fiscal policy, or the cyclical component of the Budget deficit
those aspects of the Budget that come into play to offset fluctuations in the business cycle

automatic stabilisers
elements in government spending and revenue that automatically have a moderating effect on the economic cycle

fiscal drag
the process whereby progressive income tax moderates the benefit of the rise in income to the individual by transferring a rising portion of it to the government

Table 22.3   **Phase of the business cycle**

PHASE	AGGREGATE DEMAND	AUTOMATIC STABILISER	IMPACT ON GOVERNMENT FINANCES	IMPACT ON AGGREGATE DEMAND
Economic contraction	Declining	Unemployment benefits	Increased spending: tendency to deficit	Injection of spending
Economic expansion	Increasing	Progressive income tax	Increasing revenue: tendency to surplus	Leakage or withdrawal of spending

FOREIGN COMPONENT

There is one other way to categorise Budget outcomes. Thus far, we have deliberately excluded external or overseas aspects of the Budget deficit. Our focus has been on domestic outcomes from revenue and expenditure within the Australian economy. The revenue is raised within Australia and expenditure occurs within Australia.

The overseas or external outcomes are not as important as domestic outcomes to an understanding of the main thrust of fiscal policy, but they do contribute significantly to the federal Budget deficit. The **overseas component of the Budget deficit** is made up of federal government spending overseas, less federal government revenues earned overseas. There is an overseas deficit if overseas expenditure exceeds overseas revenue.

It is wise to maintain a proper perspective on the overseas component of the Budget deficit. It has neither an expansionary nor a contractionary effect within Australia because the net effect occurs outside the domestic economy.

overseas component of the Budget deficit
occurs when federal government spending overseas exceeds federal government revenues earned overseas

EFFECTS OF THE ECONOMIC CYCLE

Figure 22.4 illustrates the history of government revenue and expenditure from 2000 to 2009 and projections to 2013. It shows how revenue and expenditure are affected by the economic cycle. The minor recession in 2001 following the introduction of the Goods and Services Tax resulted in lower tax collections, higher government spending as a percentage of GDP and a Budget deficit. The long upswing in the business cycle in the 2000s and restrained government spending led to Budget surpluses from 2002 to 2008. The massive fiscal response to the threat posed by the GFC is obvious in the chart with a large swing from surplus into deficit.

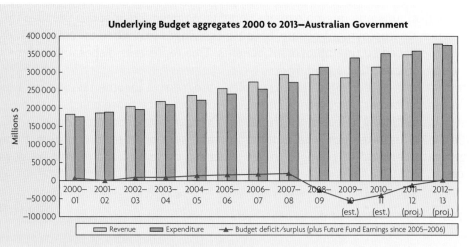

Figure 22.4
Underlying Budget aggregates 2000 to 2013

Source: Australian Treasury, Budget 2010–11, Statement Number 10, Historical Australian Government Data, Table 1, <www.budget.gov. au/2010-11/content/bp1/html/ bp1_bst10-04.htm>, accessed 28 February 2011.

underlying Budget balance
occurs through adjusting the net outcome of revenue and spending for financial transactions

The concept of an **underlying Budget balance** is the result of adjusting the net outcome of revenue and spending for financial transactions such as the sale of government-owned assets like banks, airlines and telecommunications companies. For example since 2006 earnings from the Future Fund are included as government revenue and affect the underlying budget balance. The Future Fund was established using funds from the sale of Telstra to provide earnings to cover the future costs involved in providing superannuation pensions to Commonwealth public servants.

BUDGET IMPACTS

The 2010–11 Budget contained the following forecasts and changes:

- a $40.8 billion Budget deficit
- GDP growth forecast to be 3.25 per cent, rising to 4 per cent in the following year
- unemployment forecast to fall to 5 per cent, close to the level most economists regard as full employment
- inflation expected to fall slightly from 2.75 to 2.5 per cent
- average earnings to rise by 3.75 per cent
- $9 billion from new taxes on mining companies
- $652 million in a fund to support renewable power and energy efficiency
- $66 million to boost training for the construction, infrastructure and renewable energy industries
- $1.2 billion on border protection and $1.9 billion on national security.

QUESTIONS

1. Describe the phase of the business cycle represented by these forecasts.
2. Describe some possible impacts on interest rates as a result of the Budget deficit.
3. Explain how the Budget might affect the following:
   - (a) surveillance equipment manufacturer
   - (b) self-funded retiree with a portfolio of mining shares
   - (c) unemployed person
   - (d) solar panel manufacturer.

FINANCING A DEFICIT

We have seen that the government can spend more than its revenue by going into deficit. But it still must fund its expenditure—it must continue to pay its employees and contractors, for example, and pay for equipment purchases.

In order to finance this spending, the government has to borrow. There are four sources of finance for the government when it is running a Budget deficit, namely borrowing from:

- the private sector
- the financial system
- the Reserve Bank
- overseas.

BORROWING FROM THE PRIVATE SECTOR

One method of financing a government deficit is to borrow from the private (non-government) sector. **Government bonds** are sold to the Australian public (Chapter 13). The withdrawals from private bank accounts to purchase the bonds provide money to the government for its expenditure requirements. Since these funds eventually find their way back into bank accounts, the net effect on the money supply is nil. The key aspect of this funding mechanism is that it is non-inflationary because the transfers from private sector bank accounts are offset by more government spending.

BORROWING FROM THE FINANCIAL SYSTEM

This method involves issuing securities to the financial system. The effect of this approach is to increase money supply and to enable financial intermediaries to increase their lending.

BORROWING FROM THE RESERVE BANK

Another method of financing a government deficit is for the Reserve Bank of Australia to lend money to the government. This money finds its way through the economic system to bank accounts and may enable an expansion in the money supply. As we saw in Chapter 14, the banking system can actually create credit. This is sometimes referred to as financing government spending by 'printing money' or quantitative easing. Increases in the money supply are important consequences of Reserve Bank financing of a government deficit.

BORROWING OVERSEAS

sovereign debt
*the debt owed by
governments to
foreign lenders*

Another option for financing a Budget deficit is to borrow overseas. This adds to Australia's foreign debts and the repayments are a burden on the economy. (See Chapter 24 for details.) Borrowing overseas by governments creates **sovereign debt**. **Sovereign risk** arises when investors become concerned about a government's ability to repay its debts. Investors may demand higher interest rates as the price for buying the securities issued by governments in return for funds. Or they may even demand immediate repayments. The only response for a government that has fallen out of favour is to increase taxes and to cut government spending thus reducing the need to borrow and freeing up funds to pay higher interest rates.

sovereign risk
*the risk that a
government may not
be able to repay its
debts to foreigners as
they fall due*

CONSEQUENCES OF GOVERNMENT DEBT

**net lending of all
public authorities
(NLPA)**
*summarises all
lending and
borrowings of all
government and
semi-government
organisations
in Australia in
a single year*

Budget deficits affect the **net lending of all public authorities (NLPA)**. The NLPA summarises all borrowings of all government and semi-government organisations in Australia in a single year and is an important economic indicator.

In 2008 Commonwealth loans of $32 billion offset $26.3 billion of borrowing by state governments and local authorities. In 2009 as part of the response to the GFC the Commonwealth borrowed $9 billion which together with state and local government borrowing made a total public sector debt of $40.7 billion. In summary the NLPA shifted from net lending of $5.7 billion to net borrowings of $40.7 billion.

Note that the NLPA is made up of all government borrowings—state, territory and federal. It is usually expressed as a percentage of GDP. The NLPA gives an immediate indication of governments' calls on domestic and overseas savings. Domestic savings in particular are critical. The more the government borrows, the less there is available for the private sector to borrow (see 'crowding out' opposite).

There is some debate about the level of public debt as measured by the NLPA. Many commentators raise concerns that the NLPA is too high or that the government is passing on huge debts to future generations. But remember that the proportion of public debt held inside Australia represents an asset to the holders, while it is also a liability to the public sector, and interest payments, which are spending for the public sector, are income for the holders (on which they pay tax). However, that proportion held overseas is a burden on the Australian economy in that it is a liability only to Australia and an asset for the foreign holders of the debt.

Another concern is the effect known as **crowding out**; according to this theory, borrowing by the government drains the pool of funds available for private borrowers and raises the cost of finance so that less private investment occurs. The result may be that government current expenditure is financed at the expense of private capital spending, which may make future living standards lower than they would otherwise be.

Note this final point about debt: if the debt is accumulated as a result of investment in long-term capital projects which generate economic benefits that more than pay the associated interest costs, then this is a good outcome from an economic point of view. In Chapter 1 you studied how investment can shift the production possibility curve. However, if the extra spending that generated the debt is used to provide bigger cars for ministers or more luxurious accommodation for members of parliament, then no economic benefits are created and the costs represent a burden for future generations.

crowding out
the theory that borrowing by the government drains the pool of funds available for private borrowers and raises the cost of finance so that less private investment occurs

STRENGTHS AND WEAKNESSES OF FISCAL POLICY

LEARNING OBJECTIVE 7
Outline the strengths and weaknesses of fiscal policy in Australia

Like all political decisions, the implementation of fiscal policy is a matter of debate. Policy makers who favour a small public sector prefer lower government spending in general and advocate tax cuts as a means of placing spending power in the hands of the private sector. On the other hand, policy makers who favour a large public sector prefer to use high government spending to stimulate expenditure in the economy.

STRENGTHS

Both the broad stance and the detail of fiscal policy are open to public scrutiny. This is partly because the federal Budget is a well-publicised economic event and the key components—taxation, amount of government spending, and the Budget outcome—affect all members of society. This transparency obliges governments to justify their policy measures, although the measures need not have proven economic benefits. For example, it is generally accepted that a government cannot impose a new tax unless it can justify it in parliament and to the community.

A second strength is that fiscal policy can be directed towards particular sections of the community and the economy. For example, progressive taxation is a principle embedded in fiscal policy in Australia. It ensures that low-income earners not only pay less tax as a percentage of income than high-income earners, but also gain from government expenditure on health, education and welfare.

Another strength is that the effect of fiscal policy can be immediate. Expenditure increases that consist of direct payments to individuals in the community can feed quickly into consumption spending in the economy.

WEAKNESSES

The most obvious weakness of fiscal policy is the uncertainty of its outcomes. Non-discretionary aspects create much of this uncertainty. It is clear that if Budget outcomes were more predictable, governments would resort to fiscal policy to obtain specific outcomes from their economic management.

Timing is also a weakness of fiscal policy. Policy changes are made at Budget time and perhaps one other time during the year, and then have to be processed through the parliament and public service. This limits the responsiveness and flexibility of both policy and practice.

Legislative processes may cause a delay between recognising a problem and introducing the consequent change in policy. There is also a delay between the introduction of a change and the effects of that change. Expansionary Budget policies, if financed by debt, can crowd out private expenditure, thus lowering long-term living standards.

The net effect of these strengths and weaknesses is that fiscal policy has often been implemented alongside monetary policy and wages policy in an effort to achieve the best mix of economic outcomes.

SOVEREIGN RISK IN EUROPE

LINK TO
INTERNATIONAL
ECONOMY

In mid 2010 markets fell heavily as investors became concerned about the sovereign risk attached to borrowings by members of the European Union. Even though an A$1 trillion guarantee arrangement was put in place for Greece there was a reassessment by markets of the fiscal health of many countries with high government debt to GDP ratios. These countries included Spain (11.5 per cent), Britain (12 per cent), and even the United States where the budget deficit was projected to reach 10.3 per cent of GDP in 2011.

Commentators drew attention to the problems in democratic societies where there are strong public demands for more government spending and lower taxes. Politicians find it difficult to resist these pressures in their quest for campaign funds and votes. The fiscal outcomes of ever-widening budget deficits require financing either through higher taxes or increased borrowing. In times of uncertainty the question of sovereign risk arises as investors become concerned that governments may default—that is, not be able to repay loans as they fall due and they demand higher interest rates as the price of their continuing support. In the long run the only solutions are economic reforms to increase productivity and wealth to restore government finances.

QUESTIONS

1. Explain the significance of the ratio of government debt to Gross Domestic Product.
2. Explain the meaning of the term 'sovereign risk'.
3. Define the term 'fiscal policy'.
4. Explain two options that are available to governments that find they have to act to restore the confidence of foreign lenders in their fiscal policies.

SUMMARY

1. Fiscal policy may be defined as a macroeconomic policy concerned with the effects on the economy of the receipts and expenditure of the government sector.
2. Given Australia's political structure and the nature of fiscal policy, the federal government has limited options both in managing the economy overall, and in managing aggregate demand in particular.
3. The federal government is a significant economic player, with revenue and expenditure equivalent to about one-quarter of Australia's GDP. The major source of government revenue is income tax, and the major item of expenditure is social security and welfare.
4. There are three possible Budget outcomes:
    (a) balanced: revenue = expenditure
    (b) surplus: revenue › expenditure
    (c) deficit: revenue ‹ expenditure.
5. For a particular Budget, we cannot establish its outcome by simply comparing government revenue and government expenditure. We must also consider the distribution of the impact on revenue and spending.
6. Discretionary fiscal policy (or the structural component of the Budget deficit) refers to those aspects of the Budget which the government controls, where it can deliberately change revenue or expenditure. Non-discretionary fiscal policy (or the cyclical component of the Budget deficit) refers to those aspects of the Budget that come into play to offset economic fluctuations like inflation and unemployment.
7. A Budget deficit may be financed by borrowing from any of the following:
    (a) the private (non-government) sector
    (b) the Reserve Bank
    (c) overseas.
    Any of these methods decrease the net lending of all public authorities (NLPA).
8. The strengths of fiscal policy are:
    (a) it is open and well publicised in the media
    (b) it can be directed towards particular sectors of the community and the economy (e.g. progressive taxation)
    (c) its effects can be immediate.
9. The weaknesses of fiscal policy are:
    (a) its outcomes are uncertain
    (b) there is a time-lag between decisions and outcomes (e.g. three-year tax changes)
    (c) it may have undesirable long-term effects on living standards.

KEY TERMS

automatic stabilisers	465	discretionary fiscal policy (or structural component of the Budget deficit)	465	non-discretionary fiscal policy (or cyclical component of the Budget deficit)	465
balanced Budget	460	economic management	461	overseas component of the	
budget	459	fiscal drag	465	Budget deficit	466
budgetary policy	459	fiscal policy (or budgetary policy)	459	progressive taxation	460
budgetary stance	459	government bonds	468	sovereign debt	468
Budget deficit	463	net lending of all public authorities (NLPA)	468	sovereign risk	468
Budget surplus	462			underlying Budget balance	466
crowding out	469				

REVIEW QUESTIONS

1. Identify whether the following statements are true or false. Be prepared to justify your answer.
   (a) Fiscal policy is also called budgetary policy. True or False?
   (b) Companies are the largest source of government revenue. True or False?
   (c) The main areas of expenditure for the Australian Government are social security welfare and health. True or False?
2. Distinguish between discretionary and non-discretionary fiscal policy.
3. Why is the planned Budget outcome usually different from the actual Budget outcome?
4. Explain the role of discretionary fiscal policy in economic management.
5. What is the function of progressive taxation in fiscal policy?
6. Explain three methods of financing a Budget deficit.
7. If the government wants to reduce unemployment what steps can it take using fiscal policy?
8. If Australia's balance of payment problem became serious enough to reduce the flow of overseas finance, how could the government use fiscal policy to restore Australia's credibility with lenders?
9. What is meant by the net lending of all public authorities (NLPA)? Why is it important in the Australian economy?
10. Explain 'crowding out', using examples.
11. Discuss the main strengths of fiscal policy.
12. Discuss the main weaknesses of fiscal policy.
13. What contribution does fiscal policy make to economic management?

APPLIED QUESTIONS AND EXERCISES
THE FISCAL CHALLENGES OF AN AGEING POPULATION

In 1901 the average life expectancy for women was 58.8 and for men 55.2. In 2007 life expectancy at birth for women had risen to 83.7 and for men to 79.2. The percentage of the population aged 85 and older was forecast to rise from 1.8 per cent in 2010 to 5.1 per cent in 2050.

The ageing of the population will lead to a need for greater spending on health care and pensions. Figure 22.5 illustrates a scenario for Australia given a continuation of current macroeconomic policy, which is to run a balanced Budget on average over the economic cycle.

QUESTIONS

1. Define the following terms:
   (a) balanced Budget
   (b) surplus Budget
   (c) deficit Budget
   (d) economic cycle
   (e) aggregate demand.
2. Given the scenario of an ageing population, describe two options that can be pursued by the Australian Government.
3. Describe the impacts of your suggestions on aggregate demand in Australia.

THE FISCAL CHALLENGE OF NEGATIVE GEARING

Australia is one of the few countries where the costs of owning a rental property can be offset against taxable income without limit. This means that if the rent earned from a property is less than the costs, such as the costs of holding

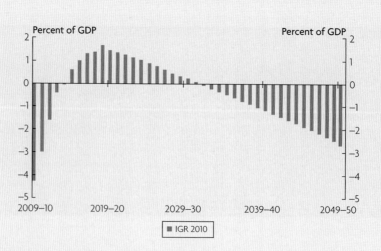

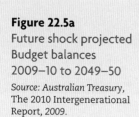

Figure 22.5a
Future shock projected Budget balances 2009–10 to 2049–50

Source: Australian Treasury, The 2010 Intergenerational Report, 2009.

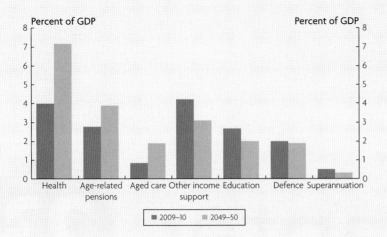

Figure 22.5b
Future shock projected
Federal Government
Spending 2009–10
to 2049–50
Source: Australian Treasury,
The 2010 Intergenerational
Report, 2009

the property (e.g. interest on borrowings, maintenance and rates), then the difference can be deducted from other income before paying tax, with no limit on the amount. This is called negative gearing.

In 2010 the average Australian household had 44 per cent of its wealth in the family home which is sheltered from capital gains tax, 16 per cent of its wealth in rental properties which benefit from negative gearing, 13 per cent in superannuation savings, 12 per cent in shares and 4 per cent in savings with financial institutions. Many argued that the house price inflation of 20 per cent in 2009–10 was partly the result of negative gearing. Some of the costs from this inflation were identified as:

- a rapid increase in household debt and repayments as a percentage of income
- intergenerational inequality as younger people were priced out of the housing market

- an excessive and destabilising degree of investment in housing as compared to other forms of capital investment
- the largest single deduction claimed by taxpayers in 2008–09 was the result of negative gearing causing a loss of revenue to the government.

QUESTIONS

1. Identify some groups in society who might benefit from negative gearing and some groups who might suffer.
2. Identify some of the effects of negative gearing on the demand for public housing funded by taxpayers.
3. Do you think negative gearing should continue to be allowed? Give two reasons for your answer.
4. Also explain the consequences of your decision on the federal Budget.

Chapter 23

Monetary policy

LEARNING OBJECTIVES

After studying this chapter, you will be able to:

1. discuss the objectives of monetary policy
2. explain how changes in interest rates affect different sectors of the economy
3. describe the instruments of monetary policy
4. explain how the Reserve Bank of Australia uses open market operations to influence the cash rate and interest rates in general
5. discuss the weaknesses and the strengths of monetary policy.

INTRODUCTION

In the 2000s monetary policy has the objective of controlling inflation. The agreed target for monetary policy is to keep inflation within a range of 2 to 3 per cent on average over the economic cycle. The Reserve Bank is responsible for formulating and implementing monetary policy. It can make decisions about monetary policy independently from the political process without consulting the government. The target range of inflation is at a level where it will not distort economic decision making by business and the community, and provides guidance for the development of expectations about future inflation rates (see Chapter 12 for details on inflation).

The objective of this chapter is to acquaint you with monetary policy as it has been applied in Australia and as it may be applied in the future.

MONETARY POLICY AND ECONOMIC OBJECTIVES

LEARNING OBJECTIVE 1
Discuss the objectives of monetary policy

The ultimate objective of monetary policy is to assist the economy to achieve economic growth and full employment with relatively low inflation. In the 2000s **monetary policy** is primarily concerned with setting the interest rate on very short-term loans in the money market. Other interest rates in the economy are affected by changes in this interest rate and thus the general cost and availability of credit is impacted. In Australia the Reserve Bank is responsible for the formulation and implementation of monetary policy.

The tools used by the Reserve Bank are called the instruments of monetary policy. The economic theory that lies behind monetary policy is not complicated. Essentially, if the overall objective of economic policy is to slow the rate of economic growth, then the instruments of monetary policy can be used to raise interest rates and thus restrict the availability of credit. On the other hand, if the objective is to stimulate economic growth, interest rates are lowered and credit becomes more readily available.

monetary policy
policy that involves setting the interest rate on overnight loans in the money market with the ultimate objective of achieving economic growth and full employment with relatively low inflation

INTEREST RATES

Before looking at the detail of monetary policy, we first consider how changes in the cost and availability of credit affect different sectors of the economy. We have examined interest rates in Chapter 13 and the circular flow in Chapter 8.

Economists generally agree that changes in interest rates are likely to affect private investment spending to a far greater extent than consumer spending.

Remember the dual nature of interest rates: they are a cost to the borrower and a return to the lender.

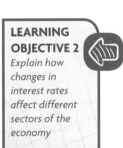

LEARNING OBJECTIVE 2
Explain how changes in interest rates affect different sectors of the economy

Effects on household spending

Lower interest rates may induce some households to save less and borrow more, thus increasing consumption spending. However, other households may have to increase their savings rate to offset the lower return from lower interest rates, in order to reach goals such as paying for children's education or retirement funding. Households with mortgages may

LINK TO BUSINESS

HOUSE PRICES AND MORTGAGE RATES

Changes in interest rates can have a dramatic effect on house prices as falling interest rates enable more people to take on mortgage finance to purchase houses. In Australia this effect is compounded by the taxation arrangement called negative gearing, which enables people investing in rental property to deduct the interest costs of their borrowing from their taxable income without limit. In 2010 in Victoria more loans were negotiated for the purchase of new investment properties than were provided for new home purchases by owner occupiers.

As interest rates fall the monthly repayments required to service the loan also fall thus a greater number of households can afford to make the repayments required. As more people seek to acquire houses, house prices will tend to rise if the demand exceeds the supply.

QUESTIONS

1. Assume you are a real estate agent. Describe two effects falling interest rates will have on your business.
2. Assume you are a bricklaying contractor. Describe two effects of rising interest rates on your business.

take advantage of lower interest rates to accelerate the rate at which they reduce their debt burden by maintaining the level of repayments. Thus it is not clear that lower interest rates necessarily lead to higher consumer spending.

Effects on business spending

The impact of interest rates on business investment spending is easier to predict because of the clear relationship between interest rates and the investment decision. A business that decides to proceed with an investment obviously expects the rate of return on the investment to exceed the cost of borrowed funds.

Factories, office buildings and capital equipment are expensive, and the dollar cost of interest charges on funds borrowed to finance these projects is a burden. Small changes in the interest rate can have a significant effect on the cash flow required to fund the repayments.

Also, a business may have the choice of committing spare funds to financial assets like commercial bills or to a potential capital investment. A general rise in interest rates may increase the attractiveness of financial assets and reduce the attractiveness of the capital investment.

instruments of monetary policy
tools used by central banks to influence the price and availability of credit

Thus monetary policy mostly affects private investment, and in this way it affects the level of output, employment and income in the economy.

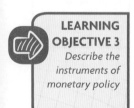

LEARNING OBJECTIVE 3
Describe the instruments of monetary policy

INSTRUMENTS OF MONETARY POLICY

The **instruments of monetary policy** are the tools used by the Reserve Bank to influence the price and availability of credit.

EVOLUTION OF MONETARY POLICY

In the period since 1980, the implementation of monetary policy has shifted from being a process involving a complex array of instruments to being a simple process involving only setting the **cash rate** via **open market operations**.

In Chapter 15 we studied the history of the regulation of the banking system during the 20th century, and saw that instruments of monetary policy included:

- reserve asset ratios, which prescribe ratios for liquidity such as the prime assets ratio
- interest rate controls on both deposit and lending rates
- directives to banks on which sectors of the economy to favour, such as farmers or exporters
- exchange controls, whereby approval from the Reserve Bank had to be gained prior to funds being moved into or out of Australia.

The changes in these instruments affected banks directly and then filtered through to the rest of the economy. Banks were subject to these controls because:

- banks are unique in their ability to create credit
- banks as a group represent the majority of financial assets in Australia
- banks hold a special position of trust as the core of the financial system.

While banks were the major players in finance markets, these controls were effective in influencing the general level of economic activity. However, during the 1960s and 1970s, banks steadily lost market share because the controls made it difficult for them to compete with other types of financial institutions, like merchant banks and building societies. Deregulation, which partly aimed to enhance the competitive position of banks, removed many of these controls. In the 1990s the main instrument of monetary policy became the open market operation and in the 2000s the focus of monetary policy is on the cash rate.

cash rate
interest rate on at call and very short-term deposits in the short-term money market

open market operations
the buying and selling of government securities—and occasionally bank-backed securities—by the Reserve Bank on secondary markets

RESERVE ASSET RATIOS

Reserve asset ratios (RARs) are ratios prescribed by the Reserve Bank to ensure that banks maintain some desired minimum level of liquidity, like a ratio of cash to deposits (see Chapter 13).

Reserve asset ratios were raised and lowered, depending on the stance of monetary policy at the time. Either they have enabled banks to increase lending by increasing their cash to deposits ratio (see Chapter 13), or they have forced banks to reduce their lending by squeezing their cash to deposits ratio.

Reserve asset ratios have not been used in Australia as instruments of monetary policy for many years; rather, they exist as a prudential measure, to ensure that banks have a reserve of highly liquid assets to meet any prospective run on their deposits. Since 1998 bank liquidity has been assessed on a case-by-case basis. Banks have to submit a liquidity management plan to the Australian Prudential Regulation Authority.

reserve asset ratios (RARs)
ratios prescribed by the Reserve Bank to ensure that banks maintain some desired minimum level of liquidity, e.g. a ratio of cash to deposits

DIRECTIVES

The Reserve Bank has the power to direct the lending policies of banks, in terms of:

- the dollar value of bank lending
- which industries or purposes are to be given priority.

Forms of Reserve Bank **directives** were known as quantitative and qualitative controls respectively. In the 1970s quantitative controls were used extensively as tools of monetary policy. At one extreme, the Reserve Bank could issue an instruction to banks telling them how much they could lend on a weekly or monthly basis. Less extreme was the concept of **moral suasion**, where the Reserve Bank used its authority as supervisor of the financial system to persuade banks to cooperate in achieving a target (for, say, new lending approvals) or in giving preference to a particular sector of the economy (such as exporters).

INTEREST RATE CONTROLS

The Reserve Bank has the power to make regulations to set interest rates for lending and deposit gathering by banks. Bank interest rates were set by the Reserve Bank until 1974, when the Trade Practices Act was passed. This made collusion between competitors illegal, and uniform interest rates were abandoned. However, up to 1980 a form of interest rate control continued in that the Reserve Bank set the maximum interest rates that could be offered and charged by banks.

Deregulation removed most interest rate controls. However, it should be noted that the Reserve Bank still has the power to set interest rates and the other controls mentioned above under the Banking Act and the Reserve Bank Act.

MONETARY POLICY IN CHINA

LINK TO INTERNATIONAL ECONOMY

In many countries, including China, the above tools of monetary policy are still used by the central bank.

In 2010 the China Banking Regulatory Commission instructed banks in Beijing, Shanghai, Shenzhen and Hangzhou to stop extending mortgages to people purchasing their third home. The CBRC also directed banks in other cities to require a deposit of 60 per cent and to charge interest at one and a half times the central bank's benchmark rate. The aim was to reduce speculation in property which was driving up prices rapidly.

QUESTIONS

1. List the types of controls being used in China.
2. Explain how these controls might affect property prices.

OPEN MARKET OPERATIONS

LEARNING OBJECTIVE 4

Explain how the Reserve Bank uses open market operations to influence the cash rate and interest rates in general

In the 2000s monetary policy decisions involve setting the cash rate, which is the rate charged on overnight loans between financial intermediaries. The official cash rate target is the average rate of interest paid on at call and very short-term deposits. The Reserve Bank Board is responsible for making decisions about changes in the cash rate target.

The Reserve Bank uses open market operations to keep the actual cash rate as close as possible to the target rate by managing the supply of funds available to banks in the money market. Transactions between banks are settled via **exchange settlement accounts (ESA)** held with the Reserve Bank. The banks are required to maintain a positive balance in these accounts at all times. The main variable affecting the balances in ESA accounts is government transactions. For example when tax payments are made funds flow out of the ESA accounts to the government. When pensions are paid funds flow from the government into ESA accounts. On any day there will be a tendency for a surplus or a deficit in the accounts. Through open market operations the Reserve Bank can influence the interest rates banks have to pay for the funds needed to maintain a positive balance in their ESA accounts.

Open market operations are the buying and selling of government securities by the Reserve Bank on secondary markets. (When a security is issued for the first time it is sold in the primary market; see Chapter 14.) Open market operations are conducted with institutions that are members of the Reserve Bank Information and Transfer System (RITS) (mainly banks).

The objective of open market operations is to ensure that the demand for and supply of ESA funds are in balance at the target cash rate.

Figure 23.1 illustrates the close relationship between the cash rate and other money market interest rates with the cash rate setting a floor for other rates for securities of longer duration and different security. In this way open market operations influence both the level of liquidity and **yields** in financial markets.

In this context the yield is the relationship between interest paid on a financial security expressed in the form of dollars relative to the purchase price. The yield is the dollars paid in interest relative to the purchase price, expressed as a percentage:

$$\text{yield} = \frac{\text{guaranteed return}}{\text{market value}}$$

In general, if the Reserve Bank wishes to reduce the availability of ESA funds it sells securities. This tends to reduce the availability of finance and raise the cash rate. Rises in the cash rate will tend to raise the general level of interest rates. Alternatively, to increase the availability of ESA funds and reduce the cash rate, the Reserve Bank purchases securities

exchange settlement accounts (ESA)
all banks are required to maintain accounts with the Reserve Bank for the purpose of settling interbank transactions. These accounts must always be in credit

yield
the interest paid on a financial security expressed in the form of dollars relative to the purchase price, expressed as a percentage

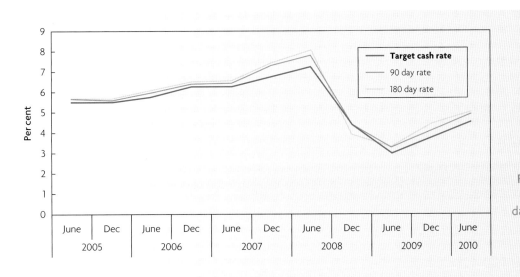

Figure 23.1
Reserve Bank cash rate target and 90 and 180 day bank accepted bills, June and December 2005–10

Source: Reserve Bank, Statistics, Table F1.

which will tend to increase the availability of ESA funds and lower the cash rate. Falls in the cash rate will tend to lower the general level of interest rates.

The impact of open market operations on the Reserve Bank Information and Transfer System participants and on short-term money markets in general can be illustrated using the following model.

Model of open market operations

We begin with some assumptions:

- Economic agents have the choice of holding their wealth in only two forms—cash or government bonds. Bonds yield interest and offer the possibility of capital gain. Cash, of course, yields nothing.
- If cash holders are offered interest and the prospect of capital gain, they will want to swap their cash for bonds.
- Government bonds are issued in the primary market with a face value of $100. The interest rate over the life of the bond is guaranteed at 10 per cent of the face value per annum. This means that, over the life of the bond, the holder will receive $10 per year, regardless of changes in the market value of the bond.

We can draw up a table that shows this point:

Table 23.1   Calculating yield on a government bond

FACE VALUE $	MARKET VALUE $	GUARANTEED RETURN $	YIELD %
100	100	10 p.a.	$\frac{10}{100}$
			= 10% p.a.

EXAMPLE 1

Let's assume that the government wishes to raise the cash rate and rates in general and reduce liquidity. To achieve this, the Reserve Bank could offer bonds for sale at a price below their face value. For instance, it could offer to sell bonds with a face value of $100 for $80. This presents new purchasers with the prospect of a $20 capital gain if they hold the bonds until maturity, when the Reserve Bank would redeem them for $100 each.

This type of sale would affect yields as follows:

Table 23.2   Reducing money supply through government bonds

FACE VALUE $	MARKET VALUE $	GUARANTEED RETURN $	YIELD %
100	80	10 p.a.	$\frac{10}{80}$
			= 12.5% p.a

The effects of such an open market operation are twofold:

- Less money is held by the banks because it has been swapped for bonds and banks may seek more funds on the short-term money market causing interest rates to tend upwards.
- Yields on government bonds have risen. Any borrowers who compete with the government for loan funds must also raise the yields they offer on their securities. This leads to a general rise in the level of interest rates in the economy.

EXAMPLE 2

Now, assume that the government decides to do the opposite and increase the availability of ESA funds. The Reserve Bank seeks to buy bonds from the banks by offering the prospect of immediate capital gain. For instance, $100 bonds could sell for $120. The effects of this move would be:

Table 23.3   **Increasing money supply through government bonds**

FACE VALUE $	MARKET VALUE $	GUARANTEED RETURN $	YIELD %
100	120	10 p.a.	$\frac{10}{120}$
			= 8.33% p.a.

Again, this open market operation has a twofold effect:

- More liquidity is held by the banks as they swap money for bonds and they will try to shed these funds by lending more on the short-term money market.
- Yields on government bonds have fallen. Borrowers who compete with the government for loan funds can reduce the interest rates payable on their securities.

Quantitative Easing

Quantitative easing was used extensively in the United States and United Kingdom as part of the policy aimed at stimulating demand following the global financial crisis (GFC). It involved the central bank purchasing a wide range of securities from the private sector including government bonds and mortgage-backed securities with the aim of injecting new money into the system and forcing down interest rates on financial assets, thus stimulating aggregate demand. It is essentially the same as the open market operation outlined above but involves a much wider range of securities and sellers. The process is often described as 'printing money' when it involves the Treasury selling government securities to the central bank to finance government expenditure because in this case the government is spending more but the private sector is not spending less. Such situations can lead to inflation and the devaluation of the currency (see Chapters 12 and 13). Quantitative easing was used extensively in the United Kingdom and the United States; however, even with interest rates at record lows and a growing money supply, business and consumers were reluctant to borrow and spend.

quantitative easing
purchases of a wide range of securities by the central bank with the aim of increasing the money supply and lowering interest rates

The theory behind the model

Changes in the cash rate and other short-term rates usually have a speedy influence on the whole structure of deposit and lending rates in Australia.

Economic theory contends that higher interest rates (costs of borrowing money) discourage borrowing for investment in capital equipment which tends to reduce the level of aggregate demand. This, in turn, tends to depress price levels and the level of employment.

Conversely, lower interest rates encourage borrowing to buy capital equipment. This raises the level of aggregate demand. Higher demand results in higher prices and a fall in unemployment. Thus the interest rate acts as a transmission mechanism for transferring changes in the financial sector to the real sector.

However it should be noted that interest rates are influenced by a range of factors including the risk tolerance of investors, the degree of competition among lenders and the international financial environment. Also, deposit and lending rates available from financial institutions do not always move in line with changes in the cash rate.

Changes in interest rates can take some time to affect economic activity because individuals and business have to adjust their behaviour to take account of the new situation. Changes in rates are transmitted to the real economy via savings and investment behaviour, the supply of credit, and the exchange rate to affect aggregate demand. The rate of inflation is to a large extent the outcome of the interaction between aggregate demand and aggregate supply (see Chapter 10).

Thus it can be seen that the effects of changes in interest rates are difficult to predict with any certainty.

Figure 23.2 illustrates the theory of the flow through of the impact of changes in interest rates.

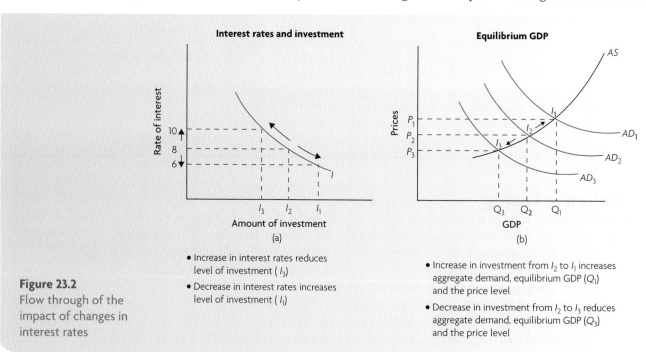

Figure 23.2
Flow through of the impact of changes in interest rates

Interest rates and investment

Amount of investment
(a)

- Increase in interest rates reduces level of investment (I_3)
- Decrease in interest rates increases level of investment (I_1)

Equilibrium GDP

GDP
(b)

- Increase in investment from I_2 to I_1 increases aggregate demand, equilibrium GDP (Q_1) and the price level
- Decrease in investment from I_2 to I_3 reduces aggregate demand, equilibrium GDP (Q_3) and the price level

Figure 23.2(a) illustrates a generalised money market with three different cash rates—6, 8 and 10 per cent.

An easing of monetary policy lowers the general level of interest rates and increases the supply of funds available for lending for investment. Figure 23(b) shows how an increase in investment will increase the level of aggregate demand and thus increase the equilibrium level of GDP (see Chapter 10). A tightening of monetary policy will increase interest rates and reduce the level of investment and aggregate demand, and thus reduce the equilibrium level of GDP. Tighter monetary policy is usually deployed with the aim of reducing demand-pull inflation.

Figure 23.3 illustrates the impact of changes in interest rates on retail sales, motor vehicle sales and private investment in dwellings. It can be seen that each of the series responds to changes in interest rates, with the response of motor vehicle sales and dwelling investment being quite dramatic. It would be expected that in most circumstances retail sales would be more stable given that a large component involves the necessities of life. However the course of the GFC can be seen in retail sales, with an increase in 2009 caused by the fiscal stimulus being sandwiched between low growth years in 2008 and 2010 (see Chapter 22).

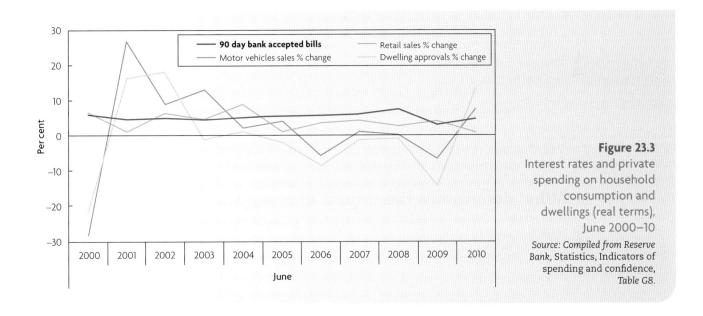

Figure 23.3
Interest rates and private spending on household consumption and dwellings (real terms), June 2000–10

Source: Compiled from Reserve Bank, Statistics, Indicators of spending and confidence, Table G8.

It can be seen that higher interest rates and then the GFC affected vehicle sales and dwelling investment from 2005 with recovery occurring in 2010.

THE EFFECTIVENESS OF MONETARY POLICY

LEARNING OBJECTIVE 5
Discuss the weaknesses and the strengths of monetary policy

The effectiveness of monetary policy can be assessed in a variety of ways. Monetary policy is used to pursue the goal of an acceptable level of inflation. Thus one way of assessing its effect is to look at how changes in monetary policy affect levels of inflation and how this affects production, employment and international competitiveness. It is difficult to determine the exact effects because monetary policy is only one of many influences on these economic indicators.

WEAKNESSES

Monetary policy can exert powerful pressures when used to slow down the rate of economic growth and reduce inflationary pressures. However, it is difficult to predict how much time will elapse between the tightening of monetary policy and the slowing of the economy. For example, research conducted by the Reserve Bank suggests that changes in mortgage interest rates continue to have an effect on the demand for housing for up to two years after the change.

Higher interest rates are unpopular because they:

- discourage investment and thus reduce long-term growth prospects
- increase the costs of production, of house purchases and add to general household costs
- increase the costs of personal borrowing, credit cards and mortgages
- increase the inflow of funds from offshore thus raising the exchange rate which adversely affects exporters and import competing industries (see Chapter 19).

The effectiveness of monetary policy is also difficult to predict when it is being used to stimulate economic activity. Some commentators describe this process as 'like pushing on a string'. That is to say, even though finance is readily available and interest rates are low, more borrowers do not necessarily appear. In the past two decades some interest rate changes had little effect on economic activity, whereas at other times the effects of changes have been dramatic.

Also, because Australian banks rely on funding from overseas to finance a substantial part of their loan portfolio, the interest rate they charge on loans is heavily influenced by international factors. This means that in some circumstances their funding costs may be higher than those indicated by the cash rate in Australia.

What determines the impact of changes

The impact of the changes in monetary policy can be influenced by the prevailing economic environment, for example:

- levels of indebtedness
- actual and expected rate of inflation
- levels of business and consumer confidence.

The attitude of banks is another factor. The effect of a looser monetary policy may be to increase the cash reserves of the banking system, but if banks are raising credit standards because of previous losses on risky lending, then fewer customers will qualify for loans. This actually occurred in the aftermath of the GFC with bank lending falling because banks were raising their credit standards, even though interest rates were progressively lowered and consumers focused on reducing their indebtedness rather than on taking on more loans.

The attitude of potential borrowers is also important. Following the 2008 GFC, in 2009 businesses reduced their borrowings in order to restore balance sheet strength and raised capital through issues of shares.

Thus, even if banks were willing lenders, the number of willing borrowers in 2009 and beyond was probably smaller than in 2007 and earlier.

Coordinating monetary policy

Monetary policy is one of the instruments available to governments to influence the state of the economy. It is likely to be more effective when it is aligned with the other instruments. For example, the effect of running an expansionary fiscal policy and a contractionary monetary policy is likely to be an increase in public sector employment and a reduction in private sector employment. This will lead to a need to increase taxation, which has the effect of reducing private sector spending, which is likely to cause further unemployment.

In the global economy it has become very difficult to conduct monetary policy in isolation from the rest of the world. Australia, with its heavy burden of private sector international debt, needs to continue to borrow each year as well as rolling over its existing debt. Interest rates in Australia must be competitive with those of other international borrowers as well as allowing for relative inflation rates and perceived country risk. Consequently, if interest rates rise in the major economies of the United States, Japan and Germany, interest rates in Australia are likely to rise in order to maintain relativities.

STRENGTHS

Monetary policy is extremely powerful when used to pursue contractionary economic policies. However, it is difficult to predict the time lag between implementing the policy and when it will take effect.

The main strength of monetary policy is the speed with which it can be changed—its flexibility. Open market operations can be carried out on a daily basis and can influence most interest rates within a matter of weeks. In contrast, fiscal policy can be delayed by debates, wrangles in the Senate, or arguments with the state governments and other pressure groups.

The other attraction of monetary policy for politicians is that its effect is more subtle and widespread than fiscal policy. Changes in fiscal policy usually produce identifiable winners and losers, whereas the effects of monetary policy are more diffuse and can be blamed on a variety of factors other than political government. Apart from emergencies, it can be expected that monetary policy will be used to contain the rate of inflation within an acceptable range over the economic cycle so as to encourage the maximum rate of economic growth compatible with a low inflation environment. Thus in the 2000s there were long periods of relative interest rate stability—a stark contrast to the previous decades.

SUMMARY

1. Monetary policy involves actions that influence the cost and availability of credit, and is carried out by the Reserve Bank. The ultimate objective of monetary policy is to control inflation thus assisting the economy to achieve economic growth and full employment.

2. The instruments of monetary policy that are available to the Reserve Bank include:
   (a) reserve asset ratios
   (b) directives
   (c) interest rate controls
   (d) open market operations
   (e) quantitative easing.

3. In the 2000s the main tool of monetary policy in Australia is open market operations. Open market operations are the buying and selling of government securities in secondary markets by the Reserve Bank in order to influence the cash rate to keep it close to the target rate.

4. The effectiveness of monetary policy is open to question. Monetary policy can exert a strong negative influence on the economy, but is much weaker when trying to stimulate economic activity. Also it is difficult to predict the time lag between the action and the outcome in the economy.

5. The effectiveness of monetary policy depends on factors such as:
    (a) levels of indebtedness
    (b) actual and expected inflation
    (c) levels of business and consumer confidence.

KEY TERMS

		instruments of monetary policy	476	quantitative easing	481
cash rate	477	monetary policy	475	reserve asset ratios (RARs)	477
directives	478	moral suasion	478	yield	479
exchange settlement accounts (ESA)	478	open market operations	477		

REVISION QUESTIONS

1. In your own words define the following terms:
    (a) monetary policy
    (b) ultimate objectives
    (c) instruments of monetary policy
    (d) interest rates
    (e) exchange settlement account.

2. Give an example of how a change in monetary policy can affect the ultimate objectives.

3. Distinguish between the effect of changes in interest rates on consumer spending and on investment spending.

4. In your own words define the following terms:
    (a) open market operations
    (b) yield
    (c) face value
    (d) market value.

5. Explain how the yield on a government bond is affected by changes in the market price in secondary markets.

6. Explain how sales of government bonds by the Reserve Bank can result in decreased availability of liquidity and higher interest rates.

7. In your own words define the following terms:
    (a) reserve asset ratios
    (b) non-callable deposits
    (c) directives.

8. Explain how higher interest rates might affect the finances of households.

9. Explain how lower interest rates might affect the finances of businesses.

10. Explain some of the difficulties in assessing the effectiveness of monetary policy.

11. Explain the weaknesses of monetary policy.

12. Explain the strengths of monetary policy.

13. Explain how the level of indebtedness and business confidence can influence the effectiveness of expansionary monetary policy.

14. Explain the main objective pursued by the Reserve Bank in seeking to stabilise the financial system.

15. Explain how open market operations can affect:
    (a) interest rates
    (b) the inflation rate
    (c) the exchange rate.

16. Discuss the meaning of the statement: 'Monetary policy is like pushing on a piece of string.'

APPLIED QUESTIONS AND EXERCISES
THE OBJECTIVE OF MONETARY POLICY

Monetary policy in Australia has the final objective of low inflation as the best contribution that monetary policy can make in the long run to growth in output, employment and living standards.

The aim is to allow the economy to grow as fast as possible, consistent with low inflation. The key elements in the monetary policy framework are:

• explicit announcements of changes in the cash rate, with explanations of the reasons for the change

- formal political support for Reserve Bank independence, as contained in the *Reserve Bank Act*, and for its 2 to 3 per cent inflation target.

  Thus monetary policy is framed in response to changes in the inflation rate, with the objective of keeping it around 2 to 3 per cent. If inflation looks like going over the target, monetary policy may be tightened and interest rates increased.

QUESTIONS

1. How would the Reserve Bank use monetary policy if it was concerned that the inflation rate was going to rise above 3 per cent?
2. Describe the effect on businesses and families with borrowings that require large repayments relative to their income.

APPLICATIONS OF MONETARY POLICY

Figure 23.4 illustrates the household savings to income ratio from 1980 to 2010. It can be seen that the ratio was close to zero or negative from 2001–08. However it had risen in 2009–10 as households seemed to be interested in saving more and borrowing less in response to their experience in the GFC.

QUESTIONS

1. Explain what is meant by an easing of monetary policy.
2. Given the ratio of household savings to income explain the likely impacts of an easing of monetary policy in:
   (a) the period 2001–08
   (b) 2010.

   In your answer refer to:
   (a) business and consumer confidence
   (b) the attitude of banks.

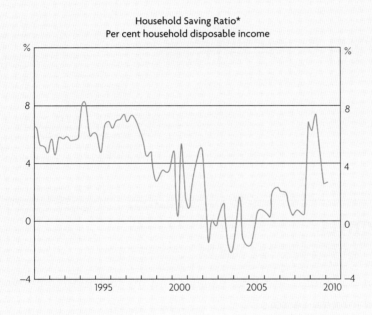

Household Saving Ratio*
Per cent household disposable income

Figure 23.4
Attitudes to debt and monetary policy

*Net of depreciation

Source: Speech by Ric Battellino, Deputy Governor, Reserve Bank, to the Moreton Bay Regional Council, Redcliffe Queensland, 'Twenty years of economic growth', 20 August 2010, Graph 7, <www.rba.gov.au/speeches/2010/sp-dg-200810.html>, accessed 19 October 2010.

Chapter 24

External policy

LEARNING OBJECTIVES

After studying this chapter, you will be able to:

1. explain what is meant by external balance and the relationship between the external and internal sectors
2. examine the main external policy measures to promote Australia's position in the external sector
3. describe the major means by which the Australian Government attempts to influence investment flows
4. describe the advantages and disadvantages of capital inflow and the major means by which the government attracts capital inflow to balance the deficits on current account
5. outline the position of the exchange rate of the Australian dollar as an indicator for the external balance and the role of the exchange rate policy in the external sector.

INTRODUCTION

As discussed in Chapter 21, external balance is one of the major macroeconomic objectives of the Australian Government. At the same time, **external policy** is one of the major instruments used by governments for promoting stabilisation and economic growth.

external policy
a government policy meant to promote external balance

International business is regarded by government as vital to the economic security and future wellbeing of every Australian. Part 7 presented in detail Australia's position in the international economy in terms of flows of goods, services and investment. It also identified the deficits on the current account of the balance of payments as a major issue for Australia's economic performance.

In this chapter we will examine the main economic policy instruments used by the government to correct the problems related to the balance of payments, which may affect the overall performance of the economy.

EXTERNAL BALANCE

LEARNING OBJECTIVE 1
Explain what is meant by external balance and the relationship between the external and internal sectors

One of the main goals of government economic management is to achieve an external balance. An external balance is a level and a pattern of transactions with the rest of the world consistent with the welfare and growth of the Australian economy. Under a floating exchange rate regime, balance is achieved through exchange rate adjustment.

External transactions, explained in detail in Chapter 18, are summed up in the balance of payments, where:

current account = capital and financial account (including 'net errors and omissions')

The current account is made up of the balance on goods and services, the net income (mainly investment income) and net current transfers.

Australia is a small open economy. Exports and imports of goods and services make up a considerable proportion of our GDP (around 21 per cent), yet the Australian economy is too small to have much impact on prices in world markets.

As noted before, exports are one of the components in the aggregate demand equation:

$$Y = C + I + G + (X - M)$$

Exports are one of the main 'injections' for the economy. A change in the value of exports can cause the level of GDP to change by a multiple of the export change (the multiplier effect; see Chapter 9). But the external sector adds another leakage to the circular flow, in the form of imports. So the multiplier effect of any increase in exports is reduced by the leakage to imports.

As explained in Chapter 18, the largest contributor to Australia's current account deficit has traditionally been 'the net income' item. This reflects the difference between the value of income, such as dividends and interest, receivable by residents from non-residents (credit) and that is payable by residents to non-residents (debit).

As Figure 24.1 overleaf shows, Australia's current account balance was consistently in deficit in the 2000s, and this has been a traditional feature throughout Australia's economic history. In effect, the balance on the current account shows the extent to which a nation is living

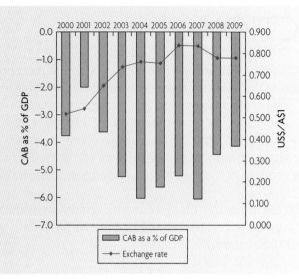

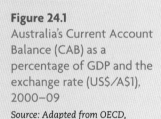

Figure 24.1
Australia's Current Account Balance (CAB) as a percentage of GDP and the exchange rate (US$/A$1), 2000–09

Source: Adapted from OECD, Economic Outlook, May 2010.

within its income; or, in terms of savings, the extent to which a nation draws on foreign savings or exports its own domestic savings. Therefore we have to rely on net financial inflows to finance that deficit, and to provide an additional source of savings for investment purposes. In other words, the huge deficits we have been running on the current account are paid for by capital and financial inflows—that is, overseas borrowings by governments and the private sector.

This accumulation of current account deficits adds up every year to the size of Australia's net foreign debt, representing by the end of June 2010 around 55 per cent of Australia's GDP.

EXTERNAL BALANCE VERSUS DOMESTIC BALANCE

External balance needs to be consistent with the maintenance of existing (or growing) levels of consumption, employment and national output over the long term. Thus we must be able to service the income flows (income balance) required by any increases in the level of our net foreign debt that is implied by inflows recorded in the financial and capital account.

The floating of the Australian dollar in December 1983 markedly changed the emphasis in achieving external balance.

Fixed exchange rate

international reserves
include the RBA's holdings of monetary gold, foreign exchange and special drawing rights (SDRs) with the IMF, which are available for use in meeting balance of payments and other needs

Before the float, under a fixed or managed exchange rate system, the fluctuations in the balance of payments were transferred to the stock of **international reserves**. In this situation, it was important to maintain an adequate level of reserves to counter any short-term fluctuations in the balance of payments. Consequently, to achieve internal balance, it was important to avoid persistent or sustained balance of payments surpluses or deficits. These would cause a persistent increase or decrease in stock of reserves.

Floating exchange rate

Since the float, fluctuations in the balance of payments have been transferred to the exchange rate. Under a freely floating exchange rate, external balance is achieved by avoiding persistent increases or decreases in the floating exchange rate.

It should be stressed that, since the float of the dollar, the exchange rate is no longer an economic policy measure that can be adjusted by the government to modify fluctuations in the balance of payments. The exchange rate is now only an economic indicator of conditions in the external sector. Figure 24.1 indicates quite large fluctuations of the Australian dollar in relation to the US dollar over 2000–09 (between US$0.51–0.84). In October 2010, the Australian dollar reached parity with the US dollar for the first time since its floating in 1983.

One should emphasise that external policy needs to influence the components of the balance of payments and the exchange rate, but without increasing inflationary pressures or decreasing the levels of production and employment in the internal sector.

Interdependence

Levels of internal economic activity or high rates of inflation influence the exchange rate. Therefore the government monetary, fiscal and incomes policies must be improved consistently so that they achieve stable economic conditions; otherwise the exchange rate will be affected.

At the same time, a lower exchange rate is encouraging exports and as publicised one in five Australian jobs is trade-related.

The interdependence between the internal and external sectors creates a major difficulty for the government when framing external policy measures. Not only do these measures influence the components of the balance of payments, but their effect influences the level of economic activity in Australia, including the general price level and the level of employment.

Two factors determine the relative prices of Australian manufactures and services in international markets: the domestic inflation rate and the exchange rate. Given that the latter depends mainly on market prices, it is obvious that Australia's competitiveness is influenced primarily by wage and price movements within the Australian economy.

Therefore it is crucial to the Australian export trade that the government adopt policies (fiscal, monetary and incomes) to:

- restrain wage rises and bring inflation and interest rates down to—or below—the rates of our major trading partners
- encourage more investment in export-expanding and import-replacing industries
- urgently improve the productivity of workplaces, transport and shipping facilities and management in order to boost exports and make imports less competitive and attractive.

In conclusion, it is important when framing external policy to give consideration to the effect of policy changes on the internal economy.

EXTERNAL POLICY OBJECTIVES

After defining the external balance and establishing its interdependence with the domestic balance, we can sum up the main objectives of external policy as follows:

- a competitive export sector to contribute to economic growth and to moderate the deficit on current account
- a steady capital and financial inflow to finance the current account deficit and to contribute to economic development
- a reasonably stable exchange rate, at a level consistent with the first two aims.

Accordingly, we shall approach external policy by investigating its influence on, and how it is influenced by, the current account, the capital and financial account, and the exchange rate.

**LEARNING
OBJECTIVE 2**
*Examine the
main external
policy measures
to promote
Australia's
position in the
external sector*

EXTERNAL POLICY MEASURES

In Australia, the Constitution put the control of international trade into the hands of the federal government. Most international trade in Australia is carried out by private firms in the business sector, but the government undertakes certain responsibilities to facilitate and encourage trade, while placing specific restrictions on it.

The economic recessions of the 1980s, early 1990s, and the global financial crisis demonstrated the vulnerability of the Australian economy to the international environment, especially our inability to industrialise our exports in line with world trends.

In the past, several Australian prime ministers promised that Australia could achieve both sustainable high growth and stabilisation of the current account deficit. The fact is that Australia's current account deficit has diminished, especially in periods of slow-down like that in the context of the GFC (e.g. financial years 2008 and 2009).

We will examine below two categories of external policies:

1. government policies to promote exports
2. government policies to promote international investment flows.

GOVERNMENT POLICIES TO PROMOTE EXPORTS

A nation's trade policies are those designed to influence its trade relations with the rest of the world in order to achieve an external balance.

The Australian Government undertakes various activities in support of Australian exports. These include:

- multilateral negotiations
- regional and bilateral initiatives
- trade promotion and publicity
- export incentives
- industry assistance.

Multilateral negotiations

A major objective of Australian foreign and trade policy, especially in the first half of the 1990s, was the liberalisation of world trade via multilateral negotiations. These were conducted within the **General Agreement on Tariffs and Trade (GATT)**, which has become the **World Trade Organization (WTO)**.

Australia has played a leading role in the international drive to reform agricultural trade through a group of 13 agricultural exporting nations, called the **Cairns Group**.

The Cairns Group has become a major 'third party' in the multilateral trade negotiations under the Uruguay Round and the Doha Round.

The Australian Bureau of Agricultural and Resource Economics estimated that a successful outcome to the Doha Round could increase Australia's agricultural exports (worth over A\$27 billion in 2006–07) by 3 to 15 per cent, or over A\$1 billion a year to farmers.

Certainly, Australia has also a lot to gain from liberalisation measures in the area of manufacturing, minerals and services, which at present, individually, provide export earnings even higher than agriculture. This is why the successful conclusion to the Doha Round of WTO negotiations remains the Australian Government's highest trade policy priority. The WTO provides Australia with the largest forum (currently 153 members)

General Agreement on Tariffs and Trade (GATT)
international treaty that committed signatories to lowering barriers to the free flow of goods across national borders and led to the World Trade Organization

World Trade Organization (WTO)
The organisation that succeeded the General Agreement on Tariffs and Trade (GATT) as a result of the successful completion of the Uruguay round of GATT negotiations. It is based in Geneva (Switzerland)

Cairns Group
a group of 13 non-subsidising agricultural exporting nations, led by Australia, which has represented a balancing force between the US and the EU in the Uruguay and Doha rounds of multilateral negotiations

through which to negotiate multilateral trade rules and market access commitments, and seek enforcement of these commitments, including through the WTO's binding dispute settlement mechanism.

Regional and bilateral initiatives

Recognising the primary importance of the Asia-Pacific region for Australia, the government has given a high priority to the creation and development of the **Asia-Pacific Economic Cooperation group (APEC)**. APEC activities involve regional consultation and economic cooperation between the 21 member countries (Australia, New Zealand, seven ASEAN countries, Japan, China, Taiwan, Hong Kong, Republic of Korea, Canada, the United States, Mexico, Papua New Guinea, Russian Federation, Peru and Chile). APEC has set deadlines for trade liberalisation for its members: developed member countries were to achieve free trade by 2010, and developing member countries by 2020.

The Australian Government has also supported the negotiation of comprehensive **free trade agreements (FTAs)** that are consistent with the World Trade Organization rules and guidelines and which complement and reinforce the multilateral trading system.

A list of Australia's bilateral FTAs is presented in Table 24.1.

Table 24.1   Australia's Free Trade Agreements (FTAs) as of October 2010

AUSTRALIAN FTAs IN FORCE (DATE OF EFFECT)	AUSTRALIAN FTAs UNDER NEGOTIATION
• New Zealand (1965, extended 1983) • Singapore (28 July 2003) • Thailand (1 January 2005) • United States (1 May 2005) • Chile (6 March 2009) • ASEAN (27 February 2009)	• FTA negotiations with China, the Gulf Cooperation Council, Japan, Malaysia, Pacific Agreement on Closer Economic Relations (PACER) Plus, Trans-Pacific Partnership Agreement. • Feasibility studies on possible FTAs with Indonesia and India.

Source: DFAT, <www.dfat.gov.au/trade/ftas.html>, accessed 28 October 2010.

According to DFAT, FTAs promote stronger trade and commercial ties between participating countries, and open up opportunities for Australian exporters and investors to expand their business into key markets. They can speed up trade liberalisation by delivering gains faster than through multilateral or regional processes.

FREE TRADE AGREEMENTS—AN AUSTRALIAN PERSPECTIVE

In April 2010, the Australian Department for Foreign Affairs and Trade (DFAT) made a submission to the Productivity Commission's Review of Australia's Free Trade Agreements (FTAs).

DFAT pointed out a number of trade and investment achievements of Australia's FTAs:

- The Singapore–Australia FTA removed restrictions on the number of wholesale banking licences available to Australian banks in Singapore.
- The Australia–United States FTA ensured access for Australian business to the United States federal and state government procurement markets for the first time.
- The Australia–ASEAN–New Zealand FTA (Anzcerta) will eliminate tariffs on 96 per cent of current Australian merchandise exports to ASEAN countries by 2020, with most of the liberalisation achieved over the next few years.
- Australian investment has grown in all of our FTAs partners considered in the submission since the entry into force (EIF) of those FTAs. Australian investment in the United States in particular

APEC (Asia-Pacific Economic Cooperation group) *a regional organisation founded in 1989 with the stated aim to increase multilateral cooperation in view of the economic rise of the Pacific nations and the growing interdependence within the region. It has 21 member economies in East Asia, Australasia, North America and Latin America*

free trade agreement (FTA) *agreement in which participants remove trade barriers among themselves, but keep a certain level of protection against trade with the outside world*

LINK TO INTERNATIONAL ECONOMY

continued ⌄

continued

picked up after 1 January 2005 and, at $394.6 billion, it was over 40 per cent higher than before the entry into force date. Overall income from Australian investment in the United States has increased following 1 January 2005—on average, income has doubled (to A$12.8 billion).
- Australian investment in Singapore and Thailand and income from such investments have grown faster than in the period prior to the conclusion of the FTAs.
- Australia's FTAs have contributed to promoting reform within Australia:
  - for instance, the Anzcerta agreement contributed significantly to the increased mobility of goods and labour
  - another series of significant domestic reforms resulted from the Australia-United States Free Trade Agreement (AUSFTA) regarding Australia's foreign investment regime.

The combination of these efforts—multilateral, regional and bilateral—creates a self-reinforcing network of commitments at a number of levels—the so-called 'cascade effect'—where each agreement, or reform, flows into building a more robust and predictable trading environment for Australia.

Trade promotion and publicity

Australian Trade Commission (Austrade)
the Australian Government's trade and investment development agency

The **Australian Trade Commission (Austrade)** was established in 1986 as a statutory authority to take over the responsibilities of export promotion and incentives.

Austrade organises trade missions and exhibitions around the world, and produces publications and advertising material to promote Australian export products.

Given the trade–investment linkage, in 2008 Austrade took over the task of attracting productive foreign direct investment (FDI) into Australia from Invest Australia. Austrade has specialist investment commissioners who promote Australia's competitive advantages as an investment destination and facilitate FDI into Australia.

Export Finance and Insurance Corporation (EFIC)
an Australian federal government agency that provides export credit and finance services to Australian exporters

The **Export Finance and Insurance Corporation (EFIC)** is another federal government agency promoting Australian exports by providing a range of financing options to assist Australian companies exporting and investing overseas.

In 2009–10 EFIC supported export contracts and overseas investments of over A$5.9 billion.

At the state level, from 1985 to 2004, the **Australian Overseas Project Corporation of Victoria (OPCV)** assisted Australian construction companies to compete for contracts in overseas development projects. OPCV has completed over 400 aid-related projects in some 50 countries and generated revenue of over $330 million for Victoria.

In 2004, OPCV was sold to Sinclair Knight Merz (SKM), a highly respected global professional services consultancy group of more than 3500 skilled personnel with offices across the United Kingdom, Australia, New Zealand, South-East Asia, the Pacific and South America.

It was hoped that the sale would enable the OPCV to operate in a fully commercial mode, putting it on the same basis as all other businesses in the Australian international aid sector.

Export incentives

The federal government provides export market development grants (EMDGs) to firms that incur expenditure in developing overseas markets for Australian goods, services and technology, and in attracting overseas tourists to Australia.

The EMDG scheme:

- encourages small and medium-sized Australian businesses to develop export markets
- reimburses up to 50 per cent of expenses incurred on eligible export promotion activities
- provides up to eight grants to each eligible participant.

To access the scheme for the first time, businesses need to have spent $10 000 over two years on eligible export marketing expenses.

Industry assistance

Industry assistance includes tariffs and quotas on imports, bounties and subsidies to selected industries, grants for research and development and taxation concessions.

As discussed in Chapter 20, as a result of structural reforms in the Australian economy, since the mid 1980s there has been a steady reduction in import protection and a shift in assistance from inefficient import-replacement industries (textiles, clothing, footwear) to export-oriented industries (e.g. the car sector).

The new strategy focus is illustrated by industry assistance schemes such as the Australian Government's 'New car plan for a greener future'.

industry assistance
government measures for assisting domestic industry including import protection, bounties and subsidies to selected industries, grants for research and development and taxation concessions

GOVERNMENT POLICIES TO PROMOTE INTERNATIONAL INVESTMENT

Before 1975, Australian investment policy, covering both FDI and portfolio investment, was mostly regulated by the Australian Government by way of its foreign exchange controls and occasional ad hoc interventions.

In 1974, the Foreign Investment Advisory Committee was established and, in 1976, it was replaced by the Foreign Investment Review Board (FIRB) to screen proposed investments.

In 1975, the Australian Government formalised for the first time its foreign investment policy through the *Foreign Acquisitions and Takeovers Act 1975* (Cwlth). This was amended in 1989 and is complemented by regulations issued pursuant to the Act in 1991.

Since the mid 1980s, there has been a trend away from protection in the design and conduct of Australian economic policy. In this context, a liberalisation of foreign investment guidelines took place. By 1987, the restrictions on foreign investments in manufacturing, services, resources processing, non-bank financial institutions, insurance, stockbroking, tourism, rural properties and primary industry (except mining) were eliminated.

Foreign investors were extended national treatment, though several industry sectors, including banking, domestic and international civil aviation, airports, media, newspapers, broadcasting and telecommunications—although not completely closed—were still subject to limitations.[1]

Foreign investment is regulated principally by the *Foreign Acquisitions and Takeovers Act* in combination with the Foreign Investment Policy issued by the Australian Government. Both are administered by the Federal Treasurer, who is assisted by FIRB.

The Act provides for the notification of investment proposals and for the prohibition of certain types of proposals that are, in the judgment of the Treasurer, contrary to the national interest.

In recognition of the contribution that foreign investment has made and continues to make to the development of Australia, the stated general stance of policy is to welcome foreign investment.

LEARNING OBJECTIVE 3
Describe the major means by which the Australian Government attempts to influence investment flows

The Act requires foreign investment proposals to be screened prior to their execution wherever they exceed the monetary thresholds specified in the *Foreign Acquisitions and Takeovers Regulations*.

The removal of restrictions has had two unfavourable effects:

- a large proportion of the investment flows (both in and out) comprise short-term speculative movements
- Australian investment abroad has increased dramatically (reaching a record US$32.8 billion in 2008).

Because direct controls, in principle, cannot be applied when the exchange rate is floating, the government has to rely on other policies to influence the amount of capital inflow indirectly:

- high domestic interest rates
- depreciating exchange rate
- domestic policies that give overseas investors confidence in the Australian economy.

Domestic interest rates that are high compared with overseas rates attract loan funds (i.e. government securities and bonds) from overseas. Therefore a firm monetary policy is necessary to maintain high interest rates. But high interest rates have the disadvantage of discouraging borrowing for investment by domestic business firms, which slows economic growth. Therefore, high interest rates maintained over a long period can have considerable disadvantages.

A depreciating exchange rate makes it cheaper to buy Australian dollars with foreign currencies, and so encourages a greater volume of capital inflow. With a flexible exchange rate, depreciation may be the result of a growing current account deficit, or of financial inflow drying up, or a combination of both.

Domestic policies that encourage financial inflows are necessary to make the Australian economy an attractive proposition for overseas investors. These include:

- reducing the current account deficit by encouraging export industries
- reducing the federal Budget deficit, which would have the effect of reducing inflationary expectations as well as the pressure on interest rates
- an incomes policy that reduces wage growth, lessens inflationary expectations and improves international competitiveness of exports.

LEARNING OBJECTIVE 4

Describe the advantages and disadvantages of capital inflow and the major means by which the government attracts investment inflows to balance the deficits on current account

One should note that notwithstanding the above progress in Australia's international investment framework, a number of analysts such as Kasper,[2] Kirchner,[3] Makin[4] and ITS Global[5] have been quite critical of the Australian Government's maintenance of some inward FDI restrictions, which—they contend—are impeding Australia's economic growth.

The above critical views seem to be supported by analysis from the OECD, which has placed Australia among the OECD's five member countries with the most restrictive FDI regimes, along with Iceland, Mexico, Austria and Canada.

ADVANTAGES OF INVESTMENT INFLOWS

Net capital inflow is necessary to finance Australia's persistent current account deficit. Net capital inflow is an injection into the economy, which compensates for the leakage in the form of the current account deficit.

The positive effects of foreign investment in Australia are:

- It provides scarce funds for our resource-rich but capital-scarce economy. Indeed, since 1959–60, there have been only three years when domestic savings exceeded investment. Even if Australia did dramatically improve the ratio of domestic savings, it would still have only limited funds for development of capital-intensive resource projects.
- It creates jobs. One estimate suggests that about 70 per cent of the new jobs in Australian manufacturing since World War II were provided by foreign-owned or controlled companies.
- It has helped build up the technological level of the economy, improve the quality of the workforce, and revolutionise management techniques. Therefore, the capital inflow contributes to economic growth and development.

net capital inflow
is an injection into the economy, which compensates for the leakage in the form of the current account deficit

DISADVANTAGES OF INVESTMENT INFLOWS

- The main disadvantage of net investment inflows, when it is in the form of loans, is the burden of the foreign debt and interest payments. As noted in Chapter 18, at the end of 2009–10, Australia's net foreign debt accounted for around 55 per cent of GDP, the highest ratio ever recorded.
- It increases the degree of **foreign ownership** and control of key sectors of our economy, particularly in manufacturing and mining. However, in recent years there have been some significant buy-backs of Australian assets. At the same time some of our biggest companies, such as BHP, have also expanded their overseas assets dramatically.
- It discourages local expenditure on research and development. The Japanese became great by importing technology and ideas and using them to produce goods more cheaply than anyone else. In other words, the technological dependence associated with foreign investment need not restrict an economy's development. Indeed it can greatly stimulate it.
- Foreign investment tends to deindustrialise Australia, because most foreign capital goes not into manufacturing, but into property and services. This argument overlooks the fact that the economy is now post-industrial: the tertiary sector (services) has the largest contribution to GDP growth in all Western countries and all newly industrialising countries. We cannot change foreign investors' decisions anyway. Multinational companies are invariably concerned with a global view of their operations. Managers may consider it in the best interest of the company to close down local branches (like Nissan-Australia or Heinz), with highly undesirable consequences for local employment. However, Australian-owned companies may also decide to close a branch or a plant overseas. It is any investor's right.

foreign ownership
ownership of domestic assets (e.g. shares, securities, real estate) by foreign companies

Because capital inflow has both benefits and costs, the government faces some dilemmas in its policy decisions. As long as there is a current account deficit, the government must obviously encourage capital and financial inflow to balance that deficit and to help to meet the demand for investment funds in the domestic capital market.

On the other hand, it should not let that inflow be so large that the foreign debt and interest payments become too much of a burden on the economy. So it must adopt policies that will reduce the need for investment inflows and thus keep it at moderate levels.

There are three ways in which the government may influence the level of net capital inflow:

- reduce the amount of its own overseas borrowings (the official capital flows), which generally the Australian government has achieved
- impose direct controls on private investment flows (politically, not sustainable)
- implement measures to influence indirectly the amount of capital inflow and outflow.

IS AUSTRALIAN INVESTMENT ABROAD HEALTHY?

LINK TO
INTERNATIONAL
ECONOMY

We particularly refer in this snapshot to Australian *direct* investment abroad, that is, investment by Australian firms that provides them with significant influence over the operations of a foreign enterprise. With regard to the above title question, many in the trade unions believe that Australian investment abroad is equivalent to 'exporting Australian jobs' and consequently the money should stay at home.

But on the evidence presented by the Industry Commission,[6] most of the increase in overseas direct investment can be taken as a positive development, with short- and long-term benefits for the Australian economy.

Where the investment is to overcome the natural barrier of high transport costs, it is clearly good for the Australian economy. It will allow Australian companies to escape the limitations of the small domestic market and cash in on higher growth in some foreign economies.

Even when the investment has been made necessary by artificial Asian trade barriers, it is still making the best of the prevailing circumstances and the Australian economy and its workers will be better off as a result of the investment.

Of course, some of the overseas investment is cost-driven (i.e. attracted by cheaper costs), but, even then, it may represent a healthy adjustment of the Australian economy. The point of opening the economy to overseas competition was to make Australian industry specialise in the things it does best. Australia should be exporting labour-intensive activities, which are better suited to the developing economies of Asia.

Only where the overseas investment represents an attempt by companies to escape artificially inflated labour costs or unnecessary restrictive regulations or some other domestic failure does it represent the 'undesirable exporting of jobs'. Of course, in that case it is the underlying economic failure that should be corrected, not the investment outflow.

One additional point is that investment overseas is one of the foreign business strategy options for any company, big or small, and that globalisation has obvious benefits for a company. Moreover the financial crisis in Asia resulted in a number of valuable assets becoming available at low prices. The acquisition of such assets (e.g. companies producing goods and services in Asian countries) is expected to strengthen the competitive position of Australian companies and to improve their profitability for the benefit of the shareholders and of the Australian economy as a whole.

For the majority of firms—Australia's Industry Commission found—Australian direct investment abroad complements exports and, in aggregate, it is also likely to enhance Australia's net export performance. The linkage between exports and foreign direct investment is very well illustrated by the case of the Australian wine industry.

From 1992 to 2009, the value of Australia's wine exports grew from $263 million to $2 271 million, an increase of 763 per cent. Australia became the world's fourth-largest exporter of wine in the world next to France, Italy and Spain, accounting for about 3 to 4 per cent of world wine exports. Overseas interests, particularly French (e.g. Moët et Chandon, Bollinger and Roederer) and

American (e.g. Constellation Brands Inc.), have invested in Australian wineries, bringing with them not only financial capital, but also technology, marketing skills and contacts in export markets in Europe, North America and Asia.

On the other hand, Foster's, along with other Australian wine companies (some of them with foreign equity) such as BRL Hardy, Southcorp and Lion Nathan, have been aggressively buying up American wine firms, largely to improve their access to the all-important distribution networks for American supermarkets.

In conclusion, the overall answer to the title question should be a resounding 'yes'.

QUESTION

What are the main arguments in favour of, and against, Australian investment abroad?

THE EXCHANGE RATE AND ECONOMIC POLICY

> **LEARNING OBJECTIVE 5**
> *Outline the position of the exchange rate of the Australian dollar as an indicator for the external balance and the role of the exchange rate policy in the external sector*

The exchange rate of the Australian dollar is an important economic indicator for the issue of external balance for four reasons:

1. The exchange rate is an indicator of the health of the balance of payments, which is also its main determinant.
2. Changes in the exchange rate affect the rate of capital inflow. Ceteris paribus, a fall in the exchange rate will encourage more capital inflow, and a rise will discourage it.
3. Changes in the exchange rate cause changes in the Australian dollar price of exports and imports. A depreciation causes increased competitiveness for exports and makes imports more expensive. The ultimate result should be an improvement in the balance of current account. An appreciating exchange rate will have the reverse effect.
4. Changes in the exchange rate, through their effect on import prices, cause changes in the domestic inflation rate.

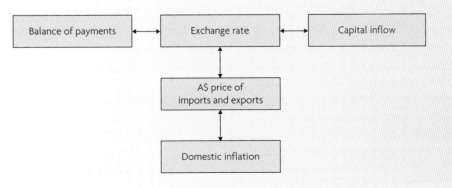

Figure 24.2
Factors affecting the exchange rate

A depreciating exchange rate brings about a rise in import prices, which comprise about 10 per cent of the basket of goods that determines the CPI. Conversely, an appreciation of the exchange rate lowers the prices of imports and reduces domestic inflation.

EXCHANGE RATE POLICY

The **exchange rate policy** is undertaken by the government, through the Reserve Bank, to attain specific macroeconomic objectives by means of influencing Australia's exchange rate. It is the method by which the government allows the exchange rate to be determined and the extent to which the government may decide to influence it.

As mentioned in Chapter 19, before the dollar was floated the government played a significant role in determining the exchange rate. Manipulation of the exchange rate under the free-floating regime established at the end of 1983 appears to be unnecessary. Theoretically, a free-floating exchange rate regime guarantees a zero net monetary movement.

Maintenance of an adequate level of international reserves is no longer a problem since banks are free to deal in foreign exchange, which they must obtain from within the foreign exchange market itself. However, the government has reserved the right to intervene in the market by way of the Reserve Bank in order to:

- smooth the course of the exchange rate where large transactions test the depth of the market
- adjust the composition of its resources
- buy or sell currency as a result of transactions with its customers.

In fact, since the Australian dollar was floated, the Reserve Bank has been active in the foreign exchange market. The usual government policy is to allow enough intervention to smooth out temporary fluctuations, because excessive volatility of the exchange rate creates costly uncertainty for firms involved in trade.

The main advantage of the floating rate is that the rate set by demand and supply is an equilibrium rate, so the market will always be cleared and there will be no surplus or deficit in the balance of payments that could affect the money supply.

Thus a floating exchange rate should give the government much more control over money supply growth than a fixed exchange rate. In other words, exchange rate targeting may be sacrificed in favour of monetary targeting, as it is not possible simultaneously to control the money supply and the exchange rate.

One should note that intervention in the foreign exchange by a central bank by buying or selling its currency is not necessarily successful (see the example of Thailand's central bank in 1997). The shift of the currency in the direction desired by the central bank can be successful only if the major players in the forex market (e.g. the large investment houses in the United States, Europe and Japan) operate (e.g. sell or buy the currency) in the same direction. Otherwise, the central bank's activities will be unsuccessful, because the big players throw larger funds on the forex market.

Another point to retain is that 'the dirty float' (e.g. central bank trading activities) is not the same thing as 'competitive devaluations' discussed in Chapter 19. In the latter case, the government undertakes a gross intervention to devalue its currency in order to provide an unfair advantage to its exporters.

SUMMARY

1. The basic aim of external policy is to achieve external balance, that is, some degree of balance between total payments (required for imports of goods and services and capital and financial outflows) and total receipts (received on account of the exports of goods and services and capital and financial inflows).
2. The main objectives of external policy are:
   (a) a competitive export sector
   (b) a steady capital inflow
   (c) a reasonably stable exchange rate.
3. The major concerns related to Australia's current account of the balance of payments are the size of the current account deficit and the growing foreign debt. Government policies meant to influence each component of the current account include:
   (a) promotion of exports (through Australia's participation in multilateral/regional/bilateral agreements)
   (b) assistance to industry
   (c) improvement in the international competitiveness of manufactures
   (d) reduction in government borrowing overseas
   (e) stabilisation of interest rates and exchange rate movements.
   It is believed that only policies to increase domestic savings would bring a fundamental solution to the problem of the current account deficit, foreign debt and net income deficit.
4. Net investment inflows are needed to finance Australia's persistent current account deficit. Investment inflow has a number of obvious advantages, but also has disadvantages. The government can influence the level of the net investment inflow through various measures, such as:
   (a) direct controls over private capital flows (politically, not sustainable)
   (b) indirect measures to encourage capital inflow (e.g. high domestic interest rates, a depreciating exchange rate).
5. A floating exchange rate gives the government more control over money supply growth than a fixed exchange rate. However, it is not possible to control both the money supply and the exchange rate at the same time.

KEY TERMS

Asia-Pacific Economic Cooperation group (APEC)	493	Export Finance and Insurance Corporation (EFIC)	494	industry assistance	495
Australian Trade Commission (Austrade)	494	external policy	489	international reserves	490
Cairns Group	492	foreign ownership	497	net capital inflow	497
exchange rate policy	500	free trade agreement (FTA)	493	net income deficit	500
		General Agreement on Tariffs and Trade (GATT)	492	World Trade Organization (WTO)	492

REFERENCES

1. B. Dyster and D. Meredith, *Australia in the International Economy in the Twentieth Century*, Cambridge University Press, Cambridge, 1990.
2. W. Kasper, *Open for Business? Australian Interests and the OECD's Multilateral Agreement on Investment*, CIS Issue Analysis 1, CIS, Sydney, 1998 and W. Kasper, *Capital Xenophobia: Australia's Controls of Foreign Investment*, CIS Sydney, 1984.
3. S. Kirchner, *Capital Xenophobia II: Foreign Direct Investment in Australia, Sovereign Wealth Funds, and the Rise of State Capitalism*, CIS Policy Monograph 88, 2008.
4. T. Makin, 'Capital xenophobia and the national interest', AOIF Paper 8, *Symposium on Australia's Open Investment Future*, Institute of Public Affairs, Melbourne, 4 December 2008.
5. ITS Global, *Foreign Direct Investment in Australia—the increasing cost of regulation*, Report by ITS Global,

9 September 2008, <www.itsglobal.net/docs/FDI_FinalReport_150908.doc>, accessed 11 November 2010.

6. Industry Commission, *Implications for Australia of Firms Locating Offshore*, Report No. 53, Australian Government Publishing Service, Canberra, 28 August 1996.

REVIEW QUESTIONS

1. Outline the meaning of external balance.
2. Discuss the relationship between external balance and domestic balance.
3. What are the main external policy objectives?
4. What are the main external policies in the area of trade? Discuss.
5. Outline the main advantages of foreign direct investment in Australia.
6. What economic policies can the government use to encourage more investment inflows (especially foreign direct investment)?
7. Name two indirect measures by which government can encourage foreign investment in Australia.
8. What is the relationship between the current account deficit and foreign debt?
9. What are the advantages of a floating currency over a fixed exchange rate? Discuss.
10. Outline some desirable solutions to the problem of a large Australian current account deficit and foreign debt.
11. Distinguish between the 'dirty float' and currency devaluation.

APPLIED QUESTIONS AND EXERCISES

1. A report on the Australian high-tech sector reveals that Australia is the second largest consumer of information technology and telecommunications products in the Asia-Pacific region, behind Japan, and accounts for 2 per cent of the world market. It is exceeded only by the United States as the world's most avid user of computers, with 26 computers for every 100 people.

   However, Australia is punching far below its weight as a producer and exporter. It accounts for less than 1 per cent of world production and about one-third of 1 per cent of world exports.

   The balance of trade in these products and services is running 4:1 against Australia.

   What government measures would you recommend in order to rectify this situation? (Your answer should be up to 500 words in length.)

2. Should Australia develop competitiveness in trade-exposed sectors only, or should it build competitiveness across the whole economy? Discuss your position on this strategy dilemma.

3. Consider this statement: 'The federal government is reluctant to put tight limits on state borrowings abroad, because the states would then seek finance in the domestic market and that would increase the crowding-out effect of public sector borrowing.'
   (a) Explain the statement in your own words.
   (b) Do you agree with the position of the government? Explain.

4. Discuss the difference between global/multilateral trade liberalisation and regional/bilateral free trade agreements. Outline a few Australian activities in each category of agreements.

5. In the context of the negotiation of an Australia-China Free trade Agreement, this is a meeting between representatives of the Australian manufacturing sector and the Australian Department of Foreign Affairs and Trade (DFAT), with the participation of a small team from the Prime Minister's Office.
   Divide the class into three teams:
   (a) the Australian manufacturing team, who will present their concerns related to the negotiation of a Free Trade Agreement with China
   (b) the DFAT team, who will defend the merits of a bilateral trade agreement with China, while taking note of the arguments raised by the manufacturing team
   (c) the Office of the Prime Minister team, who will bring its views and try to reconcile the two sets of arguments as outlined by the other two teams.

9

ECONOMIC GROWTH AND DEVELOPMENT

Chapter **25**

Economic growth

LEARNING OBJECTIVES

After studying this chapter, you will be able to:

1. examine the meaning and importance of economic growth
2. establish the ways in which economic growth is measured and identify the limitations of GDP as a measure of economic growth
3. identify the sources of growth—supply, demand and allocative factors
4. explain the classical view and some modern views of economic growth
5. review some major problems underlying the history and the future of economic growth in Australia and the Asia-Pacific region
6. explain the controversy over the benefits and costs of economic growth.

INTRODUCTION

Economic growth, economic welfare, standard of living and total welfare were central themes in Economics courses in the 1960s and 1970s.

The emergence of *stagflation* (simultaneously high levels of inflation and unemployment), following the energy crisis of 1973, turned attention to the study of economic negatives—reducing the effects of inflation, unemployment and external instability.

However, growth, welfare and quality of life are fashionable again and 'sustainable economic growth' and 'the standard of living' are prominent chapters in Economics courses. Prime ministers and treasurers boast when the figures are good, opposition leaders make critical speeches in parliament when Budget growth figures are not fulfilled.

The fast economic growth achieved by the so-called tiger economies of East Asia raised a lot of praise around the world, but also stirred a number of critics.

Economic growth can be both a cause and consequence of business investment. But it can also set off inflation and unemployment, create current account difficulties and cause currencies to shift alarmingly. Growth can provide higher standards of living for the citizens of a country. But its absence, or an unfair distribution of its benefits, is one of the basic causes of poverty in low-income developing countries.

In this chapter we will examine some of the major issues related to the concept of economic growth.

THE MEANING AND IMPORTANCE OF ECONOMIC GROWTH

LEARNING OBJECTIVE 1
Examine the meaning and importance of economic growth

economic growth
a sustained increase, over time, in the real value of the production of goods and services

Economic growth is a vital issue in economics. It is sometimes defined as a sustained increase, over time, in the real value of the production of goods and services. In a material sense, it means increasing the quantity or volume of goods and services available in the economy in order to satisfy as many wants as possible.

To achieve this, an economy needs to produce effectively and efficiently. In this way, it will maximise the satisfaction of wants. Further output of goods and services associated with economic growth converts into greater income. Expanding real income makes new opportunities available to individuals, without the sacrifice of other opportunities.

A growing economy may, for example, spend more money to clean up the environment without sacrificing levels of consumption and investment. Economic growth relaxes production constraints imposed by scarcity and allows a nation to embark on new projects without penalty.

ECONOMIC GROWTH AND THE PRODUCTION POSSIBILITY CURVE

You will recall our discussion on the production possibility curve (PPC) in Chapter 1.

Suppose the economy produces two kinds of goods—consumer goods and capital goods. The production possibility curve in Figure 25.1 overleaf shows the different maximum possible combinations of quantities of capital and consumer goods that the economy can produce if it employs fully all its available productive resources (labour, capital, land, enterprise), given the existing state of the technology.

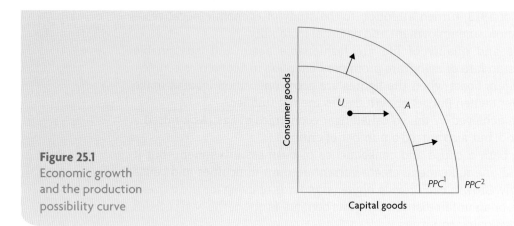

Figure 25.1
Economic growth and the production possibility curve

An increase in the quantity or quality of any of these resources, or any technological improvement, will cause an outward shift of the production possibility curve from PPC^1 to PPC^2. As a result, the economy can produce more of both kinds of goods.

Economic growth may be viewed as the continual shifting outwards of the production possibility curve, caused by growth in the quantity or quality of the economy's productive resources or by continuous technological improvement, or by some combination of both. If the economy's production possibility curve shifts outwards, the economy's capacity to produce increases. But the full benefits of this capacity will not be realised unless it stays on its production possibility frontier.

There are two main reasons why the economy may operate inside its production possibility frontier:

1. Some of the economy's productive resources are unemployed. In other words, if there is unemployment of labour resources, or if there is unused plant capacity, the economy will operate inside its frontier, as at position U in Figure 25.1. In order to remain on the frontier, the economy's aggregate demand for goods and services must grow at a rate sufficient to utilise fully the increased productive capacity provided by economic growth.
2. Some of the economy's resources are underemployed—that is, resource allocation is inefficient. When resource allocation is efficient, resources are employed in those activities for which they are best suited.

For example, although former communist countries in Eastern Europe (such as Bulgaria, Romania, Poland) had good resources for agriculture and consumer goods, they instead expanded their heavy industries for which they did not have enough raw materials or production and marketing expertise. This represented an inefficient allocation of resources and led those countries to virtual bankruptcy.

REVIEW QUESTIONS

1. What is the meaning of the term 'economic growth'?
2. Under what circumstances may the economy operate inside its production possibility frontier?
3. What is the significance of an outward shift of the economy's production possibility frontier?

MEASURING ECONOMIC GROWTH

LEARNING OBJECTIVE 2
Establish the ways in which economic growth is measured and identify the limitations of GDP as a measure of economic growth

Economic growth is an increase in the quantity of goods and services produced over time, that is, an increase in the real or constant price value of production.

GROSS DOMESTIC PRODUCT (GDP)

The indicator most often used to measure economic growth is the gross domestic product (GDP) (see Chapter 9).

The two main production statistics used to measure economic growth are:

1. **Real GDP or GDP at constant prices**. The value of annual production (GDP) is first determined in money or nominal terms; then any increase in value due to inflation is taken out to give the real GDP, or GDP at constant prices. Any percentage increase in real GDP is used in calculating the nation's annual economic growth.
2. The increase in real GDP/GNP (gross national product) per head (per capita). This indicator is largely used by international organisations such as the World Bank or the International Monetary Fund, particularly when trying to make international comparisons. The per-head measure enables a more reliable comparison of economies of different sizes and with different populations.

real GDP (GDP at constant prices)
GDP figures that have been inflated or deflated to account for price-level changes

OTHER INDICATORS

Other indicators used for measuring economic growth include:

- gross national income (see below)
- **net domestic product (NDP)**, which is GDP minus depreciation of capital equipment
- specific indicators of sources of economic growth, such as labour force size, government expenditure, growth in productivity
- productivity measures, such as output per labour hour, output per worker employed.

net domestic product (NDP)
GDP minus depreciation of capital equipment

Gross national income (GNI)

According to the World Bank, the **gross national income (GNI)** is

the sum of value added by all resident producers plus any product taxes (less subsidies) not included in the valuation of output plus net receipts of primary income (compensation of employees and property income) from abroad.[1]

This definition was used by the World Bank for the first time in the 2001 edition of its *World Development Indicators* and this terminology is in line with the 1993 United Nations System of National Accounts (1993 SNA). Some countries continue to compile their national accounts

gross national income (GNI)
the sum of value added by all resident producers plus any product taxes (less subsidies) not included in the valuation of output plus net receipts of primary income (compensation of employees and property income) from abroad

according to the System of National Accounts version 3, referred to as the 1968 SNA. For instance, GNI was previously called gross national product (GNP).

In practical terms, the major difference between GDP and GNP/GNI is made by the *net investment income*. For example, in the case of Australia, this is the difference between the income earned by Australian investors overseas and the income earned from investment in Australia by non-residents (e.g. foreign firms, governments and individuals). See Chapter 9 for more details on the GNI.

LIMITATIONS OF GDP AS A MEASURE OF ECONOMIC GROWTH

Although real GDP is the normal measure of economic growth, it has some limitations, both as a measure of economic growth and as an indicator of changes in the standard of living.

As a measure of economic growth, per capita GDP ignores:

- non-monetary incomes
- unpaid production: subsistence farming, voluntary home cleaning, personal car repairs, free government services
- the cash economy and black markets.

As an indicator of changes in the standard of living, per capita GDP ignores:

- income distribution (especially significant in countries where there are large disparities in income)
- the amount of effort (i.e. total working hours) required to produce this output
- the costs of growth, such as infrastructure bottlenecks, pollution and stress.

LEARNING OBJECTIVE 3
Identify the sources of growth—supply, demand and allocative factors

SOURCES OF ECONOMIC GROWTH

Achieving economic growth at a satisfactory rate means producing more goods and services each year. This is achieved through the combined contribution of three groups of factors: supply, demand and allocative factors.

SUPPLY FACTORS

*supply factors
the physical ability of
an economy to grow*

Supply factors relate to the physical ability of an economy to grow.

Production is the process where factors of production (land, labour, capital and enterprise) are combined by producers to provide valuable goods and services. Production can be increased by using more resources, or by using existing resources more efficiently.

Natural resources (land)

By definition, the quantity of land is in fixed supply. However, natural resources include not only the land surface and what it is used for, but also all naturally occurring resources—minerals; fossil fuels such as coal, oil and gas; timber; water. Some of these resources are abundant in Australia.

It is possible to expand land area by reclaiming land from the sea, as Singapore and the Netherlands have done. Techniques such as irrigation, exploration, reafforestation, use of fertilisers and soil conservation can improve the quality of land resources.

Human resources (labour and enterprise)

The quantity of labour can be increased over a long period by the natural growth of the population as a whole. In the short term, it can be increased by immigration. The labour force comprises all those willing to work or actively seeking work.

The size of the Australian workforce, especially in the 1950s and 1960s, was considerably increased by immigration and, starting in the 1970s, by increased participation of married women in the workforce.

Labour efficiency improves by increasing the skills of the labour force through better education and training. Research by two Americans, Schultz and Denison[2] attributed about half the growth in the GDP of the United States to improvement in human capital—better-educated workers and managers. A nation with a highly educated workforce is likely to provide the climate that encourages innovation and entrepreneurs. Emphasis on education is one of the factors behind East Asia's fast economic growth. A stable political system, the opportunity for education, access to money capital, taxation incentives, and the opportunity to profit from one's own effort and initiative will all favour the development of entrepreneurial talents.

Capital goods

Capital, in the form of items such as robots, factories and computers, increases the ability of the economy to produce goods and services and, therefore, promotes economic growth.

Modern capital tends by nature to substantially increase plant efficiency and productivity. More capital equipment, or more advanced units of capital, increases the productivity of both land and labour. Capital is a strong resource in developed countries such as Japan, the United States and Germany.

Investment, or the accumulation of real capital, holds the key to economic growth. Many capital investments in Australia have been financed through domestic savings, but capital inflow from overseas (mainly direct investment) has also brought capital assets, modern technology and managerial skills. More capital-intensive methods of production have brought economies of large-scale production, and have reduced costs and increased efficiencies in many areas of production.

DEMAND FACTORS

A growing level of aggregate demand is required to realise a nation's productive potential. This requires additional spending by individuals, companies and governments, creating increased demand for production. You will remember that aggregate demand is made up of consumption and investment, plus government spending and exports, minus imports (see Chapter 10). Any rise in the first four components tends to promote economic growth, while an increase in imports or a decrease in the first four components tends to throw the economy into reverse.

ALLOCATIVE FACTORS

To achieve its productive potential, a nation must provide not only for the full employment of its resources, but also for full production from those resources. Resources should be allocated in such a way as to make the maximum contribution to output. The **allocation of resources** refers to the way in which available factors of production are allocated to the production, distribution and exchange of goods and services.

allocation of resources
the way in which available factors of production are allocated to the production, distribution and exchange of goods and services

The supply factors and aggregate demand are the actual driving forces for economic growth. However, growth implies new methods of production as well as changes in resource supplies and consumer demand. The demand for some goods is highly sensitive to increases in real income, while demand for other goods is less sensitive. All these changes call for a realignment or reallocation of the economy's resources. Unless these changes occur with reasonable speed, the economy will not fully realise its capacity for growth.

allocative efficiency
occurs when all available resources are devoted to the combination of goods most wanted by society

Wages and prices must be flexible if an efficient allocation of resources is to be achieved. Prices of all resources (including labour) should reflect market conditions and, as a result, wages in rapidly growing industries should increase rapidly, while wages and prices of other resources in a declining industry increase at a lower rate or even decline.

Moves to promote increased competition in industry and a reduction in tariff protection can also improve **allocative efficiency** and move our economy towards its growth potential.

LEARNING OBJECTIVE 4
Explain the classical view and some modern views of economic growth

THEORIES OF ECONOMIC GROWTH

THE CLASSICAL VIEW OF ECONOMIC GROWTH

Adam Smith attributed economic growth to the 'invisible hand'—in other words, to the ability of the free market to allocate the factors of production, goods and services to their most valuable use. During the late 18th and early 19th centuries the classical British economists such as David Ricardo and Thomas Malthus painted a rather gloomy picture of the prospects for economic growth.[3]

Ricardo and Malthus argued that a nation's economic growth would inevitably lead to stagnation and a subsistence standard of living. In its simplest form, their argument rested on two basic premises:

1. the law of diminishing returns
2. the population would expand to the point where the economy's limited resources would only provide a subsistence living.

law of diminishing returns
the change in total output when the quantity of one input to a production process is increased, while quantities of all other inputs are held constant

The **law of diminishing returns** describes the change in total output when the quantity of one input to a production process is increased, while quantities of all other inputs are held constant. The law indicates that, with a given technology, the addition of successive units of one resource (labour) to fixed amounts of other resources (land and capital) will ultimately result in smaller and smaller increases in total output. One can conclude that the average output or productivity per worker will ultimately diminish as more and more labour is added. Classical economists applied this law to economic growth. They argued that, given a fixed state of technological know-how, as a larger and larger population works with a fixed amount of land and other resources, the increase in total output becomes smaller and smaller.

subsistence level
the minimum standard of living necessary to keep the population from declining

In their view, both output and population growth cease once output per capita has fallen to the subsistence level. (The **subsistence level** may be viewed as the minimum standard of living necessary to keep the population from declining.) It is this implication of such a dismal long-run equilibrium position that earned economics its designation as 'the dismal science'.)

THE NEO-CLASSICAL THEORY OF ECONOMIC GROWTH

Models by economists such as Karl Marx and Robert Solow[4] stressed the deepening of capital as a way of increasing per capita output.

In the neo-classical theory of economic growth, a number of economists, including Solow and Swan[5] argued that, when an economy is in equilibrium, growth in output is determined by the growth in the labour force and the rate of technological progress. That is, neither the level of savings nor the ratio of capital to output influences the long-run rate of growth. Both of these factors can, however, affect the rate at which an economy which is not already on its long-run growth path will move toward long-run equilibrium.

Similarly, while distortions in the economy will not affect the long-run rate of growth, they will affect the level of per capita income. So removing a distortion can result in a step-up in income, after which long-run growth resumes. In this neo-classical model, the return to investment falls as more and more capital is put in place until a point is reached where the expected return from a further increase in investment is below the financing cost. Beyond this point, investment occurs only as needed to replace existing capital as it depreciates and to complement increases in the labour force and technical progress. (For a more comprehensive exposition, see, for example, Mankiw.[6])

'ENDOGENOUS' GROWTH THEORIES

Recent theoretical and empirical research has produced the so-called **endogenous growth** theory. (The endogenous variable is a variable in an economic model whose value is determined *within* the model. An exogenous variable is one whose value is not determined by the model.) This suggests that there are economic mechanisms that can lead to a permanent increase in the rate of economic growth—increases in capital accumulation, and not just exogenous technical progress, can, under certain circumstances, increase growth. Economists embracing this theory include Paul Romer, R. Lucas, and Grossman and Helpman.[7]

endogenous growth *modern explanations of the economic growth process contending that the process of technological change is endogenous to economic growth rather than being treated as exogenous, as in the earlier Solow growth model*

The theory predicts that long-run rates of economic growth will increase on the basis of capital accumulation. It is based on the view that diminishing private returns to capital tend to be more than offset by the existence of externalities (e.g. benefits derived from an increase in the level of general education of the population) or non-rival goods such as knowledge. Thus the technology embodied in these investments drives growth.

More importantly, the new view suggests that certain types of investment will generate more externalities than others. The types of investment suggested as possible sources of endogenous growth include investments in physical capital, public infrastructure, research and development and human capital.

GOVERNMENT ROLE IN ECONOMIC GROWTH

There is considerable controversy about the optimal role for government, with empirical and theoretical support for a wide variety of possible roles.

Some economists, such as Wade,[8] argue that governments have a role in generating growth, and point to the experiences of some of the fast-growing economies of East Asia and Europe. The opposing and—until recently—dominant view is that these economies have succeeded because their governments acted to complement, rather than substitute for, market signals. According to the neo-classical growth theory, long-term economic growth is determined by factors largely outside the control of governments, which should do little more than ensure the economy is operating as efficiently as possible.

OTHER RECENT GROWTH THEORIES

social competence
the skills necessary to be accepted and fulfilled socially

British economists A. Maddison and M. Abramovitz[9] identified in their 1980s studies some convergence in economic growth rates between developed countries over the last century. A major factor behind this convergence is identified as the level of **social competence** (education, experience with large-scale production, distribution and finance) that enabled some economies to exploit advanced technology.

The new growth theories are important because they focus on the factor that is generally acknowledged to be the key to long-term economic growth: increased productivity from new knowledge produced by investment by rational, profit-seeking economic agents.

REVIEW QUESTIONS

1. What are the basic theoretical premises justifying the inevitability of stagnation in economic growth, as presented by Ricardo and Malthus?
2. What is meant by 'endogenous growth'?
3. Discuss the opposing views on government's role in economic growth.
4. What is the main factor emphasised by new growth theories as the key to long-term economic growth?

LEARNING OBJECTIVE 5
Review some major problems underlying the history and the future of economic growth in Australia and the Asia-Pacific region

ECONOMIC GROWTH IN AUSTRALIA

GROWTH BEFORE 1945

Modern Australian economic history has been characterised by sustained and stable growth, periodically interrupted by major economic setbacks. The depressions of the 1840s, 1890s and 1930s are examples of such setbacks.

As in other developing economies, Australia's economic growth began with the establishment of an export industry. It was the wool industry that first established Australia as an exporter, and diversification into the export of other primary products followed this success. In the 1850s rich deposits of gold were discovered, and quickly exploited, adding to the country's export resources. Further diversification into other types of mining and the agricultural industries soon added other minerals, and later wheat, to the list of major export commodities. Table 25.1 shows the approximate percentage growth rates during this period.

Table 25.1   **Average economic growth rates (approximate per cent per annum) in Australia, and factors contributing to economic growth, 1861–1959**

PERIOD	GROWTH RATE %	COMMENT
1861–90	About 5	Strong sustained growth supported by wool and gold production and developments in manufacturing industries.
1890s	About 1	Affected by depression in the early 1890s—good recovery in second half.
1900s	About 4	Strong sustained growth after mild recession in 1902.
1910s	About 2.5	Affected by World War I; growth of about 4 per cent average per year except for 1915 and 1916.
1920s	About 2.5	Growth higher in early 1920s but slowed after 1925 and economy in depression by 1929.

continued ↘

PERIOD	GROWTH RATE %	COMMENT
1930s	About 2	Affected by depression in early 1930s—a good recovery in second half.
1940s	About 4	Aided by production for World War II and postwar reconstruction. Large number of migrants after war.
1950s	About 4.5	Strong sustained growth in a period of strong population growth and economic development.

Source: Ken Nailon, Economic Growth and Standard of Living, No. 5, Problems in Economic Series, VCTA Publishing Pty Ltd, Collingwood, Victoria, 1992. Reproduced by permission of Macmillan Education Australia.

Typically, the next stage in the development of a young economy is the establishment of a manufacturing base. In Australia this was closely linked to the mining of gold: gold brought wealth, and wealth attracted capital investment and a new labour supply.

The huge influx of migrants attracted by the discovery of gold dramatically increased the population. This created a new market for housing, and an incentive for the government (backed by British capital) to fund capital works, such as roads, railways and water supplies. The mining industry was also a catalyst for improvement in production techniques. Alluvial mining and tunnelling techniques were developed, and these were later applied to the exploitation of other mineral resources.

Another important growth period for the Australian economy was the period between the financial crash of the 1890s and the Great Depression of the 1930s. During this period (apart from the war years, 1914 to 1918) mining and agricultural output continued to increase, and this provided a strong base on which the manufacturing industry continued to grow and expand. Iron and steel and other metal industries developed, and a strong motor vehicle manufacturing industry was established, based on the domestic supply of mineral resources.

The depressions of the 1890s and 1930s were part of a pattern that affected other Western economies, but they had a devastating effect in Australia. During the early 1930s, Australia's production fell by 25 to 30 per cent, the share of investment dropped from 20 to 5 per cent of GDP and unemployment reached 30 per cent.

Although the Depression was dramatic, recovery was swift: by the second half of the 1930s, growth was averaging almost 5 per cent a year. High wool prices, mining and more efficient production lay behind this remarkable recovery. Manufacturing rose above pre-Depression levels, and a revival in the building industry had reverberations throughout the economy.

World War II was the catalyst to further manufacturing diversification which was essential to continued development of the economy. The demand for war supplies included a wide range of products, from armaments to food and clothing. This stimulated production in a variety of industries. The resultant growth was reinforced by the need for postwar reconstruction and a new wave of immigration.

GROWTH AFTER WORLD WAR II

As Table 25.2 overleaf shows, the period from the late 1940s to the early 1970s was one of significant growth, prosperity and what economists technically consider as near full employment.

The high population growth, due to an expansion in the birth rate in the 1950s and high migration levels, had a twofold effect: first, on the size and skill of the labour force, due especially to the migrant intake; second, on the size of the domestic market, bringing increased demand and economic activity. The level of investment (capital asset growth) rose in the 1950s to nearly 30 per cent of GDP.

Table 25.2   **Factors contributing to economic growth (average growth rates per cent per annum, except where indicated)**

ECONOMIC INDICATORS	1949–60	1960–73	1973–79	1979–89
Real GDP	4.2	5.2	2.7	3.1
Population	2.4	1.9	1.2	1.5
GDP per person employed	2.2	2.5	1.7	1.2
Real wages	1.4	3.2	1.4	0.9
Inflation (CPI)	5.5	3.9	12.1	8.5
Ratio of investment to GDP %	30.0	25.4	25.4	23.0
Unemployment rate	2.0	1.9	5.0	7.5

Source: Ken Nailon, Economic Growth and Standard of Living, No. 5, Problems in Economic Series, VCTA Publishing Pty Ltd, Collingwood, Victoria, 1992. Reproduced by permission of Macmillan Education Australia.

By 1972 there were signs that the period of relative stability was ending. The economic problems of the 1970s and 1980s included stagflation (simultaneously high levels of inflation and unemployment) and external instability—expanding current account deficits in the balance of payments and increasing external debt (see Chapter 18). These problems affected economic performance and contributed to a declining growth rate.

Rates of inflation exceeded 9 per cent in most years, and rates of unemployment were more than 6 per cent from the mid 1970s, exceeding 10 per cent in the recessions of 1982–83 and 1990–91. The level of economic growth in the 1980s fluctuated considerably. Some excellent rates were achieved, but they were not sustained because of the tendency to invest speculatively for short-term profits, rather than productively in new capital assets.

The floating of the Australian dollar in December 1983, the deregulation of the financial sector and the 'Button plan' (see Chapter 20) for lowering government protection in the manufacturing sector exposed the Australian economy to world market forces. It is generally believed that the 1980s saw the globalisation of Australia's economy. Strong domestic demand expanded employment in 1987–89, but also contributed to a severe deterioration of the current account deficit and expanded external debt. For all its achievements, the 1980s ended in monetary failure: a deep economic recession provoked by interest rates of 18 per cent. Restrictive economic policies aimed at the problems of the external sector reduced the level of economic activity and the real GDP recorded negative growth (e.g. –1 per cent in 1991). Inflation went below 2 per cent but, during the 1990–91 recession, unemployment jumped to more than 11 per cent.

ECONOMIC GROWTH AFTER THE EARLY 1990s RECESSION

The period since 1991 is the longest period of growth that Australia has recorded for at least the past century. Table 25.3 shows that economic growth in Australia has recorded over some 20 years a relatively high average annual rate of 3.4 per cent, with a slow-down in the second half. Significant growth factors were:

- Part of this growth is due to an increase in population (natural growth and immigration), particularly in the last years of the 2000s.
- Australia was also well placed to take advantage of the emergence of China, both in terms of its location and the composition of its exports.
- The inflation rate was lower than in the 1980s, basically due to technology, more competition and low interest rates.

- The cumulative effect of a long period of gradually falling protection, combined with the changes in behaviour that this helped to bring about.
- Last but not least, the rise of Australia's labour productivity, especially that of its 'multifactor' productivity, which as Table 25.3 indicates was the major contributor to Australia's economic growth over the 1990s.

Multifactor productivity represents that part of the growth in output that cannot be explained by growth in labour and capital inputs. Examples of multifactor productivity growth include improved production techniques, better management practices and organisational change.

multifactor productivity
that part of the growth in output that cannot be explained by growth in labour and capital inputs.

Table 25.3   **Australia's real GDP growth (per cent per annum) and contributions to GDP growth (per cent), 1990–91 to 2008–09**

PERIODS	REAL GDP GROWTH AVERAGE ANNUAL % CHANGE	CONTRIBUTIONS TO GDP GROWTH (PERCENTAGE POINTS)*		
		LABOUR	CAPITAL	MULTIFACTOR PRODUCTIVITY
1990–91 to 2000–01	3.6	0.8	1.3	1.5
2000–01 to 2008–09	3.2	1.0	1.8	0.4
1990–91 to 2008–09	3.4	0.9	1.5	1.0

Source: Ric Battellino, Twenty years of growth, RBA speeches, <www.rba.gov.au/speeches/2010/sp-dg-200810.html>, accessed 11 November 2010.

The Howard Government's industry package of December 1997 committed government to boost growth to a sustained 4 per cent, for the first time setting a target against which to measure the government's economic performance. However, Australia has managed economic growth rates of 4 per cent and above in only four subsequent years: 1998 (5.1%), 1999 (4.5%), 2002 (4%) and 2007 (4.2%). An unfavourable global environment (e.g. the slow-down in the United States economy and other major economies, the terrorism events of 11 September 2001 and the global financial crisis) has been the major reason for lower economic growth rates In Australia.

Table 25.4 shows which sectors or industries of the Australian economy have registered a higher than average growth and consequently an increase in their share of Australia's GDP.

Following global trends, most growth industries are located (with the exception of mining) in the area of services: financial and insurance services (+3.8 percentage points); mining (+2.7 percentage points); professional, scientific and technical services; construction; transport, postal and warehousing and administrative services.

Table 25.4   **Australia's GDP by industry* per cent of total, 1991–92 and 2008–09**

INDUSTRY	2008–09 (% OF GDP)	1991–92 (% OF GDP)	DIFFERENCE (+/– %)
Financial and insurance services	10.8	7.0	+3.8
Education, health and social assistance	10.4	10.8	–0.4
Retail and wholesale trade	9.6	10.2	–0.6
Manufacturing	9.4	14.0	–4.6
Ownership of dwellings	8.0	8.9	–0.9

continued ↘

continued

INDUSTRY	2008–09 (% OF GDP)	1991–92 (% OF GDP)	DIFFERENCE (+/– %)
Administrative (including public administration and safety)	8.0	7.9	+0.1
Mining	7.7	5.0	+2.7
Construction	7.4	6.3	+1.1
Professional, scientific and technical services	6.1	4.3	+1.8
Transport, postal and warehousing	5.8	5.6	+0.2
Utilities, accommodation and food services	5.0	6.4	–1.4
Information media and telecommunications	3.4	4.1	–0.7
Rental, hiring and real estate services	3.0	3.1	–0.1
Arts, recreation and other services	2.8	3.1	–0.3
Agriculture, forestry and fishing	2.6	3.3	–0.7

Note: *GDP excludes taxes, subsidies, and the statistical discrepancy.

Source: Ric Battellino, Twenty years of growth, RBA speeches, <www.rba.gov.au/speeches/2010/sp-dg-200810.html>, accessed 11 November 2010.

In exchange, manufacturing's market share of Australia's GDP has dropped over the period by 4.6 percentage points, which is in line with trends in major developed economies.

The big question is whether an increasingly deregulated labour market will mean a trade-off between job growth and further falling living standards for the least advantaged, whose numbers in Australia have been increasing markedly. It is clear that even more sustained economic growth is needed to create better prospects for Australia's unemployed.

INTERNATIONAL COMPARISONS

Comparability of statistics from one country to another is affected by different methods of data collection, different standards of accuracy, and different definitions of what is included. Taking into account the relativity of such comparisons, we can say that Australia's growth rate compares favourably with other Western countries.

A 1991 study by A. Maddison[10] indicated that, taking a long-term view over the period 1900 to 1987, Australia held the sixth ranking among 16 OECD countries in terms of annual average compound growth rates, at 3.1 per cent.

As Table 25.5 shows, following the recession of the early 1990s Australia's growth rate has compared very favourably with that of its major trading partners and that of other OECD countries. OECD reports indicate that the Australian economy has continued to grow strongly, despite the cyclical downturn that hit most OECD countries in 2001–02 and 2008–09. As mentioned earlier, Australia and Poland were the only OECD economies to avoid a recession during the GFC of 2008–09.

Table 25.5   **Comparative economic growth in Australia, OECD, and selected industrialised countries, average annual growth rates (per cent), 1975–2009**

	AVERAGE				
	1975–85	1986–95	1996–02	2003–08	2009
Total OECD	3.2	2.9	2.9	2.4	-3.5
United States	3.4	2.9	3.5	2.4	-2.5
Euro area	2.3*	2.5	2.4	1.8	-4.0
Japan	3.9	3.2	0.8	1.6	-5.3
Canada	3.2	2.3	3.6	2.3	-2.7
Australia	3.0	3.0	3.9	3.2	0.8

Note: *European Union.

Source: Adapted from OECD, Economic Outlook, June 2003 and May 2010.

However, Australia's population growth (including immigration) has traditionally been higher than that of other OECD countries and Australia needs to maintain higher rates of economic growth in order to maintain a steady growth in living standards.

THE SIGNIFICANCE OF GROWTH RATES

LINK TO BUSINESS

The Link to Business in Chapter 21 discussed the importance of macroeconomic objectives, including economic growth, for the good performance of any individual business. But how important is the pace of economic growth?

What difference does it make whether an economy grows at 3 per cent, or 4 per cent, or 5 per cent? A great deal! A rule-of-thumb calculation known as the rule of 72 readily shows why this is so.

THE RULE OF 72

For any growth rate in real GDP, the **rule of 72** says that the number of years it will take for real GDP to double in size is roughly equal to 72 divided by the growth rate.

For example, if the economy's real GDP grows at a rate of 2 per cent, it will take approximately 36 years (72 ÷ 2) for real GDP to double. If it grows at 3 per cent, it will take 24 years to double (72 ÷ 3). If it grows at 6 per cent, real GDP will double in only 12 years (72 ÷ 6)!

Consider the implications of different growth rates for our economy. Economists tend to agree that in the 1960s the economy could grow 4 per cent each year without setting off demand-pull inflation. However, because of the slow-down in productivity growth during the 1970s and early 1980s, this figure may be more like 3 or even 2 per cent. According to the rule of 72, at a 4 per cent growth from the year 1984, this doubling would occur in the year 2002. However, if the safe growth rate needed to avoid excessive inflation is 3 per cent, real GDP would not double until approximately the year 2008, which is 24 years from 1984. If the safe growth rate is 2 per cent, real GDP would not double until the year 2020.

Suppose we start with the actual level of real GDP in 1998–99 ($590.4 billion) and project two different growth paths into the future, 3 and 4 per cent per annum. Clearly, the farther into the future we go on these two different paths, the greater the difference in the possible levels of real GDP:

- In 2005–06 the difference amounts to roughly $50.8 billion.
- By 2010–11, real GDP with 4 per cent growth is about $945.2 billion, and with 3 per cent growth it is about $841.8 billion—a difference of $103.5 billion.

Source: Adapted from R.N. Waud, A. Hocking, P. Maxwell and J. Bonnici, Economics, Harper Educational Publishers, Sydney, 1992, p. 475.

rule of 72
the number of years it will take for real GDP to double in size is roughly equal to 72 divided by the growth rate

continued

QUESTIONS

1. What is the rule of 72?
2. Calculate the average annual real GDP growth rate over the last five years. How many years will the economy need to double its real GDP at this rate?

Over the last three decades, the newly industrialised countries (NICs) in East Asia, the so-called tiger economies, have consistently exhibited higher growth rates than the established economies. The Link to International Economy at the end of this chapter (p. 520) examines the economic success of the tiger economies, the debate about their 1997 financial crisis, and their growth prospects.

The success of the Asian NICs is due to their improvements in productive capacity: high levels of investment in plant and equipment, improved labour force skills through education and training, and higher managerial efficiency. These improvements have enabled them to specialise in production for export, gradually shifting from labour-intensive manufactures—textiles, toys, footwear, clothing—to capital-intensive products, such as various types of machinery and microelectronics.

This export strategy for growth and its success in East Asian economies poses an interesting approach for Australia to consider in the context of its stated objective of transforming itself from the Lucky Country to the Clever Country. At the same time, the Asian crisis may teach Australia valuable lessons.

PURCHASING POWER PARITY

purchasing power parity (PPP)
a theory stating that exchange rates between currencies are in equilibrium when their purchasing power is the same in each of the two countries

We mentioned in Chapter 9 that a new method of calculating GDP/GNP, **purchasing power parity (PPP)**, has been used in recent years in parallel with the traditional method using international exchange rates (the so-called **World Bank Atlas method**). The PPP conversion factor is defined as the number of units of a country's currency required to buy the same amounts of goods and services in the domestic market as one US dollar would buy in the United States.

World Bank Atlas method
traditional method of calculation of GDP/GNP/GNI by using three-year international exchange rates for expressing the national indicators in national currency in US dollars and achieving comparable indicators

Purchasing power parities (PPPs) are calculated by comparing the prices of identical goods and services in different countries and applying expenditure weights of GDP. These price comparisons are made by calculating *price relatives*, which are the price of a specified good or service in one country divided by the price of the same item in another country. For example, if a 300 ml can of Pepsi costs Rp16.42 in country A and $3.24 in country B, a price relative can be calculated as 3.24 ÷ 16.42, or about 0.20. Price relatives are calculated for several hundred items covering all the final expenditure components of GDP and PPPs are then obtained as the weighted average of these price relatives. The weights used are the shares of expenditure on each item in total GDP.

Source: Asian Development Bank, <www.adb.org/documents/books/key_indicators/2009/pdf/Regional-Tables-Introduction.pdf>, accessed 12 November 2010.

In other words, the PPP method calculates the size of an individual economy on the basis of what that country actually produces and consumes, rather than on what exchange rates for the US dollar suggest it does—which can be misleading.

In Chapter 9 we presented the World Bank list of the world's largest economies using the traditional conversion of GDP in national currencies to US dollars at official exchange rates.

According to the PPP method, China's GDP in 2009 (US$8.9 trillion) was 1.8 times larger than previously thought, making it the world's second largest economy. India's economy (US$3.7 trillion) is about three times larger under the PPP method. Several industrial countries—such as Germany, France and Italy—all saw their economic output figures drop slightly with the new method. For Australia, the PPP method recorded a slightly lower GDP in 2009 (US$858 billion), compared to the traditional World Bank method based on exchange rates (US$925 billion). According to the PPP method, in 2009 Australia ranked as the 17th largest economy in the world.

COSTS AND BENEFITS OF GROWTH

LEARNING OBJECTIVE 6
Explain the controversy over the benefits and costs of economic growth

BENEFITS OF GROWTH

The chief benefit of economic growth is that it eases the basic economic problem of satisfying humanity's unlimited wants. As explained above, with economic growth there can be more for everyone. In other words, material living standards can be raised.

In terms of the production possibility curve that we have examined, economic growth pushes out the frontier and allows an economy to have more consumer goods without having to forgo important capital goods. There are, in fact, combinations that allow more of both consumer goods and capital goods.

Another benefit of growth is that it increases employment opportunities; this reduces government costs associated with unemployment benefits and other social measures connected with an ailing economy.

However, it has become increasingly apparent in the industrialised countries that there are costs to economic growth.

POLLUTION AND THE ENVIRONMENT

When the economy produces 'goods' it also produces 'bads'—smoke, garbage, junkyards, stench, noise, traffic jams, urban and suburban congestion, toxic chemicals, polluted water, ugly landscapes, and other things that detract from the general quality of life. Such problems, traditionally experienced by developed countries, are now experienced by the NICs in Asia. In fact, all output, both goods and 'bads', eventually returns to the environment in the form of waste. The more we experience economic growth, the more obvious this fact becomes.

The use of **non-renewable resources** is another serious issue. Opponents of growth view the production of many of our consumer goods and services as a wasteful use of our scarce non-renewable resources, such as oil, natural gas and minerals.

The car is cited as a prime example. Vast quantities of non-renewable resources—steel, glass, lead, copper and other metals, plastics—are used in the production and operation of cars. More than seven million cars are abandoned annually in the United States alone. In addition, a great deal of steel and concrete is used in the construction of freeways to facilitate easy movement of the car. Cropland is also shrunk by industrial and civil engineering projects. Cars are also a major source of air pollution, especially through the emission of greenhouse gases such as carbon dioxide and nitrogen dioxide.

non-renewable resources
natural resources, such as oil or minerals, that are present in finite supply and are not renewed by a natural system as quickly as they are used

GOVERNMENT AND THE ENVIRONMENT

Part of the environmental cost of growth is due to early government policy on the use of environmental resources. That is, it was usual to make no charge for the use of air, rivers, lakes and oceans. Consequently, there was no cost to the waste-maker: wastes were dispersed into the environment.

Since the 1970s specialists have expressed the view that the government has to change the conditions under which producers and consumers are allowed unrestricted use of environmental resources.

Economic principles suggest that it is necessary to equate the price charged for use of environmental resources with the cost of the damage inflicted on society by their use. The price charged may take the form of a tax on the polluting process or the purchase price of licences that allow a certain amount of pollution.

In these ways the government ensures that the polluter pays to alleviate pollution. Investment in anti-pollution equipment can become a major area for companies' budgets. This will have the effect of increasing costs for the producer and/or prices for the consumer.

Alternatively, the government may provide a subsidy to the producer not to pollute. In this case the public pays to alleviate pollution.

LIMITS TO GROWTH

The hard facts of pollution, energy shortages, urban sprawl and traffic congestion are increasingly insistent reminders that there are limits to economic growth. Shortages of skilled labour may be another downside of rapid economic growth.

Doomsday predictions, similar to the classical view of economic growth, argue that the limits of economic growth are likely to be reached some time in the latter half of the next century. Critics of these predictions contend that such a forecast is most likely wrong because it grossly underestimates the advances of science, technology and innovation, which have always been major sources of economic growth.

**LINK TO
INTERNATIONAL
ECONOMY**

EAST ASIA'S ECONOMIC GROWTH—FROM THE AFC TO THE GFC

During the three decades to 1996, the newly industrialising East Asian economies, referred to as tiger economies, enjoyed breathtaking growth (Table 25.6). Never before has any region sustained such rapid growth for so long.

Although government intervention may have played a positive role in East Asian economic growth, it is clear that economic fundamentals—stable macroeconomic management, investment in people, open markets, allowing prices to reflect economic scarcity—are the major factors in their 30 years of economic success before the 1997 crisis.

Table 25.6   **Economic growth rates in the East Asian tiger economies**

	GDP IN 2008 (US$ BILLION)	AVERAGE ANNUAL REAL GDP CHANGE (% P.A.)		
		1990–2000	2001–08	2009
Singapore	182	7.6	5.8	-1.3
Taipei*	732	6.3	4.0	-1.9

continued ↘

	GDP IN 2008 (US$ BILLION)	AVERAGE ANNUAL REAL GDP CHANGE (% P.A.)		
		1990–2000	2001–08	2009
South Korea	832	6.5	4.5	0.2
Hong Kong SAR	215	5.8	5.2	−2.8
Thailand	263	3.6	5.2	−2.3
Malaysia	192	7.0	5.5	−1.7
Indonesia	540	4.2	5.2	4.5
China	4909	10.6	10.4	8.7

Note: *PPP.

Source: Adapted from World Bank, World Development Indicators 2010; Asian Development Bank, Key Indicators 2010.

THE ASIAN FINANCIAL CRISIS (AFC): PESSIMISTS AND OPTIMISTS

As happens in any major issue, the mid 1990s slow-down and the 1997 to 1998 financial crisis in East Asia have seen the experts divided into optimists and pessimists. The pessimists, led by the United States economist Paul Krugman,[11] were unsurprised, because they thought all along that the fast economic growth was unsustainable. To them, the slow-down is structural, proving that the fast economic growth reflected the quantitative nature of the resources in tiger economies, rather than gains in efficiency. Krugman blamed the over-guaranteed and under-regulated financial institutions in East Asian countries for the many bankruptcies in their economies.

Their case was strengthened by relatively high current account deficits in countries such as Indonesia, Thailand and Malaysia, accompanied by growing foreign debt and excessive monetary growth, encouraging speculators (such as George Soros) to attack their overvalued currencies. The collapse in the value of real estate, currencies and other financial assets in countries like Indonesia, South Korea and Thailand exacerbated their economic crisis. And the economic crisis, as Indonesia showed, can turn into a deep political crisis.

The optimists thought that the slow-down was a cyclical phenomenon: given the sound macroeconomic framework and the entrepreneurial nature of East Asians, the cycle was expected to turn and the East Asian economies were expected to spring forward.

As in many controversies, the truth may be found somewhere in the middle. Krugman's opinions may be exaggerated, but the mid 1990s slow-down and the 1997 financial crisis in East Asia exposed structural problems in the tiger economies.

According to Andrew Sheng, central banker, corporate regulator, academic, and World Bank official, the Asian financial crisis (AFC) of 1997–98 and the GFC a decade later were different crises with different causes.

A difference between the Asian financial crisis and the GFC is that in the former crisis, the affected countries could export their way out of the crisis, aided by depreciated currencies. In the GFC, this was not a feasible option.

The Asian financial crisis reflected the breakdown of the 'Tokyo Consensus' (the Japanese view that industrial policy will generate growth and prosperity), and in the GFC the 'Washington Consensus' that replaced it 'was put to the stress test and found wanting'.

It is now clear that the indirect impacts of the sub-prime crisis on the region through the trade channel will be very severe. Exports have declined sharply for most economies in the region. Unemployment and related social problems have increased.

continued ⌄

In the short term, governments have vigorously used the fiscal pump, and also pursued rapid monetary easing.

In the medium term, Asian countries need to increase domestic sources of growth. Public infrastructure investment can be an important growth driver over the next three to five years.

Many Asian countries may need new regional or global assistance to facilitate the financing of public investment.

What is the future for Asian countries?

According to Angus Maddison's projections, by 2018, China will overtake the United States as the largest economy in the world, with India as number 3. By 2030, he estimates that Asia (including Japan) would account for 53 per cent of world GDP, whereas the United States and Europe would account for only 33 per cent.

These changes in Asia's share in the global economy will certainly bring a bigger role for Asia in global trade and financial matters.

Source: East Asia Forum, <www.eastasiaforum.org/tag/icrier/>, accessed 12 November 2010.

SUMMARY

1. Economic growth is defined as a sustained increase over time in the real value of the production of goods and services. It may be viewed as a continued shifting outwards of the economy's production possibility frontier, caused by growth in the quantity and quality of the economy's available resources (land, labour, capital, enterprise) and by continuous improvement in technology.
2. Gross domestic product (GDP) is the main measure of production. However, GDP has certain limitations, both as a measure of economic growth and as an indicator of changes in the standard of living.
3. The classical economists' view of economic growth was that a nation's economic growth naturally tended towards stagnation and a subsistence standard of living. Both output and population growth cease once per capita output has fallen to the subsistence level.
4. The drag on economic growth imposed by the law of diminishing returns and population growth can be overcome by technological change, and education and other forms of investment in human capital.
5. Australian history shows periods of stable, sustained growth, punctuated by some major setbacks such as the depressions in the 1840s, 1890s and 1930s. In the 1980s, when some excellent rates were achieved, they were not sustained because of the tendency to invest speculatively for short-term profits, rather than productively in new capital assets. After the recession of the early 1990s, the growth of the Australian economy compared favourably with that of other developed OECD economies. The 4 per cent growth target set by the Australian Government in December 1997 will be a challenge for the Australian economy, but probably still insufficient to cut the numbers of unemployed significantly.
6. Economic growth is beneficial in that it eases the basic economic problem. However, both industrialised countries and NICs are increasingly suffering undesirable by-products of growth—pollution, traffic jams, production bottlenecks, stress.
7. There are controversial views on the limits of economic growth. Supporters of growth argue that the advances of science, technology and innovation will continue as major sources of economic growth.

KEY TERMS

REFERENCES

1. World Bank, *World Development Indicators 2001*.

2. George Schultz was a close economic adviser to President Richard Nixon from 1968 to 1974 and Secretary of State under President George Bush. E.F. Denison is a United States expert in the theory of economic growth. See his *Trends in United States Economic Growth*, Brookings Institution, Washington, DC, 1985.

3. Adam Smith (1723–90). Smith was a Scottish economist and philosopher, regarded by many as the founder of modern economics. David Ricardo's (1772–1823) most important work was *The Principles of Political Economy and Taxation*, 1817, which dominated English classical economics for the next 50 years. Thomas Malthus (1766–1834), English clergyman and economist, wrote the famous essay on the *Principle of Population* (1798).

4. Karl Marx (1818–83), a German economist and radical journalist, published the first volume of his famous work *Das Kapital* in 1867. The remaining volumes were edited by his friend Friedrich Engels and published posthumously in 1885 and 1894. His work owed a great debt to David Ricardo, of the classical school. R.M. Solow was a distinguished United States economist and contributor to the theory of economic growth. See his 'Technical change and the aggregate production function', *Review of Economics and Statistics*, vol. 39, August 1957; and 'Growth theory and after', *American Economic Review*, vol. 78, no. 3, June 1988.

5. T. Swan, 'Economic growth and capital accumulation', *Economic Record*, vol. 32, 1956.

6. N.G. Mankiw, 'The growth of nations', *Brookings Papers on Economic Activity*, no. 1, Brookings Institution, Washington DC, United States, 1955, pp. 275–326.

7. P. Romer, 'Increasing returns and long-run growth', *Journal of Political Economy*, vol. 94, no. 5, 1986; R. Lucas, 'On the Mechanics of Economic Development', *Journal of Monetary Economics*, vol. 22, 1988; G. Grossman and E. Helpman, 'Trade, innovation, and growth', *American Economic Review, Papers and Proceedings*, vol. 80, no. 2, May 1990.

8. R. Wade, *Governing the Market: Economic Theory and the Role of Government in East Asian Industrialisation*, Princeton University Press, New Jersey, United States, 1990.

9. A. Maddison, *Phases of Capitalist Development*, Oxford University Press, 1982; M. Abramovitz, 'Catching up, forging ahead, and falling behind', *Journal of Economic History*, vol. 46, no. 2, June 1986.

10. A. Maddison, *Dynamic forces in Capitalist Development: A Long-run Comparative View*, Oxford University Press, United States, 1991, Tables 3.1 and 3.2.

11. P. Krugman, 'The myth of the Asian miracle', *Foreign Affairs*, vol. 73, no. 6, 1994.

REVIEW QUESTIONS

1. What is the main measure of production? Are there any other indicators that are not used for measuring economic growth?

2. When discussing economic growth, economists use two indicators: gross domestic product (GDP) and gross national product (GNP/GNI). Is there any difference between them or are they the same?

3. What are the main limitations of GDP as a measure of economic growth?

4. What are the three groups of factors contributing to economic growth?

5. How can the quantity and quality of human resources be upgraded?

6. What are the two main factors that should allow an efficient allocation of resources so that a nation can achieve its productive potential?

7. How does economic growth affect production possibilities?

8. What is the relationship between the level of real GDP produced in any year and the quantity of labour employed and labour productivity?

9. Which strategy produces better quality growth: mobilising more productive resources, or increasing productivity?

10. What factors have contributed to Australia's economic growth in the past? How does Australia compare with other major economies in terms of economic growth at present? Discuss.

11. How do you account for the slowdown of economic growth in Australia in the 1970s?

12. Discuss the main factors underlying the high economic growth achieved by the Asian NICs in the 1980s. Distinguish between the effects of the Asian financial crisis and the GFC on developing East Asia.

13. What are the main benefits of economic growth?

14. Discuss the role of government in regulating environmental issues.

15. What are the major limits to economic growth? Will such limits ever be reached?

APPLIED QUESTIONS AND EXERCISES

1. What is the effect on the shape and position of a nation's production possibilities curve from new management practices that can be used in all industries to improve productivity by about the same amount in all industries?

2. If we assume that the growth target set by the Howard Government in 1997 of 4 per cent per annum will be on average sustained over a long period, how many years will it take for Australia's GDP to double? (Use the rule of 72.)

3. The components of Karland's aggregate demand changed from 2009 to 2010 as follows:

Table 25.7: Aggregate demand, Karland, 2009 and 2010

COMPONENT	2009 ($ MILLION)	2010 ($ MILLION)
Private investment	150	150
Government current expenditure	100	105
Consumer demand	600	620
Imports	150	155
Government capital expenditure	130	120
Exports	170	175

4. According to the figures in Table 25.7, in 2010:
   (a) Government sector demand was above the 2009 level. True or False?
   (b) Overseas net demand was higher than private investment. True or False?
   (c) Aggregate demand was lower than in 2009. True or False?
   (d) Consumer demand made the highest contribution to economic growth. True or False?

5. According to World Bank data, the per capita GNI of the United States in 2001, based on exchange rates (World Bank Atlas method), was US$34 280. What was the per capita GNI in the United States in the same year, based on purchasing power parity (the PPP method)? Why?

6. In relation to the financial crises in East Asia, are you a pessimist or an optimist? Explain your position.

7. Search the websites of international organisations such as the World Bank ‹www.worldbank.org› and the Asian Development Bank ‹www.adb.org› and examine the evolution of economic growth after 2009 in order to update Table 26.5 on page 539. Draw your own conclusions in relation to economic growth in the East Asian tiger economies.

Chapter **26**

Economic development

LEARNING OBJECTIVES

After studying this chapter, you will be able to:

1. define the process of economic development and outline the main indicators used to estimate the level of a country's development (e.g. per capita GNI)
2. examine some general theories of development and identify the major factors that inhibit economic development in less developed countries (LDCs)
3. explain the role of agriculture, industrialisation and international trade for economic development
4. understand the contribution of Western governments and international economic organisations to the economic development of LDCs, mainly through foreign aid and foreign investment
5. explain the role of development planning in economic development, as well as its limitations
6. outline the millennium development goals.

INTRODUCTION

Since World War II, geographical boundaries and national identities have changed dramatically. Newly independent states in Asia, Latin America and Africa started to seek lines of development other than those imposed by former colonial powers, with a view to strengthening their independence and improving the welfare of their people.

With the emergence of the Communist bloc in Eastern Europe, the developed countries were anxious to demonstrate that growth in their free economies under a democratic system could surpass growth under Communism. Thus they hoped to prevent less developed nations from succumbing to Communist propaganda in their desire to accelerate growth.

The collapse of the Communist system in the former USSR and Eastern Europe after 1989, and the initiation by the former Council of Mutual Economic Assistance (COMECON) countries of economic reforms to ensure their transition to a market economic system, have made development theory a rich component of the study of economics.

LEARNING OBJECTIVE 1
Define the process of economic development and outline the main indicators used to estimate the level of a country's development (e.g. per capita GNI)

economic development
the process of lifting a nation's per capita consumption, production and income so that its people can enjoy the benefits of improved material wellbeing

ECONOMIC DEVELOPMENT VERSUS ECONOMIC GROWTH

Economic development is a fundamental goal of any nation. **Economic development** is the process of lifting a nation's per capita consumption, production and income so that its people can enjoy the benefits of improved material wellbeing.

Although a major component of economic development is provided by economic growth, we must draw a distinction between economic growth and economic development. Economic development includes not only growth, but also a political, social and cultural transformation of society that contributes to better living standards.

Almost by default, the most commonly used indicator to distinguish between the less developed countries (LDCs) and advanced countries is the gross national income (GNI) per capita. The World Bank classifies countries by GNI, but recognises that 'classification by income does not necessarily reflect development status'. While per capita GNI is a reasonably efficient measure of economic growth, it does have some limitations, both as a measure of economic growth and as an indicator of the standard of living:

- As a measure of economic growth, per capita GNI ignores non-monetary incomes and unpaid production, as well as the cash economy.
- It does not take into account income distribution and inequalities in income; it only shows a national average.
- It does not show regional variations.
- It does not take into account the local cost of living.
- It fails to measure the social and environmental cost of development (e.g. the costs of growth such as pollution, stress and infrastructure bottlenecks).
- Exchange rates can often be distorted to give a better picture of a country's economy.

GNI works on the basis of a market economy and therefore in non-market economies where there is great subsistence farming and trading, for example Kenya, a non-monetary sector has to be added.

The World Bank believes that GNI per capita figures give a better indication of relative standards of living when converted into purchasing power parity (PPP). PPP relates the average earnings to the ability to buy goods, that is, how much you can buy for your money. However, even GNI per head (PPP) does not show regional or racial variations, nor does it take into account the social and environmental costs of development.

A range of indicators can be used and in combination they enable comparisons to be made which highlight differences even where GNI per person is the same. However, as international experts on development note, it is impossible to come up with a comprehensive measure— or even a comprehensive set of indicators—because many vital dimensions of human development are non-quantifiable. Nevertheless, a range of composite measures have been introduced: the Physical Quality of Life Index, the Index of Sustainable Economic Welfare, the Human Poverty Index and the Human Development Index (HDI).

The HDI was developed by the United Nations and extends the definition of development from a narrow focus on income to one that measured the extent to which people could 'live long, healthy and creative lives'. The Human Development Index (HDI) measures the level of a country's achievement in the context of human development. The HDI comprises three indicators:

- longevity (life expectancy and infant mortality)
- knowledge (adult literacy and average years schooling)
- standard of living (purchasing power adjusted to the local cost of living).

The United Nations Development Programme (UNDP) calculates the HDI every year in its publication, *Human Development Report*.

COMPARISONS BETWEEN COUNTRIES

Since the industrial revolution, which began in Britain in the second half of the 18th century, economic history records an accelerated pace of economic development. In fact, the time required for substantial changes in the level of economic development has shrunk substantially since the industrial revolution.

Figure 26.1 presents an example of the evolution of per capita output (in effect, GNP). It appears that the United Kingdom took 58 years to double its output per person. Starting in 1839, the United States took 47 years. Starting in the 1880s, Japan did it in only 34 years. After World War II, many countries doubled their per capita output even faster than Japan, for example Brazil in 18, Indonesia in 17, South Korea in 11 and China in 10 years.

Australia took 31 years to double its real GDP per person from $6438 in 1948–49 to $12 746 in 1979–80 (at average 1984–85 prices).

The pace of progress has hastened, not only for income and material consumption, but also for other aspects of welfare such as health and life expectancy.

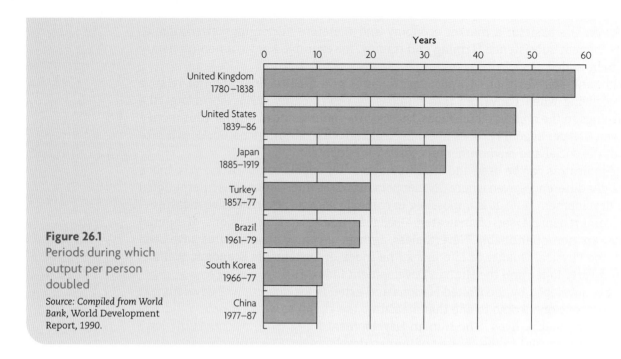

Figure 26.1
Periods during which output per person doubled

Source: Compiled from World Bank, World Development Report, *1990.*

According to the World Bank, technological progress, more than any other single factor, has fuelled this economic advance in all major economic sectors: agriculture, industry and services. Famines disappeared from Western Europe in the 1930s and from Asia in the 1970s.

green revolution
the introduction of pesticides and high-yield grains and better management during the 1960s and 1970s, which greatly increased agricultural productivity

The **green revolution** in countries like China and India was made possible by the introduction of high-yielding grain varieties, chemical fertilisers and pesticides.

Over time, countries have tended to converge with respect to some aspects of performance more than others. For instance, countries now classified as less developed have better standards of basic health than the industrial countries did when they were at a corresponding level of income.

low-income economies
according to the World Bank this category included 43 countries with GNI per capita of US$975 or less in 2009

Because of the interplay of various factors, countries differ widely in their levels of economic development. Certainly, where we draw the line between 'developed' and 'developing' is an arbitrary matter. According to the World Bank classification (Table 26.1), most developing countries would be low- and middle-income countries. Most experts agree that countries with per capita GNIs below US$3900 in 2009 are unquestionably non-industrial countries. These poor countries, classified by the World Bank as **low income** and **lower–middle income** countries, make up 96 of the 210 countries covered by Table 26.1, accounting for around 4.6 billion people (or almost 70 per cent of the world's population).

lower–middle income economies
include 55 countries with 2009 GNI per capita between US$976 to US$3855

Table 26.1   **Classification of world's economies by country income group, number of countries, population, and GNI per capita range/average in 2009, US dollars/capita**

upper–middle income economies
consist of 46 countries with 2009 GNI per capita between US$23 856 to US$11 905

WORLD REGIONS/ INCOME GROUPS	NUMBER OF ECONOMIES	POPULATION (MILLION PEOPLE)	GNI PER HEAD RANGE/ AVERAGE (ATLAS)
Low income	43	846	US$975 or less
Middle income	101	**4812**	US$976–11 905
• Lower–middle income	(55)	3810	US$976–3855
• Upper–middle income	(46)	1002	US$3856–11 905

continued ↘

WORLD REGIONS/ INCOME GROUPS	NUMBER OF ECONOMIES	POPULATION (MILLION PEOPLE)	GNI PER HEAD RANGE/ AVERAGE (ATLAS)
Low and middle income	144	**5659**	US$975–11 905
• East Asia and Pacific	(23)	1944	3143*
• Europe and Central Asia	(24)	404	6793*
• Latin America and Caribbean	(29)	572	6936*
• Middle East and North Africa	(13)	331	3594*
• South Asia	(8)	1568	1088*
• Sub-Saharan Africa	(47)	839	1096*
High income	66	1116	US$11 906 or more
WORLD	210	6775	8741*

Note: *GNI per head average (World Bank Atlas method).

Source: Adapted from The World Bank, <http://info.worldbank.org/etools/tradesurvey/LPI2010_World_classification_table.pdf>, <http://siteresources.worldbank.org/DATASTATISTICS/Resources/POP.pdf> and <http://siteresources.worldbank.org/DATASTATISTICS/Resources/GNIPC.pdf>, accessed 15 November 2010.

In calculating gross national income (GNI—formerly referred to as GNP) and GNI per capita in US dollars for certain operational purposes, the World Bank uses the **Atlas conversion factor**. The purpose of the Atlas conversion factor is to reduce the impact of exchange rate fluctuations in the cross-country comparison of national incomes.

The Atlas conversion factor, for any year, is the average of a country's exchange rate (or alternative conversion factor) for that year and its exchange rates for the two preceding years, adjusted for the difference between the rate of inflation in the country, and through 2000, that in the G5 countries (France, Germany, Japan, the United Kingdom and the United States). For 2001 onwards, these countries include the Euro Zone, Japan, the United Kingdom and the United States. A country's inflation rate is measured by the change in its GDP deflator.

According to the Atlas method, in 2009 Burundi had the lowest GNI per capita (US$150), while the highest income per capita was recorded by Monaco (approximately US$203 300).

As discussed in the previous chapter, the World Bank, like other international organisations, also uses an alternative method for calculating the GNI per capita, the so-called purchasing power parity (PPP). The per capita income according to the PPP method has varied between US$290 (Liberia) and US$57 740 (Luxembourg).

According to the Atlas method, in 2009 Australia was ranked 24th in the world with an income per capita of US$43 370, while its rank under the PPP method was 25th (US$38 210).

high income economies
include 66 countries with GNI per capita of US$11 906 or more

Atlas conversion factor (method)
the average of a country's exchange rate (or alternative conversion factor) for that year and its exchange rates for the two preceding years, adjusted for the difference between the rate of inflation in the country, and through 2000, that in the G5 countries (France, Germany, Japan, the United Kingdom, and the United States). For 2001 onwards, these countries include the Euro Zone, Japan, the United Kingdom, and the United States

GENERAL THEORIES OF DEVELOPMENT

HISTORICAL STAGES OF DEVELOPMENT

Many economic experts (including Karl Marx) have tried to read into economic history a linear progression through inevitable stages of development, such as primitive economy, feudalism, capitalism and some form of Communism.

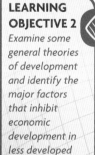

LEARNING OBJECTIVE 2
Examine some general theories of development and identify the major factors that inhibit economic development in less developed countries (LDCs)

The facts have not confirmed such timetables. The mixed economies that dominate the Western world were not predicted, while Communism collapsed in the former USSR and Eastern Europe.

THE VICIOUS CIRCLE

The primary causes of underdevelopment are so closely interconnected that together they have been said to form a **vicious circle** (Figure 26.2). One part of the vicious circle that perpetuates stagnation and poverty is the gap between savings and investment.

According to the vicious circle theory:

- Productivity is low because investment is low.
- Investment is low because savings are low.
- Savings are low because income is low.
- Income is low because productivity is low.

The theory concludes that, in effect, poor nations are poor because they are poor.

vicious circle

theory of economic development which contends that the primary causes of underdevelopment (low productivity, low investment, low savings and low income) are so interconnected that together they form a vicious circle

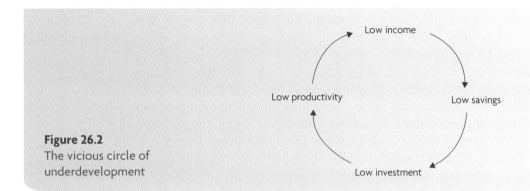

Figure 26.2
The vicious circle of underdevelopment

Critics of the theory challenge the assumption that a low level of savings in LDCs is inevitable. They argue that people of widely different ages and cultures have demonstrated the ability to save. For instance, they have diverted considerable resources from present consumption needs in order to:

- build extravagant monuments: the pyramids in Egypt, the Taj Mahal in India, the Acropolis in Greece, the Aztec temples in Mexico, the numerous cathedrals of Europe and Spanish America, the presidential palace on the Ivory Coast
- celebrate long national or religious holidays
- sustain high population growth rates
- maintain unequal distribution of income.

All these can be interpreted as signs of the possibility of untapped savings.

A great economic statistician, Simon Kuznets of Harvard, found that in the period of their most rapid growth, most developed countries experienced net savings ratios of 10 to

20 per cent of national income. At present, net savings rates for money in LDCs average only 5 to 10 per cent of national income.

LUMP SUM CAPITAL AND VENT FOR SURPLUS

Some economists, like Kindleberger[1] see the small size of the market as one major cause of underdevelopment. He suggests that large sums of capital are needed to build up the infrastructure before development can take place.

Improving the infrastructure (including roads, public transport, communication systems, water and power supplies) creates markets of regional and national size, where economies of scale can take place and innovation and competition is encouraged.

Critics, however, point out that infrastructure need not be completed overnight, nor embrace the newest technology. By tempering future aspirations with present realities, the immediate need for capital can be reduced. Others note that development takes place in cities, not rural areas, thus further weakening the importance of an extensive infrastructure.

An alternative to lump sum capital is represented by increased exports, which expand the size of a country's market. In classical theory, increased export demand is called **vent for surplus**. It results in the utilisation of otherwise idle resources, permits greater specialisation and facilitates increased export demand and development.

vent for surplus
increased export demand

In many LDCs increased exports result from expansion of old techniques to new areas; no qualitative change in production takes place.

BALANCED VERSUS UNBALANCED GROWTH

Studies of development have often been fascinated with **balanced growth**. Some experts argue that investment must take place in all parts of the economy at once to overcome the small size of the market, and to increase income and demand. New industries increase the demand for each other's products and lower the cost of their inputs. Integration of investment also ensures the training of a broader pool of labour, from which all industries benefit.

balanced growth
approach on economic growth recommending investment in all parts of the economy at once to overcome the small size of the market, and to increase income and demand

Critics of this theory maintain that if a country had the resources to launch a program of balanced growth, it would not be underdeveloped in the first place. They favour a concentration of scarce capital and labour resources in key industries to take advantage of size. Insufficient internal demand for the industry's output could then be supplemented by demand for exports. Economic history shows that the United States first developed by specialising in agricultural exports, while Belgium first specialised in glass and woollen production.

The desire for balanced growth has led to costly mistakes. With its second five-year plan, India embarked on a program to speed development of heavy industry. The plan was criticised for stressing an area that relied heavily on imported capital and foreign technicians, while providing few jobs domestically. This emphasis on heavy industry (investment per worker in heavy industry was five times higher than in lower priority light industry) forced cutbacks in other crucial areas of the economy, such as education and agriculture.

LEARNING OBJECTIVE 3
Explain the role of agriculture, industrialisation and international trade for economic development

AGRICULTURE IN THE DEVELOPMENT PROCESS

Agriculture has several important functions in the development of a country.

- As the largest employer or occupation, the agricultural sector is the source of workers for industrialisation.
- The agricultural sector supplies raw materials to industry and food to urban industrial workers.
- The agricultural sector provides foreign exchange to import machinery and raw materials needed by infant industries in LDCs.

Since a large share of national income is generated in agriculture (see Table 26.2), agriculture must become a major source of savings for investments needed by industrialisation programs.

Table 26.2   **Importance of agriculture in selected developing economies—employment in agriculture as a percentage of total employment and value added in agriculture as a percentage of total value added, 1990 and 2009**

ECONOMY	EMPLOYMENT IN AGRICULTURE (% OF TOTAL EMPLOYMENT)		VALUE ADDED IN AGRICULTURE (% OF TOTAL VALUE ADDED)	
	1990	2009	1990	2009
China	60.1	38.1	27.1	10.3
Indonesia	55.9	41.2	19.4	15.3
Malaysia	26.0	13.5	15.0	9.3
Pakistan	51.1	45.1	26.0	21.6
Philippines	44.9	32.3	21.9	14.8
Sri Lanka	46.8	34.0	24.2	12.6
Thailand	63.3	39.0	12.5	11.6
Vietnam	72.1	51.9	38.7	20.9

Source: Compiled from Asian Development Bank (ADB), <www.adb.org/Documents/Books/Key_Indicators/2010/xls/RT-1-11.xls> and <www.adb.org/Documents/Books/Key_Indicators/2010/xls/RT-2-04.xls>, accessed 12 November 2010.

Table 26.2 shows the dependence of various developing countries on agriculture. It appears that, as a result of their industrialisation, the selected economies have reduced their dependence on agriculture in terms of both share of employment and share of GDP.

LAND TENURE AND REFORM

land tenure
the mode of holding rights in land

One of the major problems of agriculture in LDCs is **land tenure**. In many countries, a relatively small percentage of the population owns a disproportionately large share of the arable land.

LINK TO
BUSINESS

Land may be owned by individuals, private and public companies, cooperatives or government. Large areas of land are worked by landless labourers. The Food and Agriculture Organisation (FAO) has identified Asia (64.5 per cent of the world's landless), Africa (19.3 per cent) and Latin America (10.2 per cent) as areas with large numbers of landless labourers; the problem is particularly severe in Bangladesh, India and Indonesia. With profits accruing to the landlord, the farmer is poorly motivated and agricultural productivity is frequently low.

The food shortages of a number of LDCs are partly a result of patterns of land ownership where large areas of land are owned by few people who choose not to use it, or use it for non-food crops like cotton, jute and tobacco. Land reform is difficult to implement however, because of entrenched interests and strong political opposition.

A 2003 World Bank report titled *Land policies for growth and poverty reduction* indicates that land policies are at the root of social conflicts in countries as diverse as Cambodia and Colombia, Zimbabwe and Côte d'Ivoire. Yet a growing number of countries (e.g. China, Mexico, Thailand, Uganda and some transition countries in Eastern Europe), are successfully addressing land policy issues in ways that benefit everybody.

AGRICULTURAL TECHNOLOGY AND THE GREEN REVOLUTION

Agricultural technology adds greatly to farm productivity. Organic and synthetic fertilisers have improved average yields dramatically and helped to compensate for land deficiencies. Pesticides and insecticides have expanded the average area a single farmer can tend by reducing the time needed to disinfect the crop. Irrigation has allowed for double cropping in many countries where formerly one harvest was standard. New methods of rotating cereal crops with legumes restore lost nutrients to the soil and help to maintain the land's productivity. New high-yielding varieties of grain seeds significantly increase yields.

The remarkable progress in agricultural productivity has been called the green revolution. It started in the mid 1960s and has contributed to a significant expansion of grain crops such as wheat, maize and rice in LDCs such as India, China, Pakistan, Mexico, the Philippines, Sri Lanka and Kenya.

OBSTACLES TO CHANGE

It is difficult to transform peasants into commercial farmers open to technological innovations in agriculture. Farmers in LDCs are traditionally suspicious of the people in the best position to help them with technical advice: the young, the college-educated, the foreign (e.g. consultants from international organisations).

Peasants fear new technology because innovation means risk, and they know only too well that the price of failure is famine. New agricultural technology is also expensive and it is necessary to make it more accessible to peasants. At the same time, technology needs to be adapted to local conditions because, in many cases, success in one geographic area has led to disaster for farmers in other areas.

It is believed that agricultural technology is generally more difficult to transfer from one country to another than industrial technology.

THE FOOD CRISIS

The 'food crisis' was a popular concept in the 1960s, when most experts were pessimistic about the future of the food supplies of the world, especially in Asia. Despite alarmist predictions by Malthus or 'neo-Malthusianists', the historical evidence suggests that the growth of the productive potential of global agriculture has so far been more than sufficient to meet the growth of effective demand, due to a combination of technological progress in farming, migration from food-deficient areas to areas of food surplus and increased international trade.

Table 26.3 confirms that over the last two decades or so, the world's agricultural production has managed to outpace the world's population growth overall and in selected developing countries. At the same time it was reported that developed countries try to reduce farm output surpluses.

Table 26.3   **Agricultural production and population growth, average annual per cent rate, 1990–2000 and 2000–08**

COUNTRIES	AGRICULTURAL OUTPUT GROWTH (AVERAGE % P.A.)		POPULATION GROWTH (AVERAGE % P.A.)	
	1990–2000	2000–08	1990–2000	2000–08
Brazil	3.6	4.2	1.4	1.4
Bangladesh	2.9	3.2	2.0	1.6
China	4.1	4.4	1.0	0.7
Egypt	3.1	3.3	1.9	1.9
India	3.2	3.2	1.9	1.6
Indonesia	2.0	3.3	1.5	1.3
South Africa	1.0	1.7	2.0	1.3

continued ↘

COUNTRIES	AGRICULTURAL OUTPUT GROWTH (AVERAGE % P.A.)		POPULATION GROWTH (AVERAGE % P.A.)	
	1990–2000	2000–08	1990–2000	2000–08
Thailand	1.0	2.5	1.0	1.0
Vietnam	4.3	3.9	1.7	1.3
Philippines	1.7	3.8	2.2	1.9
World	2.0	2.5	1.4	1.2

Source: Compiled from World Bank, World Development Indicators, 2010 and United Nations, population database, <http://data.un.org/Data.aspx?d=SOWC&f=inID%3A78>, accessed 15 November 2010.

The 2009 issue of the *The State of Food Insecurity in the World* estimated that, as a result of the global financial crisis, for the first time since 1970, more than one billion people— about 100 million more than in 2008 and around one sixth of all humanity—are hungry and undernourished.

The recent crisis is historically unprecedented, with several factors converging to make it particularly damaging to people at risk of food insecurity.

- First, the GFC overlapped with a food crisis, where, even after some relaxation, commodity prices remained high by recent historical standards and were volatile.
- Second, the GFC-related food crisis is affecting large parts of the world simultaneously. Previous economic crises that hit developing countries tended to be confined to individual countries, or several countries in a particular region. As such, the scope of instruments used in the past to face the effects of the crisis (e.g. currency devaluation, borrowing or increased use of official assistance) becomes more limited.
- Third, with developing countries today more financially and commercially integrated into the world economy than they were 20 years ago, they are far more exposed to shocks in international markets, with many countries experiencing across-the-board drops in their trade and financial inflows, and a serious drop in their export earnings, foreign investment, development aid and remittances.

Research by the Food and Agriculture Organisation shows that the world, as a whole, has the production potential to cope with food demand over the next three decades or so. However, developing countries are expected to become more dependent on agricultural imports, and food security in many poor areas will not improve without substantial increases in local production. The potential for a food crisis is still there and the situation should be monitored on an on-going basis.

INDUSTRIALISATION AND DEVELOPMENT

Industrialisation is the process whereby industrial activity (particularly manufacturing) assumes a greater importance in the economy of a country or region. It is a basic dimension of development.

LDCs view industry as the leading sector essential for strong rates of present and future growth and development. They rely on industry:

- to train labour and absorb it into high-paying jobs
- to relieve serious unemployment and underemployment in agriculture
- to satisfy growing demand for manufactured goods which they cannot import because of balance of payments difficulties
- for reasons of national security and pride.

TYPE OF INDUSTRY

Having decided that industrialisation is essential, LDCs face many choices concerning the type of industry to stimulate. They have to find the proper balance between:

- heavy and light industry
- the public and private sectors
- large-scale and small-scale operations
- production of new and traditional products
- import-substitution and production for export
- industries that maximise output or employment.

Heavy industry refers to large-scale operations using capital-intensive modern technology to produce basic products, mostly used as inputs in other industries. Some examples are steel and industrial machinery and tools. Light industries produce simple labour-intensive consumer goods, such as textiles, glassware and bicycles.

In India, the decision to manufacture steel (a heavy industry) was justified by the large size of the domestic market, abundant coal and high quality iron ore deposits, the availability of technical assistance and India's inability to pay for imports of steel and capital equipment.

Public sector (i.e. government) investment has been justified in many LDCs, when external economies are present. External economies are advantages that a firm acquires when its industry grows in size in a particular area, resulting in increased efficiency and lower unit costs (e.g. improved services). The public sector is also preferred when the private sector lacks market information, and when huge amounts of capital, not available in the private sector, are required.

Large-scale industry refers to huge operations employing thousands of workers, usually with relatively capital-intensive techniques and modern technology, producing either a basic product such as steel or a mass consumption good such as cars. It would be inefficient (i.e. the unit cost would be much higher) to produce these products in small firms.

Small-scale firms generally produce traditional products—shoes, furniture, bricks, textiles. These firms are usually driven out of business when industrialisation begins, because large-scale, lower-cost firms begin to produce the same items more cheaply.

LDCs frequently prefer large-scale operations in order to take advantage of economies of scale, but they often create few employment opportunities and result in one firm satisfying the limited domestic market (monopoly).

In view of the unemployment problem in most LDCs, it would perhaps be better in the first place to set up small-scale industries to produce new products rather than replace traditional ones. However, in the real world many LDCs prefer to replace traditional products with an imported substitute (where the market is already existent and evident) than to produce new products for export.

Many of these choices are closely interrelated and often must be made simultaneously.

Import-substitution

The process of **import-substitution** on a wide scale, as a deliberate policy for industrialisation, was started in the 1930s by LDCs such as Argentina, Brazil and Turkey, and spread after World War II to other countries such as India, Indonesia and Pakistan.

Among the reasons for import-substitution we can mention:

- The presence of manufactured imports indicates the existence of a domestic market for those particular manufactures.
- Protection against foreign competition can be easily provided (e.g. import tariffs).
- It is hoped that import-substitution will eventually relieve balance of payments problems.

Protection was provided mostly by import tariffs which became progressively higher with higher stages of processing. This was done to encourage, first, the assembly of foreign parts, in the hope that later more and more of these parts and intermediate products could be produced domestically (backward linkage). It also encouraged foreign firms to establish so-called 'tariff factories' to overcome the tariff wall.

However, import-substitution generally results in inefficient industries that produce at high prices and thus discourage local demand. Many such industries have an excessive capital intensity and provide limited employment opportunities. Dependence on imported raw materials and parts for capital plants creates further problems for the balance of payments.

import-substitution
a deliberate policy for industrialisation with import protection provided mostly by tariffs which become progressively higher with higher stages of processing

Industrial exports

Some LDCs realised the need to specialise their industries to produce manufactured goods for exports. These are known as newly industrialised countries (NICs), LDCs that are rapidly expanding their manufacturing output.

Countries referred to as NICs include South Korea, Taiwan, Singapore, China, Malaysia, Indonesia, Thailand, Mexico and Brazil. In all these countries manufacturing has a major share in both the gross domestic product and exports.

Table 26.4   **Manufactured exports of selected newly industrialising countries as a percentage of the world's manufactured exports**

COUNTRY	1963	1983	1990	2008
South Korea	0.0	2.1	2.5	5.1
Taipei, Chinese	0.2	2.1	2.6	2.2
Singapore[a]	n/a	1.0	1.6	2.4
China	n/a	1.2	1.9	13.5
Indonesia	0.0	0.1	0.4	0.6
Malaysia	0.1	0.3	0.7	1.3
Thailand	0.0	0.2	0.6	1.3
Brazil	0.1	0.8	0.7	0.7
Mexico	0.2	0.7	1.1	2.1

Note: (a) includes re-exports.

Source: Compiled from World Trade Organization, International Trade, 1995, 2002, 2010.

For instance, the share of manufacturing in the GDP of NICs in most cases is between 30 and 40 per cent, while the corresponding share in low-income countries like Bangladesh, Ethiopia, Mozambique, Benin and Ghana is between 0 and 10 per cent. In 1988, Taiwan, Hong Kong and South Korea entered the ranks of the top 15 of the world's exporters of manufactures, and Singapore, Brazil and Mexico were in the top five. In 2001 the nine NICs in Table 26.4 (p. 537) had more than tripled their share of the world's exports of manufactures to almost 30 per cent, compared to only 8.5 per cent in 1983.

When LDCs produce manufactured goods for export, they overcome the smallness of the domestic market and can take advantage of economies of scale. Production of manufactured goods for export requires international competitiveness and stimulates efficiency throughout the economy.

THE ROLE OF TRADE IN DEVELOPMENT

In general, nations tend to specialise in what they do best. This is called the principle of comparative advantage. According to this principle, a nation has a comparative advantage in those commodities that are produced with the factors of production (labour, capital, land, enterprise) that are relatively abundant and cheap in that nation. In economic terms, trade based on comparative advantage contributes to the basic goal of increasing the efficiency with which a nation uses its factors of production to raise its standard of economic development.

TRADE AS AN ENGINE OF GROWTH

According to many economic experts, international trade can be an 'engine of growth'. This view is supported by historical facts. For instance, in the 19th century, exports led growth in Britain and several other non-advanced countries, and since World War II exports have led growth in Western Europe and Japan.

The same is true of the NICs of East Asia. In 1995 Singapore, Taiwan, Malaysia, Thailand, Hong Kong, South Korea and China exported goods worth about US$700 billion, or about 14 per cent of the world's merchandise exports. In 2009, China became the world's number one exporter of goods and the 5th largest global exporter of services. Asia as a whole has increased its exports of goods over 1999–2009 by 2.5 times to almost US$4 trillion, accounting in 2009 for over 30 per cent of global merchandise exports. The exceptions are provided by low income LDCs, where exports were not able to contribute to self-sustaining growth. This happens when a dynamic export sector has only few linkages with the rest of the economy.

This is the case with the mineral sectors in various LDCs in Asia, Africa and Latin America, which share the following features:

- Mineral exports (e.g. copper in Chile and Zambia) were developed in these countries during the 19th century by foreign investors who provided the capital, technology, management and markets.
- The production process is capital-intensive (therefore it employs few local workers).
- Most other inputs (machinery, tools, supplies) are imported.
- Most minerals show slow growth of demand and weak export prices compared with manufactured goods.

Taken together, these factors explain why such an export sector has minimal effects on growth.

A number of international economic organisations have a specific role in assisting the trade and development of LDCs. The United Nations Conference on Trade and Development (UNCTAD) provides:

- assistance for commodity exports from LDCs
- export marketing assistance
- debt relief measures for low-income countries.

The World Trade Organization (WTO) has special provisions to promote the trade of LDCs.

FOREIGN AID AND FOREIGN INVESTMENT

LEARNING OBJECTIVE 4
Understand the contribution of Western governments and international economic organisations to the economic development of LDCs, mainly through foreign aid and foreign investment

A major factor in the economic development of new industrial countries is represented by public foreign aid (**official development assistance**). This refers to the flow of resources and technical assistance to LDCs directly from the governments of more advanced countries and from international organisations such as the World Bank. Foreign aid can be divided into various categories:

- bilateral (from the government of a developed nation to the government of an LDC) or multilateral (from an international organisation such as the World Bank)
- tied (restricted to be spent in the donor nation) or untied
- general purpose or for a specific project
- loan or grant
- financial or in kind (food aid or technical assistance).

From 1980 to 2002, official development assistance tended to decline both in real terms and as a percentage of the GNP/GNI of donor countries (Table 26.5).

official development assistance
the flow of resources and technical assistance to LDCs directly from the governments of more advanced countries and from international organisations such as the World Bank

Table 26.5   **Official development assistance (ODA) by donor country, average 1991–92 and 2008**

Donor country	ASSISTANCE (ODA) (US$ MILLION)		ODA AS % OF GNP/GNI	
	1991–92	2008	1991–92	2008
United States	11 186	26 254	0.20	0.19
Japan	11 152	8 502	0.31	0.19
United Kingdom	3 322	12 134	0.32	0.43
France	7 728	10 122	0.62	0.39
Canada	2 260	4 635	0.46	0.32
Australia	1 132	2 834	0.37	0.32

Source: Compiled from Development Co-operation Directorate (DAC), Statistical Annex of the 2003 Development Co-operation Report, Organisation for Economic Cooperation and Development, 12 January 2004; World Bank, World Development Indicators 2010, Section 6, Global Links.

INTERNATIONAL AID INSTITUTIONS

The most important aid institutions are the World Bank (formerly the International Bank for Reconstruction and Development or IBRD) and its affiliates, the International Development Association (IDA) and the International Finance Corporation.

The United Nations extends technical assistance through a number of specialised agencies, such as:

- Food and Agriculture Organization (FAO)
- United Nations Industrial Development Organization (UNIDO)
- United Nations Development Programme (UNDP).

THE ROLE OF FOREIGN AID

Foreign aid can supplement domestic savings and at the same time assure the importation of required goods from abroad. The history of foreign aid indicates that some LDCs have limited ability (due to lack of technicians and infrastructure) to absorb foreign capital efficiently. In any event, foreign aid is most useful when it acts as a catalyst in stimulating greater domestic development efforts.

PRIVATE FOREIGN INVESTMENT AND LOANS

Private foreign investment can be direct or portfolio:

- Direct investment occurs when a business enterprise in an industrial country acquires interests in an LDC. It involves managerial control.
- Portfolio investment refers to the purchase of securities and does not involve foreign control of the enterprise.

Private loans to LDCs are mostly short-term commercial export credits extended by advanced countries to encourage their own exports. The rapid growth of such loans over the last two decades has helped development but has also increased the debt repayment burden of many LDCs.

EXTERNAL DEBT

The external (foreign) debt is the amount of money (including interest) which is owed by a domestic economy to overseas lenders. Between 1995 and 2008, the total external debt of the low- and middle-income countries doubled (see Table 26.6). This huge external debt has been incurred mostly by middle-income developing countries, particularly in Latin America, Asia and Eastern Europe.

Among the world's largest debtors (in excess of US$100 billion) in 2008 one can identify countries such as:

- Russian Federation—US$402 billion
- China—US$378 billion
- Turkey—US$277 billion
- Brazil—US$255 billion
- India—US$230 billion
- Poland—US$218 billion
- Mexico—US$203 billion

- Indonesia—US$150 billion
- Argentina—US$128 billion
- Romania—US$105 billion.

Table 26.6   **External debt of low- and middle-income countries, and total debt service as a percentage of GNI and exports of goods and services, by region, 1995, 2008**

DEVELOPING REGION	TOTAL EXTERNAL DEBT (US$ BILLION)		TOTAL DEBT SERVICE AS % OF GNI		TOTAL DEBT SERVICE AS % OF EXPORTS OF GOODS AND SERVICES	
	1995	2008	1995	2008	1995	2008
Low and middle income	1872	3718	38.1	22.1	17.1	9.5
East Asia and Pacific	455	628	35.5	13.7	12.7	3.9
Europe and Central Asia	290	1399	32.5	37.3	10.6	18.6
Latin America and Caribbean	598	894	35.2	21.8	25.4	14
Middle East and North Africa	140	131	53.5	15.1	19.7	5.3
South Asia	152	326	32.2	21.3	25.6	8.4
Sub-Saharan Africa	236	195	76.2	21.2	15.9	3.3

Source: Compiled from World Development Indicators, 2010, *Section 6, Tables 6.10 and 6.11.*

Table 26.6 indicates that from 1995 to 2008, the debt service as a percentage of the GNI of the group of developing countries tended to decline. At the same time the total debt service of developing countries in 2008 tended to account for a smaller ratio (about half) of exports of goods and services.

When repaying money borrowed abroad, LDCs face the double problem of savings and foreign exchange. If payment of US$25 million is due on a loan, the country must withdraw that amount from current consumption or cut back investment by that amount. If the loan has been used productively to increase output, the withdrawal of US$25 million does not hurt the economy because it has generated enough income to cover the cost of the loan. But if the loan is unproductive, repayment will result in a reduction in the current standard of living.

Foreign exchange is another problem. Usually the loan must be paid back in the lender's currency, so the borrower must increase export earnings to raise the necessary foreign exchange. If the loan was used in the foreign trade sector to promote exports or import-substitutes, repayment may not be difficult. But if the loan was used for domestic industry, raising sufficient foreign exchange could be a problem.

We can conclude that developing economies showed a better external financial performance prior to the GFC. A short-term deterioration was an expected outcome during the GFC, but the favourable trend may resume with recovery from the crisis.

LEARNING OBJECTIVE 5

Explain the role of development planning in economic development, as well as its limitations

development planning

the preparation of blueprints for the entire economy, or parts of it, together with direct and indirect provisions for their implementation

DEVELOPMENT PLANNING

Development planning refers to the preparation of blueprints for the entire economy, or parts of it, together with direct and indirect provisions for their implementation.

There are different types of planning. At one extreme is central planning, with complete government control over the economy down to the lowest level. At the other extreme is indicative planning, where the government, in cooperation with the private sector, provides projections and voluntary economic guidelines. Development planning generally falls somewhere in between.

In Indonesia, a state-dominated, centralised economic system was developed after independence under President Sukarno, but it was replaced in 1969 by the 'New Order' of President Suharto, based on a series of five-year plans ('Repellita') designed to build an agriculture-based economy capable of supporting simultaneous development of large-scale industrial projects and smaller consumer- and export-oriented processing industries. Indonesia's second 25-year development program started on 1 April 1994.

Economic planning has played a crucial role in Taiwan's economic growth. Since 1953, the government has implemented a series of economic development plans. Taiwan's blueprint for economic and infrastructure development into the 1990s was its Six-Year National Development Plan (1991–96). The plan, devised by the Council of Economic Planning and Development, called for a spending program of US\$303 billion on infrastructure projects which included urban mass transit systems, public housing, digital communications networks, and pollution control. It aimed to produce annual average economic growth of 7 per cent. The actual rate was about 6.2 per cent. (Unlike Indonesia, Taiwan had been only slightly affected by the Asian crisis.)

MALAYSIAN DEVELOPMENT

LINK TO INTERNATIONAL ECONOMY

Malaysia has traditionally used a number of development plans: two 10-year Outline Perspective Plans (1981–90 and 1991–2000 inclusive) and eight Malaysia Plans, with the Eighth Malaysia Plan covering the period 2001 to 2005.

The Malaysian economy encountered serious difficulties during the first half of the 1980s. It made a spectacular turnaround from 1987 as a result of a far-reaching program of liberalisation and structural reforms, with greater emphasis on the private sector as the main engine for growth. The vigorous recovery was clearly manifested in the rapid growth rates of an average of 9.1 per cent per annum during the last three years of the Fifth Malaysia Plan, 1988–90.

This high economic growth was not without problems. It revealed deficiencies in the transport system, and a major share of Malaysia's development expenditure had to be devoted to removing transport bottlenecks. The transport problems and constraints on manufacturing capacity aroused fears of inflation. In the mid 1990s a growing shortage of skilled labour in the manufacturing sector created upward pressure on wages. Air and water pollution in the big industrial area became a major concern.

With the downturn in Asian economies, Malaysia's currency, the ringgit, lost more than 30 per cent of its value between August 1997 and February 1998. Investment funds dried up. Malaysia's central bank announced that GDP had slumped 1.8 per cent in the first quarter of 1998, raising doubts about Malaysia's hope of achieving at least 2 per cent growth for the year.

In response, the Prime Minister at the time, Dr Mahathir, said Malaysia would 'prioritise' expenditure to favour industries of the future, including a project called the Multimedia Super Corridor or Cyberjaya. Malaysia pledged to invest US$10 billion in infrastructure for the corridor, including a high-speed telecommunications backbone. Malaysia hopes the corridor will become an Asian Silicon Valley, a centre not just of high-technology manufacturing, but also of electronic service industries. As a test bed for multimedia products and services, it has drawn investment commitments from high-technology and telecommunications multinationals including Motorola Inc., Lucent Technologies Inc., Siemens Ag and NTT.

Malaysia's government body responsible for development planning is the Economic Planning Unit (Jabadana Perdana Menteri). Its stated objectives are to:

- enhance Malaysia's socioeconomic development towards achieving developed nation status by the year 2020
- improve the quality of life of all Malaysians and promote balanced and sustainable development through effective development planning
- strengthen internal resilience and international competitiveness
- promote optimum utilisation of available resources.

The 1990s decade has seen a deepening and widening of Malaysia's industrial base as well as the further development of its services sector. As such, a strong foundation has been laid for the economy to move forward into the new globalised environment.

In the first decade of this century, an important policy component in Malaysia's development plans was to enhance the knowledge content of the economy to increase production capacity in all sectors. The next 10 years will see human resource enhancement and intensive research and technology development that will transform Malaysia into a regional hub of knowledge-based economy.

In November 2006, the Comprehensive Development Plan (CDP) was revealed. Under the plan, five 'flagship zones' in the 221 134.1 hectares (2 211.3 square kilometres) of land covered are identified as developmental focal points. Four of these flagship zones are found in the 'special economic corridor' of Nusajaya-Johor Bahru-Pasir Gudang. The corridor—which includes the significant ports of Tanjung Pelepas, Pasir Gudang, and Tanjung Langsat—is prioritised for development in the Comprehensive Development Plan, with particular focus on Nusajaya.

The economic growth plan of the CDP consists of:

- a strategic economic thrust for immediate implementation
- a future growth scenario, 2005–25, for long-term application.

Both of these were developed bearing in mind the region's economic strengths in manufacturing and services, with 60 per cent of value-added manufacturing derived from electrical and electronic, chemical and chemical products (petrochemical, plastics, oleo chemicals) and food processing sub-sectors.

Malaysia is an important trade and investment partner for Australia. Two-way trade in goods and services in 2009 was worth in excess of A$10 billion placing the trading relationship with Malaysia 11th overall. Major Australian exports included copper, aluminium, agriculture and food (milk and cream), non-monetary gold, medicaments, education and tourism.

Australian direct investment in Malaysia is relatively low, at around A$300 million. However, a stronger Malaysian domestic sector, the move up the value chain for exporters, and progressive freeing-up of restrictions, could well be associated with a revival of foreign direct investment into domestic as well as export industries. Australia's experience in telecommunications provides opportunities for Australian high-tech companies to export to or to invest in Malaysia.

continued ↘

continued

The completion of the bilateral free trade agreement between Australia and Malaysia, on top of the agreement Australia has already signed with the ASEAN group, will provide a solid basis for the expansion of international trade and investment between the two nations.

QUESTIONS
1. Explain the role of trade in Malaysia's economic growth since 1985.
2. Discuss the reasons why Malaysia has chosen to develop a multimedia super corridor.

LIMITATIONS OF PLANNING

Development planning faces serious limitations, both in preparation and implementation. First, most LDCs do not have sufficient data to draw up a comprehensive and realistic development plan. Many also lack the expertise and facilities required to draw up the plan. Problems of implementation result from the limited range and effectiveness of the policy instruments at government disposal and from the difficulty of enlisting the active support and enthusiasm of millions of isolated and uneducated people.

Despite its shortcomings, the planning exercise is useful for LDCs:

- It helps to expose unrealistic and overambitious targets.
- It can point to inconsistencies in intersectoral flows and identify bottlenecks in the economy.
- It can help to achieve a more efficient allocation of development resources in general.

LEARNING OBJECTIVE 6
Outline the millennium development goals

THE MILLENNIUM DEVELOPMENT GOALS

A framework of eight goals, 18 targets and 48 indicators to measure progress towards the millennium development goals was adopted by a consensus of experts from the United Nations Secretariat and IMF, OECD and the World Bank.[3]

The millennium development goals summarise and give substance to the commitments embodied in the Millennium Declaration, adopted unanimously by the members of the United Nations in September 2000. They reinforce the paramount task of development as improving the welfare of all people on Earth—to help us realise our human potential, to reduce insecurity and increase opportunity, and to ensure that the benefits secured in the current generation are sustained and augmented in the next. The eight goals are as follows:

1. Eradicate extreme poverty and hunger
2. Achieve universal primary education
3. Promote gender equality and empower women
4. Reduce child mortality
5. Improve maternal health
6. Combat HIV/AIDS, malaria and other diseases
7. Ensure environmental sustainability
8. Develop a global partnership for development.

The millennium development goals grew out of the agreements and resolutions of world conferences organised by the United Nations in the 1990s. The first seven goals are mutually reinforcing and are directed at reducing poverty in all its forms. Better healthcare increases school enrolment and reduces poverty. Better education leads to better health. And increasing income gives people more resources to pursue better education and healthcare and a cleaner environment. The last goal—global partnership for development—is about the means to achieve the first seven.

Now widely accepted as a framework for measuring development progress, the goals focus the efforts of the world community on achieving significant, measurable improvements in people's lives. They establish yardsticks for measuring results—not just for developing countries, but also for rich countries that help to fund development programs and for the multilateral institutions that help countries implement these programs.

SUMMARY

1. Economic development is different from economic growth: economic development includes not only growth, but also a political, social and cultural transformation of society which contributes to better living standards.

2. Despite obvious limitations, GNI per capita is the most commonly used indicator to distinguish between the LDCs and the developed countries. Countries with per capita GNIs below US$2900 in 2002 are regarded as non-industrial countries. These poor countries, classified by the World Bank as low-income and lower-middle income economies, account for 118 of the 208 countries listed in Table 26.1. They account for about 4.9 billion people (or almost 80 per cent of the world's population).

3. LDCs must overcome many obstacles to achieve a satisfactory rate of economic growth, especially in per capita terms. The situation of many low-income countries has been aptly described as a vicious circle—they are poor because they are poor.

4. Despite some improvements in farm production following the green revolution in the mid 1960s, the growth of population in many LDCs has outpaced the growth of food production. Difficulties in the transfer of agricultural technology, the conservatism of farmers, and especially lack of reform in land ownership, increase the number of unemployed and underemployed people in agriculture.

5. Emphasis on industrial development, especially when oriented towards import-substitution, resulted in insufficient industries in some LDCs. However, newly industrialising countries (NICs) in East Asia, which have established export-oriented industries, have achieved high rates of economic growth.

6. A major factor for the economic development of new industrial countries is the official development assistance (ODA) provided to LDCs by governments of developed nations and international organisations such as the World Bank. Unfortunately, over the last two decades, the share of ODA in GNP/GNI of donor countries has tended to decline. The rapid growth of private loans from developed nations to LDCs to encourage the latter's exports has helped development but has also increased the debt burden of many LDCs.

7. Development planning is a useful instrument for LDCs in directing their development process. Although development planning faces serious difficulties both in preparation and implementation, the planning exercise itself can be useful.

8. The millennium development goals summarise and give substance to the commitments embodied in the Millennium Declaration, adopted unanimously by the members of the United Nations in September 2000. The millennium development goals set specific targets for improving income poverty, education, status of women, health, the environment and global development cooperation.

KEY TERMS

REFERENCES

1. Peter H. Lindert and Charles P. Kindleberger, *International Economics*, Irwin, Illinois, US, 1982.
2. World Bank, *World Development Indicators*, 2002 and 2003.
3. Report of the Secretary-General, *Road Map Towards the Implementation of the United Nations Millennium Declaration*, A/56/326 United Nations General Assembly, 6 September 2001.

REVIEW QUESTIONS

1. How would you describe the natural resource situation in LDCs? In what ways do price fluctuations affect LDC exports? Is a weak natural resource base an obstacle to economic growth?
2. Outline some strategies adopted to promote growth and development in LDCs.
3. How did the Asian financial crisis affect economic development in Asia?
4. Explain the difference between 'economic growth' and 'economic development'.
5. Is per capita GNP a representative indicator for the level of a country's development? Explain.
6. What other concepts are used to estimate the level of economic development?
7. What is the main factor behind the economic advance in all major economic sectors (e.g. agriculture, industry, services)?
8. What is the vicious circle argument? How is it criticised?
9. Describe briefly the lump sum capital argument.
10. What is the most common criticism of the balanced growth approach to development?
11. What is the role of agriculture in the development process?
12. What are the obstacles to change in agriculture?
13. Discuss the relationship between population growth and the food crisis in LDCs.
14. Name three main choices that LDCs face in the industrial area.
15. Exports led the growth of several non-industrial countries in the 19th century. Why, then, did exports fail to lead the growth of many LDCs in the 20th century?
16. What are the two major sources of public foreign aid (official development assistance)?
17. What is the role of foreign aid?
18. Discuss the distinction between direct and portfolio investments.
19. How does foreign debt affect the economies of developing countries? Briefly discuss.
20. What is development planning? Discuss its advantages and its limitations.
21. What is the main objective of the first seven millennium goals?
22. Do you think the millennium goals are achievable? Why or why not?

APPLIED QUESTIONS AND EXERCISES

1. Table 26.7 shows the changes in indices of agricultural production per capita in 10 selected developing countries. From the point of view of food security, which country has achieved the best improvement over the period? Briefly explain.

Table 26.7: Agricultural production per head (1999–2001 = 100)

COUNTRIES	1994–96	2007
Brazil	89	120
Argentina	89	117
Bangladesh	85	102
China	83	120
India	96	108
Indonesia	103	125
Mexico	94	112
Thailand	96	114
Vietnam	79	116
Philippines	99	111

Source: FAO, Statistical Yearbook, 2009.

2. Select five newly industrialising countries (NICs) and collect information on their progress on manufacturing exports and inward FDI from:
   (a) WTO database at ‹http://stat.wto.org/Home/WSDBHome.aspx›.
   (b) UNCTAD World Investment report at ‹www.unctad.org/wir›.

   Outline the progress achieved by the selected NICs over the most recent 10 years.

3. Online exercise—Collect data on bilateral trade and the investment relationship between Australia and Malaysia from the most recent editions of:
   (a) DFAT, Composition of trade, ‹www.dfat.gov.au/publications/stats-pubs/composition_trade.html›
   (b) ABS 53520—International Investment Position, Australia: Supplementary Statistics, ‹www.abs.gov.au/AUSSTATS/abs@.nsf/DetailsPage/5352.02008?OpenDocument›
   (c) International Trade Centre UNCTAD/WTO, ‹www.intracen.org/menus/products.htm›.

   Draw a few conclusions regarding the evolution of the bilateral relationship between the two nations over the most recent five years.

4. Research project—The aim of this project is to extend your knowledge and understanding of the differences between developed countries and LDCs. You may present your findings as a report (1500 to 2000 words); it may also be summarised in a class talk with audiovisual back-up.

   Your report should contain the following:

   (a) **Introduction**
      Define economic development, and outline the scope and purpose of the report.

   (b) **Country profile**
      Select an LDC in Asia (per capita GNI under US$2900 in 2002) and a high-income country (over US$9076). Use statistics and other research to create a socioeconomic profile for each country. Sources include the International Monetary Fund, UNCTAD, WTO, Asia Yearbook and the World Bank.
      Suggested headings are:
      (i) production indicators: GDP/GNP; size; growth; structure
      (ii) capital resources
      (iii) population and demographic indicators
      (iv) labour resources
      (v) agriculture and arable land
      (vi) product composition of international trade
      (vii) political institutions.

   (c) **Strategies**
      Give advice to the government of the LDC on strategies to promote economic development:
      (i) reliance on central economic planning or the market
      (ii) self-reliance
      (iii) import-substitution or export orientation
      (iv) incentives to foreign investors.

   (d) **Conclusion**
      List the benefits and possible problems for accelerated development.

   (e) **References**

5. Online exercise—Collect data from the websites of ABS and DFAT on bilateral trade and investment between Australia and Malaysia and analyse the progress made by the two nations in their business relationships over the most recent decade.

GLOSSARY

A

Absolute advantage The ability of a country to produce a good using fewer resources than another country

Adjustable rate mortgage Mortgages with a low initial rate of interest where the interest rate is reset after a period of time usually at a higher rate, with a link to some indicator rate like the 10-year government bond rate

Aggregate demand The total expenditure on domestically produced goods and services

Aggregate demand curve The amount of goods and services—real domestic output—that domestic consumers, private businesses, the government and foreign buyers will collectively want to purchase at each possible price level

Aggregate supply (AS) The total value of all goods and services produced within the economy in a particular time period

Aggregate supply curve A graphical representation of the relationship between real production and the price level

Algorithmic computerised share trading Where computers trade directly with each other

Allocation of resources The way in which available factors of production are allocated to the production, distribution and exchange of goods and services

Allocative efficiency Occurs when all available resources are devoted to the combination of goods most wanted by society

Amplitude The size of any one movement in the business cycle, whether peak or trough

APEC (Asia-Pacific Economic Cooperation group) A regional organisation founded in 1989 with the stated aim to increase multilateral cooperation in view of the economic rise of the Pacific nations and the growing interdependence within the region. It has 21 member economies in East Asia, Australasia, North America and Latin America

ASEAN (Association of South-East Asian Nations) A regional organisation formed in 1967 to promote regional stability

Asset Wealth which might take the form of bank deposits, shares, property, antiques and jewellery

Asset classes The four major types of assets that could form part of a typical investment (cash or short-term money market securities, fixed-income securities or bonds, properties, and shares)

Asset demand for money People have to choose between holding money in the form of cash or financial assets such as bank accounts

Atlas conversion factor (method) The average of a country's exchange rate (or alternative conversion factor) for that year and its exchange rates for the two preceding years, adjusted for the difference between the rate of inflation in the country, and through 2000, that in the G5 countries (France, Germany, Japan, the United Kingdom, and the United States). For 2001 onwards, these countries include the Euro Zone, Japan, the United Kingdom, and the United States

Australian Prudential Regulation Authority (APRA) The prudential regulator for banks, life and general insurance companies, superannuation funds, building societies, credit unions and friendly societies

Australian Securities and Investments Commission (ASIC) The body charged with protecting retail investors from fraudulent practices and other unfair activities

Australian Trade Commission (Austrade) The Australian Government's trade and investment development agency

Authoritarian capitalism An economic system that has a high degree of government control and direction combined with private ownership of resources

Automatic stabilisers elements in government spending and revenue that automatically have a moderating effect on the economic cycle

Average revenue Total revenue divided by the quantity sold

B

Balance of payments A record of the economic transactions between Australian individuals, businesses and governments, and their counterparts in other nations throughout the world for a given period of time

Balance on goods The difference between the value of exports free-on-board (f.o.b.) and the value of imports f.o.b.

Balanced Budget Occurs when expenditure is equal to revenue

Balanced growth Approach on economic growth recommending investment in all parts of the economy at once to overcome the small size of the market, and to increase income and demand

Bank concentration Consolidating delivery points for banking services in large regional centres

Bank Interchange Transfer System (BITS) An inter-bank electronic funds transfer mechanism for high-value transactions

Bank margin The differential between what a bank pays for their liabilities and charges for their assets

Banks As the major repositories of savings and operators of the payments system, Australian banks are licensed by the government (however, many organisations perform many of the same functions but do not call themselves 'banks')

Barriers to entry Means of preventing new firms entering an industry through legal, economic, financial or technical means

Base period The year that is regarded as 100 in the calculation of a price index

Base year The year containing the reference price level and output relative to which price levels or outputs in other periods are measured

Basic economic problem The questions of what to produce, how to produce and for whom to produce arise because of scarcity

Break-even point The level of activity at which total revenues equal total costs

Broad money M3 plus deposits lodged with non-bank financial institutions, less non-banks' holdings of currency and bank deposits

Bubble Rapid inflation in the price of assets like housing or commodities such as gold and shares in particular industry sectors. The dotcom bubble of the early 2000s involved a massive inflation of shares in companies in the information technology sector

Budget A statement of intended income and expenditure

Budget deficit Occurs when expected expenditure is higher than expected revenue

Budgetary policy Involves government expenditure and revenue to pursue macroeconomic policy objectives

Budgetary stance The current state of government fiscal policy (i.e. expansionary, contractionary or neutral)

Budget surplus Occurs when expected revenue is higher than expected expenditure

Building societies NBFIs whose primary function is the provision of mortgage finance for owner-occupied housing by accumulating the funds of members into loans for housing

Business cycle The recurrent 'ups and downs' in the level of growth in economic activity that extend over a period of several years

Business sector Consists of the individual firms that undertake the production of goods and services

C

Cairns Group A group of 13 non-subsidising agricultural exporting nations, led by Australia, which has represented a balancing force between the US and the EU in the Uruguay and Doha rounds of multilateral negotiations

Capital Any good used in the production process to produce other goods

Capital account Comprises primarily capital transfers, including certain aid flows and transfers of migrants' wealth, and entries for the acquisition (less disposal) of non-produced, non-financial assets such as patents and copyrights

Capital adequacy requirement (CAR) Banks are required to hold a certain amount of capital, usually expressed as a ratio, against credit and market risk

Cartel Firms that enter into collusive agreements or engage in other discriminatory practices

Cash Notes, coins and investments in assets such as short-term money market instruments

Cash rate Interest rate on at call and very short-term deposits in the short-term money market

Central bank The bank at the top of a financial system, responsible for conducting monetary policy and ensuring the stability of the payments system

Centralised decisions All economic decisions are handled by the central planning authorities

Centrelink A statutory authority reporting to the Minister for Family and Community Services (DFACS)

Ceteris paribus All things being equal

Circular flow model A diagram representing the flow of products and resources between businesses and households in exchange for money

Closed economy An economy that is isolated from the rest of the world

Collateralised debt obligations (CDO) Similar to mortgage backed securities but divided in to sub-classes based on risk, with interest and principal repayments being allocated to the senior class first

Collective goods Another name for public goods

Collective welfare The state decides which goods and services will be produced and allocates them equitably among the members of the economy as a whole

Collusion Where the firms in an oligopolistic market make an arrangement regarding the price of the product or somehow agree on how to divide the market share between them

Command (centrally-planned) economy All economic decision making is planned and managed by a central planning authority

Commercial bills Issued to a lender by a borrower as evidence of a lender's debt and the borrower's asset, and can be sold to another party during the life of the debt

Comparative advantage The ability of a country to produce a good at a lower opportunity cost than another country

Competition policy A set of principles and measures meant to facilitate effective competition in the interests of economic efficiency, while accommodating situations where competition does not achieve economic efficiency or conflicts with other social objectives

Complementary goods Two or more products are said to be complementary goods when an increase in the price of one causes a decrease in demand for the other

Completely elastic supply Where supply of the good will cease when the price decreases

Compound interest Interest that is calculated on the initial deposit but also takes into account interest that is reinvested

Conditions of demand Factors that may cause the demand curve to shift

Conditions of supply Factors that may cause the supply curve to shift and lead to an increase or decrease in supply

Consumer price index (CPI) The measurement of quarterly changes in the price of a 'basket' of goods and services that account for a high proportion of expenditure

Consumption The process of using up goods and services

Contractual savings institutions (e.g. insurance companies) Where a person makes periodic payments for life insurance on the basis of a contract that specifies if the person dies certain benefits will be paid to a nominated person

Contribution margin (CM) The amount of revenue remaining after deducting variable cost

Corporatisation Opening a government business enterprise (GBE) to elements of the private sector while the government maintains statutory ownership

Cost-push inflation If wages increase faster than the rate of increase in productivity, companies may find it necessary to raise prices to maintain profitability

Credit creation The process by which bank deposits are created as a result of the lending ability of banks

Credit multiplier The number of times an initial deposit can multiply in the process of credit creation

Credit rating agencies Agencies that rate the financial soundness of companies issuing financial securities

Credit unions NBFIs in which membership is restricted to individuals who share some common bond, generally similarity of employment

Cross elasticity of demand Measures how the quantity demanded of one good responds to changes in the price of another good

Cross-subsidisation Subsidising the delivery costs of free or low-cost products through higher charges on other products

Crowding out The theory that borrowing by the government drains the pool of funds available for private borrowers and raises the cost of finance so that less private investment occurs

Currency appreciation When the value of a nation's currency moves upwards from the initial exchange rate

Currency depreciation The downward valuation of a nation's currency against a foreign currency

Current account Measures exports and imports of goods and services, a country's income earned by and from the rest of the world, and current transfers

Cyclical unemployment Unemployment caused by the lack of jobs during a contraction/recession

D
Decentralised decisions Decision making is left to the individual and there is no government intervention in the market

Deficit unit An economic agent that spends more than it receives in current income

Deflation A situation of falls in the general price level

Demand schedule Shows the amount of a commodity that would be purchased over a range of prices at a particular time

Demand-pull inflation When suppliers of labour, goods and services seek to take advantage of excessive demand in the domestic economy by raising their prices

Deposit-taking financial institutions Those that obtain most of their funds in the form of deposits from savers (e.g. banks and credit unions)

Deregulation The removal of regulations, usually government regulations, that restrict certain types of activities in the market

Determinants of aggregate demand An assortment of ceteris paribus factors other than the price level that affect aggregate demand, but which are assumed constant when the aggregate demand curve is constructed

Determinants of aggregate supply An assortment of ceteris paribus factors, other than the price level, that cause changes in the short-run and long-run aggregate supply

Development planning The preparation of blueprints for the entire economy, or parts of it, together with direct and indirect provisions for their implementation

Direct financing When economic agents such as businesses and governments borrow by issuing their own securities such as shares or government bonds without help from a financial intermediary

Direct investment When an individual undertakes the task of developing and executing their own financial investment strategy

Directives Directions about bank business, issued to banks by the Reserve Bank

Discretionary fiscal policy, or the structural component of the Budget deficit Those aspects of spending and taxation in the Budget over which the government exercises control

Diseconomies of scale Cost increases per unit of output which result from increasing production

Disequilibrium A situation where the total injection of funds in the economy is out of balance with the total leakage of funds

Disequilibrium conditions All situations other than market equilibrium

Disposable income Income available for a household to spend

Diversification Spreading investments across a range of asset classes

Double-entry bookkeeping A system where each transaction is recorded as two offsetting entries

Dynamic analysis Assumes that the amount of resources will change over time

E

Economic development The process of lifting a nation's per capita consumption, production and income so that its people can enjoy the benefits of improved material wellbeing

Economic growth A sustained increase, over time, in the real value of the production of goods and services

Economic management The use of the full range of policies, such as monetary and fiscal policy, to achieve economic objectives

Economic system The way a nation organises its economic activities to solve the issue of scarcity and the basic economic problems

Economies of scale When total production costs increase at a slower rate than the increase in the quantity of output

Effective demand The amount of a commodity that will be purchased at a given price by consumers at a point in time

Effective rate of assistance Is 'a measure of the net assistance to an industry divided by its unassisted value added'—that is,

the net assistance to an industry relative to its contribution to the economy

Efficiency Using resources to produce the goods and services on which we place the highest value

Elaborately transformed manufactures (ETMs) Identified by the ABS as finished, or value-added, goods

Elastic demand Where a change in price leads to a more-than-proportionate change in quantity demanded

Elastic supply Where the quantity supplied changes more than proportionately to the change in price

Electronic Funds Transfer at Point of Sale (EFTPOS) A system that allows purchases to be funded directly from a bank account via a computer link

Emerging market economies Economies in a process of transition from being command economies to being more market-oriented in their approach to answering the basic economic questions

Endogenous growth Modern explanations of the economic growth process contending that the process of technological change is endogenous to economic growth rather than being treated as exogenous, as in the earlier Solow growth model

Enterprise The ability to combine the three other factors of production to produce goods and services to satisfy consumption demands

Equilibrium Refers to a situation where the quantity demanded and the quantity supplied is in balance at a particular price

Equilibrium in circular flow A situation where total injections in the economy are equal to total leakages (the outflows and inflows are in balance)

Equilibrium price The price at which the quantity demanded is equal to the quantity supplied

Equilibrium quantity The quantity demanded and supplied at the equilibrium price

Equity The equal distribution of goods and services to all members of a command economy

Excess demand When the price of a good falls below the equilibrium level

Excess supply When the quantity supplied is greater than the equilibrium level

Exchange rate The price of one currency in terms of another currency

Exchange rate policy Undertaken by the government, through the Reserve Bank, to attain specific macroeconomic objectives by means of influencing Australia's exchange rate

Exchange settlement accounts (ESA) All banks are required to maintain accounts with the Reserve Bank for the purpose of settling interbank transactions. These accounts must always be in credit

Exclusion principle People who do not pay for a good or service can be excluded from consuming it

Exclusive dealing The supply of goods to a purchaser on the condition that it does not deal with the supplier's competitor(s), nor stock the competitor's goods

Export Finance and Insurance Corporation (EFIC) An Australian federal government agency that provides export credit and finance services to Australian exporters

Exports (X) Expenditure on domestically produced goods and services by overseas governments, firms and individuals

External balance An absence of substantial deficits on the current account of the balance of payments, and a relatively stable exchange rate

External policy A government policy meant to promote external balance

Externalities (spillovers) The negative by-products of production

F

Factor endowment A country's share of factors of production

Factors of production The resources (land, labour, capital and sometimes enterprise) used to produce goods and services

FDI flows (outflows and inflows) Outflows of FDI represent the flow of FDI out of the country, while FDI inflows refer to the flow of FDI into the country

FDI stock (outward and inward) Presents a static picture of a given moment in time of the accumulated value of foreign-owned assets over the years

Final goods and services Finished goods and services that are being purchased for final use

Finance companies NBFIs that provide businesses and individuals with services such as personal credit, leasing, factoring and wholesale financing

Financial account Covers the direct investment, portfolio investment, other investment and reserve assets categories

Financial conglomerates Financial services organisations providing a full range of financial services to meet the needs of their customers

Financial intermediaries Institutions that accept funds from depositors and lend them to borrowers

Financial investment Activity conducted by individuals, funded by saving primarily to increase their individual wealth

Financial markets networks of traders using telephones and computers to buy and sell assets such as shares, bonds, securities and foreign exchange

Financial planner/adviser Provides services such as the preparation and management of investment plans to suit an individual

Financial sector This third sector of the economy has savings as a leakage from the flow of income and investment as an injection in the flow of income

Financial system Those institutions and arrangements that allow individuals and businesses to store savings, receive financial advice and assist in the settlement of financial transactions

Fiscal drag The process whereby progressive income tax moderates the benefit of the rise in income to the individual by transferring a rising portion of it to the government

Fiscal policy Involves government expenditure and revenue to pursue macroeconomic policy objectives

Fixed costs Costs that the firm incurs irrespective of any level of output

Fixed exchange rates Exchange rates for which the values are determined by government decision

Fixed income security Type of loan whereby the lender makes the funds available in return for a legal debt instrument

Floating exchange rate The value of a currency in terms of other currencies is set by the market forces of demand and supply, and it can rise or fall depending on market conditions

Foreign (external) debt The total amount of money Australian residents have borrowed from overseas residents

Foreign direct investment (FDI) A category of investment that reflects the objective of establishing a lasting interest (more than 10 per cent of ordinary shares) by a resident enterprise in one economy (direct investor) in an enterprise (direct investment enterprise) that is resident in an economy other than that of the direct investor

Foreign exchange risk The risk that borrowers of foreign currency may face falls in the value of local currency, requiring more local currency to purchase the foreign currency needed to repay the loan

Foreign ownership Ownership of domestic assets (e.g. shares, securities, real estate) by foreign companies

Free-rider effect The provision of public goods (e.g. military forces, police, street lighting, street cleaning), from which people cannot be excluded from consuming just because they have not paid

Free trade agreement (FTA) Agreement in which participants remove trade barriers among themselves, but keep a certain level of protection against trade with the outside world

Frictional unemployment Unemployment caused by the normal search time required by workers with marketable skills who are changing jobs, initially entering the labour force, or re-entering the labour force

Full employment A main macroeconomic objective geared towards a full employment zone or target, which allows for a relatively small proportion of unemployment

Functions of money Money performs the functions of a medium of exchange, measure of value, store of wealth and standard for deferred payments

G

GDP deflator A measure of inflation calculated on a broad range of prices at various stages of the economic system

GDP (E) A version of GDP which measures GDP as the sum of all the expenditures involved in taking that total output off the market

GDP (I) A version of GDP which measures GDP as the sum of income derived or created from the production of the GDP, the main source of data being tax returns

GDP (P) A version of GDP measured at the point where goods and services leave the producers

General Agreement on Tariffs and Trade (GATT) International treaty that committed signatories to lowering barriers to the free flow of goods across national borders and led to the World Trade Organization

General risk The possible variations in returns, the potential to suffer losses in the value of your capital sum, or the possibility that you will not meet your investment goals

Goods and Services Tax (GST) Indirect tax at a rate of 10 per cent imposed on both goods and services, introduced in Australia on 1 July 2000

Government bonds Securities issued by the government in return for funds loaned by individuals and corporations

Government Business Enterprises (GBEs) Government-owned enterprises

Government Businesses Advice Branch (GBAB) Provides advice to the Australian Government relating to its Government Business Enterprises (GBEs) and other commercial entities

Government purchases of goods and services (G) Component of aggregate demand, which consists of government consumption (also known as G^1) and government investment (known as G^2) and excludes all government transfer payments

Government sector This fourth sector in the five-sector economy involves governments influencing the equilibrium level of national income by the use of taxation (T) which is a leakage and government spending (G) which is an injection

Green revolution The introduction of pesticides and high-yield grains and better management during the 1960s and 1970s, which greatly increased agricultural productivity

Gross capital formation Outlays on additions to fixed assets of the economy (e.g. land improvements, machinery and equipment purchases, construction works), and net changes in inventories

Gross domestic product (GDP) The market value of all final goods and services produced in the economy during a year

Gross national expenditure (GNE) Equals the sum of domestic consumption, investment and government expenditures ($C + I + G$).

Gross national income (GNI) comprises the total value produced within a country (i.e. its gross domestic product) together with its income received from other countries (notably interest and dividends), less similar payments made to other countries

Gross private investment expenditure (I) Expenditure by the private sector on capital goods and services (*not* including the transfer of paper assets or second-hand tangible assets)

Group of 20 Established in 1999 in the wake of the Asian financial crisis the G20 includes all major developed and developing nations and aims to promote financial stability and sustainable economic growth and development

H

Heterogeneous products Products that have been differentiated from each other and can in most cases be clearly identified with a particular firm

'Hidden unemployed' People who are willing to work but are not actively seeking employment, because of the depressed state of the labour market or the lack of adequate facilities or services

High income economies Include 66 countries with GNI per capita of US$11 906 or more

Hilmer Report Released in 1993, the report—formally *The National Competition Policy Report*, commissioned by the Prime Minister and undertaken by a committee chaired by Professor Fred Hilmer—argued for greater competition among government-owned entities and made extensive recommendations on the adoption of competition policy in Australia on a new scale

Home equity loans Loans based on the value of the borrower's property with the security deriving from the rising value of the property

Homogeneous product A standardised product whose producer is indistinguishable from other producers

Horizontal agreements Agreements between firms in the same industry at the same level of production, designed to limit competition

Household sector Owns all the resources (labour, land, capital, enterprise), sells them to the business sector and earns a factor income (e.g. wages, rent, interest, profit) for contributing resources to production

I

Implicit price deflator (IPD) A broadly based measure of the average level of prices in the economy based on consumer goods and services, investment goods and services, goods and services purchased by the government, and goods and services exported and imported

Implicit price deflator index (IPDI) A measure of inflation calculated on a broad range of prices at various stages of the economic system

Imports (M) Expenditure by domestic consumers on goods and services produced overseas

Import-substitution A deliberate policy for industrialisation with import protection provided mostly by tariffs which become progressively higher with higher stages of processing

Income effect The effect of changes in income on people's ability to spend

Income elasticity of demand Measures the responsiveness of quantity demanded for a particular product to changes in a person's income

Indexation Adjusting cash payments in line with changes in the CPI

Indirect financing When finance is arranged through an intermediary

Individual demand curves Individuals normally exhibit different demand curves, reflecting different and varied scales of preference for a product at various prices

Individual supply curves Producers normally exhibit different supply curves, reflecting preferences about the quantities of production at various price levels

Industry assistance Government measures for assisting domestic industry including import protection, bounties and subsidies to selected industries, grants for research and development and taxation concessions

Inelastic demand Where a change in price causes a less-than-proportionate change in the quantity demanded

Inelastic supply Where the quantity supplied is relatively unresponsive to price changes

Inferior goods Those that we decrease our consumption of when our income increases

Inflation a persistent increase in the general level of prices

Inflows Injections into the flow of income (e.g. investments, government spending, exports)

Instruments of monetary policy Tools used by central banks to influence the price and availability of credit

Intangible assets Non-physical assets like know-how

Intellectual property Knowledge embedded in the workforce

Interest rate effect The impact on total spending (real GDP) caused by the direct relationship between the price level and the level of interest rates

Interest rates Compensation to the lender for giving up liquidity, expressed as the ratio between dollars of repayments per year and the amount borrowed

Internal balance Stability of prices (a minimal rate of inflation), and stability of employment (a minimal rate of unemployment)

International reserves Consist of Australia's holdings of foreign currency and gold

International trade The exchange of goods and services between two interested parties, located within different national boundaries

Investment The process of increasing capital; therefore, it represents that part of production which is not used for current consumption

Investment objectives The purpose for which you are saving money

J

J-curve effect The tendency of a nation's trade balance to first deteriorate before improving as a result of a devaluation or depreciation in the nation's currency

Job Network A national network of over 100 private and community organisations dedicated to finding jobs for unemployed people, particularly the long-term unemployed

K

Kinked demand curve The demand curve in oligopolies may be kinked or bent due to price changes and the behaviour of the other firms in the industry

L

Labour Any productive physical and mental activity

Labour force All persons aged 15 years and over who, during the reference week, were employed or unemployed (as defined)

Labour force participation rate For any group, the labour force expressed as a percentage of the civilian population in the same group

Land Any naturally occurring endowment that an economy has at its disposal

Land tenure The mode of holding rights in land

Law of demand There is an inverse (indirect) relationship between price and the quantity demanded

Law of diminishing returns If you hold one factor of production constant while adding more of the variable factors of production, then output per unit of input will initially increase before output begins to decrease per unit of input

Law of supply The quantity supplied will vary directly with the price of the product

Leverage Borrowing to invest in assets that are expected to produce a rate of return greater than the cost of the borrowing

Liability A form of negative wealth where you owe something to someone else (e.g. a car loan, gambling debts, mobile phone bill)

Liquidity A consumer's ability to make purchases

Liquidity of the asset The ability to convert the asset into cash

Loan to valuation ratio Ratio of the amount of the loan to the valuation of the property

Long run The time period sufficient for a firm to be able to vary the quantities of its factors of production

Long-run aggregate supply (LRAS) Represents the relationship between the price level and output in the long run, when both prices and average wage rates can change

Long-term (hard-core) unemployment When a person is unemployed for 12 months or more

Lower–middle income economies Include 55 countries with 2009 GNI per capita between US$976 to US$3855

Low-income economies According to the World Bank this category included 43 countries with GNI per capita of US$975 or less in 2009

M

Macroeconomic policies Government policies that affect the aggregate level of economic activity (including total production, income, expenditure and employment)

Managed float The system where the central bank (RBA) intervenes and adjusts the TWI-based value of the domestic currency when economic conditions require it

Managed funds These accumulate the funds of many individuals into large parcels for investment purposes

Managed investment An investment handled by a financial intermediary

Margin loan Loan secured against a holding of shares

Marginal cost The addition to total cost through producing one additional unit

Marginal propensity to consume (MPC) The proportion of any change in disposable income that is consumed

Marginal propensity to save (MPS) The proportion of any change in disposable income that is saved

Marginal revenue The addition made to total revenue by the sale of one additional unit

Market demand curve A summation of all the individual demand curves in a particular situation

Market economy An economy where resources are allocated and goods and services distributed with minimal control and regulation

Market failure Occurs when the market system itself may fail to provide adequately for all members of society

Market power The ability to exert control over the price or quantity side of the marketplace

Market socialism An economic system that combines public ownership of resources with increasing reliance on market forces to coordinate economic activity

Market structures Different types of markets, identified by factors such as number of buyers and sellers, nature of the product, availability of information, ability to enter and leave, forms of competition and mobility of resources

Market supply curve The sum or aggregate of individual supply curves

Mergers Where two or more firms join together to become one firm

Microeconomic policies Government policies that affect individual components of the economy (consumers, firms, industries, markets)

Misuse of market power Using market power in ways that will lessen competition, acting to damage or eliminate competitors, prevent entry into the market or deter a person from engaging in competitive market behaviour

Mixed economy An economy with a mixture of private enterprise and government intervention

Monetary policy Policy that involves setting the interest rate on overnight loans in the money market with the ultimate objective of achieving economic growth and full employment with relatively low inflation

Money A generally acceptable medium of exchange for goods and services

Money base Private sector holdings of notes and coins plus deposits of banks with the RBA and RBA liabilities to the private non-bank sector

Money income The actual amount of money a consumer has in dollars and cents

Money-market corporations NBFIs that almost exclusively service the corporate sector and operate in the short-term wholesale finance market

Monopolistic competition Where a large number of firms produce close, but not perfect, substitutes

Monopoly A situation where there is one seller or one buyer in the market

Moral suasion A situation where the Reserve Bank uses its authority to persuade banks to cooperate in achieving a target or in giving preference to a particular sector of the economy

Mortgage backed securities (MBS) Securities which result from the packaging of a collection of mortgages as a financial asset. The underlying value is based on property values and the mortgage repayments

Mortgage companies Companies that trade in mortgages either by on-lending funds to borrowers for housing or by packaging mortgage loans for sale in the wholesale finance market

Multifactor productivity That part of the growth in output that cannot be explained by growth in labour and capital inputs.

Multiplier effect The chain reaction that results from changes in the level of expenditure

N

National Socialism A right wing political ideology that tried to amalgamate elements of both left- and right-wing ideologies into an economic and political structure

National turnover of goods and services (NTGS) The total market supply of final goods and services ($GDP + M$)

Needs Things that are necessary for our survival: food, shelter and clothing

Negative gearing Using borrowed money to invest in assets like property and shares in the hope that the returns from the investment will be greater than the costs of interest and loan repayments. In Australia investors can deduct the net losses arising from the costs of owning negatively geared assets, including the interest costs of their loan, from their total income for tax purposes. Australia is unusual among advanced economies because there is no limit on the amount that can be claimed as a loss for tax purposes on negative gearing arrangements

Net capital inflow Is an injection into the economy, which compensates for the leakage in the form of the current account deficit

Net domestic product (NDP) GDP minus depreciation of capital equipment

Net exports effect Impact on total spending (real GDP) caused by the inverse relationship between the price level and the level of exports

Net income deficit The balance of income coming into a country minus the income going out

Net lending of all public authorities (NLPA) Summarises all lending and borrowings of all government and semi-government organisations in Australia in a single year

Net overseas migration The addition (or loss) to the population of Australia arising from the difference between those leaving permanently or on a long-term basis, and those arriving permanently or long term

Ninja loans Loans to people who have no income, no job and no assets

Nominal GDP GDP measured at current prices (e.g. dollars of the period)

Nominal interest rate The face value paid to the lender, or by the borrower

Nominal value The dollar-value of a good or service

Non-cyclical unemployment Unemployment that is not related to any phase of the business cycle (includes such forms as frictional, structural and seasonal unemployment)

Non-discretionary fiscal policy, or the cyclical component of the Budget deficit Those aspects of the Budget that come into play to offset fluctuations in the business cycle

Non-price allocative mechanisms Distributing a limited amount of goods and services among unlimited wants through means other than price (e.g. making people wait in line for them)

Non-productive transactions Transactions where no production of goods or services occurs (e.g. purely financial transactions, and second-hand sales)

Non-recourse lending Where there is no recourse to the borrower if he or she is unable to continue to service the loan. The lender takes possession of the property and the borrower walks away with no obligation

Non-renewable resources Natural resources, such as oil or minerals, that are present in finite supply and are not renewed by a natural system as quickly as they are used

Non-structural reforms Those that do not alter the decision-making environment or incentives

Normal goods Those that we consume more of when our income increases

O

Official development assistance The flow of resources and technical assistance to LDCs directly from the governments of more advanced countries and from international organisations such as the World Bank

Oligopoly Where a market has relatively few suppliers

Open economy A five-sector economy (i.e. one with an external sector) where imports are a leakage and exports are an injection to the income flow

Open market operations The buying and selling of government securities—and occasionally bank-backed securities—by the Reserve Bank on secondary markets

Opportunity cost The sacrifice, or forgone alternatives, in choosing to satisfy one need or want rather than another

Outflows Leakages from the flow of income (e.g. savings, taxes and imports)

Overdraft An extension of a line of credit to a bank customer

Overseas component of the Budget deficit Occurs when federal government spending overseas exceeds federal government revenues earned overseas

P

Payments system the means by which debts are settled between economic agents, facilitated in Australia by banks

Peak The phase of the business cycle during which the economy reaches its maximum after rising during an expansion

Perfect competition A hypothetical model of an economy which provides the basis of many economic theories and models

Period of the cycle A complete business cycle, experienced when the level of economic activity has fluctuated between peak and peak, or conversely, between trough and trough

Personal consumption expenditure (C) Expenditure on locally produced as well as imported final goods and services

Point method Used to find the elasticity coefficient, which shows what kind of elasticity a product has

Portfolio investment Covers investment in equity where the investor holds less than 10 per cent of the ordinary shares or voting stock of an enterprise and investment in debt securities

Price A means of allocating limited goods and services among unlimited wants according to consumers' ability to purchase

Price discrimination When a supplier charges different purchasers different prices for goods of the same grade and quality

Price elasticity of demand The degree of responsiveness of demand quantity for a product to a change in the price of that product

Price elasticity of supply Measures the responsiveness of producers to any price changes

Price fixing A horizontal arrangement that arises when firms in an industry agree on a recommended price for the goods

Price indices Measurements of the changes in prices over time

Price maker A firm is a price maker when it is able to set the price in the marketplace

Price taker A firm is a price taker when it cannot influence the price in the marketplace

Price war Involves the use of pricing as a competitive weapon

Primary boycotts Agreements between two or more competitors to refuse to deal, or limit their dealings, with another supplier or class of competitors

Primary market where new issues of government bonds or shares, for example, are purchased for the first time

Primary sources of money The primary sources of money are the net effects of governmental and international transactions on the money supply inside Australia

Private goods Goods that are consumed by those individuals who are willing and able to pay for them; if you cannot pay for them you cannot consume them

Private ownership The factors of production can be possessed by individuals as their private property (the evidence of which is a legal title) and others can be denied the use of these assets

Privatisation Changing the ownership of a public enterprise by selling it to the private sector

Product differentiation The process whereby real or imagined differences are created in products that are in effect identical

Product market Where households are the buyers of goods and services and business firms are the sellers

Production The process of combining the resources of land, labour, capital and enterprise to produce goods and services

Production possibility frontier A line indicating the maximum output levels on a production possibility graph (also known as the production possibility curve)

Production possibility schedule A table showing the various amounts of two goods that can be produced, given the five assumptions

Productivity A measure of what can be produced for each hour of work

Profit Revenue minus cost

Progressive tax The higher your income, the greater percentage of it you must pay as tax

Progressive taxation As individual incomes rise, the percentage of income deducted as income tax rises

Property Real estate (e.g. houses, apartments, factories, office buildings)

Prudential regulation Involves the creation of rules for financial institutions aimed at minimising the risk of market failure

Prudential supervision Prudential supervision involves checking that the regulations are being observed

Public goods Goods that cannot be withheld from one individual without withholding them from the society as a whole

Purchasing power parity (PPP) A theory stating that exchange rates between currencies are in equilibrium when their purchasing power is the same in each of the two countries

Q

Quantitative easing Purchases of a wide range of securities by the central bank with the aim of increasing the money supply and lowering interest rates

R

Ratchet effect The result of the tendency for prices of both products and resources to be individually 'sticky' or inflexible in a downward direction, leading to a loss in the downward flexibility of the general level of prices

Rate of return Ratio of dollars gained or lost relative to the cost of the investment

Real balances or wealth effect The impact of changes in the price level on consumer wealth and ultimately on consumer spending and aggregate demand

Real GDP (GDP at constant prices) GDP figures that have been inflated or deflated to account for price-level changes

Real income The purchasing power of money income

Real interest rate The nominal rate adjusted for the effects of expected inflation

Real value The value of a good or service once the nominal (dollar-value) has been adjusted for inflation

Reallocation of resources When land, labour and capital are put to a different use. The government can determine reallocation through tax policies and incentives, subsidies and other forms of intervention

Recession A period where growth rates in the levels of output decline over two or more successive quarters

Redistribution Intervention by the government to transfer income from high to low income earners through progressive income tax and cash transfer payments (social security)

Regressive tax The lower your income the greater the percentage you pay in tax

Regulation Involves the creation of rules for the conduct of business activities under the umbrella of legislation

Resale price maintenance When a supplier directly sets a price below which a retailer cannot sell goods, or acts indirectly by threatening to cut off supply if the retailer sells below that supplier's stated price

Reserve asset ratios (RARs) Ratios prescribed by the Reserve Bank to ensure that banks maintain some desired minimum level of liquidity, e.g. a ratio of cash to deposits

Reserve Bank of Australia (RBA) Australia's central bank, responsible for monetary policy and financial system stability

Resource (factor) market Where households are the sellers of resources and business firms are the buyers

Resources Inputs used in the production of goods and services for consumption to satisfy our needs and wants

Restrictive trade practices Any actions by a firm that aim to restrict or limit competition

Retail thrifts Offer deposit and loan services that essentially complete with banks; include building societies and credit unions

Risk The chance of bad consequences

Risk mitigation The steps you might take to reduce the impact should particular risks actually happen

Rule of 72 The number of years it will take for real GDP to double in size is roughly equal to 72 divided by the growth rate

S

Savings A leakage or withdrawal from the circular flow of income defined as that part of household income not spent on current consumption

Scarcity The relationship between unlimited needs and wants and the limited supply of resources available to satisfy those needs and wants

Seasonal unemployment Unemployment resulting from a seasonal down-turn in business activity that is independent of the business cycle

Secondary boycotts Actions that hinder supplies to or from a firm where it is intended to damage the firm substantially or bring about a lessening of competition in the market

Secondary market Where traders buy and sell shares that were originally issued in the primary market

Secondary source of money Increasing money supply through credit creation

Securitisation The collecting of assets like mortgages into a pool to create a new financial security, the value of which is backed by the assets and cash flows deriving from the underlying mortgages. It is a method used by many financial institutions to pass the risk embedded in their lending portfolio on to those who purchase the securitised assets

Self-interest Maximising individual economic welfare at the expense of any attempts to directly maximise collective welfare

Shadow banking system Non-bank financial institutions which are usually intermediaries channelling funds from investors to borrowers. These institutions do not accept deposits and are thus usually not subject to regulation

Shareholder equity Value of the assets of the business after all debts have been paid

Shares (equities) Represent a unit or part ownership of a company and entitle an investor to a proportion of the company's profits in the form of dividends

Short run The time period whereby a firm is not able to vary its inputs of factors of production

Short-run aggregate supply (SRAS) Total real production available in the economy when prices in the economy can change, but the prices (e.g. nominal wages) and productivity of all factor inputs (e.g. wage rates, labour productivity and technology level) are assumed to be held constant

Simple (or flat rate) interest Interest rates calculated on the initial sum deposited or borrowed

Simply transformed manufactures (STMs) The opposite of ETMs, these are goods with a low level of processing, for example bauxite and cotton fabric

Social competence The skills necessary to be accepted and fulfilled socially

Sovereign debt The debt owed by governments to foreign lenders

Sovereign risk The risk that a government may not be able to repay its debts to foreigners as they fall due

Spread The difference between the interest rate margins that banks offer customers for their deposits and the rates that banks charge borrowers

Stabilisation Pursuing economic growth under minimal business cycle fluctuations, providing more scope to attain satisfactory reallocation and redistribution (the two other goals of macroeconomic policies)

Stability of employment A macroeconomic objective to achieve a minimal rate of unemployment

Stability of prices A macroeconomic objective to achieve a minimal rate of inflation, through productivity improvements (mainly due to technological progress) and increased competition

Stagflation A situation of simultaneously rising unemployment and inflation

State ownership In a command economy, the state owns the productive resources

Static analysis Assumes a fixed amount of resources at a given point in time

Structural change When a shift in the pattern of production in the economy results in an improvement in the overall level of output and productivity

Structural policy (microeconomic policy) Includes those measures taken at the microeconomic level to make the economy perform better in terms of creating real income from the available inputs

Structural reforms Those changes to the environment of decision making that induce decisions leading to greater efficiency

Structural unemployment Unemployment caused by a mismatch of the skills of workers out of work and the skills required for existing job opportunities (often referred to as 'technological unemployment')

Sub-prime mortgage The most risky form of mortgage lending to people with a history of not being able to make loan repayments on a consistent basis

Subsistence level The minimum standard of living necessary to keep the population from declining

Substitute goods Goods that serve a similar purpose to a desired good and are able to satisfy a similar demand

Substitution effect As the price of a good changes, consumers will cease purchasing it and buy closely related or substitute goods

Superannuation Requires people to save a proportion of their income over a long period of time with no withdrawals

Supply The ability and willingness of producers to offer for sale a good or service at a certain price at a certain point in time

Supply factors The physical ability of an economy to grow

Supply schedule Shows the amount of a good that producers are willing and able to supply at various prices

Surplus unit An economic agent that spends less than its current income

Systematic risk Risks associated with movements in the whole market

Systemic risk The risk of failure of an entire system, such as a national financial system, resulting from the failure of a key component such as a large bank becoming unable to meet its financial obligations to other banks

T

Tangible assets Assets that have a physical existence like buildings

Taxation A compulsory payment to government; therefore, a leakage of funds from the circular flow of income

Technological change The introduction of new technologies, resulting in changes to production techniques and the development of new products

Terms of trade The ratio of the price index of a nation's exports of goods and services to the price index of the nation's imports of goods and services

Total cost The addition of fixed and variable cost for each level of output

Total revenue The total amount of revenue that a firm receives from selling a given quantity of goods

Total revenue method Finds total revenue by multiplying the quantity sold by the selling price

Transactions demand for money The desire to use money for cash transactions such as buying an ice-cream

Triple A rating Securities with almost no risk of default

Trough The phase of the business cycle in which the economy reaches its minimum after falling during a recession

U

Underemployment When people who have part-time jobs would prefer to work more hours, or full-time

Underlying Budget balance Occurs through adjusting the net outcome of revenue and spending for financial transactions

Unemployment A situation where some people are willing and able to work, but are unable to find paid employment

Unemployment rate The percentage of people in the labour force who are without jobs and are actively seeking jobs

Unit elasticity of demand Where a change in price leads to an equal change in quantity demanded

Unit elasticity of supply Where a change in price leads to a proportionate change in quantity supplied

Unsystematic risk Movements arising in particular industries or individual companies

Upper–middle income economies Consist of 46 countries with 2009 GNI per capita between US$23 856 to US$11 905

Utility The satisfaction provided through goods and services

V

Value added The market value of a firm's output less the value of its intermediate goods and services

Variable costs Those costs directly associated with the level of production

Vent for surplus Increased export demand

Vertical agreements An agreement between firms involved in different stages of the production process, designed to limit competition

Vicious circle Theory of economic development which contends that the primary causes of underdevelopment (low productivity, low investment, low savings and low income) are so interconnected that together they form a vicious circle

W

Wants More complex commodities that improve the quality of our lives

Wealth An individual, household, business or nation's accumulation of assets

Wealth creation Increasing the value of your assets and protecting against the effects of both inflation and taxation

Wholesale financial intermediaries Include finance companies, money-market corporations, mortgage companies and managed funds, and usually on-lend money loaned to them by corporations such as banks

World Bank Atlas method Traditional method of calculation of GDP/GNP/GNI by using three-year international exchange rates for expressing the national indicators in national currency in US dollars and achieving comparable indicators

World Trade Organization (WTO) The organisation that succeeded the General Agreement on Tariffs and Trade (GATT) as a result of the successful completion of the Uruguay round of GATT negotiations. It is based in Geneva (Switzerland)

Y

Yield The interest paid on a financial security expressed in the form of dollars relative to the purchase price, expressed as a percentage

Yield curve The relation between the interest rate (or cost of borrowing) and the time to maturity of the debt for a given borrower in a given currency

INDEX

The abbreviation 'vs' is used in the index for 'versus'.
Page numbers in *italic* refer to figures in the text.

quantity, 7
    determinant of aggregate supply,
        216–17
    static production possibility model,
        11–12
restrictive trade practices, 141–5
    penalties, 144
retail clothing industry, price controls, 94
retail clothing trade, 93–4
retail thrifts, 295
return on investment, 329–30
revenue, 460
    perfect competition, 103–5
Ricardo, David, 4, 133, 353, 510
risk
    conservative investments, 346
    defined, 330
    mitigation, 330
    related to
        asset class, 333–5
        interest rates, 279
        rate of return, 329–30
RITS see Reserve Bank Information and
    Transfer System
Romer, Paul, 511
Rule of 72, 517
Russia
    ban on wheat exports, 252
        effect on wheat price, 56

S

Sachs, Jeffrey, 5
Samuelson, Paul, 133
satisfaction see utility
savings, 155–6, 389–90
    vs growth, 161
    see also marginal propensity to save (MPS)
Say, Jean Baptiste, 5, 198
scarcity, 6–8
    production possibility theory, 11–14
    related to economic systems, 18–19
seasonal unemployment, 232
secondary boycotts, 144
secondary financial markets, 297
secondary income, national accounts, 381
secondary source of money, 274–7
securitisation, 319
segmental performance, 346–7
self-interest, 20
services see goods and services
shadow banking sector, 320
share market, 334
shareholder equity, 334

shares, 334
    asset class, 332
    associated risk, 333
short-run aggregate supply (SRAS), 214
short run costs
    perfect competition, 105–6
        schedule, *107*
short run profit, maximisation, 109–14
shortage, and disequilibrium, 42–3
simple interest, 336
simply transformed manufactures (STMs), 359
skiing industry, elasticity of supply and
    demand, 81–2
Smith, Adam, 4, 353
social competence, 512
social objectives, 451–3
Solow, Robert, 161, 511
sovereign debt, 468
sovereign risk, 468
    Europe, 470
spending, 460
spillovers see externalities
spreads, 312–13
SRAS see short-run aggregate supply
stabilisation of resources, 445
stability
    employment, 446
        vs economic growth, 448–9
        vs external stability, 449
        vs price stability, 448
    exchange rate, 447
    prices, 446
        vs employment stability, 448
    see also economic stability
stagflation, 242, 250
standard of living see living standards
state ownership, 21
    means of controlling monopolies, 138
static analysis, 11
static production possibility model, 11–13
sticky prices model, 215
sticky wage model, 214
Stiglitz, Joseph, 5
STMs see simply transformed manufactures
structural change, 417–19
    Australia, 425–42
        competition policy, 429–30
        government business enterprises,
            433–6
        protection, 425–7
        telecommunications, 430–3
    international factors, 425
    protection, 425–7
    reasons, 419–25

structural policy, 418
structural production, 418
structural reforms, 418–19
structural unemployment, 231–2
    causes, 240–1
structure of demand, 208–9
sub-prime mortgages, 319
subsistence level, 510
substitute goods, 36
    availability, and price elasticity
        of demand, 74–5
    oligopolies, 95
    price changes
        and conditions of demand, 46–7
substitution effect, 36
Super System Review, 339
superannuation, 336–40
    final lump sums, 338
superannuation funds, 304
superannuation schemes, 337–8
supply, 36–7
    capacity to create demand, 212
    defined, 37
    elasticity see price elasticity of supply
    excess
        defined, 41
        and disequilibrium, 40–2
    law of, 37
    related to demand, 39–44
supply curve, 38–9
supply factors, 508–9
supply schedule, 37
surplus
    defined, 41
    and disequilibrium, 40–2
surplus units, 285
Swan, T., 511
systematic risk, 330
systemic risk, 320, 321

T

tangible assets, 334
tariff protection see protection
taxation, 157, 336
    effects
        long-run aggregate supply, 219
        on private investment spending,
            205
        redistribution of income, 135
    progressive taxes, 135
    reform, 436–7
    regressive taxes, 135
    related to MPC, 188

technological change
  defined, 420
  effect on
    conditions of demand, 45, 49
    conditions of supply, 51
    employment, 240, 241
    private investment spending, 206
  related to
    economic advance, 528
    structural change, 420
telecommunications services, 430–3
  broadband, 433
  competition, 431–2
  prospects, 433
  shift to mobile services, 432–3
terms of trade, 361–4
  effect of floating exchange rate, 402
total cost, 106–7
total revenue, perfect competition, 105
total revenue method
  measurement of price elasticity of
    demand, 64–7
trade
  engine of growth, 538–9
  liberalisation, 492–4
  promotion and publicity, 494–5
  role in development, 538–9
Trade Practices Act 1974 (Cwlth)
  Cabcharge breach, 147
  penalties, 144
trade theory *see* international trade,
  theories
trade weighted index (TWI), 395–8
transactions demand for money, 277
transition economies *see* emerging market
  economies
troughs in business cycles, 184–5
TWI *see* trade weighted index

U

unbalanced growth, 531
underemployment, 232–3

underlying Budget balance, 466
unemployment
  causes, 240–3
    Keynesian analysis, 240
    structural unemployment, 240–1
    technology, 240, 241
  changes, 236–40
  criteria, 230–1
  definition, 228–30
  economic costs, 243
  effect of technology, 240, 241
  effects, 243–4
  measurement, 233–40
    direct measures, 234
    indirect measures, 235–6
    trend changes, 236–40
  outlook, 244
  related to inflation, 242
  social costs, 244
  targets, 446
  types, 231–3
unemployment rate, 233
  males and females, 237
unit elasticity, 62–3
unit elasticity of supply, 71
unit trusts, 286
United Kingdom, investment in Australia,
  369
United States, global financial crisis, 319–21
unsystematic risk, 330
upper-middle income economies, 528
utility, 20

V

value added, 168
value-at-risk (VaR), 347
VaR *see* value-at-risk
variable costs, 106
vent for surplus, 531
vertical agreements, 142
vicious circle
  economic development, 530–1

W

Wade, R., 511
wages, determinant of aggregate supply, 218
Wallis Committee, 297, 318
wants, 7
  characteristics, 7–8
  satisfaction, 8
water, elasticity of supply and demand, 79
wealth, 327
  creation, 327–40
    approaches, 328
    defined, 327
    history, 327–8
wealth effect, 201
WEF *see* World Economic Forum
Weil, David, 162
welfare programs
  effect on unemployment, 241
  indexation of payments, 270
White Paper on Full Employment
  (1945), 445
wholesale financial intermediaries, 295
Work Choices, 437–8
worker misperception model, 215
Workplace Relations Amendment Act 2005
  (Cwlth), 437–8
World Bank Atlas method, 518
World Economic Forum (WEF)
  Global Competitiveness Report (GCR),
    422–4
World Trade Organization (WTO), 492–3
WTO *see* World Trade Organization

Y

yield, 479
yield curves, 345
  and risk of conservative investments,
    346

Z

Zimbabwe, financial crisis, 271